Strauss's Handbook of Business Information

Strauss's Handbook of Business Information

A Guide for Librarians, Students, and Researchers

Second Edition

Rita W. Moss

LIBRARIES UNLIMITED

A Member of the Greenwood Publishing Group

Westport, Connecticut • London

Library of Congress Cataloging-in-Publication Data

Moss, Rita W.
    Strauss's handbook of business information : a guide for librarians, students, and
    researchers / Rita W. Moss.—2nd ed.
        p. cm.
    Rev. ed. of: Handbook of business information / Diane Wheeler Strauss. 1988.
    Includes bibliographical references and index.
    ISBN 1–56308–520–8 (alk. paper)
    1. Business—Reference books—Bibliography—Handbooks, manuals, etc. 2. Business
information services—United States—Handbooks, manuals, etc. 3. Government
publications—United States—Handbooks, manuals, etc. 4.
Business—Databases—Handbooks, manuals, etc. 5. Business—United States—Electronic
information resources—Handbooks, manuals, etc. I. Title: Handbook of business
information. II. Strauss, Diane Wheeler. Handbook of business information. III. Title.
Z7164.C81S7796 2004
[HF 1010]
016.33—dc21   2003054569

British Library Cataloguing in Publication Data is available.

Library of Congress Catalog Card Number: 2003054569
ISBN: 1–56308–520–8

First published in 2004

Libraries Unlimited, 88 Post Road West, Westport, CT 06881
A Member of the Greenwood Publishing Group, Inc.
www.lu.com

Printed in the United States of America

The paper used in this book complies with the
Permanent Paper Standard issued by the National
Information Standards Organization (Z39.48–1984).

10 9 8 7 6 5 4 3 2 1

Contents

Part I: Formats of Business Information

Part II: Fields of Business Information

Chapter 12: Stocks (*Cont.*)

Chapter 13: Bonds and Other Fixed-Income Securities

Chapter 14: Mutual Funds and Investment Companies

List of Figures

Introduction

Since the first edition of this book appeared a revolution has occurred in the availability and format of business information. Since 1988 more and more information has become available both electronically and as full text. The true revolution began, however, with increasingly capable Web browsers that provided user-friendly access to online databases, plus the access to free information provided by companies, institutes, associations, and governments.

On first analysis it might appear that this explosion of readily available information would render obsolete the position of the business librarian, but of course it has only changed the complexity of the questions and raised the levels of patron expectations.

In recognition of this sea change in information retrieval techniques a great deal of emphasis has been placed in this new edition on the Internet as a source of reliable, accurate, and timely information. Nevertheless, the print resources have not been neglected, as these still provide a strong foundation for most collections.

Another notable change in resource material that has occurred in recent years is the increasing international scope of business information that has paralleled the globalization of corporations and economies, so international resources are featured in each chapter.

Despite the changes, the basic organization of this work is the same as that developed by Diane W. Strauss. The *Handbook* is divided into two main parts. The first seven chapters cover business information according to the formats in which it is made available: guides, bibliographies and quick reference sources; directories; periodicals, and newspapers; loose-leaf services; government documents; statistics; and examples of different types of electronic resources. The second part of the book covers specific topics within the area of business. Chapter 8 focuses on both the area of marketing and specific resources for that area. Chapter 9 covers the different types of accounting and the basic concepts of the subject as well as the main sources of information. Chapter 10 concentrates on money, credit, and banking and the major organizations and information resources covering those topics. Chapters 11 through 15 cover the varying aspects of investment, ranging from stocks through bonds, mutual funds, and futures and options. Chapters 16 and 17 cover insurance and real estate and once more provide basic information on the concepts within the subject area as well as descriptions of information resources.

I would like to thank Diane W. Strauss and also my colleagues in the Reference Department of Walter Royal Davis Library of the University of North Carolina at Chapel Hill for their support and encouragement.

I

Formats of Business Information

1

Basic Business Reference Sources

Accurate, timely business information is vital. Executives contemplating a plant relocation, for example, must consider such factors as corporate income tax rates, availability of and average weekly wages of workers, cost of living, climate, and community resources before making their decision. A marketing department will want to learn all it can about the economic and social characteristics of specific regions of the country so that it can decide how to boost sales or where best to launch a new product. Proprietors of new businesses may want to find out what kinds of financial assistance are available from government agencies and prospective investors, and to learn all they can about the recent successes (or failures) of related companies. Each of these situations illustrates the importance of information in business decision making, planning, and problem solving, and each question is answerable to a very large extent by consulting library business collections.

Librarians and researchers seeking business information, in fact, are confronted with an overwhelming number of books, periodicals, newspapers, government documents, databases, and other sources from which to choose. Examination of these sources will reveal that their quality varies considerably; some are superb, others are marginal at best. To succeed, the librarian or researcher must decide not only where to go for the desired information but also how to select the best sources from the many that are available. This chapter lists and describes important business guides, bibliographies, and other fact-finding aids that identify some of the best and most widely used sources of business information. Also included in this chapter are major reference sources—dictionaries, almanacs, encyclopedias, and handbooks—that can be used to answer requests for quick, factual information.

Guides

Bibliographic guides to business literature are abundant. Some focus on specific business activities such as marketing and accounting, and others attempt to survey the entire range of business activities, but the best have certain characteristics in common. They provide an overview of the area being covered; they frequently describe characteristics typical of research in the field; and they list, annotate, and sometimes evaluate relevant sources in a variety of formats. This section describes bibliographic guides that encompass the entire range of business activities. More specialized, subject-oriented guides are presented in the chapters that follow.

Types of Business Guides

Business guides can be classified in a number of ways (see figure 1.1). They can, for example, be categorized by the breadth of coverage they provide. General guides cover many fields of business and may include handbooks and basic textbooks as well as reference sources. Selective guides, on the other hand, may exclude from discussion all but reference materials or may omit coverage of certain subjects. A selective guide might, for example, exclude insurance, international trade, or operations research or might focus only on databases. Dictionary guides are compilations of research materials in highly specialized areas such as robotics or beekeeping. Although their level of subject specificity is valuable, dictionary guides lack the subject background provided by general and selective bibliographic guides. Finally, other guides are written with specific user populations in mind. They are written for managers and executives, researchers, women, business students, or novice library users. Each is written for a designated user group and describes the basic sources and research techniques most likely to be of interest to that group.

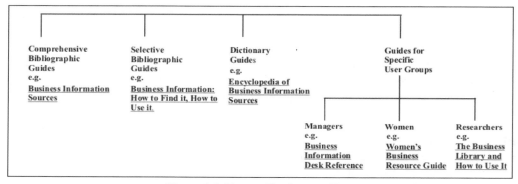

Figure 1.1. Types of business guides.

No single guide, no matter how thorough or well written, can possibly serve all needs. Therefore, representative examples of each type of guide are essential sources in all but the smallest and most selective business reference collections. Some of the most important guides are described below.

General Bibliographic Guides

Business encompasses so many different activities and is characterized by such rapid change that a truly comprehensive, up-to-date printed guide to the literature is impossible. There are, however, a few guides that provide thorough coverage of standard business reference sources and important texts, handbooks, and related works.

Daniells, Lorna M. **Business Information Sources**. 3rd ed. Berkeley: University of California Press, 1993. 725p.

Popovich, Charles J., and M. Rita Costello. **Directory of Business and Financial Information Services**. 9th ed. Washington, D.C. Special Libraries Association, 1994. 471p.

Business Information Sources is widely acknowledged to be the most comprehensive guide available, indispensable to librarians and researchers alike. Written by Lorna Daniells, who has been both business bibliographer and head of reference at Harvard Business School's prestigious Baker Library, *Business Information Sources* (frequently referred to as "Daniells") lists and annotates an impressive array of books, periodicals, documents, databases, and other sources. It is divided into two main parts. The first, comprising the opening nine chapters, describes basic business reference sources. It begins with a description of the types of libraries in which business reference services are provided; proceeds to identify sources of quick reference information; and discusses such basic reference formats as bibliographies, indexes and abstracts, government publications, doctoral dissertations, databases, microforms and cassettes, handbooks, and loose-leaf services. Subsequent chapters discuss publications that track current business and economic trends and present domestic, foreign, and industry statistics. Also covered in this section are directories and investment sources.

The second part focuses on specific management functions, covering such topics as accounting, corporate finance and banking, international management, insurance and real estate, and marketing. Coverage in this section includes textbooks, collections of readings, and books written for the practicing manager as well as reference sources and key trade and professional associations. Entries provide essential bibliographic information and succinct, but thorough, annotations. Pagination is included for books and pamphlets, and entries for each periodical include the frequency of publication and the names of the indexing and abstracting services in which its articles are listed.

Business Information Sources is further enhanced by "A Basic Bookshelf," a chapter that lists and describes essential reference titles appropriate to a personal or small business library collection, and by a comprehensive author, title, and subject index.

Not all business publications, however, are included in Daniells. The emphasis is on English-language works published primarily in the United States. Two categories of materials, published proceedings and business casebooks, are specifically omitted, and coverage of government documents, databases, and materials suitable for vertical file collections is far from inclusive. Even so, this guide's scope and the quality of the information it contains are extraordinary. Its usefulness as a reference tool and as an aid to collection development is difficult to overestimate. As this latest edition has eliminated some materials included in previous volumes, it is necessary to keep older editions.

The *Directory of Business and Financial Information Services* is a reliable and useful tool providing a variety of current resources that can be consulted in the decision-making process. This directory, with its emphasis on services, complements Daniells. *Directory of Business and Financial Information Services,* in its ninth edition, contains an expanded list of sources available in print and electronically as either in CD-ROM or an online service. The *Directory* lists by title 1,249 selected business and financial services issued by nearly 370 vendors. Each source document in the alphabetical portion is given an entry number, which is cross referenced in the separate publisher's, master title, and subject indexes. The main emphasis is again on resources from the United States, but about 150 titles are foreign in origin.

Selective Business Guides

The distinction between general and selective business guides is an arbitrary one. No guide is all-encompassing, but some, notably Daniells, are more comprehensive than most. Others limit their coverage by subject, information format, or type of library or information setting to which the listed source is appropriate. Guides emphasizing specific subject areas are included in many of the upcoming chapters. The titles listed below, however, selectively present sources relevant to several different fields of business.

Lavin, Michael. **Business Information: How to Find It, How to Use It.** 2nd ed. Phoenix, Ariz.: Oryx Press, 1992. 499p.

Karp, Rashelle S., ed., and Bernard S Schlessinger, assoc. ed. **The Basic Business Library: Core Resources**. 4th ed. Westport, Conn.: Oryx Press, 2002. 288p.

One of the best selective guides is Michael Lavin's *Business Information: How to Find It, How to Use It.* As its subtitle indicates, the guide emphasizes research techniques and basic business concepts as well as information sources. Lavin first introduces business information and basic finding aids, not only covering standard reference sources but also identifying major characteristics of business information and the organizations from which it typically is available. The various published sources of company data are also considered, with chapters on business directories; registered trademarks; corporate finance; and basic investment information, advice, and analysis. Another section focuses on statistical information. In addition to chapters that identify general economic and industry statistics with descriptions of many of the sources that contain them, it includes an extremely useful and interesting introduction to statistical reasoning in population estimates and projections. This is illustrated through an excellent discussion of the decennial Census of Population and Housing. Finally, four special topics—local area information, business and labor law, marketing, and taxation and accounting—are treated at length. Title and subject indexes are also included.

Business Information is different from other guides in many important respects. Each chapter begins with an outline of the topics to be covered and the major sources to be discussed and is followed by an explanation of the concepts necessary to understand each source. Although far fewer titles are covered than in most other guides, those that are included are treated more thoroughly. Annotations, which vary in length from a single paragraph to more than a page, are thorough and are sometimes supplemented with reprints from the sources being discussed. Finally, each chapter concludes with a brief, annotated list of titles for further reading. The second edition includes new topics and additions to those previously included in the first edition. Other changes include a much updated and enlarged coverage of electronic products.

Although it is useful for identifying some of the best business reference resources appropriate to medium-sized business library collections, the Lavin book is perhaps even better for its clear and well-written descriptions of basic research techniques and business concepts. It belongs in every business collection.

The Basic Business Library similarly seeks to identify business resources essential for small and medium-sized libraries. It presents an alphabetical, annotated list of core reference titles and a core list of business journals suitable for a small library. There is a bibliography on business reference and business librarianship and a series of essays on such topics as marketing business libraries, acquiring business books, developing a business reference collection, and evaluating investment and online resources. The overview of business librarianship and library practices and the several lists justify the acquisition of *The Basic Business Library* for most business reference collections.

The comprehensive and selective guides described above are most useful for descriptions of standard business publications and for general surveys of business literature. The librarian or researcher in quest of statistics on paper bag production or in need of information on the olive oil industry, however, will need to consult sources that provide more detailed subject indexing. Dictionary guides are particularly useful in such situations.

Dictionary Guides

A dictionary guide is a computer-generated list of publications, databases, and other information sources, usually arranged by very narrow and precise subject headings. The titles that follow are representative.

Woy, James, ed. **Encyclopedia of Business Information Sources**. 12th ed. Detroit: Gale Research, 1970– . Frequency varies.

Starer, Daniel. **Who Knows What: The Essential Business Resource Book**. New York: Henry Holt, 1992. 1239p.

Long the standard dictionary guide, the *Encyclopedia of Business Information Sources* lists a wide variety of published reference sources, databases, trade and professional associations, research centers and institutes, and other information sources on over 1,100 business-related subjects. It is arranged alphabetically by topic, from "Abbreviations" and "Abrasives Industry" to "Zinc" and "Zoning." Each topic is subdivided into types of information sources available (e.g., almanacs, abstracts, bibliographies, encyclopedias, handbooks, financial ratios, and price and statistics sources), with full bibliographic citations and prices for most of the items listed. E-mail addresses and Web site URLs have been provided when they are available. Also included are the addresses and telephone numbers of publishers. The entry for the box industry, shown in figure 1.2, is typical.

BOX INDUSTRY
See also: PAPER BOX AND PAPER CONTAINER INDUSTRIES

DIRECTORIES
National Paperbox Association Membership Directory. National Paperbox Association. Annual. $125.00.

FINANCIAL RATIOS
R M A Annual Statement Studies, Including Comparative Historical Data and Other Sources of Composite Financial Data. Robert Morris Associates: The Association of Lending and Credit Risk Professionals. Annual. $125.00. Median and quartile financial ratios are given for over 400 kinds of manufacturing, wholesale, retail, construction, and consumer finance establishments. Data is sorted by both asset size and sales volume. Includes a clearly written "Definition of Ratios," a bibliography of financial ratio sources, and an alphabetical industry index.

ONLINE DATABASES
PIRA. Technical Centre for the Paper and Board, Printing and Packaging Industries. Citations and abstracts pertaining to bookbinding and other pulp, paper, and packaging industries, 1975 to present. Inquire as to online cost and availability.

PERIODICALS AND NEWSLETTERS
Boxboard Containers International. Intertec Publishing Corp. Monthly. $28.00 per year. Formerly *Boxboard Containers.*

Paperboard Packaging. Advanstar Communications, Inc. Monthly. $35.00 per year.

PRICE SOURCES
PPI Detailed Report. Bureau of Labor Statistics, U.S. Department of Labor. Available from U.S. Government Printing Office. Monthly. $37.00 per year. Formerly *Producer Price Indexes.*

STATISTICS SOURCES
Fibre Box Industry Statistical Report. Fibre Box Association. Annual.

United States Census of Manufactures. U.S. Bureau of the Census. Quinquennial. Results presented in reports, tape, CD-ROM, and Diskette files.

TRADE/PROFESSIONAL ASSOCIATIONS
Fibre Box Association. 2850 Golf Rd., Rolling Meadows, IL 60008. Phone: (847) 364-9600. Fax: (847) 364-9639.

National Paperbox Association. 801 N. Fairfax St., Suite 211, Alexandria, VA 22314-1757. Phone: (703) 684-2212. Fax: (703) 683-6920. E-mail: boxmaker@paperbox.org • URL: http://www. paperbox.org

Pacific Coast Paper Box Manufacturers' Association. P.O. Box 60957, Los Angeles, CA 90060-0957. Phone: (213) 581-1183. Fax: ((213) 581-1183.

Wirebound Box Manufacturers Association. 3623 Sprucewood Lane, Wilmette, IL 60091. Phone: (847) 251-5575. Fax: (847) 251-5898.

Figure 1.2. Typical entry in *Encyclopedia of Business Information Sources*.
From *Encyclopedia of Business Information*, 13th edition. Edited by James Woy. Gale Research, 1999.
Copyright © 1999. Reprinted by permission of the Gale Group.

Who Knows What: The Essential Business Resource Book, compiled by Daniel Starer, can be used as an inexpensive supplement to the *Encyclopedia of Business Information Sources*. Thousands of information sources are arranged by subject, and each entry includes addresses, telephone and fax numbers, and a brief description of the services offered. The information in *Who Knows What* can also be found in other popular tools, including the *Small Business Sourcebook* and the *Washington Information Directory*. However, the consolidation of information into one volume, and a competitive price, distinguish it from other sources. When the book budget does not permit purchase of the *Encyclopedia*, *Who Knows What* is a useful alternative.

To this point, the guides that have been presented have been intended for an array of prospective users. Other guides are written with specific user populations in mind.

Guides for Specific User Groups

People who might benefit most from using a business library or consulting business information sources are often unaware of the range and availability of such resources. Accordingly, guides to sources of business information and to the libraries that contain them can serve an important function. Some are written specifically for business people and business students, others for researchers. The following titles represent the guides intended for business professionals and students.

Freed, Melvyn N., and Virgil P. Diodato. **Business Information Desk Reference: Where to Find Answers to Business Questions**. New York: Macmillan, 1991. 513p.

Maier, Ernest L., and others. **The Business Library and How to Use It: A Guide to Sources and Research Strategies for Information on Business and Management**. 6th ed. Detroit: Omnigraphics, 1996. 329p.

Littman, Barbara. **The Women's Business Resource Guide; A National Directory of More Than 800 Programs, Resources and Organizations That Help Women Start or Expand a Business.** 2nd ed. Chicago: Contemporary Books, 1996. 302p.

Business Information Desk Reference is intended primarily for professional business people in need of information. The writers do not assume that users have an understanding of research procedures or any knowledge of sources. The book is arranged in eight sections, with the first two parts giving information on selecting and evaluating sources and then linking the needed information to a source that supplies the answer. Section C supplies sources to specific questions posed in two dozen business areas ranging from accounting and financial analysis to taxation. The format is columnar, with questions on the left of the page and suggested sources on the right. Frequently more than one source is suggested so that the user has a better chance of finding answers in a wide variety of libraries and information centers. Each entry in this section is cross-referenced to a descriptive profile of printed sources in. Section D. Sections E and F follow the same plan for electronic resources. The *Desk Reference* profiles more than 500 print sources and 400 online databases as well as supplying directories of business and trade organizations and federal departments and agencies. The *Desk Reference* is by no means comprehensive, and the authors recognize that it should be used as an entry point for the research process. Nevertheless, the focus on the application of sources to actual questions and the clear and concise annotations provide a useful finding aid and a practical perspective on the importance of specific tools.

The Business Library and How to Use It is a practical guide for librarians, students, and researchers. Divided into 16 chapters presented in four sections, the book presents a methodical approach to research in the library. The first section instructs readers in basic library skills, including the Library of Congress and Dewey Decimal Classification systems and the use of the card catalog, while sections two and three focus on specific information formats (periodical literature, databases, handbooks and yearbooks, directories, financial and investment services, and government publications). Chapters generally begin with a survey of the types of materials to be covered, followed by lists of relevant reference works with brief annotations. The fourth section provides some guidance and cites helpful sources for creating reports using the information gathered. As with the *Desk Reference, The Business Library and How to Use It* is not written with the sophisticated researcher in mind. Its annotations and introductory remarks, however, can be useful to librarians and general library users as well as to more specialized business clientele.

The purpose of *The Women's Business Resource Guide* is to direct women entrepreneurs to women's and general business organizations and agencies that recognize their special needs and circumstances. The *Guide* contains information on resources to help women with training and technical assistance and business financing. One section of particular interest is "Selling to the Government," which provides step-by-step instructions on breaking into this lucrative market. Although some of the listings would benefit anyone starting a business, the emphasis is on programs, loans, and resources directed specifically at women.

Other guides are written for experienced researchers, who are already familiar with library materials and resources, and with many basic reference techniques. Coverage in these publications is usually more intensive, and often the focus will be on a specific aspect of business research rather than the whole gamut of available business information. The following titles typify guides that belong in this category.

How to Find Information About Companies. Part 1. 13th ed. Washington, D.C.: Washington Researchers, 1997. 666p.

How to Find Information About Companies. Part 2. 5th ed. Washington, D.C.: Washington Researchers, 1997. 517p.

How to Find Information About Companies. Part 3. 5th ed. Washington, D.C.: Washington Researchers, 1997. 604p.

Fuld, Leonard M. **The New Competitor Intelligence: The Complete Resource for Finding, Analyzing, and Using Information About Your Competitors**. New York: John Wiley, 1995. 482p.

Washington Researchers (http://www.washingtonresearchers.com), a private information brokerage and consulting firm, has parlayed its experience and expertise into a series of helpful publications for researchers, executives, and information specialists. *How to Find Information About Companies* is now a three-part publication that contains strategies, methods, and sources for researching information. The first part, also listed as the 13th edition, is the original book that was also published under this title and remains an excellent practical guide to corporate information sources. It begins with a brief description of the why and how of company research, but the real emphasis is on information available from print and online sources, the Internet, federal and state government agencies, local and regional sources, trade and professional associations, and what are listed as "people sources." Three sections focus on resources available in libraries and information centers. The first, "Print Sources," contains an annotated publications list compiled by Lorna Daniells. The second, "Online Data Bases," includes a brief description of database searching, a listing of relevant database vendors, gateway systems, and a matrix of the top 39 databases used for business intelligence, followed by an annotated description of 166 databases. The third section features "Company Intelligence On Disc," which contains a very basic description of CD-ROM technology and an annotated list of CD-ROMs. The second part of *How to Find Information About Companies* is organized by type of information and shows how to research a target. Beginning with "Your Research Strategy," this part also supplies sources for industry information, labor force data, corporate culture including strengths and weaknesses, marketing and financial intelligence, and management and product information. Examples and checklists embellish this whole section and will be of practical assistance to anyone conducting research. The third volume includes resources, processes and techniques for researching private companies, divisions and subsidiaries, business units, foreign firms, service companies, acquisition candidates, and executives.

How to Find Information About Companies is expensive, especially when bought as a three-volume set, but the volumes are also available individually, and those libraries with earlier editions will find that these remain useful, especially for basic research. Washington Researchers produces other volumes whose coverage includes subsidiaries, divisions, service companies, and industries. At the company Web page (http://www.washingtonresearchers. com) they also maintain lists of Web links available under the heading "free resources."

The New Competitor Intelligence: *The Complete Resource for Finding, Analyzing, and Using Information About Your Competitors* describes specific tools and techniques that can be used to acquire information about companies. It treats information gathering as a two-step process. The first begins with establishing a foundation (understanding intelligence, assembling a research team, understanding the difference between basic and creative information sources, the traits of a good information gatherer, and developing a library of information sources) and proceeds to discussions of research techniques. Several research checklists for beginners are included, illustrating typical research projects and presenting, in order of priority, sources worth checking. The second section focuses on both basic and nontraditional or creative information sources. These are resources that are likely to be available in business libraries, including databases and publications. Fuld then proceeds to creative information sources, showing readers how items as diverse as corrugated boxes, boxcars, technical manuals, help-wanted ads, and telephone yellow pages can be used to learn about companies that might otherwise be difficult to research. The third section uses "actual but disguised" cases to outline the patterns of analysis, and the fourth part outlines ways for the reader to establish an ongoing information-gathering system. The text is supplemented with charts, graphs, case histories, and the addresses and telephone numbers of publishers and database producers.

The above guides and others like them are invaluable. They provide readers with an introduction to basic business sources, concepts, and research techniques, and help to acquaint them with business information needs. They are not, however, intended to be nor should they be used as the sole sources of information about business publications and databases. Bibliographies are also important.

Bibliographies

Business bibliographies come in a variety of formats and serve an assortment of users. Some provide retrospective lists of significant publications in all languages. Others list only the most recent publications and are limited by country. Some cover relatively narrow fields, such as agribusiness or costs of living, while others include titles for all fields of business.

This section focuses on bibliographies that present information on current English-language publications primarily issued by American publishers. Some are aimed at librarians and others at library users.

Librarians seeking to build or improve business collections can begin by consulting the guides previously mentioned. In many instances, they will also refer to some of the bibliographies listed below.

New York Public Library. Research Library. **The Bibliographic Guide to Business and Economics**. New York: R. R. Bowker, Reed Elsevier Inc. 1975– . Annual.

Baker Books. Boston: Baker Library, Harvard Business School, September 1998– . Monthly. Available at http://www.library.hbs.edu/bakerbooks/. (Formerly issued monthly in paper as *Recent Additions to Baker Library*. Boston: Baker Library, Harvard Business School, v. 13– , 1973–1998.)

Baker Library. **Core Collection: An Author and Subject Guide**. Boston: Baker Library, Harvard Business School, 1969– . Annual.

The Bibliographic Guide to Business and Economics is a comprehensive listing, by author, title, and subject, of books, reports, conference papers, and miscellaneous publications in business, economics, finance, labor, and related fields cataloged by the Library of Congress and the New York Public Library. It is most useful for large business and research libraries wanting to assess their business holdings but is generally too costly and too inclusive to be practical for smaller libraries.

More current information is available at *Baker Books*, a free monthly acquisitions list at http://www.library.hbs.edu/bakerbooks/. Arrangement is by broad subject area. A fairly detailed record is given for each title, and a hot link to other resources in the Baker collection is provided for subject headings and authors. A hot link is also provided to amazon.com for those books included in the company's inventory. Baker Library also issues the annual *Core Collection,* which lists all titles currently housed in the Baker Library Reading Room. Although both *Recent Additions to Baker Library* and *Core Collection* are useful, many of the titles listed are most suitable for academic business libraries and large research collections.

Of more practical benefit to small and medium-sized libraries are the bibliographies and resource guides that are available free of charge on many library Web sites. Many of these bibliographies are annotated and can be used not only for instruction but as a collection tool. A good starting point would be the Business Reference Services at the Library of Congress. (http://lcweb.loc.gov/rr/business/index1.html). As more libraries share their resources in this way and as more use is made of searching other institutions' online catalogs, smaller libraries with more limited budgets will be able to access the same bibliographic information as larger repositories. Furthermore, this information can be supplemented by accessing publishers' lists via the Web.

Other useful sources for annotated bibliographies include the following.

"Best Business Books [Year]," **Library Journal.** Annual feature, published in March.

Wynar, Bohdan S. **American Reference Books Annual**. Littleton, Colo.: Libraries Unlimited, 1970– . Annual.

Every year, *Library Journal* lists and annotates some of the best books of the year in a survey of the past year's trends in business publishing. Written by a subject specialist (in recent years Susan S. DiMattia, a business information consultant), "Business Books" lists by subject both circulating and reference titles judged by the author to be superior or significant.

The emphasis is different in *American Reference Books Annual (ARBA)*. First, only reference works are included. Second, whereas "Business Books" is a selective, subjective list of the most highly acclaimed titles, *ARBA* includes publications of varying quality. Some are first-rate; others are clearly inferior. What makes *ARBA* so useful are the detailed, critical reviews, some of which discuss the strengths and weaknesses of specific titles at considerable length. Each review is signed, and citations to earlier reviews in library journals are included. By including both so-called good and bad titles accompanied by thoughtful evaluations, *ARBA* allows librarians to make informed decisions about publications to avoid as well as those to collect. *ARBA* is one of the many publications that is also online. This service, available at http://www.ARBAonline.com, includes coverage from 1997 until the present and contains over 500 subject areas and titles from more than 400 publishers. Being available online makes an invaluable collection development tool more user-friendly and more current.

Although standard library publications such as *Library Journal, Choice*, and *Wilson Library Bulletin* publish reviews of current business publications, the following periodicals are particularly useful for tips on business research techniques and for information about relevant publications.

Special Libraries Association. Business and Finance Division. **BF Bulletin.** Los Angeles: The Division. 1988– . Triannual.

Business Information Alert: Sources Strategies, and Signposts for Information Professionals. Chicago: Alert Publications, 1996– . Web version available at http://www. alertpub.com/hpbia.html. (Former title: *Business Information Alert: What's New in Business Publications, Databases, and Research Techniques,* by the same publisher.)

The *BF Bulletin* is the official newsletter of the largest division of the Special Libraries Association. Like most such publications, it includes news of Division activities and of its members, but what makes it most useful is its collection of articles, bibliographies, and suggestions for locating difficult-to-find information. An issue may, for example, explain business concepts such as market share and beta coefficients and then proceed to identify sources that contain them. The articles cover topics as diverse as "Using the Business Pages of the *New York Times*," "Selected Sources of Time Series and Forecasts," and "Tracking Emerging Equity Markets on the World Wide Web." A regular column, "Recent U.S. Government Publications of Interest to Business and Finance Librarians," lists and annotates selected documents. The emphasis throughout is on practical information.

Readers are encouraged to share their experiences, both good and bad, in looking for specific types of information or in using new business publications. Occasionally, the Division's publisher relations committee will correspond with publishers about titles with which librarians are dissatisfied or that are essentially recycled versions of earlier works, and frequently the publishers' responses are printed in the *Bulletin*. Other features include descriptions of specific business libraries and reprints of bibliographies from contributing special, academic, and public libraries. The *Bulletin,* which is included with Division membership and is available to nonmembers at a nominal price, is a forum where business and finance librarians from a wide range of library settings can share their common interests and concerns. It is well worth the subscription price. For members of the division the newsletter is online at the Web page at http://www.slabf.org/.

Business Information Alert (http://www.alertpub.com/hpbia.html) has an intended audience of business information professionals and researchers and is as much a guide as a bibliography. Each issue is not long, but each page contains either analyses of sources, reviews of both electronic and hard copy information, or tips and techniques to help researchers. The regular columns include "From the Editor," "News & Trends," and "New Sources" as well as a leading article, which in the past has ranged from "Small Business: Where to Find Company Information" to "Cross-border Competitive Intelligence." The contributors are from a variety of companies, universities, and libraries, and the information shared is both timely and carefully researched. For those interested in seeing the contents of the publication, the tables of content are viewable at http://www.alertpub.com/contents_bia.html, and one may request a sample copy. It may be advisable to check the sample as the publication is expensive although very informative.

The titles described above are basic reference sources that enable librarians and researchers alike to identify business publications relevant to their interests. Equally important, however, are reference sources that provide quick, factual information. This chapter concludes by examining five major categories of quick reference tools: dictionaries, almanacs, encyclopedias, handbooks, and subject Web pages.

Dictionaries

Business vocabulary can at times be baffling to the uninitiated. The librarian confronted for the first time with such terms as *market segmentation, convertible debentures,* and *beta coefficient* or with such slang as *highlighting, Fannie Mae,* and *golden parachutes* may feel with some justification that standard English and business English are two different languages. Not only librarians but also most business people need to be familiar with terms outside their usual areas especially as functions become blurred and management terminology becomes more cross-disciplined. Many standard dictionaries are, in fact, weak in their coverage of business jargon. As a result, specialized dictionaries are essential to all business collections and must be updated regularly as business terms change frequently. Dictionaries are available for each field of business. There are, for example, dictionaries of insurance, accounting, finance, and real estate. Many of these specialized dictionaries are discussed in the chapters that follow.

General Business Dictionaries

Other business dictionaries provide more general coverage. Some of the best and most widely used general business dictionaries are listed below.

Rosenberg, Jerry M. **Dictionary of Business and Management**. 3rd ed. New York: John Wiley, 1993. 374p.

Terry, John V. **Dictionary for Business and Finance.** 3rd ed. Fayetteville: University of Arkansas Press, 1995. 405p.

Cross, Wilbur. **Prentice Hall Encyclopedic Dictionary of Business Terms**. Englewood Cliffs, N.J.: Prentice Hall, 1995. 472p.

The *Dictionary of Business and Management*, compiled by Jerry M. Rosenberg, defines some 7,500 terms from different fields of business, ranging from accounting to warehousing. Slang and acronyms are included in addition to standard business terms, and definitions are clear and succinct. The emphasis, as in most business dictionaries, is on current usage, and as a result this edition has removed many terms defined in earlier volumes, most of them clustered in the computer and transportation fields. Appendixes present equivalent measures, interest and income tables, and foreign currencies. Although this edition is less comprehensive, it still remains a standard dictionary for business collections.

The third edition of Terry's *Dictionary for Business and Finance* has added more than 200 terms, keeping it current with business usage. Incorporated into the vocabulary lists is the area of business for which the definition is used, for example, statistics, or even whether the same definition is used in more than one field, for example, statistics, economics. This is one of the more comprehensive dictionaries available and also one of the cheapest.

Prentice Hall Encyclopedic Dictionary combines short definitions of terms with more extensive clarifications of what are considered major concepts. In all instances the entries have been chosen because of practical connections with business. Also included are five essays covering management, resources available to an organization, procedures and regulations within an organization, the nature and uses of money, and communications. More than a dictionary but far short of an encyclopedia, the *Prentice Hall Encyclopedic Dictionary* may prove more useful, as a ready reference tool, for the student or business person than for a librarian.

The general business dictionaries discussed thus far are U.S. publications. For coverage of British terms, some of which are considerably different from American usage, at least one British dictionary will prove useful. One of the most recent and inclusive titles is listed below.

The Oxford Dictionary for the Business World. New York: Oxford University Press, 1993. 996p.

The Oxford Dictionary is perhaps more scholarly than other business dictionaries, providing the etymology and usage of terms, brief profiles of leading figures in the business world, and a listing of abbreviations frequently used in business. In addition to the main body of the dictionary are eight appendixes that contain information ranging from world time zones to the cost of mailing a package in England.

Business vocabulary reflects the constant change characteristic of business. In addition, it makes frequent use of specialized jargon and slang, which are also subject to change. As a result, it is important that a collection of business dictionaries be as current as possible. The librarian who does not regularly update business dictionaries is doing library users a disservice. However, although there is no dearth of new business dictionaries, not all are worth collecting. Accordingly, librarians will want to consult many of the bibliographies and guides mentioned in the previous sections to identify some of the best and most useful dictionaries.

Multilingual Business Dictionaries

Although this book emphasizes U.S. business practice, this will often involve interaction with foreign companies and agencies, so it would be derelict to ignore dictionaries that present business terms in a variety of languages. Unlike their general business counterparts, these dictionaries do not include definitions. They are used instead by business people who need to determine the English equivalent of a foreign term or the foreign version of an English phrase.

Harrap's Five Language Business Dictionary. Bromley, Kent: Harrap Books Ltd., 1991. 448p.

Harrap's Five Language Business Dictionary brings together English, German, Spanish, French, and Italian business terms. Each page is arranged in six columns. In the first column are arranged the multilingual integrated alphabetical listings, and this is followed by a column for each of the five translations. This enables the user to get all the translations for each word. The dictionary provides 80,000 translations based on 20,000 words and phrases.

For more intensive coverage of foreign business vocabulary, dictionaries that pair English terms with their equivalents in a specific foreign language are useful. A wide variety of such publications are available; there are, for example, English/German and English/Spanish dictionaries as well as similar works in other languages. A comprehensive collection of all such dictionaries in every language is generally impractical, but each library's collection should, of course, reflect the interests and needs of its own users. Robert Beard of Bucknell University began an excellent site devoted to dictionaries, which has now been transformed into a commercial site providing free dictionaries, language and language-related services, and links to translating services. This is available at http://www.yourdictionary.com/about.html.

Acronyms and Abbreviations Dictionaries

The language of business has its own unique vocabulary, filled with jargon and slang. It also makes frequent use of abbreviations and acronyms, and although some of these designations are commonly recognized, others can be baffling to the librarian or researcher new to the field. Offhand references by patrons to M1, NASDAQ, GNMA, or CFTC are not unusual, and often a librarian must refer to a list of acronyms or abbreviations to comprehend fully a request for assistance. A comprehensive list is available in the following standard reference work.

Bonk, Mary Rose, and Regie E. Carlton. eds. **Acronyms, Initialisms & Abbreviations Dictionary**. 24th ed. Detroit: Gale Research, 1998. 3v.

Acronym Finder. 1988–2003. http://www.acronymfinder.com/. (August 18, 2003).

The *Acronyms, Initialisms & Abbreviations Dictionary* lists over 450,000 acronyms, initialisms, abbreviations, contractions, alphabetic symbols, and other condensed words or phrases. Although all disciplines and fields are represented in the *Dictionary*, many of the items listed are drawn from business and trade or are directly relevant to it. The *Dictionary* is issued in three volumes. The first, which actually consists of three volumes, alphabetically lists acronyms and abbreviations and the words or phrases that they represent. Volume 2, *New Acronyms, Initialisms & Abbreviations*, comprises an inter-edition supplement to volume 1, and the third volume is a *Reverse Acronyms, Initialisms & Abbreviations Dictionary*. By consulting this most comprehensive of acronyms dictionaries, the full-text counterparts of most such business designations can be readily identified.

Acronym Finder is free on the Web at http://www.acronymfinder.com/. It contains about 300,000 terms, not all related to business, and is easily searchable by full or partial entry. For those libraries and individuals not able to afford the *Acronyms, Initialisms & Abbreviations Dictionary,* this may be an adequate substitute.

Almanacs

Almanacs are an essential part of any reference collection, making it possible to find quickly current information about a wide range of subjects. They may, for example, include summary country information, lists of award and prize winners, demographic and economic statistics, chronologies, and directories.

Alsop Ronald., ed. **The Wall Street Journal Almanac.** New York: Ballantine Books, 1998– . Annual.

Godin, Seth. **The Information Please Business Almanac.** Boston: Houghton Mifflin, 1994– . Annual

The *Wall Street Journal Almanac* combines essays and analysis written by the leading journalists from *The Wall Street Journal* with an impressive array of useful statistics. Using it, readers can review the past year's business events, assess the recent performance of specific industries, identify the largest companies in the Dow Jones Indexes, or find the largest announced mergers and acquisitions.

Although some of the information presented is original, most of it has been culled from other sources such as business and trade journals and government documents. Many of these primary sources are, in fact, found in most libraries. Researchers in need of the most current information would do well to consult the original source. The *Almanac* remains extremely useful, however, for finding quick factual information and for identifying the sources in which more detailed or more current information may be found. It is a basic business reference source.

The Information Please Business Almanac also contains a compendium of business facts and statistics ranging from the levels of service and the pricing structure of UPS to financial ratios for selected industries. Included are maps for some of the largest U.S. cities and even a section on the "best times to fly." Additional useful resources are recommended throughout the almanac.

Encyclopedias

Although many disciplines are represented by comprehensive, multivolume encyclopedias, business is not one of them. Instead, the emphasis is on single-volume works that deal with specific fields of business. Some of the best known of these publications are the *Encyclopedia of Banking and Finance*, the *Encyclopedia of Accounting Systems*, and the *Encyclopedia of Investments*. These and several other specialized encyclopedias are discussed in later chapters, but it may be useful to consider here some titles that have more general applications.

Greenwald, Douglas. **Encyclopedia of Economics**. 2nd ed. New York: McGraw-Hill, 1994. 1093p.

Maurer, John G., et al. **Encyclopedia of Business**. Detroit: Gale Research. 1995. 2v.

As was mentioned previously, there is considerable overlap between business and economics. The *Encyclopedia of Economics*, which contains articles written by 191 authors on over 300 different topics, reflects this overlap. In addition to articles on economic theory, it includes many that are directly relevant to business, covering specific investment media, basic statistical measures of economic and business well-being, government agencies responsible for the regulation of business activities, and other topics. "Bond Rating Agencies," for example, describes the history of, basis for, and importance of such ratings and compares the rating categories used by Standard & Poor's and Moody's (Mergent). Much has changed in the field of economics since the publication of the first edition, and as a result some topics have been dropped, new ones have been added, and all entries have been updated. Each article is signed, and frequently suggestions for further reading are included. Subject and contributor indexes are also included.

The objective of the *Encyclopedia of Business* was to create a practical and comprehensive reference book that would provide information on concepts, theories, models, practices, techniques, and ideas used in the business world. The book is written, as far as possible, in nontechnical language, and covers a broad range of subjects readily understandable even to the lay reader. Entries are signed, and all include a further reading list. The *Encyclopedia of Business* is expensive, and smaller libraries may prefer to buy the cheaper specialist volumes.

Handbooks

The difference between single-volume encyclopedias and business handbooks is often negligible. Both are good sources of quick, factual information, but as a rule handbooks tend to cover fewer topics at greater length than do encyclopedias and often presuppose a basic understanding of the subject. The following title represents handbooks that survey business activities.

Hampton, John J., ed. **AMA Management Handbook**. 3rd ed. New York: AMACOM, 1994. Various pagings.

The American Management Association (AMA) is the premier professional association of managers in this country. Among other services, it offers several well-written and useful business titles through its publishing agency, AMACOM. The *AMA Management Handbook* is typical. Although the *Handbook* emphasizes management, it covers other topics as well, including manufacturing; purchasing, transportation, and physical distribution; marketing; information systems and technology; packaging; cost control; and public relations. In this third edition some authors have changed from the previous edition, but the traditional management concepts have been retained. New ideas have been introduced to reflect changing technologies and emerging trends that reflect the changing environment encountered by management organizations. Each chapter is written by an expert and includes graphs, charts, and sample forms. A detailed index is appended. Although the *Handbook* is somewhat more technical than the encyclopedias listed above, it also provides more thorough treatment of the subjects being discussed.

Most handbooks focus on specific business activities such as insurance and accounting. Several specialized handbooks are discussed in chapters 9 through 18; still others can be identified by consulting standard business bibliographies and guides.

Internet Resources

No one business Internet site will answer all questions, and despite the belief that "everything is on the Web," libraries and researchers still need print products. This section provides a description of several Web sites that provide free information and links to other sources. The products discussed here are search engines and general sites; other more specific sites are listed in the following chapters. Not included are subscription databases.

Google. 1998. http://www.google.com/. (Accessed August 17, 2003).

CNNmoney. ©2001. http://money.cnn.com/. (Accessed August 17, 2003).

According to its Web page, The Google search engine at this time searches 3,083,324,652 pages for results when a query is entered. Everyone knows the basics of searching in Google: Put in words and links to Web pages will appear. But Google also allows one to search for images, within news groups, and for pdf documents, often a rich source of business information. For detail on the various ways of searching and using special options such as the translator and tool bar, information is provided at http://www.google.com/about.html. Google also provides lists of U.S. and international news services as well as a directory listing that somewhat resembles that of Yahoo (http://www.yahoo.com). In the business directory listing there are 51 topics ranging from accounting to wholesale trade.

CNNmoney is one of the best known business news services, with enough information on the site to keep researchers current with today's business material. The site supplies breaking news and commentaries as well as stock quotes, links to calculators, and basic guides to everything from investing in mutual funds to the best way to finance a new car.

Most university libraries have always prepared bibliographies and guides for their own students to use. Now almost all libraries in the world have a Web presence, making it easier to find and use these materials. The links in figure 1.3 are an example of guides and Web links maintained by academic libraries.

Rutgers Business Cyber Library	http://business.rutgers.edu/cyber/
American University Library	http://www.library.american.edu/subject/business/index.html
Gelman Library, George Washington University	http://www.gwu.edu/gelman/ref/readyref/
Goizueta Business Library, Emory University	http://business.library.emory.edu/researchaids/researchaids_index.html
UT Libraries Online (Austin)	http://www.lib.utexas.edu/refsites/business.html
Lippincot Library @ Wharton	http://gethelp.library.upenn.edu/guides/business/businesswebsites.html
New York Public Library	http://www.nypl.org/research/sibl/index.html

Figure 1.3. Some subject guide collections and Web links maintained by academic libraries.

Also provided by libraries and librarians are the various "Quick Reference" or "Virtual Reference" desks. These are frequently assessed for content and free material and are a good place to begin research on the Web. Figure 1.4 is an example of a service provided by a research library.

REFERENCE DEPARTMENT — DAVIS LIBRARY

Quick Reference - Business & Economics

General Topics

Area & Cultural Studies

Arts & Humanities

Government Information

Science & Technology

Social Sciences

Accounting and Taxes
Banking
Bankruptcy
Bonds
Business & General Forms
Codes
Company Directories
Company Financial
Economic Indicators
Economics
Electronic Journals
Exchanges

Futures, Options, Commodities
Industry
Initial Public Offerings (IPOs)
Insurance
International Business Resources
Journals & Newspapers
Market Analysis
Market Indices
Marketing/Advertising
Mergers & Acquisitions
Mutual Funds
News Services

Non-Profit Organizations
Patents, Trademarks & Standards
Personal Finance
Real Estate
Small Business
Statistics
Stock Quotes
Stock Research
Ticker Symbols

Can't Find What You Are Looking For? How Can We Help You?

Figure 1.4. Quick Reference maintained by the reference staff of Davis Library, University of North Carolina at Chapel Hill. http://www.lib.unc.edu/reference/quick/.
Reproduced courtesy of the Walter Royal Davis Library.

Each of these headings is connected to no more than 12 annotated Web links (see figure 1.5).

REFERENCE DEPARTMENT — DAVIS LIBRARY

Quick Reference - Business & Economics - Stock Research

Historical Stock Prices -- Silicon Investor. Prices back to 1968
> For stock information by industry - click on stocktalk. For news about the market click on Market Insight. For historical stock information enter, in the search box, the name of a company. Current information appears but check directly above where this begins - there are links for historical prices, insider trading activity and expected earnings.

Hoover's StockScreener
> Choose your criteria to create your own lists of stocks.

RiskGrades
> Check the risk values of one stock or a portfolio. "What-if scenarios let you see whether... [certain trades] would improve your risk/return and diversification profile". (Forbes Web Review)

Stock Research Sites on the Web -- Foster Business Library, University of Wahington
> "This site contains evaluations of free stock research sites on the Web. There has been no attempt to apply any qualitative or quantitative ranking to the sites, rather, this lists the features available on the different sites along with some evaluative comments on usability and design.

Stock Splits and Stock Dividends Equity Analytics, Ltd.
> Stock splits and dividends back to 1996. Plus a calendar of upcoming splits.

Figure 1.5. Annotated links in the Stock Research Section of Quick Reference.
Reproduced courtesy of the Walter Royal Davis Library.

Although the basic reference sources described in this chapter are important, they are by no means the only useful sources of business information. The next six chapters treat business information available in other formats, including directories, periodicals and newspapers, loose-leaf services, government documents, statistics, databases, and Internet resources.

2

Directories

Background

Among frequently asked business reference questions are those involving the identification of the manufacturers of particular products, the addresses and telephone numbers of specific companies, the names of their key executives, and a listing of their key competitors. Directories, which supply the answers to these and many other questions, are of prime importance in business reference. At a minimum, a good business directory will include the names, addresses, and telephone numbers of the companies it lists as well as the names of their chief executives and, often, a phrase or code describing the products or services offered by each company. Directories are now available in diverse formats from a variety of vendors. The original publishers, for the most part, still issue the directories in hard copy but may also deliver them as a CD-ROM and as a Web product. They may also be available as part of packages compiled by the publishers and as contracts made with independent vendors such as Dialog and LexisNexis. These are the "established" directories that many of us have become used to handling. Although most of the electronic products have added features to enhance searching and retrieval of information, the format chosen will depend on available funding, licensing arrangements, and technical considerations. More recent additions in this area are free and "for fee" Web products from both what we think of as established publishers and from Web-only producers. Although not everything is on the Web, a good supply of consistent information is now freely available.

Business Establishments Not Listed

Many questions requiring the use of business directories are easy to answer. Verifying the address of Union Carbide's corporate headquarters or the name of the president of General Electric is reference service at its most basic. Not all such seemingly simple requests for business information, however, are so quickly satisfied. It is an inescapable fact of reference life that frequently the company about which you need to find information is not listed in the "standard," printed commercial directories. According to Figure 710 of the 2002 *Statistical Abstract,* there were in 1998 some 17.4 million business enterprises in the United States,[1] and according to the same figure there were over 218,000 new startups from 1996 to 1998. (See figure 2.1, page 22.)

No. 710. Number of Returns, Receipts, and Net Income by Type of Business: 1980 to 1998

[8,932 represents 8,932,000. Covers active enterprises only. Figures are estimates based on sample of unaudited tax returns; see Appendix III. Minus sign (-) indicates net loss]

Item	Number of returns (1,000)			Business receipts [2] (bil. dol.)			Net income (less loss) [3] (bil. dol.)		
	Nonfarm proprietorships [1]	Partnerships	Corporations	Nonfarm proprietorships [1]	Partnerships	Corporations	Nonfarm proprietorships [1]	Partnerships	Corporations
1980	8,932	1,380	2,711	411	286	6,172	55	8	239
1985	11,929	1,714	3,277	540	349	8,050	79	-9	240
1989	14,298	1,635	3,628	693	524	10,440	133	14	389
1990	14,783	1,554	3,717	731	541	10,914	141	17	371
1991	15,181	1,515	3,803	713	539	10,963	142	21	345
1992	15,495	1,485	3,869	737	571	11,272	154	43	402
1993	15,848	1,468	3,965	757	627	11,814	156	67	498
1994	16,154	1,494	4,342	791	732	12,858	167	82	577
1995	16,424	1,581	4,474	807	854	13,969	169	107	714
1996	16,955	1,654	4,631	843	1,042	14,890	177	145	806
1997	17,176	1,759	4,710	870	1,297	15,890	187	168	915
1998	17,409	1,855	4,849	918	1,534	16,543	202	187	838

[1] In 1980, represents individually owned businesses, including farms; thereafter, represents only nonfarm proprietors, i.e., business owners.   [2] Excludes investment income except for partnerships and corporations in finance, insurance, and real estate before 1998. After 1997 finance and insurance, real estate, and management of companies included investment income for partnerships and corporations. Starting 1985, investment income no longer included for S corporations.   [3] Net income (less loss) is defined differently by form of organization, basically as follows: (a) Proprietorships: Total taxable receipts less total business deductions, including cost of sales and operations, and certain capital expensing, excluding charitable contributions and owners' salaries; (b) Partnerships: Total taxable receipts (including investment income except capital gains) less deductions, including cost of sales and operations and certain payments to partners, excluding charitable contributions, oil and gas depletion, and certain capital expensing; (c) Corporations: Total taxable receipts (including investment income, capital gains, and income from foreign subsidiaries deemed received for tax purposes, except for S corporations beginning 1985) less business deductions, including cost of sales and operations, depletion, certain capital expensing, and officers' compensation excluding S corporation charitable contributions and investment expenses starting 1985; net income is before income tax.

Source: U.S. Internal Revenue Service, *Statistics of Income*, various publications.

Figure 2.1 Number of Returns, Receipts, and Net Income by Types of Business: 1980 to 1998.
Reproduced from the Bureau of the Census, *Statistical Abstract,*
http://www.census.gov/prod/2002pubs/01statab/business.pdf.

One of the standard business directories found in most reference collections, Dun & Bradstreet's *Million Dollar Directory,* lists about 1 percent of U.S. enterprises. Two of the more comprehensive listings of American businesses are described below.

References USA Business. Omaha, Neb.: infoUSA, 1999– . CD-ROM. (Information available at http://www.referenceusa.com/ for all subscriptions.)

D&B International Business Locator. New Yoek: Dun & Bradstreet, n.d. CD-ROM. (Also available as a Web product from Dun & Bradstreet and as an online service from Dialog, where it is known as Dun's Market Identifiers, File 516.)

Reference USA Business covers about 12 million U.S. businesses and organizations compiled from nationwide yellow pages and other sources. The *International Business Locator* covers a total of 28 million businesses.

So, at least some of the time, print and electronic directories will not answer what initially seem to be very simple requests for directory information.

In some instances, a company may not be listed because it is too small. A two-person accounting firm in Oshkosh, Wisconsin, is not likely to be included in any of the standard print or electronic business directories. Neither are enough people employed nor enough money earned for the firm to be included in a national or even a state directory. Furthermore, it provides a service rather than a product, and directory listings for businesses in the service sector are generally more difficult to find than for those in the manufacturing sector.

Public and Private Companies

Another important distinction must be kept in mind when searching for company information: the difference between public and private companies. A public or publicly traded company is one that sells stock to the public and is in effect publicly owned. The federal government and most state governments have very strict laws about information that these companies must provide, both to the government and to stockholders. As a result, information on these companies is relatively easy to find. If, however, the company operates only in one state, then information is required to be provided only to that state. In such a case there will be no national listing and so availability of data will depend on state regulations.

A private or privately held company, also referred to as a closely held company, is one that does not sell stock to the public. It is usually exempt from the detailed reporting required of public companies and, as a result, information about many of these companies will be difficult to find. Some directories include information about the larger private companies, but as a rule, private companies are less often listed in directories than are public companies.

Parent Companies, Subsidiaries, Divisions, and Affiliates

Failure to find a company listing in a major national directory does not mean that no listing exists. Although the firm might be a small, privately held company about which nothing in print can be found, it is also possible that it is a subsidiary or a division of another, larger company. The librarian looking for the address of Rohr, Inc., an aerostructures manufacturer, is contending with this problem. One might reasonably expect to find it listed in all of the major national business directories. Not all directories include it, however, because it is a subsidiary of a larger company, the BFGoodrich Company, Inc. Thus, in these days of corporate takeovers and conglomerates, it is entirely possible that the company being sought is owned by yet another company. And while some subsidiaries and divisions are cited separately in basic business directories, not all of them are.

A parent company is a company that operates and controls other separately chartered businesses. Smithfield Foods, Inc., is the parent company of Gwaltney of Smithfield, Ltd., and Sunnyland Inc., for example, and Sony Corporation is a parent company that owns and operates several separately chartered companies, including Sony USA.

A subsidiary is a company that, although separately chartered, is owned or controlled by another company. Normally, the parent company owns at least 50 percent of its subsidiary's stock. If all of the stock is owned by the parent company, the subsidiary is referred to as wholly owned. Sony Electronics Inc. is a subsidiary of Sony USA because, although it is a separately established business, Sony USA owns and controls it. Subsidiaries began as separate businesses and have been acquired, taken over, or spun off by the parent company. Columbia Pictures, for example, was incorporated in New York in 1924, acquired by Coca Cola in 1982, and then in 1989 taken over by Sony Corp. To further complicate matters, subsidiaries often have subsidiaries of their own. Sony Corporation USA, for example, has several subsidiaries, ranging from Sony Electronics Inc., to Sony Music Entertainment Inc. Although major subsidiaries may be listed separately in some of the basic business directories, often it is necessary to consult special directories of subsidiaries to find information about them.

A division is a functional area or activity within the company. Unlike a subsidiary, it is not a separately chartered business. LifeSavers Co. and Fleischmann's Foods, for example, are divisions of Nabisco Foods Group.

Finally, an affiliate is a separately chartered business whose shares are owned by one or more companies, with the level of ownership by any one company generally less than 50 percent.

Most of the time, directory inquiries will be for large companies that can be easily located. If, however, a company name does not sound familiar or if a search for it has proven unsuccessful, answers to the following questions should be sought:

1. How big is the company? Many publishers require that a company's assets, sales, or number of employees meet certain minimum standards for it to be listed.

2. Is the company public or private? Private companies are often not included in business directories; public companies usually are.

3. What is the company's business? Companies that manufacture or sell products are generally better represented in directories than are those that sell services.

4. Is the company a subsidiary, a division, or an affiliate of another company, or a foreign holding? If so, it may be necessary to consult a directory that lists these separately or links them with the appropriate parent companies.

With the answers to these questions in hand, the information search strategy can be modified, and other more specialized directories can be consulted, online directory files can be accessed, or the information can be sought from government agencies and other organizations.

To reiterate: Most directory questions are simple to answer. With a few exceptions, usually caused by one or more of the above factors, they can be answered using the directories described in this chapter.

SIC and NAICS Systems

In addition to listing company addresses, telephone numbers, and officers, many directories also categorize companies by the activities in which they are engaged. Often these activities are designated by the use of a government-devised system of numeric codes. Since the late 1930s these definitions have been taken from the Standard Industrial Classification system (SIC), which was updated through revisions although manufacturing remained as its base. The last *Standard Industrial Classification Manual* was issued in 1987. Now North America has a new system for classifying businesses and reporting industry statistics, the North American Industry Classification System (NAICS.) This is a complete and fundamental revision of the system used to classify businesses by industry and was developed jointly by the United States, Canada, and Mexico to standardize data listing throughout North America. This new system has been devised to include new technologies and the growing influence of the service sectors, which have become more influential in the economy than manufacturing.[2]

The Standard Industrial Classification System

The SIC attempts to classify all business establishments by the types of products or services they make available. Establishments engaged in the same activity, whatever their size or type of ownership, are assigned the same SIC code.

SIC Hierarchy

The Standard Industrial Classification system is divided into 11 broad divisions, such as "Construction," "Retail Trade," and "Agriculture, Forestry, and Fishing." These divisions are subdivided into 99 two-digit major groups. "Major groups" are subdivided into three-digit "individual groups," and individual groups into four-digit "industry codes," which is the designation most often used in directories. As figure 2.2 indicates, the classification becomes more precise as more digits are added.

SIC Code	Categories	Division, Group, and Industry
Division E	Division	Transportation, Communications, Electric, Gas, and Sanitary service
48	Major group	Communications
481	Individual group	Telephone Communications
4812	Industry	Radiotelephone Communications

Figure 2.2. Example of the SIC hierarchy.

For example, one can move from Division E, "Transportation, Communications, Electric, Gas, and Sanitary service," to major group 48, "Communications," to individual group 481, "Telephone Communications," to industry code 4812, "Radiotelephone Communications," the SIC for establishments "primarily engaged in providing two-way radiotelephone communications services, such as cellular telephone services" (see figure 2.3, page 26).

Someone seeking to identify the major manufacturers of these services would simply turn to the SIC section of the directory and compile a list of all of the companies grouped under SIC code 4812.

Although SIC 4812 is the proper designation for radiotelephone communications, it is not safe to assume that all companies grouped in directories under that code operate this service. They do not. They may specialize in providing telephone paging and beeper services or in leasing telephone lines or other methods of telephone transmission, such as optical fiber lines and microwave or satellite facilities, or reselling the use of such methods to others.. Librarians should keep these multiple-product entries in mind when using directories, realizing that in many instances a four-digit SIC code may be misleading. Good reference practice requires not only that the proper SIC code be identified but also that any other products sharing the same SIC code be noted. Often, a four-digit SIC code may include too many different products to be really useful.

Division E: Transportation, Communications, Electric, Gas, And Sanitary Services

48: Communications

481: Telephone Communications

4812: Radiotelephone Communications

Establishments primarily engaged in providing two-way radiotelephone communications services, such as cellular telephone services. This industry also includes establishments primarily engaged in providing telephone paging and beeper services and those engaged in leasing telephone lines or other methods of telephone transmission, such as optical fiber lines and microwave or satellite facilities, and reselling the use of such methods to others. Establishments primarily engaged in furnishing telephone answering services are classified in Services, Industry 7389.

Beeper (radio pager) communications services

Cellular telephone services

Paging services: radiotelephone

Radiotelephone communications

Figure 2.3. Example of the SIC hierarchy.

Taken from the *Standard Industrial Classification Manual* hierarchy, http://155.103.6.10/cgi-bin/sic/sicser5.

Although most directories that feature SIC listings also include a brief list and description of the SIC codes, by far the most detailed information can be found in the *Standard Industrial Classification Manual*, a basic business reference source.

U.S. Office of Management and Budget. **Standard Industrial Classification Manual**. Springfield, Va.: National Technical Information Service, 1987. 703p.

The *SIC Manual* consists of lists and descriptions, arranged by divisions, of industries, products, and services. Figure 2.3 is the *SIC Manual's* entry for SIC 4812.

An alphabetical index lists all products and services featured in the main part of the Manual, including for each item its SIC code and the division to which it is assigned. Using it, one can determine the appropriate SIC for a particular product or service. If a description of the code itself is essential, or if one wants to find out what other products or services have been assigned the same SIC code, one can turn to the front of the volume. Taking advantage of the Web, one can use http://www.osha.gov/oshstats/sicser.html to search the 1987 version of the *SIC Manual* by keyword, to access descriptive information for a specified four-digit SIC, and to examine the manual's structure.

The North American Industry Classification System

On April 9, 1997, the Office of Management and Budget (OMB) announced the adoption of a new industry classification replacing the Standard Industrial Classification (SIC). The objectives for the 1997 revision were to identify new industries and to reorganize the system according to a more consistent economic principle, according to types of production activities performed rather than the mixture of production-based and market-based categories in the SIC.

Some of the main reasons that NAICS is considered a better system are identified in a flier published by the Economic Classification Policy Committee:

Relevancy   NAICS identifies more industries that contribute to today's economy; over 350 new industries and nine new service industry sectors. The Manufacturing sector is restructured to recognize new high tech industries.

Comparability   NAICS was developed by the United States, Canada, and Mexico to produce comparable data.

Consistency   NAICS uses a consistent principle: businesses that use similar production processes are grouped together.

Adaptability   NAICS will be reviewed every five years, so classsifications and information will keep up with the changing economy.[3]

Within the NAICS system the names of the groupings are different than those in the SIC system. NAICS calls the highest level of aggregation in the system a sector; the SIC referred to this grouping as a division. Other changes have been made, as shown in figure 2.4.

NAICS		SIC	
2-digit	Sector	Division	Letter
3-digit	Subsector	Major Group	2-digit
4-digit	Industry Group	Industry Group	3-digit
5-digit	NAICS Industry	Industry	4-digit
6-digit	National	N/A	N/A

Figure 2.4. NAICS versus SIC: Structure and names.
Taken from http://www.census.gov/epcd/www/naicsdev.htm.

NAICS Hierarchy

NAICS uses a six-digit coding system to identify particular industries and their placement in the hierarchical structure of the system. The longer code accommodates the larger number of sectors and allows more flexibility in designating subsectors. The first two digits identify with the sectors, the third denotes the subsector, the fourth designates the industry group, the fifth defines the NAICS industry, and the sixth digit signifies the national industry. The international NAICS agreement fixes only the first five digits of the code. The sixth digit adapts to user needs in the three countries. Thus at the five-digit level the United States, Canada, and Mexico will use the same codes, and any differences will be reflected in the sixth digit. (See figure 2.5, page 28.)

NAICS level	Example #1		Example #2	
	NAICS code	Description	NAICS code	Description
Sector	31-33	Manufacturing	51	Information
Subsector	334	Computer and electronic product manufacturing	513	Broadcasting and telecommunications
Industry group	3346	Manufacturing and reproduction of magnetic and optical media	5133	Telecommunications
Industry	33461	Manufacturing and reproduction of magnetic and optical media	51332	Wireless telecommunications carriers, except satellite
U.S. Industry	334611	Reproduction of software	513321	Paging

Figure 2.5. Two examples of the NAICS hierarchy.
Reproduced from http://www.census.gov/epcd/www/naicscod.htm.

Figure 2.6 shows the differences between the SIC and the NAICS. A six-digit system was adopted for NAICS to provide for increased flexibility.

Division title	Sector title
Agriculture, Forestry, and Fishing	Agriculture, Forestry, Fishing, and Hunting
Mining	Mining
Construction	Construction
Manufacturing	Manufacturing
Transportation, Communications, and Public Utilities	Utilities
	Transportation and Warehousing
Wholesale Trade	Wholesale Trade
Retail Trade	Retail Trade
	Accommodation and Food Services
Finance, Insurance, and Real Estate	Finance and Insurance
	Real Estate and Rental and Leasing
Services	Information
	Professional, Scientific, and Technical Services
	Administrative and Support and Waste Management and Remediation Services
	Educational Services
	Health Care and Social Assistance
	Arts, Entertainment, and Recreation
	Other Services (except Public Administration)
Public Administration	Public Administration
None (previously, categories within each division)	Management of Companies and Enterprises

Figure 2.6. SIC divisions versus NAICS sectors.
Taken from http://www.census.gov/epcd/www/pdf/naicsdat.pdf.

NAICS United States is the first classification system that is production based, that is, units that have similar production processes are grouped in the same industry. NAICS provides 1,170 detailed industry classifications, which is a 15 percent increase in classifications from the 1987 SIC system. The NAICS system also replaces or revises some 60 percent of the previously accessible SIC industries. "It provides 358 new industries the SIC did not identify, 390 that are revised from their SIC counterparts, and 422 that continue substantially unchanged. The result is expanded and revised industry classifications that mirror businesses in our modern economy."[4] (See Figure 2.7.)

```
Semiconductor machinery manufacturing
Fiber optic cable manufacturing
Reproduction of computer software
Manufacture of compact discs except software
Convenience stores
Gas stations with convenience food
Warehouse clubs
Food/health supplement stores
Pet supply stores
Pet care services
Cable networks
Satellite communications
Paging
Cellular and other wireless communications
Telecommunication resellers
Credit card issuing
Temporary help supply
Telemarketing bureaus
Interior design services
Industrial design services
Hazardous waste collection
HMO medical centers
Continuing care retirement commmunities
Casino hotels
Casinos
Other gambling industries
Bed and breakfast inns
Limited service restaurants
Automotive oil change and lubrication shops
Diet and weight reducing centers
```

Figure 2.7. Selected new U.S. industries being identified in NAICS.
Taken from htttp://www.census.gov/epcd/www/naicsind.htm.

For more detailed material about the NAICS system and a forthcoming North American Product Classification System (NAPCS), updated information is available on the Web page at http://www.census.gov/epcd/www/naics.html and also at http://www.naics.com. Although there is an online searchable index to the NAICS codes and descriptions at http://www.census.gov/epcd/naics02, the *NAICS Manual* is available in hard copy and like the *SIC Manual* will probably prove indispensable.

North American Industry Classification System: United States, 2002. Washington, D.C.: Executive Office of the President, Office of Management and Budget, [Lanham, Md.: Bernan Press; Springfield, Va.: National Technical Information Service, distributor; Washington, D.C.: Superintendent of Documents, Government Printing Office, distributor], 2002. 1419p.

NAICS 2 is a revision of the original NAICS. It includes substantial changes in the construction and wholesale trade classifications. New entries have been created for Internet service providers and Web search portals, as well as Internet publishing and broadcasting. NAICS will be reviewed every five years, so that classifications keep up with changing industries.

Although the Standard Industrial Classification system has been officially replaced by the NAICS system, it has not yet been fully implemented, especially by commercial publishers. SIC codes are still frequently used in standard business directories, although many are now combining both systems. It is therefore still necessary to understand and be able to use both systems.

Basic Business Directories

There are several standard business directories with which most reference librarians are familiar: *Standard & Poor's Register of Corporations, Directors, and Executives*, the *Million Dollar Directory*, and *Thomas Register of American Manufacturers and Thomas Register Catalog File*. *CorpTech* is another well-known directory that publishes data on one of America's strongest business segments, high-tech manufacturing, development, and services; companies that make, develop, and provide services related to everything from lasers to computers, and from biotech products to advanced materials. Also very popular since its inception in 1991 are the series of *Hoover's Handbooks*, which contain reliable company information including in-depth profiles. Titles include *Hoover's Handbook of American Business, Hoover's Handbook of World Business, Hoover's Handbook of Emerging Companies, Hoover's Handbook of Private Companies, Hoover's Handbooks Index, and Hoover's Master List of Major U.S. Companies.* Although not quite so well known, *the Standard Directory of Advertisers* is also helpful and is used heavily by those who are familiar with it. There are other directories that concentrate on certain subjects ranging from banks and insurance companies to investment managers and security dealers. All of these business directories deserve close examination. Some are examined in this chapter, and others are explored in the more subject-specific chapters.

Standard & Poor's Register of Corporations, Directors, and Executives. New York: Standard & Poor's, 1928– . 3v. Annual, with supplements.

This publication is also offered as a CD-ROM, a diskette, magnetic tape, a batch access product, and a Web product. On the Web it is available as part of *Standard & Poor's NetAdvantage,* which brings together in one easy-to-use interface 10 of Standard & Poor's products: *Stock Reports, Industry Surveys, Corporation Records, The Register, Stock Guide, Bond Guide, Earnings Guide, The Outlook, Mutual Fund Reports,* and *Dividend Record.* The *Register* is also marketed through the online vendors Dialog, CompuServ, and LexisNexis.

Standard & Poor's Register of Corporations, Directors, and Executives is a three-volume annual, updated by three cumulated supplements. Volume 1 lists, by company name, some 75,000 businesses. Although a number of Canadian and international businesses are included, the emphasis is on U.S. companies. Each listing includes company name, address, and telephone number; names and titles of principal officers; the names of the company's primary accounting, bank, and law firms; a description of and the SIC codes for the company's major products or services; and, when available, annual sales and number of employees. In addition, if the company is publicly held, the exchanges on which the company's stock is traded are also noted. Finally, divisions and subsidiaries are listed under the parent name unless they are so large that they merit a separate entry.

Volume 2 is a biographical directory, which includes brief company affiliation and biographical information on 437,500 company officers, directors, and other principals. Usually included are year of birth, college attended and date of graduation, current position and business address, home address, e-mail address, fraternal memberships, and organizations and/or companies of which the individual is a director.

The third volume comprises indexes listing Standard Industrial Classification codes and the companies categorized under each code; a geographic index; lists of new additions to the directory, an obituary section; and a corporate family index that lists parent companies, divisions, subsidiaries, and affiliates.

Although the *Register* lists fewer companies than the *Million Dollar Directory* or *Thomas Register*, it lists many companies that the other directories do not contain. In addition, it often includes officers who are ranked farther down the executive hierarchy than president or vice president. This can be particularly useful when looking for the name of a company sales director or purchasing officer.

D & B Million Dollar Directory. Bethlehem, Pa.: Dun & Bradstreet, 1959– . 5v. Annual.

Dun & Bradstreet also offers many choices for accessing information. The *Million Dollar Directory* is alternatively available as *D&B Million Dollar Database, D&B Million Dollar Directory®—Top 50,000 Companies, D&B Million Dollar Disc™,* and the *D&B Million Dollar Disc Plus™.*

The *Million Dollar Directory* is another standard business directory, whose scope and arrangement have changed several times during the past decade. At present, it consists of five volumes. The first three volumes alphabetically list some 160,000 American public and private companies, which must meet one of the following criteria: they must be a headquarters or single location having a tangible net worth exceeding $500,000, 250+ employees at the location, or $25+ million in sales volume. The fourth and fifth volumes are geographic and industry indexes. The *D&B Million Dollar Directory®—Top 50,000 Companies* is a subset of this material and can be bought individually. The *D&B Million Dollar Disc* supplies data on 240,000 leading public and private U.S. companies with sales of more than $5 million or 100+ employees or branch locations with more than 500 employees. *D&B Million Dollar Disc Plus* provides access to information on 400,000 leading public and private U.S. companies. The criteria for inclusion are sales exceeding $3 million or 50+ employees and branch locations with more than 500 employees. The CD-ROM version of this product also contains a more complete listing of directors as well as key executives' biographies. Both CD-ROMs are issued quarterly or annual updates are available. The *Directory* is also a Web product.

Each company listing in the *Million Dollar Directory* includes the name, address, and telephone number of the company; the company's state of incorporation; titles and names of key executives; categories of products and services offered; SIC code(s); approximate annual sales; and number of employees.

The first index, or "Series Cross-Reference by Geography" volume, lists businesses geographically by state and then by city or town. With this one can identify all of the major businesses in any city, ranging from New York to Hoople, North Dakota.

The second index volume, which lists businesses by industry classification, is equally important. By using it, one can identify the major manufacturers of specific products; by checking under SIC code 2067 one can compile a list of the major manufacturers of chewing gum in the United States.

Librarians are sometimes surprised to learn that Dun & Bradstreet does not actually sell its directories to subscribers; rather, it leases them. Unless special arrangements are made, the superseded editions must be returned to the publisher as soon as the new editions are received. Libraries that can make a strong case for retaining superseded editions—generally academic or research libraries that emphasize their importance for scholarly or historical research—are usually allowed to keep them. Each library must, however, receive permission from the publisher to do so. If the publisher agrees, the library must sign a contract promising that the superseded volumes will not be sent to other libraries and that they will be returned to the publisher should the subscription be canceled.

This leasing arrangement is worth noting because, to some extent, it limits a library's options; subscribing to the *Million Dollar Directory* and other Dun & Bradstreet publications is an all or nothing proposition. Either they must be leased on an annual basis or not at all; a library cannot choose to receive them every second or third year only. This may not be a problem with the *Million Dollar Directory* because most libraries would choose to update it annually in any event, but it can be a problem with some of the other more specialized Dun & Bradstreet directories for which annual updating may not always be feasible.

Thomas Register of American Manufacturers and Thomas Register Catalog File. New York: Thomas Publishing, 1905– . 33v. Annual. (Available also as a CD-ROM product and at http://www.thomasregister.com.)

Thomas Register of American Manufacturers and Thomas Register Catalog File is a multivolume annual that provides information on American manufacturers, distributors, and suppliers. The hard copy is arranged in three main parts. Volumes I through 24 make up the "Products and Services" section, with 63,000 sectors grouped by product and then by state and city. Thomas uses an arrangement called the modified noun system. Companies manufacturing animal cages, for example, are listed under "Cages: Animal," and those making tool chests are listed under "Chests & Cabinets: Tool." Sometimes a product may have several divisions. Collar manufacturers, for example, are grouped under 41 categories, including Collars: Aluminum, Collars: Casing, Collars: Cervical, Collars: Dog & Cat, Collars: Drill, Collars: Float, Collars: Hinge, Collars: Lock, Collars: Self-Locking, Quick Release, Collars: Shirt, Collars: Threaded Bore and Collars: Vacuum!

The three company profiles volumes alphabetically list more than 158,000 companies. Compared to the other directories already discussed, the information given is rather brief, including only company name and address, telephone number, and products. In some instances, a code rating the company's tangible assets is also featured. (Tangible assets are defined as anything that has physical, material substance, such as property, machinery, laboratory equipment, or stocks and bonds.)

Although company entries in both the "Products and Services" and "Company Profiles" volumes are normally rather brief, some companies have paid additional fees to include company logos or fuller product descriptions with their listings. Even more detailed information can be found in the "Catalog File," volumes 27 through 33, which features the catalogs of 2,600 different companies. Information provided varies from company to company but usually includes photographs, product specifications, and other data that can be extremely useful to suppliers, distributors, salespeople, and marketing specialists.

The multiple CD-ROM set contains more than 8,000 catalogs on seven discs, as well as the information contained in the books. Searching is by any variation of the product or service description trademark and can be limited by state, area code, zip code, and word search.

The greatest service performed by Thomas is to offer the complete publication free (registration is required) on the Web at http://www.thomasregister.com. Searching is simple and can be performed using a word search such as "dog collars" rather than the listing "collars: dogs" (see figures 2.8 and 2.9).

Product Headings Found

Search Path: collars
Displaying 1 - 25 of 45 product headings found

		Companies	Catalogs & Websites	Orders & RFQs	CAD Drawings	Send E-mail
1	Collars	83	33	17	4	60
2	Collars: Aluminum	17	9	5	1	15
3	Collars: Casing	4				
4	Collars: Cervical	22	2			3
5	Collars: Custom	13	5	1		10
6	Collars: Dog & Cat	60	8	3		10
7	Collars: Drill	26	6	1		9

Search ThomasRegister
I'm looking for a:
Product or Service
Company Name
Brand Name
Containing the words:
Find It
Want help with your search? Try our Search Tips.

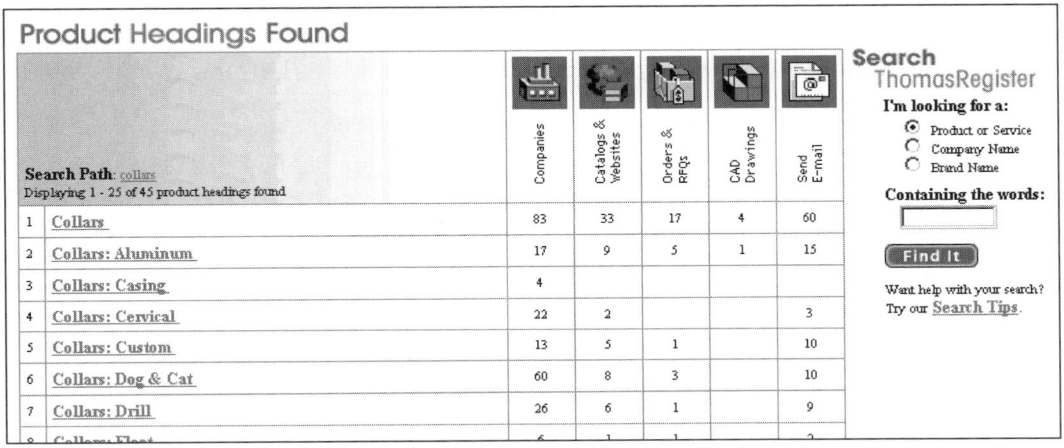

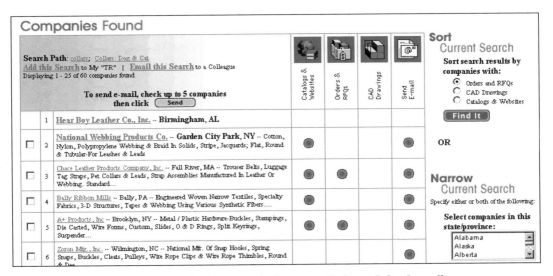

Figure 2.8. List of entries after search for collars. http://www.thomasregister.com.
Reproduced courtesy of the *Thomas Register.*

From the retrieved search list one can link directly to the company's Web site and catalog. There is also information on the accessibility of online ordering and a direct e-mail link.

Companies Found

Search Path: collars; Collars: Dog & Cat
Add this Search to My "TR" | Email this Search to a Colleague
Displaying 1 - 25 of 60 companies found

To send e-mail, check up to 5 companies then click Send

			Catalogs & Websites	Orders & RFQs	CAD Drawings	Send E-mail
	1	Hear Boy Leather Co., Inc. -- Birmingham, AL				
☐	2	National Webbing Products Co. -- Garden City Park, NY -- Cotton, Nylon, Polypropylene Webbing & Braid In Solids, Stripe, Jacquards; Flat, Round & Tubular-For Leashes & Leads	●			●
☐	3	Chace Leather Products Company, Inc. -- Fall River, MA -- Trouser Belts, Luggage Tag Straps, Pet Collars & Leads, Strap Assemblies Manufactured In Leather Or Webbing. Standard...	●	●		●
☐	4	Bally Ribbon Mills -- Bally, PA -- Engineered Woven Narrow Textiles, Specialty Fabrics, 3-D Structures, Tapes & Webbing Using Various Synthetic Fibers....	●			●
☐	5	A+ Products, Inc -- Brooklyn, NY -- Metal / Plastic Hardware-Buckles, Stampings, Die Casted, Wire Forms, Custom, Slides, O & D Rings, Split Keyrings, Suspender...	●	●		●
☐	6	Zoron Mfg., Inc. -- Wilmington, NC -- National Mfr. Of Snap Hooks, Spring Snaps, Buckles, Cleats, Pulleys, Wire Rope Clips & Wire Rope Thimbles, Round				●

Sort Current Search
Sort search results by companies with:
Orders and RFQs
CAD Drawings
Catalogs & Websites
Find It
OR
Narrow Current Search
Specify either or both of the following:
Select companies in this state/province:
Alabama
Alaska
Alberta

Figure 2.9. Sample list of companies from result of search for dog collars. http://www.thomasregister.com. Reproduced courtesy of the *Thomas Register.*

For those libraries that find the S & P *Register* and the *Million Dollar Directory* too expensive for their budgets, the following volumes issued by Hoover's may be adequate for their needs.

Hoover's Handbook of American Business. Austin, Tex.: Hoover's Business Press, 1991– . 2v. Annual.

This two-volume set contains in-depth profiles of 750 influential U.S. companies. including more than 50 of the largest privately owned companies. Included is an overview of the company, historical background, officers, key competitors. and a small amount of financial information.

Hoover's Handbook of Emerging Companies. Austin, Tex.: Hoover's Business Press, 1993– . Annual.

The latest edition covers 500 of the most dynamic American companies, with in-depth profiles of 100 of these. All of the companies in the book are public or are expected to go public shortly. A majority of the companies covered have sales between $10 million and $1 billion, and include both Internet businesses and recent initial public offerings (IPOs).

Hoover's Handbook of Private Companies. Austin, Tex.: Hoover's Business Press, 1994– . Annual.

Includes 750 nonpublic U.S. enterprises with revenues in excess of $600 million, and also includes both large industrial and service corporations.

Although the primary focus of Hoover's is the Internet, it maintains a link to its publishing roots by issuing its information in book and CD-ROM form. The three titles above are a small part of the hard copy collection that can be checked by clicking on the Hoover's Publications button at htt://www.hoovers.com.

In 1995 Hoover's (http://www.hoovers.com) launched its Internet site, and according to its mission statement, it endeavors to "produce business-information products and services of the highest quality, accuracy, and readability. . . . to make that information available whenever, wherever, and however our customers want it through mass distribution at affordable prices." Hoover's does provide high-quality information at a reasonable price and also provides the company "capsules" free. Using only the free services, one can connect to the nearly 15,000 capsules, which in turn will connect to the company annual report, 24 hours delayed SEC filings, and even information on key officers. Also available free are insider trades reports, earnings estimates, and selected news stories. One can also elect to buy research reports from vendors such as Dun & Bradstreet or Experian. A paid membership includes company profiles, in-depth financials, historical financials, full lists of officers, full lists of competitors, real time SEC filings, and the "Business Boneyard," a listing of companies that no longer exist. Individual memberships are available and also commercial licensing. Hoover's continues to expand its offerings through alliances with a variety of data providers such as News Alert and Transium. Hoover's also has distribution agreements with several partners, including AOL, AOL's CompuServe subsidiary, Bloomberg, Dow Jones Interactive, GO.com, LEXIS-NEXIS, Microsoft Investor, Reuters, and Yahoo!

Although there are many Internet portals available, Hoover's continues to provide excellent information at a reasonable price and access to other producers and services on one convenient desktop application. Although only the company section of of the Hoover's publications has been described, the Web page also includes sections on industry, careers, initial public offerings, investment news, and business travel.

CorpTech EXPLORE Database on CD-ROM. Woburn, Mass.: U.S.A.: Corporate Technology Information Services, ©1997– . Quarterly updates.

CorpTech EXPLORE DatabaseGOLD on CD-ROM. Woburn, Mass.: U.S.A.: Corporate Technology Information Services, ©1997– . Quarterly updates.

CorpTech Explore Database. Woburn, Mass.: U.S.A.: Corporate Technology Information Services, ©1997– . Continuously updated.

CorpTech publishes profiles of some 50,000 U.S.-based manufacturers and developers of technology products, including public and private companies in 17 industries: Factory Automation, Biotechnology, Chemicals, Computer Hardware, Defense, Energy, Environmental, Manufacturing Equipment, Advanced Materials, Medical, Pharmaceuticals, Photonics, Computer Software, Subassemblies & Components, Test & Measurement, Telecommunications & Internet, and Transportation. The profiles in the *CorpTech EXPLORE Database on CD-ROM* are the "Standard Profile" compiled by the publisher. This consists of general directory information with a short description of the companies' activities; sales and employment levels; some executive names, titles, and responsibilities; and product listings.

Extended profiles are offered in both the Web product (information available at http://www.corptech.com) and in the *CorpTech EXPLORE DatabaseGOLD on CD-ROM*. These consist of a Standard Profile, a table like that in the "Rankings" report, a "Family" list of the parent company and all operating units, up to four years of sales and employment history, and up to ten years of corporate and executive changes that *CorpTech* has detected as a result of its regular data updating process. One can also link to competitors within the product areas designated to the original company reviewed. Company capsules are provided free at http://www.corptech.com.

Standard Directory of Advertisers: Classified Edition. Wilmette, Ill.: National Register Publishing, 1915– . Annual.

Researchers should be aware that although there is considerable overlap in coverage, each directory has its own unique features, and each lists companies not found in the other directories. The *Standard Directory of Advertisers* is not nearly as well known as the *Million Dollar Directory* or *Standard & Poor's Register* and lists far fewer companies. It is important, though, because it includes companies and organizations not listed in the other directories. The criterion for inclusion in the *SDA* is that the companies must allocate at least $200,000 in annual appropriations for either national or regional advertising campaigns. Companies that are too small to be included in the other basic business directories and some nonprofit organizations that advertise extensively are included in the *Standard Directory of Advertisers*. Featured is information not found in the other directories, including where available, annual advertising appropriations and type(s) of advertising media used, the advertising agency representing the company, and the names of key executives. Companies are arranged by broad industry categories such as "Farm Equipment & Supplies" and "Financial Services," with access facilitated by a company name index.

Another useful feature is the brand name index, which lists brand names and the companies that own them. Since many business reference requests involve identifying the company that manufactures a specific brand, this list of 63,000 trade names can be very helpful. Using it, one can determine that Knob Creek is the trade name for bourbon produced by Fortune Brands Inc., that Pim is the name for a line of hosiery manufactured by the Sara Lee Corporation, and that Goobers candy is manufactured by Nestle.

Plunkett Research publishes one series of specialized directories that deserves mention. These directories concentrate on a specific industry and include an overview of the industry as well as a listing of the companies within that industry. So far publications have been issued for 12 industries, including Engineering & Technology, Entertainment & Media, Energy, Finance & Investments, Retail, Internet & Telecommunications, and Health Care. *Plunkett's Retail Industry Almanac*, for example, includes a short glossary of retail industry terms; markets, statistics, and trends of the retail industry; contacts and Web sites for important government agencies, retail organizations and trade groups; a section on the use of the Internet to sell products; a discussion on the trends in malls with the addresses of major developers and managers; and individual listings for 500 companies.[5]

These directories are only some of the many available, but they are the more generally well known. There are also many specialist directories, some of are described below.

Internet Directories

Although Web sites have been mentioned in descriptions of the directories already described, these were sites for directories already available, at least partially, in other formats. There are other company directory Internet sites that can be used to access a startling amount of information and at least for the moment are free to the user. Discussed here are some of these directories

CorporateInformation (http://www.corporateinforamtion.com) started out as a personal collection of sites and links built and maintained by George Regnery of the Winthrop Corp., but it has grown to be one of the best meta sites for finding information on private companies, as well as for international firms. One can search by industry or country and by state in the United States, or simply by company name. Included are links to corporate information from 127 countries. Choosing the country Argentina leads one to 34 links with economic, stock, and industry information as well as a list of the top10 companies by market capitalization, which then links directly to the research reports from *Wright Investors' Service*.

The Small Business Administration compiles the *PRO-Net Database* (http://pro-net.sba.gov/pro-net/search.html), an Internet-based database of information on more than 171,000 small, disadvantaged, and women-owned businesses.. Businesses profiled on the *Pro-Net* system can be searched by SIC codes, key words, location, quality certifications, business type, and ownership race and gender. Results include company names and contact information, name of owner, annual revenues, and status of owner such as, black, Asian, and Hispanic.

Pharmaceutical Online (http://www.pharmaceuticalonline.com/) is a Web portal that serves the needs of pharmaceutical professionals. The site includes a searchable directory that gives not only an address but frequently a contact person, along with a full list of the company's products. As well as full or partial company name entry, searching is also possible by both broad and narrow product category.

Biospace (http://www.biospace.com/) is an excellent source for information on the biotechnology industry. This site contains a searchable database and a geographic listing of company information. Another useful addition is the ability to search the database to find job postings within biotechnology companies.

Guides to Directories

Several of the basic business reference sources described in chapter 1 include information about directories. Other, more specialized directories are included in chapters devoted to specific subject areas such as accounting and banking. The *Encyclopedia of Business Information Sources* lists highly specialized as well as general directories. Using it, one can identify such diverse sources as the *Bee Researchers Directory, Wines and Vines Annual Directory,* and *American Blue Book of Funeral Directors.* Although the titles are not annotated, price information is usually included in addition to standard bibliographic citations.

DesJardins, Dawn Conzett, ed. **Directories in Print**. 18th ed. Farmington Hills, Mich.: Gale Group, 2000. 2v. [Updated between editions by supplements.]

Klein, Barry T., and Bernard Klein, eds. **Guide to American Directories**. 14th ed. Nyack, N.Y.: Todd Publications, 1999. 465p.

Directories in Print, subtitled "A Descriptive Guide to Print and Non-Print Directories, Buyer's Guides, Rosters and Other Address Lists of All Kinds," groups directories under 26 broad subject categories such as "General Business," "Manufacturing Industries and Commercial Services," and "Management, Employment, and Labor". In addition to annotations, entries include the publisher's address; e-mail addresses and URLs, when available; frequency of publication; number of pages; price; former titles; and available alternative formats.

The *Guide to American Directories* now combines the former *Guide to American Directories: A Guide to the Major Directories of the U.S. with Major Foreign Directories Included* and an earlier publication, *Guide to American Scientific and Technical Directories.* This integrated volume lists nearly 11,000 directories and guides published in the United States and 1,000 major international and foreign directories. Each entry includes a brief annotation and the price of the directory at the time of publication. As with *Directories in Print*, arrangement is by subject classification, but with much narrower categories totaling about 150.

Examination of these guides will soon make one thing abundantly clear: Few libraries have comprehensive or even representative directory collections listing all products, geographic areas, and types of companies. Such collections would be impossible for even the largest and most affluent of business libraries. However, certain types of specialized directories are fairly common; these are considered next.

Subsidiaries, Divisions, and Affiliates

Some company divisions and subsidiaries do not merit separate entries in standard business directories. This is worth reemphasizing because many users give up after unsuccessfully checking the standard business directories for specific companies. Failure to find a company listed in one of the basic directories does not mean that the desired information is not close at hand in a more specialized source. In many instances, the next logical step will be to check one or more of the directories that specialize in information about subsidiaries, divisions, and affiliates.

Directory of Corporate Affiliations Library. New Providence, N.J.: National Register Publishing, 1967– . 5v. Annual.

America's Corporate Families and International Affiliates. Parsippany, N.J.: Dun & Bradstreet, 1983– . 3v. Annual.

Two of the most heavily used sources for checking corporate family connections are the *Directory of Corporate Affiliations* and *America's Corporate Families*. Although there is considerable overlap between them, each features some companies that are not included in the other.

The *Directory of Corporate Affiliations* is a five-volume set containing two index volumes in which one may search by company name, SIC codes, geography, brand names, or corporate responsibilities; a volume listing 4,100 U.S. public companies along with 42,000 worldwide affiliates, subsidiaries, and divisions; a volume that includes 8,800 privately held U.S. corporations as well as 12,150 U.S. and international subsidiaries; and a final volume listing 2,450 parent companies and 52,000 subsidiaries for international public and private enterprises. Requirements for inclusion are described in the front as being "flexible" but generally U.S. companies are required to have revenues greater than $10 million or more than 300 employees, whereas foreign companies must have revenues larger than $50 million. The five volumes are only available for purchase as a complete set. For those who need operational functionality the directory is also available as a CD-ROM or Web service, *Corporate Affiliations Plus,* and as an online service, *Corporate Affiliations Online*, from the Dialog Corporation (file 513). All electronic formats are updated quarterly. The information in this source is obtained from questionnaires sent to companies and from follow-up telephone calls.

The other perennial favorite for tracing corporate linkage is Dun & Bradstreet's *America's Corporate Families and International Affiliates,* which also lists about 15,000 corporations and 1000,000 subsidiaries, divisions, and branches. One of the major differences in *Directory of Corporate Affiliations* is that one may buy separately the two volumes that include the U.S. corporations or the one volume that covers the foreign ultimate parent companies. All companies are cross-referenced geographically and by industry classification. Corporations operating wholly and exclusively within the United States or within countries outside the United States are not covered. To be included companies must have two or more business locations, have 250+ employees at that location, exceed $25 million in sales volume, or have a tangible net worth greater than $500,000; inclusion is limited to only those multinational corporate families having at least one U.S. family member and at least one foreign family member. D & B also offers a Web product, *Family Tree Finder*, with which one can determine relationships within large corporate entities and research or build hierarchical family trees.

Who Owns Whom. London: Dun & Bradstreet International, 1976– . 8v. Annual.

Directory of American Firms Operating in Foreign Countries. 10th ed. New York: Uniworld Business Publications, 1999. 3v.

Directory of Foreign Firms Operating in the United States. 10th ed. New York: Uniworld Business Publications, 1999. 856p.

Other directories treat corporate ownership of multinational and foreign companies. A series called *Who Owns Whom* lists parents and subsidiaries in separate volumes for North America, the United Kingdom and Ireland, Continental Europe, and Australasia and the Far

East. *Who Owns Whom* contains information on the corporate structure of approximately 310,000 parent companies and their 890,000 subsidiaries. It covers all the major business locations of the world. Approximately 70 percent of the companies in *Who Owns Whom* are based in Europe, 20 percent in North America, and 10 percent in the rest of the world. Information for each full company entry includes name, address and global region, business activity, status as either a parent or subsidiary, year of incorporation, and parent information. Global ultimate parent entries also include a full hierarchical listing of subsidiaries and the number of companies in the corporate family.

The *Directory of American Firms Operating in Foreign Countries* and the *Directory of Foreign Firms Operating in the United States* are not only used for standard subsidiary information but are also very popular with patrons interested in seeking employment abroad.

Foreign Companies

More and more in this time of globalization librarians will be asked to provide information on foreign companies. If the request is for an address for the corporate headquarters of a foreign company with American-based subsidiaries, the *Directory of Foreign Firms Operating in the United States* and the *Directory of Corporate Affiliations* or *America's Corporate Families and International Affiliates*, mentioned in the preceding section, will be useful.

If, however, the company has no U.S. subsidiaries, or if the information needed is a list of foreign companies manufacturing a particular product, consulting foreign or international directories will be necessary. Two of the major publishers of foreign business directories are Dun & Bradstreet and Kompass. Dun & Bradstreet International, Ltd., publishes directories for Great Britain and Europe.

Kompass presently issues 67 directories for 17 countries, including Estonia, the Ivory Coast, and Croatia. This company also produces 32 individual country and 8 multicountry CD ROMs. Since these directories typically cost over $300 each, only the most affluent libraries can afford comprehensive collections. Now, however, at http://www.kompass.com the *Kompass Worldwide Database* is available through two access levels. The first is free and will typically provide address, some executives, a little financial information, a full listing of products and services, and, where available, addresses of subsidiaries and other locations. Some of the added features a subscription will provide are a full-text search in the company profiles of all companies, manufacturing or distributing, importing or exporting, in several languages in any of the 70 countries for which there are data; an e-mail function; Kompass Classification Codes; and a corporate activity sheet. The database consists of 1.5 million companies worldwide, about 50,000 product and service codes, 23 million product and service references, 2.9 million executives' names, and 600,000 trademarks and brand names.

Because it is so expensive to collect information on so many individual countries, many libraries will choose instead to collect consolidated directories. Two of the most popular publications from Dun & Bradstreet are described below.

Principal International Businesses. New York: Dun & Bradstreet International. 1974– . Annual.

D&B Europa. High Wycombe, England: Dun & Bradstreet Ltd.: Dun & Bradstreet International, 1989– . 4v. Annual.

Principal International Businesses is a directory of the world's leading 50,000 firms, covering all types of businesses in 140 countries, ranging from Albania to Zimbabwe. The main section lists companies by country and then alphabetically by company name. Each entry includes company name and address, cable address or telex number, sales volume and number of employees (when this information is available), SIC code(s), and the name of the company's chief executive. If the company is a subsidiary, or if it imports or exports products, this information is also included. This single-volume resource is cross-referenced alphabetically, geographically, and by industry classification. Dun & Bradstreet also presents this information in an annual CD-ROM available in three levels of coverage: *Principal International Businesses Disc—Basic,* which offers coverage of 100,000 leading companies outside the United States; *Principal International Businesses Disc—Expanded,* which covers 250,000 leading companies outside the United States; and *Principal International Businesses Disc, Expanded Plus,* which carries coverage of 500,000 leading companies outside the United States. The other D&B product listed above, *D&B Europa,* covers 60,000 top European companies in 23 countries. Each company listing gives contact details, names of executives, and job functions and lists the ultimate parent company, net worth, profit, annual sales, and number of employees. Included are details on the top 5,000 companies ranked by sales and employee numbers, the top 10 percent of companies in each main business activity ranked by sales, and statistical sales profiles for each country. A CD-ROM version of *Europa*, containing information on over 135,000 public and private companies across Europe, is also available.

Another major publisher of international directories is Graham & Whiteside (http://www.gale.com/graham&whiteside/index.htm), a London-based company that is now an imprint of the Gale Group. Some of the titles it publishes both in CD-ROM and hard copy are *Major Companies of Africa South of the Sahara, Major Companies of the Arab World 2000, Major Companies of Central & Eastern Europe & the CIS, Major Companies of the Far East & Australasia,* and *Major Companies of Latin America & the Caribbean*

State and Local Directories

Many requests for business information require the use of directories that have far narrower geographic foci than international or even national directories provide. State and local directories can be tremendously useful for locating information on companies too small to be included elsewhere. State industrial directories are published by a number of different organizations; state government agencies, trade associations, and commercial publishers are the most common. Although coverage will vary from one state to another, most directories include company name, address and telephone number, name of president or chief executive officer, approximate number of employees, and SIC or other product designation. Although format is not always consistent, most directories usually include sections that arrange companies by city or county, by SIC or product, and by company name.

For many libraries, the collection of state directories will be limited to their own state's directory. Larger business reference collections may include additional directories representing neighboring states or the most heavily industrial states. Some of the country's major business libraries include directories for all 50 states.

Harris Publishing (http://www.harrisinfo.com) produces hard copy, Web, and CD-ROM directories that are the leading low-cost reference tools profiling manufacturing establishments. At the Web site one can search and retrieve, for no cost, basic address information for nearly 400,000 manufacturing establishments. *Selectory Online* from the same company is a Web product that operates on a subscription or pay-as-you-go system.

InfoUSA (http://infousa.com) also provides information at the state level. As the information is taken from the yellow pages, this includes not only manufacturing but also service industries, including retail outlets. This company is also well known for its compilations of mailing lists. Details of all the products, in hard copy, on CD-ROM, and on the Web are listed on the company Web site.

It was observed previously in this chapter that some companies only operate in one state and so must file public documents with the secretary of state and not the Securities and Exchange Commission. Itemized in figure 2.10 are the 25 states that offer Web access to these records at this time. It is to be expected that in the future other states will also make their directories Web accessible.

Alabama	http://www.sos.state.al.us/sosinfo/inquiry.cfm
Alaska	http://www.dced.state.ak.us/bsc/CorpStart.cfm
Arizona	http://www.cc.state.az.us/corp/filings/index.htm
Arkansas	http://www.sosweb.state.ar.us/corps/
Florida	http://ccfcorp.dos.state.fl.us/index.html
Georgia	http://www.sos.state.ga.us/corporations/corpsearch.htm
Hawaii	http://www.ehawaiigov.com/breg/new/
Idaho	http://www.idsos.state.id.us/corp/corindex.htm
Illinois	http://www.sos.state.il.us/cgi-bin/corpname
Iowa	http://www.sos.state.ia.us/corpweb/
Kansas	http://www.ink.org/public/corps/
Kentucky	http://www.sos.state.ky.us/corporate/entityname.asp
Louisiana	http://www.sec.state.la.us/crpinq.htm
Maine	http://www.state.me.us/sos/corpinfo.htm
Maryland	http://www.mdbusiness.state.md.us/
Missouri	http://168.166.2.55/missouribusinesses/
New Mexico	http://www.nmprc.state.nm.us/ftq.htm
North Carolina	http://scc035.sips.state.nc.us/sec/corp/
Nevada	http://sos.state.nv.us/default.asp
Rhode Island	http://www.sec.state.ri.us/corporations/
Texas	http://open.cpa.state.tx.us/
Utah	http://www.dced.state.ut.us/busdev/dbi/bizdir99.htm
Vermont	http://170.222.200.66/seek/CORPSEEK.HTM
Washington	http://dor.wa.gov/index.asp?/prd/
Wyoming	http://soswy.state.wy.us/corps1.htm

Figure 2.10. State company directories.

Lists of Largest Companies

Librarians receive frequent requests for lists of largest companies. Since several sources rank companies by size, generally these questions are answered easily. The librarian, however, should first determine how the company's size is to be measured. Criteria used for ranking companies by size include annual sales, assets, profits, and number of employees; list makers use different criteria for compiling their lists. Some of the most frequently used lists are published as special issues of various business magazines.

When the need is for a ranked list of more than the top 100 or 500 companies, however, few of those in magazines or journals are adequate. Although one may compile customized lists from most of the electronic directories already mentioned, there is also available a hard copy source popular with many librarians.

D & B Business Rankings. Bethlehem, Pa.: Dun & Bradstreet, 1982– . Annual.

This was formerly known as *Dun's Business Rankings*. This publication ranks over 25,000 of the nation's leading private and public businesses by size as measured by sales volume and number of employees. These indicators are also used to rank these businesses within each state, within industry categories, and within the private/foreign-owned designation.

Trade Directories

Many of the directories that already have been discussed list major companies under broad industry classifications. The business person seeking to identify companies under narrower product or service designations may need to consult a trade directory specializing in a particular industry or trade. Literally hundreds of such special directories are in print, each focusing on a specific industry. Some, such as those dealing with the petroleum, paper, textiles, and food industries, feature directories that rival standard business directories in size. Others are considerably smaller, issued as paperbacks or even as pamphlets. Trade directories can be identified by using the guides to directories such as *Directories in Print* and the *Encyclopedia of Business Information Sources,* mentioned previously.

Employment Directories

Business people and consumers are not the only ones who make frequent use of business directories. Another group comprises people in the job market who seek employment in the world of business. Frequently they use standard business directories to identify prospective employers. One can also fully explore the Web pages of different companies to find detailed information about them. These sources, however, do not always include the names and titles of human resources officers or information about employee training programs or benefits. Such information can usually be obtained by consulting the following special employment directories.

The Career Guide: D&B Employment Opportunities Directory. Parsippany, N.J.: Dun's Marketing Services, 1983– . Annual.

The Almanac of American Employers. Galveston, Tex.: Plunkett Research, 1985– . Annual.

Plunkett's Companion to *The Almanac of American Employers*: **Mid-Size Firms**. Galveston, Tex.: Plunkett Research, 1998– . Biennial.

The *Career Guide* contains information on 5,000 companies. Each entry includes an overview of the company itself, a list of the disciplines hired, a description of career development opportunities within the company, and employee benefits as well as employers offering work-study or internship programs. Also included is the address to which employment inquiries should be sent and, in many instances, the name and title of the person to be contacted. Sections that list employers geographically and by broad industry category, employer branch locations, and personnel consultants by state supplement the main company listing section. Brief articles on job-hunting strategies and statistics indicating current employment patterns complete the directory.

The Almanac of American Employers is an inexpensive alternative to The *Career Guide*. It covers 500 rapidly growing firms of 2,500 or more employees, listing and ranking salaries and employee benefits and assessing their financial stability. Each item of information about a company receives a point score. Companies are also assigned a composite score and rank. Salaries and benefits are also included, rated on a scale of 1 to 5. The *Almanac* is useful for its description of the type of business and number of employees, the contact information provided, and general information about women officers or directors and apparent minority officers or directors. The *Companion* volume focuses on mid-sized firms, from 300 to 2,500 employees. These volumes also include a section on major trends affecting the job market and a separate index by industry. A CD-ROM version accompanies the hard copy.

Since 1988 Harvard Business School has been publishing a series of guides, including *Careers in the Nonprofit Sector, Careers in Management Consulting, Careers in Finance,* and *Careers in Marketing.* Each book describes its industry's varying career opportunities and includes up-to-date profiles of leading companies; a mailing list of recruiting contacts; and a selective bibliography of relevant books, directories, Web sites, and other resources compiled by the Harvard Business School career resources librarian. Ordering information is available from the publisher's site at http://www.hbsp.harvard.edu/products/press/.

The Internet is again an enormous source of information. As well as being able to search company Web sites, most of which list employment opportunities, there are sites directed especially to those searching for employment or employees. New graduates may register at petersons.com (http://www.petersons.com/career/) and post their resume. At *America's Job Bank* (http://www.ajb.dni.us/) one may post a resume, create cover letters, track job searches, and find contact information for individual employers. Those searching for a job with a federal agency will want to check the *Federal Jobs Digest* at http://www.jobsfed.com, whereas those searching for a job in an academic institution will search *The Chronicle of Higher Education* at http://chronicle.com/jobs/.

There are so many accessible employment Web sites that it may be best to start with a gateway such as Monster.com (http://www.monster.com) or CareerPath.com (http://www.careerpath.com). Most features are offered free of charge to the job seeker, except that posting a resume on Monster.com entails a small fee. Employers are charged to post opportunities, and the fee increases with the number of categories in which the job is registered. Both Web sites include help on building resumes and career advice for all levels and areas.

A meta site known to many librarians is *The Riley Guide* (http://www.dbm.com/jobguide/), which was the first guide to use the Internet to aid in job searches. Although this page has fewer "bells and whistles" than many sources, it provides a thorough guide to the many accessible online sites and services.

The Internet has some well-known publications for job help. A reference classic is the *Occupational Outlook Handbook,* now available free at http://www.bls.gov/oco/home.htm. Each biennial publication provides a summary of working conditions, the training and education needed, earnings, and expected job prospects in a wide range of occupations. A companion volume is *Career Guide to Industries,* at http://www.bls.gov/oco/cg/. The *Career Guide* reports on over 42 industries and gives information on "working conditions, employment, occupations in the industry, training and advancement, earnings and benefits, employment outlook, and lists of organizations that can provide additional information."

Biographical Directories

Sometimes the need may be for information about an individual rather than a company. A salesman may want all of the data he can gather about a prospective client, a toastmaster may need personal background information to introduce an honored guest, or a small business woman may want to compile a mailing list of prominent business people in a particular location or industry. Standard biographical directories such as *Who's Who in America* and the Who's Who geographical series (*Who's Who in the Midwest, Who's Who in the South and Southwest,* etc.) include information about prominent executives, but other more specialized biographical directories that focus solely on the world of business are also available and may list people not included in general biographical directories. In addition, Standard & Poor's *Register of Corporations, Directors, and Executives*, described in the section on basic business directories, incorporates a biographical directory as volume 2 of the three-volume set.

Reference Book of Corporate Management. Parsippany, N.J.: Dun's Marketing Service, 1967– . 4v. Annual.

Who's Who in Finance and Industry. Chicago: Marquis Who's Who, 1936– . Biennial.

Dun & Bradstreet also publishes a biographical directory, the four-volume *Reference Book of Corporate Managements*, which provides brief biographical information on thousands of principal officers and directors of more than 12,000 leading companies. Arrangement is by company name; volume 4, the "Cross-Reference" volume, includes an index of executives as well as the geographical and SIC indexes that are standard Dun & Bradstreet directory features.

Another widely used biographical business directory is *Who's Who in Finance and Industry*, a biennial that lists both North American and international business executives. Each biographical profile includes educational background; career history; political, civic, and religious affiliations; special achievements; and personal data. A professional index, which lists biographees under professional designations such as "Agriculture", makes it possible to identify key executives in a particular industry or field.

Other Special Directories

The *Encyclopedia of Business Information Sources* and *Directories in Print*, mentioned in the "Guides to Directories" section, list an almost overwhelming number of special business directories. These guides should be consulted whenever attempting to identify special industry and service-oriented directories. A few special directories are so regularly used, however, that they merit mention.

Encyclopedia of Associations. Farmington Hill, Mich.: Gale Group, 1956– . 4v. Annual.

Business Organizations, Agencies, and Publications Directory. 11th ed. Farmington Hill, Mich.: Gale Group, 1986– . Annual.

The *Encyclopedia of Associations* features brief information on nearly 23,000 "nonprofit American membership organizations of national scope," and includes sections on trade, business and commercial organizations, commodity exchanges, chambers of commerce, and other types of organizations relevant to business. Each entry includes the organization's address and telephone number, the name of the chief officer, founding date, and the number of members and staff. In addition, most entries include brief descriptions of the organizations and lists of name changes, conference dates, and major publications. Also available for five different regions is the *Encyclopedia of Associations: Regional, State and Local Organizations*, for those librarians or researchers who do not have the need for a national directory. The *Encyclopedia of Associations: International Organizations* covers about 21,000 multinational and national organizations for countries ranging from Afghanistan to Zimbabwe. This whole set of directories is available as either a CD-ROM or an Internet product. One can buy the whole unit of 440,000 entries or purchase only the modules needed. The *Encyclopedia of Associations* is also available from GaleNet, Dialog, and LexisNexis.

Less essential than the *Encyclopedia of Associations* but still very useful is the *Business Organizations, Agencies, and Publications Directory*. Much of the information included in this directory is compiled from other sources, including the *Encyclopedia of Associations*, other Gale publications, and government documents. Although not a primary information source, it offers the undeniable convenience of access to a single directory rather than to several, disparate sources that may not all be close at hand. Large business reference collections and, alternatively, small libraries lacking access to the sources from which the information was gathered, may feature this directory in their collections.

Research and Technology

Biotechnology Guide U.S.A. 5th ed. Basingstoke; New York: Macmillan, [Distributed by Grove's Dictionaries Inc.], 1999. 710p.

Although standard business directories list many companies that sponsor corporate research and development, these directories do not, as a rule, list company research and development centers, research laboratories, and their staff.

In recent years, publishers have begun to compile even more specialized directories of high technology firms. The best known are the *Corporate Technology Directory* (described previously) and *Biotechnology Guide U.S.A.*, which includes an analysis of the industry as well as alphabetical company listings. Also incorporated are indexes by company areas of interest and biotechnology areas such as cell therapy and bioinformatics. Included as well are details of major company mergers that occurred between 1995 and 1999. A companion volume, *The Biotechnology Guide 2000,* covers over 9,500 organizations in 84 countries and presents over 5,800 profiles of commercial biotechnology companies, universities, institutes, and research organizations.

Available on the Web is the Biotechnology Industry Organization's list of members, at http://www.nbif.org/industry/register.html. It is searchable by U.S. region or company, and there is also an alphabetical listing. Included in each company entry is the address, and Web page listing.

A favorite book of many librarians was the publication *Directory of American Research and Technology*. Unfortunately Bowker has decided to no longer publish this title and as yet it has not been picked up by anyone else.

Consultants

Only the largest consulting firms are listed in standard business directories. To identify individuals or organizations that offer consulting services, it is usually necessary to refer to special directories. Two such sources are in common use.

Consultants and Consulting Organizations Directory. 21st ed. Farmington Hill, Mich.: Gale Group, 1973– . 2v. Annual.

D&B Consultants Directory. Bethlehem, Pa.: Dun & Bradstreet, 1986– . Annual.

The *Consultants and Consulting Organizations Directory* features over 22,000 firms, individuals, and organizations arranged in 14 fields of consulting activity. Each entry includes the name of the principal executive(s), location of headquarters and branch offices, the organization's purpose, and recent mergers and former names. Subject, geographical, and consulting firms indexes enhance access to the main section of the directory. A mid-year supplement issued between editions brings the *Consultants and Consulting Organizations Directory* up-to-date.

D&B Consultants Directory lists 30,000 consulting firms within more than 1,000 activities, ranging from "Abuse, Misuse" to "Zoning." Although it lists more consultants than the *Consultants and Consulting Organizations Directory*, its entries include somewhat less information. Another difference is that the Gale publication is arranged by broad subject categories, whereas the Dun & Bradstreet directory's main point of access is by consultant's name. Each, however, contains indexes that cross-reference the main section. Further, while there is considerable duplication between the sources, each contains listings that are unique. As a result, many libraries will choose to acquire both directories.

At this time many consulting firms have a Web presence. One easy way to find companies is to use Yahoo! (http:www.yahoo.com) to search in the company section for consulting. Yahoo compiles a fairly inclusive listing of companies that are on the Internet. For those who need recommendations to a specific consultant, the best thing is still to contact the professional organization in the area in which one needs help.

Trade Names

Brands and Their Companies. 20th ed. Farmington Hill, Mich.: Gale Group, 1976– . Annual.

Companies and Their Brands. 20th ed. Farmington Hill, Mich.: Gale Group, 1976– . Annual.

International Brands and Their Companies. 4th ed. Farmington Hill, MI: Gale Group, 1990– . Biennial.

As mentioned previously in this chapter, inquiries often involve linking a specific brand name with the company that owns it. Two sources of this information have already been described: the *Thomas Register of American Manufacturers* and the *Standard Directory of Advertisers.* Another important source is the *Brands and Their Companies* and the *Companies and Their Brands* series from Gale Group, which lists almost 258,000 U.S. consumer brands and 80,000 manufacturers, importers, or distributors associated with them. A companion directory, *International Brands and Their Companies,* has material on 84,000 products in countries other than the United States and includes listings for 28,000 manufacturers and distributors.

The directories discussed in this chapter are but a few of the hundreds of business directories in print.

Online Business Directories

Electronic directory databases continue to grow in number and importance. Many libraries, however, still collect hard copy for a variety of reasons. The first of these is probably cost. Although the online and CD-ROM databases provide added searching functionality and often more information, this usually means an added cost and smaller libraries, which want to provide a selection of directories, will probably continue to buy hard copy for the time being. A second problem that looms large for research libraries is the provision of historical information. Online versions of directories tend to be current only, and superseded CD-ROMs may be used only if the library also keeps the software that runs them. This is updated with the receipt of each new disk, so a concentrated effort must be made to keep each software edition. Another problem arises with CD-ROMs when the vendor builds in an expiration date and the disk will not function after this is reached. These and certain licensing restrictions are problems to be resolved before most libraries can fully commit to electronic versions of directories.

Notes

1. "Number of Returns, Receipts & Net Income, by Type of Business1980 to 1998," *Statistical Abstract of the United States* (Washington, D.C.: Government Printing Office, 2001), 473 (Table 710).

2. Economic Classification Policy Committee, *Calibrating a New Economy.* Available at http://www.census.gov/epcd/www/pdf/naicsbch.pdf (Accessed August 23, 2003).

3. Ibid.

4. Economic Classification Policy Committee. 1993. *Criteria for Determining Industries.* Available at http://www.census.gov/epcd/naics/issues4 (Accessed August 23, 2003).; Economic Classification Policy Committee. No date. *New Data for a New Economy.* Available at http://www.census.gov/epcd/www/pdf/naicsdat.pdf (Accessed August 23, 2003).

5. *Plunkett's Health Care Industry Almanac, Plunkett's Telecommunications Industry Almanac, Plunkett's E-Commerce & Internet Business Almanac, Plunkett's Retail Industry Almanac, Plunkett's Financial Services Industry Almanac, Plunkett's On-Line Trading, Finance & Investments Web Sites Almanac, Plunkett's Energy Industry Almanac, Plunkett's Entertainment & Media Industry Almanac, Plunkett's InfoTech Industry Almanac,* and *Plunkett's Engineering & Research Industry Almanac.* Details available from http:www. plunkettresearch.com.

3

Periodicals and Newspapers

The world of business is not static. In the course of a year, many things can happen. Interest rates may skyrocket and stock prices plummet; new technologies emerge and old products become obsolete. Executives may retire, be fired, or abscond with company funds. Companies themselves may be victims of hostile takeovers or may in turn acquire companies. As a result, although directories and other reference books provide valuable information about fixed points in time, they are seldom completely up-to-date. For current information, business people turn to online databases, loose-leaf services, periodicals, and newspapers. Of these, newspapers and periodicals are the most commonly used, either in hard copy or accessed via the Internet. This chapter seeks to examine various types of business periodicals and newspapers as well as representative examples of each and the indexes, abstracts, online databases, and Internet resources that provide access to them.

Types of Business Periodicals

There are six main types of business periodicals: general business, trade, scholarly, consumer, government, and regional (see figure 3.1).

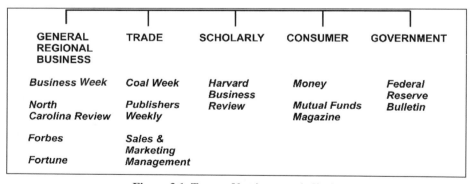

Figure 3.1. Types of business periodicals.

General Business Periodicals

General business periodicals provide broad coverage of the state of the economy and of commerce and industry. Although specific articles may treat different fields of business separately, the focus is broad, emphasizing overall trends and developments. *Business Week, Fortune,* and *Forbes* are general business periodicals. They are important and popular and can be used to supplement standard business reference sources. Many of these publications are available electronically. Some will appear full text in online databases, and most have some type of Web presence with at least some of the information available at no charge.

Business Week. New York: McGraw-Hill, 1929– . Weekly. Web version available at http://www.businessweek.com/.

Although *Business Week* may not, as its publishers advertise, show its readers how to "develop a silver tongue, a golden touch, and a mind like a steel trap," it does provide them with coverage of current conditions in national and international business and finance. It is the business manager's *Time* or *Newsweek*, with concise, interesting, and frequently entertaining articles supplemented by statistics, graphs, photographs, and illustrations.

Cover stories focus on subjects as diverse as artificial intelligence, capitalism in China, computer software, and baby boomers. Weekly news briefs include news with both analysis and commentary, international business, social issues, finance, management, information technology, media, marketing, and government. Also included each week are book reviews, editorials, and personal business advice. *Business Week* enjoys tremendous popularity; with a circulation of 990,000 it is "the most widely read of all business periodicals."[1]

In addition to the statistics that accompany many of its articles, *Business Week* also provides two pages of financial statistics in each issue. "Investment Figures of the Week" presents information on markets in both the United States and major foreign markets and includes technical market indicators, "leader" and "laggard" industry groups, and foreign exchange. Data include weekly, monthly, and annual figures and are usually for the period two weeks prior to the date of the issue being consulted. Strongest and weakest stocks are also identified.

Business Week also features a series of recurring articles and issues. Annual articles include surveys of cigarette and liquor sales, labor negotiations, personal income, pensions, and industry forecasts. Although these articles are seldom more than three or four pages long, the information they contain is useful and may not always be readily available elsewhere. For example, the annual "Industry Outlook" article generally discusses factors responsible for growth or decline in industry in this country and points to some of the ways in which changes may be made. In a recent "Outlook" summaries and graphs were included on the auto, energy, and building industries. If someone wants an idea of where industries may make changes, this is a place to start.

In addition to these annual surveys, *Business Week* produces a "Corporate Scoreboard" series, which provides information on domestic and foreign corporate and industry performance. For those who want to check the online edition for this information a simple search, using the word "scoreboard" will retrieve a list of all that are on the Web site. The series includes the following:

> *Bank Scoreboard:* Ranks the top 100 U.S. banks by assets.
>
> *CEO and Executive Compensation Scoreboard*: Annual survey of executive pay, usually issued in April.
>
> *Corporate Scoreboard*: Includes balance sheet data (assets and debts), with companies grouped by broad industry categories.

Hot Growth Companies Scoreboard: Includes balance sheet data. Usually issued in June.

International Bank Scoreboard: Lists the top 50 worldwide banks ranked by assets.

Investment Outlook Scoreboard: Annual review of the outlook for both personal and institutional investment. Lists for each of the companies include stock price, dividend rate, earnings per share, and other detailed stock performance information.

IT 100/200: Data and contact information for the top 200 global information technology companies. Includes balance sheet data.

Mutual Fund Scoreboard: Reviews the investment performance for equity, fixed-income, and closed-end funds.

Quarterly Corporate Scoreboard: Reviews financial performance (sales, profits, and growth) of some 900 U.S. companies, arranged by broad industry category. Also lists the 10 most profitable and least profitable companies and industries.

Reference departments lacking immediate access to current issues of *Business Week* may order and buy online, from the *Business Week* Web site, the special reports needed.

Fortune. New York: Fortune Magazine, 1930– . Biweekly. Web version available at http://www.fortune.com/.

Fortune is the glossiest of the general business periodicals. Its popularity in the business community is undisputed; it is a key source of current information on all aspects of management, business, finance, and the economy. Each issue contains regular sections such as "Techno File," "Smart Managing," and "Fortune Investor," as well as several special articles on such varied topics as farm price supports, abstinence, and baseball. Articles in *Fortune* are signed and generally longer than those appearing in *Business Week* but are less likely to contain statistical data. Also missing are regular business and financial statistics pages.

As does *Business Week, Fortune* publishes several special issues. Best known are the annual lists of largest companies. Other issues include "Deals of the Year" in January," America's Most Admired Corporations" and "U.S. Business Hall of Fame" in March, and "What CEOs Really Make," in June.

Unlike *Business Week, Fortune* provides most of these special lists for no charge at its Web site. Although *Fortune* is generally less useful than *Business Week* for answering statistical business reference questions, its profiles of up-and-coming executives and entrepreneurs, as well as of those elected to its business hall of fame, make it particularly useful as a source of current biographical information.

Forbes. New York: Forbes, 1917– . Biweekly. Web version available at http://www.forbes.com/.

Forbes is another important general business periodical. Like *Fortune* and *Business Week*, it includes regular columns and features such as management strategies and trends, profiles of prominent business people, and investment commentary. Again, the scope is rather broad. However, whereas *Fortune* and *Business Week* are intended primarily for business professionals, Forbes is written with the investor in mind. As a result, the focus is somewhat different. Rather than a single column on personal investments, for example, *Forbes* features several such columns of commentary and advice, each dealing with a specific investment medium and each written by an acknowledged expert in the field.

Like *Business Week, Forbes'* articles are frequently supplemented with statistics, and it, too, contains regular statistical features dealing with business and finance. The first of these is the "Forbes Index," which presents general business and economic statistics. It charts for a 14-month period eight main economic indicators: new housing starts, industrial production, manufacturers' new orders, manufacturers' inventories, personal income, unemployment claims, retail store sales, consumer prices, and consumer installment credit. The Forbes Index, which is a composite of these indicators, is charted for the past 10 years, with a close-up for the past 12-month period.

The "Forbes/Barra Wall Street Review" charts stock price indexes over 12-month and 10-year periods, includes a brief summary of recent stock market activity, and provides a close-up of equity markets and tables for the best and worst performing industry factors. *Forbes* publishes several special issues. In addition to its list of largest companies, the "Forbes' 500," it publishes an annual mutual fund survey, industry surveys, company growth predictions, a list of America's wealthiest individuals and families, and a special report on multinational corporations. The lists are available from the Web site and can be sorted, using various provided criteria, and then printed.

Taken together, *Business Week, Fortune,* and *Forbes* are the three most important general business periodicals and are essential to business collections in all libraries.

Trade Periodicals

General business periodicals are useful because they provide an overview of current business and economic conditions, but they seldom provide the depth of coverage required by a business researcher seeking detailed descriptive and analytic data for a particular industry. Someone looking for statistics pertaining to the meat-packing industry, for example, or for the latest information on packaging and advertising of prescription drugs, would find little of value in *Fortune* or *Forbes.* In such situations, trade journals are often the best sources of information.

Almost every business endeavor is represented by at least one trade journal. "If there were just two guys in the world collecting and selling turkey buzzard eggs," writes Dick Levin, "you can be sure that one of the two would start a monthly Turkey Buzzard Egg Dealers Journal and start selling it to the other."[2] Although turkey buzzard eggs are not yet actually covered in depth by any trade journal, the poultry business is well represented by such publications as *Poultry Digest, Poultry and Egg Industry, Commercial Egg Management from Farm to Market , Turkey World,* and *Poultry Times.* There are, in fact, hundreds of trade journals, each one dealing with a specific business, industry, or profession. Some are issued by commercial publishers, others by trade and professional organizations. Most contain news of current developments in the field, reviews of past performance and forecasts for the future, descriptions of key companies and personalities, and buyers' guides and directories. They are, in short, veritable gold mines of highly specialized information, and can be invaluable to librarians and researchers seeking elusive statistics or information. Typical examples of trade journals are *Beverage World, Cosmetics and Toiletries, Pit and Quarry, Sludge,* and *Sales & Marketing Management.*

Breadth and depth of trade journal hard copy collections vary considerably from library to library. Electronic access is becoming easier. Because of license agreements ʾh companies such as Ebsco, Gale Group, and LexisNexis, many articles from trade ʾnals appear full text on electronic databases shortly after publication. Associations also feature at least part of their journals on their Web pages, and there are meta web sites available for news and magazines, such as http://www.newsdirectory.com, maintained by *NewsDirectory.com*.

A corporate information center may still subscribe to all of the trade journals that reflect its company's interests, and a public library may collect those relating to community industries and businesses, while an academic library may subscribe to those that support its curricula.

Scholarly Journals

Scholarly business periodicals focus on ideas rather than on the brief descriptions of present conditions, the recent past, or the near future found in general business periodicals and trade journals. Signed articles, based on research findings, are frequently lengthy and may include bibliographies. They may be theoretical or may suggest new ways of dealing with existing business problems. They are publications of substance, whose value endures long after the somewhat ephemeral information in trade and general business periodicals has ceased to be of widespread interest.

Scholarly periodicals are often published under the sponsorship of learned societies, professional associations, or colleges and universities. Academic libraries are the heaviest subscribers to scholarly publications. Although collections of these journals may be somewhat limited in special and public libraries, one such publication, the *Harvard Business Review,* is found in almost every library setting.

Harvard Business Review. Boston: Graduate School of Business Administration, Harvard
  University, 1922– . Bimonthly.

The *Harvard Business Review* is preeminent among scholarly business periodicals. Its popularity derives from the quality of its articles, authored by highly regarded scholars and business practitioners, and by their relevance to current business problems. Both its publisher and its readers view it as a continuing education tool for business executives. It is noted for the diversity of its articles, the eminence of its authors, and a combination of both the practical and the innovative. The *Harvard Business Review* is included in most of the business indexes and abstracts that are described later in this chapter. It publishes its own annual author and subject index, as well as 5- and 10-year cumulative indexes. It can also be searched online and retrieved as full text through EBSCO, a major database vendor.

Consumer Periodicals

Consumer-oriented periodicals, also known as personal finance magazines, are aimed at the general public. Usually glossy, these periodicals court their readers with articles describing how to invest in stocks, bonds, and mutual funds; buy real estate; speculate in commodities; save money; and pay lower taxes. Often included are articles on successful investors, entrepreneurs, and self-made millionaires.

Although these periodicals are directed to the general public, they are particularly valuable to reference librarians because of regular articles that describe investment media and the mechanics of investing in nontechnical terms. They list major information sources, particularly investment advisory publications. *Kiplinger's Personal Finance Magazine* (http://www.kiplinger.com/magazine/) is one of the oldest of these periodicals, and *Mutual Funds Magazine* (http://www.mutual-funds.com/mfmag/) is one of the newest. Perhaps the most popular of all, however, is *Money.*

Money. New York: Time, 1972– . Monthly. Web version available at http://money.cnn.com/.

In addition to regular columns and features that include recent developments on Wall Street and a Fund Watch, *Money* includes articles describing the best brands of chocolates, ski gear, and other consumer goods as well as discussing subjects as diverse as computer software, facelifts, the latest automobiles, and advice from financial planners and investment analysts . Each issue of *Money* also monitors mortgage loan rates, credit card interest rates, and mortgage rates. In addition to its weekly features *Money* annually rates the "Best 100 Mutual Funds" and the "Best Places to Live."

The Web version of *Money,* which is from the editors of both CNN and *Money* magazine, is one of the most comprehensive sites for the general investor. Articles are featured along with guides on budgeting and saving and *Money*'s popular features such as "Best Places to Live." One can also check on the dates of the release of economic information from the government or set up a personal portfolio. A section on calculators includes one for estimating retirement, one to estimate the costs of mortgage refinancing, a savings calculator, and a fund screener.

Reading or checking *Money*, in any format, will help librarians anticipate user demand for specific information and, in some instances, will help to identify publications that should be added to the collection. *Money's* explanation in lay terms of the newest investment media can also help librarians keep abreast of recent trends and developments.

Government Periodicals

Business periodicals published by the federal government may at first glance seem to be drab cousins of their colorful, commercially published counterparts. Appearances to the contrary, however, they contain a wealth of information and can be of significant reference value to librarians and researchers. However, the character of government publications has changed considerably in the last few years. Many of the publications have ceased or have been converted to Web versions, so a researcher now needs to think in terms of sources of information rather than titles of publications. A few sources are described in this section, and many more are available. They can be identified by consulting the following booklets.

Geahigan, Priscilla C., and Robert F. Rose, eds. **Business Serials of the U.S. Government**. Chicago: American Library Association, 1988. 86p.

Key Business Sources of the U.S. Government. [Compiled by] Steven W. Staninger, Susan Riehm Goshorn, and Jennifer C. Boettcher. Chicago: Reference and User Services Association, American Library Association, 1998. 81p.

Business Serials of the U.S. Government lists and annotates over 180 titles, chosen for inclusion on the basis of their usefulness as business reference sources. Arrangement is by broad subject category. Each entry includes a standard bibliographic citation as well as Superintendent of Documents classification and serial numbers; the Library of Congress card number; and an annotation that includes the source(s) in which the title is indexed, pagination, the kinds of illustrations typically included, the sources of the data reported, and a description of scope and coverage. Some of the journals included in this listing are no longer published, and some are now only Web publications. Much of the statistical information and some of the articles from federal publications are available on the appropriate agency Web site.

Key Business Sources of the U.S. Government originally started as an update to *Business Serials of the U.S. Government,* but because of unprecedented changes in the way the U.S. government information was produced and circulated it was difficult to confirm which items would continue and which would be eliminated. As a result, it was decided that the approach should be to include "key" sources of business information available from the U.S. government. This volume contains an annotated list of books, serials, CD-ROMs, microforms, and Internet sites and is a useful first step in finding essential information.

The following publications, which are among the most highly regarded and heavily used, are at this time still available in paper copy, although Web versions also exist.

U.S. Council of Economic Advisers. **Economic Indicators**. Washington, D.C.: Government Printing Office, 1948– . Monthly. Web version available at http://www.access.gpo.gov/congress/cong002.html.

U.S. Department of Commerce. Bureau of Economic Analysis. **Survey of Current Business**. Washington, D.C.: Government Printing Office, 1921– . Monthly. Web version available at http://www.bea.doc.gov/bea/pubs.htm.

The federal government is the world's largest collector and publisher of statistics, and many of them are published in government periodicals such as *Economic Indicators, Monthly Labor Review,* and the *Survey of Current Business*. Of these, the most widely used is the *Survey of Current Business*, published monthly by the Commerce Department's Bureau of Economic Analysis (see figures 3.2 and 3.3, page 56).

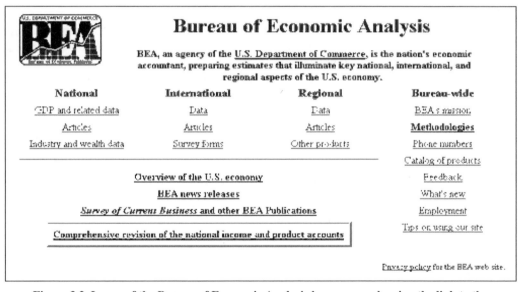

Figure 3.2. Image of the Bureau of Economic Analysis home page, showing the link to the *Survey of Current Business.* http://www.bea.doc.gov/bea/pubs.htm.

Each issue is a comprehensive report on business activity and estimates and analyses of U.S. economic activity and includes, in addition to articles on the national, regional, and international economic accounts and related topics, a column describing the current business situation and statistical tables highlighting national income and product accounts. The statistical section consists of tables for about 270 series and charts for about 130 series.

Note: Beginning with the January 1998 issue, the *Survey* is available in pdf format free of charge on BEA's Web site at http://www.bea.doc.gov/bea/pubs.html. It is also once more available, since January 2002, as a print copy.

Description	Title	Source	Format
International transactions	Annual Revision of the U.S. International Accounts, 1993-2001	*SCB*, July 2002	PDF (274kb)
	U.S. International Transactions, First Quarter and Year 2002	*SCB*, July 2002	PDF (3.2 Mb)
	Selected Issues in the Measurement of U.S. International Services	*SCB*, June 2002	PDF (546kb)
	An Ownership-Based Framework of the U.S. Current Account, 1989-99	*SCB*, April 2002	PDF
	Reconciliation of the U.S.-Canadian Current Account, 1999 and 2000	*SCB*, November 2001	PDF (702kb)
	U.S. International Services: Cross-Border Trade in 2000 and Sales Through Affiliates in 1999 (Corrected, December 6, 2001)	*SCB*, November 2001	PDF (2.4Mb)
	Cross-Border Trade in Services, 1986-2000	*SCB*, October 2001	PDF (417kb)
	U.S. International Transactions: Revised Estimates for 1989-2000	*SCB*, July 2001	PDF (148kb)
	U.S. International Transactions, Fourth Quarter and Year 2000 (Tables 1-10 in PDF format)	*SCB*, April 2001	PDF (494kb)

Figure 3.3. Typical international data listing, *Survey of Current Business*, copied from the Web page (August 2002). http://www.bea.doc.gov/bea/pubs.htm.

U.S. Department of Labor. Bureau of Labor Statistics. **Monthly Labor Review**. Washington, D.C.: Government Printing Office, 1915– . Monthly. Web version available at http://stats.bls.gov/opub/mlr/welcome.htm.

U.S. Board of Governors of the Federal Reserve System. **Federal Reserve Bulletin**. Washington, D.C.: Board of Governors of the Federal Reserve System, 1915– . Monthly. Web version available at http://www.federalreserve.gov/pubs/bulletin/default.htm (articles only).

Other government periodicals are more specialized. The *Monthly Labor Review*, for example, includes articles and statistics on employment and unemployment, work stoppages, prices and price indexes, and wages. The *Federal Reserve Bulletin* concentrates on money and banking, featuring articles and detailed banking, financial, and monetary statistics.

The federal government is not the only government publisher of periodicals. Although space does not permit their inclusion, it should be noted that state, foreign, and international agencies also issue business periodicals that can be of considerable research value.

Regional Periodicals

The categories of periodicals previously discussed provide information on the national and international level. Economic statistics in government periodicals such as the *Survey of Current Business* are primarily for the United States. Corporations covered in general business periodicals such as *Fortune* are usually nationally prominent blue-chip companies.

Frequently, however, librarians are asked to provide information about small, private companies, or about state and local economic conditions. One valuable source of such information is the growing number of local, state, and regional business publications, categorized here as regional periodicals. Some, such as the *Boston Business Journal* and *New Orleans City Business*, focus on specific cities; others, such as *Business North Carolina* and *Texas Business*, provide statewide coverage. Such publications typically include profiles of locally prominent business people, companies, and industries, and state and local economic indicators. At a minimum, a good business collection will include periodicals for the city and state in which it is located, and it may extend to regional periodicals as well. The City and Regional Magazines Association maintains links to online editions at http://www. citymag.org/links.html. Access to regional business periodicals is also available through such database vendors as EBSCOhost, Gale, ProQuest, and Dialog.

Periodical Directories

Literally hundreds of business periodicals are published every year. Some of the most popular, such as *Business Week*, *Money*, *Harvard Business Review*, and *Survey of Current Business*, are familiar to almost everyone. Others are not nearly so well known, and often librarians may be asked to help identify or provide information on such titles. For example, a business person may want to identify trade magazines in which he can advertise his new line of waterbeds, or he may want to find the source that will best enable him to keep up with the latest developments in the home heating industry. In these situations, librarians frequently turn to periodical directories; the following are used often.

Ulrich's International Periodicals Directory. New York: Bowker, 1932– . 5v. Annual.

The Standard Periodical Directory. New York: Oxbridge Communications, 1964/1965– . Biennial.

Gale Directory of Publications: An Annual Guide to Newspapers, Magazines, Journals, and Related Publications. Detroit: Gale Research, 1880– . Annual.

Ulrich's is the most commonly used periodical directory. The 36th edition contains information on over 156,00 periodicals from around the world, arranged in 856 broad subject classifications. In addition to a "Business and Economics" section, which includes listings for accounting, banking and finance, economic situations and conditions, and investment, as well as general business and economics publications, *Ulrich's* also includes categories for specific industries and trades, such as building and construction, the clothing trade, and paints and protective coatings. Other fields of business such as advertising and public relations and real estate are listed separately.

Each entry includes title, frequency of publication, the publisher's name and address, and Dewey Decimal Classification. In addition, the entry usually includes the ISSN (International Standard Serial Number), circulation, subscription price, year first published, language of the text, the presence of advertising and book reviews, and the names of the indexing and abstracting services in which the periodical is covered. A bullet symbol (•) is used to identify availability as an online database, and frequently the name(s) of the online vendor is listed as well. *Ulrich's* also includes, in volume 4, a cross-index to subjects, a list of periodicals that have ceased publication, a title index, a title change index, and an ISSN index. Volume 5 includes a listing of serials on CD-ROM, serials available online, and an index to publications of international organizations, as well as various guides and indexes to newspapers. This publication is also available as *Ulrich's Plus*, a CD-ROM database and since the year 2000 as an Internet edition at http://www.ulrichsweb.com. Other providers include Dialog as File 480, Ovid Technologies, and in the BUSINESS library of LexisNexis.

Although *The Standard Periodical Directory* contains only some 75,000 compared to *Ulrich's* 156,000, its coverage is limited to the United States and Canada. As a result many more periodicals published in these countries are included than are in *Ulrich's*. Titles listed include business, consumer, and trade magazines, newsletters, house organs, selected daily and weekly newspapers, yearbooks, and directories. As in *Ulrich's*, arrangement of titles is by subject, with many general business, trade, and industry categories. In addition to the information contained in *Ulrich's, The Standard Periodical Directory* annotates the titles it lists and includes information on the physical characteristics of periodicals; the names of their advertising, circulation, and art directors; and the prices of single issues.

The *Gale Directory of Publications*, formerly the *IMS/Ayer Directory of Publications*, lists newspapers, magazines, and trade journals published in the United States, Puerto Rico, and Canada. Unlike *Ulrich's* the *Gale Directory* arranges serial titles by state and city rather than by broad subject classification. The beginning of each state entry includes a brief description of the state, with demographic and publishing statistics, and is followed by city listings. All periodicals published in each city are listed alphabetically regardless of subject content. The listing for Milwaukee, Wisconsin, for example, includes titles as diverse as *The Milwaukee Journal Sentinel*, one of the city's daily newspapers; *American Christmas Tree Journal; Building Operating Management; New Car Prices; Quality Management Journal; Sanitary Maintenance;* and *Spare Time.* The arrangement of the *Gale Directory* requires several cross-indexes. They include a master name and keyword index; separate subject lists of agricultural, college, foreign language, Jewish, fraternal, black, religious and women's publications; newsletters; general circulation magazines; daily newspapers; daily periodicals, free newspapers, and shopping guides; and trade and technical publications. Entries are not quite as comprehensive as those in the *Standard Periodical Directory* but are useful for advertising rates and specifications for specific titles.

Each of the directories mentioned above can be used to access major business and trade publications. Each has its strengths. *Ulrich's* includes more foreign-language titles and lists indexing and abstracting services in which specific periodicals are indexed. *The Standard Periodical Directory* features the most detailed descriptions of content and includes some advertising information, and *Gale* includes even more detailed information about advertising specifications and rates.

Other, more selective, publications are also useful.

Fulltext Sources Online. Medford, N.J.: Information Today, 1989– . Biannual. Web version available at http://www.fso-online.com/.

Endres, Kathleen L., ed. **Trade, Industrial, and Professional Periodicals of the United States**. Westport, Conn.: Greenwood Press, 1994. 467p.

Oxbridge Directory of Newsletters. New York.: Oxbridge Communications. 1979– . Annual

MediaFinder: Oxbridge Directories of Print Media and Catalogs on CD-ROM. New York: Oxbridge Communications, 1997– . Web version available at http://www.mediafinder.com.

Endres, Kathleen, L. **Trade, Industrial, and Professional Periodicals of the United States.** Westport, Conn.: Greenwood Press, 1994. 467p.

Fulltext Sources Online covers over 17,000 periodicals, newspapers, newsletters, newswires, and TV/radio transcripts found online in full text. Because database providers are often selective in their inclusion of articles, full text does not mean that all of the articles printed in a journal are provided online. Full text also means, in most cases, text only, and tables and images will be missing. In most cases, for the journals listed, the dates of coverage and the file name or number are given. Details are also provided on the currency of the listing and also the lag time before it appears in the specified databases. The arrangement is alphabetical, but the directory also contains subject and geographical indexes, and an added bonus is the listing of journals with free archives on the Web. Those who purchase the print volume also receive an ID and password to access the online list of archived journals. Nonsubscribers can search for free, but full records are displayed only to registered users. (See figure 3.4.)

Financial Times (United Kingdom)

FT Profile has the UK first edition by 0:00 hours British
Standard Time on day of publication, and all editions (UK
and International) by 3:00 hours British Standard Time on
day of publication. Lexis-Nexis distributes outside of
Europe and has the Frankfurt edition from 1982-1985 and
the UK and International editions from mid-1986 to
present. Dialog and Dow Jones distribute the UK (early
edition) and International editions outside of Europe.

http://www.ft.com	Update file
Span: 30 day	
DataStar: BIDB: BUSINESS & INDUSTRY	11/94 - 08/98
Dialog: 622: FINANCIAL TIMES	01/86 - 08/98
Dialog: 9: BUSINESS & INDUSTRY DB	11/94 - 08/98
Dow Jones: PUB LIBRARY (FTI)	01/93 - 09/98
FT Profile: BAI	11/94 - Pres.
FT Profile: FT	01/82 - Pres.
Freq: Daily. Lag: 24 hr	
FT Profile: TFT	Update file
Freq: Daily; Lag: None: Span: 1 day	
Nexis: NEWS (FINTIME)	01/82 - Pres.
Freq: Daily; Lag: 24 hr	
Reuters: RBB	09/96 - Pres.
Westlaw: DIALOG ON WEST (FTF)	1986 - 08/98
Westlaw: DOW JONES ON WEST	01/93 - 09/98
Freq: Daily; Lag: None	

Figure 3.4. Typical entry from *Fulltext Sources Online*.
Copyright ©1998. Reproduced courtesy of *Information Today, Inc.*

The *Oxbridge Directory of Newsletters*, with over 20,000 listings, is the largest consolidated collection of newsletters, loose-leaf publications, bulletins, and fax letters. The book has a subject arrangement extending from "Accounting" to "Water Supply, Power & Waste," but also includes indexes for titles, title changes, publishers and publishers by state. Each entry includes the publisher's name, address, and e-mail when available; key personnel; a short editorial description; and circulation and subscription information.

The Oxbridge publications available on the *MediaFinder* CD-ROM include *Standard Periodical Directory, Oxbridge Directory of Newsletters, National Directory of Magazines,* and the *National Directory of Mailing Lists*. The CD-ROM has 90,000 listings of print media and catalogs and searchable fields that include title, publications that rent their lists, printing specifications, subscription price, and circulation. The Web version of *Mediafinder* (http://www.mediafinder.com) describes itself as "a transactional service center—offering the ability to request subscriptions, advertising, and list rental rates—for over 90,000 magazines, catalogs, newsletters, newspapers and more" (Web page). A free search is provided by words in a title in the Online Search box, or a list of journals by subject can be retrieved.

Trade, Industrial, and Professional Periodicals of the United States lists and annotates about 100 specialized business publications. Although it includes far fewer titles than the general periodical directories described above, it provides considerably more information for those it lists. In addition to a descriptive essay about the publication, each entry includes a full publication history including title changes (and the dates each title was in effect) and printed and online indexing services in which the title is included. This title is in the series Historical Guides to the World's Periodicals and Newspapers, issued by Greenwood Press. Earlier useful volumes include *Financial Journals and Serials: An Analytical Guide to Accounting, Banking, Finance, Insurance and Investment Periodicals* and *Business Journals of the United States,* both edited by William Fisher.

Guides to Special Issues

Fortune, *Forbes*, and *Business Week* were previously mentioned as periodicals that publish regularly recurring special issues. Many business, trade, and technical periodicals publish such issues, which normally fall into one of five broad categories: directories and buyers' guides, convention and exhibit reports, statistical reviews, industry reviews, and industry forecasts. The information these special issues contain is often unique or difficult to locate elsewhere; as a result, they can be enormously helpful to librarians and researchers. Many can be purchased separately, making it possible to order key issues and keep them close at hand in the reference collection.

Uhlan, Miriam, and Doris B. Katz, eds. **Guide to Special Issues and Indexes of Periodicals**. 4th ed. New York: Special Libraries Association, 1994. 223p.

Directory of Business Periodical Special Issues. Austin, Tex.: Reference Press, 1995. 162p.

The Grey House Directory of Special Issues. Millerton, N.Y.: Grey House Publishing, 2001. Annual.

The *Guide to Special Issues and Indexes of Periodicals* and the *Directory of Business Periodicals Special Issues* list major business, consumer, and trade journals alphabetically by title. For each entry, publisher's address, frequency of publication, and annual subscription rate are given in addition to a listing of special issues and the months in which they appear. *The Grey House Directory* includes the special issues and buyer's guides for over 1,800 business and trade magazines.

Users of these special directories should be forewarned that publishers may change the months during which specific special issues are published. Failure to find a special issue in the month indicated in either of these directories, therefore, does not necessarily mean that it is no longer being published.

With Internet access one is able to find most of the compiled lists from these issues, and this has been made easier with the help of Gary Price, a researcher and consultant. Mr. Price compiles *Price's List of Lists,* which contains all the unrestricted lists on the Internet; it is available at http://www.specialissues.com/lol/ (see figure 3.5). The list is accommodated at this site by Trip Wyckoff, who maintains *Specialissues.com* (http://www.specialissues.com/), a Web site that tracks special issues of trade and industry magazines.

Specialissues.com currently reports on the special issues of 2,880 trade and industry journals and includes "industry outlooks, overviews, or surveys; statistical issues; company ranking lists; buyers guides; salary surveys; product/industry focus issues; membership directories; who's who registers; and tradeshow specials" (taken from the Web site). Full pricing information is available at the site, and there are details about free trials along with a full journal list.

Periodical Indexes and Abstracts

Indexing and abstracting services provide access to literally hundreds of general trade, scholarly, consumer, government, and regional business periodicals, enabling users to find recent information on a wide range of subjects. Some of the most popular business periodicals are indexed in general indexes such as *Readers' Guide to Periodical Literature* and *Public Affairs Information Service Bulletin*. Business indexes such as *F&S Index United States*, *Business Periodicals Index,* and *Business & Industry* cover a broad range of business titles, while specialized indexes such as *Accounting & Tax Index* (formerly *Accountants' Index*) has a narrower focus. Chapters to come will cover specialized periodical indexes and some of the full-text databases now available: Commonly used business and general periodical indexes are discussed below. Readers should note that the following titles are by no means a complete listing of all indexes and abstracts in which business periodicals are cited; for more comprehensive listings, consult *Business Information Sources* or the listing of periodical indexes in *Ulrich's International Periodicals Directory*. Business indexes have changed greatly over the past several years, and even the smallest libraries often have access to databases that include some full text, but for historical research and for those times that electronic full-text databases fail to meet our needs, basic indexes and abstracts can create a much appreciated comfort zone.

Gary Price's List of Lists

Health Care and Social Assistance

Magazine	Article	Year
DrugTopics	Top 200 Brand and Generic Drugs By Units In 2001	2002
DrugTopics	Top 200 OTC/HBC Brands In 2001	2002
DrugTopics	Top 200 Brand and Generic Drugs By Retail Sales	2002
DrugTopics	Top 200 Drugs By WAC for Hospitals In 2001	2002
DrugTopics	Annual Rx Survey for 2001	2002
Health Care's Most Wired Magazine	Most Wired on a Budget	2002
Health Care's Most Wired Magazine	The Most Improved	2002
Healthcare Informatics	Top 100 Healthcare Information Technology Companies (ranking includes: vendor profiles, up and coming companies, market consolidation discussions, where hospitals are spending IT dollars)	2002
Healthcare Informatics	Up & Comers	2002
Healthcare Purchasing News	Hospital Ranking	2002
HomeCare Magazine	Top Home Medical Equipment Companies	2003
Hospitals & Health Networks	Annual Top 100 Most Wired Hospitals and Health Systems Survey (1998)	2002
Modern Healthcare	Surveys	2002
Modern Healthcare	Annual Contract Management Survey (1978)	2002

Figure 3.5. Extract from Healthcare and Social Assistance Section of *Price's List of Lists*.
Reprinted with permission of the author.

Readers' Guide to Periodical Literature. New York: H. W. Wilson, 1900/1904– . Semimonthly with annual cumulations. Also available as *Readers' Guide Abstracts, Readers' Guide Abstracts Full Text Mega Edition* and *Readers' Guide Abstracts Full Text Mini Edition.* (All Wilson products are now available as WILSONDISC, WILSONTAPE, and WilsonWeb as well as in the familiar print editions.)

PAIS Bulletin. New York: PAIS, 1915– . Semimonthly with periodic cumulations. (Formerly *Public Affairs Information Service Bulletin.*) (*PAIS International* is available online, on CD-ROM, in print, on tape, and via the Internet. *PAIS Select* is a CD-ROM product that provides selected full-text journal articles.)

The Readers' Guide to Periodical Literature indexes general interest periodicals published in the United States. Included among the business serials it indexes are *Black Enterprise, Business Week, Changing Times, Forbes, Fortune, Money, Monthly Labor Review,* and *Nation's Business.* In addition, many of the other periodicals it indexes also feature articles relating to business. As a result, *Readers' Guide* is a good source to consult when looking for popular, general interest business articles written with the layperson in mind. Indexing is by author and subject. A separate book review section is also included.

PAIS Bulletin, is more specialized and more scholarly than *Readers' Guide*. It focuses on current economic, social, and political considerations, and it indexes books, documents, conference proceedings, pamphlets, and reports in addition to periodicals. Arrangement in *PAIS* is by subject, with numerous cross- references. *PAIS* is useful not only for the articles indexed but also for its annual listing of directories and for its indexing of free and inexpensive pamphlets. *PAIS Select* offers selected full-text articles that include tables and charts from the journal.

Business Periodicals Index. New York: H. W. Wilson, 1958– . Monthly, except July, with periodic cumulations. (Also available as *Wilson Business Abstracts Full Text and Wilson Business Abstracts* on tape, CD-ROM, and the Internet, and through the Dialog corporation.)

F&S Index United States. **F&S Index Europe. F&S Index International.** Farmington Hills, Mich.: The Gale Group, 1960– . Weekly, with monthly, quarterly, and annual cumulations.

F&S Index Plus Text. Farmington Hills, Mich.: The Gale Group, 1972– . Monthly. CD-ROM/Web.

Business Periodicals Index is the basic print business index, the one that has been published longest, is most popular, and is most likely to be found in a variety of library settings. It is a subject index and covers such fields as accounting, advertising and marketing, banking, chemicals, construction, cosmetic and drug industries, economics, electronics, finance and investment, industrial relations, insurance, management, personnel administration, purchasing, retail trade, and specific businesses, industries, and trades. Also included are entries for prominent executives and companies and a separate book review section. *BPI* indexes over 520 business periodicals, ranging from *ABA Banking Journal* to *World Oil*. Most are general business periodicals; trade journals are not well represented. *Wilson Business Abstracts Full Text* includes full-text coverage of more than 240 periodicals back to January 1995. *Wilson Business Abstracts* includes abstracting of periodicals from June 1990 and indexing from July 1982.

BPI's strength is its coverage of general business and management matters. It is less useful for the latest news on product and industry developments or for information on specific companies, particularly those not well known. Many librarians turn to *F&S Index* for such information.

F&S indexes over 1,000 periodicals. In addition to such general business titles as *Business Week* and *Fortune,* it also features business-oriented newspapers such as the *Wall Street Transcript*, special reports, and an array of trade publications including *Appliance Manufacturer* and *Health Industry Today*. *F&S*'s strengths are new products and technological developments, corporate acquisitions and mergers, and social and political factors affecting business. The index is divided into two main sections, "Industries and Products" and "Companies."

The "Industries and Products" section reports on new products, product demand and use, sales, market data, and general economic factors. Arrangement is by a numerical coding system, based roughly on the Standard Industrial Classification system described in chapter 2. The code, however, contains more numbers and is thus more precise than its SIC counterpart. The *Standard Industrial Classification Manual*, for example, assigns SIC code 3714 to automotive brakes. Brakes, however, are not the only items listed. "Motor Vehicle Parts and Accessories," SIC 3714, includes over 50 different products, ranging from axles to windshield wipers. Although *F&S* begins with the same four-digit code, by adding two additional digits it is able to create a code, 371432, that is unique to automotive brakes. The advantages of such a system are obvious. Rather than having to read through entries for many different items, the researcher immediately is able to identify those for a specific product. In addition to greater specificity, the *F&S* codes are also more current and reflect the development of new products and technologies in a way that the SIC and NAICS codes, which are infrequently revised, cannot. A section in the front of each issue contains an alphabetical index to the *F&S* codes that are used.

The "Companies" section includes articles relating to mergers, sales and licensing agreements, company analyses, and forecasts of company sales and profits. Although arrangement is by company name rather than by *F&S* code, in all other respects the entries are similar to those found in the "Industries and Products" section.

Business Periodicals Index and *F&S Indexes* are all extremely useful. *BPI*'s strength is in its coverage of management concepts and general business developments, while *F&S* is strongest for coverage of specific products and companies. Someone seeking articles on quality circles or on strategic planning, for example, would find *BPI* more useful, whereas someone interested in medical lasers or frozen yogurt would be wise to turn first to *F&S*.

Another index that has become very popular in recent years is *Business & Industry*. This is an alternative to *F&S* and also has a global focus on companies, products, and industries. It is now produced by Gale Group, which also publishes *F&S*. Most librarians will need to check the overlap between the two and decide which will be most valuable for the collection.

Newspapers

Sometimes monthly, biweekly, or even weekly periodicals are not recent enough to satisfy current information needs. Although most business developments are eventually described in periodicals, they appear first in newspapers. The categories to which newspapers can be assigned roughly parallel those for periodicals. They include regular daily newspapers with business sections or pages, and special business and financial, trade, government, and employment opportunity newspapers (see figure 3.6).

It is impossible to write about newspapers without discussing Web-based products. As of July 19, 2002, NewspaperLinks.com listed, and linked to, all electronic versions of newspapers available worldwide. Internet versions of newspapers give researchers access that was never before possible to international, national, and local news. Most news sites are value added, with links not only to news on business and technology but also to stock quotes, information on mutual funds, and investment research. The Internet has revolutionized how people receive and process information, and newspapers will continue to offer online access to compete with other media.

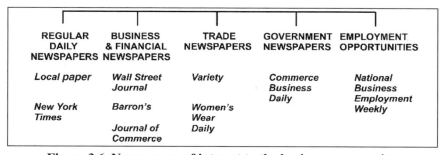

Figure 3.6. Newspapers of interest to the business community.

Regular Daily Newspapers

Even the most modest daily newspaper includes a page or two of business information, usually consisting of news and feature articles about local businesses and tables of trading and price statistics for selected stocks, bonds, mutual funds, and commodities. Coverage is selective, with greatest emphasis being given to businesses and companies headquartered in the area. Some of the larger daily newspapers, such as the *Chicago Tribune* and the *Washington Post*, have excellent business sections. Coverage in the *New York Times* is outstanding. In addition to its lengthy business section in Sunday editions, the *Times* also publishes in its daily editions a compilation of news, features, tables, and advertisements that fills most of the paper's second section. Coverage ranges from brief statements of corporate and executive news to detailed analyses of major financial developments and specific industries. In many instances, the *New York Times* fills the need for news on industry trends, stock prices, and corporate developments. It is a resource that should not be overlooked.

Business and Financial Newspapers

In addition to regular daily newspapers, most libraries subscribe to papers that specialize in providing in-depth coverage of current business, economic, and financial conditions. The *Wall Street Journal* is the best known and most important of these business and financial newspapers.

Wall Street Journal. New York: Dow Jones, 1889– . Daily, except Saturdays and Sundays. Some free information available at http://online.wsj.com/public/us.

Investor's Business Daily. Los Angeles: Investor's Daily, 1984– . Daily, except Saturdays and Sundays. Some free information available at http://www.investors.com/.

The *Wall Street Journal* is considered indispensable by most people looking for information. Its coverage of political, social, economic, and financial news makes it required reading for executives, business people, investors, and business reference librarians. With an estimated readership of over 2 million, the *Journal* is an integral part of the daily business scene; every reference librarian should be familiar with it.[3] The *Wall Street Journal Interactive Edition* provides not only the entire contents of the print *Journal* but also a "Personal Journal," where one can set up a personalized news profile and portfolio, which can include stock, bond, and mutual fund quotes. Once the profile is set, whenever the *Journal* publishes news or columns that meet the criteria, these will be included in the personalized edition. The criteria may be updated as needed. This is a fee-based service, with a reduction in price to those who receive the paper copy. At this time the service is free to those with an educational subscription.

The daily *Journal* is divided into four sections. The first section contains major news articles, features, spot news, special reports, and the editorial page. Also included in the first section are regularly recurring articles on inflation, unemployment, government announcements, Federal Reserve policy, economic forecasts, leading economic indicators, and business statistics. Although these statistics will be covered in chapter 5, it is worth noting here that government agencies and private organizations regularly compile statistics on such activities as capital spending, business failures, domestic car sales, and consumer prices. The second section of the *Journal* covers the marketplace and includes a series of special reports for each day of the week: Monday is "eWorld," Tuesday is "Managing Your Career," Wednesday is "Work & Family" or "Business & Race," Thursday is "Personal Technology," and Friday is "Health Journal." In addition, the second section includes corporate, executive, and industry profiles, and columns such as the "Digest of Corporate Earnings Reports."

The third section contains statistical tables for stocks and other investment media as well as such well-known columns as "Ahead of the Tape."

Among the statistics covered are the following:

    Dow Jones averages

    New York Stock Exchange (NYSE),

    American Stock Exchange (AMEX)

    NASDAQ national market issues

    Dow Jones global indexes

    Futures

    Foreign currency

    Options

    Bonds

To the uninitiated, many of these tables can seem overwhelming. The print is small, numbers dense, and explanations cryptic (see figure 3.7). Fortunately, many secondary sources provide detailed explanations of the most important of these tables. For example, chapters 11 through 15 of this book include lengthy descriptions of stock, bond, mutual fund, futures, and options tables. In addition, the *Journal's* publisher, Dow Jones, makes available a series of explanatory and promotional brochures describing information contained in the *Journal*.[4]

1	2	3	4	5	6	7	8	9	10
High	Low	Stock	Div	PE	100s	High	Low	Last	Change
113/4	63/4	XXX	.40	14	237	113/4	107/8	11	+1/8

Columns 1 & 2   represent the highest and lowest price over the past 52 weeks.

Column 3   shows the stock name

Column 4   shows the annual rate of dividend based on the companies most recent declaration. XXX company is showing a dividend of .40, which means that for every 100 shares owned one will collect $40.

Column 5   represents the price earnings (P/E) ratio. This is the stock price divided by declared earnings-per-share for the last four quarters. A low P/E can indicate a flat stock (possibly with declining profits), while a high P/E can be a sign of rapid growth or increased volatility.

Column 6   represents the volume of shares (in 100s) traded the day before.

Column 7 & 8   shows the highest and lowest trading price the previous day.

Column 9   shows the price per share at closing the day before.

Column 10   shows the difference in the closing price (per share) to the last trade of the preceding day.

Figure 3.7. Interpreting a stock market table compiled for a fictional company XXX.

The fourth section of the revamped *WSJ* is "Personal Investing." This the part that now contains the mutual funds listing as well as columns on subjects such as home equity loans and personal taxes. Dow Jones established an Educational Service Bureau in 1947 to promote the use of the *Wall Street Journal* by college educators. Since then, the Educational Service Bureau and the publications it offers have grown significantly. There are now five regional offices, each making pamphlets available to librarians and educators. (Address information is available at http://info.wsj.com/college/.) A guided tour of the *Journal* is available on the Web under the title "How to Read the Wall Street Journal," at http://info.wsj.com/college/guidedtour/index.html.

Although the *Wall Street Journal* remains the undisputed favorite, a relatively new business daily continues to enlarge its popularity. The *Investor's Business Daily*, which began publication in 1984, was conceived to provide both succinct and thorough coverage of business, financial, economic, and national news. It features potential successful stocks before they receive broad attention and offers evaluative tables, screens, and graphs (also available online at http://www.dailygraphs.com/). Its emphasis is on investor information, and it includes some data not available in the *Journal*. Its daily stock tables, for example, include an earnings-per-share rank for each stock and measure its relative price strength and changes in its trading volume. Each issue of *Investor's Business Daily* begins with "IBD's Top 10," a brief synopsis of important business news of the day, and then continues with political, social, and public policy topics. Also included are articles on companies creating new products, implementing new ideas, and using innovative management strategies. *Investor's Business Daily's* "Computers & Technology" page is designed to supply the latest developments in the fields of computer networking, the Internet and online services, intranets and private networks, communications, software, hardware, peripherals, and support services. Also included are pages that include evaluative articles on the economy and stocks.

In libraries in which neither user demand nor the materials budget is sufficient to accommodate two daily business newspapers, the *Journal* is still the best choice. The *Investor's Business Daily*, however, is a worthwhile addition to most larger business collections.

Wall Street Journal Index. New York: Dow Jones, 1958– . Monthly, with annual
  cumulations. (Also available as an annual purchase.)
The Journal is indexed in the *Wall Street Journal Index*, a monthly that provides subject and company name access to the final Eastern Edition. The index is divided into two main parts, "General News" and "Corporate News." The general news section uses subject and personal name headings, and entries under each heading provide brief synopses of the articles indexed. Researchers should be aware that sometimes the subject headings used in the general news section are too broad to be very useful. Someone looking for information on self-regulation in the accounting profession, for example, would have to scan through all of the articles indexed under "Accounting" (including articles on specific accounting firms, accounting principles and standards, and companies audited by accountants) to identify those on self-regulation. Subject indexing is not a strength of the *Wall Street Journal Index*.

The corporate news section is more useful. In addition to article summaries, entries in this section also include earnings and dividend information. *The Index* also includes closing Dow Jones averages for the month or year being indexed, and since 1981 the annual volumes have also included an index to *Barron's,* another important Dow Jones publication.

The *Wall Street Journal* is now also indexed in most major electronic indexes, but the full text of articles is available electronically only in the *Wall Street Journal Online Edition* (http://online.wsj.com/public/us) or the Factiva databases and for libraries via Bell & Howell's *Proquest Direct* and also in CD-ROM format.

Barron's National Business and Financial Weekly. New York: Dow Jones, 1921– . Weekly. Web version available at http://www.barrons.com/.

Just as the *Wall Street Journal* is the most widely read business daily, so its sister publication, *Barron's*, is the most popular business weekly. Aimed primarily at investors, *Barron's* focuses on various investment media and covers political, economic, and social news as it affects investments.

Barron's is divided into three main parts. The first consists of articles and regularly featured columns. The articles may include interviews with prominent financial analysts, investment officials, executives, or government leaders, or they may analyze the prospects for specific companies. The second part of *Barron's*, titled "Market Week," consists of statistics for the past week's market transactions. These weekly statistics are one of the most comprehensive collections of current statistics available. The second section contains not only weekly statistics for traditional investments but also regularly featured columns. The columns, written by specialists, deal with different aspects of finance and investment. They include:

"Up and Down Wall Street": Focuses on trends in finance and investment.

"The Trader": Summarizes the past week's stock market activities.

"The International Trader": Covers foreign markets and the corporate, monetary, and political developments that affect them.

"Commodities Corner": Discusses one or two specific commodities.

"Current Yield": Covers capital markets.

"The Striking Price": Discusses options and financial futures.

The final part of *Barron's* provides news and analysis of the "Mutual Fund" section. As with the *Wall Street Journal*, the Dow Jones Educational Service Bureau makes available pamphlets that describe *Barron's,* promote its use, and explain some of its recurring features and statistics. Ordering information is available at http://ads.barrons.com/college/.[5]

Wall Street Transcript. New York: Wall Street Transcript, 1963– . Weekly. Web version available at http://www.twst.com/.

Quite a different approach is offered by the *Wall Street Transcript*, a weekly that consists of transcripts of roundtable discussions of specific industries and selected reports on individual companies prepared by brokers and securities analysts. Although no tabular statistics are included, many of the reports on specific companies include tables, charts, and statistics. An overview of recent issues is available online at http://www.twst.com/hotline.html.

Journal of Commerce. New York: Twin Coast Publishers, 1827– . Daily except Saturdays and Sundays. We version available at http://www.joc.com/.

The *Journal of Commerce* is a specialized business newspaper. Emphasis in the *Journal* is on news and statistics pertaining to commodities such as coffee or fuel oil and on foreign trade and freight transport. Although the *Journal* is not common to all libraries, those that subscribe to it should make full use of it for its detailed data on shipping and specific commodities. Listings of inbound and outbound ships and their scheduled ports of call, for example, and the weekly shipping timetable to world ports make it particularly useful for the business person who is interested in international trade. The Web site, at this time, includes free information on logistics, shipping, and trade.

The above business and financial newspapers, although important, are but a sample of such papers presently being published. Others can be identified by consulting bibliographic guides and directories and by conducting a Web search. A list of electronically accessible business dailies is available at http://newslink.com/.

Subscription to any newspapers will, of course, be determined by the scope of the library's business collection, its users, and, not incidentally, the size of its materials budget.

Trade Newspapers

Trade papers, like their trade magazine counterparts, include news, statistics, and descriptions of developments in particular industries and trades that may be virtually impossible to locate elsewhere. Two of the best known are *Variety* (http://www.variety.com), the entertainment industry's trade paper, and *Women's Wear Daily* (http://www.wwd.com), which covers retailing of women's and children's apparel and accessories. As can trade magazines, many can be identified by using the *Gale Directory of Publications*.

Government Newspapers

Although the *Congressional Record* is the best known of the government-published newspapers, it is by no means the only one. Another, *Commerce Business Daily*, is of considerable interest to the business community.

FedBizOpps. n.d. [January 2002?].http://www.fedbizopps.gov/. (Accessed August 23, 2003).

Commerce Business Daily offered opportunities to business firms seeking to sell products or services to the federal government. Each day, it listed government procurement invitations, subcontracting leads, sales of surplus government property, and foreign business opportunities. In addition, it identified government contracts that had already been awarded to specific companies and described research and development projects in which specific federal procurement officers may be interested. This publication has been discontinued in the print format, and the information is now available as part of the online service *FedBizOpps* (see figure 3.8).

```
PART: U.S. GOVERNMENT PROCUREMENTS (MODIFICATION)
SUBPART: SUPPLIES, EQUIPMENT AND MATERIAL
CLASSCOD: 31--Bearings
OFFADD: Defense Supply Center Richmond, 8000 Jefferson Davis
  Highway, Richmond, VA 23297-5000
SUBJECT: 31--BEARING PLAIN, SELF-ALIGNING
SOL SP0441-99-R-0729
DUE 113099
POC Buyer: Mimi Kirkland/BW200/804-279-3508 Contracting Officer
  Carolyn Altizer/BW001/804-279-3527
DESC: ARG98266046501 for an IQC is hereby changed to YPG99293000826
  for a Firm Fixed Price Contract. This requirement is for 80 each with 100% quantity option
  provisions. All other conditions remain unchanged.
LINKURL: www.dscr.dla.mil
LINKDESC: DSCR Homepage
EMAILADD: mkirkland@dscr.dla.mil
EMAILDESC: Contact the buyer via e-mail
CITE: (W-309 SN398491)
```

Figure 3.8. Typical listing, *FedBizOpps*, http://www.fedbizopps.gov/.

Employment Opportunities Resources

National Business Employment Weekly. New York: Dow Jones, 19uu– . Weekly.

An increasing number of newspapers and tabloids are devoted solely to the job market. The *National Business Employment Weekly*, for example, combines articles on such general topics as employment interviews and job search techniques with sections that list opportunities in a designated profession, such as engineering or marketing, or that include advertisements for franchising and distributorship opportunities.

A free site for executive, managerial and professional jobs is http://www.careerjournal. com/Default.asp.. The content comes from the editorial resources of the *Wall Street Journal,* and the *Journal's Online Edition*, both published by Dow Jones. This site also includes a database of thousands of positions and an e-mail alert service for new positions. More general information on resumes and issues in human resources, as well as relocation guides, are also available. For those who need more local job information, the classifieds sections of online newspapers are very functional.

For those interested in working for the federal government, http://www.fedworld.gov/ jobs/jobsearch.html is a first-stop search page for current positions. FedWorld downloads source files from the FJOB bulletin board system. It provides searching by state, grade, and merit position. It must be noted that not all jobs are automatically included, as some are advertised only on agency Web pages. A good source to use in finding these agencies is at http://www.fedworld.gov/gov-links.html.

News Services

For current awareness there are many services on the Web that are both subscription and free. One of the simplest ways to get current updates of news is to use a free service such as http://dir.yahoo.com/News_and_Media/, http://www.excite.com/ and http://money. cnn.com, where one can personalize a news page. Another free service is http://www. newsindex.com/, which contains a free e-mail awareness service, a customized news ticker service for your computer, and a keyword searchable index. This service provides a list of the more than 300 sources indexed and fairly detailed instructions for setting up the service.

Periodicals, Newspapers, and Indexes Available Online

Although printed newspaper and periodical indexes are still staples in many libraries, the use of online bibliographic databases to access articles has become increasingly commonplace.

Online databases are considered at length in chapter 8. It is worth mentioning here, however, that many of the publications that have been discussed in this chapter are available as online databases. *Barron's, Commerce Business Daily, Harvard Business Review, Investor's Business Daily*, and the *Wall Street Journal* can all be searched online as full-text databases, and other publications give some information free on the Web. In addition, computerized versions of *Business Periodicals Index*, *F&S Index*, and several other printed indexing services are available. To remain current with not only the type of information available but also the formats in which this is published, the librarian and researcher must constantly check the publishers' Web pages.

All of the databases mentioned above and other, similar databases make it possible to search in minutes a wide range of periodicals and newspapers that might not otherwise be available in every library setting.

Notes

1. *Business Week* circulation figures were taken from the 1999 edition of *Ulrich's International Periodicals Directory* (New York: Bowker, 1932– . 5vs. Annual.).

2. Dick Levin, *The Executive's Illustrated Primer of Long-Range Planning* (Englewood Cliffs, N.J.: Prentice-Hall, 1981), 182.

3. For more thorough analysis of the *Wall Street Journal* see Michael B. Lehmann, *The Irwin Guide to Using The Wall Street Journal*, 5th ed. (Chicago: Irwin Professional Publishing, 1996).

4. Educational publications from the *Wall Street Journal* are available at http://info.wsj.com/college/teaching/index.html. *Wall Street Journal* educational representatives are listed at http://info.wsj.com/college/sales.html.

5. Publications available from *Barron's Educational Edition* (order form at http://ads.barrons.com/college/):

- *A User's Guide to Barron's.* A 32-page introduction to the financial tables and statistics and a critical guide to *Barron's* features and columns. Limit 50 copies. Free.

- *Talk Like a Pro.* A quick, easy-to-use guide to stock tables and various Dow Jones averages that provides students with a handy reference to key financial data and commonly used symbols. Limit 50 copies. Free.

- *How Professors Use Barron's in the Classroom.* A booklet full of tested ideas using the information in *Barron's* for courses in finance, economics, real estate, accounting, management, and business administration. Free.

4

Loose-leaf Services

Coverage of business reference sources in the preceding chapters has focused on information available in traditional formats, whether in print or electronically, such as bibliographies, directories, periodicals, and newspapers. They are formats common to all subject disciplines, as likely to be found in the humanities and social sciences as in business. Although these types of publications are important to the business community as well, they fail to meet one of its most important requirements, the need for detailed, current information pertaining to fields that are heavily dependent on statutory, administrative, and judicial rulings. An accountant needing to keep abreast of the most recent amendments to the tax law or a personnel director in search of recent court decisions regarding dismissal of employees, for example, would find that neither *Business Week*, the *Wall Street Journal*, nor any of the other sources described in the preceding chapter would provide the level of detail required. Loose-leaf services, however, satisfy the need for such highly specific, up-to-date information. They are all but unique to the fields of business and law and, in fact, often combine the two. There are many different types of loose-leaf services on a variety of topics, but there are some features common to most services. Loose-leaf services include indexes to the materials within them. They also contain a current awareness feature, such as current reports or a highlights section, summarizing recent developments in that topic.

Technology is creating new ways to access information formerly only available through loose-leaf publications. Thus many looseleaf services are now available in CD-ROM format or Web versions, or through online vendors such as LexisNexis and WESTLAW. This chapter focuses on what are generally known as loose-leaf services and the differing formats in which they are now obtainable.

History and Development

Enactment of the federal income tax law in 1913, followed by the creation of the Federal Trade Commission in 1914, gave the first real impetus to the development of loose-leaf services. In each case, lawyers, accountants, and business people were required not only to know the law as it was originally enacted but also to keep abreast of subsequent amendments, court cases, administrative regulations and rulings, and other developments. Loose-leaf services, which culled relevant sections from multiple primary sources such as the U.S. Code, court decisions, the Code of Federal Regulations, and the *Federal Register*, and which could be revised simply by inserting or removing specified pages from loose-leaf binders, were ideal. They were both more up-to-date and more convenient to use than traditionally bound materials and, in some instances, made information accessible that was not otherwise widely available.

Reform legislation enacted during the New Deal era in the 1930s provided another spur to the growth of loose-leaf services. Passage of such laws as the Social Security Act of 1935 and the Fair Labor Standards Act of 1938, as well as the creation of such government agencies as the Securities and Exchange Commission, the National Labor Relations Board, and the Federal Deposit Insurance Corporation, all had profound effects on the practice of business, leading to increased regulation of business and economic activity by the federal government. This expansion of the government's role was reflected in a corresponding increase in the volume of legislative, administrative, and judicial rulings, all of which changed frequently. Again, loose-leaf services proved the ideal format for coping with both the volume and frequency of changes in the law relating to these fields. Services covering labor, securities, social security, and bankruptcy were among those inaugurated during the New Deal.

More recent legislation has focused on consumer and employment regulations, protection of the environment, telecommunications, international licensing, and the privacy of both individual and company records. Again, initial enabling legislation has been supplemented by amendments, court decisions, and rulings from government regulatory organizations. As in earlier years, new loose-leaf services were created to help business people and professionals keep informed and up-to-date.

Today there are literally hundreds of loose-leaf services, many of them falling into the categories shown in figure 4.1. Scope and arrangement vary from publisher to publisher and from title to title, but some generalizations about loose-leaf services can be made. First, they represent areas, such as taxation and labor, that are heavily regulated by government and in which changes are commonplace and frequent. Second, each specialized field covered by a

Accounting and auditing	Labor and employee relations
Banking	Legislation
Bankruptcy	Occupational safety and health
Commercial credit	Pensions and compensation
Consumer credit	Product liability
Corporations	Profit sharing
Energy	Real estate
Environment	Securities
Estates	Social Security
Fair employment	Taxation
Foods, drugs, and medical devices	Trade regulations

Figure 4.1. Some fields represented by loose-leaf services.

loose-leaf service is treated comprehensively. Included are all relevant primary source materials, such as legislation, agency rulings and interpretations, judicial decisions, executive orders, and administrative rulings. Third, loose-leaf services often include secondary data such as lists of pending legislation, citations to relevant periodical articles and books, editorial commentary, and the latest news on developments in the field. Fourth, the arrangement and detailed indexing of information in loose-leaf services make them more convenient and easier to use than the myriad of primary sources from which the information is gathered. Loose-leaf publishers, in fact, point out that many of the government agencies responsible for issuing rules and regulations and administering the law are among their best customers. Finally, the relative ease and frequency with which loose-leaf services are updated often make them the first place in which changes are reported. They are essential to libraries serving patrons who must keep abreast of statutory and regulatory business law.

Format and Contents

Although many different loose-leaf publishers are represented in law library collections, in business reference settings three publishers are dominant. They are the Bureau of National Affairs (BNA), Commerce Clearing House (CCH), and Research Institute of America (RIA). Each issues services on a wide range of subjects, most of which are quite expensive and many of which essentially duplicate similar services published by the other companies. Unless the business reference collection is unusually comprehensive or affluent or serves a community of users in which comparing coverage in different services is important, usually one publisher predominates. Both CCH and RIA, for example, publish federal tax reporters, but many business libraries subscribe to only one tax service. (See figure 4.2.)

Bureau of National Affairs (BNA) http://www.bna.com/	Commerce Clearing House (CCH) http://www.cch.com	Research Institute of America (RIA) http://www.riahome.com/
Banking Report	Business Franchise Guide	Federal Tax Coordinator
Bankruptcy Law Reporter	Capital Changes Reports	2d
Construction Labor Report	e Law Monitor	Pension & Benefits Expert
Disabilities Law Library on CD	Federal Energy Regulatory Commission Reports C Opinions, Orders, Decisions	RIA Federal Tax Regulations
Electronic Commerce & Law Report		U.S. International Taxation
Intellectual Property Library on CD	Federal Energy Regulatory Commission Reports C Statutes and Regulations	
International Licensing	Guide to State Telecommunications Law	
Labor Relations Reporter (complete service)	Standard Federal Tax Reporter	
	State Tax Reporters	

Figure 4.2. Some loose-leaf services available in paper or electronic format from three major publishers.

Loose-leaf services may be organized in one of two ways: interfiled or newsletter style. A newsletter style loose-leaf is issued as one or more topical newsletters each week or month. These newsletters are filed in a binder behind topical dividers for reference. Usually, there will be a cumulative index to the series of newsletters. Most services published by the Bureau of National Affairs (BNA) are newsletter style.

An interfiled service consists of two main parts: a series of binders and the accompanying perforated sheets to be inserted in them. Beyond that, arrangement varies. Although some publishers use a cumulating method in which new sections are simply added to the old without any concurrent substitution or removal of pages, most services are kept up-to-date by adding new pages and removing those that are no longer current. Such loose-leaf services are often called reporters. Depending on the complexity of the field being covered, a reporter may consist of a single loose-leaf volume or several volumes. The *Standard Federal Tax Reporter* from CCH, for example, consists of 22 volumes. At a minimum, most loose-leaf services consist of the following parts: a "how to" section, the basic text, new matter, and a series of indexes and finding aids.

Almost every reporter begins with several pages of instruction and description, which explain the scope of the reporter, its arrangement, and how to use it most effectively. Loose-leaf services are complex, filled with legal and business jargon, and their text presupposes basic familiarity not only with the subject matter but also with the ways in which the publishers have chosen to arrange it. Many of the questions concerning the contents and use of a specific loose-leaf service can be answered simply by reading the introduction, which should be required reading for business reference librarians, serious researchers, and for those responsible for filing loose-leaf services.

The bulk of each service is composed of the basic text, consisting of statutes, regulations, rulings, court decisions, and editorial commentary. Subjects in sections are divided by guide cards identifying each unit's contents. A table of contents appears at the beginning of each division, outlining the subjects to be found; in these contents pages as in the indexes, references are made to paragraph numbers rather than page numbers.

Although frequent changes are made to the basic text to keep it up-to-date, most reporters also include supplementary "current matters" sections in which new developments are reported. These sections vary from one service to another, but generally include a regular bulletin or newsletter, lists of and status reports on new and pending legislation, and texts or summaries of recent court decisions and regulatory agency rulings and opinions. This layering of basic text material with separate sections containing the most recent information is also reflected in the indexing characteristic of loose-leaf services.

Indexes provide immediate access to specific divisions and paragraphs. Most reporters include a basic subject index, supplemented by a current index, issued between revisions of the basic index. In some instances, the current index will be supplemented by yet another, even more up-to-date index. For example, a full Commerce Clearing House index may consist of three separate parts, a "Topical Index," a "Current Topical Index," and "Latest Additions to the Current Topical Index." Clearly, a thorough subject search will require that all topical indexes be consulted.

Additional finding aids provide alternative means of accessing information. Most loose-leaf services include case tables, which can be searched by case name; citator tables, which list court decisions by name and include references to subsequent rulings and decisions in which prior court decisions have been cited; and numeric tables, which make it possible to search by public law numbers, ruling numbers, and other official numeric designations. In most instances, these sections include detailed explanations of their use; the astute researcher will read these as well as the service's introductory section before beginning work.

Electronic Publishing

Loose-leaf services have traditionally been the major tool for discovering the statutes, regulations, rulings, and cases that together form federal laws and regulations that affect business. Until recently the only alternative to housing large collections of loose-leaf services was to use LexisNexis or Westlaw. But as the online charges for Lexis and Westlaw were high, especially for publications that need to be accessed continually, only the largest firms tended to use these online services on a regular basis. But now, available to everyone, are both CD-ROM titles and Web products, provided by the companies who first made loose-leaf services available. A CD-ROM has the capacity to store huge amounts of data. With current technology, one compact disc can hold about 550 megabytes of data, which is the equivalent of about 100–120 volumes of law books or 255,000 pages of printed text. This solves enormous storage problems both for large libraries and small establishments. "In talking to publishers who have converted products to the Internet, the consistent off the record comment is that the bulk of their new sales are Internet products while the number of print sales is steadily declining."[1] Publishers are continually adding to the products available electronically and some, in fact, such as BNA's *Disabilities Law Library on CD,* are only available in this format, although some sections may be available in print.

The three publishers mentioned previously (BNA, CCH and RIA) all have a wide array of both paper and electronic products. In this section the online Web products are surveyed. For further information, the publishers' Web pages provide extensive reports on all their publications in all formats.[2]

RIA is a New York–based business unit of Thomson Tax and Accounting (TTA) and was formed by joining the Research Institute of America (RIA), Computer Language Research (CLR), and Warren, Gorham & Lamont (WG&L). The Web product from RIA is called *Checkpoint.*

The opening screen contains five research areas: Federal, State & Local, International, Pension & Benefits, and Estate Planning, which are displayed in a drop down box. One can choose the section to search and enter keywords, or choose from previously selected keywords, or choose to do a citation search. For those who prefer an hierarchical approach or simply know which materials they wish to search, clicking on the database button will display a complete listing of the titles contained in the chosen set so that one can choose a narrower spectrum of information to search. Retrieved documents are heavily cross-referenced with hyperlinks to related documents.

CCH, a Chicago-based wholly owned subsidiary of Wolters Kluwer U.S., has always been well known for its services, especially the *Standard Federal Tax Reporter.* Many CCH products are available on CD-ROMs and also as Web products. One very useful extra for those libraries and companies who still have holdings only on CD-ROM is that it is possible to use the access passwords provided for the discs to gain access to the Internet versions of the products to which they subscribe. As many of the CD-ROMs are only updated quarterly, this gives the user recourse to updates before the disc is received. The Web version is entered by choosing from four libraries: Federal and State Tax; Business and Finance; Health, Medical and Entitlements; and Human Resources. Within the library one may perform a simple or power search or a citation search.

The Bureau of National Affairs, Inc., was founded in 1926 and incorporated in 1947 as a wholly employee-owned company. BNA produces more than 200 news and information services and numerous dailies, including the *Daily Environment Report* and the *Daily Report for Executives.* Once the service has been logged into, one will choose a section (called an "infobase" by BNA) and this will display the "table of contents." Within each database one can also perform a free text or quote search, and some databases allow for truncation and proximity searches.

Although legal and business materials are generally the best known loose-leaf services, many industries and professions use media that can be classified as such. One well-known service is that generally known as the *Dodge Reports*, which provides advance information on current and pending construction jobs. In the past libraries collected the *Dodge Building Cost Calculator & Valuation Guide* and the update supplements known as the *Calculator Valuation Guide.* These were further reinforced with weekly updates and the daily *Dodge Construction News Greensheets.* Although these can still be purchased, Dodge has amalgamated all the information on a Web page at http://www.fwdodge.com/. One can receive the latest information on construction projects and the services needed as well as accessing information on over 850,000 construction-related firms.

The replacement of loose-leaf services by electronic access can bring greater efficiency to a collection of materials. Although loose-leaf services were always regarded as the most recent information on regulations and laws, most of the updates were received weekly and then staff time had to be allocated to file the materials. There was always the problem of missing pages and the complications of replacing them. Now one may access information that is updated on a daily basis and news as it is breaking. Many libraries still collect the paper services, but the ease of use and the timeliness of electronic collections are making these services very appealing to the user.

Directories

Although loose-leaf services are listed selectively in some of the basic business guides described in chapter 1, such listings are far from comprehensive. The librarian seeking information about the availability of loose-leaf services on a particular subject or the contents of a specific reporter may turn to the *Directory of Business and Financial Information Services* or *Legal Looseleafs in Print.*

Popovich, Charles J., and M. Rita Costello, eds. **Directory of Business and Financial Information Services.** 9th ed. New York: Special Libraries Association, 1994. 471p.

Legal Looseleafs in Print. Teaneck, N.J.: InfoSources Publishing, c1981– . Annual.

The *Directory of Business and Financial Information Services*, first published in 1924, lists and annotates 1,249 different services, many of which are published in loose-leaf format. Entries are arranged by title, with subject, publisher, and master title indexes. Each listing includes the publisher's name and address; a descriptive annotation; and an indication of format, size, and frequency of publication. Although prices are also included, they are useful primarily as benchmark figures, since they represent prices quoted prior to publication in 1994.

Legal Looseleafs in Print provides a complete listing by title of the loose-leaf services currently in publication in the United States. Included is a topical index to make it easy to find a service in a particular area.

Although electronic access is now available for many of the publications that used to be available in loose-leaf many libraries and companies still prefer to collect these subject areas in print. But whatever the format, these services are still generally known as loose-leaf services.

Notes

1. Howard W. Wolosky,"What's New in Tax and Accounting Research?" *The Practical Accountant* 31, no 6 (June 1998): 47–52.

2. BNA, http://www.bna.com; CCH, http://www.cch.com; RIA, http://www.riahome.com.

5

Government Information and Services

The preceding chapter on loose-leaf services touched on the government's role as regulator and overseer of many commercial activities. The scope of this chapter is considerably broader, encompassing the broad range of information and services made available to business by federal and state government agencies. The value of such government support cannot be overestimated. Agencies compile and publish data, supply personal expertise, and, in many instances, provide financial assistance to individuals and organizations. The aim of this chapter is to provide an overview of the major types of business-related government information and services and of the print and electronic sources that identify them.

Federal Government Information

The federal government is widely acknowledged to be the world's largest gatherer and publisher of information. Once primarily available in paper copy, that information is now published in other formats as well, including microfiche, computer tape, CD-ROM, and on the Internet. Whatever the format, much of this information can be tremendously useful to the business community. In fact, there are many business fields in which government documents are the most comprehensive information source available; no private, commercial publisher, for example, can possibly match the detailed demographic and socioeconomic data routinely gathered and published by the Census Bureau. Government documents play an indispensable role in answering business-related inquiries, whether they be about the cost of living in Chicago, or forecasts for the steel industry, or the number of families in Memphis living in air-conditioned houses. There are Department of Labor publications on the outlook for specific occupations; congressional hearings on trade regulations and the national debt; Interstate Commerce Commission statistics on trucking; and Small Business Administration documents on how to establish, operate, and promote small businesses. There are, in fact, very few subjects about which the federal government has not issued publications. Unfortunately, except for a few standard reference works such as the *Statistical Abstract* and the *Government Manual*, documents are often overlooked by patrons and sometimes even by librarians as important information sources. There are also publishers who recompile and in some cases add value to the basic information and sell it in a variety of formats.

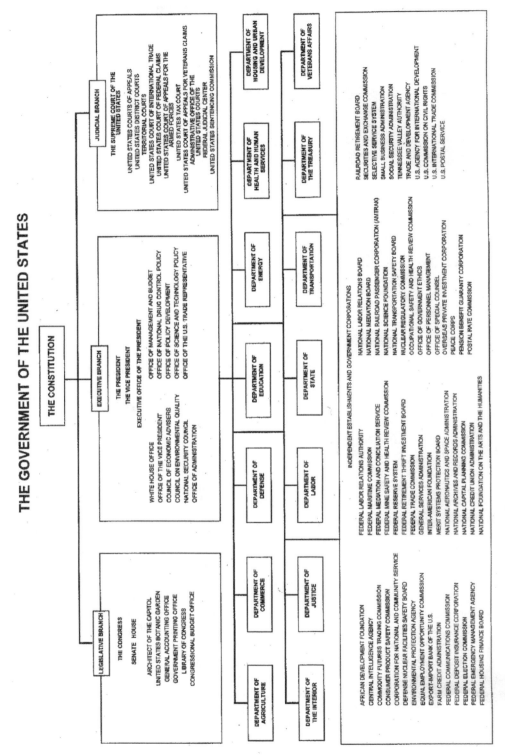

Figure 5. 1. Branches of the federal government. Reproduced from page 21 of the *Government Manual* at http://www.gpoaccess.gov/gmanual/browse-gm-02.html.

Structure of the Government

Effective promotion and use of federal documents begins with an understanding of the organizational structure of the government. The Constitution created three branches of government: legislative, judicial, and executive. In addition, although not set forth in the Constitution, an unofficial fourth branch, comprising independent agencies and government corporations, is commonly recognized (see figure 5.1).

Legislative Branch

The legislative branch consists of both houses of Congress and support organizations, such as the General Accounting Office, the Library of Congress, and the Government Printing Office. The publications of each reflect their varying purposes.

Congressional documents, for example, provide a record of information gathered and opinions shared and debated as well as laws enacted. The work of preparing and considering legislation is done largely by committee, and congressional committee publications such as committee prints (background information and studies prepared by staff for committee use), hearings, and reports contain a wealth of information. While there are few congressional committees whose activities do not affect business in one way or another, some, listed in figure 5.2, are particularly important. Copies of current committee prints, hearings,

HOUSE	SENATE
Agriculture	Agriculture, Nutrition & Forestry
Energy and Commerce	Banking, Housing & Urban Affairs
Financial Services	Commerce, Science & Transportation
Science	Environment & Public Works
Small Business	Finance
Transportation and Infrastructure	Health, Education, Labor & Pensions
Ways and Means	Small Business

Figure 5.2. Congressional committees pertaining to business.

and reports can usually be obtained by contacting the Senate Document Room or by writing or calling the documents clerk of the committee itself. Since congressional documents are printed in limited supply, it may be necessary to borrow older ones from nearby depository libraries or to acquire reprints from commercial publishers. These publications, from the 101st Congress onwards, are also available from http://thomas.loc.gov/. This site includes a searchable index of reports and bills plus a calendar of committee meetings.

Support organizations in the legislative branch include the Congressional Budget Office, the Office of Architect of the Capitol, and the U.S. Botanic Garden. The agencies in this category with most relevance to business, however, are the General Accounting Office, the Government Printing Office, and the Library of Congress.

The General Accounting Office (GAO) is an independent, nonpolitical agency responsible for auditing government agencies and for making recommendations to Congress on how to improve the efficiency and effectiveness of government programs. The GAO generates reports in response to legislation that specifically directs it to analyze and evaluate specific programs and also to requests for assistance from congressional staff; its findings are published in reports to Congress, many of which are publicly available.[1] Reports can cover broad topics, such as foreign investment in the United States and the financial condition of American agriculture, or they may focus on narrower topics such as income security and corporate financial audits and standards.

The Government Printing Office (GPO) executes printing and binding orders placed by Congress and by other government agencies. In addition, it produces and distributes federal government information publications and provides public access to government information online. Its activities are more fully described in the section on government publishers that follows.

Although the Library of Congress was established to serve the information needs of Congress, its considerable resources are also available to the public. These include collections that make it the world's largest library, and access to a number of services, some of which are listed later in this chapter.

The now defunct Office of Technology Assessment (OTA) was created by the Technology Assessment Act of 1972 to "help Congress anticipate and plan for the consequences of technology." Its basic function was to provide congressional committees with studies that identified the social, economic, and physical consequences that may accompany various policy decisions relating to the use of specific technologies, such as nuclear power and alternative fuels. This office was closed in September 1995, but an archival CD-ROM[2] of all the reports is available from the Superintendent of Documents, and an archival Internet site is maintained by The Woodrow Wilson School of Public and International Affairs at Princeton University (http://www.wws.princeton.edu/~ota/).

Judicial Branch

The judiciary is composed of the Supreme Court, the U.S. Courts of Appeals, and District and Territorial Courts. In addition, it includes national courts such as the U.S. Tax Court and the U.S. Court of International Trade. Finally, two support agencies, the Administrative Office of the U.S. Courts and the Federal Judicial Center, complete the roster of organizations in this branch.

Compared to the legislative and executive branches, the judicial arm of the government is not a prolific publisher. The documents it issues are primarily court decisions. While these decisions can have tremendous impact on how business is conducted, requests for the legal information they contain are generally handled by law libraries and in documents departments rather than in more general library settings. This may be changing because of the availability of federal decisions from such services as http://thomas.loc.gov/ and the accessibility of state information through the Internet.

Executive Branch

The executive branch consists of the president, the Executive Office of the President, the vice president, and 14 cabinet departments. While the duties of the president and vice president themselves require no discussion, the other executive agencies merit examination.

The Executive Office of the President is composed of various advisory and administrative support agencies. Those that are particularly important to business are the Council of Economic Advisers, the Council on Environmental Quality, the Office of Management and Budget, and the Office of the U.S. Trade Representative. For a full list of agencies and information about them, go the White House Web site at http://www.whitehouse.gov/government/.

The Council of Economic Advisers (http://www.whitehouse.gov/cea/) is responsible for analyzing the economy and for advising and recommending policies to the president that promote economic growth and stability. It also assists in the preparation of two very important recurring documents, *Economic Indicators*, a monthly compilation of economic statistics prepared for the Congress's Joint Economic Committee, and the annual *Economic Report of the President*. The council's own annual report, not incidentally, is bound with the president's report and comprises the bulk of the document. In 1999, for example, the president's report was 4 pages long, and the council's, 443 pages.

The main purpose of the Council on Environmental Quality (http://www.whitehouse. gov/ceq/) is to formulate and recommend national policies to improve the environment. These recommendations are based on a continuing analysis of the environment, and the changes or trends that affect it, as well as a review and appraisal of the ways in which government programs and regulations contribute to sound environmental policy. Nearly all federal activities affect the environment in some way, and before federal agencies make decisions they must have information about the potential impact of their actions on the quality of the environment. Many of these findings are published, and in recent years Council documents have covered such topics as urban sprawl, energy alternatives, forging conservation partnerships with farmers, blocking offshore oil drilling, and clean water. Like that of the Council of Economic Advisers, its annual report is filled with an impressive array of information and statistical data, ranging from the pollutant standard for urban air quality to the status of whale stocks. As are most other Council on Environmental Quality publications, the annual report is available from the Government Printing Office.

The Office of Management and Budget (http://www.whitehouse.gov/omb/) is charged with several responsibilities. They include reviewing the organization and management of the executive branch, developing and promoting interagency coordination and cooperation, helping the president prepare the budget, and supervising and controlling its administration. In addition, OMB is responsible for planning program performance evaluations and for keeping the president informed of work proposed, initiated, and completed by government agencies. Although it produces documents on a wide range of subjects, the most heavily used title is the *Budget of the United States Government* (http://www.whitehouse.gov/ omb/budget/) and its satellite documents, such as the *Citizen's Guide to the Federal Budget* and *Analytical Perspectives,* which is usually part of the final budget .

The Office of the U.S. Trade Representative (http://www.ustr.gov/) is responsible for administering trade agreements and coordinating trade policy. It periodically issues documents such as the *U.S. National Study on Trade in Services and A Preface to Trade*, a good introduction to U.S. international trade policy and policy making.

In addition to the agencies mentioned above, the president establishes several commissions, committees, boards, and task forces periodically to conduct fact-finding missions. Most publish their findings, and many relate to business and the economy.

Although the Departments of Commerce, Labor, and Treasury are particularly important, each of the 14 executive departments affects business in some way. Appendix B lists the departments, their primary responsibilities relating to business, and selected agencies and publications. Each department publishes a wide array of reports, periodicals, statistics, and information for the general public, most of which are available from the Government Printing Office and many of which are also available on their individual Web sites. Each department also employs a complement of subject specialists who are generally quite willing to share their expertise and, in addition, each has at least one public affairs or information office.

Many departments have regional or field offices, established to provide assistance to designated regions of the country. The Department of Labor's Bureau of Labor Statistics, for example, has regional offices in 8 different cities, the Census Bureau in 12. One of the easiest ways to determine the location of the closest field office is by consulting the *United States Government Manual,* or if one has access to the Internet, each government agency lists offices and contacts on its Web page.

Independent Agencies and Government Corporations

The *United States Government Manual* (http://www.gpoaccess.gov/gmanual/index.html) lists over 50 different independent government organizations authorized by the president or by Congress. Some, such as the Federal Trade Commission and the Nuclear Regulatory Commission, are regulatory agencies. In many instances, the activities they oversee and regulate are commercial ones; as a result, these agencies touch on business in a very real and constant way. Others, such as the Federal Deposit Insurance Corporation, are government-established corporations. Whatever their designation, these agencies comprising the unofficial fourth arm of the government routinely gather and publish statistics, research findings, and agency regulations and decisions. They are prolific publishers. The agencies with greatest impact on business activities are listed in appendix C.

This overview of federal government structure attests to its complexity and diversity. There are literally hundreds of government departments, committees, bureaus, commissions, and agencies. Most are described in the official directory of federal organization, the *United States Government Manual.*

U.S. National Archives and Records Administration. Office of the Federal Register. **United States Government Manual**. Washington, D.C.: Government Printing Office, 1935– . Annual. Web version available at http://www.gpoaccess.gov/gmanual/index.html.

The *United States Government Manual* provides comprehensive information on independent, legislative, executive, and judicial agencies. The address and telephone numbers for each agency and district office are provided, as well as a brief description of its history, programs, and activities, and a list of its principal officials. In addition, each entry features a section that lists the names and telephone numbers of departments responsible for public information, contracts and grants, publications, and employment. Organization charts for major departments and agencies are included, and a list of abolished and transferred agencies is appended. Name, subject, and agency indexes complete the *Manual*. This inexpensive directory is, in fact, a treasure trove of information, an indispensable guide to the federal government and, although much of the information is now available on the Internet, it still belongs in every reference collection.

Although the *Manual* provides an overview of the legislative branch, it is not the most comprehensive congressional information source. That distinction belongs to another federal publication, the *Official Congressional Directory*.

U.S. Congress. Joint Committee on Printing. **Official Congressional Directory**. Washington, D.C.: Government Printing Office, 1809– . Annual. Web version available at http://www.gpoaccess.gov/cdirectory/index.html.

Prepared for the use of Congressional members and their staff, the *Official Congressional Directory* (http://www.gpoaccess.gov/cdirectory/index.html) is useful to anyone who requires information about the legislative branch of the government or about executive, judicial, independent, and private organizations whose activities affect Congress. It includes a listing of congressional committees and subcommittees, their staff, and the members of Congress who serve on them; a biographical section arranged by state; and an alphabetical listing of legislators, their office addresses and telephone numbers, and the names of their administrative and executive assistants. Information on embassies, diplomats, and international organizations is also included. Using the *Directory*, one can find the name of the ambassador to Botswana, determine when a senator's term of office will expire, and compile a list of OECD member countries. Like the *United States Government Manual*, the *Official Congressional Directory* is a basic reference source. Together they provide detailed and comprehensive access to most government organizations.

In government as in business, however, change is commonplace. Programs and responsibilities are reassigned, new departments and agencies are created, and old ones are reorganized or even abolished. Thus, as with many annual business directories, these government directories sometimes lag behind. One solution is to supplement them with commercially published directories issued more frequently. Following are two of the most commonly used commercial publications.

Carroll's Federal Directory: Executive, Legislative, Judicial.. Washington, D.C.: Carroll Publishing, 1980– . Bimonthly.

Federal Yellow Book. New York: N.Y. Leadership Directories, 1976– . Quarterly.

Carroll's Federal Directory and the *Federal Yellow Book* provide directory access to federal agencies and key executives. Both are also available electronically either as a CD-ROM or through the Internet. Although much of the information is garnered from federal telephone directories and the *United States Government Manual,* the commercial products' advantage is their relative currency. One is updated bimonthly, the other quarterly, and as a result they sometimes reflect more accurately current government organization and staffing than do the government annuals. Both issue quarterly CD-ROMs, and the Web product is updated daily. *Leadership Directories* provides some of this information free, at http://www.leadershipdirectories.com/ . Subscriptions to these books, or to the online services, cost several times the purchase price of the *United States Government Manual* and the *Official Congressional Directory*.

Federal Government Publishers

The federal government, as we have seen, is complex and diverse, and each government agency produces documents for public information and use. Documents take many different forms, and their intellectual content varies widely, but most are made available (in print or CD-ROM versions) through the two major government publishers, the Government Printing Office and the National Technical Information Service. With the advent of the Internet more information is being made available in an electronic format by the issuing agencies, although print versions may still be available from the GPO. Consideration of these and of the other federal publishers is in order.

Government Printing Office

Although it began as the printer for Congress and is officially an agency of the legislative branch, the Government Printing Office's activities have long since expanded to make it the primary source for printing, distribution, and sale of federal government documents. Each year it publishes thousands of items and makes many of them available through a network of depository libraries and a sales program.

Today the GPO is at the vanguard in providing government information through a wide range of formats, including printing, microfiche, CD-ROM, and online through *GPO Access* (http://www.gpoaccess.gov).

Depository Libraries

The GPO distributes many of the documents it publishes, in various formats, to over 1,350 depository libraries, at least one in each congressional district. The depository system was created to ensure public access to documents, and each depository library "is designated to receive, without charge on a deposit basis, government publications issued by governmental agencies, except those determined by the issuing agencies to be required for official use only or for strictly administrative or operational purposes . . . [or] classified for reasons of national security."[3] Four points should be emphasized. First, depository libraries do not pay for the documents they receive. Second, although housed in the library, the documents do not really belong to the library; they are there "on deposit." The federal government has the right to ask for their return at any time. Third, the depository program exists to make documents available to the public. Although definition of public availability varies from one depository library to another, at a minimum it means that anyone has the right to use, on site, any document held by the library. Fourth, not all GPO-published documents are sent to depository libraries; a distinction is made between nondepository documents, which are not sent to depositories, and depository documents, which are.

There are two types of depository libraries, regional and selective. The country's 50 regional depositories are required to receive and keep permanently all documents that have been designated as depository items. In addition, regional depository staffs are expected to provide interlibrary loan and reference service and other types of assistance, both to the public and to other libraries in their region. Many regionals have been depositories since the late nineteenth or early twentieth centuries. As a consequence of their extensive collections and their strong service orientation, they are usually excellent providers of information, advice, and assistance.

Selective depository libraries can choose the documents that they want to receive; unlike the regionals, they are not required to accept and house every depository document published by the Government Printing Office. In addition, with the approval of the regional depository library in their area, they can discard unwanted documents. As a result, there is considerable variation in the breadth and depth of selective depository collections. Some rival regional depositories in size and scope; others are considerably narrower. There are presently some 1,300 selective depository libraries in the United States and, like their regional depository counterparts, they provide access to and assistance in the use of their documents collections.

Although most nondepository library business reference collections include a core of basic business sources published by the federal government, depository libraries provide access to more specialized sources and to GPO titles that are no longer in print. Library staff and users would do well to become acquainted with collections, service policies, and documents librarians at nearby depository libraries. They constitute a rich information source, one that can be of particular benefit to business librarians and researchers. A complete list of selective and regional depository libraries can be obtained by writing to the Government Printing Office or by checking the Web page at http://www.gpoaccess.gov/libraries.html (see figure 5.3).

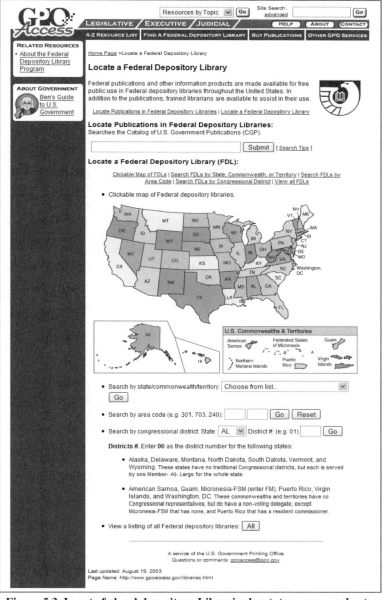

Figure 5.3. Locate federal depository Libraries by state or area code at http://www.gpoaccess.gov/libraries.html.

GPO Sales Program

Nondepository libraries wishing to build documents collections of their own or to acquire specific government publications usually purchase them from the Government Printing Office's Superintendent of Documents.

There are 24 GPO bookstores in cities across the United States, each of which stocks and sells approximately 1,500 of the GPO's most popular titles. (Bookstore locations are listed at http://bookstore.gpo.gov/locations/index.html). In addition, librarians can acquire federal documents through commercial book dealers, jobbers, and document delivery services. Usually, however, the choice is to order documents from the GPO by mail or by telephone. Another alternative is the Online Bookstore at http://bookstore.gpo.gov/index.html.

Many libraries no longer buy print editions of documents but use the online products provided by the GPO. The core documents, ranging from the Gettysburg Address to three years of *Economic Indicators,* are available at http://www.gpoaccess.gov/su_docs/locators/coredocs/index.html.

Public Law 103–40, known as the Government Printing Office Electronic Information Enhancement Act of 1993, stated that free electronic access should be provided to information products produced by the federal government. *GPO Access* (http://www.gpoaccess.gov/) was established by this law and began operations in 1994. It provides easy, one stop, no fee access to information from all three branches of the government. The information provided is the official, published version, and the material retrieved from *GPO Access* can be used without restriction, unless specifically noted. *GPO Access* provides free online use of over 1,000 databases ranging from the *Budget of the United States Government* to the *Federal Register.* (See figure 5.4.)

The *Federal Bulletin Board* (FBB) (http://fedbbs.gpoaccess.gov/) is another component of the GPO. Federal agencies use the *FBB* as a means to distribute electronic files in various file formats to the public. Information is available from the White House and executive branch agencies, including independent agencies, such as the Department of State and Treasury and the Federal Labor Relations Authority. Data vary from *Daily Treasury Statements* to *Free National Export Strategy Documents.* (See figure 5.5.)

GPO Bibliographies and Lists

Consulting one or more of the GPO's bibliographies and lists, available in differing formats, can identify documents published by the Government Printing Office. Among the most important are the *Monthly Catalog of United States Government Publications, U.S. Government Books, New Books, Subject Bibliographies,* and *Government Periodicals and Subscription Services, Price List 36.* Each merits attention.

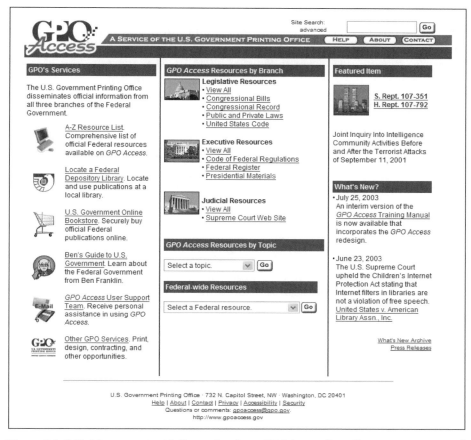

Figure 5.4. Official government information from *GPOAccess* (http://www.gpoaccess.gov/).

Figure 5.5. Materials available from the *Federal Bulletin Board* (http://fedbbs.gpoaccess.gov/).

U.S. Superintendent of Documents. **Monthly Catalog of United States Government Publications**. Washington, D.C.: Government Printing Office, 1895– . Monthly, with monthly and annual indexes. (Records since January 1994 are available at http://www.gpoaccess.gov/cgp/index.html and also as a CD-ROM product.)

"The Monthly Catalog," writes Yuri Nakata, "is to government publications what the Cumulative Book Index is to general book publications."[4] It records and indexes documents received by the Government Printing Office from all arms of government-legislative, judicial, and executive branches, and independent and regulatory agencies as well. Arrangement of documents included in the *Monthly Catalog* is by issuing agency. All Department of Commerce publications, for example, are grouped together regardless of subject, as are those of the Department of Labor, the Federal Trade Commission, and other agencies. Entries are brief, but the full bibliographic records are available on the online version and the CD-ROM version. The preliminary pages of each issue of the *Monthly Catalog* describe its contents and use in some detail. (See figure 5.6.)

SuDocs Call No.:	A 62.15:IN 7
Title:	1995 crop insurance handbook (CIH) : underwriting and actual production history (APH) standards for Federal Crop Insurance Corporation employees and reinsured companies.
Author:	Federal Crop Insurance Corporation. Underwriting Division.
Published:	[Washington, D.C.] : U.S. Dept. of Agriculture, Federal Crop Insurance Corporation, Underwriting Division,
Date:	[1995]
Description:	viii, 327 p. : ill. ; 28 cm.
Item No.:	0071-C
Subject:	Insurance, Agricultural -- Crops -- United States -- Handbooks, manuals, etc.
Entry No.:	95-19379

Figure 5.6. Sample short entry from the online version of the *Monthly Catalog* (http://www.gpoaccess.gov/cgp/index.html).

One should be aware of two additional pieces of information before calling upon depository libraries for assistance. As mentioned earlier, not all GPO-published documents are designated as depository documents. Those that are include heavy black dots, or bullets, in the main listing next to the item number. Regional depository libraries, required to receive and keep all depository documents, should have all of these bulleted documents. Selective depository libraries, on the other hand, may have only a limited number of such publications. In addition, many documents formerly published in paper copy are now available only in microfiche or via the Web. Finally, it is never safe to assume that a particular document, simply because it is not a depository item, will be unavailable at depository libraries. Many depositories have extensive holdings of nondepository documents collections purchased from commercial publishers such as Readex and Congressional Information Service.

The Marcive company (http://www.marcive.com) has worked consistently with libraries to make the *Monthly Catalog,* from 1976, available in electronic format. Many institutions choose to load the tapes from Marcive directly into the online catalog to make available an integrated collection of all library holdings, but there are also available both Web versions and CD-ROMS. More information is available at the company Web page.

When the choice is to acquire documents rather than to borrow them from another library, other information is necessary. In many instances, documents can be ordered from the Superintendent of Documents; their availability from the GPO at the time of printing is usually indicated in the main record by an entry stating "For sale by the U.S. G.P.O., Supt. of Docs., Congressional Sales Office." Mail order forms are included in the preliminary pages of each issue of the *Monthly Catalog,* or one may order at the Online Bookstore at http://bookstore.gpo.gov/index.html.

A document's inclusion in the *Monthly Catalog* does not guarantee its availability from the Government Printing Office. Some must be ordered from the issuing agencies themselves or may be freely available on agency Web pages.

Since the main section of the *Monthly Catalog* is arranged by government agency, there is a title keyword index available. The online MOCAT (http://www.gpoaccess.gov/cgp/index. html) is searchable by keyword, title, SuDoc number, item number, stock number, or date, or one can perform a multiple field search. The CD-ROM is indexed by keyword, author, title, series/report number, subject, stock number, contract number, and classification number.

Although the *Monthly Catalog* is the most comprehensive listing of GPO publications, it is not always the best source for building business reference collections, particularly in small and medium-sized libraries. In these settings, other sources, such as *New Products from the U.S. Government*, and the GPO's *Subject Bibliography* series, may be more helpful.

New Products from the U.S. Government. Washington, D.C.: U.S. Government Printing Office, Superintendent of Documents, 1994– . Bimontly.

New Products is a catalog of popular government books, periodicals, and databases. Entries are arranged by government agency and include title, date of publication, formats available, number of pages, GPO stock number, and price. Also included are lists of best sellers and new releases. This publication is available free from the Superintendent of Documents.[5]

U.S. Superintendent of Documents. **Subject Bibliography Index**. Washington, D.C.: Government Printing Office, 2000. 15p. (Available through links at http://bookstore.gpo. gov/sb/sale180.html).

The Government Printing Office also publishes a series of brief bibliographies that list popular pamphlets and brochures by subject. At present, there are over 160 areas covered in these bibliographies, all of which are listed in the *Subject Bibliography Index*. Bibliographies of particular interest to the business community include the titles shown in figure 5.7.

Accounting and Auditing	*Labor-Management Relations*
Agricultural	*Marketing*
Banks and Banking	*New Independent States*
Business	*Occupational Safety and Health*
Employment and Occupations	*Patents and Trademarks*
Energy	*Personnel Management*
Financial Institutions	*Securities and Investments*
Foreign Country Studies	*Small Business*
Insurance	*Statistics*
International Trade	*Taxes*

Figure 5.7. *Subject Bibliography* **list.**

For each document listed, the *Subject Bibliography* includes its title, date, pagination, Superintendent of Documents number, GPO stock number, and price. Many titles are annotated. Although the *Subject Bibliographies* and the *Index* are depository items and available in most documents collections, individuals and other libraries can acquire their own free copies by writing to the Superintendent of Documents. The latest issues of *Subject Bibliographies* is available on the Internet at http://bookstore.gpo.gov/sb/index.html. Selections from a patents and trademarks bibliography are shown in figure 5.8.

Home | Privacy | Site Search | Help | Comments
Site Contents | What's New | *Online Bookstore* | Finding Aids | Library Services

Subject Bibliography

Patents and Trademarks (021)

Attorneys and Agents Registered to Practice Before the United States Patent and Trademark Office...

2000, As of December 22, 2000. BOOK. 2001. 665 p. 0-16-050741-3

S/N 003-004-00693-5 -- $52.50 Add to Cart

2002, As of December 21, 2001. BOOK. 2002. 608 p. 0-16-051103-8

S/N 003-004-00696-0 -- $53.00 (Out of Stock)

Basic Facts About Trademarks. BOOK. 2000. Describes the registration process and filing requirements for trademarks. Contains sample written applications, drawings, and specimens. Also includes blank application forms, a list of patent and trademark depository libraries, information about trademark processing and service fees, and a one page summary of the International Schedule of Classes of Goods and Services. 22 p.; ill.

S/N 003-004-00694-3 -- $3.50 Add to Cart

Code of Federal Regulations, Title 37, Patents, Trademarks, and Copyrights, Revised July 1, 2002. BOOK. 2002 0-16-068231-2.

S/N 869-048-00130-1 -- $47.00 Add to Cart

Microfiche of the above. MICROFICHE. 2001.

S/N 869-047-00130-5 -- $2.00 Add to Cart

General Information Concerning Patents, 1997. BOOK. 2001. Intended for inventors, prospective applicants for patents, and students. Provides general information about patents and the operations of the Patent and Trademark Office. 34 p.

S/N 003-004-00695-1 -- $5.00 Add to Cart

Index of Patents Issued From the United States Patent and Trademark Office:

1993, Part 2, Index to Subjects of Inventions. BOOK. 1993. (Clothbound) 624 p.
0-16-045396-8
C 21.5/2:993/PT.2

S/N 003-004-00671-4 -- $57.00 Add to Cart

1994:

Part 1, List of Patentees, Volumes 1-2. BOOKS. 1995. (Clothbound) 2 bks. (4487 p.) 0-16-045356-9

Figure 5.8. *Subject Bibliography* **example: Patents and trademarks (021).**

An arrangement of government Internet sites in the same topic areas as those of the *Subject Bibliographies* is compiled at http://www.library.okstate.edu/browsetopics/index. html. This is of particular help to the novice searcher who may not know which agency to access for information.

U.S. Government Subscriptions Catalog. Washington, D.C.: Government Printing Office, 1974– . Quarterly. Web version available at http://bookstore.gpo.gov/subscriptions/ index.html.

Government Periodicals and Subscription Services is a catalog that lists serial titles and subscription services available from the Government Printing Office, including such titles as *Economic Indicators, Monthly Labor Review*, and *Commerce Business Daily*. Entries are arranged by title and usually include current prices, stock numbers, Superintendent of Documents classification, and, when applicable, the bullet symbol used to identify depository items. (See figure 5.9.)

CONSTRUCTION REPORTS:

Statistical data covering all areas of construction, such as ownership, location, type of structure, units completed and under construction, sold and for sale prices, contracts and permits, and other useful information.

C30. Value of New Construction Put in Place
LIST ID CRCA
File Code 2M
SuDocs Class Stem C 3.215/3:

> **Monthly.** Reports on value of new construction put in place, by type. Price listed is for a one-year subscription. Shipped first class.
>
> - **S/N:** 703-040-00000-4
> - **Price:** $42.00 ⊌Add to Cart
>
> NOTE: The May issue is available by contacting the GPO Order Desk at 866-512-1800 (Toll-free) or 202-512-1800 (DC Metro area).

Figure 5.9. Sample Entry in *U.S. Government Subscriptions Catalog* for construction reports, at http://bookstore.gpo.gov/subscriptions/subs004.html#022.

The availability of most of this information via *GPOAccess* at http://www.gpoaccess.gov/ has made collection of and quick access to materials easier for people without recourse to a convenient depository library.

Although the Government Printing Office is the principal printing agency of the federal government, it does not publish and sell all federal documents. Other government agencies are also involved in the publication of documents, usually more specialized than those available through the GPO. One of the most important of these agencies is the National Technical Information Service.

National Technical Information Service

The National Technical Information Service (NTIS), an agency of the Department of Commerce, is the central source for public sale of government-sponsored research, development, and engineering reports, and for sales of technical reports prepared by foreign governments and by local government agencies. (See figure 5.10.)

NTIS Product Families & Types

Below are links to pages that focus on specific collections within the NTIS Web site.

Product Families	Product Types
▶ Business Collection *Business and International Trade Online Bookstore*	▶ Audiovisual/Multimedia
	▶ Computer Products
▶ Environmental Collection	▶ Databases
▶ Health Collection	▶ Publications & Reports
▶ Military Publications & Manuals	▶ Subscriptions
▶ Toxic Substances Control Act Unpublished Reports	

Figure 5.10. NTIS product families and types: Business collection, at
http://www.ntis.gov/products/families/business.asp?loc=4–3–1.

When compared to the GPO, however, the NTIS has a much narrower focus. No congressional hearings or government regulations or consumer-oriented publications are included. There are other differences between the agencies. The GPO sells only current titles. The possibility of obtaining a 10- or even 5-year-old document from the GPO is remote. The National Technical Information Service, on the other hand, offers access to all of the documents received since its inception. Another difference is that the GPO subsidizes the printing and sale of its documents, which are very inexpensive. The NTIS, in contrast, is required by law to operate on a cost-recovery basis. As a result, there is considerable difference between the prices of NTIS and GPO documents. Finally, whereas the Government Printing Office has established a network of designated depository libraries, there is no NTIS equivalent. Although many research and technical libraries comprehensively collect NTIS documents, their collections are not part of a government-sponsored system.

NTIS documents are available in a wide variety of formats, including paper copy, microfiche, and microfilm, and various electronic formats. Orders can be placed by mail or by telephone; documents can be purchased from the NTIS sales unit in Springfield, Virginia; or one can search for publications and order online at http://www.ntis.gov/. If a document is available online one may purchase a downloadable version, which speeds up the process and makes information available when it is needed (See figure 5.11).

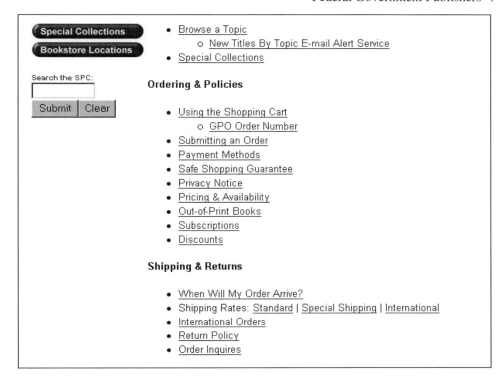

Figure 5.11. Ordering online from NTIS at http://bookstore.gpo.gov/support/index.html.

Although there are available paper indexes to find documents, NTIS has posted an electronic catalog at http://www.ntis.gov/search. This includes more than 400,000 government publications as well as data files, CD-ROMs, and audiovisuals issued by NTIS since 1990. Searching capability is limited to titles and topics, and most records do not include product summaries. If one is searching specifically for business information, this can be easily retrieved from the product family search page for "Business and International Trade" at http://www.ntis.gov/products/families/business.asp?loc=4–3–1. This is a collection of more than 20,000 titles specifically chosen with the business community in mind. There are drop down boxes featuring specific commercial publishers, government, or nonprofit organizations, or one can search the entire business collection. There are also browsable lists of NTIS bestsellers, audiovisual business products, computer business products, and online databases.

Both the Government Printing Office and the National Technical Information Service have extensive and wide-ranging publishing programs. Although the GPO is the government's major publisher and the NTIS the major information clearinghouse, they are by no means the only collectors and disseminators of government information. There are approximately 300 additional federal information clearinghouses, information centers, and depository programs. Most focus on specific research or program areas, such as energy, aging, or education, and many collect and print both government and private sector publications. Two of the best known clearinghouses are the Educational Resources Information Center and the National Criminal Justice Reference Service; two of the best known depository programs are those administered by the Patent and Trademark Office and the Census Bureau.

Of particular interest to business is the information available from the U.S. Patent and Trademark Office at http://www.uspto.gov/. Included at this Web site are booklets such as *Basic Facts about Trademarks, General Information Concerning Patents,* and the *Examiner's Handbook,* and downloadable forms and instructions for patent and trademark applicants. There is also a searchable database of registered patent attorneys and agents. The USPTO also offers free searchable databases to trademarks and patents. The patents, available from 1976 on, are offered in full image format.

Trends in Federal Publishing

Publishing activities of the federal government change from year to year and, more notably, from one administration to the next. Emphasis in recent years has been on reducing federal expenditures, which has been reflected in the government's publishing program. Many documents formerly available in paper copy, for example, are now available only on the Internet or in microfiche, or have been discontinued. Many titles have been "privatized." This means that commercial publishers bear the brunt of publishing costs but are also entitled to earn profits from the government titles they publish. Understandably, documents librarians are concerned about such changes, which mean that many formerly available documents are priced for profit rather than to cover costs.

In the April 2000 edition of *Administrative Notes* (http://www.access.gpo.gov/su_docs/fdlp/pubs/adnotes/), the newsletter of the Federal Depository Library Program, there is an update on the published formats of government information. This details the fact that the most popular dissemination medium in the Federal Depository Library Program is now online. (See figure 5.12.)

Media	Titles	Copies	% of FDLP Titles
Online (GPO Access)	4,173	n/a	16.4
Online (links to other agency sites)	8,956	n/a	35.2
Subtotal for Online	13,129	51.6	
Paper (includes USGS maps)	5,178	2,400,292	20.4
Microfiche	6,826	3,026,140	26.8
CD-ROM	290	107,235	0.1
Subtotal for Tangible	12,294	5,533,667	48.4
Grand Total	**25,423**	**5,533,667**	**100.0**

Figure 5.12. Summary of the online and tangible titles added to the FDLP from October 1999 through February 2000. From http://www.access.gpo.gov/su_docs/fdlp/pubs/adnotes/.

Commercially Published Guides, Bibliographies, and Periodicals

Guides

The volume and scope of published federal information can overwhelm the uninitiated at times. One good way to begin the quest for such information is by consulting a guide to federal documents. Three of the best are *Introduction to United States Government Information Sources, Using Government Information Sources,* and *Tapping the Government Grapevine.*

Morehead, Joe. **Introduction to United States Government Information Sources**. 6th ed. Englewood, Colo.: Libraries Unlimited, 1999. 491p.

Robinson, Judith Schiek. **Tapping the Government Grapevine: The User-Friendly Guide to U.S. Government Information Sources**. 3rd ed. Phoenix, Ariz.: Oryx Press, 1998. 286p.

Sears, Jean L., and Marilyn K. Moody. **Using Government Information Sources: Print and Electronic.** 2nd ed. Phoenix, Ariz.: Oryx Press, 1994. 539p.

A proper understanding of documents and documents librarianship begins with an understanding of the structure of the government and federal publishing programs. Although both have been covered briefly in this chapter, *Introduction to United States Government Information Sources*, which is used as a textbook in many documents courses, treats them in greater depth. It describes the publications and activities characteristic of each branch of the government as well as the history, responsibilities, and role of the Government Printing Office and the Superintendent of Documents. Depository libraries and legal and technical report literature are also covered. *Introduction to United States Government Information Sources* provides an authoritative overview of federal production and distribution of documents, in all available formats, as well as of the types of publications issued by specific government agencies. It is a basic documents information source that is useful for students, librarians, and researchers.

Tapping the Government Grapevine is a highly readable text that explains the intricacies of government information and how to find sources that meet specific research needs. Chapters feature search and access tips, tables and illustrations, and detailed coverage of Internet resources and directories of World Wide Web addresses. Addresses for agencies, Web sites, and lists of free publications appear at the end of relevant chapters.

Using Government Information Sources focuses more on practical search strategies and research techniques used to locate documents on specific subjects. Each chapter deals with a different topic; those particularly relevant to business include Foreign Countries, Occupations, Selling to the Government, Business Aids, Tax Information, Economic Indicators, Business and Industry Statistics, Income, Earnings, Employment, Prices, Consumer Expenditures, Foreign Trade Statistics, Projections, Budget Analysis, Technical Reports, Patents and Trademarks, and Standards and Specifications. Each chapter is grouped into subcategories of similar or related material, each with a checklist of titles providing full bibliographic information and Superintendent of Documents classification numbers. Narrative descriptions of the titles are included in each section, and many chapters are enhanced by the use of sample pages from the documents cited. Relevant indexes, databases, and other specialized sources are also listed.

Using Government Information Sources and *Tapping the Government Grapevine* are particularly helpful to librarians and researchers confronted for the first time with inquiries about subjects with which they have only limited familiarity; *Introduction to United States Government Information Sources*, on the other hand, is most useful for developing a sense of the types of publications that are available from the government, of the basic indexes used to identify them, and of the history and development of various federal publishing programs. Taken together, they provide an outstanding introduction to documents and to the types of business-related reference and research inquiries that documents can answer.

Bibliographies

Commercial publishers also publish documents bibliographies. Three of the most popular are the *Guide to Popular U.S. Government Publications, Government Reference Books*, and the *Subject Guide to U.S. Government Reference Sources.*

Hardy, Gayle J., and Judith Schiek Robinson. **Subject Guide to U.S. Government Reference Sources.** 2nd ed. Englewood, Colo.: Libraries Unlimited, 1996. 358p.

Hoffman, Frank W., and Richard J. Wood. **Guide to Popular Government Publications**. 4th ed. Englewood, Colo.: Libraries Unlimited, 1997. 285p.

Government Reference Books. Littleton, Colo.: Libraries Unlimited, 1968/1969– . Biennial.

The *Subject Guide to U.S. Government Reference Sources* selectively lists and annotates key government reference sources, regardless of format, available through depository libraries, the Internet, and occasionally as free copies from either the GPO or individual agencies. Arrangement is by broad subject category, such as social sciences or science and technology, and each entry includes full bibliographic information; an annotation; and when applicable, Superintendent of Documents classification, Library of Congress, and Dewey classifications.

Guide to Popular Government Publications provides information about documents by topics. Those of special interest to business include Business and International Trade; Consumer Information and Protection; Copyrights, Patents and Trademarks; and Labor and Employment. Each annotated entry includes Superintendent of Documents classification, stock numbers, and prices.

Government Reference Books is a biennial listing of key reference sources issued by the Government Printing Office, an annotated guide to atlases, bibliographies, catalogs, dictionaries, directories, guides, handbooks, indexes, manuals, and other reference publications issued during the two-year period covered. Most titles are grouped together by subject; the section on economics and commerce, for example, includes titles categorized by such subject designations as employment and labor and government assistance and procurement. In addition to the bibliographic citation and annotation, each entry includes the Superintendent of Documents classification, *Monthly Catalog* entry number, stock number, and price. Most of the titles listed are depository documents.

The federal government is committed to providing public access to its information. In addition to being one the world's largest publisher of printed sources, the federal government is also one of the world's largest producers and suppliers of electronic information, either through the Internet, as CD-ROMs, as magnetic tape, or as diskettes. Some federal databases are available through standard online database vendors. Still others can be accessed through government agencies, their contractors, or designated centers, or they can be purchased outright from the federal government. One way to identify such government-produced data files is through use of the *Federal Data Base Finder.*

Lesko, Matthew. **Federal Data Base Finder**. 4th ed. New York: Gale Research, 1995. 1253p.

Although now in need of updating, the *Federal Data Base Finder* gives information about databases, computer tapes, and microcomputer disks available from the government and private contractors. Each entry includes the name of the database; a description of its contents and scope; price; and contact information including the agency address, telephone number, and, in many instances, the name of an information or subject specialist. One way to update this information is to use the *Government Information Locator Service* (GILS) (http://www.access.gpo.gov/su_docs/gils/), a new way to identify, locate, and describe publicly available federal information resources, including electronic information resources. GILS is a decentralized collection of agency-based information locators that directs users to relevant information resources within the federal government. Not all agencies have provided information on the location of their GILS records, so it cannot yet be considered a comprehensive database.

Periodicals and Indexes

Although periodicals published by the Government Printing Office are listed in the *Monthly Catalog*, their contents are not. Accordingly, many documents departments and large research libraries subscribe to a commercially published index to federal serial titles.

Index to U.S. Government Periodicals. Chicago: Infordata International, 1970–1987. Quarterly, with annual cumulations.

LexisNexis Government Periodicals. Bethesda, Md.: CIS, 1988– . Quarterly updates.

The discontinued hard copy *Index* lists articles by author and subject, with each entry featuring a standard bibliographic citation. As the electronic versions only begin coverage in 1988, these volumes are still needed in collections to trace older articles. *CIS Government Periodicals Universe* is a continuation of CIS's *US Government Periodicals Index on CD-ROM* (now discontinued) and covers articles in approximately 170 current federal publications. It includes retrospective coverage through 1988 of over 70 additional federal publications that have major research, reference, or general interest value. The index provides detailed access by subject and author.

Some of the most popular government periodicals, such as the *Federal Reserve Bulletin*, *Survey of Current Business,* and *Monthly Labor Review*, are also included in standard indexes such as *ABI/INFORM* and *Public Affairs Information Service* (*PAIS.*)

For a listing of government titles available on the Web one should check *GPOAccess* at http://www.access.gpo.gov/su_docs/, or for government periodicals one can check an alphabetical listing provided by the Documents Department at Auburn University, http://www.lib.auburn.edu/madd/docs/govperiodicals.html.

In addition, there is a specialized documents periodical that identifies important new documents and trends in government publishing. The final issue of the year contains a list of notable documents

Journal of Government Information: An International Review of Policy, Issues and Resources. New York: Pergamon Press, v. 9– . 1974– . Bimonthly. (Formerly *Government Publications Review*.)

Government Publications Review is a bimonthly scholarly journal devoted entirely to international, foreign, federal, state, and local documents; their production and distribution;

and documents librarianship. Tables of contents from 1973 are available electronically at http://www.lib.auburn.edu/madd/docs/jgi/contents.html.

For up-to-date information on documents one should access the ALA Government Documents Round Table (GODORT) Web page at http://sunsite.berkeley.edu/GODORT/.

To this point this chapter has focused on published information sources. Equally important, however, are the large number of government services available to business people, many of which are described in the following section.

Federal Government Services to Business

The federal government spends billions of dollars annually, much of it for the accumulation of information and specialized expertise. The budget for publicizing the availability of such information and knowledge, however, is negligible. As a result, information and services that might contribute to productivity and profit are underutilized. There are literally hundreds of special programs and services available to business, ranging from counseling to special loans.

The government is often viewed, with some justification, as a vast, bureaucratic maze, complicated, confusing, and intimidating. For librarians and researchers in search of special information or assistance, the first question often is not where to find it, but rather how to find out where to find it, preferably with a minimum of telephone calls or Web searches. Sometimes it is difficult to determine just which agency to contact. In such a situation it may be best to begin with the *U.S. Business Advisor* at http://www.business.gov/ (see figure 5.13). Federal agencies worked together to build the *U.S. Business Advisor*, maintained and funded by the U.S. Small Business Administration as a one-stop electronic link to all the in-

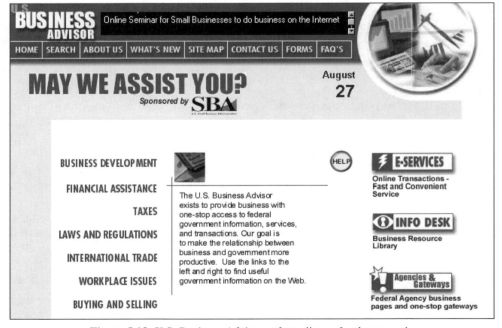

Figure 5.13. *U.S. Business Advisor* at http://www.business.gov/.

formation and services government provides for the business community. This is also now part of *FirstGov* at http://www.firstgov.gov/. Through a series of links one may access information on business development, financial assistance, taxes, laws and regulations, international trade, workplace issues, and buying and selling. Buying and selling, for example, is a good place to start if one wants to sell goods to either federal or state government agencies or needs to check on property for sale. This Web resource provides access not only to business information but also to electronic transactions; education, training, and counseling online; and networks of buyers and suppliers.

Federal Libraries

The government also offers specialized assistance through federal libraries. These represent a tremendous information asset, offering unique collections and resources and highly skilled staff. Most routinely answer mail and telephone inquiries, and many are open to the public. Particularly important to business people and business librarians are the Commerce Department, Census Bureau, Labor Department, and Treasury Department Libraries, and the Library of Congress. A listing of *WWW Sites of Federal Libraries* is available at http://lcweb.loc.gov/flicc/fliccmem.html.

Experts

"For any problem that you may face either professionally or personally," writes Matthew Lesko, "there is likely to be a free expert on the federal payroll who has spent years studying the very same subject."[6] These experts provide special assistance that, were it being sought from a private consultant, might cost hundreds or even thousands of dollars. Their areas of expertise range from stratospheric research to health care; for business, the most frequently consulted experts are those specializing in industry analysis, foreign markets, and the collection and analysis of statistical data.

Many industry analysts are employed by the Census Bureau; others are employed by the Commerce Department's International Trade Administration. At this time the easiest and most up-to-date method to find a contact is either to check the agency Web page or to seek out experts by using the list at http://www.census.gov/contacts/www/contacts.html.

Although experts can be found in almost every government agency, the ones most often consulted by business people are found in such Department of Commerce organizations as the International Trade Administration and the Bureau of Economic Analysis, as well as in the Departments of Labor, Agriculture, and the Treasury, and in the Small Business Administration.

Loans and Financial Assistance

More than 1,000 different federal assistance programs are available to individuals and organizations, over 200 of which are intended to promote the development and continued financial well-being of business enterprises. These include loans from the Small Business Administration, grants from the Economic Development Administration, and insurance from the Overseas Private Investment Corporation. Such programs are listed and described in the following sources.

U.S. Office of Management and Budget. **Catalog of Federal Domestic Assistance**. 2000. http://www.cfda.gov/ (Accessed August 23, 2003).

The most comprehensive listing of federal assistance programs is contained in the *Catalog of Federal Domestic Assistance*. The *Catalog* is the basic reference source for financial assistance programs, including grants, loans, loan guarantees, scholarships, mortgage loans, insurance, and nonfinancial assistance and services. The *Catalog* describes all 1,424 federal domestic assistance programs. It contains information on all financial and nonfinancial assistance programs administered by the departments and establishments of the federal government. The General Services Administration (GSA) publishes the *Catalog* twice a year, in June and December.

Other sources of loan information are *U.S. Business Advisor* (http://www.business.gov/) and *FirstGov* (http://www.firstgov.gov/), where one can obtain information about loan guarantees, equity capital, trade financing, and surety bond guarantees.

Government Purchase of Goods and Services

In 1955, the U.S. government adopted a policy of relying on private industry whenever possible to supply needed goods and services. Agency requirements vary tremendously, ranging from high technology weaponry to painting and dry cleaning. There are two main categories of government purchasing. The first includes general items, such as office equipment and janitorial services, items for which the General Services Administration is the main purchaser. The second category consists of special, mission-oriented goods and services required by individual agencies.

Again the main place to gain information on opportunities to do business with the government is the *U.S. Business Advisor* (http://www.business.gov/), by clicking on the buying and selling section.

State Government Information and Services

State government agencies, like their federal counterparts, are key providers of information and services to business. They publish statistical compendia, research findings, market surveys, annual reports, and other documents; provide access to information about locally based companies; and offer counseling and technical assistance to new and relocating businesses. Unfortunately, such sources and services are underutilized by those who might most benefit from them.

Published Information

Publishing programs and policies regarding document distribution and sales vary from state to state. Most, however, publish a wide range of titles. Blue books, legislative handbooks, and statistical abstracts are the most commonly used state document reference sources, but others can make equally valuable contributions to business reference. Most states generally publish employment and unemployment statistics and economic indicators monthly or at least several times a year. In addition, glossy brochures designed to lure prospective businesses and tourists combine propaganda with useful information, and directories provide access to government officials, state manufacturing industries, and trade and professional associations. Although there is significant variation from one state to another, most have designated specific libraries as state document depositories. Often the state library is named the official depository, and it distributes duplicate copies of the documents it receives to other in-state depository libraries, usually large research and public libraries. In addition, some of these same libraries collect documents from other states.

One of the ways in which documents used to be chosen by libraries was by using the *Monthly Checklist of State Publications* issued by the Library of Congress. This long-standing serial title was discontinued in 1994, and its mission was taken up by librarians at the University of Illinois at Urbana-Champaign. This group produces *StateList: The Electronic Source for State Publication Lists,* accessible at http://gateway.library.uiuc.edu/doc/ StateList/check/check.htm. The Internet site offers centralized access to state checklists and/or shipping lists that are currently available on the Internet for a total of 32 states.

Meta-indexes for *State and Local Governments* and a complete listing of all states with links to their first level of Web pages is available via the Library of Congress at http://lcweb.loc.gov/global/state/stategov.html. Piper Resources is a company that maintains an updated page of links to *State and Local Government on the Net* at http://www.piperinfo.com/state/index.cfm. The criterion for inclusion is that servers must be controlled and managed by state agencies or local government agencies.

Services to Business

Services offered to business by state agencies parallel those offered by the federal government.

Although not perhaps thought of as a service, there is much state statistical information available from state agencies and also from the federal government. One way to begin the search for statistics is to use http://www.fedstats.gov/. More than 70 agencies in the U.S. federal government produce statistics of interest to business and the public. The Federal Interagency Council on Statistical Policy maintains this site to provide easy access to the full range of statistics. One can search by state and deepen the search to individual counties.

State regulation of business activities requires that many businesses and corporations file reports with the government. Although many of these reports are not published as documents, they are available to the public at the state agency that collects them. Each state, for example, requires that a company file articles of incorporation that include information about the company, its location, and the nature of its business in order to incorporate. Other government filings include insurance company financial reports, complaints about companies or specific consumer products, environmental impact studies, and franchise information. Facilities for reading and often for copying some of these unpublished documents are available. Although some corporate directories are appearing on various state Web pages, the majority of the information just mentioned is still only available after a personal visit to an agency.

Information from and about the states is becoming easier to access. Many business librarians work in settings in which only a few key documents reference sources are collected, but with electronic access the level of service provided can be as complex as that of any large research library. One can retrieve tax documents for all states, check on licensing regulations, and eventually even be able to check on all state filings. In addition, although not covered in this chapter, international, foreign, and local government documents can provide information that is unique, timely, and relevant to business research.[7]

Conclusion

Government information continues to be one of the major resources used by business librarians. We may use the raw data produced by the agencies or opt for a repackaged format from a vendor such as Gale, but whatever we use, the numbers have been compiled by either federal, state, or local governments. Moreover, it is becoming easier to access at least current information because of the Internet. The main problem that could arise is the loss of older materials as these are dropped from Web pages by agencies. There must be some provision for this information to remain accessible in whichever format is appropriate.

Notes

1. GAO reports are available at http://www.gao.gov/.

2. OTA CD-ROM set (S/N 052-003-01457–2) is available for $23.00 through the Superintendent of Documents, P.O. Box 371954, Pittsburgh, PA 15250-7974.

3. Yuri Nakata, *From Press to People: Collecting and Using U.S. Publications* (Chicago: American Library Association, 1979), 15.

4. Ibid.

5. You may submit your order to the Government Printing Office via the Internet, phone, fax, postal mail, or teletype. Payment must accompany your order.

Internet *GPO Access* Online Bookstore
Phone (202) 512-1800 between 7:30
A.M. and 4:30 P.M., Eastern Time
Fax (202) 512-2250

Mail Superintendent of Documents
P.O. Box 371954
Pittsburgh, PA 15250-7954
Teletype (710) 822-9413;
ANSWERBACK USGPO WSH

6. *Information USA* (New York: Viking, 1983), 38.

7. Links to 220 world governments on the Web are at http://www.gksoft.com/govt/en.

6

Statistics

Statistics are vital to decision making. They are particularly important in management, accounting, marketing, finance, and any field of business where there is a need to assess past performance, compare and appraise current activities, and make predictions about the future. Market researchers, for example, use statistical data to compare sales of one brand with another and to predict consumer demand for new products. Union leaders use them to justify a case for increased wages to keep up with spiraling living costs, and personnel managers, to measure labor turnover and absenteeism. Statistics are, in fact, so essential to business that the ability to identify, provide access to, and, in some instances, assess the relative merits of statistical data is fundamental to good business reference service. This chapter considers basic business-related uses of statistics, some of the major compilers and publishers of statistical data, key types of business and economic statistics, and the sources that contain them. In addition, it examines some of the pitfalls common in using such data.

Major Compilers and Publishers of Statistics

The cost of collecting primary statistical data, particularly on a large scale, is so great that usually only the largest or wealthiest organizations can afford to do so. Most businesses depend on secondary statistical data generated by government agencies, trade associations, commercial publishers, and private research firms. Each of these organizations regularly compiles, analyzes, and publishes statistics. Familiarity with their statistics-gathering programs and representative publications is an important first step in providing statistical reference assistance.

Federal Government Agencies

The federal government is the greatest single supplier of statistics. The 70 agencies that compile and publish statistical data report expenditures of at least $500,000 per year in statistical pursuits.[1] These data provide information on the population, agriculture, energy and the environment, employment and earnings, money supply, foreign and domestic trade, industrial activity, health, education, and many other subjects. Responsibility for collecting and analyzing such data is assigned to several different agencies within the government. Some major statistical analyses, such as labor force statistics, are carried out by agencies, such as the Bureau of Labor Statistics, whose sole missions are statistical. In other cases, agencies have developed statistical programs that support their operational planning and evaluation functions as an outgrowth of their administrative responsibilities. Federal statistical organization, in essence, is decentralized, with the diverse statistical activities of all agencies coordinated by the Office of Management and Budget's Office of Information and Regulatory Affairs. The full report *Statistical Programs of the United States Government*, prepared by the OMB, is available at http://www.whitehouse.gov/omb/inforeg/02statprog.pdf.

Agencies fall into three broad categories according to their principal statistical activities and responsibilities (see figure 6.1).

Central Coordinating Agency
Office of Management and Budget's
Office of Information and Regulatory Affairs

GENERAL PURPOSE STATISTICAL AGENCIES	ANALYTICAL AND RESEARCH AGENCIES	ADMINISTRATIVE AND REGULATORY AGENCIES
Bureau of the Census	Bureau of Economic Analysis	Environmental Protection Agency
Bureau of Labor Statistics		
National Center for Education Statistics	Council of Economic Advisers	Federal Trade Commission
National Center for Health Statistics	National Agricultural Statistics Service	Securities and Exchange Commission
Bureau of Justice Statistics		Internal Revenue Service

Figure 6.1. Some statistical organizations of the federal government.

Statistical Agencies

More than 70 agencies in the U.S. federal government produce statistics of interest to the public. The Federal Interagency Council on Statistical Policy maintains a Web site, *FEDSTATS* (http://www.fedstats.gov/), to provide easy access to the full range of statistics and information produced by these agencies for public use.

These agencies collect, compile, and make available statistics in specific fields for general use. Businesses, private organizations, government bodies, and individuals in many different settings use the data they supply. Demographic statistics published by the Census Bureau, for example, enable companies to gauge future demands for their products based on the race, age, sex, occupation, and educational levels of different segments of the population. They are also used to help companies decide where to relocate, to measure population growth and decline in different parts of the country, and to document significant changes in the composition of the population.

The Bureau of the Census is the largest agency, responsible for the collection, compilation, and publication of demographic and economic statistics. Its statistical programs fall into two main categories: (1) current programs, which produce the monthly, quarterly, and annual data contained in such publications as the *Current Population Reports* series and *County Business Patterns*, and (2) periodic censuses and programs mandated by law.

As a rule, data contained in the periodic censuses, which can be as much as 5 or even 10 years old, are updated by current Census Bureau publications. The *Census of Manufactures*, for example, is brought up-to-date by the *Annual Survey of Manufactures*, the *Current Industrial Reports* series, *Survey of Plant Capacity*, and *Manufacturers' Shipments, Inventories, and Orders*.[2] Although useful, the current publications lack the detailed geographic, product, and demographic coverage common to censuses. In addition to censuses and surveys, the bureau also publishes such basic statistical compilations as the *Statistical Abstract of the United States* and the *County and City Data Book*.

Keeping up with census publications, the types of statistics they contain, and the formats in which they are available is no easy task. Fortunately, several guides and lists are available to help identify and simplify access to specific census statistics sources.

U.S. Bureau of the Census. **Census Catalog and Guide.** Washington, D.C.: Government Printing Office, 1946– . Annual. Web version available at http://www.census.gov/prod/www/abs/catalogs.html.

————. **Monthly Product Announcement**. Washington, D.C.: Government Printing Office, 1981–2000. Monthly. Web version available at http://www.census.gov/mp/www/mpa.html. (Replaced by *Census Product Update* at http://www.census.gov/mp/www/cpu.html.)

————. **Catalog of Publications, 1790–1972**. Washington, D.C.: Government Printing Office, 1974. 591p.

U.S. Bureau of the Census. **Guide to the 1997 Economic Censuses**. Washington, D.C.: n.d. http://www.census.gov/epcd/www/guide.html. (Accessed August 25, 2003).

The annual *Census Catalog and Guide* lists and annotates data products in all formats. Web page availability is also cited. The latest edition (1998) is designed to be a companion to the 1997 edition. The main section contains abstracts of products issued by the Census Bureau from October 1996 through December 1997 (see figure 6.2, page 108). The products are grouped first by media and then by subject. The special section of the 1997 *Catalog* lists key sources of data and assistance whereas that of the 1998 *Catalog* leads users through the Internet programs and services of the Census Bureau. This reflects the strong public use of the Census Bureau Internet site.

The *Monthly Product Announcement* was a free list of recently released publications and data. Arrangement is by format, then by subject. Each listing included the title, series number, price, and, when available, the correct URL to access the document. This information is now available at http://www.census.gov/mp/www/cpu.html.

The first census publications were issued almost 200 years ago. Since then, the breadth and depth of census enumerations have increased considerably. In addition, titles and frequency of census data collection have changed, and specific items have been added to or deleted from successive census questionnaires. Statistics about American agriculture, for example, were once included as part of the Census of Population; today, they comprise a separate census. Similarly, data on religious affiliation included in early censuses are no longer gathered and published. The retrospective *Catalog of Publications, 1790–1972* is useful for identifying specific publications and what they contain.

Construction

CURRENT CONSTRUCTION
REPORTS

Index for construction reports:
<http://www.census.gov/prod/www/
titles.html#contsvy>

300

C20. Housing Starts

Frequency of issue—Monthly.

*Geographic areas covered and
subject content*—See abstract
No. 412 in the 1997 Catalog.

9-21 pp. Monthly. Annual
subscription: $22. GPO S/N 703-
015-00000-0. List ID "CRHS."
Use the GPO order form.

Abstract site: <http://www. census.
gov/prod/www/abs/mscho04a.html>

List of the issues: <http://www.
census.gov/prod/1/constr/c20/
c20.html>

Figure 6.2. Sample entry, *Census Catalog and Guide.* Reprinted from U.S. Census Bureau,
*Census Catalog and Guide,*1998 (http://www.census.gov/prod/www/abs/catalogs.html).

Finally, the Census Bureau also publishes guides to specific censuses. One of the most useful for business librarians and researchers is the *Guide to the Economic Censuses*, which contains descriptions of the censuses that, taken together, comprise the Economic Census. A new edition is published for each census. The latest guide is available only on the Internet.

At this time the best source for information on Census programs, publications, and statistics is the Web page maintained by the Bureau at http://www.census.gov.

The Bureau of Labor Statistics (BLS) (http://www.bls.gov/) is the principal source of information on labor economics and, as does the Census Bureau, the BLS makes its statistics available in a wide range of formats; much of the data now appears on its Web page. Available from this site are statistics on employment and unemployment, prices and living conditions, compensation and working conditions, productivity and technology; links to surveys and programs; background papers on *Issues in Labor Statistics*; *BLS Research Papers;* and other publications such as the *Occupational Outlook Handbook*.

The Bureau of Economic Analysis is an agency of the Department of Commerce and along with the Census Bureau and *STAT-USA* is part of the Department's Economics and Statistics Administration. The mission of BEA is to produce and circulate accurate, timely, relevant, and cost-effective statistics that provide a comprehensive, up-to -ate picture of economic activity. BEA's economic accounts present basic information on such key issues as U.S. economic growth, regional economic development, and the United States' position in the world economy. A summary of BEA's current estimates usually appears first in news releases, which are available to the public in a variety of forms: online through BEA's Web site at http://www.bea.doc.gov/, on recorded telephone messages, and in printed BEA reports. BEA information is also available online through *STAT-USA's Economic Bulletin Board* and by fax through *STAT-USA/FAX*. For a detailed description of BEA's economic programs, consult the *Catalog of Products* at http://www.bea.doc.gov/bea/uguide.htm. The *Catalog* listings are by subject area or product number. A typical listing will include product number, price and listing, and when available a direct link to any free downloads. (See figure 6.3.)

Business Inventories (12 Installments) NLS-0166	N	Printout	$108.00
Contains the underlying estimates for business inventories, including estimates of the change in book value, inventory valuation adjustment, and the change in business inventories in current and chained dollars; the estimates are in greater detail than those published in national income and product accounts tables 5.10 and 5.11. Also included are monthly and quarterly estimates of real manufacturing trade inventories, sales, and inventory-sales ratios, in detail similar to that published quarterly in the *Survey of Current Business.* Contains the latest 12 quarters or 8 months and 4 quarters of estimates.			

Motor Vehicle Output (12 Installments) NLS-0251	N	Printout	$108.00
Contains details separating domestic and foreign auto and truck purchases (quarterly only); Canadian auto imports, Mexican auto imports, and total auto imports (quarterly only); unit sales (including trucks), inventories, and production (monthly and quarterly); average expenditure per car (monthly and quarterly). These estimates underline national income and product accounts tables 8.8U and 8.9U. Each table contains the latest 2 years and 10 quarters of estimates.			

Figure 6.3. Typical listing from the *Catalog of Products*.
Reproduced from the BEA's *Catalog.* (http://www.bea.doc.gov/bea/uguide.htm#subj).

Government-produced statistics are used frequently by business researchers. Although data collected by the other statistical agencies may be used less widely, they also have direct business applications. At the Web page of *FEDSTATS.gov* (http://www. fedstats.gov/) one may list agencies by the subject area in which they produce statistics. This listing provides one a link to the agency Web page as well as to statistical lists and contacts, complete with telephone numbers or -email addresses (see figure 6.4).

Bureau of Economic Analysis measures, presents, and interprets Gross Domestic Product (GDP), personal income, corporate profits, and related items in the context of the National Income and Product Accounts. BEA also maintains personal income and related measures for States and localities, the U.S. balance of payments accounts, and the foreign direct investment accounts.	• **Contact Information** • **Key Statistics**
Census Bureau provides information on retail and wholesale trade and selected service industries; construction activity, such as housing permits and starts, the value of new construction, residential alterations and repairs, and quarterly price indexes for single-family houses; quantity and value of industrial output-e.g., manufacturing activities; shipments, inventories, and orders; capital expenditure information; foreign trade-including imports, exports, and trade monitoring; and state and local government activities. The Census Bureau also maintains the Standard Statistical Establishment List that is used for statistical frames and the production of aggregate data on County Business Patterns.	• **Contact Information** • **Key Statistics**
Customs Service collects and verifies tariff and trade data, which are tabulated, analyzed, and disseminated by the Census Bureau.	• **Contact Information**
Directorate for Information Operations and Reports (DIOR) in the Department of Defense (DOD) collects DOD contract information in support of national economic indictors and the Small Business Competitiveness Demonstration Program. DIOR also produces statistics on DOD purchases from educational and nonprofit institutions, and state and local governments.	• **Contact Information** • **Key Statistics**
Economics and Statistics Administration (ESA) in the Department of Commerce carries out Congressionally-mandated studies, such as the annual assessment of foreign direct investment in the United States. ESA disseminates current economic statistics through an electronic system known as STAT-USA.	• **Contact Information**

Figure 6.4. Some agency listings for economic statistics.
Taken from *FEDSTATS* at http://www.fedstats.gov/programs/economic.html.

Administrative and Regulatory Agencies

Finally, although statistics gathering and dissemination are not their primary functions, almost every administrative or regulatory agency produces valuable statistics as a by-product of its administrative operations. The *Statistics of Income* series published by the Internal Revenue Service, for example, is extremely useful to market researchers attempting to assess corporate and personal income. The Statistics of Income (SOI) program now has its own Web page at http://www.irs.ustreas.gov/prod/tax_stats/, where one can consult data files compiled from tax and information returns on subjects such as corporations, partnerships, or sole proprietorships

The statistical resources of the federal government are extensive and varied. Although once difficult to access, their identification has been considerably simplified by their widespread availability via the Internet using such search engines as *FEDSTATS* and the commercially available *Statistical Universe*.

State Government Agencies

State agencies generally operate independently of the federal government in determining and carrying out their statistical programs. As a consequence, there is considerable variation in the scope of state statistical programs. Much information is, in fact, collected by state and local government organizations and then submitted to the federal government for compilation and publication.

Still other statistics-gathering and publishing activities remain the sole province of state agencies. Although state publishing programs vary, at a minimum most publish statistical compendia as well as specialized statistics focusing on industrial development, employment and unemployment, and the state's economy. Piper Resources has Web links to all state and local government sites at http://www.piperinfo.com/state/index.cfm. This provides convenient access to a wide variety of links to information from specific states.

Trade Associations

Charged with keeping their members apprised of industry trends and developments, trade associations constitute another major supplier of statistics. These data are usually collected from association surveys or from reports submitted by member firms and are published as annual, monthly, and even weekly statistical compilations. Although coverage varies, most include information on industry production, inventories, shipments, sales, and prices. The Association of Home Appliance Manufacturers (http://www.aham.org/), for example, issues an annual *Major Appliance Industry Fact Book,* occasional reports on specific appliances, performance standards, spec books, and a monthly statistical press release, *Major Appliance Factory Shipments.* Many trade associations also include free statistical information on their Web sites and so are excellent sources of industry information.

Although these publications are intended primarily for association members, they can be invaluable to librarians and researchers in need of detailed industry data. Although a few association publications are distributed only to members, some are available free of charge to educational institutions, and many can be purchased from the associations themselves, trade publishers, or other sources. Not all association statistics are published, however. When printed sources fail to provide the information being sought, the association staff should be contacted for assistance.

To find out if associations have a Web presence one can use a subject directory such as Yahoo, which has a listing of Web addresses at http://dir.yahoo.com/Business_and_Economy/ Organizations/Trade_Associations/ or access the Open Directory Project at http:// dmoz.org/Business/Resources/Associations/.

Commercial Publishers

Commercial publishers issue a wide range of statistical data, some gathered through original research, but most culled from government agencies and trade associations.

Infrastructure Industries USA.. Farmington Hills, Mich.: Gale Group, 2001– . Biennial.

Manufacturing and Distribution USA.. Farmington Hills, Mich.: Gale Group, 2000– . Annual.

Information, Finance and Services USA. Farmington Hills, Mich.: Gale Group, 2000– . Biennial.

Gale Group is particularly adept at combining federal and commercial sources and presenting the result in an easily understood format. Much of the information in these volumes is drawn from the *County Business Patterns* and *Economic Census* series, *Input-Output* statistics from the Department of Commerce, Department of Labor statistics, and *Ward's Business Directory of U.S. Private and Public Companies*. Although many libraries may own or be able to access electronically these materials, it is the concise way in which the data are extracted and presented that makes the Gale Group series a worthwhile purchase.

Trade journals are important sources of such information, often including both general business and economic statistics and highly specialized industrial data. *Beverage World*, for example, features annual rankings of soft drinks, beer, and bottled water at their Web site, http://www.beverageworld.com/. One can access, among other things, statistics on top brands, regional consumption, and beverage category breakdowns. As well as statistics there is also a daily news roundup, news archives, and classifieds of interest to those involved in the industry. *American Banker* (http://www.americanbanker.com) publishes lists of the largest banks, credit unions, and foreign banks operating in the United States. Direct Contact Publishing's *jumpstation* (http://www.imediafax.com/jumpstation/) is a good starting point to check on business publications Web pages. It lists more than 3,000 publications arranged by industry category.

In addition to statistics contained in periodicals and newspapers, many commercial publishers also issue statistical fact books and directories. One of the most widely used compilations is the loose-leaf *Statistical Service*, published by Standard & Poor's.

As America has become increasingly statistics-conscious, the market for popular statistics sources has also grown. Most of these sources draw on statistics generated and originally published by government agencies. Some repackage the government data, making them simpler to use by providing explanations and tables that are easier to understand. Others use these data to publish guides to high-paying jobs, safe cities, and locations where quality of life is better than average.

Finally, some commercial publishers make detailed and highly sophisticated economic and business information available to their customers, either in print or, more commonly, as online databases, computer tapes, or CD-ROMs.

Other Organizations

In addition to data gathered and published by federal and state government agencies, trade associations, and commercial publishers, statistics are also published by university research centers; independent research organizations such as the Conference Board (http://www.conference-board.org/); the Tax Foundation (http://www.taxfoundation.org/); and business organizations such as stock and commodity exchanges, banks, accounting firms, and publicly traded companies.

Basic Statistical Concepts

Familiarity with key statistical concepts enables librarians to understand more clearly requests for specific kinds of statistical information and to anticipate problems that may arise when seeking or supplying such information. This section considers four statistical concepts-sampling, time series, forecasts and projections, and index numbers-that are basic to business statistics.

Sampling

Data about the population or some designated segment of it are tremendously important to business researchers, government agencies, and others. Ideally, such data should accurately reflect information collected from examination of each person in the population being studied. Surveying an entire population, however, is generally too time consuming, difficult, and costly to be practical or even effective. As a result, researchers usually select a smaller, representative segment of the population for studies and analysis and use the data gathered to make inferences about the entire population. This process is called sampling, and the representative segment of the population being measured is known as a sample. Sampling is not confined to demographic study; it is used whenever the universe being measured is too large to lend itself to analysis of each of its constituent units. Sampling techniques are often employed in the study of production, wages, sales, and other business-related activities as well as in analysis of the population.

The Census Bureau employs sampling as a means of gathering detailed information about the social and economic characteristics of the population. Every 10 years, for example, it sends questionnaires about population and housing to every household in the country. Most receive brief questionnaires, but others receive a lengthier document that solicits additional information. Thus, while some portions of the Census of Population reflect enumeration or counting of almost every household in the United States, other parts are statistical inferences based on the results of the Census Bureau's sample of households.

Other census publications are completely based on samples, for example, *American Housing Survey,*[3] a special study issued periodically as part of the *Current Population Reports* series. When a sample is being used, reputable statistical publications will describe its composition and, in many instances, point out its limitations. Thus, the Census Bureau's introduction to the *American Housing Survey* includes the following information:

> The data come from a Census Bureau nationwide sample survey in odd-numbered years for national, regional, and metropolitan/non-metropolitan data, and from surveys in 47 metropolitan statistical areas over a multi-year cycle. These data detail the types, size, conditions, characteristics, housing costs and values, equipment, utilities, and dynamics of the housing inventory; they describe the demographic, financial, and mobility characteristics of the occupants; and give as well some information on neighborhood conditions.

As with all types of statistical information, careful perusal of the introductory textual matter and footnotes is essential to determine the scope and limitations of the data being presented.

Time Series Analysis

Sometimes statistics are gathered and published on a one-time basis. A market research firm, for example, may be commissioned to collect data on consumption of and preferences for different types of peanut butter. Such data meet specific needs, reflecting conditions at a fixed point in time. They result from a single research effort and are not updated on a regular basis.

Most situations call for regularly collected statistical data that reflect changes over time. Such numbers are called time series and are used to analyze changes in business conditions and the economy, including such items as income, prices, production, and consumption. Most time series consist of monthly, quarterly, or annual observations, and many are produced by the government. Such data are analyzed to identify patterns and, in some instances, to make forecasts about the future.

Many time series that are published weekly, monthly, or quarterly reflect predictable seasonal changes, caused by such factors as climate and school openings and closings. Building construction, for example, regularly shows a slowdown in winter months due to adverse weather conditions and increases during temperate months. Retail sales are influenced by such holidays as Christmas and Valentine's Day, and unemployment rates generally increase during the summer when school is closed and decrease when school reopens.

Time series that are subject to such predictable seasonal variations are often presented in two different ways: unadjusted and seasonally adjusted. Unadjusted time series present data as they are collected without regard to fluctuations caused by regular seasonal changes. Seasonally adjusted time series, on the other hand, are "deseasonalized" so that, as near as possible, predictable seasonal changes are eliminated through statistical manipulation. The resulting seasonally adjusted data reflect changes not caused by normal seasonal variation, changes that are sometimes difficult to identify using unadjusted data.

Many statistical publications present both unadjusted and seasonally adjusted time series. The *Survey of Current Business*, for example, includes both. To be effective, librarians must be clear about which type of information is being sought and label the time series data they supply as either seasonally adjusted or unadjusted.

Forecasts and Projections

Informed speculation about the future is essential for business executives, who must regularly decide whether to increase production of existing products, develop new ones, or otherwise prepare for anticipated changes. Thus, while they often consult time series to assess recent trends and developments, they also use them to make predictions about the future, in the form of forecasts and projections. Although these terms are often used interchangeably, there is a difference between the two. Forecasts are short-term predictions based on the recent past, generally extending no more than two years into the future. Since they draw on information about current conditions, which often do not change appreciably over a two-year period, forecasts can be quite accurate. Projections are predictions made about the distant future. The Census Bureau, for example, has already published population projections for the year 2100. Projections cover a greater time span, which may include technological developments, man-made and natural disasters, and other events that may not have been anticipated at the time the projections were made. As a result, projections are more speculative and prone to error than forecasts:

Extrapolations are useful, particularly in that form of soothsaying called fore-casting trends. But in looking at the figures or charts made from them, it is necessary to remember one thing constantly: The trend-to-now may be a fact, but the future trend represents no more than an educated guess. Implicit in it is "everything else being equal" and "present trends continuing," and somehow everything else refuses to remain equal, else life would be dull indeed.[4]

Business forecasts and projections are published by a wide variety of sources, including government agencies, private research organizations, corporations, commercial publishers, and others, and are contained in many of the publications that are described later in this chapter.

Index Numbers

One way in which researchers can consider changes over time is by comparing statistics for one time period with another. They can, for example, compare the number of automobiles manufactured in the United States in 1998 with the number for 1988, or they can contrast the cost of a haircut or rent or groceries or other consumer goods for one period with another. One way to do this is to count the actual number of units being measured, dollars spent for rent or number of cars rolling off the assembly line. Often, however, index numbers are used instead.

In its simplest sense, an index number is the ratio of one quantity to another, expressing a given quantity in terms of its value relative to a base quantity. Index numbers frequently are used to compare percent change over time, to measure relative changes in quantity, price, or value of an item or series of related items compared with a designated time, known as the base period or base year. The base period has a value of 100, and any changes from it represent percentages. Upon consulting the *Statistical Abstract of the United States*, the researcher learns that the Consumer Price Index uses 1982–1984 as the base year, and that the index in 1998, for all items, was 163.0. This means that the CPI rose 63 percent from the base year. In other words, any number over 100, the number assigned to the base year, reflects an increase; anything less than 100, a decrease. Had the CPI been 90, it would have meant that costs had declined by 10 percent since the base year. Although months or groups of years are sometimes used for base periods, the most commonly used base period is a year. Base years are chosen to provide a good basis for comparisons and are thus relatively stable years economically. In the example used above, 1982–1984 is the base period, and government tables showing this and other consumer prices include this notation: [1982–84 = 100]. Base years sometimes change. Librarians comparing index numbers for 1977 with 1996 must first determine that the base year being used for both sets of data is the same. *Historical Statistics of the United States*, described later in this chapter, presents data using constant base years.

The index number consulted most frequently in libraries is the Consumer Price Index (CPI). This is a composite of indexes relating to the prices of specific consumer goods and services, used as a primary measure of inflation. Since some misunderstanding on the part of library users about the nature and application of the *CPI* exists, further discussion of this important index is in order.

The Consumer Price Index is a monthly measure of the change in average prices over time of a fixed list (usually called a market basket) of goods and services. It is based on the average prices of different items purchased for daily living, items such as shoes, fuel, dairy products, bus fares, newspapers, and dental services. Each item is assigned a weight to account for its relative importance in consumers' budgets. New cars, for example, may account for 4 percent of the index, whereas shoes may be less than 1 percent.

Each month, BLS data collectors visit or call thousands of retail stores, service establishments, rental units, and doctors' offices all over the United States to obtain price information on thousands of items used to track and measure price change in the CPI. Roughly 80,000 prices are recorded each month, and these represent a scientifically selected sample of the prices paid by consumers for the goods and services purchased. The Bureau of Labor Statistics now publishes two official Consumer Price Indexes, known as the CPI-U and the CPI-W.[5] Each month, BLS releases thousands of detailed CPI numbers to the media. However, the media usually focus on the broadest, most comprehensive CPI. This is "The Consumer Price Index for All Urban Consumers (CPI-U) for the U.S. City Average for All Items, 1982–84=100." These data are reported on either a seasonally adjusted or not seasonally adjusted basis. It is possible now by accessing the Bureau of Labor Statistics *Most requested Series*" at http://data.bls.gov/cgi-bin/surveymost?cu to retrieve selected data for selected areas and thus to compile tables only for the data needed. Figure 6.5 displays monthly data from the Consumer Price Index-All Urban Consumers, Medical Care Services, from 1992 until 2002.

Consumer Price Index - All Urban Consumers

Original Data Value

Series Id: CUUR0000SAM2
Not Seasonally Adjusted
Area: U.S. city average
Item: Medical care services
Base Period: 1982-84=100

Year	Jan	Feb	Mar	Apr	May	Jun	Jul	Aug	Sep	Oct	Nov	Dec	Annual	HALF1	HALF2
1992	184.6	186.4	187.4	188.1	188.9	189.7	191.1	192.2	192.9	194.2	195.2	195.6	190.5	187.5	193.5
1993	197.5	199.1	199.7	200.7	202.0	202.6	203.8	204.5	205.0	206.2	206.8	207.1	202.9	200.3	205.6
1994	208.4	209.8	210.4	211.4	212.0	212.6	213.8	214.7	215.4	216.8	217.5	218.2	213.4	210.8	216.1
1995	219.8	221.3	221.8	222.4	223.0	223.5	224.6	225.6	226.1	226.9	227.4	227.8	224.2	222.0	226.4
1996	229.3	230.3	230.7	231.1	231.6	231.9	232.9	233.4	233.6	234.2	234.9	235.0	232.4	230.8	234.0
1997	236.3	237.1	237.7	238.1	238.5	238.7	239.2	239.8	240.0	240.5	241.2	241.8	239.1	237.7	240.4
1998	242.9	244.2	244.8	245.4	245.9	246.5	247.4	248.2	248.4	249.0	249.3	249.6	246.8	245.0	248.7
1999	251.3	252.6	253.1	253.5	254.0	254.6	255.5	256.2	256.6	257.1	257.7	258.5	255.1	253.2	256.9
2000	260.1	262.0	263.2	263.9	264.4	265.6	266.7	268.0	268.7	269.4	269.8	270.4	266.0	263.2	268.8
2001	273.0	274.9	275.9	276.8	277.3	278.3	278.9	280.5	281.0	282.0	283.0	283.5	278.8	276.0	281.5
2002	286.2	287.7	288.9	290.2	291.2	291.7									

Figure 6.5. The Consumer Price Index for all urban consumers (CPI-U) 1982–84 = 100: Medical care services. From http://data.bls.gov/cgi-bin/surveymost?cu.

The CPI affects the income of about 90 million persons as a result of statutory action: 47.8 million Social Security beneficiaries, about 22.4 million food stamp recipients, and about 4.1 million military and federal civil service retirees and survivors. Changes in the CPI also affect the cost of lunches for 26.7 million children who eat lunch at school, while collective bargaining agreements that tie wages to the CPI cover almost 2 million workers.

However, using the CPI to compare one city's cost of living with that of another is virtually meaningless. This is because each measures price change only in the designated area. So if the 1999 CPI for New York is 177, this means that prices have increased by this amount in that area only since 1982–1984. Only the increase is measured, and this does not reflect the prices for 1982–1984. It could still cost more to live in a different city even if the CPI is lower. Fortunately, another source permits comparisons between cities.

American Chamber of Commerce Researchers Association. **ACCRA Cost of Living Index.** Louisville, Ky.: ACCRA, 1992– ; ACCRA, 1981– . Quarterly.

The *ACCRA Cost of Living Index,* formerly known as the *Inter-City Cost of Living Index* and the *Inter-City Cost of Living Indicators Project,* measures current prices for consumer goods and services in 310 urban areas. This empowers researchers to compare living costs in one city with another or to compare the actual dollar amounts paid for specific items, such as hamburger, haircuts, and apartment rent in several locations. Since the *ACCRA Cost of Living Index* is published specifically to permit comparison between cities, it is extremely useful to companies and individuals contemplating moving to another part of the country.

Three important differences between the *Consumer Price Index* and the *ACCRA Cost of Living Index* should be noted. First, the CPI measures change over time, with the base year equaling 100. The *Cost of Living Index,* on the other hand, measures change between locations rather than change over time, with a national city average of 100 used as the base for comparison. A CPI of 250, in other words, means that it now costs 150 percent more to buy the same goods and services as it did in 1982–1984 (or in any other base year designated), while an *ACCRA Cost of Living Index* of 116 means that it costs 16 percent more than the current national average to live in a specific city or town.

Second, while comparison of Consumer Price Indexes between specific cities is impossible, comparison of two or more cities to the national average using the *Cost of Living Index* is simple. Using it, a researcher can determine that Huntsville's index of 93.2 means that it would cost 6.8 percent less than the national average to live there, and that Flagstaff's index of 112.3 represents living costs 12.3 percent above the national average. Further, someone moving from Huntsville to Flagstaff could expect to pay approximately 19.1 percent more for consumer goods and services.

The *Inter-City Cost of Living Index* is not without its flaws. One of the most significant is that many large urban areas are not represented; a recent issue omitted Chicago and New Orleans. In addition, the list of cities represented does not always remain constant from one year to the next. Thus, simply because a city is included in one issue, it is not safe to assume that it will be listed in subsequent issues. Despite these drawbacks, the *Index* is a popular, much-used, and generally reliable source that belongs in most business reference collections.

In addition to indexes that permit comparison between cities, the *ACCRA Cost of Living Index* includes a section that lists actual dollar amounts paid for specific consumer goods, ranging from the average cost of a movie and a pizza to a six-pack of beer and a bottle of aspirin.

Another important BLS index, the *Producer Price Index,* is used to measure price changes in goods at various stages of production, ranging from raw materials such as logs and timber to finished products, such as furniture. Like the Consumer Price Index, the Producer Price Index appears in many different statistics sources, including the *Survey of Current Business, Statistical Abstract of the United States,* and *STAT-USA.*

Other privately produced price indexes are considerably more fanciful. The Big Mac Index, for example, is based on the theory of purchasing-power parity, the notion that a dollar should buy the same amount in all countries. The Big Mac purchasing power parity is the exchange rate that would mean hamburgers cost the same in America as abroad. Comparing actual exchange rates with purchasing power parities indicates whether a currency is under- or overvalued. The Christmas Price Index measures changes from one year to the next in the prices paid for items mentioned in the popular "Twelve Days of Christmas" carol, including partridges, turtle doves, and gold rings.

Economic Indicators

In business libraries, some of the most frequently requested statistics are those used to assess the state of the national economy. Dozens of statistics are commonly used for this purpose, but among the most important are the Gross Domestic Product, Industrial Production, Leading Indicators, Personal Income, the Consumer and Producer Price Indexes, Retail Sales, Employment, and Housing Starts. All are issued on a regular basis by the government and are reported in newspapers, periodicals, statistical reference sources, online news services, and online government releases. The economic indicators listed above, however, are by no means the only ones. Keeping abreast of such statistics, their frequency of issuance, and the sources in which they appear is not always easy. Fortunately, in recent years several fine directories to economic time series data have been published. Some are listed below. Many indicator data sets have moved to the Web, and those sites that may be more permanent are listed at the end of this section.

Darney, Arsen J, comp. and ed. **Economic Indicators Handbook: Time Series, Conversions, Documentation.** Farmington Hills, Mich.: Gale Group, 1992– . Biennial.

Johnson, David B. **The Black Book of Economic Information: A Guide to Sources and Interpretation**. Sun Lakes, Ariz. : Thomas Horton and Daughters, 1996. 512p.

O'Hara, Frederick M., Jr., and F. M. O'Hara III. **Handbook of United States Economic and Financial Indicators.** Rev.ed. Westport, Conn.: Greenwood Press, 2000. 395p.

Lehmann, Michael B. **The Irwin Guide to Using the *Wall Street Journal*.** 6th ed. New York: McGraw-Hill, 2000. 366p.

In the 2000 edition of *Economic Indicators Handbook* there are 266 statistical time series commonly used for measuring the economy of the United States. The data came from the U.S. Department of Commerce, the U.S. Department of Labor, the American Stock Exchange, the National Association of Securities Dealers, the New York Stock Exchange, and the Conference Board. Most of the data were obtained by special arrangement with these groups rather than from already published sources. Each section begins with a clear explanation of the series covered, including how they are calculated, any revisions to the data, and a short bibliography of further resources. The series covered include Gross National Product as well as Gross Domestic Product, Business Cycle Indicators such as Index of Industrial Production, Cyclic Indicators, such as personal income, Economic Series, Consumer Price Index, Producer Price Index, and Selected Stock Market Price Indexes. An added bonus to the section on the Consumer Price Index is the inclusion of historical data at the city level. This book is especially useful for researchers and students who are unsure about statistics, who will appreciate that the explanations and the statistical compilations are contained in one volume.

The *Black Book of Economic Information* is a mixture of handbook and encyclopedic dictionary written for anyone who is "overwhelmed, bored or bedazzled" by economic data. Each topic or series covered begins with a "snapshot" about the data, including the correct name, the agency or institution that issues the series, the publications that carry the information, publication frequency, and a telephone number for further inquiries. This is followed by a short explanation of the series and then, for those who need it, there is a more detailed explanation. Some data sets are included, but not as many as in the *Economic Indicators Handbook*. It is, however, an inexpensive volume that is readily affordable for most libraries.

The *Handbook of United States Economic and Financial Indicators* lists 284 different time series, ranging from "Advisory Sentiment Index" to the "Wiltshire Small-Cap Index." Although entries are not long, they include a definition, an explanation of the derivation of the statistic, comments on its applications, and list its frequency, publisher, and the publication(s) in which it is announced. Indicators published by trade associations, consulting firms, financial publishing companies, and other private organizations are also included. An appendix of nonquantitative indicators is also provided and is particularly helpful to librarians confronted with questions about such purported measures of economic and financial well-being as the "Short-Skirt Index," which holds that rises and falls in women's hemlines are accompanied by similar actions in the stock market; the "Surly Waiter Index"; and the "Drinking Couple Count."

Many economic statistics are first issued in government news releases. After the initial release, many are subsequently published in the *Wall Street Journal*, a good source of current economic indicators. The *Irwin Guide to Using the Wall Street Journal* focuses on some of the key statistics reported, describing what they measure, how they are computed, and when they appear in the *Journal*. In addition, the *Guide* provides information on how each statistic is used to track the economy and includes excerpts from *Wall Street Journal* articles that illustrate the context in which specific statistics are used.

Government periodicals such as the *Survey of Current Business* (http://www.bea.doc.gov/bea/pubs.htm) and *Monthly Labor Review* (http://stats.bls.gov/opub/mlr/mlrhome.htm) are prime sources of economic statistics. *Economic Indicators* (http://www.access.gpo.gov/congress/cong002.html), a monthly publication prepared by the Council of Economic Advisers for the Congress's Joint Economic Committee, includes historic as well as current data. The State of the Nation section of *STAT-USA* provides current and historical economic and financial releases and economic data. This segment contains newly circulated data in "Today's Hot Releases," "Daily Releases," "Current Versions of America's Top Fifty Releases," and the "State of the Nation Library," which contains *STAT-USA*'s collection of over 3,000 files of domestic economic information.

Reliability of Statistics

Users, writes Joe Morehead, sometimes attribute "the power and value of holy writ"[6] to statistics. No statistics, whatever their air of authority, deserve unquestioning acceptance. Some, in fact, are deliberately misleading. The advertising cliche, "nine out of ten doctors surveyed prefer Brand X," is a good example. Clearly, sampling techniques were employed. The advertisers, however, do not document sample size in their commercial, nor do they describe how the sample was selected. Although the advertisement implies that a preponderance of all doctors prefer Brand X, it is entirely possible that the sample consisted of only 10 doctors, all of whom were employees of or stockholders in the company manufacturing Brand X. Further, the advertisers do not list the options the doctors could choose from when selecting Brand X. They might have been given alternate brands of the same product, or they might have been presented with choices that clearly were unacceptable. The numbers themselves are suspect, with the mention of doctors lending an air of credibility and respectability by flaunting what Darrell Huff, author of *How to Lie with Statistics*, calls the "O.K. name":

> Anything smacking of the medical profession is an O.K. name. Scientific laboratories have O.K. names. So do colleges, especially universities, especially ones eminent in technical work. . . . When an O.K. name is cited, make sure that the authority stands behind the information, not merely somewhere alongside it.[7]

The Pentagon's body counts during the Vietnam War and public opinion polls commissioned by politicians are also examples of statistics that are deliberately misleading. These examples lead to the first questions that astute librarians and researchers ask when reviewing statistical data: Where did the data come from? Is the source unbiased, or does it have a vested interest in supplying data that will lead to one conclusion rather than another? Are the statistics self-serving?

When, as near as possible, statistical objectivity has been ascertained, methodology must be examined. Most librarians are not statisticians, but by reading the table headers, footnotes, and any additional documentation, they can learn about some of the more obvious limitations of the data being presented:

> It is important that users, whether primary or secondary users, know just how the data for a particular table were collected and analysed, what was included, and what was omitted. For instance, firms with under a certain number of employees may be omitted from tables of production or employment statistics, and certain industries may for one reason or another be omitted from more general tables. In regular tables the content or classification may change at some time; and errors or later information may mean that some regular tables (foreign trade statistics, for instance) are corrected in the cumulated figures published in the next or even a later issue. A new base year for time series will mean that one cannot use earlier tables of index numbers in the same context. Figures may be rounded up or rounded down in a table or series of tables, and if these figures are added together they can result in an inaccurate figure. Time series may be amended to allow for seasonal or other variations. Misinterpretations can be avoided if care is taken to read the explanatory notes or other matter which statisticians usually take trouble to provide in an effort to overcome these and other dangers.[8]

Statistics, in short, require careful scrutiny to determine both their reliability and their applicability to the research situation at hand. Such assessment presupposes the existence of statistical data, and this chapter concludes with consideration of some of the most important sources of statistical information.

Statistical Publications

Statistical inquiries are an intrinsic component of the driving force of business reference. More and more they comprise the bulk of day-to-day business reference work in most libraries. Many statistical reference questions are simple to answer, requiring only the use of an almanac or some other basic reference source. Others are considerably more difficult, calling for perseverance and ingenuity. A few are impossible to answer, either because the data do not exist or because they are inaccessible to libraries. Privately commissioned market research studies, usually because of high prices, fall into the last category. In most instances, though, statistics are available and can be identified by consulting the following sources.

Dictionaries and Encyclopedias

Theory has it that a good reference librarian can answer inquiries in any field without benefit of the appropriate educational background or even rudimentary knowledge of the subject being studied. No reference librarian, however, can answer an inquiry unless he or she understands the question being asked. This is particularly true in the area of business and economics statistics, where jargon is commonplace and terminology foreign to the uninitiated. Fortunately, several dictionaries and other sources define basic terms and concepts and are useful for definitions of less commonplace terms and concepts. Three publications are listed below.

Marriot, F.H.C. **A Dictionary of Statistical Terms**. 5th ed., New York: John Wiley, 1989. 223p.

Shim, Jae K., and Joel G. Siegel. **Dictionary of Economics**. New York: John Wiley, 1995. 373p.

Vogt, Paul W. **Dictionary of Statistics & Methodology: A Nontechnical Guide for the Social Sciences**. 2nd ed. Thousand Oaks, Calif. : Sage Publications, 1999. 318p.

Since the publication of the first edition in 1957, *A Dictionary of Statistical Terms* has gained widespread acceptance as the standard dictionary of current statistical terminology. Nearly 3,500 entries are included, featuring brief definitions and, in many instances, equations and formulas. The focus in *A Dictionary of Statistical Terms* is on terms in current usage. The *Dictionary of Economics* is more general in coverage and designed for laypeople who want to understand terminology in publications such as *Business Week* and the *New York Times*. The explanations are clear and frequently illustrated. The *Dictionary of Statistics & Methodology* is also designed to give, as far as possible, nontechnical explanations of terms and concepts. The emphasis is on understandable terms and definitions that may be easily appreciated by the nonpractitioner. Any of these publications will give the librarian or researcher a fair grounding in unfamiliar terms or concepts.

Guides and Indexes

Some of the publications described in previous chapters can be particularly helpful in identifying and locating statistical data. Lorna Daniells's *Business Information Sources*, for example, devotes separate chapters to basic U.S. statistical sources, industry statistics, and foreign statistics and economic trends, and identifies additional statistical publications in chapters focusing on such business operations as accounting and marketing. Michael Lavin's *Business Information: How to Find It, How to Use It* includes a whole section on statistical information, with chapters on statistical reasoning, the Census of Population and Housing, population estimates and projections, general economic statistics, and industry statistics. The *Encyclopedia of Business Information Sources* offers a greater level of subject specificity, listing published sources of statistics pertaining to such topics as honey and zinc production, carpet imports, and peanut stocks. In addition, *Data Sources for Business* and Market Analysis, described in chapter 9, devotes considerable attention to both government and privately generated statistics sources. In addition to the titles listed above, several specialized statistical guides and indexes are also available. Although space does not permit consideration of them all, some of the most useful are listed below.

Berinstein, Paula. **Finding Statistics Online: How to Locate the Elusive Numbers You Need**. Medford, N.J.: Information Today, 1998. 356p. (Updated at http://www.berinsteinresearch.com/stats.htm.)

O'Brien, Jacqueline Wasserman, and Steven Wasserman, eds. **Statistics Sources**. 23rd ed. Farmington Hills, Mich.: Gale Group, 1999. 2v.

American Statistics Index. Washington, D.C.: Congressional Information Service, 1973– . Monthly, with annual cumulations.

Statistical Reference Index. Washington, D.C.: Congressional Information Service, 1980– . Monthly, with annual cumulations.

Index to International Statistics. Washington D.C.: Congressional Information Service, 1983– . Monthly, with annual compilations.

LexisNexis Statistical. 1987– . http://www.lexisnexis.com/academic/universe/statistical. Bethesda, Md.: LexisNexis Academic Library Solutions. (Accessed August 20, 2003).

Finding Statistics Online is both a guide showing how to find statistics and a desktop reference. It explains how to locate statistical data through professional systems and services and the Internet. The book includes information on the nature of statistics and how to evaluate their validity. Chapters 1 through 4 cover searching tips; explanations of the types of statistics and methodologies used for assembling them; and examples of government agencies, associations, institutions, and private organizations that produce statistical sources. The remaining 14 chapters list available statistical sources by subject area. Much of the information in the online update duplicates that found in the companion book, but not everything that is in the book appears on the Web page. A nice feature of the update is that the Web-based information is hot linked for easy access. This book is one that most researchers will find extremely useful.

Statistics Sources, described by its publisher as a finding guide to statistics, provides subject access to data contained in compilations such as the *Statistical Abstract of the United States* and the *United Nations' Statistical Yearbook;* basic statistical publications from many organizations; and special statistical issues of professional, technical, and trade journals. Arrangement is alphabetical by subject, with over 20,000 subjects, covering such areas as advertising earnings and industry in Zimbabwe. One of the strengths of *Statistics Sources*, like its companion publication, the *Encyclopedia of Business Information Sources*, is the level of subject specificity it provides. Using it, one can determine sources of statistics for shipments of lawnmowers, beer production in Angola, and the rate of injuries in the textile industry. Coverage is international, and although U.S. government and United Nations publications predominate, many private, commercial, and foreign government publications are also included. Each entry features the name of the issuing organization, the publication title, and, when applicable, its date. Page numbers are not given. Another useful feature is the extensive list of available "Federal Statistical Databases" and the addresses given for the sources of nonpublished data.

Statistics Sources provides quick access to statistical publications, but it does not describe their contents. A series of statistical indexes published by Congressional Information Service remedy this lack. The first of these, the *American Statistics Index*, made its debut in

1973, considerably simplifying work for documents and business librarians and for researchers seeking federal statistical data. The *American Statistics Index*, or *ASI*, is a master guide to statistical publications of the federal government. The print version is published in two parts, an Index Section and an Abstracts Section.

The *ASI* Index Section contains a variety of separate indexes. The main index lists sources by subject and name. Index entries include brief notations of content, frequently cite the title of the publication in which the statistics are presented, and always provide an accession number for reference to the *ASI* Abstracts Section and to microfiche reproductions of those publications sold by Congressional Information Service. Numerous cross-references to related index terms are also included.

In addition to the main subject index, the *ASI* Index Section also features an Index by Categories, which includes references to all publications that contain comparative tabular data broken down into designated geographic, economic, and demographic categories. Although the main subject index provides more detailed subject access, the Index by Categories is useful when more specific information is being sought. General information on the national labor force, for example, is identified more easily through the Subject Index, whereas the Index by Categories is more helpful to identify publications pertaining to women in the workforce.

Once publications and their corresponding accession numbers have been identified, the Abstract Section can be consulted. Entries are arranged by accession number and include many of the features common to entries in the *Monthly Catalog of United States Government Publications,* such as Superintendent of Documents classification, item number, and when applicable, the *Monthly Catalog* entry number and/or the NTIS number. As in the *Monthly Catalog*, depository documents are designated by a bullet.

Information in *ASI*'s Abstract Section, however, is considerably more detailed than that in the *Monthly Catalog*. Every publication is annotated and, in many instances, specific tables or articles are listed and described separately. Each annotation provides full bibliographic data, describes the publication, and lists tables and articles.

Microfiche copies of publications listed in *ASI* are available from the publisher. Libraries can order *ASI* Microfiche Library collections that include all of the publications indexed. Alternatively, they can select fiche copies of nondepository publications only.

Finally, each volume of the *American Statistics Index* includes a lengthy introduction that describes the types of publications that are indexed, explains their arrangement, and presents search strategies highlighting effective use of this index.

Arrangement is similar in the second major Congressional Information Service index, the *Statistical Reference Index (SRI)*. As is the *American Statistics Index, Statistical Reference Index* is divided into index and abstract sections, with subject and category indexing provided in the Index Section, and publication descriptions in the Abstract Section. The *SRI*, however, indexes and abstracts statistics contained in publications not issued by the federal government. It includes statistics published by 1,000 private concerns such as trade associations, corporations, commercial publishers, and independent and university-affiliated research organizations, as well as approximately half of all state governments in the United States. Each entry includes an accession number, bibliographic information, a description of contents, and information for requesting or purchasing copies from the issuing source.

As with *ASI*, many of the publications listed in *SRI* are available from the publisher. However, while *ASI* documents are copied in their entirety, not all SRI publications are. Some are limited to designated statistical excerpts, and some are not available as part of the SRI Microfiche Library and must be ordered directly from the original publisher. However, in spite of these limitations, the *SRI* Microfiche Library permits access to many publications that otherwise would be difficult or time consuming to acquire.

A third Congressional Information Service index, the *Index to International Statistics*, provides abstracts and indexes of some 2,000 indispensable titles from 100 international intergovernmental organizations, including the United Nations, the European Union, and the Organization for Economic Cooperation and Development, and descriptions of statistical publications of international intergovernmental organizations. Before the advent of easy Web searching this was an indispensable way to find statistics for countries other than the United States.

LexisNexis Statistical brings together the *American Statistics Index, Statistical Reference Index*, and *Index to International Statistics* and links them to available full-text documents from 1995 to the present. Libraries can subscribe to one, two, or all three components, and there are also options to subscribe to part of each component. Each library or researcher will need to check the options available at http://www.lexisnexis.com/academic/ universe/Statistical/ to see which components will best suit their needs. Key documents will always be available, as they are stored in permanent data archives by the company. Abstracts link directly to individual tables, figures, and charts.

LexisNexis Statistical comprises several modules that can be purchased individually and added to as the budget allows. The *Base Editon* includes over 30,000 statistical tables. With the addition of the *Research Edition Table Collection* the subscriber can add an extra 100,000 indexed tables. Other optional modules include the online version of *ASI, SRI,* and IIS, with links to available full-text documents.

Searching is easy. From the first screen choices can be made to search all or parts of collections by clicking the appropriate boxes. Then either keywords or subject headings can be chosen to limit the search further. (See figures 6.6 and 6.7.)

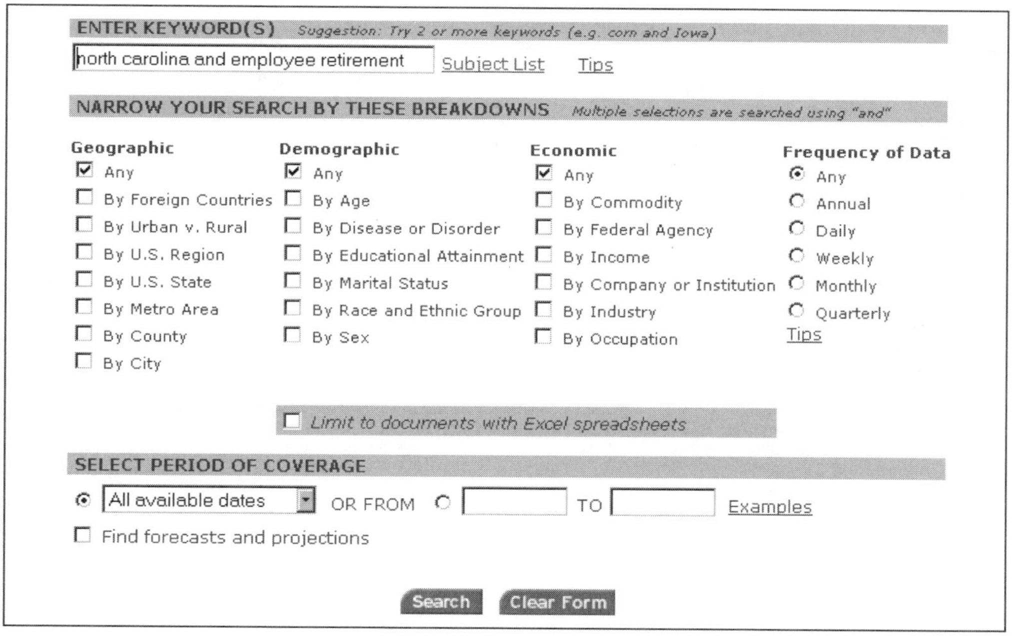

Figure 6.6. Opening search screen of *LexisNexis Statistical*. Reprinted with the permission of LexisNexis, a division of Reed Elsevier, Inc.All documents in *LexisNexis Statistical* are available as ASCII text with GIF images; pdf files for viewing and printing of facsimiles of official printed publications; and spreadsheets of key time series statistics so data can be manipulated and large documents that are divided into smaller, more manageable sections.

Search Terms: north carolina and employee retirement

FOCUS™ [   ]   Search Within Results   Edit Search

Print   Email

Document List   **Table View**   ‹‹previous Table 4 of 7. next››

Find More Like This

Copyright © 2002, Congressional Information Service, Inc.

Finances Of State And Local Public **Employee Retirement** Systems For The U.S., Virginia, And Surrounding States: 1997

Report Title: Virginia Statistical Abstract, 1999-2000 Edition (Full Document...)
Issued By: University of Virginia--Weldon Cooper Center for Public Service
Publication Date: 1999
Table on Page(s): 426-427

(GIF 29K)

TABLE 11.7A
**Finances of State and Local Public Employee Retirement
Systems for the U.S., Virginia, and Surrounding States: 1997**

| | Receipts | | | Payments | | |
| | Contributions | | | | | |
	Employee	Government	Investment Earnings	Benefits Paid	With-drawals	Other Payments
United States	$20,788,148	$44,932,265	$158,969,044	$68,940,706	$3,399,195	$3,355,122
Virginia	106,129	1,027,691	5,786,919	1,170,066	89,243	147,794
Delaware	29,761	93,216	600,494	162,968	1,986	16,674
District of Columbia	48,342	291,626	428,815	415,776	2,436	13,070
Florida	128,543	3,309,498	4,678,975	1,930,579	20,440	128,847
Georgia	341,470	1,116,018	3,402,913	1,248,967	57,255	52,720
Kentucky	369,246	618,891	1,555,603	829,074	51,115	18,603
Maryland	123,784	871,878	5,326,861	1,297,408	45,013	221,548
North Carolina	609,250	753,320	2,695,385	1,293,839	107,182	7,861
South Carolina	347,267	437,267	1,346,151	684,036	60,043	11,119
Tennessee	176,180	495,267	2,265,217	756,409	28,222	26,271
West Virginia	110,616	306,958	266,328	310,911	12,483	3,749

(GIF 25K)

TABLE 11.7A   *continued*
**Finances of State and Local Public Employee Retirement
Systems for the U.S., Virginia, and Surrounding States: 1997**

SOURCE:

U.S. Department of Commerce, Bureau of the Census. "Employee Retirement Systems of State and Local Government." (http://www.census.gov/govs/www/per.html) April 6, 1999.

NOTES:

In thousands of current dollars. Data are statistical in nature and thus do not represent an accounting statement.

These data cover retirement systems sponsored by a recognized unit of state or local government whose membership is comprised primarily of public employees compensated with public funds and which holds identifiable assets to finance retirement and associated benefits. Excluded are "pay-as-you-go" retirement programs (i.e. direct payments to retired or disabled employees from appropriation of general funds), plans not identified as contributory, and payments to private trustees or insurance carriers who administer the investments and benefits.

Subject Descriptors: State and local employees;Civil service pensions;

‹‹previous Table 4 of 7. next››

Figure 6.7. Example of a document retrieved from *LexisNexis Statistical*. Reprinted with the permission of LexisNexis, a division of Reed Elsevier, Inc.

Statistical Compilations

One of the best ways to begin the search for data is by consulting a statistical compilation. Comprising data culled from many other sources, such publications can provide direct answers to many statistical reference inquiries and indirect access to sources that will answer others. International, foreign, federal, and state government agencies; commercial publishers; and other organizations publish statistical compendia. The following such compilations are basic to business reference.

U.S. Department of Commerce. Bureau of the Census. **Statistical Abstract of the United States.** Washington, D.C.: Government Printing Office, 1878– . Annual. Web version available at http://www.census.gov/statab/www/. (Also available in CD-ROM.)

U.S. Department of Commerce. Bureau of the Census. **Historical Statistics of the United States, Colonial Times to 1970.** Washington, D.C.: Government Printing Office, 1975. 2v. (Also available on CD ROM from Cambridge University Press.)

Mitchell, B. R. **International Historical Statistics: Africa, Asia & Oceania, 1750–1993.** 3rd ed. London: Macmillan Reference, 1998. 1113p.

Mitchell, B. R. **International Historical Statistics: the Americas, 1750–1993.** 4th ed. London: Macmillan Reference, 1998. 830p.

Mitchell, B. R. **International Historical Statistics: Europe, 1750–1993.** 4th ed. London: Macmillan Reference, 1998. 959p.

At every minute of every working day, hypothesizes one writer, a librarian somewhere is using the *Statistical Abstract of the United States*. Although this observation falls into the realm of an unsubstantiated statistic, there is no doubt that the *Statistical Abstract* is one of the most heavily used reference sources in any business or general reference collection. Published since 1878, the *Statistical Abstract* is the standard summary of social, political, and economic statistics for the United States. It is a compendium of data collected from over 220 different government and private agencies, with information grouped together by broad subject categories such as "Population," "Labor Force, Employment, and Earnings," and "Business Enterprise." Each chapter begins with a description of the data being presented, definitions of key terms and concepts, and, in many instances, consideration of the limitations and the general reliability of the data being presented. Sources providing information on earlier years and/or for local areas are frequently cited as well (see figure 6.8, page 126). Although the *Statistical Abstract* is available in electronic format, it is much easier and more efficient to use in hard copy.

Since the chapters are usually several pages long, the most efficient way to identify the specific table needed is to consult the subject index. Unlike subject indexes in many government publications, that of the *Statistical Abstract* is superb. Using it, tables can be located that provide statistics on shipments and value of microwave ovens, volume of trading on the New York Stock Exchange, prices received by fishermen for tuna and cod, and hundreds of other subjects. When a fairly broad subject is being presented, subheadings are frequently used for greater precision.

The tables themselves provide basic statistics and, as shown in figure 6.9 (page 126), frequently include definitions of terms or concepts as well as the source from which the statistics were derived.

Section 27

Accommodation, Food Services, and Other Services

This new section presents statistics relating to services other than those covered in the previous few sections (22 to 26) on domestic trade, transportation, communications, financial services, and recreation services. Many of the tables were previously covered in the former Section 27, Domestic Trade and Services in the 2000 edition of the *Statistical Abstract*. Data shown for the services are classified by kind of business and cover sales or receipts, establishments, employees, payrolls, and other items. The principal sources of these data are from the Census Bureau and include the *1997 Economic Census* reports, annual surveys, and the *County Business Patterns* program. These data are supplemented by data from several sources such as the Economic Research Service of the U.S. Department of Agriculture on food sales (Table 1268), the American Hotel & Motel Association on lodging (Table 1266), and McCann-Erickson. Inc. and Publishers Information

the *North American Industry Classification System,* called NAICS (see below). All Census Bureau tables in this section are utilizing the new NAICS codes, which replaced the Standard Industrial Classification (SIC) system. NAICS makes substantial structural improvements and identifies over 350 new industries. At the same time, it causes breaks in time series far more profound than any prior revision of the previously used SIC system. For information on this system and how it affects the comparability of retail and wholesale statistics historically, see text, Section 15, Business Enterprise, and especially the Census Web site at <http://www.census.gov/epcd/www/naics.html>.

The *Accommodation and Food Services sector* (NAICS sector 72) comprises establishments providing customers with lodging and/or prepared meals, snacks, and beverages for immediate consumption. The *Other Services (Except Public Admin-*

Figure 6.8. Part of a typical introductory section to a chapter, *Statistical Abstract of the United States*. Reprinted from the 2001 *Statistical Abstract of the United States*, http://www.census.gov/prod/2002pubs/01statab/services.pdf.

No. 1341. Selected International Economic Indicators by Country: 1980 to 2000

[Data cover gross domestic product (GDP) at market prices. Gross fixed capital formation covers private and government sectors except military. Savings data are calculated by deducting outlays—such as personal consumption expenditures, interest paid, and transfer payments to foreigners—from disposable personal income]

Year	United States	France	Germany	Italy	Netherlands	United Kingdom	Japan	Canada
Ratio of gross fixed capital formation to GDP (current prices):								
1980	19.9	23.8	22.6	25.2	22.9	18.8	31.7	23.1
1985	19.2	20.3	19.5	21.8	21.0	18.1	27.7	19.8
1990	17.0	22.6	20.9	21.5	22.3	20.6	32.2	20.8
1995	17.5	18.8	22.4	18.3	20.3	16.3	27.8	17.0
1998	19.4	18.4	21.3	18.5	21.5	17.4	26.9	19.3
1999	20.0	19.1	21.3	19.0	22.2	17.7	26.2	19.5
2000	20.7	19.7	21.4	19.6	22.3	17.7	26.0	19.3
Ratio of savings to disposable personal income:								
1980	10.2	15.8	14.2	25.1	7.8	11.7	17.9	15.5
1985	9.2	13.8	12.8	21.0	5.6	9.1	19.0	15.7
1990	7.8	13.1	14.7	18.4	11.6	7.4	13.9	12.9
1995	5.6	16.0	11.2	16.6	14.9	10.3	12.3	9.2
1998	4.2	15.6	10.2	12.8	13.4	5.8	11.8	4.4
1999	2.2	15.4	9.9	11.5	10.6	5.2	11.1	4.2
2000	-0.1	15.9	9.8	10.3	9.4	4.5	11.1	3.9

Source: U.S. Dept. of Commerce, International Trade Administration, Office of Trade and Economic Analysis, based on official statistics of listed countries.

Figure 6. 9. Sample table from section 30, *Statistical Abstract of the United States*. Reproduced from the 2001 *Statistical Abstract of the United States,* http://www.census.gov/prod/2002pubs/01statab/intlstat.pdf.

The appendixes include a guide to sources of statistics, a list of state statistical abstracts and foreign statistical abstracts, a description of metropolitan areas, and a list of current metropolitan areas and their components.

Most tables present information for the past 5 or 10 years; historical information is seldom presented. Someone who wanted to show how prices paid for consumer goods in 1888 compared with those paid in 1988, for example, would find that the *Statistical Abstract* lacked the necessary historical information. It would be found, however, in *Historical Statistics of the United States, Colonial Times to 1970*. Issued by the Census Bureau as a supplement to the *Statistical Abstract*, *Historical Statistics* also serves as a reference source and finding aid. Like the *Statistical Abstract*, it footnotes the sources from which tables are compiled and includes introductory remarks in most chapters that describe methodology employed and limitations, if any, of the data as presented. Data later than 1970 are presented for some of the series in the annual issues of the *Statistical Abstract,* and there is a special historical appendix beginning with the 1975 issue.

The *International Historical Statistics* series is an attempt to pull together in one place all the major statistical series for all countries for which information is available. The series provides the researcher with mainly economic statistical data, with the sources of information identified and an extensive set of explanatory footnotes. These are very detailed statistics, enabling one to identify information anything from the output of wheat in Estonia in 1919 to the English Consumer Price Index for 1781. This is a worthwhile series for most collections but especially for any institution that supports an interest in economic history.

Although important, the above sources are by no means the only collections of statistical data. Other more specialized sources are equally important. Although space precludes listing them all, some important representative examples of more specialized statistical compilations are described below. Other sources are included in the subject-oriented chapters that follow.

County and City Extra: Annual Metro, City, and County Data Book Lanham, Md. : Bernan Press, 1992– . Annual.

Gaguin, Deidre A., and Richard W. Dodge, eds. **Places, Towns and Townships**. 2nd ed. Lanham, Md.: Bernan Press, 1998. 924p.

Handbook of U.S. Labor Statistics: Employment, Earnings, Prices, Productivity, and Other Labor Data. 3rd ed. Lanham, Md.: Bernan Press, 1999. 395p.

U.S. President. **Economic Report of the President**. Washington, D.C.: Government Printing Office, 1947– . Annual. Web version available at http://w3.access.gpo.gov/eop/.

Handbook of International Economic Statistics. Washington, D.C.: Central Intelligence Agency, Directorate of Intelligence. 1992– . Annual. (Statistical tables available in both pdf and Excel format at http://www.odci.gov/cia/di/products/hies/.)

Data on state, city, and metropolitan areas are available in two Census Bureau publications issued periodically as supplements to the *Statistical Abstract*: the *County and City Data Book* and the *State and Metropolitan Area Data Book*. Unfortunately the *County and City Data Book* is published infrequently, the last edition appearing in 1994. The *State and Metropolitan Area Data Book* is also published intermittently, last appearing for 1997–1998. This edition appears in pdf. format at http://www.census.gov/statab/ www/smadb.html. The two listed Bernan publications luckily contain much of the same data. Bernan is also now the publisher of such well-known favorites as *Business Statistics of the United States, Agricultural Statistics, Housing Statistics of the United States,* and the *Handbook of U.S. Labor Statistics.*

The *County and City Extra* is a compilation of statistics taken from government and private agencies. Data are arranged by subject in five tables according to the geographic designations shown below.

Table	Geographic Coverage
A	Includes state level data
B	Includes state and county level data
C	Includes data for metropolitan areas
D	Data for cities with a 1990 population of 25,000 or more
E	Data for congressional districts of the 106th Congress

County and City Extra is a convenient collection of frequently looked for local and state data. Information is clearly organized and well presented, making the book useful for reference collections in public, college, and university libraries. Each table represents a different geographic area but covers a wide range of subjects including population, health, housing, the labor force, income and personal taxes, wholesale and retail trade, and federal funds and grants. Appendixes describe concepts and FIPS (Federal Information Processing Standards) codes and include maps and source notes.

A companion volume, *Places, Towns and Townships*, provides data on smaller communities of the United States. It presents population and housing statistics for every city, town, village, and township covered by the 1990 census, with population updates for 1996. It includes data on manufacturing, trade, services, employment, construction, crime, and government finances.

Someone seeking statistics for a specific state, county, or city would be well-advised to consult the statistical handbook or abstracts issued by the appropriate states and also to check the appropriate state Web pages. Although many contain data derived almost exclusively from the statistical compendia described above, others offer statistics that are not available elsewhere.

As has already been shown, one way in which statistical compendia can reflect specialization is by limiting the data to specific geographic areas. Another type of specialization is by subject. Many government agencies and departments as well as commercial publishers issue statistical handbooks and yearbooks reflecting their special interests and responsibilities. One of the most useful of such publications for business research was the *Handbook of Labor Statistics*, last published by the Bureau of Labor Statistics in 1989 and since 1997 issued by Bernan Press under the title *Handbook of U.S. Labor Statistics: Employment, Earnings, Prices, Productivity, and Other Labor Data.*

The *Handbook*, which contains data from many BLS and Census Bureau publications, includes information on employment and unemployment, hours and earnings, occupation employment statistics, worker productivity, compensation, prices and living conditions, work stoppages, occupational injuries and illnesses, and foreign labor and price statistics. It also includes special labor force data on such subjects as work experience, educational attainment, alternative work arrangements, and marital and family characteristics of the labor force. Technical notes are included for each of the subjects covered, and footnotes are appended to most tables. Those needing more recent information should refer to such BLS periodicals as the *Monthly Labor Review*, the Web page of the Bureau of Labor Statistics, or the *Economic Report of the President*.

In addition to the president's annual message to Congress on the state of the economy and an accompanying report by the Council of Economic Advisers, the *Economic Report of the President* includes detailed tables of supplementary statistics on national income, production and business activity, prices, money stock, government finance, corporate profit and finance, agriculture, and international economic activity. Sources are cited, and many of the figures date back 40 years or more.

The *Handbook of International Economic Statistics* presents basic worldwide economic statistics for comparing the economic performance of major countries and regions. The data in the handbook are for 1970, 1980, and every year between 1990 and 1997. Topics covered include energy, agriculture, minerals and metals, chemicals and manufactured goods, foreign trade and aid, and the environment. Graphs and charts are used to present data on food consumption, measures of energy efficiency, electricity production, imports and exports, economic indicators, agricultural production, labor force, gross domestic product, and inflation. This is especially useful because the charts, maps, and tables are available on the Internet at http://www.odci.gov/cia/di/products/hies/hies.pdf.

The titles described above cover fairly broad subject areas. Other compendia, particularly those issued by trade associations and commercial publishers, focus on narrower subject fields. Many are discussed at length in later chapters on marketing, accounting, banking, and investments, but three are listed below.

Berinstein, Paula. **The Statistical Handbook on Technology**. Phoenix, Ariz. : Oryx Press, 1999. 304p.

Bentley, Linda Holman, and Jennifer J. Kiesl. **Investment Statistics Locator**. Rev. ed. Phoenix, Ariz.: Oryx Press, 1995. 275p.

BP Amoco Statistical Review of World Energy. 2003. http://www.bpamoco.com/centres/energy/index.asp. (Accessed August 23, 2003).

More and more people need and want statistics on the field of technology. The *Statistical Handbook on Technology* is a well-designed compendium grouped into 13 subject areas and with more than 250 tables, charts, and graphs. Each of the book's 13 chapters includes a short essay about the topic and the statistics in that area. A listing of tables and figures by chapter and a subject index make access simple.

Although the *Investment Statistics Locator* does not contain the actual statistics, it does index 53 widely held sources reporting economic and investment data. The Internet has made many of the current statistics more readily available, but this volume is still a convenient and fast way to locate resources in print publications and is especially handy for those who may be looking for older investment statistics that are not available on the Web.

BP Amoco issues on the Web the *Statistical Review of World Energy*, an excellent source of energy industry information. This publication contains approximately 10 years of data, taken from government sources and published data, and can be downloaded in Excel format or printed in pdf. The full PowerPoint slide collections are also available for each subject area. One has the option to download to view either the full report or the individual sections, which include oil, natural gas, coal, nuclear energy, and hydroelectricity. Although this is also available in print, the added advantage for researchers using the Internet edition is the ability to download using Excel.

Compilations and Search Engines on the Web

Knowing that the statistics one may need are out there somewhere on the Web is often as frustrating as the search and time taken to find them. Fortunately there are shortcuts to much of this information. Listed below is just a sampling of major statistics finding aids.

American Fact Finder, http://factfinder.census.gov/servlet/BasicFactsServlet. Demographic and economic information.

FEDSTATS, http://www.fedstats.gov/index.html. Official Web site for all statistics from federal agencies.

Economagic.com:Economic Time Series Page, http://www.EconoMagic.com/. Meant to be "a comprehensive site of free, easily available economic time series data useful for economic research, in particular economic forecasting." There are approximately 100,000 data sets. Charts are included.

FREDII, http://www.stls.frb.org/fred2/. Provides historical U.S. economic and financial data, including daily U.S. interest rates; monetary and business indicators; exchange rates; balance of payments; and regional economic data for Arkansas, Illinois, Indiana, Kentucky, Mississippi, Missouri, and Tennessee.

National Bureau of Economic Research, http://www.nber.org/data_index.html. The National Bureau of Economic Research is a private, nonprofit, nonpartisan research organization dedicated to promoting a greater understanding of how the economy works. Information at the Web site includes macro, industry, and individual data.

ECONData, http://inforumweb.umd.edu/Contents.html. A source of economic time series data from Inforum, at the University of Maryland. Several hundred thousand economic time series, produced by a number of U.S. government agencies, can be found here. These series include national income and product accounts (NIPA), labor statistics, price indexes, current business indicators, industrial production, information on states and regions, and international data

SSDC, http://odwin.ucsd.edu/idata/. The Social Science Data Center at the University of California, San Diego looks to provide easy access to raw numeric data, which is free over the Internet. It also provides links to other data archives and catalogs of materials.

Statistical Data Locators, http://www.ntu.edu.sg/lib/stat/statdata.htm. This site, maintained by staff of the library at Nanyang Technological University in Singapore, offers a very extensive list of international data sites on the Internet. It is organized by region: Asia, Oceania, North America, Europe, Africa, International, Latin America, and Others.

Notes

1. Reported on the *FEDSTATS* Web page at http://www.fedstats.gov/.

2.   Economic Census: Manufacturing Sector, http://www.census.gov/econ/www/ma0100.html

   Annual Survey of Manufactures, http://www.census.gov/econ/www/ma0300.html

Current Industrial Reports, http://www.census.gov/cir/www/alpha.html

Manufacturers' Shipments, Inventories, and Orders, http://www.census.gov/indicator/www/m3/

Survey of Plant Utilization, http://www.census.gov/cir/www/mqc1pag2.html

3. U.S. Bureau of the Census, *American Housing Survey: 1997* (Washington, D.C.: Government Printing Office, 1997). Also available at http://www.census.gov/hhes/www/ahs.html.

4. Darrell Huff, *How to Lie with Statistics* (New York: Norton, 1954), 140.

5. Until 1978, when the Consumer Price Index for All Urban Consumers, or CPI-U, was introduced, the Consumer Price Index was limited to prices paid by urban wage earners. The pre-1978 Consumer Price Index, in other words, is roughly analogous to the Consumer Price Index for Urban Wage Earners and Clerical Workers, or CPI-W.

6. Joe Morehead, "The Uses and Misuses of Information Found in Government Publications," in *Collection Development and Public Access of Government Documents* (Westport, Conn.: Meckler, 1981), 62.

7. Huff, *How to Lie with Statistics,* 123.

8. Joan Harvey, "Statistical Publications for Business and Management," in *Information Sources in Management and Business,* 2nd ed. (London: Butterworths, 1984), 136.

7

Selected, Consolidated Electronic Business Information

Technology is now woven into the fabric of civilization in every corner of the globe. During the last 25 years, in the United States, computer usage has changed from a few researchers, scientists, and engineers using large mainframes to a general population in which more than one-third own at least one personal computer. In the fall of 1984, 7.9 percent of American households reported owning a computer, in contrast to 2001, when 56.5 percent reported owning one.[1] Seven of every eight households with computers (88.1 percent) also subscribed to the Internet. By 1997 nearly 50 per cent of employees in the United States were using computers at work.[2]

Public interest in and enthusiasm for electronic information has increased tremendously along with familiarity with computers, and the Web has become the platform for innovation in information collection. End users have come to expect current information to be dynamic, fluid, and freely available. Academic and public libraries have purchased individual databases, and in some states there are statewide agreements with vendors to supply access to their databases via the Internet.[3] Business faculty and students, managers, small business people, market researchers, and individuals frequently log into online computerized databases and access the Internet to gather information for different projects. Publishers have also become part of the transformation by organizing access to information through a variety of customized interfaces that feature materials needed by companies, libraries, and individuals.

Online databases, offered through vendors such as Dialog, were at one time the type of electronic information with which librarians were most familiar, but this changed with the steady introduction of the CD-ROM and was revolutionized with the introduction of the Internet. This chapter examines electronic information in a variety of formats, ranging from CD-ROMs to suites of information available from vendors and free Web portals, and discusses some publications that help in their identification.

Online Business Databases

Online databases used to be stored on magnetic tape and required the use of mainframe computers housed at remote locations. When libraries and information centers began accessing these online databases they did so by using telephone lines and computer terminals or microcomputers with modems and telecommunications software. With the advances in technology most databases are now stored on magnetic discs and are available through an Internet connection or are in a CD-ROM format.

Database Producers, Vendors, and Aggregators

Organizations that are responsible for creating databases are known as database producers, although a broader term that has come into wide use is *content developer*. A database producer gathers information, edits it, and reproduces it in much the same way as traditional publishers do. Many databases, in fact, were preceded by and continue to have printed counterparts. As a result, most business publishers have also become business database producers. Dun & Bradstreet, Standard & Poor's, and Gale Research are major publishers of business materials and now offer both electronic and print versions of the data they collect. In the past many producers did not market their databases to either libraries or the public; instead, they leased or sold them to database vendors such as Dialog or LexisNexis, who made them available. But in another major change in the industry, both traditional and nontraditional producers are offering their own products for lease or sale.

Database vendors used to be the suppliers of the necessary hardware and software, that is, the mainframe computers and the programs to run them. In addition, they provided a certain level of standardization among the databases they offered, marketing them to the public and supplying customers with database descriptions, instructions, and training in their use. Searching databases through a vendor meant paying for both the time spent online and the documents retrieved. While using a vendor service is still more economical for highly specialized databases or those that one uses infrequently, it is easier now for the end user to access information, without an intermediary, by using databases available on CD-ROMs and via the Internet.

Database producers now license their products directly to libraries and corporations, and as a result information is now more freely available. The problem with this is that many users believe that these products are "free" because they are accessing them through the Internet. There are also still some problems with standardization in terms of basic commands and search protocols, but there is no longer the sense of urgency if a mistake is made searching as one is no longer paying for access time.

Content aggregators compile listings from various sources into one database. Perhaps the best known aggregated databases are those that provide selected full-text periodical content.[4] Those well known in the library community are Dow Jones, EBSCO, Gale, LexisNexis, OCLC, and ProQuest (see figure 7.1); they provide some of the better known aggregated databases such as *ABI/INFORM Global*, *LexisNexis Academic,* and *Business Source Elite*.

These aggregators are in many cases also database providers and vendors, and in fact the distinction among these terms is becoming blurred. One example of this is the option to choose the databases one wishes to license and have these appear on one screen as individual searchable units, with the choice also given to search all those purchased as a whole unit.

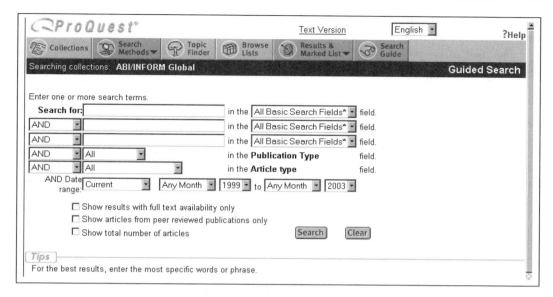

Figure 7.1. Guided search screen for a ProQuest database.

With the development of the Internet other companies and choices have appeared as both aggregators and vendors of periodical articles. Current awareness and document delivery services are available from such enterprises as *ingenta* (http://www.ingenta.com/) and *Emerald* (http://www.emeraldinsight.com/). Both provide an updating service that is of great value to the individual, and in both cases many academic libraries carry a subscription so that campus users can use the service without an individual subscription.

Not only have terms become blurred with the expansion of the Internet, but mergers between companies and services appear to be happening almost daily. Any business researcher or librarian who needs to keep abreast of current developments can do so by checking various publications, especially *Information Today* , *ONLINE, Econtent,* and *Searcher.*[5]

Business databases cover a wide range of subjects and can be categorized either by the type of information provided or by the vendors who supply them. Other chapters contain descriptions of some databases from commercial publishers, such as directories or periodicals and newspapers, so this chapter will concentrate on aggregated collections and what are being termed Web "portals." Some of the portals described in this chapter are produced by commercial vendors and charge a fee, and some cover material available free on the Web.

Portals

The terms *portal, horizontal portal,* and *vertical portal* occur frequently in articles, but unfortunately there does not seem to be a consensus about what exactly each one means. Any dictionary will describe a portal as a "gateway," and this seems to be the general meaning accepted in the Web world. Yahoo! (http://www.yahoo.com/) is a good example of a horizontal portal, as it provides access to a variety of information available in directory format and via search engine. Some articles also classify services such as Yahoo! as horizontal portals because they cover more than one subject area. One would then guess that a vertical portal covers only one subject area, as *cnnmoney* (http://money.cnn.com/) does, but perhaps a vertical portal could also cover only one aspect of business, such as mutual funds, rather than all business. A vertical portal can also exist within an organization to provide information only to its members.

One way of looking at the differences between the types of portals is to use a magazine analogy. *Newsweek* would be a horizontal portal as it covers all types of news, whereas *Business Week* would be a vertical portal because it concentrates on business news.

Selected Commercial Products

Electronic information has fundamentally changed since it was first used in the mid-1970s. Innovation has become the keyword. Electronic resources are now not only for business specialists but can also be used by the general consumer. Some of the major decisions that face researchers and librarians at this time are not only whether to buy or license a product but in which form it will be provided. Desktop delivery is popular in the business world, but this site licensing may be beyond the funding available to academic institutions, especially large institutions, when the pricing system is based on full time enrollment (fte). It is often difficult to convince vendors that only a small percentage of the students will be interested in highly specialized business databases, and that not everyone in the medieval history or comparative literature departments will be eager to access the specialized business information provided.

The following descriptions are divided into resources accessible "via" the Internet and those "on" the Internet. Because so often the Web is used as a vehicle for many commercial products, library patrons feel that they are getting the information at no cost and do not realize the price paid by the institution for value-added features such as full text and searchable indexes. Nevertheless the Internet provides access to a wealth of material that is freely distributed, and there are many sites that act as indexes and directories to this information.

Information "via" the Internet

Periodicals and Newspapers

Serials are well represented online. Most fall into three categories: electronic versions of the serials themselves; collections of electronic versions of periodicals; and indexing, abstracting, and full-text services.

Like all major aggregators or vendors, EBSCO tailors its offerings to the client. One can choose from an extensive collection of business periodical databases including: *Business Source, Business Source® Elite, Business Source® Plus, Business Source™ Premier* and *Hoover's Company Profiles.*

Business Source, available only as a CD-ROM, supplies searchable full text for about 50 publications, abstracts and indexing for over 570 business-related journals, and coverage of 50 business newspapers; *Business Source Plus*, available as part of the online version EBSCOhost and as a CD-ROM, gives cumulative full text for nearly 260 journals, including *Forbes, Fortune, The Economist*, and more than 40 regional publications, and provides abstracts and indexing for another 700 business journals. *Business Source Elite*, offered on EBSCOhost, DVD-ROM, and CD-ROM, supplies cumulative full text for over 960 journals, including *Business Week, American Banker, Forbes, Fortune, The Economist,* and hundreds of peer-reviewed journals; full text for more than 40 regional business publications; and abstracts and indexing for 1,650 business journals. Offered only in EBSCOhost, the online service, *Business Source Premier* carries cumulative full text for about 2,800 journals and abstracts and indexing for nearly 3,335 business journals.

Hoover's Company Profiles contributes in-depth profiles of more than 3,400 public and private companies in the United States and around the world and includes *Hoover's Company Capsules,* which provides information on more than 13,500 public and private companies. The capsules but not the profiles are available free at *HOOVER'S ONLINE* (http://www.hoovers.com).

The choices are designed to fit differing needs, but the search mechanisms and some searchable fields remain the same across databases so that switches can be made without users even being aware of the change. EBSCO also provides specialized services to corporate and special libraries via *Corporate ResourceNet,* which combines information from nearly 2,120 full-text sources, abstracts and indexing for 2,790 sources, plus 100,000 selected Web links.

Some full-text newspaper coverage is supplied by EBSCO in a separate database called *Newspaper Source.* This supplies the full text of *The Christian Science Monitor,* with coverage from January 1995; abstracts and indexing of the *New York Times,* the *Wall Street Journal,* and *USA Today,* all dating from 1995; and abstracts from the *New York Times Magazine* and the *New York Times Book Review.* Full-text articles from 105 contributor newspapers to the Knight-Ridder/Tribune Business News and briefs from six newswires are also included. As with most newspaper coverage in databases, obituaries (other than famous people), sports tables, classifieds, stock prices, and the weather are not included.

EBSCO offers a variety of periodicals and newspapers, with the option to download, print, or e-mail full-text articles. Other features of the databases include publisher information for individual journals, including publishers' addresses and the cost of the publications.

Another well-known aggregator/vendor is ProQuest Inc., formerly known as Bell & Howell. Since the early 1990s, the name ProQuest has been associated with a suite of electronic databases serving the library and the educational community, and in 2000 it was attracting two million page hits per day via the Internet. The major business databases available from Proquest are *ABI/INFORM Global, Accounting & Tax Database, Banking Information Source, Business Periodicals, Business Periodicals Global, ProQuest Asian Business, ProQuest European Business, ProQuest Computing,* and *ProQuest Telecommunications.*

ABI/INFORM provides in-depth coverage of business conditions, trends, corporate strategies and tactics, management techniques, competitor and product information, and a wide variety of other topics. It provides informative indexing and substantive abstracts to articles from more than 1,000 leading business and management publications, including over 350 English-language titles from outside the United States, and is especially useful for retrieving articles on strategic business and management issues. *ABI/INFORM* has always been available only in electronic format and has abstracts available from 1971. In its initial format one could search and retrieve abstracts via distributors such as Dialog, and then it became more widely available on CD-ROM. Now, on ProQuest, it provides complete articles, in full text, page image, or in a text + graphics format for more than 1,000 of the most popular and important sources. (See figure 7.2, page 138.)

Accounting & Tax Database features cover-to-cover indexing and abstracts to 300 key publications in accounting, auditing, and financial management from the United States and overseas. Also included are citations to relevant articles from over 800 newspapers, business journals, dissertations, and news magazines. Coverage is 1990+ for all publications.

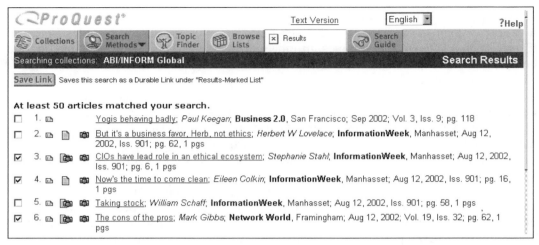

Figure 7.2. *ABI/INFORM Global* result list showing retrieval formats available.

Banking Information Source provides information about the financial services industry, banking trends, topics, issues, and operations, with comprehensive coverage of important industry sources. Complete bibliographic information, including abstracts, is available for more than 220 industry publications, newsletters, Bank Marketing Association's Golden Coin Awards competition entries and Stonier Theses, plus the citations of banking-related articles from *American Banker*, the *Wall Street Journal*, and the *New York Times*. Full-text articles are included for selected high demand titles. Coverage is 1981+ for citations, with full-text coverage beginning with 1994 material.

Business Periodicals provides the most authoritative coverage of business and management publications available, with three different editions to choose from. The database links full images of articles from the most important and popular *ABI/INFORM* sources. Each edition contains abstracts and indexing to articles from top publications, plus cover-to-cover page images from about half of the cited journals. Coverage for current subscriptions begins in 1992, with backfile availability to 1971. Full-image coverage begins in 1988.

Business Periodicals Global contains abstracts and indexing to articles from more than 1,000 publications, including almost 400 English-language titles from outside the United States. Full images are available for about half the indexed titles. *Business Periodicals Research* contains abstracts and indexing to articles from over 800 publications, half of which are available in full image.

Business Periodicals Select provides abstracts and indexing to articles from about 350 publications, with full-image availability for about one third of those titles.

ProQuest Asian Business is designed for students and faculty at business schools, offering the latest business and financial information for researchers at all levels. It can be used as a standalone resource for regional Asian business news, or in conjunction with *ABI/INFORM Global*. More than 50 key titles are included, all in fully searchable ASCII full-text format, many with article-pages images. Popular titles include *Far Eastern Economic Review*, *Asiaweek*, and *Fortune*.

ProQuest European Business is also produced for students and faculty at business schools, offering current business and financial information for researchers at all levels. It can be used as a single source for regional European business news, or for more comprehensive coverage in conjunction with *ABI/INFORM*. More than 100 key titles are included, all in fully searchable ASCII full-text format, many with article-pages images. Popular titles include *The Economist, Fortune,* and *European Business Journal.*

ProQuest Computing features the largest selection of computer-related journals found online, with daily updates. Among the 200 top journals are *Journal of the Association for Computing Machinery, Communications of the ACM, Byte, Computer Reseller News, Computerworld,* and *InfoWorld.* Records include full bibliographic citations and abstracts. ASCII full text is provided for some 95 percent of the titles.

ProQuest Telecommunications features the best collection of telecommunication journals online, selected by a panel of academic and corporate librarians who helped identify the 65 leading journals. They include *America's Network, Telecommunications, Telephony, European Broadband Networking News,* and *Journal of Broadcasting & Electronic Media.* Citations, abstracts, and ASCII full text are provided for each record.

ProQuest also provides in some of its databases aids such as citation guides and tables of contents. Customized journal title lists can be compiled by selecting the required database from http://www.proquest.com/division/tl-title.shtml.

One of the most useful newspapers provided by ProQuest is the *Wall Street Journal,* available in full-text format. Like all ProQuest full-text newspapers, it is fully searchable, with additional fields including section, page, and special feature. Subscriptions include full-text coverage from 1995 onward, with indexing available from 1989 to the present. The *Wall Street Journal Europe* is also available, providing European business news with coverage from 1990 onward. The *Asian Wall Street Journal* offers coverage beginning with 1991 material. More general full-text newspapers such as the *New York Times, USA Today,* and the *Washington Post* are also available.

Another leading publisher of library materials is the Gale Group. Among its products are a variety of well-known and authoritative directories and the *InfoTrac* (IAC) family of online search and retrieval products, which are described in this section.

General BusinessFile ASAP International contains 100,000 company profiles, more than 50,000 full-text Investext research reports, as well as full-text journal articles and a 30-day backfile of newswires. One can perform a search by subject or keyword or utilize a Boolean strategy. Gale is not only presenting full-text journals and newspapers in this product but is also including research reports and one of the company directories that it owns. It is not a full suite of business information, which will be discussed later in this chapter, but it incorporates the three sets of highly desirable information into one searchable unity and thus is an excellent place to start for company and industry information.

At the same time as producers and aggregators such as ProQuest, EBSCO, and Gale are refining and improving their products, they are also licensing their products to other nontraditional information services such as Northern Light.

Northern Light (http://www.northernlight.com) supplies information obtained from several sources, including ProQuest (see figure 7.3, page 140). This material is included in its *Special Collection* of 7,000 full-text journals, books, magazines, newswires, and reference sources. Search results may be different using this service because one does not use strict Boolean methods, and the results are ranked by an algorithm. This is not to say that the results obtained are not as good, because they may in certain cases be better. The added advantage is that single articles are fairly inexpensive for an individual to purchase from the service.

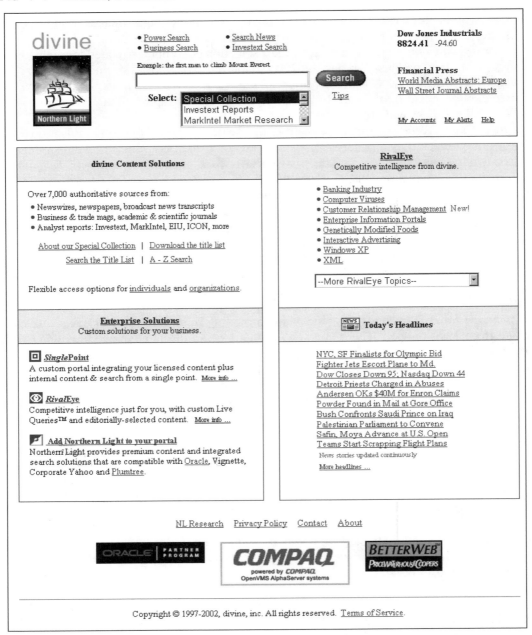

Figure 7.3. Home page of Northern Light.
Reproduced with permission of Northern Light Technology, Inc.

The online services discussed in this section are collections of journals and newspapers. Other services for business may be more specialized.

Business Suites

Every database has a producer that is distributing files in a variety of ways. They may be available directly from the producer, or they may be available to be searched via a commercial vendor such as LexisNexis. In other cases, like that of Gale, publishers are becoming their own online vendors and amalgamating various products into suites of information. This section provides information on some of the largest online collections of business information.

Business & Company Resource Center. 2000– (updated daily). The Gale Group (Producer). http://www.galegroup.com. (Accessed August 17, 2003).

Factiva. 2000– (updated several times daily). Dow Jones Reuters Business Interactive LLC. Trading as Factiva. (Producer). http://djinteractive.com. (AccessedAugust 17, 2003).

LexisNexis. 1998– (updated several times daily). LexisNexis. (Producer). http://www.lexisnexis.com. (Accessed August 17, 2003).

Business & Company Resource Center offers integrated access to a wide variety of Gale and Thomson Financial business resources, including those that cover company, industry, investment, and consumer information. The *Center* offers access to 20-minute delayed stock quotes, journals, news and press releases, consumer marketing data, corporate chronologies and histories, emerging technology reports, *First Call* consensus estimates, insider buying and selling activity, major shareholders, product and brand records, industry information, and more than 8,000 associations. This comprehensive suite of information enables a user to access information from traditional Gale hard copy materials such as the *International Directory of Company Histories* and also from specialized sources as *CDA/Investment* insider buying and selling activity, *CDA/Spectrum* major shareholders information, and *Investext Select* records. Once an initial search has been executed, a results tab bar appears across the top of the screen. One can then move easily from the company profile information to other materials such as investment reports, financials, rankings, or news and magazine stories. (See figure 7.4.) Several extra modules are available at an added cost. These are *Investext Plus, PROMT,* and *Newsletters ASAP;* others are expected to be added at a later date.

Figure 7.4. Directory information and tab "navigation" options in
Business & Company Resource Center. Reprinted with permission of The Gale Group.

Another business suite or portal is *Factiva.com,* which is a customizable, enterprise-wide business news and research solution that includes content from top national newspapers, Dow Jones & Reuters newswires, business journals, market research reports, analyst reports, and Web sites. With *Factiva,* one gets content from 118 countries, written in 22 languages. This encompasses information from 8,000 sources, including local and regional newspapers, trade publications, business newswires, company profiles, television and radio transcripts, business journals, and over 10,000 Web sites.

Using the basic search screen, one can run one search across the entire *Factiva.com* collection, which includes print sources, newswires, Web sites, pictures, and company reports. All content is universally indexed, with company, industry, geographical and news subject codes from *Factiva's* "Intelligent Indexing," which includes over 300,000 company codes, 720 industry codes, 340 news subject codes, and 370 geographical codes. The indexing is set up so that the user can choose the desired terms; after clicking on "Done" they will appear in the search box. Additional words or terms can be added to the search box before clicking on "Run Search". A "Company Quick Search," which will pull together both news and financial reports, is also available.

Some of the special features are both company and news tracking, the ability to build a personalized source list, and the option to store information in a briefcase for up to 30 days. The intelligent indexing provides a thesaurus approach to searching that guarantees a meaningful result with useful information. Boolean operators are supported, plus additional power searching connectors such as w/n, atleast, near, and same.

The Lexis service, which began in 1973, was the first commercial, full-text legal information service, available to help legal practitioners research the law. The companion service Nexis, which covers news and business information, was launched in 1979. Since that time, the Nexis service has grown to become one of the largest news and business online information services and includes comprehensive company, country, financial, demographic, market research, and industry reports. Access is provided to worldwide newspapers, magazines, trade journals, industry newsletters, tax and accounting information, financial data, public records, legislative records, and data on companies and business executives. The online version of *LexisNexis* (http://www.lexisnexis.com) , available via the Web and dial-up services, contains more than 13,500 sources, including regional, national, and international newspapers, newswires, magazines, trade journals, business publications, and public records.

LexisNexis Academic, a subset of the full blown LexisNexis service, is increasingly used by university students all over the world. No other comparable system offers the breadth and depth of business, news, and legal information from one service. One of the most crucial aspects of the contract offered to subscribers is the content loss threshold clause. The database has experienced significant fluctuations in level of content since it was set up. Some of the most significant deletions were made in August 1998, when 443 titles from *Business Dateline* and 345 titles from *ABI/ INFORM* were removed, a 13.7 percent reduction in titles, a number of which were scholarly journals. Also in August 1998, *Ulrich's International Periodicals Directory, Books in Print,* and the *Encyclopedia of Associations* were no longer accessible. In the summer of 1999, 1,923 titles were removed by the Gale Group, including titles like *The Academy of Management Review*, the *Public Relations Quarterly*, the *International Journal of Advertising*, and the *British Medical Journal.* Titles have been added to replace some of the lost material. A content advisory board has been created to monitor the database's content quality and to examine guidelines for quality content. This board consists exclusively of librarians from selected institutions. Major deletions are also announced, and monthly additions and deletions are published in *Universe News*, a monthly newsletter available electronically from http://www.lexisnexis.com/academic/newsletter/universeNewsMnu.htm.

Despite its innovations and technical changes, LexisNexis must be fighting a rearguard action against free Web news feeds, Web directories, and the wealth of financial information available free on the Internet; however, its strength lies in ease of use and the consolidation of information, including substantial backfiles, within one service.

Other services not described in this section but in other chapters include those from the publishers Dun & Bradstreet (http://www.dnb.com) and Standard & Poor's (http://www.standardandpoors.com/) and the vendor SilverPlatter (http://www.silverplatter.com/). These publishers have always been a part of traditional online services, whether offering separate databases through vendors such as Dialog or providing CD-ROMs. They are also examples of publishers who have transferred most of their traditional hard copy offerings to electronic versions. Like the services described in more depth, they have built databases that combine comprehensive coverage with the advantage of great historical depth. SilverPlatter has always been well known for its CD-ROM offerings, but it has also transformed itself into a global leader in providing comprehensive and seamlessly integrated electronic database collections of scholarly reference information. These are distributed over the Internet, through campus and corporate intranets, and on CD-ROM.

Formerly known as Moody's Financial Information Services, Mergent has been publishing, in print, detailed business descriptions, corporate histories, and financial statements since 1900. The electronic version of Mergent, previously known as *FIS Online,* is global in scope and includes, in the advanced search, the option of user-defined search features and report compilation. Extra modules include insider trades, institutional holdings found in *Mergent Equity Portraits,* and *Mergent Corporate Bond Portraits,* which were added to the online database in 2001. *Mergent Equity Portraits* contains stock price, volume, and other data, plus in-depth industry analysis, on over 10,000 companies. *Mergent Corporate Bond Portraits* contains up-to-date terms and conditions data and detailed issuer financial analysis on over 40,000 corporate bonds. Several years of annual reports from 27,000 global companies have also been added.

Traditional publishers and vendors have not vanished; they have instead followed the maxim "evolve or die," and they appear to have done this well. As long as they follow the criteria put forward by Bob Littell[6] for evaluating Web sites of "consolidate; filter and simplify; prioritize; content; categorize; convenience and cost," they should remain competitive.

Resources "on" the Internet

Business Collections

How big is the Web, really? One calculation, from *Alexa Internet* (http://www.alexa.com/), estimated that there are more than 20 million "content areas" on the Web, that 1.5 million new pages are added to the Web every day, and that the Web doubles in size every eight months.

It is hardly a secret that there is all kinds of free information on the Internet. It used to be that librarians and researchers were wary of much of that information, and although it is true that there is an awful lot of "junk" still cluttering the Web, many companies and librarians have taken up the challenge of arranging some of this vast array of "information" into usable bites. Business researchers have been most fortunate with the amount of "free" information issued by reputable publishers and producers. There are Web versions of newspapers, journals, product reviews, stock research, white papers, working papers, and statistics as well as guides to business information and even Web pages created by professors for their students. Although the Internet appears at times to be a huge, unstructured morass, the improvement in search engines and the numerous collections of data have made data collection somewhat easier. Included here are short descriptions of some consolidated sites and portals that concentrate on business information and also provide a fair amount of free information or links.

Most portals of choice are the customizable search engines such as Yahoo! (http://www.yahoo.com), which has over 20 country-specific sites and allows users to assemble their own pages using their own favorite sites. A good place to start is with *Yahoo! Finance.*

Yahoo! Finance. ©2003. Yahoo! Inc. (Producer). http://quote.yahoo.com/. (Accessed August 18, 2003).

Often regarded as the most customizable page on the Web, *Yahoo! Finance* enables the user to create multiple portfolios, customize news, check weather and traffic, and set up an address book. Data can also be synchronized to *MS Outlook Express* or a palm pilot. By entering a stock symbol one can receive a company capsule, charts, financials, headlines, upcoming events for the chosen company, and useful Web links. Yahoo! includes on the front page of this site updates on the stock market, with direct links to the exchanges and indexes, a quick quote search, and the subject divisions of information. The user can check such areas as *U.S. Markets*, *World Markets,* and *Financial News* as well as use the *Yahoo! Bill Pay and Banking Center* to check on personal finances. *Yahoo! Finance* supplies not only links to its own services and to others on the Web but also information to advise and inform the user. For example, if the Loan Center is checked a user can find substantive information on mortgages, including "understanding the loan process," "what kind of loan should you get?" and "loan purchase strategies in today's market," as well as links to obtaining a copy of your credit report.

Another subject area site that can be customized by selecting what is wanted, removing what is not, and adding favorite links that are missing is http://www.ceoexpress.com.

CEOExpress. ©1999–2003. CEOExpress Company (Producer). http://www.ceoexpress.com. (Accessed August 18, 2003).

CEOExpress was first developed by a busy CEO, Patricia Pomerleau, who believes in the "80/20 rule."[7] In 1996 she founded AlphaSight Online Strategists, a consulting company focused on helping senior executives understand and utilize the Internet for strategic advantage. Out of this experience came *CEOExpress,* which gathers on a single page links to daily news, search engines, stock and business research, and references. It logically organizes most major classes of resources so that they look uncluttered and are easy to read. This is an excellent quick reference tool to easily access frequently used sites for news, financial quotes, business, technology, travel, and much more. The list is highly selective, and the resources found here are tested to ensure their substance and quality. Some categories on this site are Daily News, Business Magazines, Newsfeeds, Business News, Tech Magazines & News, International News, Financial Markets, Quotes and Market News, Online Investor Services, and Company Research. Another much appreciated feature is the emphasis on information and not on slow-loading graphics. (See figure 7.5.)

Figure 7.5. Home page of *CEOExpress* at http://www.ceoexpress.com.
Reprinted with permission of CEO Express Company.

Figure 7.5 (*Cont.*)

Office Tools & Travel | Industry Center | Research Tips | CEO@Home | Ask an Expert 💡 | 10 Questions | ExecuDiva ⏴ ▲Top

Office Tools: Anonymizer | Calculators Online | Currency Calculator | Postage Calculator | Salary Calculator | Skytel | **Maps:** MapQuest | Subway Navigator | **Tax Info:** IRS Forms: Federal | IRS Forms: State | *More...*

Speech & Writing: Citing Sources | Common English Errors | Elements of Style | Guide to Grammar & Writing ✔ | PresentationTips | Press Release Guide | **Famous Quotes:** Bartlett's Quotations | QuoteLand | *More...*

Reference: Britannica | CIA World Facts | Consumer Info Center | Encyclopedia.com | Fast Facts | RefDesk | Translation Site | **Dictionaries:** "One Look" | Multi-Lingual | Thesaurus | Webster's Dictionary | **Libraries:** Internet Public Library | Library of Congress ✔ | National Archives | **Misc:** **Homework Help** ✔ | eHow | HowStuffWorks | Public Records Database | World Public Holidays | *NewsResource Center* | LibrarySpot | Technology Encyclopedia | *More...*

Directory Search: AnyWho ✔ | Area Code Finder | Switchboard | Int'l Dialing Codes | 800 Directory | Yellow Pages | Zip Code Finder | Zip Code Finder (Business)

Essential Downloads: Acrobat Reader | Download.com | Kid's Software ✔ | Shockwave | Software Library | TUCOWS ✔ | WinZip | **AntiVirus:** McAfee | Norton | **Browsers:** Internet Explorer | Netscape | Opera | **Security:** Microsoft Security Patches | VirusAlerts | *More...*

Tech Tools: Computerworld Quickstudy | Internet Traffic Report ✔ | List of ISPs | NetMechanic | PhotoFinder | **Website Design Advice:** Ask Tog | Alertbox | **Standards:** World Wide Web Consortium

Airlines: Airlines (World Wide) | Airline Phone #s | Airport Directory | Flight Arrivals and Departures ✔ | **Schedules:** America West | American Airlines | Continental | Delta | Jet Blue | Midwest Express | Northwest | Southwest | United | US Airways | **Flight Information:** Airline Safety | Airline Seat Maps ✔ | Airport Delays | Real Time Flight Tracker | *More...*

Travel: Express Travel Center | **Ticketing:** Expedia | Orbitz | Travelocity | **Discount Travel:** Priceline | Site59 | **General:** AAA | AmEx Travel | BizTraveler | CNN City Guide | Fodors | Frommer's | Concierge | Airplane Safety | **International:** Health Information | Legal Assistance | Passport Services | Travel Warnings | World Travel Guide ✔ | **Driving:** Driving Directions | Road Traffic & Construction | **Trains:** Amtrak | Subway Navigator | **Accommodations:** Bed and Breakfast | Find A Room | Small Luxury Hotels | *More...*

Breaktime | Industry Center | Research Tips | CEO@Home | Ask an Expert 💡 | 10 Questions | ExecuDiva ⏴ ▲Top

Sports: CBS Sportsline | ESPN | Fly Fishing | Golf Course Locator | Golf Search | Maritime Links ✔ | MySportsGuru | Sports Illustrated | NFL.com | *More...*

Real Estate: HomeAdvisor | Nat'l Real Estate Investor | Realtor.com | **Relocation:** Monster Moving | School Locator | *More...*

Leisure: Citysearch | Epicurious | Movie Reviews ✔ | Movie Showtimes | Playbill | Ticketmaster | Way Back Machine ✔ | Zagat Dine | *More...*

Unwind: Bartleby Library | Blue Mountain Arts ✔ | Civil War Archives | Dave Barry | Dilbert Zone | History Channel | LyricServer | Periodic Table of Elements ✔ | Project Gutenberg | Skeptic's Dictionary | Top Ten Lists | TV Listings | *More...*

Autos: Autobytel.com | Car & Driver | Carpoint | Edmunds Auto Info | Hemmings | Intellichoice | Kelley Blue Book | Yahoo Automotive | **Safety:** Automotive Recalls ✔ | Car Safety Ratings ✔ | Lemon Laws

Shopping: Express Biz Shopper | Express Personal Shopper | Books: Amazon ✔ | Barnes & Noble | Powell's Books | **Rare & Used Books:** Alibris | **Computers/Software:** Dell | **Gourmet Food, Flowers & Gifts:** 1-800-Flowers | GiftCorp | Great Posters ✔ | Hallmark | zChocolat ✔ | **Music/Movies/Tickets:** Amazon | CDNow | Sold-Out Tickets

Learn more about upgrading to CEOExpressSelect℠: **Take a Peek | Upgrade Now**

Business Office: 470 Atlantic Ave, 4th Floor, Boston, MA 02210 | voice - (617) 482-1200 | fax - (617) 273-8033

©1999-2002 CEOExpress Company   Boston   webmaster@ceoexpressmail.com

Figure 7.5 (*Cont.*)

cnnmoney.com. ©2003. CNN America, Inc. (Producer). http://money.cnn.com/. (Accessed August 18, 2003).

The *CNN financial network* site is the home of much information about money and business. News is a big part of this site. But the site goes beyond just the news, with numerous articles on the world of finance. There's a strong focus on personal money management, along with many references and tools to help make that management easier. For surfers in "cyberwaters," the staff at *CNNfn* have charted a course through what they feel are the essential Web sites. As well as being able to track stocks and get information on bonds and mutual funds and breaking news, one can open an online account with the broker Morgan Stanley Dean Witter. There are also available free tools and information that delivers to your e-mail a complete roundup of each day's trading activity from all the major stock and commodities exchanges, as well as breaking business news and feature stories and *The Bottom Line,* which allows one to receive analysts' reports thrice weekly.

Business.com. ©2001. Business.com Inc. (Producer). http://www.business.com/. (Accessed August 18, 2003).

Business.com is a portal that provides news, statistics, company profiles, financial data, and product and service directories. The huge online library profiles 10,000 companies and indexes over 400,000 listings. The owners have authorized a taxonomy created by a team of 50 research analysts, who have checked the Web for relevant business sites to be annotated and then included. The directory is divided into 25 groups that contain 25,000 industry subcategories, and it also features a search engine that has indexed more than 200 million Web pages.

The major groups on the top level page contain links to subcategories with functional information that is relevant across many types of industries. The Information Technology link leads to information from areas such as outsourcing, data mining, and consulting services. In the data mining category there are, at this time, 39 links to information, ranging from articles to white papers and from processes to available equipment. All components of the Web page are searchable in the *Business.com* directory.

Business.com is a powerful and essential tool that gives anyone the ability to find the business information needed, quickly and efficiently, from a single source. *Business.com* could become one of the most comprehensive online business portals, providing the resources needed to find business information. Where this Web site shines is in providing selected sites compiled into subject trees so that the user can browse and search. Of course it is no drawback that all the information is free.

Hoover's Online: The Business Network. ©2003. Hoover's Inc. (Producer). http://www.hoovers.com/free. (AccessedAugust 18, 2003).

Hoover's Online consolidates and filters a lot of useful information in one easy-to-use package (see figure 7.6). It is included in this section, despite the fact that there is a fee-based component, because of the abundance of free information provided as well. *Hoover's* mission is "to produce business-information products and services of the highest quality, accuracy, and readability" and "to make that information available whenever, wherever, and however our customers want it through mass distribution at affordable prices." One can assemble a fairly comprehensive report on a company or industry by using the free resources, but more information is provided to subscribers for a very reasonable fee. This is yet another service where one can customize a personal page to filter the information received.

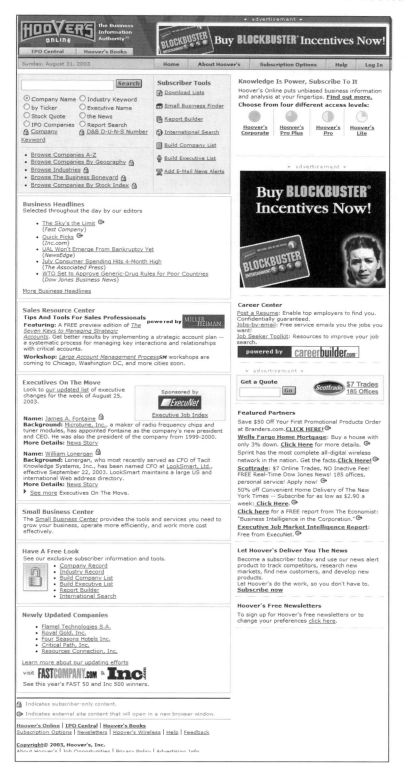

Figure 7.6. Home page of *Hoover's Online* **(http://www.hoovers.com).** Courtesy of Hoovers.com.

The opening screen gives one the option of searching directly by company name or choosing a "button" to access one of the following information segments or folders: *Companies & Industries, Hoover's IPO Central,* and the *News Center.*

The search box enables the user to enter a company name and then directly access the company capsule. Over 14,000 of these are provided free by *Hoover's* and are considered the core of the free section. The capsules cover about 14,000 public and private enterprises in the United States and around the world. This includes every company traded on the New York Stock Exchange, American Stock Exchange, NASDAQ National Market System (NASDAQ), and NASDAQ Small Cap Market, about 3,400 of America's largest, fast-growing private companies with annual revenues greater than $500 million and more than 2,500 of the most influential non-U.S. companies. Each capsule contains directory data, a link to the company's Web site, a company description, information on the top officers, names of the top three competitors, and news stories. From the capsule page one can link directly to financial information that includes the annual report and real-time SEC filings, insider trades reports, and earnings estimates. There are also direct links to patents and trademarks and Internet domains. From the company capsule the user can also link to news stories.

Industry information covers more than 300 industries broken into 28 sectors and includes lists of the major companies in each section. It also contains links to one or more "Industry Snapshots," which take an in-depth and historical look at nearly 50 different industry groups.

The question remains, if so much of the site is advertising driven and so given free to users, why take out a membership? The answer is, of course, the premium content marked with the key. This includes full company profiles, full lists of competitors, in-depth and historical financials, and the "Business Boneyard," which contains detailed profiles of companies that have either disappeared or been part of a merger or acquisition.

In August 2000 Hoover's, Inc., acquired Powerize.com, Inc., a developer of content integration and syndication technology and operator of a business research Web site with more than 600,000 registered members. Content suppliers for Powerize.com include Gale (*PROMT*), Bell & Howell (*ABI/INFORM*), EBSCO Information, *Investext, PR Newswire,* and COMTEX *News Network*, while company information comes from Disclosure, First Call, and Zacks. This added even more content to the Web site of *Hoover's* and further reinforced its utility as a first stop in the information retrieval process.

In 2003 Hoover's was purchased by Dun & Bradstreet, and further changes can be expected.

E-Books

E-books are shaking up publishing business models that have remained unchanged for years. Many libraries and universities are exploring the concept of supplying e-books to their users so that they can be checked out and read online. *netLibrary*, for example, is a major supplier of e-books to libraries.

Business books are among the offerings from netLibrary (http://www.netlibrary.com/), but there is one company that is concentrating on e-books for business. MeansBusiness Inc. (http://www.meansbusiness.com/) provides access to the concepts in books on business management. The concepts are chosen from each chapter within the selected book by an editorial team, which includes both MBAs and librarians, and are excerpted in up to seven paragraphs quoted in the author's own words.

The approach is hierarchical, with the subject areas broken down into nine categories, which are then further divided into nine subcategories. A third tier leads to a set of "Concept Suites," which contain the excerpts from the books. The first tier, the basic unit, is called a "Concept Extract" and consists of one or more directly quoted passages, which deals with an issue, idea, or problem from a business book. This level leads next to the "Concept Book Summary," which is a consecutive sequence of direct quotes, or "Concept Extract." These excerpts represent the author's primary perceptions and theories. An average of 10 "Concept Extracts," all focused on a single business concept, are then collected from the available books and formed into a "Concept Suite." This gives the user a variety of opinions, on one subject, in one package. Users can either drill down through the categories or perform a natural language search across the whole database.

Browsing and searching are free, and the options for payment are by transaction or subscription. Every item purchased or viewed is stored in the "Transaction History" section and is never deleted, thus enabling the user to build an online collection or personal library. This service is designed to appeal to business people anxious to access distilled information from a desktop. Another useful addition is an interactive reference desk manned by an editor.

This is just one of the latest examples of an entrepreneur seeing a gap in the market and seeking to fill it.

Aids to Finding Electronic Resources

There are many ways to try to keep track of changes in electronic offerings. These range from continually checking the Web pages of publishers to reading specialized journals such as *Searcher* and *E-Content*. There are also some reference books available in most large libraries, of which the most comprehensive is the *Gale Directory of Databases*.

Gale Directory of Databases. Farmington Hills, Mich.: The Gale Group, 1993– . 2v. (Also available electronically through the online services Data-Star, ORBIT Search Service, and Questel.)

Gale Directory of Databases was formed by the merger of *Computer-readable Data Bases*; *Directory of Online Databases*; and *Directory of Portable Databases*. It profiles almost 14,000 databases available worldwide in a variety of formats. Entries include producer name, contact information, a description of the database, where it is available, the update frequency, and the cost. The first volumes describe online databases, with both Internet and dial-up access information. Volume II covers CD-ROM, diskette, magnetic tape, batch access, and handheld products. The *Directory* also includes full contact and contents information on more than 3,600 producers and 2,500 online services, vendors, and distributors. The *Directory* is essential for librarians looking to enhance their database offerings and other information providers seeking the best sources for competitive intelligence.

Exploring the Web can be frustrating, but there are many useful guides and services to help one solve problems or simply choose the engine that is most comfortable. The choice in searching is whether to use a directory such as Yahoo! or *Business.com* or a search engine, which creates its lists by crawling the Web. In the latter case one must decide which engine is best for the intended inquiry. This choice is made simpler by *Search Engine Showdown* (http://searchengineshowdown.com), developed to share information about search engines, and which now includes a search engine chart to help with evaluation, reviews, statistical analysis, and strategies) (see figure 7.7, page 152). Search engines are constantly changing and upgrading, so it is useful to be able to keep abreast of developments by checking this site.

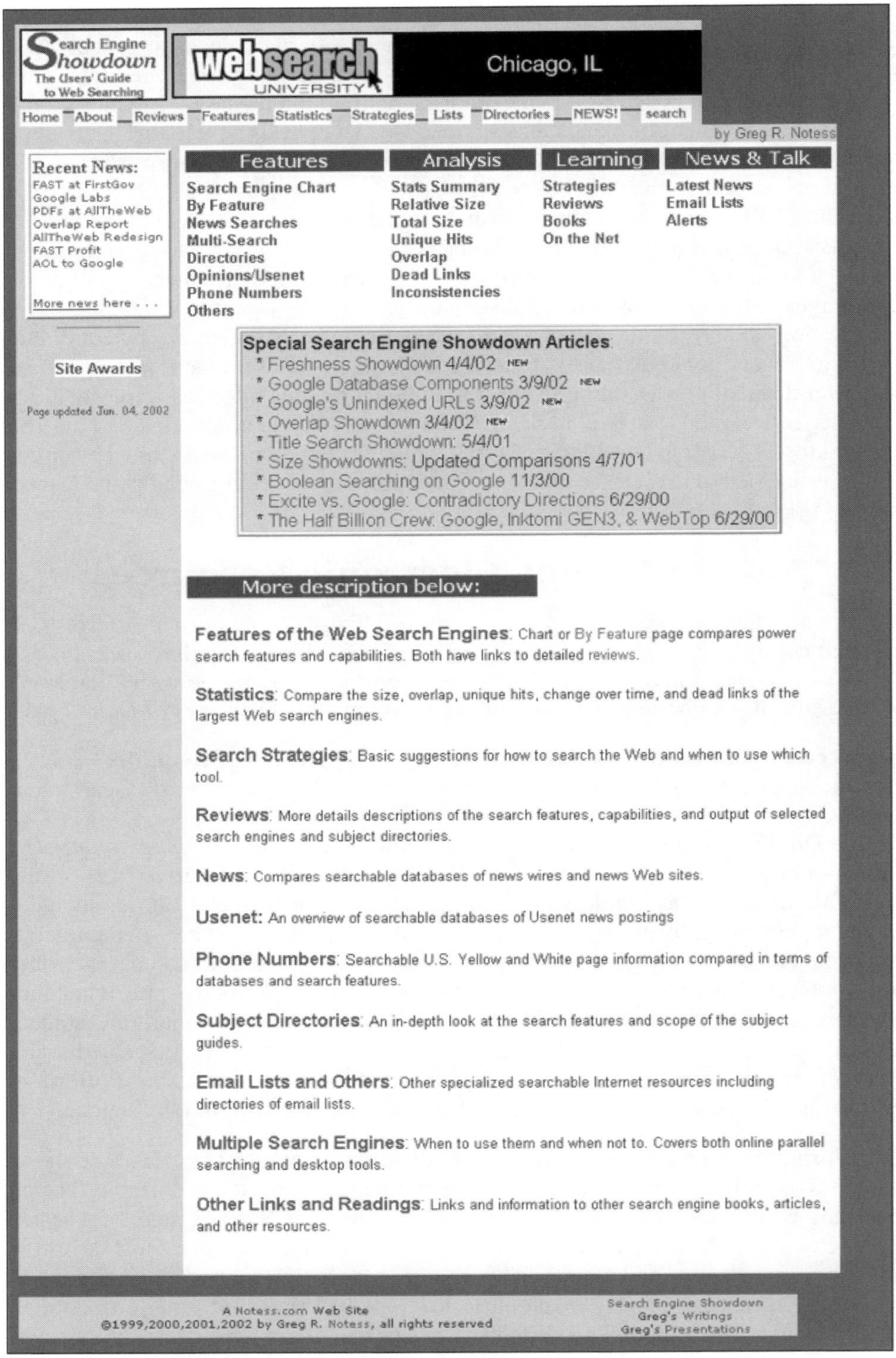

Figure 7.7. Home page of *Search Engine Showdown* (searchengineshowdown.com).
Reprinted with permission of Search Engine Showdown, http://searchengineshowdown.com.

Another possibility is to use one of the many books available that list business Web sites. This is much more problematic than using a search engine or Internet directory because of the lag time between writing or compiling and publishing print publications. One book that tends to minimize this problem is Euromonitor's listing of Web sites.

World Directory of Business Information Web Sites. 3rd ed. London: Euromonitor plc., 1999. 225p.

This directory contains details on more than 1,500 sources of business data free on the Internet. Global in scope, it contains official statistics, trade association statistics, market research reports, online surveys, company rankings, and company and brand information. Each entry contains the name of the publisher or producer and the type of organization as well as the URL and a short description of the site. The sites are arranged geographically, first by region and then by country. There are cheaper publications available, but none appears to be as global in scope.

Electronic resources, whether "on" or "via" the Internet, contain an incredible wealth of quality information that has the power to drive business and provide the consumer with needed data in a way that has changed the information retrieval habits of most people.

Notes

1. Bureau of Labor Statistics, *Monthly Labor Review*: *The Editor's Desk,* http://www.bls.gov/opub/ted/1999/Apr/wk1/art01.htm.

2. Department of Commerce, Bureau of the Census, "Workers Using Computers on the Job: 1993 and 1997," *Statistical Abstract of the United States* (Washington, D.C.: U.S. Government Printing Office).

3.Examples:

> GALILEO, http://www.galileo.peachnet.edu/

> NCLIVE, http://www.nclive.org

> OhioLINK, http://www.ohiolink.edu/

> ILLINET/OCLC, http://www.cyberdriveillinois.com/library/isl/oclc/oclc.html

> TexShare, http://www.texshare.edu/

4. For an article on comparisons of full-text offerings, see the "Poster Session" presented by Carol Franck and Holly Chambers at the ALA annual conference, Washington, D.C., June 27, 1998. Available at http://www2.potsdam.edu/LIBR/franckcr/ALA.html.

5. Tables of content and some free full text are available at

> Information Today, http://www.infotoday.com/

> ONLINE, http://www.onlinemag.net/

> Econtent, http://www.ecmag.net/

> *Searcher: The Magazine for Database Professionals,* http://www.infotoday.com/searcher/

6. Robert S. Littell, "Information Management," *Journal of Financial Service Professionals* (March 1999): 24–26.

7. Vilfredo Pareto, a 19th-century economist, found that 80 percent of production volume generally comes from only 20 percent of the producers. This rule has been applied by *CEOExpress* dynamic to the World Wide Web. Information on the Pareto principle is available at http://www.wikepedia.org/wki/Pareto_principle.

II

Fields of Business Information

8

Marketing

Marketing Basics

Marketing is a mix of activities, beginning with estimating the demand for products and progressing to their development, pricing, distribution, and promotion. These activities can be reduced to four broad categories: product, price, place, and promotion.

Marketing Activities

Product planning involves the product itself as it is designed to appeal to a predetermined group of users or potential users. It includes decisions about package design, brand names and trademarks, warranties, and the development of new products. In 1995, for example, Kraft began test marketing a new product to see if user response merited full production and distribution. The product was DiGiorno pizza.

The test results were positive, and the pizza became an official product that, by 1996, was available in about 80 percent of the United States.

Marketers must also make a series of decisions relating to *pricing,* setting profitable and justifiable prices for their products. Other factors are at work here as well. The product's image is important and may be affected by its price. It would not do, for example, to set too low a price for a perfume intended for affluent consumers; they might ignore it or think it inferior and turn instead to more costly brands. Market demand and competitors' prices must also be considered. Finally, pricing is closely regulated and is subject to considerable public scrutiny.

Promotion involves personal selling, sales promotion, and advertising using print, broadcast, and other media. Even as DiGiorno, the pizza, was being test marketed, decisions were being made about how to promote it. Marketers settled on "It's Not Delivery, It's DiGiorno" as the advertising campaign slogan, and the target market for the product was men and women, ages 25 to 54, who bought carry-out pizza.

Place refers not only to the geographic area in which the product is marketed but also to the channels and marketing intermediaries through which the product moves, as well as the transportation employed en route to the final user.

157

Marketing has grown increasingly important in the current competitive environment, and marketing activities are undertaken by manufacturers of both industrial and consumer products and by companies that sell services. Importantly, marketing is increasingly commonplace in nonprofit organizations such as libraries, art museums, charities, and political parties. Whatever the nature of the product or service, good marketing helps.

Small businesses also depend on effective marketing to keep ahead. They, even more than large corporations, can ill afford costly errors based on faulty marketing decisions or inadequate information. Good marketing does not guarantee business success, but it eliminates unnecessary gambling and improves the odds.

Market Segmentation

Not all people want or can afford all products or services. Someone in the restaurant supply business, for example, would be as disinclined to buy an industrial lathe as an adolescent would be to buy a Barbie doll, and while that same teenager might yearn for a Ferrari, it is unlikely that he or she would be able to buy one. Marketers define their markets by attempting to identify particular segments of the population that are likely to want to buy the product. Moreover, these should be people with "purchasing power and the authority to make purchase decisions."[1] This process is called *market segmentation*; that is, dividing a larger, somewhat diverse market into smaller markets in which demand for a particular product or group of products is likely to be greater:

> Firms that can identify buyers with similar needs may be able to serve those market segments quite profitably. The market consisting of people who use toothpaste (almost everyone), for example, can be divided into a number of smaller segments, each consisting of people who have more in common: children who want a toothpaste that tastes good, parents who want one that will reduce cavities, young adults who seek sex appeal and so on. The smaller, more homogeneous submarkets and serving those submarkets with your product, is called market segmentation.[2]

Although any characteristic that describes and distinguishes buyers may be useful for market segmentation, those most commonly used are geographic, demographic, psychographic, and sociographic.

Geographic

Consumers in different geographic regions may exhibit different buying behavior. Market research by automobile manufacturers has shown that certain styles and colors are more popular in some parts of the country than in others. Tastes may also vary. Campbell Soup Company, for example, makes its nacho cheese soup spicier for Texas and California than for other parts of the country. Campbell has, in fact, placed considerable emphasis on geographic segmentation.

Climate, political boundaries, and population density are some of the factors considered in geographic market segmentation.

Demographic

Demographic information is of key importance to marketers, who often segment their markets using such demographic variables as age, sex, race, income, marital status, and family size. A real estate developer considering sites for an exclusive retirement community, for example, would be particularly interested in the number of affluent adults aged 65 and older. Although current data would be important, so also would be historical statistics and projections for the future, reflecting past and anticipated trends. If statistics for the last 10 years showed an absolute decline in the number of adults 65 and older in a particular region, the developer would probably eliminate that region from the list of prospective sites for the retirement community.

Advertisers use demographic information to segment their markets as well. They identify, the demographic characteristics of the people most likely to buy their products and then direct their advertising to these people through the media that will most effectively reach them:

> Therefore, if demographic analysis shows that the heaviest usage for our product is by women who are married and under 35 years of age, with 2 or more children under 8 and a blue collar occupation by the head of the household, then we know who our market is and from this we can determine what appeals in our advertising will be most effective. Finally, we can find out those advertising media with similar demographics to reach our market most effectively with our message.[3]

Psychographic

Psychographic segmentation looks at the values, activities, interests, and opinions of the population, what we often call lifestyle. As with geographic and demographic segmentation, the variables are quantitatively measured, but unlike them, the numbers are not as easily (or as inexpensively) available. According to Marvin I. Mandall, its value is in its ability to overcome deficiencies in both demographic and geographic data:

> For some purposes, geographic and demographic market segmentation may leave something to be desired. For example, age is a commonly used demographic classification. From it, advertisements have defined the "youth market." However, the youth market may need a new definition. Is it really an age group, or is it a state of mind? The youth market overflows the traditional age brackets and today can be defined more meaningfully in terms of those who think young in any age bracket -that is, in terms of youthfulness, not youth. Even among youth within the demographic age bracket there is a wide range of differences.[4]

Sociographic

Finally, sociographic segmentation looks at the social environment, including social class and culture, peer and reference groups, and family structure and decision making.

Usually marketers use a mix of geographic, demographic, psychographic, and sociographic factors to identify their market segment. As a result, marketing research, which gathers and analyzes such data, is extremely important.

Marketing Research

Marketing research covers a whole gamut of activities but, in essence, is the process of systematically gathering and analyzing information about marketing problems and potentials for use in making marketing decisions.

Marketing research includes various subsidiary research: product research, which involves market testing for new products (such as DiGiorno pizza); studies of package effectiveness; and identifying new markets for existing products. It also includes market analysis, the study of the size, location, and other characteristics of the markets themselves. In measuring markets, market share analysis, which compares sales for one product brand against total sales for all brands of the product, is particularly important.

Sales research is another important component of marketing research and includes such activities as evaluating sales policies, setting sales quotas, and measuring the effectiveness of the sales staff. Consumer research documents consumer attitudes, reactions, and preferences, and advertising research evaluates the advertising program used to promote products, including copy and media research as well as the evaluation of advertising effectiveness. Finally, corporate and economic research programs are used to consider the relevance of the product in the context of the company itself, which in turn is examined in the context of the economy as a whole.

Primary and Secondary Data

Researchers use both primary and secondary data. Primary data are original and gathered for the specific problem being considered. Although the fit between data and problem is good, this advantage is offset by the time, cost, and skill it takes to collect primary data. Secondary data, on the other hand, are data that already exist. They are useful because they are often inexpensive and easy to obtain, but they, too, have drawbacks. The fit between marketing problems and secondary data may be none too good, and in some instances the validity of the data may be questionable. They may be outdated, or collected in an unreliable or biased manner.

Keeping these warnings in mind, market researchers will find secondary information is the most cost-effective data in most cases. Secondary information is provided by the government, by trade organizations and associations, and by commercial publishers. Most libraries are particularly strong in these areas and constitute a rich source of secondary marketing information. Some major secondary information sources are described later in this chapter.

More specialized than the rather general secondary sources listed above are "off-the-shelf" market research studies. Although not tailor-made to meet a particular company's specific market research needs, they are often highly specialized and can be extremely useful, particularly to companies not prepared to embark on expensive primary research. Several types of off-the-shelf studies can be identified, including standard research reports, reports produced by securities analysts, and off-the-shelf surveys and audits. Most frequently, librarians will be asked to help locate standard market research reports.

Standard market research reports are generally produced from secondary information sources available at many libraries—census data and trade publications, for example—and from primary data gathered from interviews and investigation. The reports, which are generally 100 to 200 pages long, may cost as little as $200 or as much as $15,000 or more, depending on depth of coverage, data used, and expertise needed to compile the reports. Clearly, the cost of these publications will preclude their addition to most libraries. Nevertheless, even though these reports mostly fall outside the scope and budget of collections, librarians should be able to help patrons identify them. Some trade publications and periodical indexes list selected reports, but one of the most comprehensive print listings is contained in the following publication.

FINDEX: The Worldwide Directory of Market Research Reports, Studies and Surveys. Bethesda, Md.: Kalorama Information, 1979– . Annual, with mid year supplement. (Also available on CD-ROM.)

FINDEX includes consumer, market, and industry studies, polls, audits, and company reports from 1,000 publishers. Arrangement is by broad industry and subject category, and each entry features title, description, publisher, date, number of pages, and price. Since most of the publications listed in *FINDEX* are not available in libraries, some librarians fear that its presence will confuse and ultimately frustrate library users. Whether or not librarians choose to add this title to their own collections, they should be aware that it exists, and that it can be found in many large business reference collections. *FINDEX* is also available as an online database, which can be searched free at http://www.MarketResearch.com/. One also has the option of ordering, and paying for, specific reports online either for immediate electronic delivery or as a print copy that will be mailed to the requester.

MarketResearch.com (http://www.MarketResearch.com/) is one of the leading providers of global market intelligence products and services. Presently they are offering over 40,000 research publications from more than 350 top consulting and advisory firms. Access can be immediate through the Web service. The company began in 1998 with the formation of Kalorama Information, LLC, and the acquisition of FIND/SVP's published products division. In 1999 the catalog distribution business was moved online, and Kalorama Information launched Kalorama Academic, offering previously unaffordable full-text market research reports to top business schools for the first time. In 2000 Kalorama Information became incorporated as *MarketResearch.com*. One of the attractions of this commercial Web site is the ability to search the database at no charge and then buy information "by the slice." One is no longer obligated to purchase full reports but can select only the chapters or sections that are of interest and so cut costs. A full list of market research publishers, complete with a description of their activities and links to their Web sites, is available from the *MarketResearch.com* site. (See figures 8.1 and 8.2, page 162.)

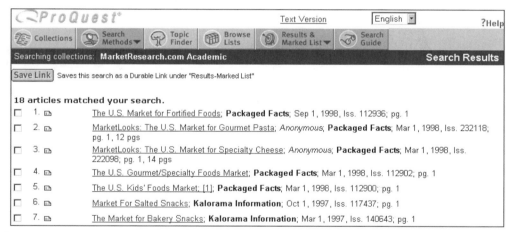

Figure 8.1. Selected results for a search in *MarketResearch.com Academic*. Reproduced with permission. Copyright 2002, All Rights Reserved, MarketResearch.com (http://www.marketresearch.com).

The company also provides academic subscriptions, via ProQuest, to time-delayed reports. These reports are not the latest edition, but for an annual fee libraries can now afford to make them available to faculty and students. In addition, *MarketResearch.com Academic* also provides current MarketLooks, which are accessible the same month the reports are published. MarketLooks are concise summaries of full-length market research reports that provide quick information on a specific market segment.

If neither secondary nor off-the-shelf studies are sufficient, firms may need to generate primary research data. Techniques used for gathering primary data include surveys, observations, and field experiments:

1. **Surveys.** Answers to questions are sought through telephone or personal, face-to-face interviews, or through the mail. Generally, a specific list of questions or a questionnaire is prepared and mailed. Validity and reliability of these surveys are vital considerations.

2. **Observation.** Here the consumer is observed in the act of purchasing. Sometimes films are taken and analyzed. Candid camera is actually an observation technique.

3. **Field experiments.** These may involve the survey method, the observation method, or both. The main characteristic is a more rigorous research design, often using sample control groups and sophisticated statistical techniques.[5]

Although large companies with highly skilled marketing staff may elect to do their own primary marketing research, often they hire other companies to do it for them. A. C. Nielsen (http://www.acnielsen.com/) and Frost & Sullivan (http://www.frost.com/) are two well-known groups that compile reports in a variety of areas ranging from automobiles to pharmaceuticals.

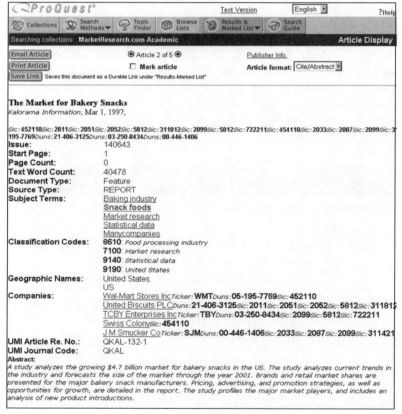

Figure 8.2. Sample report: Market for bakery snacks, produced by Kalorama Information, a division of MarketResearch.com. Reproduced with permission. Copyright © 2001, All Rights Reserved, MarketResearch.com.

Marketing Associations

Marketers are interested in the activities of two major types of associations: trade and professional. Trade associations represent diverse and wide-ranging industries. The Advanced

Medical Technology Association (http://www.advamed.org/), for example, serves manufacturers of medical devices, the National Association of Brick Distributors (http://www.building.org/texis/db/bix/+hwwrmwtEedrbxmwxNeExww/profile.html) represents distributors and dealers of bricks and other clay products, while the National Association of Diaper Services (http://www.diapernet.com/) is composed of owners of diaper rental and laundry services. What these associations have in common in addition to the other services that they provide is that they commonly collect and compile data from their members that are extremely useful to market researchers. Sometimes the information collected is published and made available commercially, as in the *Annual Statistical Report* published by the American Iron and Steel Institute both in print and CD-ROM.

Often large trade associations have divisions or sections that focus on marketing, and then there are some industries represented by associations whose sole function is marketing. Some of these associations are the American Floral Marketing Council, the Bank Marketing Association, and the Automotive Market Research Council.

Trade associations provide unique and highly specialized information about specific industries and should not be overlooked by the conscientious market researcher or the librarian seeking to build a comprehensive collection in a particular industry or group of industries. Since standard bibliographic works do not ordinarily include these publications, it may be necessary to identify issuing associations using the *Encyclopedia of Business Information Sources* or the *Encyclopedia of Associations.* Many trade associations now have a Web presence and issue many of their statistics and some reports free through the Internet. One way to easily find some of these is to search the association directory at *business know-how.com* (http://www.businessknowhow.com/associations/search_associations.asp). Entering "marketing" as a keyword reveals 36 associations such as the American Petroleum Institute and Hospitality Sales & Marketing Association International. Another alternative is to use a Web search engine.

Professional marketing associations promote advertising and marketing, conduct research, set standards, and, in many instances, publish journals, directories, and bibliographies. Among these associations are the Marketing Science Institute, the Business/ Professional Advertising Association, and the Association of National Advertisers. Two of the most important are the American Marketing Association and the Advertising Research Foundation.

The American Marketing Association has some 45,000 members in 100 countries, including educators, marketing and marketing research executives, advertisers, and sales and promotion specialists. It offers conferences and seminars to its members, fosters research, and promotes the interests of its members. In addition, it publishes several periodicals, including the scholarly *Journal of Marketing Research;* the *Journal of Marketing*, which includes both scholarly and applied research; the *Journal of International Marketing;* and a biweekly newsletter, *Marketing News.* It also publishes occasional books, monographs, and pamphlets on marketing as well as a series of bibliographies on key marketing topics such as marketing distribution, selling, and small business marketing. The AMA, the leading professional marketing association, includes 400 U.S. chapters and over 400 worldwide collegiate chapters, in addition to the activities conducted at the national level.

The Advertising Research Foundation (http://www.arfsite.org/) is a nonprofit organization whose membership is composed of advertisers, advertising agencies, the media, and colleges and universities. Its purpose is to promote the highest quality research in business and consumer marketing, advertising, and the media by developing guidelines and standards and by providing objective and impartial technical advice and expertise. The Foundation organizes conferences, compiles statistics, and publishes the *Journal of Advertising Research* as well as bibliographies, monographs, and reports.

Founded in 1938, the International Advertising Association (http://www.iaaglobal.org) is an international partnership of advertisers, agencies, the media, and corporations. Its purpose is to advocate for freedom in advertising.

Regulation of Marketing

Marketing is regulated at the federal, state, and local levels. Federal laws prohibit price fixing, false or misleading advertising, and deceptive packaging and labeling. Several agencies administer these laws and exercise some measure of control over marketing. Prime among these are the Federal Trade Commission (FTC), the Food and Drug Administration (FDA), and the Federal Communications Commission (FCC).

Federal Trade Commission

The Federal Trade Commission (http://www.ftc.gov) was established in 1914 as an independent administrative agency:

> The Federal Trade Commission enforces a variety of federal antitrust and consumer protection laws. The Commission seeks to ensure that the nation's markets function competitively, and are vigorous, efficient, and free of undue restrictions. The Commission also works to enhance the smooth operation of the marketplace by eliminating acts or practices that are unfair or deceptive.[6]

The FTC issues advisory opinions, sets industry guidelines, and establishes trade regulation rules. It has jurisdiction over false and misleading advertising and has a number of ways of dealing with advertisers involved in deceptive advertising:

> A simple procedure without formal complaint and hearings is to obtain a letter of voluntary compliance from an advertiser stating that the advertisement in question will be discontinued. After a formal complaint has been issued by the Commission, a consent order may be published in which the advertiser agrees to stop the practice without an admission of guilt. If, through formal hearings, the FTC finds the advertiser guilty of deception, the FTC may issue an order to cease and desist from such practice. The Commission also publicizes the complaints and cease and desist orders it issues. This adverse publicity for the advertiser proves to be an important weapon for the FTC. When dealing with alleged deception in advertising, the FTC considers a number of questions. At each point, a decision is made to either drop the matter or to proceed to another decision point until the matter is finally settled.[7]

In 1997, for example, the FTC issued a consent order to William E. Shell, M.D, who was at that time chairman of the board of Interactive Medical Technologies, Ltd., and Effective Health, Inc. The complaint involved the product Lipitrol, which was advertised as a weight control substance. Advertising implied or represented that:

- **A.** Lipitrol provides weight loss benefit.
- **B.** Lipitrol lowers blood cholesterol levels.
- **C.** Lipitol reduces, or reduces the risks associated with, high cholesterol including clogged arteries, high blood pressure, diabetes, breast cancer, and heart disease.
- **D.** Lipitrol can be used, beneficially and safely, in amounts or with frequency sufficient to cause diarrhea.

It was further ordered that such claims be corroborated by competent and reliable scientific evidence that substantiated the representations.[8]

The FTC publishes a number of consumer guides and guidelines for business people to use. The FTC Businesses series (http://www.ftc.gov/ftc/business.htm), for example, includes guidelines on franchise and business opportunities, appliance labeling rules, and advertising policy statements and guidance. The business publications section contains a link to consumer education, business education, guides, policy statements, and rules and acts related to advertising. Some of these publications are listed in figure 8.3.

Advertising : Business Information

A Business Checklist for Direct Marketers	[TEXT]	
Advertising and Marketing on the Internet: The Rules of the Road	[TEXT]	[PDF]
Advertising Consumer Leases	[TEXT]	[PDF]
Advertising Retail Electricity and Natural Gas	[TEXT]	[PDF]
Big Print. Little Print. What's the Deal? How to Disclose the Details	[TEXT]	[PDF]
Businessperson's Guide to the Mail and Telephone Order Mdse Rule	[TEXT]	[PDF]
The Cachet of Cashmere: Complying with the Wool Products Labeling Act	[TEXT]	[PDF]
Clothes Captioning: Complying with the Care Labeling Rule	[TEXT]	[PDF]
Complying with the Environmental Marketing Guides	[TEXT]	[PDF]
Complying with the Made In the USA Standard	[TEXT]	[PDF]
Dietary Supplements: An Advertising Guide for Industry	[TEXT]	[PDF]
Disclosing Energy Efficiency Information: A Guide for Online Sellers of Appliances	[TEXT]	[PDF]
Down...But Not Out: Advertising & Labeling of Feather & Down Products	[TEXT]	[PDF]
Dot Com Disclosures: Information About Online Advertising	[TEXT]	[PDF]
Environmental Marketing Claims	[TEXT]	[PDF]
Frequently Asked Advertising Questions: A Guide for Small Business	[TEXT]	[PDF]
How to Advertise Consumer Credit: Complying with the Law	[TEXT]	
How to Comply With The Children's Online Privacy Protection Rule	[TEXT]	[PDF]

Figure 8.3. List of business publications provided online by the FTC at http://www.ftc.gov/bcp/menu-ads.htm.

Food and Drug Administration

The Food and Drug Administration (http://www.fda.gov) is a scientific regulatory agency that acts to ensure consumer protection against a broad range of products, primarily food, drugs, cosmetics, and medical devices. As is the Federal Trade Commission, the FDA is concerned with preventing deception through misrepresentation of these products. The FDA, however, concentrates on false labeling and misrepresentation, whereas the FTC focuses on false advertising. Labeling includes not only the physical label but also any printed material accompanying the product. The FDA approves labeling for prescription medicines to ensure that physicians are fully informed about the drugs they prescribe and, in recent years, has issued regulations requiring nutrition labeling on many foods. In addition, the FDA now requires that the ingredients used in cosmetics be listed on the product labels. It also requires that warnings be included on the labels of products that are potentially hazardous. In 1979, for example, it required that warnings be included on the labels of permanent hair dye products containing an ingredient found to cause cancer in laboratory animals.

Compliance guides and manuals are available at http://www.fda.gov/ora/compliance_ref/default.htm, while listings of recalls and safety alerts are available at http://www.fda.gov/opacom/7alerts.html.

Although the FDA will not take action to correct individual complaints, it will attempt to correct the situation that causes them. The following is a warning released by the FDA about a thigh cream:

THIGH CREAMS

Various products have been promoted in the skin care market as thigh and stomach slimmers. Some advertising claims also promise the reduction of "cellulite", waffly looking or orange-peel type skin caused by fatty deposits.

Aminophylline, an approved prescription drug used in the treatment of asthma, is an ingredient used in many of these thigh cream products that marketers claim will dissolve the fat and smooth the skin. Since some individuals suffer from allergic reactions to ethylenediamine, a component of aminophylline, the FDA is concerned about the use of this ingredient in cosmetics.

Consumers need to be aware of this potential for developing an allergic reaction and carefully read product labels and follow directions. Persons who suffer from asthma may wish to avoid these products so that they don't develop a sensitization (become allergic) to aminophylline.

Drugs, unlike cosmetics, alter the structure or function of the body and are subject to an intensive review and approval process by FDA before their release to the public. Thigh creams may more appropriately be classified as drugs under the Food, Drug, and Cosmetic Act since removal or reduction of cellulite affects the "structure or function" of the body.

Figure 8.4. Warning reproduced from the Web page of the Center for Food Safety and Applied Nutrition at http://www.cfsan.fda.gov/~dms/cos-202.html.

The FDA has an informative Web site that contains primary information and publications, including reports, studies, pamphlets, and guides for its primary constituency: consumers, business people, physicians, and others involved in the production, prescription, and consumption of drugs, medical devices, food, and cosmetics.

Federal Communications Commission

The Federal Communications Commission (http://www.fcc.gov) was established in 1934 as an independent federal agency. The Act charges the Commission with establishing policies to govern interstate and international communications by television, radio, wire, satellite, and cable. There are seven operating bureaus and ten offices within the organization. The bureaus' responsibilities include processing applications for licenses and other filings, analyzing complaints, conducting investigations, developing and implementing regulatory programs, and taking part in hearings. The offices provide support services and advice.

The Mass Media Bureau (MMB) ensures that consumers have access to interference-free radio and television services that operate in the public interest. Specifically, it concerns itself with the quality of advertising and seeks to prevent obscene, profane, fraudulent, and deceptive advertising, all of which are obviously not in the public interest, convenience, or necessity. For the same reason, it also concerns itself with the quantity of time devoted to advertising.

The FCC may suspend the license of any radio or television station that is transmitting profane or obscene words. This severe threat largely eliminates any violation of this sort, but it should be noted that profanity and obscenity are constantly subject to redefinition as social mores change. Fraudulent and deceptive radio and television advertising, on the other hand, is generally handled by the FTC's taking action against the advertiser. When the FCC receives complaints against advertisers, it notifies the station, and the station usually sees that the advertiser corrects the situation. If the station ignores the complaint, the FCC takes this fact into consideration when the license comes up for renewal.

Other Government Agencies

Although the FTC, FDA, and FCC are the major agencies involved in the direct regulation of marketing activities, other federal agencies are involved as well. The Postal Service (http://www.usps.com/), for example, not only regulates "obscene, scurrilous, or otherwise offensive" mail but also regulates against the use of the mails to defraud.

The Bureau of Alcohol, Tobacco, and Firearms (http://www.atf.treas.gov/) of the Treasury Department reviews proposed advertisements and labeling of alcoholic beverages for its approval or disapproval. If advertisements that raise its disapproval are not corrected to the bureau's satisfaction, it can revoke the producer's license to sell alcoholic beverages. In addition, considerable adverse publicity can be attached to these activities.

State and local laws also regulate marketing activities. These laws vary considerably from one locale to another in their content, quality, and depth of coverage, and as a result can be confusing. They are important, however, because most federal laws come into effect only when interstate commerce is involved.

Marketing Reference Sources

Marketing reference sources are abundant. They include many different types of materials: statistical sources, government documents, directories, and databases. Two of the places to identify these items are the bibliographic sources listed below.

Guides and Bibliographies

There are several guides to the literature and resources of marketing, including the following.

Frank, Nathalie D., and John V. Ganly. **Data Sources for Business and Market Analysis**. 4th ed. Metuchen, N.J.: Scarecrow, 1983. 458p.

Marketing Information: A Professional Reference Guide. 3rd ed. Atlanta: Georgia State University Business Press, 1995.

The third edition of *Data Sources for Business and Market Analysis* lists virtually all of the major sources of external secondary marketing information. It includes chapters arranged by issuing organization (e.g., Census Bureau, professional and trade associations) and by publication type, such as services and directories. The work remains a valuable annotated bibliography of a wide range of market research and statistical data sources. Publications of the federal government make up a major portion of the book, but regional and local sources, foreign publications, professional and trade association publications, and periodicals are also included. There are indexes by title, issuing agency, subject, and geographic area.

Marketing Information is intended as both a directory and a sourcebook for all areas of marketing. Part 1 is the directory, a guide to associations and organizations, arranged by broad subject classification such as "Marketing Associations" and "Research Centers." Although some of the information this section contains is available in such standard reference works as the *Encyclopedia of Associations* and the *United States Government Manual*, other parts include information that may not be readily available in small or medium-sized business reference collections.

Part 2 lists and briefly annotates books, manuals, directories, periodicals, newsletters, databases, and nonprint materials, arranged by subject areas such as pricing, global marketing, and sales promotion. While the Frank and Ganly book's strength lies in its more thorough consideration of specific sources, replete with explanations and background information, *Marketing Information's* value comes from the detailed subject categories under which specific information sources are identified. Together, these guides provide almost comprehensive access to major sources of secondary marketing information and to the organizations that generate this information.

The library of the AMA has some details of its collection online at http://www.marketingpower.com/. The topics link to selections in such areas as: "Marketing Research," "B2B Marketing," and "Consumer Marketing." Although not as comprehensive as the volumes mentioned previously, the site does give a librarian or researcher a place to begin research into available materials.

With the fast pace of globalization and communication growth it has become increasingly important to be able to locate sources of advertising and marketing information worldwide. The following publications provide a guide to international sources in the advertising and marketing arenas.

Reed, Gretchen. **International Advertising and Marketing Information Sources**. 2nd ed. Washington, D.C.: Special Libraries Association, 2000. 114p.

World Directory of Marketing Information Sources. 3rd ed. London : Euromonitor plc, 2000. Biennial.

The SLA publication is arranged by country and region and, where available, listings include associations, publications, media expenditures, and ad tracking services. This is an inexpensive source of information that is widely available.

The *World Directory*, distributed in the United States by Gale Research, provides a summary of key business research organizations in 75 countries, alphabetically listed. Included is full contact information for official organizations, trade development bodies, libraries and market research companies, trade associations, publications, and databases. Entries are compiled by Euromonitor researchers, who contact the organizations included. This is an excellent resource that provides information on countries as diverse as Sri Lanka and the Ukraine.

Dictionaries and Encyclopedias

Although most standard business dictionaries include definitions of key marketing terms, there are special dictionaries that focus solely on marketing or on some aspect of marketing, such as advertising.

Koschnick, Wolfgang J. **Dictionary of Marketing**. Aldershot, Hants, England; Brookfield, Vt.: Gower, c1995. 647p.

Mercer, David. **Marketing: The Encyclopedic Dictionary**. Oxford, England; Malden, Mass.: Blackwell Business, 1999. 422p.

Wiechmann, Jack G. **NTC's Dictionary of Advertising**. Lincolnwood, Ill.: NTC Business Books, c1993. 222p.

Baker, Michael John. **The IEBM Encyclopedia of Marketing.** London: International Thomson Business, 1999. 928p.

McDonough, John, ed. **The Encyclopedia of Advertising.** Chicago: Fitzroy Dearborn, 2001. 3v

Beacham, Walton. **Beacham's Marketing Reference**. Washington, D.C.: Research Publishing, 1986. 2v.

Sidney J. Levy, George R. Frerichs, and Howard L. Gordon, eds. **The Dartnell Marketing Manager's Handbook**. 3rd ed. Chicago: Dartnell Corp., 1994. 1432p.

Bushko, David. **Dartnell's Advertising Manager's Handbook.** 4th ed. Chicago: Dartnell Corp., 1997. 484p.

The *Dictionary of Marketing* defines over 5,000 marketing terms, ranging from "A" Board to zoning, explained as zone delivered pricing. It is an attempt to collect an exhaustive range of marketing and related terms and to provide explanations and definitions where needed.

Designed more for use by the practitioner or marketing student, on the other hand, is *The Encyclopedic Dictionary*. Topics deemed of interest to practitioners, such as "product or service positioning," are lengthy, with suggested further readings. The volume includes numerous cross-references.

Advertising has such an extensive vocabulary of its own that several advertising dictionaries have been published. *NTC's Dictionary of Advertising* provides concise definitions of over 5,000 terms and acronyms currently used in advertising, marketing, and communications, drawn from the daily working vocabulary in agencies and corporations.

Global in scope, the *IEBM Encyclopedia of Marketing* contains essays that explain the theoretical foundations of marketing. This work covers both marketing theory and practice.

An international group of more than 200 advisors and contributors have compiled the 600 entries in *The Encyclopedia of Advertising*. Subject areas include the history of important advertising agencies and biographies of the people who worked in them; a history of major marketers and the campaigns they conducted; and important issues affecting advertising such as brand building, the commission system, and mass communications theory.

Although dated, *Beacham's Marketing Reference* is still useful to practitioners and laypeople. It contains a collection of articles by experts. In all, some 200 different topics are covered, ranging from subliminal advertising to brand awareness, from market segmentation to channels of distribution. Each article follows a standard format, presenting an overview of the topic, followed by examples, discussion of benefits, implementation, evaluation, and a conclusion. In addition, small business applications are described, and relevant references, software, and databases are identified. Related topics and terms are also listed. This is still a publication well worth using.

An extremely useful handbook filled with valuable strategies on every aspect of marketing is the *Dartnell Marketing Manager's Handbook*. It provides commonsense theory and practical guidelines to help the researcher plan both effective and profitable marketing strategies and programs. The 112 contributors include both scholarly authors and practitioners in the field of advertising, and the topics range from the scope of marketing through developing and putting a plan into execution and the steps in promoting products and services. The 71 chapters are designed to cover every key aspect of marketing. This is an essential part of any library's marketing collection.

Dartnell's Advertising Manager's Handbook is a comprehensive guide containing real-life case studies, models, strategies, techniques, and guidelines designed to help managerial decision making. Chapters include strategy research, creative concept, media, copy, design, measurement, communicating with value, human resources, global advertising, and advertising on the Internet.

There are a couple of online glossaries available. One is from the Department of Advertising, University of Texas at Austin (http://advertising.utexas.edu/research/terms/), and others are at the *Glossarist* (http://www.glossarist.com/glossaries/business/advertising.asp).

Information about successful marketing campaigns is useful to researchers aiming to target customers and prospects. There are, as already mentioned, marketing plans that one can buy or identify using a service such as *FINDEX*. But for those libraries unable to afford them, there are now collections of plans available from Gale Research.

Encyclopedia of Major Marketing Campaigns. Detroit: Gale Group, 2000. 2063p.

Major Marketing Campaigns Annual. Farmington Hills, Mich. : Gale Research, 1999– . Annual.

The *Encyclopedia* looks at 500 major marketing and advertising campaigns of the twentieth century. Each chapter looks at the campaign from an historical perspective, then explores the target market, competition, marketing strategy, and finally the outcome. In this volume one can read about the debacle of "new Coke" or find out why "snap, crackle, pop" became such a generational pleaser.

Major Marketing Campaigns Annual presents more recent campaigns in the same format as the *Encyclopedia* and is an excellent addition to it. Both titles contain campaign illustrations and interesting snippets of information such as why the mysterious "33" is featured on the back of the Rolling Rock beer bottle.

Directories

Most of the standard business directories described in chapter 2 will be of interest to marketers. For example, sales, distribution, and market research staff heavily use the *Million Dollar Directory* and *Thomas Register of American Manufacturers*.

Since standard business directories were discussed at length in chapter 2, this section focuses on titles that deal specifically with marketing and advertising.

American Marketing Association. New York Chapter. **Green Book: International Directory of Marketing Research Houses and Services.** New York: The Association, New York Chapter, 1963– . Annual. Web version available at http://www.greenbook.org/.

American Marketing Association. New York Chapter. **Green Book: Worldwide Directory of Focus Group Companies and Services.** New York: The Association, New York Chapter, 1992– . Annual. Web version available at http://www.greenbook.org.

Standard Directory of Advertising Agencies. Wilmette, Ill.: National Register Publishing, 1917– . Annual.

Standard Directory of International Advertisers and Agencies. Wilmette, Ill.: National Register Publishing, 1992– . Annual

One of the best known of these publications is the *Green Book: International Directory of Marketing Research Houses and Services.* The *Green Book* lists and describes services offered by major marketing firms. Foreign as well as U.S. marketing research firms are entered alphabetically in a single listing. Each entry includes the firm's address and telephone number, the names of its key officers, and a brief description of the services it offers. The directory contains listings by company name, research services offered, market specialties, industry specialties, computer programs, trademarked products and services, geographic location, and key personnel.

The *Green Book: Worldwide Directory* lists and describes organizations that offer facilities, recruiting, moderating, and transcription services. The listing is by city within state and identifies firms involved in marketing research, direct marketing, merchandising, audiovisual communications, and health care marketing.

The New York AMA also makes this information available in searchable form at http://www.greenbook.org. A search will result in a list of companies with links to their Web pages or a description of their services. Users of this information should be aware that it is not taken from published sources but is supplied directly by the businesses listed.

The Standard Directory of Advertising Agencies, also known as the *Agency Red Book*, contains current information about 9,000 American advertising agencies and their branches, including their names and addresses, specialization, major accounts, and over 59,000 key staff members. The listing criteria are national and regional advertising agencies, spending a minimum of $200,000 annually on paid media.

In addition to the main section, which is arranged alphabetically by advertising agency, the directory has geographical listings of agencies by states and by foreign countries, a list of the largest advertising agencies, and a special market index, which lists agencies in special fields such as the African American and Hispanic markets, business to business, food service, and entertainment. It is an essential resource for those directly involved in advertising and can be found in many business reference collections.

Equally important is the *Standard Directory of Advertisers*, a companion directory that focuses on companies and other organizations that advertise, and includes trade names, the types of media used for advertising, the advertising agencies employed, and, frequently, annual advertising budgets.

A companion product is the *Advertiser and Agency Red Books Plus,* available on CD-ROM. With more than 20 search criteria, the contents of all three *Red Books,* with more than 24,000 advertisers, 13,500 agencies, and 70,000 top advertising professionals worldwide, are made easily accessible. An online subscription service is also available at http://www.redbooks.com/.

Periodicals

Marketers turn to periodical literature to keep current with news about specific industries of interest to them, with developments in marketing and allied fields, and with the economy generally. Some may subscribe to one or two key publications, while others have extensive periodical collections at their disposal. This section begins by mentioning the indexes and abstracts used to identify relevant articles and concludes with a discussion of some major periodicals in the field.

For the most part, American marketers and librarians seeking articles on specific marketing topics will need to consult general business indexes (see chapter 3) such as *General BusinessFile International, ABI/INFORM Global,* or *Business Source Elite. General BusinessFile International,* for example, includes relevant articles found in the subject area of marketing under the headings "Analysis," "Hospitals," and "Statistics" as well as under headings relating to sales and specific industries. It also links to articles about marketing for specific companies.

One of the best indexes for all-around market coverage, however, is the *F&S Index*. Its international coverage of industries, products, and specific companies is excellent. Materials are arranged by industry and product groups using Product Codes (PC), which are based on the Standard Industrial Classification Codes (SIC). The Gale Group *F&S Index* provides data on "new products, new capacities, product demand, end users, and market data." It is available in print, on CD-ROM, and online.

A similar product is the Gale Group's *Business & Industry,* which also has a strong global focus on product and industry information. This index also contains unique marketing terms such as distribution channels and co-branding in its indexing terms. *Business & Industry* is available only online.

Marketing periodicals are abundant. Some deal with specific aspects of marketing, such as *Industrial Distribution* (http://www.manufacturing.net/magazine/ind/), *Journal of Consumer Research* (http://www.journals.uchicago.edu/JCR/home.html), and *Direct Marketing Magazine*. Some, such as the *Journal of Marketing Research* (http://www. marketingpower.com/), are scholarly journals, and others, such as *Advertising Age* (http://www.adage.com/), *Sales & Marketing Management* (http://www.salesandmarketing. com/salesandmarketing/index.jsp), and *Women's Wear Daily* (http://www.wwd.com) are trade publications. Libraries may not collect all of these serials, but many subscribe to *Advertising Age* and *Sales & Marketing Management,* and some information is given free at most of the Web sites.

Advertising Age. Chicago: Crain-Communications, 1930– . Weekly. Web version available at http://www.adage.com.

Sales & Marketing Management. New York: Bill Communications, Inc., 1918– . 16/year. Web version available at http://www.salesandmarketing.com/salesandmarketing/index.jsp.

Advertising Age is a newspaper that provides current coverage of advertising and marketing news. It includes descriptions of current advertising campaigns, news of decisions by government regulatory agencies, consumer trends, and personnel changes in the industry. *Advertising Age* is particularly useful for the special issues it publishes, including those with information on leading ad agencies and market research firms. The Web page contains some freely available features. These include special reports such as that on the history of television, or advertising at the super bowl, and a weekly report on Web traffic and advertising from *Nielsen/NetRatings* and *Ad Age*. There is also a searchable database of 400 advertisers that will give the names and countries of agencies representing a product.

AdAge Global (http://www.adageglobal.com/) is also available both in print and online. This publication delivers the latest worldwide marketing news, including marketing statistics, information on the hottest new commercials, the media, and Internet pages. As with *AdAge.com,* free registration enables one to access further material and activate e-mail alerts on breaking news.

Sales & Marketing Management covers all aspects of marketing, product development, packaging, place decisions, promotion, and pricing. It is a major publication and includes articles on specific marketing activities and on individual companies as well as personnel changes and trade news. Free resources accessible from the Web page at http://www.salesandmarketing.com/smmnew/ include a directory of sales marketing and customer service software, links to the magazines advertisers and their products and services, news about conferences, and book reviews. Another piece of useful information tucked away in the media kit is the advertising rates for the site.

As with many magazines and newspapers, even if the library or individual does not hold a subscription, it is well worth checking the Internet site for free information.

Statistics

Good marketing research is based on current and reliable statistical data. Market segmentation, for example, requires the use of statistics to define geographic, demographic, psychographic, and sociographic boundaries for market segments. The selection of a new plant site will be influenced by statistics on population and labor conditions, while the final decision about the location of a new business such as a pizza franchise or a computer store may in large part be based on statistics regarding the location of other, similar businesses in the area and the age, income, and educational levels of the population. Effective marketing strategies are based on planning. Planning involves assessing historical and current market conditions, setting objectives, developing marketing programs, and analyzing the results. Collection and analysis of data about markets and customers is an important part of the process. Factors such as sales trends, size and growth of a market, product life cycles, market share data, seasonality, profits, and industry capacity can be analyzed to develop marketing strategies. Using primary and secondary data, researchers can identify marketing opportunities. Statistics are, in short, vital for effective marketing research.

Marketing statistics fall primarily into two main categories: demographic and economic. Although trade associations and commercial publishers make statistical data available, their major producer is the federal government.

Federal Government Statistics

Almost every statistic that the government publishes is significant for research relating to industrial and consumer markets. The ones that will be most consistently useful and most heavily applied fall into four main categories: population, income, employment, and sales.

Population statistics, gathered, compiled, and published by the Bureau of the Census, are available in great detail and are basic to most marketing research. The Census Bureau, both in decennial census publications and in special reports and studies, also makes available income statistics, which indicate the buying-power of consumers. *Series P-60* of the *Current Population Reports*, for example, deals solely with consumer income, while *Series P-23* frequently includes studies that feature income and socioeconomic data. The most detailed information, however, is published in the decennial censuses.

The Bureau of Labor Statistics, the Internal Revenue Service, and the Bureau of Economic Analysis all publish income data as well. The Bureau of Labor Statistics and the Census Bureau primarily produce federal employment statistics, and sales statistics are most frequently taken from the *Economic Censuses*, the *Survey of Current Business*, and related reports. Sales and employment statistics are indicators of company performance and market size and can be put to many uses, such as the measurement of sales effectivenes.

One of the best ways to identify and locate federal statistical data, which are made freely available on the Web, is by using *FEDSTATS* (http://www.fedstats.gov/) or *American FactFinder* (http://factfinder.census.gov/servlet/BasicFactsServlet).

FEDSTATS provides access to official statistics collected and published by more than 100 federal agencies without the user having to know in advance which agency produces them. It provides linking and searching capabilities down to the county level within states. Information includes statistical profiles to the county level, published collections of statistics available online, and a subject listing.

American FactFinder is designed to make information easily accessible. The opening screen contains links to "Basic Facts" where one can find Quick Tables and Geographic Comparison Tables for Population and Housing data, Quick Reports for Economic data, and predefined Thematic Maps. It also contains search functions to help quickly locate any type of information that's available in *FactFinder*. (See figure 8.5.)

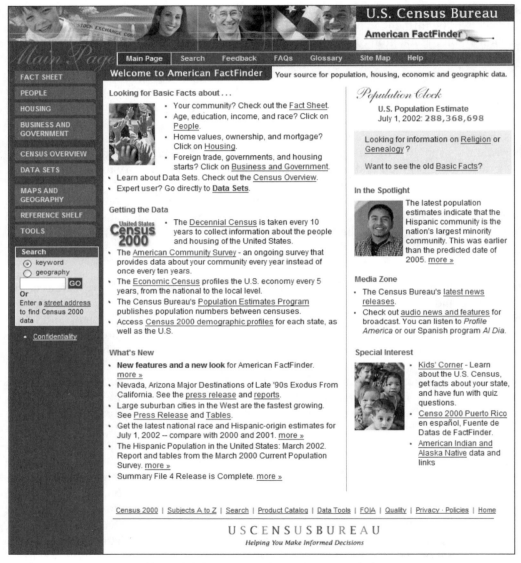

**Figure 8.5. Home page of *American FactFinder*
(http://factfinder.census.gov/servlet/BasicFactsServlet).**

There is also a major commercial guide providing access to specific government statistics, the *American Statistics Index*, which indexes, lists, and annotates statistical sources published by the federal government (see chapter 6). This is also available as *LexisNexis Statistical Universe*, a commercial database in many academic libraries.

So even though the match between the problem and the data is not likely to be exact with secondary research, there are some significant benefits, mostly financial and time related.

Commercial Statistical Publications

Government publications are unrivaled for their depth and breadth of statistical information; no commercial publisher comes close to matching them. However, some of the needed information simply may not be available from the government. Commercially published marketing guides, based on government statistics, are often supplemented with publisher-generated statistical estimates, which are extremely useful. Many are available, but the titles listed below are particularly important and can be found in most business reference collections.

Editor & Publisher Market Guide. New York: Editor & Publisher, 1924– . Annual.

Sales & Marketing Management. **Survey of Buying Power**. New York: Bill Communications, 1929– . Annual. (September Issue).

Demographics USA: County Edition. Wilton, Conn.: TradeDimensions, 1993– . Annual.

Demographics USA: Zip Code Edition. Wilton, Conn.: TradeDimensions, 1993– . Annual.

Demographics USA on CD-ROM. Wilton, Conn.: TradeDimensions, 1993– . Annual.

The Lifestyle Market Analyst. Wilmette, Ill. : Standard Rate & Data Service, 1989– . Annual.

Consumer USA. London : Euromonitor, 1988– . Irregular.

The *Editor & Publisher Market Guide* is an annual that gives detailed statistical data for U.S. and Canadian cities publishing one or more daily newspapers. It is divided into six main sections. The first section is a compilation of market ranking tables, based on publisher estimates for the current year, showing population, disposable income, total retail sales, total food sales, and income per household. Within each category, entries are arranged by size. Thus, by consulting the "Disposable Income per Household" table, it is possible to identify those metropolitan statistical areas estimated by *Editor & Publisher* to have the highest disposable income (personal income less taxes) per household.

The second section is individual market surveys for U.S. cities, arranged alphabetically by state and then by city. A state map introduces the survey for each state and pinpoints the location of daily newspaper cities, the state capital, county seats, and metropolitan statistical areas. The city market data, however, are most heavily used.

It is easy to see why this publication is so popular. Not only does it collect and present statistical data from many government publications, but it also includes data gathered and prepared by the publisher, for example, the names of specific retail stores and shopping centers. Sections follow for population, sales, income population, and income. The publication concludes with a list of Canada's provinces and newspaper cities and some abbreviated surveys for that country.

The Survey of Buying Power, another key marketing guide, is a special issue of *Sales & Marketing Management*. It contains geographically oriented demographic, income, retail sales, and media statistics for metropolitan areas and counties. It also includes regional and state summary data, tables that rank metropolitan areas by population (general, specific ethnic groups, and specific age groups), number of households, effective buying income (EBI) of households, total retail sales, and sales for retail store groups.

Although the categories used in the population and retail sales tables are self-evident, those used in the income table may need some explanation. "Effective Buying Income," or

"EBI," is a classification developed by *Sales & Marketing Management* and first used in 1948 (but similar in concept to disposable income, a designation used in the *Editor & Publisher Market Guide* and in many other publications), and is defined as personal income less personal tax and non-tax payments. In other words, EBI equals spending money, what is left to pay bills, invest, and buy consumer goods after taxes and other unavoidable payments—fines and fees—have been paid.

The Effective Buying Income tables also include a "Buying Power Index" or "BPI." The BPI is one of the *Survey*'s most widely used single market measures, particularly useful in estimating demand for mass market products.

The *Survey* also includes five-year projections for population, income, and retail sales by metropolitan areas and media markets.

In 1977, *Sales & Marketing Management* began publishing the *Survey of Buying Power Data Service*. This is now published (since 1993) by TradeDimensions under the title *Demographics USA,* with data available at both the county and zip code level. Information is much more detailed in this publication. Whereas the *Survey of Buying Power* lists the adult population by broader age group categories (18–24, 25–34, 35–49, 50 and over), using *Demographics USA* one can determine the number of people, by sex, in nine different groups (0–5, 6–11, 12–17, 18–24, 25–34, 35–44, 45–54, 55–64, 65–74, 75 and over).

The information on the CD-ROM version of *Demographics USA* is fully importable into any program that accepts dBase files and so allows the user to search, sort, rank, map, and manipulate data.

Another publisher, ESRI Business Information Solutions, also issues both county and zip code demographic data. These publications are known as the *Sourcebook of County Demographics* and the *Sourcebook of Zip Code Demographics. A* CD-ROM titled *Sourcebook America* is also issued. All products include 2001 updates and 2006 forecasts and spending potential indexes for 20 product and service categories. The *County Demographics* also includes 80 demographic variables for each U.S. county, while the *Zip Code* edition contains dominant ACORN lifestyle segmentation type for each zip code. ACORN is a neighborhood segmentation system that classifies the data into 43 clusters and 9 summary groups and can be used to distinguish the spending patterns and lifestyle choices of consumer behavior.

One can search for market profiles using the abovementioned publications, but to find a lifestyle market one would need to check in *Lifestyle Market Analyst*. This volume correlates demographic characteristics with consumer behavior patterns and can be used to learn more about the interests, hobbies, and favorite activities of consumers so that market plans can be better targeted. Interests, as defined by *LMA*, include a wide variety of activities: Bicycling, fishing, grandchildren, gambling, dieting, motorcycles, and bible reading are included. *LMA* combines lifestyle, demographic, and geographic data to provide comprehensive profiles by market, lifestyle, and consumer segment. Each profile provides comprehensive demographic information about the defined market segment. It also includes a list of the top 10 lifestyle interests for the market and a ranking and index for 60 lifestyle interests.

For more specific buying habits one should investigate *Consumer USA*. This volume, like so many others, contains an overview of the U.S. economy and market and trends in retailing and personal finance. But unlike other marketing publications. this will provide sales statistics (and forecasts) on much narrower product divisions. Examples of these are hard cheese, soft cheese, sugarless gum, mineral water, watches, personal care items, televisions. and even financial or personal business software. Euromonitor (http://www.euromonitor.com) operates internationally to produce the same marketing information for many countries ranging from Asia to the Middle East. All carry the consumer designation, such as *Consumer Japan, Consumer Latin America,* and *Consumer Eastern Europe.*

Euromonitor also produces a CD-ROM and Internet version, *World Consumer Markets,* which provides volume and value sales statistics for over 300 products from 52 countries. None of these publications is inexpensive, but any large library that serves an international business community will have some of them.

New Strategist is a publisher that specializes in publications on market segments. A full list of the books, complete with tables of contents, is listed at http://www.newstrategist.com/booklist.cfm. Among the books listed is *American Marketplace: Demographics and Spending Patterns,* which has eight chapters, including "Spending Trends," available for free download. Subjects covered by this publisher include demographics of: consumer demand; home ownership; attitudes, and information on different generations.

There are several products available that allow one to explore buying habits of people based on their media habits. Mediamark Research (http://www.mediamark.com/) conducts audience samples that are then offered in reports containing comprehensive demographic, lifestyle, product usage, and advertising media information. With these reports one can target an audience that watches a certain television program and buys a certain food. If one wants to know who watches *Friends* and eats Hershey kisses, these are the reports to check. Once again, these are very expensive, but the company does allow academic libraries to purchase reports that are two to three years old at a much reduced price. These are now available only on CD-ROM, as *Mediamark Reporter.* Similar reports from Simmons (previously issued in book form as *Simmons Survey of Media and Markets.*) are available as *Simmons Choices II.*

Zenith Media (http://www.zenithmedia.com) issues several publications for the advertising sector. These are international in scope and include a series of market and media fact books. Typical data included are household penetration of television channels, advertising revenue over time, peak time advertising rates and ratings, and total television advertising spending. Countries covered include those of Eastern and Western Europe, Latin America, Asia, the Pacific, and the United States.

Market Share

One of the statistical requests that business reference librarians regularly encounter is for information on the market share for a particular product or company. "What is the market share for Coca Cola?" a patron may ask, or "What is Kellogg's share of the market for cold cereals?" Market share is, quite simply, the ratio of sales for one company's product or product line to the total market sales of that product or product line, expressed as a percentage of the market. Market share can be for a specific brand, Fruit Loops versus Cheerios, for example, or for one company's product line, Kellogg's share of the market for cold cereals versus General Foods' market share. The concept is not a difficult one; market share can be calculated whenever total sales and specific product (or company) sales information are available. Market share can be computed for local, state, national, and even international markets as long as the necessary sales information is at hand.

Off-the-shelf market studies described earlier in this chapter frequently contain detailed market share data, but the latest publications are too expensive for most libraries. Other sources, more likely to be found in libraries, contain only selective market share information. *Advertising Age,* for example, regularly features market share data for some nationally advertised brands. *TableBase,* which is discussed later, also links to reports available in journals and magazines. *Ward's Business Directory of Largest U.S. Companies* and *Dun's Business Rankings* include sales data by SIC codes for public and some private companies. Although these directories do not give actual market share, it can be calculated easily by dividing the sales figure for a specific company into the total sales for the SIC category of which it is a part. Researchers should be forewarned, however, that this is an approximate figure at best. Many large companies are involved in the sale of a multitude of products and services, and sales figures presented are for the company as a whole rather than for the product(s) assigned the SIC code under which a company is listed. In addition, many companies too small to be included in the directories may also sell the same product or service. As a result, market shares derived from these publications are really little more than ballpark estimates. Although the sources mentioned above are useful, they have some drawbacks. Market share data are given for only a limited number of products and brands in *Advertising Age*, and the directories do not include market share for specific brands or for the market as a whole.

Market share for specific products or brands may also be included in periodical articles, which can be identified using some of the indexes already discussed and may also be available in the following publications.

Business Rankings Annual. Farmington, Mich.: Gale Group, 1989– . Annual.

Market Share Reporter. Farmington, Mich.: Gale Group, 1991– . Annual

World Market Share Reporter. Farmington, Mich.: Gale Group, 1995– . Biennial.

Market Share Tracker. London: Euromonitor, 2000. 203p.

International in scope, *Business Rankings Annual* lists the top business companies and provides information on such topics as "top cable programs by ad revenue." The comprehensive index is excellent.

The most well known and widely available of these items is the *Market Share Reporter*, which is a compilation of reports from periodical literature such as *Advertising Age*, *Appliance Manufacturer,* and *Supermarket Business*. The basic arrangement of the chapters is by two-digit SIC codes and then within the chapters the arrangement is by four-digit SIC. Each of the more than 2,000 entries is also given a number. For example, entry 985 in the 2001 volume tells us that Sony is the top producer of CD players. The table of contents is arranged by SIC number, and accompanying this is a table of products. The several indexes include listings by company and product and refer the user to an entry number. *Market Share Reporter* covers companies and products in Canada, Mexico and the United States. A collateral volume, *World Market Share Reporter,* contains over 1,600 entries for 360 geographic locations.

Euromonitor, a major international provider of marketing information, provides information for the top 15 consumer segments across 30 countries in the *Market Share Tracker*. Products ranging from alcoholic drinks to soft drinks are ranked within each country. If one needed to know the top-selling snack in Argentina, this would be a good source to check.

Market share for a specific brand or product is influenced significantly by the effectiveness of the advertising that promotes it. Selection of the appropriate medium in which to advertise is an important part of the marketing process. The next section considers various advertising media and the sources relating to them.

Advertising Media

Selection of the best media in which to advertise is no simple task. Each medium has special characteristics that the advertiser must keep in mind. However, before these characteristics are considered and an advertising plan drawn up, the following questions should be answered:

- *What do I want my advertising to accomplish?* The objects of advertising should be to increase awareness of a business and to attract new customers.

- *What is the target audience?* Determine the demographics of the intended audience and the products and services that may be useful to them.

- *What is the advertising message?* The message must be targeted to the demographic group that must be attracted

- *What advertising medium should be used?* The basic choices are television, radio, magazines, outdoor, direct mail, and the Internet.

The prospective advertiser, in other words, needs to segment his or her market and then consider the best ways(s) of reaching it.

Descriptions of four main categories of advertising media follow: print, broadcast, direct mail, and the Internet.

Print Media

The two main types of print media are newspapers and magazines. Both are used heavily by advertisers, but newspapers lead magazines and all other media in terms of advertising dollars spent. In 1999, for example, it was estimated that $46.582 billion was spent by newspaper advertisers, of which $40.640 billion was for local advertisements, and $5.942 billion for national advertising.[9]

Prospective newspaper advertisers usually want to know two things: the characteristics of the newspaper readers and/or the area in which they live, and the cost of advertising in specific newspapers. Both types of information are readily available.

Characteristics of newspaper readers in a city are likely to be similar to the population as a whole. Although this is somewhat less true of cities in which more than one newspaper is published, it is axiomatic that the socioeconomic and general demographic characteristics of the population served by a newspaper will be of great interest to those who are considering advertising in it.

Such local information may be closer at hand, either in government publications or in such statistical guides as the *Editor & Publisher Market Guide*, which gives demographic and trade information for daily newspaper cities. The other main factor affecting a marketer's decision to advertise in a specific newspaper is the cost of advertising in that newspaper. Since newspaper circulation is the basis for advertising rates and a major consideration in selecting a newspaper, credible circulation figures are essential. As a result, many newspaper publishers belong to the Audit Bureau of Circulations (http://www.accessabc.com/), a nonprofit association whose purpose is to audit and ascertain the veracity of circulation figures for newspapers and magazines published by its members. The letters "ABC" in the *Editor & Publisher Market Guide* and other publications indicate that the circulation figures presented have been verified by the Audit Bureau of Circulations. There are two other groups, the Business Publications Audit of Circulation, or BPA (http://www. bpai.com/), and the Verified Audit Circulation Corporation (http://www.verifiedaudit. com/), that audit circulation figures,

General circulation and readership statistics can be found at the Web page of the Newspaper Association of America (http://www.naa.org/). This site also provides links to information on advertising expenditures, media usage habits, and industry forecasts. Newspaper circulation figures can also be found in many publications, but coverage is most complete in the following source.

SRDS: Circulation. Wilmette, Ill.: Standard Rate & Data Service, 1957– . Annual.

SRDS: Circulation covers the circulation of 1,400 dailies, over 200 newspaper groups, and 25 consumer magazines, organized by metro area, TV market, and county penetration. Although some general market area and demographic data are included, it is the circulation analysis that makes this a useful reference source. Entries include daily and Sunday circulation figures, by MSA or county, for each newspaper. In addition, market data (households, consumer spending income, retail sales, and circulation) are featured. Although some advertising rates are included, an advertiser would be well advised to turn to the following companion publications for more detailed information.

SRDS: Newspaper Advertising Source Wilmette, Ill.: Standard Rate & Data Service, 1919– . Annual.

SRDS: Community Publications Advertising . Wilmette, Ill.: Standard Rate & Data Service, 1945– . Semiannual.

Newspaper Advertising Source is a monthly SRDS publication that includes rates for daily and weekly newspapers as well as for individual ethnic groups; colleges and universities; and international newspapers, comics, and newspaper magazines. A similar SRDS publication, *Community Publications Advertising*, gives advertising rates and specifications for 3,000 shopping guides and weekly newspapers.

Magazines, the other print medium, can be divided into three main categories: consumer, farm, and trade publications. Each of these, in turn, has many different subdivisions. Standard Rate & Data Service, for example, lists 81 classification titles for consumer magazines and 216 classifications for trade publications.

As for newspapers, circulation, characteristics of the reader population, and advertising costs are the major factors considered. Advertising rates vary widely, based on the magazine selected and the type of advertisement to be placed; a full-page, four-color ad will, naturally, cost more than a 14-line black-and-white ad. A nationally circulated periodical with many readers will charge more than one with more limited circulation or more limited subject interest. In 2001, for example, it cost approximately $203,000 to place a full-page color ad in *Sports Ilustrated*, which has an ABC verified circulation of over 3 million, but only $13,365 to place a similar ad in *Bass Times*, which has a more limited readership. For local magazines, advertising rates are often comparable to those for newspapers.

Standard Rate & Data Service also publishes two main titles covering consumer, farm, and trade magazines.

SRDS: Consumer Magazine Advertising Source. Wilmette, Ill.: Standard Rate & Data Service, 1919– . Monthly.

SRDS: Business Publication Advertising Source. Wilmette, Ill.: Standard Rate & Data Service, 1919– . Monthly, plus 4 quarterly issues of international data.

Both *Consumer Magazine* and *Business Publication* provide detailed information about magazines, including circulation, advertising rates, mechanical requirements, special issues, and advertising deadlines.

While advertising rates are significant and will be a major consideration in magazine selection, equally important is choosing one in which reader characteristics most closely match the target market identified for the product. The decision made to advertise a new line of cosmetics in certain women's magazines rather than, say, in automotive or fishing magazines may be a fairly simple one, but the next step must be to select the most appropriate women's magazines. Would *Vogue* or *Redbook* be better, or *Cosmopolitan* or *Working Woman*? To help advertisers decide, many magazines survey their readers for information about their income, occupations, education, and geographic location as well as about their attitudes toward and use of specific products. An ad in SRDS for *CIO Magazine* highlights some salient readership characteristics for prospective advertisers. Its subscribers, claims *CIO*, control IT budgets worth $85 million and have total company revenues of $3.86 billion.

Broadcast Media

Radio and television are highly effective advertising media. Broadcast advertising offers several advantages over print advertising. Radio and television programs are aimed at specific segments of the population, and the advertising that accompanies them can be aimed at these audiences. Broadcast media are also more flexible than print media, being more responsive to quick changes.

The human voice, with its capacity to establish rapport with listeners and to convey urgency, is sometimes more persuasive than print. Finally, broadcast advertising is, in a sense, more democratic, making it possible for small as well as big businesses to establish the images they want to present.

Broadcast advertising is not without its disadvantages, however. Frequent repetition of advertisements is necessary; since potential customers can be reached only during the few seconds the message is being transmitted. Copy must be both brief and effective. Finally, planning for broadcast advertising is somewhat more difficult than for print since there is little standardization between broadcast stations. Nevertheless, these disadvantages are offset by the potential that broadcast ads offer for reaching a market and for saturating it with promotional messages.

Broadcast advertisers attempt to reach prospective buyers by selecting the media, station, program, and time most likely to reach the most appropriate audience. When considering a station, advertisers look at its coverage and its audience. Coverage refers to the geographical area where the station's signal can be heard, and audience refers to the number of people who actually watch or listen to that station or to a particular program on that station.

Just as verified circulation figures are crucial for print advertisers, so also are accurate audience statistics for broadcast advertisers. Several firms offer audience measurement services; key among these are the Arbitron Ratings Company and the A. C. Nielsen Company.

Advertisers distinguish between network and spot announcements, or spots. Network announcements require buying air time from the network; spot announcements are bought on a station-by-station or market-by-market basis.

Radio advertising is appealing for many different reasons. It is less expensive than television and, because radio programming is designed to segment audiences, a much more closely defined audience can be reached than when using print media, particularly newspapers.

Radio rates are based partially on radio coverage and audience. Another factor affecting rates is time of day. Radio is primarily a daytime and early evening medium, and categories, based on when most people are likely to be listening, have been assigned to different parts of the day. Although these categories are not standardized among all stations, the classification shown in figure 8.6 is typical, with highest rates being charged for AA time slots, and lowest for D.

Class AA	Morning drive time	6:00 A.M. to 10:00 A.M.
Class B	Home worker time	10:00 A.M. to 4:00 P.M.
Class A	Evening drive time	4:00 P.M. to 7:00 P.M.
Class C	Evening time	7:00 P.M. to midnight
Class D	Nighttime	midnight to 6:00 A.M.

Figure 8.6. Radio time slots.

The most current information on radio stations is available from the following source.

SRDS: Radio Advertising Source. Wilmette, Ill.: Standard Rate & Data Service, 1929– . Quarterly.

This publication profiles over 10,000 stations. Each issue includes SRDS's usual estimates of state, county, city, and metro area market data as well as profiles of the individual stations themselves.

Another very useful publication is *Broadcasting & Cable Yearbook,* a standard reference work and a comprehensive directory to all aspects of broadcasting.

Broadcasting & Cable Yearbook. New Providence, N.J. : R. R. Bowker, 1935– . Annual.

The *Broadcasting & Cable Yearbook* includes sections that survey the broadcasting industry; profile television and cable stations; and focus on programming, professional services, technology, advertising and marketing, and satellites.

The television section of *Broadcasting & Cable Yearbook* lists all U.S. and Canadian television stations. In addition to these individual station entries, the *Yearbook* includes metro area maps showing in which counties metro area stations are viewed and a listing of television systems including Spanish-language and independently owned. The technology section lists equipment manufacturers and distributors. Using it, one can identify manufacturers of studio monitors, cameras, and lighting systems. Similarly, by consulting the "Brokers & Professionals" section, one can find television brokerage services, research specialists, consultants, and attorneys specializing in communications law.

Television advertising is big business. According to the 2000 *Statistical Abstract,* more than 98.4 percent of homes in this country have at least one television set, and, 91.9 percent of the population watch television an average of 1,575 hours each per year. Small wonder that advertisers turn to TV to promote their products. Television advertising, however, is usually very expensive.

According to the Television Bureau of Advertising (http://www.tvb.org), the average prime time 30-second commercial costs $82,3000. An estimated 130 million people watched the 2001 Super Bowl telecast, during which 30-second announcements cost over $2 million. These costs are very different from a local cable spot, which can be anything from $1 to $15,000.

Obviously knowing one's market and the shows that reach the designated audience is extremely important. *TelevisionAdvertising.com* at http://televisionadvertising.com/ offers some guidance for the small business person on choosing types of advertising. As in radio, television stations divide their broadcasting day into parts, based on when people are most likely to be watching. The categories and terms they employ, however, are different; they generally call their classifications daytime, early news, early fringe, prime, late news, late fringe, and weekend.

Time of day is one of the variables determining television advertising rates. Another has to do with the station's coverage and its audience. Broadcasters and advertisers may refer to a station's rating or to its audience share. Both are measures of its effectiveness and are based on the households using televisions index, or HUT. The HUT is simply the percentage of households in a designated area with the television set turned on. In a sample of 2,000 households with television, if 800 of these sets are turned on, the HUT would be 40. A station's rating is the percentage of households in a sample turned to a specific station at a specific time. If 400 households out of the sample of 2,000 reports turn to a particular station during the specified time period, that station would have a rating of 20 percent, usually expressed as 20.0 rating points. Finally, a station's share of audience, or share, is calculated by dividing the individual station's rating by the HUT. Thus, using the above example, dividing the station's rating of 20.0 by the HUT of 40.0 yields an audience share of 50 percent for the station. These concepts are employed for specific programs as well as for stations, with prime-time network programs ranked by rating and audience share.

One of the most heavily used listings of commercial television stations and broadcasting services is from Standard Rate & Data Service, one of the leading providers of all types of media rates and data to the advertising industry.

SRDS: TV and Cable Source. Wilmette, Ill.: Standard Rate & Data Service, 1947– . Monthly.

TV and Cable Source profiles individual television stations, state networks and groups, and national networks and groups. Also included are sections on sports networks listings for Latin America, and a section on public television.

Direct Mail

Direct mail, which includes all forms of advertising sent through the mail, has certain advantages over other media. One of the most important is that it offers the advertiser the potential for selling to individuals, identifiable by name and address and possibly other characteristics, rather than to broad groups of potential buyers having certain demographic or psychographic characteristics in common. Using carefully chosen mailing lists, compiled by the advertiser or purchased or rented from mailing list brokers, one can target the advertising to specific individuals. Print and broadcast advertising are scattergun media; direct mail, in contrast, is a pinpoint medium.

Greater selectivity in a target audience is not the only advantage. Another is greater flexibility: Direct mail advertising does not have the same limits on space or format as other media and can be mailed at any time. The advertiser is not constrained by publishing deadlines or broadcast schedules. Finally, some claim that direct mail advertising receives more attention since it is a single message rather than one in a series of competing messages in print or broadcast media.

Effective direct mail advertising begins with a good mailing list. Although some prefer to compile their own, many others use lists supplied to them by mailing list companies or mailing list brokers. For example, although a local, independently owned hardware store might construct its own mailing list, composed of previous customers and neighborhood residents, the manufacturer of a line of hardware supplies intended for national distribution might purchase or rent a mailing list of hardware wholesalers. The manufacturer might limit the list further to directors of purchasing or sales managers working for hardware wholesalers. Many libraries provide access to products such as *InfoUSA* (description provided at http://www.infousa.com) with which one can compile mailing lists.

When the decision is not to compile an in-house mailing list, advertisers must then consider outright purchase of a list from a mailing list company that compiles and sells its own list, or rent it from a mailing list broker who offers lists compiled by other organizations. These may include lists of subscribers, for example, and membership lists. For business people interested in direct mail advertising, one publication is particularly important.

SRDS: Direct Marketing List Source. Wilmette, IL.: Standard Rate & Data Service, 1967– . Bimonthly.

SRDS: DirectNet. Wilmette, Ill.: Standard Rate & Data Service, 2002– .

Mailing list compilers and brokers can be identified using *Direct Marketing List Source*, which profiles detailed descriptions of over 30,000 lists in 223 market classifications. Relevant lists can be more quickly found in the online version, where one can search by keyword or classification system, list source, and gender selection. Information provided in both services includes a description of the list and contact information.

There are many other SRDS publications, including the *Out of Home Advertising Source,* which details many nontraditional settings such as the cinema, taxis, bus shelters, and billboards. For a full description of these products the researcher should check the publisher's Web page at http://www.srds.com. Accompanying a print subscription is one password to access the product online. There are some licensing restrictions with its use, so not every library will have access to the electronic product. SRDS is, however, in the process of making all of its publications into Web products.

Advertising Expenditures

Data on advertising expenditures by companies with big advertising budgets are readily available. Some of the sources already described include such information. *Advertising Age*, for example, lists leading national advertisers and their annual advertising expenditures, and the *Standard Directory of Advertisers* often includes figures on media expenditures for each company. Another series of publications, formerly known as the LNA (Leading National Advertsiers), is described below.

Company/Brand $. New York: Competitive Media Reporting, 1974– . Quarterly.

Class/Brand $. New York: Competitive Media Reporting, 1974– . Quarterly.

Ad $ Summary. New York, Competitive Media Reporting, 1973–. Quarterly.

The first of the titles in this series is *Company/Brand $*, which lists company (and some brand) expenditures for advertising in 10 different media: consumer magazines, Sunday magazines, newspapers, outdoor, network television, spot television, syndicated television, cable TV networks, network radio, and national spot radio. The criteria for inclusion are brands that spend $25,000 or more per year in the 10 media measured. For companies that advertise several different products, there may be separate listings for each product.

The second title, *Class/Brand $,* provides quarterly and year-to-date expenditures per medium and the 10-media total for each brand, company, and classification. Media include magazines, newspapers, television, radio, and outdoor. In this publication, brands are grouped alphabetically within each of the Leading National Advertisers' (LNA's) product classes, showing brand expenditures for each medium. *Class/Brand $* is particularly useful when one wishes to compare advertising expenditures for different brands of the same product.

Arrangement in *Ad $ Summary* is alphabetical by brand name. Whereas its companion volumes, *Company/Brand $* and *Class/Brand $*, list advertising expenditures for each medium as well as total media expenditures, *Ad $ Summary* lists only total media expenditures. Types of media used to advertise each product, however, are designated. The publication includes listings of the top 100 companies in each of the 10 media.

Many libraries will not purchase the quarterly publications but instead will have the annual YTD volumes. The publisher, Competitive Media Reporting, is one of the leaders of strategic information provided mostly to advertising agencies. Information about the company and its products is available at http://www.cmr.com/.

Online advertising is becoming a revenue generator. More and more homes have access to the Internet, and time spent on it is rising. Although most sites have some advertising, it is apparent that there is still an untapped potential audience. The company or person who needs information about this advertising medium will most likely search online for data and news. There are many sites that are excellent starting points. Some are listed below.

- **I Advertising** (http://www.i-advertising.com/). A community for Internet advertising and marketing professionals. Includes "how to" articles, links to products and services, and a discussion forum.

- **CyberAtlas** (http://cyberatlas.internet.com/). Gathers online research from the best data resources to provide a complete review of the latest surveys and technologies available. Contains a section on Web advertising and statistics.

- **AD RESOURCE** (http://adres.internet.com/advertising/). Contains "how to" guides, descriptions of the different types of advertising, links to sample rates, and statistics on the top visited sites and companies on the Internet.

- **Nanyang Technological University Library** (http://www.ntu.edu.sg/library/mktg/ecomm.htm). A bibliography of international Web sites useful for Internet marketing.

Geographic Information Systems

More and more enterprises are using geographic software to analyze business trends and to make key decisions about locating new branches and designing marketing programs. GIS allows users to analyze data in spatial terms and so create a map of potential users within, for example, 10 miles of a possible new store location. Strategies such as target marketing, micromarketing, and relationship marketing require more and more information about consumers that GIS can provide. Firms such as Arby's, Burger King, The Olive Garden, Popeyes, Red Lobster, and others use GIS for market analysis, franchisee selection and placement, site location analysis, and demographic profiling.[10]

Many libraries now contain collections of GIS data and software packages, and the researcher should be aware of its potential in the marketing area. One of the most popular desktop packages, *ArcView*, is produced by Environmental Systems Research Institute, Inc. (ESRI) (http://www.esri.com/index.html). ESRI also conducts a virtual campus (http://campus.esri.com/) where one can register for a fee-based, six-module course on using *ArcView GIS* for successful marketing. From the home page one can also access a free magazine, available services, and free data downloads. For anyone just beginning to use or think about using GIS, the ESRI online site contains much useful information and assistance. ESRI is only one company involved in the expansion of GIS into the marketing field, but it is the service most often available in libraries and is also the service used by local governments.

There are many books available on GIS business applications, and the simplest way to find these is to search an online service such as amazon.com (http://www.amazon.com). To learn more about GIS and how it might be used, the librarian or researcher can also check the *About Geographic Information Systems* page (http://gis.about.com/science/gis/cs/learninggis/), which has 700 links to tutorials, software, data, and courses available through universities and other institutions.

Databases and Web Sites

Marketing activities are so pervasive that there are few bibliographic and full-text business databases in which the subject is not covered. General business files such as *ABI/INFORM* and *Business Source Elite* contain a wide range of articles, both general and scholarly, relating to the field. For more specific advertising and marketing statistical data the best database is *TableBase*, which is international in scope and covers more than 90 industries.

TableBase. Detroit: Gale Group, 1996– . Daily updates.

TableBase specializes exclusively in tabular data on topics such as market share, company and brand rankings, industry and product forecasts, production and consumption statistics, imports and exports, usage and capacity, number of users/outlets, trends, and demographics. It features indexing with concept terms, such as Ad budget, Consumption, Market Share, and Generation Y; industry terms like Broadcasting; and marketing terms like Community Advertising. Special features include the custom written unique titles that describe content and precise indexing at the table level as well as full-text searching. Originally introduced by Responsive Database Services Inc., this product is now owned by the Gale Group. It is also available as a CD-ROM and through Dialog (http://wwww.dialog.com)

If you need serious information about advertising and want to use the Web as a resource, one of the best ways to begin is to use *Advertising World* from the University of Texas at Austin (http://advertising.utexas.edu/world/). It is billed as "the most extensive collection of advertising-related links on the Web," and this claim is easy to understand when one scans the index. It appears as if every marketing and advertising link that exists is there. The Web sites are concisely annotated and are organized in alphabetical order. (See figure 8.7.)

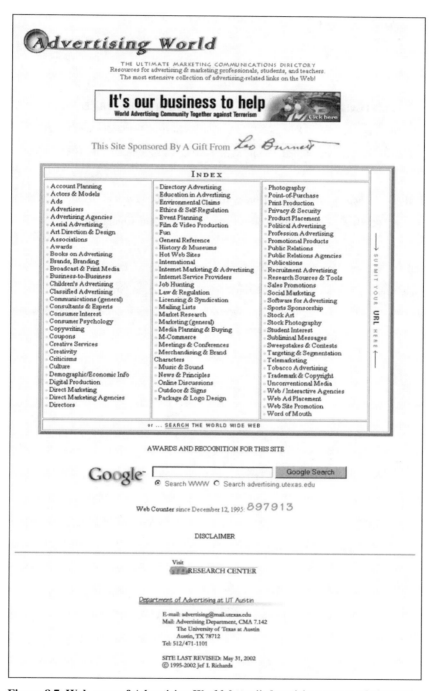

Figure 8.7. Web page of *Advertising World*, http://advertising.utexas.edu/world/.
Reprinted with permission.

For an excellent site on the history of advertising, including advertisements that can be downloaded, the researcher should check the *Emergence of Advertising in America: 1850–1920 Project* (http://scriptorium.lib.duke.edu/eaa/). Included in this collection are the J. Walter Thompson Company "House Ads" from 1889–1925. The collection contains over 9,000 images that represent the emergence of the advertising industry in the United States.

Notes

1. Louis E. Boone and David L. Kurtz, *Contemporary Marketing* (Hinsdale, Ill.: Dryden Press, 1974), 112.

2. Frederick A. Ross and Charles A. Kirkpatrick, *Marketing* (Boston: Little, Brown, 1982), 109.

3. Marvin I. Mandall, *Advertising*, 4th ed. (Englewood Cliffs, N.J.: Prentice-Hall, 1984), 146.

4. Ibid., 147.

5. William T. Ryan, *A Guide to Marketing* (Homewood, Ill.: Learning Systems Company, 1981), 12.

6. Taken from the FTC mission statement at http://www.ftc.gov/ftc/mission.htm.

7. Mandall, *Advertising*, 92.

8. U.S. Federal Trade Commission, Federal Trade Commission Actions, http://www.ftc.gov/os/.

9. Taken from a brokerage report issued on March 9, 1999, by Salomon, Smith Barney.

10. C. Battista, "Competition in the Food Chain," *Business Geographics* 3, no. 3 (1995): 32–34.

9

Accounting and Taxation

This chapter introduces basic concepts and terminology in accounting and taxation that apply to the use of publications, databases, and other sources in libraries and information centers. Although they are covered in separate sections, it should be noted that accounting and taxation are closely related, and that the study of one almost inevitably requires consideration of the other. Both have profound and long-lasting effects on the daily conduct of business and, as a result, are of interest to business and laypeople as well as accountants and tax professionals.

Accounting Basics

Accounting provides information used to assess the financial status of businesses and other economic entities, including government agencies and nonprofit organizations. Although it is frequently confused with bookkeeping, the latter is but one aspect of the entire accounting process. Accounting is, in fact, a financial information system. It begins with determining the raw data to be collected; proceeds to gathering, recording, analyzing, and verifying them; and culminates in communicating the data to interested parties. An important aspect of accounting is the objectivity with which the information is presented:

> The essence of accounting is its special quality of neutrality. Accounting is financial map-making. It organizes, maps, and presents complex transactions and financial interrelationships in a reliable fashion. Not all information is necessarily useful. Of equal or greater importance is the accountant's assurance that the information is verifiable, objective, accurate, and has been compiled in an unbiased way.[1]

Accounting information is used within an organization to make decisions about finance, resource allocation, production, and marketing. It is also used externally by creditors, other businesses, investors, and government agencies charged with monitoring business activities and organizations. Accounting, which has been called the language of business, is quantitative and is usually expressed in monetary terms.

Types of Accounting

The three major fields of accounting are private, public, and government accounting. *Private accounting* is carried out within a single organization, such as a corporation. It includes such specialties as managerial, financial, and tax accounting. Managerial accounting develops, produces, and analyzes data to be used for internal management decisions. It includes cost accounting, which concentrates on determining various unit costs, and internal auditing, which checks for fraud and waste and helps to ensure that proper accounting procedures are being followed. Financial accounting gathers and reports information for inclusion in published financial statements such as balance sheets and income statements. These are included in corporate annual reports to shareholders, stock exchanges, and the Securities and Exchange Commission. Finally, tax accounting refers to recording and reporting corporate and income tax and tax liability. It is a complicated specialty that requires knowledge of current and past tax legislation, court rulings, and administrative decisions, as well as accepted accounting practices that will minimize corporate tax liability.

Although private accounting is essentially for the benefit and under the purview of a single organization, *public accounting* is, either directly or indirectly, for the benefit of the public. It offers independent professional accounting assistance to the public and consists of three main specialties: auditing, management services, and tax services. The most important of these is auditing, the base upon which most public accounting rests.

Private accountants employed by companies and other organizations are responsible for preparing and documenting financial statements. It is the responsibility of the independent public accountant to examine these financial statements and verify their accuracy, completeness, and compliance with generally accepted accounting principles. This process, called auditing, includes several different steps. In addition to checking figures for accuracy, it may also involve reviewing contracts, agreements, minutes of directors' meetings, and other corporate documents. In addition, it may require interviewing or corresponding with bankers and other creditors or conducting inventories. Upon completion of this process, the public accountant reaches a conclusion that becomes the auditor's report, expressed as an opinion. These opinions, more fully described in the section on basic accounting concepts, are accepted as authoritative by executives and managers within the company, and by creditors, stockholders, investors, and other interested parties. Only certified public accountants (CPAs) are allowed to conduct external financial audits for their clients.

Management services, another public accounting specialty, offer independent reviews of clients' accounting and management systems, with suggestions for their revision and improvement. Accountants may assess the availability and prudent use of financial and statistical information within the client's organization, monitor internal control systems devised to prevent losses through theft or waste, review internal accounting procedures for efficiency and effectiveness, consult on how to manage cash resources more profitably, or install or modify computerized accounting systems.

Finally, just as private accountants provide tax advice and assistance to the organizations for which they work, public accountants offer similar services to their clients. They prepare income tax returns, consult on tax problems, and help to plan tax programs. In addition to providing professional assistance with income taxes, public accountants also offer services pertaining to other types of taxes and tax-related issues, including property, foreign and franchise taxes, and estate planning.

Public accounting firms range in size from sole practitioners to huge, multinational companies employing thousands of workers. The largest of these firms, now known as the Big 4, dominate the accounting marketplace and enjoy high visibility and prominence. The largest companies at this time are Deloitte & Touche, Ernst & Young, Pricewaterhouse Coopers, and KPMG (Klynveld Peat Marwick Goerdeler).

The third field of accounting is government accounting. Government agencies at all levels employ accountants in a wide range of positions. Their responsibilities parallel those of private and public accountants: They may prepare financial statements; audit the records of their own or other government agencies, contractors, or private citizens; or gather and present data that will help managers decide how best an agency should operate to meet its mandated responsibilities. At the federal level, for example, accountants in the Internal Revenue Service (IRS) audit personal and corporate income tax returns, while those employed by the Defense Contract Audit Agency examine the records of private defense contractors. The General Accounting Office (GAO) assists in investigations to determine the compliance of federal agencies with government policies and regulations and monitors the expenditure of public funds. Similar accounting activities are carried on at the state and local levels.

In summary, private, public, and government accounting are the three broad fields into which the profession is distributed. Although there is some overlap between the work performed in these areas, each has its own specialties. For all three fields, however, the generally acknowledged indication of professional competence is the CPA certificate, which is described in the following section. Not all CPAs are employed by Big 5 accounting firms or practice as public accountants. Many work as private accountants for corporations and nonprofit organizations, and still others are employed by the government. CPA status, in other words, designates a certain level of competency and adherence to professional standards and ethics and does not necessarily mean that an accountant works in the field of public accounting.

Certified Public Accountants

The right to practice as a CPA is governed by individual state boards of accountancy. Although the rules vary, particularly as they relate to minimum educational and experiential requirements, all require that candidates must pass the Uniform CPA Examination. The exam, which is given in every state and U.S. territory each May and November, is prepared by the Board of Governors of the American Institute of Certified Public Accountants (AICPA) (http://www.aicpa.org/). To pass it, candidates must prove competence in the application of accounting and auditing standards, procedures, and principles to practical accounting problems, and they must demonstrate an understanding of professional responsibilities. The two-day examination is rigorous, and many candidates do not pass it the first time. Each section, however, is graded separately, and candidates are permitted to take subsequent examinations until passing grades are achieved for all parts.

Libraries can assist prospective CPAs by acquiring publications that will help them prepare for and pass the examination or by knowing where to direct them to find resources. Some of the most useful sources are those published by the American Institute of Certified Public Accountants. Others are commercially published.

American Institute of Certified Public Accountants. **Information for Uniform CPA Candidates**. 17th ed. New York: AICPA, 1970– . Annual.

————. **Uniform CPA Examination: Official Questions and Unofficial Answers.** New York: AICPA, 1972– . Semiannual.

————. **Uniform CPA Examination: Selected Questions and Unofficial Answers Indexed to Content Specification Outlines 1900s–2000.** New York: AICPA, 19uu– . Annual.

Whittington, O. Ray, and Patrick R. Delaney. **Wiley CPA Examination Review**. New York: John Wiley, 1983– . 4v. Annual.

Many candidates begin their preparation for the Uniform CPA Examination by consulting *Information for Uniform CPA Candidates*, a booklet that discusses the format and focus of each section of the exam.[2] In addition, it includes a statement on the purpose and general objectives of the Uniform CPA Examination, describes how the exam is compiled and graded, and suggests how to prepare for it. The current edition also includes some sample questions.

Uniform CPA Examination: Official Questions and Unofficial Answers consists of all questions included in a specific exam, accompanied by unofficial answers and study references. *Uniform CPA Examination* includes detailed instructions for candidates taking the test and lists future examination dates. An index by content specification, which enables readers to identify by number all of the questions dealing with a specific subject, is also included.

The American Institute of Certified Public Accountants publishes a cumulative subject index to topics covered in earlier exams, *Uniform CPA Examination: Selected Questions and Unofficial Answers Indexed to Content Specification Outlines*. The index is particularly useful to candidates who are weak in certain areas and would like to improve their skills by studying the questions that focus on their weaknesses. It also helps candidates to determine topics emphasized during past exams and to anticipate the direction future exams might take.

In addition to the publications issued by the AICPA, several commercially published sources are available. Typical of these is the *Wiley CPA Examination Review*, an annual, four-volume work that includes study guides, suggestions for test taking, and other information in addition to the CPA questions and unofficial answers. Libraries in which there is heavy demand for materials relating to the Uniform CPA Examination can make a good case for acquiring one or more of the commercially published sources in addition to the official AICPA publications. In libraries where the demand is not so great, however, the AICPA titles should receive first consideration.

American Institute of Certified Public Accountants (AICPA)

The American Institute of Certified Public Accountants (http://www.aicpa.org/index.htm) is the oldest and largest association of professional accountants in the United States. Governed primarily by boards and committees composed of AICPA members, it promotes and maintains high professional and ethical standards; supports research; and represents the public accounting profession to government, the business community, and the general public. As was mentioned in the preceding section, it also prepares the uniform examination given to all CPA candidates. In addition, the AICPA publishes a wide range of professional accounting materials, including the *Journal of Accountancy*, which is indexed online from 1996 to 1999 and is full text from 2000 at http://www.aicpa.org/pubs/jofa/joaiss.htm. Also online at the AICPA Web site are various newsletters and exposure drafts from different AICPA groups and committees (http://www.aicpa.org/pubs/index.htm).

Basic Accounting Concepts

Although it is beyond the scope of this book to delve deeply into accounting principles, practices, and procedures, three accounting concepts and their application to business reference service should be considered. These are the basic financial statements included in corporate reports, the standards followed by the accounting profession in presenting and interpreting data, and the financial ratios used to assess and compare one company with others in the same industry.

Key Financial Statements

Although corporate annual reports and the financial statements extracted from them are common to library business collections, and ready access to them from the Web is established, not all librarians and researchers are familiar or comfortable with the data they contain. This section focuses on two basic financial statements, the balance sheet and the income statement, as well as on the notes and auditor's report that accompany them.

The balance sheet is a status report that describes the financial condition of a company at a fixed point in time. It is important to remember that the data being presented reflect conditions on the specified day only:

> As a snapshot on a certain day, it can be "managed". Companies will pick the best day in their year to take the snapshot, and always remember that they have 364 days notice of that day arriving! It may well be as like the business for the rest of the year as our passport photographs represent true and fair views of us!"[3]

Balance sheets present assets, or the company's financial resources. These assets include cash, buildings, property, supplies, and money owed to the company. Also presented are liabilities and stockholders' equity. Liabilities are debts and other corporate obligations and may include such items as long- and short-term debt and income tax. Stockholders' equity is the total interest that shareholders have in a corporation. It is the company's net worth, derived by subtracting liabilities from assets, and is what stockholders would earn if the company were liquidated at its balance sheet value. (See figure 9.1, page 194, for an example of a balance sheet.)

Three points about balance sheets are worth noting. First, the assets and the liabilities and equity are equal; they always balance. Balance sheets are, in fact, based upon the following equation: Assets = Liabilities + Equity or, rearranging, Assets - Liabilities = Equity.

Second, most balance sheets include information for the preceding as well as the current year. Finally, the notes that follow the balance sheet are an integral part of it, and should not be overlooked.

The second basic financial statement is the income statement. Also known as the earnings report or the profit and loss statement, it shows how much money a company made, or lost, during the fiscal year being reported. Where the balance sheet highlights financial conditions on a given date, the income statement reflects the entire year's activities and frequently includes data for earlier years. Taken together, the historic and current information in an income statement can be used to assess the company's progress and to make predictions about its future. As a result, investors frequently consult income statements.

The two major items included in an income statement are revenues and expenses. Revenues consist of the money received or anticipated for goods and services sold by the company. Revenues can include sales or interest received. Expenses usually consist of overhead costs such as salaries, interest paid on loans, taxes, and other costs associated with the company's business. (See figure 9.2, page 195.)

MONTANA CLAY & CASTING, INC.
BALANCE SHEETS
December 31,

	1995	1996
① ASSETS:		
② Current Assets:		
③ Cash	0.1	5.2
④ Accounts Receivable $29.9 and $34.0		
⑤ Less: Allowance for doubtful accounts of $2.0		
Net Accounts Receivable	27.9	32.0
⑥ Inventory	24.3	26.1
⑦ Prepaid Expenses	0.5	0.5
Total Current Assets	52.8	63.8
⑧ Fixed Assets:		
Land	10.0	10.0
Buildings and Equipment, $55.8 and $65.8 at cost,		
less Accum. Depreciation of $30.7 and $34.7	25.1	31.1
Total Property & Equipment	35.1	41.1
⑨ Notes Receivable	2.0	1.5
⑩ Other Assets	2.0	2.0
⑪ Total Assets	91.9	108.4
⑫ LIABILITIES:		
⑬ Current Liabilities		
⑭ Accounts Payable	50.3	48.0
⑮ Accrued Expenses	2.0	2.4
⑯ Notes Payable - Term Loan	0.0	2.4
⑰ Current Portion LTD	0.0	2.0
Total Current Liabilities	52.3	54.8
⑱ Long Term Liabilities		
⑲ Notes Payable	0.0	10.6
⑳ Note-Payable - shareholder	53.5	0.0
Total Long Term Liabilities	53.5	10.6
㉑ Total Liabilities	105.8	65.4
㉒ EQUITY:		
㉓ Common Stock	2.0	2.0
㉔ Paid in Capital	0.0	53.5
㉕ Retained Earnings	(15.9)	(12.5)
Total Equity	(13.9)	43.0
㉖ Total Liabilities and Equity	91.9	108.4

Figure 9.1. Balance sheet example. Image taken from the Web page of the Small Business Administration at http://www.onlinewbc.gov/docs/finance/fs_balmap1.html.

Example of items in an Income Statement

STATEMENT OF INCOME
(in thousands)

OPERATING INCOME

Interest income
Interest expense

Net Interest Income

Less: Provision for loan losses

Net Interest Income After Provision

Financially related services
Other operating income

Total Operating Income

NET OPERATING INCOME

OTHER INCOME (EXPENSE)

Patronage income
Other income/(Expense)
Income tax benefit (Expense)

Total Other Income (Expense)

NET INCOME

Figure 9.2. Items in an income statement.

By comparing revenues with expenses, the income statement reflects net profit or loss for the company for the year being reported. In addition, net earnings per share of common stock is usually included.

Detailed notes that clarify, qualify, and supplement data presented in the balance sheet, income statement, and other financial statements are also included in annual reports and 10K and 10Q filings with the Securities and Exchange Commission. Most offer information not contained in the text and should be examined carefully. Frequently they summarize significant accounting principles followed in preparing the financial statements, provide information on corporate operations and employee benefits, and describe pending lawsuits.

Following the notes that accompany the financial statements is a brief report submitted by the public accounting firm responsible for auditing the company's financial records.

Just as physicians presented with the same set of symptoms may diagnose different ailments, so also may public accountants auditing the same financial statements reach different conclusions. For this reason, auditors' reports are presented as opinions. Usually the opinion is that the financial statements are fair, and that they have been prepared in conformity with generally accepted accounting principles. If circumstances warrant, the auditors can qualify their opinions about an exception taken or state an adverse opinion. It is rare, however, for a report to be issued with an adverse opinion. External audits, as mentioned previously, are always conducted by independent CPAs in public accounting practice and, in the case of large, blue-chip companies, are usually conducted by one of the big accounting firms.

Corporate financial statements are included in annual reports, and they are also reproduced in such commercially published sources as the Mergent *Manuals*. As a result, familiarity with basic terms, concepts, and applications can be extremely helpful to librarians in understanding requests for assistance and in providing information to business researchers. One way to gain such familiarity is by studying the tutorial provided by the Small Business Association for people starting a business. The tutorial describes balance sheets and income statements and explains their constituent parts and provides examples. Part 1 (see figure 9.3) covers the balance statement, and each section is linked to a more comprehensive explanation (see figure 9.4). Part 2 describes the profit and loss statement, and Part 3 looks at ratios and quality indicators. Although it is designed for the small business operator, it is easy to understand and covers all the basic questions.

PART 1 - BALANCE SHEET	
Balance Sheet Introduction	Operating Cycle
ASSETS	Current Assest
Accounts Receivable	Analyzing A/R
Inventory	Inventory Cycle
Minimum Inventory	Notes Receivable
Other Current Assets	Non-Current Assets
Fixed Assets	Intangibles
Other Assets	Total Assets
LIABILITIES	
Current Liabilities	Account Payable
Accrued Expenses	Notes Payable
Current Portion Long Term Debt	Long Term Debt
Officer Loans	Contingent Liabilities
EQUITY	Total Liabilities and Equity

**Figure 9.3. Table of contents for SBA balance statement,
http://www.onlinewbc.gov/docs/finance/fs_incstmt1.html.**

Fixed Assets.

Fixed assets represent the use of cash to purchase physical assets whose life exceeds one year. They include assets such as:

- Land
- Building
- Machinery and Equipment
- Furniture and Fixtures
- Leasehold Improvements

Calculating Net Fixed Assets. When a fixed asset is purchased for use in operations of the business it is recorded at cost. As the asset wears out, an amount is charged to expense and accumulated annually in a contra-account known as accumulated depreciation. Accumulated depreciation is the cumulative sum of all the years' worth of wearing out that has occurred in the asset. The gross fixed asset (purchase price) less the accumulated depreciation equals the Net Fixed Asset Value (also known as book value).

Gross Fixed Assets (Purchase Price)	- Accumulated Depreciation	= Net Fixed Assets (Book Value)

Figure 9.4. Further explanation of fixed assets provided by the SBA, http://www.onlinewbc.gov/docs/finance/fs_balsheet1.html#fixed.

Another helpful online service, again directed to the small business owner, is the Toolkit provided by Commerce Clearing House at http://www.toolkit.cch.com/. The section "Managing Your Business Finance" (http://www.toolkit.cch.com/text/P06_0100.asp) provides not only explanations but also Excel templates, which are useful for both business owners and students.

Most libraries will have books on understanding financial statements, such as the Wiley publication *How to Read a Financial Report* or accounting handbooks and textbooks.

Accounting Principles and Standards

Accounting principles are human creations. They are not, writes Stephen Moscove, "like the immutable laws of nature found in physics and chemistry,"[4] but are instead rules developed by the accounting profession to serve the needs of the business community, investors, and government. Also known as *standards*, accounting principles are fundamental guidelines that help to determine whether specific choices of ways to record accounting information are acceptable. Their purpose is to ensure that the financial statements prepared by accountants are relevant, reliable, and comparable.

Accountants use the phrase *generally accepted accounting principles*, or GAAP, to refer to the body of conventions, rules, and procedures that define accounting practices at a particular time. Thus, an auditor's assurance that the financial statements examined present information fairly and in accordance with generally accepted accounting principles means that the financial accounting procedures followed reflect the consensus of accountants and officials regarding proper accounting practices at the time the report was prepared.

The inculcation of the principles and any changes to them is greatly influenced by government agencies; professional organizations in accounting and related fields; and academicians, securities analysts, bankers, other professionals, and major corporations.

Although many organizations have affected the formulation of accounting principles, the most important today are the Securities and Exchange Commission and the Financial Accounting Standards Board.

In 1934 the Securities and Exchange Commission (SEC) was established by Congress to regulate the nation's securities markets and to ensure that investors have adequate information on which to base their investment decisions. Among other things, Congress empowered the SEC to establish the accounting principles to be followed by publicly traded companies in reporting their financial condition. Although the SEC has chosen to delegate much of that responsibility to professional accounting organizations such as the Financial Accounting Standards Board, its role in helping to set and enforce those principles should not be underestimated.

Although the Securities and Exchange Commission has statutory authority to establish standards of financial accounting and reporting, it is the Financial Accounting Standards Board (FASB) (http://www.fasb.org) that is primarily responsible for setting generally accepted accounting principles for financial reporting. Established in 1973, the FASB consists of a substantial research staff and seven full-time board members appointed by the Financial Accounting Foundation. Like the foundation, the Financial Accounting Standards Board is independent of all other business and professional organizations. Its standards are recognized as authoritative and official by the SEC, the AICPA, and other organizations.

The FASB issues three main types of accounting pronouncements. *Statements of Financial Accounting Standards* (SFAS) are authoritative statements that spell out current accounting standards. More than 145 SFAS have been issued, each dealing with a specific accounting topic. SFAS 45, for example, deals with accounting for franchise fee revenue, and SFAS 142 with goodwill and other intangible assets. A listing and summary of all statements can be found at http://www.fasb.org/st/. In addition, the FASB issues *Statements of Financial Accounting Concepts*, publications that describe ideas and concepts that will guide the development of future accounting standards and that may provide the groundwork for a philosophical framework for financial accounting and reporting. Finally, as their name implies, *Interpretations of Statements of Financial Accounting Standards* explain, clarify, and sometimes amend previously issued statements of standards and reports in Accounting Research Bulletins and Opinions. In addition, the FASB publishes Exposure Drafts, Discussion Memoranda, and special research reports. All can be purchased separately from the FASB or acquired through subscription plans. The FASB Web page (http://www.fasb.org) provides summaries of much of the material and full-text downloads of Exposure Drafts and Bulletins.

Prior to the creation of the FASB in 1973, the AICPA (http://www.aicpa.org) was responsible for the promulgation of generally accepted accounting principles. From 1939 to 1959, the AICPA issued over 50 Accounting Research Bulletins (ARBs) and Accounting Terminology Bulletins through its Committee on Accounting Procedures. In 1960, the institute established the Accounting Principles Board (APB) to issue authoritative opinions and to publish research studies. Before its dissolution in 1973, the APB issued 31 Opinions, which were later adopted by the FASB as part of generally accepted accounting principles.

A wide range of publications is available to keep accountants apprised of FASB and AICPA official pronouncements. Some of the most widely used are listed and discussed below.

FASB. Financial Accounting Research System (FARS). Norwalk, CT : Financial Accounting Standards Board, 1996– . CD-ROM. (Updates approximately 6 times a year.)

Williams, Jan R. Miller Comprehensive GAAP Guide. New York: Harcourt Brace Jovanovich, 1974– . Annual.

FARS includes FASB and AICPA Pronouncements, FASB Statements, Interpretations, Technical Bulletins, and Concepts Statements; APB Opinions and Statements; and AICPA Accounting Interpretations and Terminology Bulletins. Also included is an abstract for each issue discussed by the FASB's Emerging Issues Task Force since its inception in 1984 and questions and answers from FASB Special Reports. The issuing of the CD made it easy for even the smallest library to now own a complete set of Standards for what is a very reasonable price. For full information on prices and subscriptions check the Web page at http://www.fasb.org.

The *Miller Comprehensive GAAP Guide* presents generally accepted accounting principles in current use. Miller has been rewritten to eliminate jargon and increase comprehension by using what its authors describe as "plain, understandable English."

Auditing Standards

Another acronym common to accounting is GAAS, or generally accepted auditing standards. While GAAP refers to rules and conventions followed in presenting financial information, GAAS refers to the rules followed by public accountants in auditing clients' financial records. Generally accepted auditing standards are developed by the Auditing Standards Board of the AICPA, the senior technical body of the institute, responsible for issuing pronouncements on auditing matters. All CPAs are required to follow the rules and procedures set forth by the Auditing Standards Board. Just as an auditor's report verifies that GAAP have been followed, so also does it indicate that the auditor preparing the report has followed GAAS when reviewing the statements for accuracy. Both GAAS and GAAP are important. The auditor's statement that a financial report has been examined in accordance with GAAS and has been found to conform to GAAP is, as one writer notes, "about as nice a compliment as you can pay a financial statement."[5] Publications dealing with auditing standards are abundant. Some that are widely used are listed below.

AICPA Professional Standards. Chicago: Commerce Clearing House, 1974– . 2v. Loose-leaf. Updated annually.

Bailey, Larry P. **Miller GAAS Guide.** New York: Harcourt Brace Jovanovich, 1982– . Annual.

Epstein Barry J., and Abbas Ali Mirza. **IAS Interpretation and Application of International Accounting Standards.** New York: John Wiley, 2002. 1014p.

Ordelheide, Dieter, and KPMG, eds. **Transnational Accounting (TRANSACC).** 2nd ed. New York : Palgrave, 2001. 3v. + supplement.

U.S. Auditing Standards, the first volume of *AICPA Professional Standards*, deals with auditing standards and guidelines. It includes Statements on Auditing Standards issued by the Auditing Standards Board, covering such subjects as the training and proficiency of independent auditors, adherence to principles, and the circumstances under which auditors may issue adverse opinions. A topical index and appendixes are also included.

Like its *GAAP* counterpart, *Miller GAAS Guide* restates auditing standards in basic, jargon free English. Arranged to correspond to the types of auditing or accounting services that CPAs provide to their clients, the annual paperback offers an inexpensive alternative to the more comprehensive and up-to-date service published by Commerce Clearing House

With the globalization of markets, a solid understanding of the accounting practices of other countries is needed, and this is supplied by the *IAS Interpretation and Application of International Accounting Standards*. International Accounting Standards (http://www.iasb.org.uk/cmt/0001.asp) are going to be enforced by 2005 by the European Union, and already many other developing and emerging countries are adopting them. The *IAS Interpretation and Application* is a quick guide to all the standards issued and revised and includes examples and explanations.

TRANSACC analyzes and describes what are regarded as the most important regulatory systems of accounting and financial reporting systems of the world. For each country covered the information provided includes forms of business organization, general principles, special accounting areas, auditing and financial reporting areas, and national databases. This book is intended as a working tool for practitioners, academics, and students to compare accounting practices country by country.

Ratio Analysis

Until now, discussion of basic accounting concepts has focused on accounting and auditing standards and on two important financial statements, the balance sheet and income statement. This section considers another basic concept, ratio analysis, and examines some of the sources that contain information used in ratio analysis.

Sometimes managers and executives, government officials, investors, and others use financial information just as it is presented in financial statements. Frequently, however, they convert it into ratios to facilitate comparison. A ratio is simply one number expressed in terms of another. Ratio analysis is the study of relationships between and among various items on financial statements. Each ratio relates one item on the balance sheet (or income statement) with another or, more often, relates one element from the balance sheet to one from the income statement. Financial ratios are measures of corporate performance and are particularly useful when compared with similar ratios for earlier years or with ratios for other companies in the same industry.

As shown in figure 9.5, a number of financial ratios are in common usage, each serving as a yardstick against which a company can compare one aspect of current performance to earlier years or to the industry norm. When historical standards are used, the company's ratios are compared from one year to another. By looking at changes over time, it is possible to identify trends and to appraise current performance in the light of historical relationships. Data used in historic ratio analysis for a specific company can be obtained from its annual reports or from commercially published sources, such as those issued by Standard & Poor's, Mergent (Moody's), and Value Line.

Industry standards, in contrast, involve a comparison of a particular company's ratios to those of other companies in the same line of business. Standards of comparison include ratios calculated from the financial statements of similar companies or average ratios for an industry. Industry ratios are available in several different sources, some of the most well known of which are discussed below.

LIQUIDITY—These measure the company's capacity to pay its debts as they come due.

Current Ratio: ratio between all current assets and all current liabilities.

Current Assets
Current Liabilities

1:1 means that the company has equal assets and liabilities. A better liquidity ration would be higher than 1:1

Quick Ratio: ratio between all assets *quickly* convertible into cash and all current liabilities. Excludes inventory.

Cash + Accounts Receivable
Current Liabilities

Shows if current liabilities can be met without the sale of inventory. Usually a ratio of 1:1 indicates that bills can be met.

SAFETY—Shows a businesses resistance to risk.

Debt to Equity: ratio between money invested by the owners and the money borrowed.

Debt
Equity

The higher the ratio the higher the risk to creditors.

Figure 9.5. Examples of financial ratios.

RMA's Annual Statement Studies. Philadelphia: Risk Management Association, 1923– . Annual.

Troy, Leo. **Almanac of Business and Industrial Financial Ratios**. Englewood Cliffs, N.J.: Prentice-Hall, 1971– . Annual.

Dun & Bradstreet Credit Services. **Industry Norms and Key Business Ratios: Desk Top Edition.** New York: Dun & Bradstreet, 1982/1983– . Annual.

Risk Management Association (formerly Robert Morris Associates), the national association of bank loan and credit officers, has long been noted for its extensive work in ratio compilation and analysis. Each year, it collects financial statements submitted to member banks from current and prospective borrowers in many different industries. The statements are then compiled by industry category and are published as *RMA's Annual Statement Studies*. Although it is designed primarily for commercial bankers who need to compare one company's performance with the industry norm to determine whether the company is a good credit risk, *Annual Statement Studies* is also used by business people, executives, researchers, students, and librarians.

Annual Statement Studies contains composite financial data on manufacturing, wholesaling, retailing, service, and contractor industries. Arrangement is by broad category, such as manufacturing, and then by line of business. For example, there are pages for "Bottled and Canned Soft Drinks and Carbonated Water"; "Flavoring Extracts and Syrups"; and "Wines, Brandy, & Brandy Spirits." Each line of business is represented by a page-long entry that includes detailed financial information and financial ratios (see figure 9.6, pages 202–3).

MANUFACTURERS—APPAREL & ACCESSORIES, NEC SIC# 2389

Current Data Sorted By Assets / Comparative Historical Data

0-500M	500M-2MM	2-10MM	10-50MM	50-100MM	100-250MM	# Postretirement Benefits / Type of Statement	4/1/93-3/31/94 ALL	4/1/94-3/31/95 ALL
1	1	6	7		3	Unqualified		
3	7	8	1			Reviewed		
3	5	6	1			Compiled		
						Tax Returns		
2	1	4	4	1	2	Other		
	23 (4/1-9/30/97)		43 (10/1/97-3/31/98)					
9	14	24	13	4	2	**NUMBER OF STATEMENTS**		
%	%	%	%	%	%	**ASSETS**	%	%
	9.9	4.5	2.5			Cash & Equivalents	D	D
	19.7	29.3	26.2			Trade Receivables - (net)	A	A
	36.7	46.0	40.6			Inventory	T	T
	3.4	1.9	.8			All Other Current	A	A
	69.7	81.7	70.1			Total Current		
	25.2	13.6	15.4			Fixed Assets (net)	N	N
	1.9	2.0	10.0			Intangibles (net)	O	O
	3.3	2.7	4.5			All Other Non-Current	T	T
	100.0	100.0	100.0			Total		
						LIABILITIES	A	A
	10.8	21.7	21.9			Notes Payable-Short Term	V	V
	4.1	5.2	2.6			Cur. Mat.-L/T/D	A	A
	14.3	18.2	12.1			Trade Payables	I	I
	.0	1.9	.2			Income Taxes Payable	L	L
	7.7	11.4	9.4			All Other Current	A	A
	36.9	58.3	46.2			Total Current	B	B
	18.4	10.2	20.1			Long Term Debt	L	L
	.1	.5	.3			Deferred Taxes	E	E
	1.9	.5	5.2			All Other Non-Current		
	42.7	30.7	28.2			Net Worth		
	100.0	100.0	100.0			Total Liabilities & Net Worth		
						INCOME DATA		
	100.0	100.0	100.0			Net Sales		
	33.0	28.7	29.1			Gross Profit		
	31.9	23.4	23.1			Operating Expenses		
	1.1	5.3	6.0			Operating Profit		
	.8	2.2	3.0			All Other Expenses (net)		
	.3	3.1	3.0			Profit Before Taxes		
						RATIOS		
	3.1	2.2	2.4					
	1.5	1.4	1.6			Current		
	1.3	1.1	1.2					
	1.0	.8	1.3					
	.7	.5	.7			Quick		
	.5	.4	.3					
13	29.2	26	14.0	55	6.6			
32	11.5	39	9.3	63	5.8	Sales/Receivables		
47	7.7	68	5.4	76	4.8			
22	16.9	70	5.2	74	4.9			
111	3.3	118	3.1	111	3.3	Cost of Sales/Inventory		
174	2.1	135	2.7	183	2.0			
9	40.9	17	21.9	21	17.4			
37	9.9	32	11.5	30	12.2	Cost of Sales/Payables		
72	5.1	76	4.8	62	5.9			
	3.7	5.4	3.6					
	7.8	12.1	6.6			Sales/Working Capital		
	28.5	31.6	16.1					
	3.9	4.5	7.8					
(12)	1.6	(22) 2.5	2.7			EBIT/Interest		
	-.5	1.4	1.3					
		13.6				Net Profit + Depr., Dep.,		
		(12) 1.4				Amort./Cur. Mat. L/T/D		
		1.1						
	.1	.2	.2					
	.5	.5	.4			Fixed/Worth		
	1.2	1.3	-2.3					
	.6	1.5	1.2					
	1.7	3.0	2.1			Debt/Worth		
	3.7	5.4	-8.1					
	26.4	52.4				% Profit Before Taxes/Tangible		
(13)	9.0	(23) 19.2				Net Worth		
	-3.3	13.1						
	8.7	13.3	10.5			% Profit Before Taxes/Total		
	3.6	4.6	6.0			Assets		
	-4.5	2.0	1.1					
	46.6	43.4	19.1					
	14.6	22.8	13.7			Sales/Net Fixed Assets		
	6.2	9.2	8.0					
	3.4	2.9	1.8					
	2.6	2.2	1.7			Sales/Total Assets		
	1.3	1.6	1.4					
	.7	.6	1.0					
(12)	1.6	1.2	(11) 2.2			% Depr., Dep., Amort./Sales		
	4.6	2.6	3.6					
						% Officers', Directors', Owners' Comp/Sales		
12148M	44700M	280111M	493609M	521542M	547352M	Net Sales ($)		
2915M	17401M	122787M	289437M	298682M	322552M	Total Assets ($)		

© RMA 1998 M = $ thousand MM = $ million

Figure 9.6. Entry from *RMA's Annual Statement Studies*. © "2002" by RMA—The Risk Management Association. All rights reserved. No part of this table may be reproduced or utilized in any form or by any means, electronic or mechanical, including photocopying, recording or by any information storage and retrieval system without permission in writing from RMA—The Risk Management Association. Please refer to www.rmahq.org for further warranty, copyright and use of data information.

MANUFACTURERS—APPAREL & ACCESSORIES, NEC SIC# 2389

Comparative Historical Data				Current Data Sorted By Sales					
			# Postretirement Benefits						
			Type of Statement						
	8	18	Unqualified	1		1	3	4	9
	9	16	Reviewed		6	2	2	6	
	11	15	Compiled	2	5	2	4	1	1
	6	3	Tax Returns	3					
	15	14	Other		1	1	2	5	5
					23 (4/1-9/30/97)		43 (10/1/97-3/31/98)		
4/1/95-3/31/96 ALL	4/1/96-3/31/97 ALL	4/1/97-3/31/98 ALL		0-1MM	1-3MM	3-5MM	5-10MM	10-25MM	25MM & OVER
	49	66	NUMBER OF STATEMENTS	6	12	6	11	16	15
%	%	%	ASSETS	%	%	%	%	%	%
DATA NOT AVAILABLE	5.8	6.1	Cash & Equivalents		7.9		4.6	5.3	2.9
	26.5	26.3	Trade Receivables - (net)		22.6		28.5	21.7	30.3
	38.3	40.6	Inventory		39.8		43.0	46.8	37.7
	1.3	1.8	All Other Current		4.0		3.9	.6	1.1
	71.9	74.7	Total Current		74.4		80.0	74.3	72.0
	20.8	16.3	Fixed Assets (net)		20.9		15.4	14.9	15.0
	3.6	4.6	Intangibles (net)		1.6		1.8	7.3	8.0
	3.7	4.4	All Other Non-Current		3.0		2.9	3.5	4.9
	100.0	100.0	Total		100.0		100.0	100.0	100.0
			LIABILITIES						
	17.4	18.2	Notes Payable-Short Term		15.6		24.6	18.1	16.2
	4.1	3.8	Cur. Mat.-L/T/D		4.6		6.8	3.3	2.7
	13.7	13.8	Trade Payables		13.3		13.4	18.1	10.2
	.6	.8	Income Taxes Payable		.0		1.1	1.6	.6
	7.4	9.9	All Other Current		5.2		8.8	14.8	10.6
	43.2	46.4	Total Current		38.8		54.7	55.9	40.3
	14.6	15.2	Long Term Debt		20.0		6.0	12.8	16.5
	.3	.3	Deferred Taxes		.1		.1	.7	.3
	2.9	3.0	All Other Non-Current		2.8		1.4	.7	9.0
	38.9	35.1	Net Worth		38.3		37.8	30.0	33.9
	100.0	100.0	Total Liabilities & Net Worth		100.0		100.0	100.0	100.0
			INCOME DATA						
	100.0	100.0	Net Sales		100.0		100.0	100.0	100.0
	35.0	30.1	Gross Profit		25.0		34.4	32.9	25.4
	30.6	25.7	Operating Expenses		22.3		29.8	26.8	21.6
	4.3	4.4	Operating Profit		2.7		4.6	6.1	3.7
	1.4	2.1	All Other Expenses (net)		1.9		1.5	2.5	3.1
	3.0	2.2	Profit Before Taxes		.8		3.1	3.6	.6
			RATIOS						
	2.6	2.5			4.6		1.6	2.1	3.2
	1.7	1.6	Current		1.5		1.4	1.3	2.3
	1.3	1.2			1.4		1.1	1.1	1.2
	1.2	1.3			1.5		.7	.7	1.5
	.8	.7	Quick		.7		.5	.5	1.3
	.5	.4			.5		.4	.3	.8
	22 16.5	**24** 15.1			**19** 19.2		**30** 12.2	**20** 18.5	**46** 7.9
	46 8.0	**41** 9.0	Sales/Receivables		**35** 10.4		**38** 9.6	**37** 10.0	**63** 5.8
	61 6.0	**65** 5.6			**51** 7.1		**68** 5.4	**59** 6.2	**76** 4.8
	44 8.3	**54** 6.7			**44** 8.3		**74** 4.9	**72** 5.1	**70** 5.2
	99 3.7	**104** 3.5	Cost of Sales/Inventory		**69** 5.3		**118** 3.1	**107** 3.4	**101** 3.6
	146 2.5	**152** 2.4			**183** 2.0		**126** 2.9	**183** 2.0	**146** 2.5
	14 25.2	**12** 29.3			**6** 61.8		**17** 21.5	**18** 19.9	**11** 33.8
	25 14.4	**29** 12.7	Cost of Sales/Payables		**18** 20.2		**33** 11.1	**30** 12.1	**18** 20.2
	49 7.5	**54** 6.7			**62** 5.9		**41** 8.9	**64** 5.7	**48** 7.6
	4.6	4.4			4.0		6.3	4.9	3.6
	8.4	7.6	Sales/Working Capital		6.6		13.2	16.4	4.5
	17.6	19.4			15.2		18.3	99.3	11.0
	5.5	4.3			3.7		4.3	4.2	6.9
	(45) 2.3	(61) 2.1	EBIT/Interest		(10) 1.7		(10) 2.5	(15) 2.5	2.8
	1.3	1.1			.5		1.0	1.4	.6
	3.0	3.0							
	(15) 1.9	(25) 1.6	Net Profit + Depr., Dep., Amort./Cur. Mat. L/T/D						
	.9	1.2							
	.2	.2			.1		.1	.3	.2
	.5	.4	Fixed/Worth		.5		.4	.6	.2
	1.4	1.4			4.9		1.3	2.8	−3.7
	.8	.9			.6		1.4	1.8	.8
	1.7	2.2	Debt/Worth		2.3		2.2	3.7	1.3
	7.0	6.8			13.3		3.2	11.4	−11.0
	46.0	31.9			27.8		20.5	53.5	33.9
	(44) 17.2	(56) 18.0	% Profit Before Taxes/Tangible Net Worth		(10) 7.1		18.0	(14) 22.3	(11) 23.3
	1.9	5.6			−1.7		13.1	6.2	12.1
	10.5	11.6			7.8		13.0	12.5	11.1
	6.0	5.0	% Profit Before Taxes/Total Assets		3.6		6.1	4.4	6.0
	1.2	.8			−1.7		3.1	2.0	−4.3
	45.8	34.0			125.3		54.3	28.4	25.6
	19.6	17.6	Sales/Net Fixed Assets		18.1		22.9	13.9	16.7
	7.1	9.9			6.0		10.1	9.1	9.7
	3.1	3.0			3.7		3.3	3.0	2.2
	2.1	2.0	Sales/Total Assets		2.2		2.4	1.9	1.7
	1.7	1.6			1.2		1.6	1.6	1.6
	.7	.6			.4		.4	.8	.8
	(42) 1.3	(61) 1.4	% Depr., Dep., Amort./Sales		(11) 1.5		1.1	(15) 1.8	(13) 1.3
	2.1	2.8			3.8		1.9	3.1	3.1
	2.8	2.1							
	(22) 5.3	(20) 3.0	% Officers', Directors', Owners' Comp/Sales						
	10.4	4.1							
	990693M	1899462M	Net Sales ($)	4000M	24034M	26322M	74167M	266279M	1504660M
	531217M	1053774M	Total Assets ($)	2118M	12371M	12878M	34155M	137198M	855054M

M = $ thousand MM = $ million

Figure 9.6 (*Cont.*)

As shown in figure 9.6, a typical entry in *Annual Statement Studies* consists of several vertical and horizontal columns and an almost bewildering array of figures. One of the easiest ways to understand the information that each entry contains is by using the center column to divide the left and right sides of the page, and to draw an imaginary horizontal line between the top of the page and the horizontal columns labeled "Ratios." Keeping these divisions in mind, some generalizations can be made about the information included for each industry.

The top part of the page begins with the name and SIC/NAICS[6] code of the industry being reported. In figure 9.6, for example, the industry is Manufactures, Apparel & Accessories and the SIC is 2389. Most of the information presented in the top half of the page is taken from balance sheets ("Assets" and "Liabilities") and income statements ("Income Data"). Instead of being expressed in dollars and cents, however, each item is expressed as a percentage. Thus, 40.6, the number shown in the "Inventory" column for all companies reporting, indicates that corporate inventories constitute 40.6 percent of total corporate assets for the 66 apparel and accessories manufacturers reporting.

Other divisions on the page should also be noted. Data to the right of the first page, for example, are historic; data to the left, current sorted by sales. The second page shows historic and current asset size. In addition, each page is categorized by size, grouped into six categories, ranging from companies with sales of less than $1 million to those with sales of $25 million and those with assets ranging from $0–$500,000 to $250 million. Thus, of the 66 manufacturers of apparel and accessories reporting in 2000, 9 had assets of less than $500,000, 14 had assets of more than $500,000 but less than $2 million, 24 had assets of between $2 and $10 million, 13 had assets of more than $10 million and $50 million, 4 had assets between $50 and $100 million, and 2 were in the top category. These categories are important because they permit comparison between companies of roughly comparable size.

Also included in the "Current Data" section at the top of the page is an indication of the financial periods being reported. The notations "23(4/1–9/30/97)" and "43(10/1/97–3/31/98)" indicate that 23 of the financial statements had fiscal dates falling between April 1 and September 30, 1997, and that the remaining 43 had fiscal dates falling between October 1, 1997, and March 31, 1998.

Columns to the right and left present consolidated historical data from earlier years. Note that historic financial information is not categorized by asset size of reporting companies and that the number of companies may vary from one year to another.

The bottom part of the page consists primarily of 16 different financial ratios, ranging from Current Ratio to a ratio of officers' compensation divided by net sales. The ratios, their derivation, and applications are described in the preliminary pages of *Annual Statement Studies*; only the names of the ratios are listed, with accompanying data, in the entry for each industry.

For each ratio, three different values—the upper quartile, median, and lower quartile —are given. Risk Management Association describes the methodology used for computing these values:

> For any given ratio, these figures are calculated by first computing the value of the ratio for each financial statement in the sample.................
>
> The array of values are then divided into four groups of equal size. The three points that divide the array are called quartiles.................
>
> The upper quartile is that point at which 1/4 of the array falls between the strongest ratio and the upper quartile point. The median is the middle value and the lower quartile is that point at which 3/4's of the array falls between the strongest ratio and the lower quartile point. [7]

Risk Management Association uses medians and quartiles instead of average figures to better reflect the full range of ratio values within an industry. Median and quartile values are always shown in this order: upper quartile, median, and lower quartile. For companies manufacturing apparel and accessories with assets between $10 and $50 million, for example, the array for one ratio, Current Ratio, is 2.4, 1.6, and 1.2. In other words, 1.6 is the median Current Ratio, 2.4, the upper quartile, and 1.2, the lower quartile. Just as with the variety of asset size classes for companies in a particular industry, the three different ratio categories make it possible to more thoroughly assess corporate performance.

Additional numbers are presented in boldface type for three of the ratios relating to sales. For example, the entry for the Sales/Receivable Ratio (in the current data sorted by sales) for manufacturers of apparel and accessories with assets of between $1 and $3 million is:

19	19.2
35	10.4
51	7.1

The numbers in boldface, which are always to the left of the ratios to which they refer, are for days. Using the example shown above, the median Sales/Receivable Ratio, which measures the company's ability to collect its accounts receivable, is 10.4, the number of days, 35. The 10.4 ratio means that the median company has annual sales equal to 10.4 times its receivables. The boldface number to the left of the ratio represents a conversion of the Sales/Receivable Ratio into days. In the case of the Sales/Receivable Ratio, the days' receivable figure represents the number of days that pass, on average, between company billing and the receipt of payment. In the example shown above, the company collects its money approximately 35 days after billing.

Some of the columns are empty. In the current data sorted by sales no data are given for the column 3–5 million. RMA omits the ratio values whenever there are fewer than 10 statements in a sample.

In addition to the data presented for each industry, *Annual Statement Studies* includes explanations of balance sheet and income data, definitions of ratios, a listing of SIC/NAICS codes covered, and a bibliography of sources of composite financial information for industries not included.

For the more than 600 industries covered, *Annual Statement Studies* is the most detailed information source of composite financial information available. It is a basic business reference tool; the time invested in learning what it contains and how to use it will reap ample returns. Risk Management Association cautions that the *Annual Statement Studies* be regarded only as a general guideline and not as an absolute industry norm. This is due to limited samples within categories, the categorization of companies by their primary SIC number only, and different methods of operations by companies within the same industry. For these reasons, RMA recommends that the figures be used only as general guidelines in addition to other methods of financial analysis. The data are also available in CD-ROM and online formats.[8]

Risk Management Association is now producing a companion volume to the *Annual Statement Studies*. This new volume, *Industry Default Probabilities and Cash Flow Measures,* now includes "average probability of Default Estimates, Cash Flow Measures, and Change in Financial Position information categorized by industry for 450 industries." This volume is being marketed as an extension of the *Annual Statement Studies.*

The *Almanac of Business and Industrial Financial Ratios* is another basic source. Compiled annually from data collected by the Internal Revenue Service, the *Almanac* provides 50 performance indicators on more than 179 different lines of business. Compared to the *Annual Statement Studies*, the *Almanac* covers fewer businesses and presents fewer ratios. Further, where *Annual Statement Studies* presents three different values (upper quartile, median, lower quartile), the *Almanac* includes only the industry average for each ratio. Finally, although both the *Almanac* and *Annual Statement Studies* are published yearly, data in the *Statement Studies* are more current. In contrast, information in the *Almanac* may be as much as four years old.

If these were the only differences between the publications, the *Almanac* would be of negligible value. However, although the *Annual Statement Studies* covers more industries in greater depth, it lacks some of the features available in the *Almanac*. First, a greater number of companies in each line of business are represented in the *Almanac*, which is based on tax returns rather than on financial statements submitted to banks. The industry composite for manufacturers of apparel in *Annual Statement Studies,* for example, is based on data from 66 firms, while the composite in the *Almanac* is based on tax returns from 861 companies. In addition, the *Almanac* uses a greater number of asset size categories. In all, 12 different categories are used, ranging in size from "zero assets" to "$250 million and more." The *Almanac* also distinguishes between profit-making companies and those that are not. Each entry is two pages long, with the first page presenting composite data for all companies in the industry, and the second page limited to companies that earned a profit for the year being reported. In many instances, these features result in even greater precision than is possible with *Annual Statement Studies*. Consequently, most business libraries subscribe to both publications.

A third basic source, *Industry Norms and Key Business Ratios: Desk Top Edition,* presents composite financial information for over 800 different lines of business, arranged by SIC. Based on data collected by Dun & Bradstreet for its credit reporting service, entries for each business include balance sheet and income statement information and 14 financial ratios. Although *Industry Norms and Key Business Ratios* does assign the same values to ratios as *Annual Statement Studies*, it does not categorize companies by asset size and generally includes less information for each line of business than either *Annual Statement Studies* or the *Almanac of Business and Industrial Financial Ratios*. Its real strengths are its timeliness and the wide array of industries it covers.

Only general data are supplied in the *Desk Top Edition*. Although Dun & Bradstreet also publishes a series of industry volumes that include detailed geographic and asset-size breakdowns and offers multiple formats, they are costly and are not available in most libraries.

The three titles discussed above are among the most important sources of composite financial information, but they are by no means the only ones. Others include the Census Bureau's *Quarterly Financial Report for Manufacturing, Mining and Trade Corporations* (http://www.census.gov/prod/www/abs/qfr-mm.html). The composite industry sources listed above are not inclusive. Not every industry is covered. "If," as Dick Levin writes, "you manufacture corrugated steel pipe, maple flooring, or fabricated roof trusses, or if you install ceiling tiles,"[9] the composite sources may not be particularly useful. In such instances, the best recourse is to identify sources of financial and ratio information for a single industry or group of related industries. Trade associations, accounting firms, large corporations, government agencies, and universities commonly issue such publications. Of these, trade associations are perhaps the most important providers of financial data, covering businesses and industries that are not included elsewhere. A sample of titles indicates the scope and diversity of these publications. The *NP&PA Key Business Ratios*, for example, is published by the National Paperbox Association, while the Merchandising Association offers *Key Indicators to Success: NAMA Operating Ratio Report for Vending Operators*. Most trade associations have a Web presence and can be found using a Google search or through the listings on Yahoo! at http://dir.yahoo.com/Business_and_Economy/Organizations/Trade_Associations/.

Not all libraries stock these specialized sources of financial information and accounting principles and standards. A number of more general publications are discussed below.

Sources of Accounting Information

The literature of accounting is voluminous. It includes numerous handbooks, loose-leaf services, periodicals, documents, and online sources, some written for accounting practitioners and others for nonaccountants. This section considers many of the types of accounting information sources generally consulted and lists and describes representative publications in each category. Readers should, however, keep in mind that the literature of accounting reflects continuing and continuous changes. As accounting theories, practices, and principles change, so also do many accounting sources.

Guides, Bibliographies, and Dictionaries

For librarians and researchers confronted for the first time with an accounting research problem, one of the best ways to gain familiarity with the literature is by referring to guides and bibliographies.

Daniells, Lorna. "Accounting/Control and Taxation." in **Business Information Sources**. 3rd ed. Berkeley: University of California Press, 1993, 313–38.

Although *Business Information Sources* is dated, it continues to be a major source of information. The chapter "Accounting/Control and Taxation" lists and annotates accounting handbooks and textbooks, periodicals, indexes and abstracts, loose-leaf services, and basic reference sources; it also features sections that deal with specific types of accounting such as management, government, and financial statement analysis and auditing. Also included are sections on accounting services, surveys of accounting practice, and accounting for multinational enterprises. Using the listed publications as a base it is easy to check for new editions and publications.

U.S. Superintendent of Documents. **Accounting and Auditing**. Washington, D.C.: Government Printing Office, 2000. (Subject Bibliography 42). 56p.

Accounting and Auditing, a bibliography published irregularly by the Superintendent of Documents, lists and annotates selected relevant federal documents in all formats. As with other bibliographies in the Superintendent of Documents' Subject Bibliography series, entries include annotations, Superintendent of Documents classification numbers, GPO stock numbers, prices, and ordering information. Although the emphasis is on government accounting, other subjects are also covered; accounting and auditing practices for small business, for example, are well represented. Like the other GPO Subject Bibliographies, *Accounting and Auditing* may be purchased online, or a free copy can be requested. [10]

The accounting profession has its own vocabulary and conventions. It includes many unique words and, in addition, uses familiar words in unique ways. As a result, most business reference collections supplement standard business dictionaries with specialized accounting sources. There are many different dictionaries available, some are more encyclopedic in scope and are usually available in academic libraries, and now there are also some available via the Web that may satisfy the needs of some researchers.

Abdel-Khalik, A. Rashad, ed. **Blackwell Encyclopedic Dictionary of Accounting.** Malden, Mass.: Blackwell, 1997. 308.

Siegel, Joel G., and Jae K. Shim. **Dictionary of Accounting Terms**. 3rd ed. Hauppauge, N.Y.: Barron's Educational Series, 2000. 488p.

Investorwords.com. **AccountingWords**. n.d. http://www.investorwords.com/cgi-bin/ bysubject.cgi?1. (Accessed August 18, 2003).

AICPA. **Glossary of Terms, Acronyms and Abbreviations**. n.d. http://www.aicpa.org/ members/glossary/a.htm. (Accessed August 18, 2003).

The *Blackwell Encyclopedic Dictionary* includes both definitions and explanations of major accounting terms. More than 100 contributors have compiled authoritative and comprehensive entries for terms ranging from "accounting for defeasance" to "warrants," many of which also include extensive bibliographies. The volume is extensively indexed and cross-referenced. This volume belongs in all libraries that support an accounting program.

Less comprehensive in the length of its entries but also possibly less intimidating to casual users, the *Dictionary of Accounting Terms* offers clear and concise definitions of 2,500 accounting terms and concepts, both those regarded as standard and new expressions. In addition, if examples are required for clarity, they are included. The *Dictionary* provides cross-references when appropriate and a list of acronyms and abbreviations in the appendix. This is another dictionary that should be in all libraries.

Investorwords began with an initial dictionary for investors but has since developed smaller Web compilations by subject. For those needing to occasionally check words, *Accounting Words* is a handy free tool. The company provides site licensing for a small fee.

Although the *Glossary of Terms, Acronyms and Abbreviations* contains many terms internal to the organization other more general terms are also included.

Handbooks and Encyclopedias

When more information is required than can be found in dictionaries, researchers frequently turn to handbooks and encyclopedias. Several such publications are available. Some deal with specialized fields of accounting and others are more general. Some are written for accountants, and some for managers, small business people, and others lacking accounting expertise.

Tracy, John A. **Accounting for Dummies**. 2nd ed. Foster City, Calif.: IDG Books Worldwide, 2001. 388p.

Understanding basic accounting concepts, applications, and vocabulary greatly enhances the ability of managers and business people to communicate with accountants and to assess corporate strength. *Accounting for Dummies* is not written for those who want to practice accounting but is an excellent aid for those who want to read and understand financial and accounting reports. Concepts are made easier to understand because of the many examples, templates, and worksheets.

Bragg, Steven M. **Accounting Reference Desktop**. New York: John Wiley, 2002. 615p.

Plank, Tom M., and Lois R. Plank. **Accounting Desk Book**. 11th ed. Englewood Cliffs, N.J.: Prentice Hall, 2000. 712p.

Handbooks for the professional accountant are equally abundant. Generally they come in two sizes: desk books, intended for quick reference, and detailed, comprehensive sources that are often published in more than one volume. The *Accounting Desk Book* and the

Accounting Reference Desktop, for example, are two such ready reference sources, each highlighting topics of wide interest and appeal.

Coverage in these handbooks varies, but each treats in depth the theory and practice of accounting and their application to business problems and includes references to major accounting pronouncements, including those of the AICPA and FASB.

More specialized handbooks and encyclopedias are also available. Some deal with accounting practices as they relate to specific industries; others reproduce accounting forms, letters; and reports, and still others present mathematical tables and formulas. Two volumes available in most libraries are described below.

Plank, Tom M., and Lois R. Plank. **Encyclopedia of Accounting Systems**. 2nd ed. ed. Englewood Cliffs, N.J.: Prentice-Hall, 1994. 2v.

Lipkin, Lawrence, Irwin K. Feinstein, and Lucille Derrick. **Accountant's Handbook of Formulas and Tables.** 3rd ed. Englewood Cliffs, N.J.: Prentice-Hall, 1988. 627p.

The *Encyclopedia of Accounting Systems* examines accounting practices and systems as they relate to specific industries, businesses, professions, and nonprofit organizations. Each chapter covers a separate industry and includes a general overview of the industry as well as a description of the basic design of the accounting system, data processing procedures, cost and payroll systems, plant and equipment records, and many other special features relating to the industry. The chapter on construction contractors, for example, includes a section on the functional peculiarities of the business, a chart of accounts for general contractors, and an example of a "percentage-of-completion" financial table. The *Encyclopedia* covers a wide assortment of industries and professions, ranging from aquaculture and funeral directing to scuba diving stores and real estate. It is one of the most comprehensive compilations of industry specific accounting systems and is widely used.

Accountants are frequently required to draw upon tables, formulas, and computations in performing their work. Most accountants and financial managers will use computer programs for mathematical problems and calculations, but the *Accountant's Handbook of Formulas and Tables* is still useful for those who need to check on a formula before performing a calculation or incorporating it into a computer program. The *Handbook* includes examples for many formulae and presents data on many topics in 17 different tables, including present value, square roots and reciprocals, sample size, and random decimal digits. Although the book is now out of print, it is held by many libraries and is still a worthwhile item in collections.

Directories

Representation of accountants and accounting firms in the standard business directories discussed in chapter 2 is rather sparse. Although thousands of companies are included in the *Million Dollar Directory*, only about 400 are listed under SIC 8721, the designation for accounting services. While *Standard & Poor's Register of Corporations, Directors and Executives* includes the names of the principal accounting firms representing many of the companies it lists, it has fewer than 75 entries for accounting firms themselves. To identify accounting firms or locate accountants, it is usually necessary to consult specialized directories.

CPAFirms.com. **List of CPA Firms.** n.d. http://www.cpafirms.com/Firmlist/. (Accessed August 18, 2003).

Emerson's Directory of Leading US Accounting Firms. Bellvue, Wash.: Emerson Company, 1998–. Annual

Who Audits America. Menlo Park, Calif.: Data Financial Press, 1976– . Semiannual.

List of CPA Firms indexes individual accounting practitioners, firms, and corporations whose partners are members of the American Institute of Certified Public Accountants. Searching is by region, state, area code, and name of accounting firm. The entries are brief, limited to name, address, and firm specialty, but there are links to Web pages when available.

Emerson's Directory of Leading US Accounting Firms has changed its focus from earlier editions and now concentrates on only the largest 500 firms. The information is more in depth than in earlier editions, and for each firm there is a history, a list of the top officers, the primary industry segments served, and consulting services offered. Included are various compilations of the 500: companies arranged by number of employees, by state and city, and by primary segments served, as well as an alphabetical listing of the top officers.

Who Audits America is a directory of publicly traded companies and the accounting firms that audit them. The first part of the directory focuses on the companies being audited. In addition to standard directory information, it provides the company's ticker symbol, the industry code for the primary product or service being sold, number of employees, corporate assets and sales, and the name of the accounting firm performing the audit for the period being covered. In addition, this section lists companies that have merged, been acquired, or changed their names since the last edition was published. The second part of *Who Audits America* focuses on auditors. It is arranged in several different parts, including a ranked listing of auditors by total sales of audited companies.

Periodicals

The importance and pervasiveness of accounting in almost every facet of business is reflected in articles appearing in general business periodicals and newspapers. Accounting is also well represented by specialized periodicals, which are particularly valuable for their presentation of current accounting theory and practice.

Journal of Accountancy. New York: American Institute of Certified Public Accountants, 1905– . Monthly.

The official journal of the American Institute of Certified Public Accountants, the *Journal of Accountancy* serves as the principal medium for the exchange of information and ideas by and for accounting practitioners. It includes articles on accounting, auditing, management advisory services, taxation, and related fields. Regular features include columns on computer applications, recent tax developments, and government and professional news. In addition, the *Journal* prints the complete texts of official pronouncements issued by the AICPA and the Financial Accounting Standards Board. Although the *Journal* is included in most business and some general periodical indexes frequently with the full text of the articles, it is also available from 1997 onward at the Web site, http://www.aicpa.org/pubs/index.htm. It is arranged by month and by year and is searchable in separate author and subject indexes at the site.

Other AICPA magazines and newsletters freely available from http://www.aicpa.org/pubs/index.htm are *The CPA Letter*, *CPA Exam Alert*, *In Our Opinion*, *The Practicing CPA*, *The Tax Advisor,* and recent accounting and auditing standards.

Periodical Indexes and Abstracts

Major accounting periodicals are either indexed or available full text in such standard business sources as *ABI/INFORM Global* and *Business Source Elite*. One specialized index, held in most major business reference collections, is also available.

Accounting & Tax Index. Ann Arbor, Mich.: UMI, 1992– . Quarterly, with 4th issue an
  annual cumulation.

In 1921, the AICPA Library published the *Accountants' Index*, an author, title, and subject index to English-language books and periodicals received by the library since 1912. Following publication of the original volume, supplements were issued every two or three years until 1971, when it became an annual. In 1992 this title was superseded by *Accounting & Tax Index,* which is issued quarterly with the fourth issue being the annual cumulation, and its coverage consists of 300 accounting and tax publications, including government documents, published proceedings, and official releases from the AICPA and FASB, as well as periodical articles. Fields covered include accounting, auditing, data processing, financial reporting, financial management, investment, and taxation. Cross-references are common. This is also available as the *Accounting & Tax Database,*[11] which contains full-text articles for more than 200 journals from 1991.

Loose-leaf and Electronic Services

Frequent changes in accounting practices, which in turn reflect changes in laws, regulations, and professional standards, make this a field in which loose-leaf services are still abundant despite the proliferation of online services. Many deal exclusively with accounting standards and principles; key examples have already been discussed in the sections on generally accepted accounting principles and auditing standards. Others on taxation are cited later in this chapter. Many of the well-known services such as Commerce Clearing House (http://www.cch.com), RIA (http://www.riahome.com/), and BNA (http://www.bna.com) provide both print and online products and services. It is impossible to mention more than a few of the products available, so for further information on the hundreds of products published it will be necessary for the researcher or librarian to check the product catalogs available at the company Web pages.

SEC Accounting Rules. Chicago: Commerce Clearing House, 1968– . Loose-leaf.

Although the Securities and Exchange Commission has delegated much of its responsibility for setting the standards for financial reporting and accounting, it nonetheless remains active in this sphere, issuing several series that affect financial accounting practice. Some of its most important publications are those from the Division of Corporate Finance and the Staff Accounting Bulletins, all of which are included in the *Accounting Rules,* which continuously updates all SEC rulings. This product is also available as a CD ROM or via the Internet.

Other services, aimed primarily at smaller accounting firms and individual practitioners, present practical information and advice and are really the loose-leaf equivalents of handbooks.

Guide to Managing an Accounting Practice. Fort Worth, Tex.: Practitioners Publishing Company, 1975– . 3v. Loose-leaf.

AICPA Technical Practice Aids. Chicago: Commerce Clearing House, 1975– . 2v. Loose-leaf.

Behrenfeld, William, and Andrew R. Biebl. **Accountant's Business Manual**. New York: American Institute of Certified Public Accountants, 1987– . Loose-leaf.

The *Guide to Managing an Accounting Practice* is a three-volume loose-leaf service that provides practical guidance and articles on developing an accounting practice and on administration, personnel, keeping pace with technology, and management data. It includes forms, sample letters, worksheets, and other illustrations and, in addition, presents financial ratios, balance sheets, and financial statements about accounting firms of various sizes, so that performance and profitability can be evaluated. Practitioners Publishing Company (http://www.ppcnet.com/eCatalog) also produces more specialized guides for accountants, including *Preparing Financial Statements*, *Real Estate Taxation*, and *Practical Estate Planning*. All products are available in loose-leaf, on CD-ROM, or as a Web service.

Technical Practice Aids, published by Commerce Clearing House for the AICPA, provides practical guidance for dealing with specific accounting and auditing problems in conformity with current standards and procedures. It covers financial statement presentation, assets, liabilities and deferred credits, capital, revenue and expense, audit fieldwork, auditors' reports, and specialized industry and organizational problems. The second volume includes Statements of Positions issued by both the AICPA Accounting and Auditing Standards Divisions and Lists of Issues Papers published by the AICPA Accounting Standards Division.

The *Accountant's Business Manual* focuses on an array of general business, legal, and financial topics relevant to accounting practice rather than on accounting and auditing per se. Topics covered include individual and corporate tax changes, obtaining financing, investment vehicles, insurance, employment regulations, cash management, business plans, unemployment insurance, and human resources. With the manual comes a CD-ROM that contains worksheets, sample agreements, checklists, and other forms that can be tailored to fit the user's needs.

Government Documents

Federal documents on accounting generally fall into three broad categories: "how to" booklets and pamphlets for small business people and nonaccountants, procedural manuals for the audit of private government contractors, and studies and audits of government agencies themselves.

The most prolific publisher of accounting aids for nonaccountants is the Small Business Administration, and most of its publications are available in both Microsoft Word and pdf format. Not only does the SBA publish short guides, but it also evaluates accounting software at http://www.onlinewbc.gov/docs/finance/acct_softw.html and offers links to shareware at http://www.sba.gov/library/shareware room.html#accounting.

Some of the publications offered by the SBA are *Understanding Cash Flow*, *Audit Checklist for Growing Businesses,* and *Record Keeping in a Small Business,* all of which can be downloaded from http://www.sba.gov/library/pubs.html#eb-7. All of these publications contain examples.

Companies doing business with the Department of Defense may be interested in publications issued by the Defense Contract Audit Agency, or DCAA.

U.S. Defense Contract Audit Agency. **DCAA Contract Audit Manual**. Washing on, D.C.: Government Printing Office, 19uu– . Loose-leaf.

Established in 1965, the Defense Contract Audit Agency (http://www.dcma.mil/) has the right to audit the books and records of any private contractor having a negotiated contract with the Department of Defense. Its *DCAA Contract Audit Manual* prescribes auditing policies and procedures and presents guidelines and techniques for DCAA personnel. Although the *Manual* is far too specialized for most library collections, librarians and researchers should be aware that such a publication exists and is available in most regional depository libraries and that some sections are available through a search on the Web at http://web2.deskbook.osd.mil/default.asp.

The General Accounting Office (http://www.gao.gov/), an agency of the legislative branch, is responsible for investigating and carrying out legal, accounting, auditing, and cost settlement functions of government programs and operations as assigned by Congress. Each year, it issues hundreds of reports and other publications that describe its findings, and these are now available from 1995 onward at the GAO Web page. GAO publications are also included in the *Monthly Catalog of United States Government Publications*.

Electronic Resources for Accounting/Taxation

Accounting is a discipline in which regular updates of materials are essential, and this has resulted in the proliferation first of loose-leaf products, and since the early 1990s, of CD-ROM and Internet accessible products. The accountant is now provided with much more timely information in the form that it is needed. The growth of international accounting has also increased the demand for quickly available information, and the following products supply a vast array of facts and analysis.

AICPA's reSOURCE ONLINE. New York: American Institute of Certified Public Accountants, 199?– . Internet.

BNA Tax Management. Washington, D.C.: Bureau of National Affairs, 1990s– . Internet.

CCH Incorporated. **CCH Internet Tax Research Network** Chicago: CCH, 1990s– . Internet.

RIA Group. **RIA Checkpoint.** New York: RIA, 1990s– . Internet.

reSOURCE ONLINE contains AICPA's professional standards, technical practice aids, financial reporting trends, and standard-setting guidance. The titles included are *AICPA Professional Standards, AICPA Technical Practice Aids, Accounting Trends & Techniques*, all current AICPA Audit and Accounting Guides, and all current Audit Risk Alerts. The database is updated monthly. For information on pricing check http://www.cpa2biz.com/, the online store for the AICPA.

BNA Tax Management covers U.S. income, estate, gifts and trusts, state, and foreign taxation. The service is divided into two libraries; the first covering foreign and U.S. and the second states. As with all the accounting resources online, content in *BNA* can be customized, and the areas for which there is no subscription paid appear in a lighter color. Subscription areas available in this service are *Portfolios Plus,* which provides practice tools and analysis for U.S. income, estate, gifts and trusts, and foreign income and journals and special reports; *Tax Practice,* which includes practice tools, analysis, and client letters for every area of taxation; and *State Tax,* which includes analysis, handbooks, legislation and regulation summaries, journals, and special reports for all U.S. state jurisdictions. Information on other products and prices is available at http://www.bna.com/.

CCH Internet Tax Research Network provides access to all of CCH's federal state and global products, which can be bought in modules and added on as the need arises or as money becomes available. As with all the online products guides, news, journals and Reporters are included, and all are searchable individually or as a group. Entries within search results are cross-linked, with the same symbol used in the loose-leaf files, and navigating within the service is relatively easy. Tax information is available, by year, from 1978 onwards. Pricing and contact information is at http://www.cch.com.

RIA Checkpoint is a database of U.S. federal, state, and global tax information. It contains primary federal tax resources such as the *Internal Revenue Code* and also a number of RIA full-text publications such as the *Federal Tax Coordinator* and the *RIA Federal Tax Handbook*. It also includes Warren, Gorham, and Lamont financial reporting and management resources such as the *Handbook of SEC Accounting and Disclosure* and several BNA products. More information is available at http://www.riahome.com/.

It is impossible in a short description to include all the features of any database, and this is especially true of the collections summarized above. The Web pages of each describe the wealth of materials included in each service and also give details about different subscription packages.

Most academic libraries will subscribe to at least one of these services, but because of licensing agreements they may not be available to the public. For this reason libraries may continue their subscriptions to some loose-leaf services.

Tax Basics

Librarians in almost every setting are called upon to provide information concerning taxation. This may range from supplying current federal and state income tax forms to stocking and providing access to, and assistance with, loose-leaf or online services that present and analyze the most recent tax laws, rulings, regulations, and coexistence or amount of sales tax levied in another city or town. Whatever the nature of such requests for assistance, the librarian's ability to understand and communicate with researchers about them will be enhanced by an understanding of the tax system and some of the key tax reference resources. This section briefly describes major types of taxes collected in this country, the government agencies responsible, and some of the tax sources most frequently consulted by laypeople and tax professionals.

Governments levy taxes to promote certain economic and social objectives such as economic growth and full employment, to finance their operations, and to provide such public goods and services as education, a system of national defense, and a network of roads and highways. In the United States, taxes are imposed by state and local governments as well as by the federal government. As a result, there is considerable variety in the tax structures and tax rates levied in different places by different levels of government.

Kinds of Taxes

As shown in figure 9.7, there are two basic kinds of taxes, excise and property. Excise taxes are directly imposed on manufacturing, selling, or using certain merchandise or products, or on certain occupations or activities, such as obtaining a license or transferring property. An excise tax is a fixed, absolute charge, a fee that is levied regardless of the taxpayer's financial status or ability to pay. Anyone in the same tax district who buys a gallon of gasoline or a quart of whiskey, for example, can expect to pay the same tax regardless of his or her economic status. Estate, gift, and sales taxes are all excise taxes.

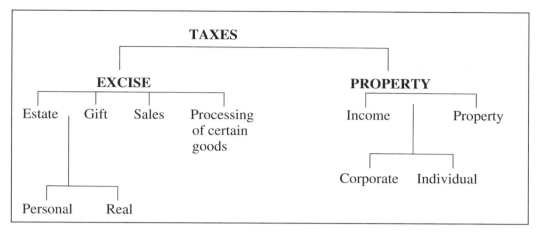

Figure 9.7. Types of taxes imposed by governments.

Property taxes are imposed on the basis of the value of certain property, whether it be real estate, personal property, or individual or corporate income. Such taxes are also called ad valorem taxes to indicate that they constitute a percentage of the value of the items being taxed.

As mentioned earlier, the tax structures for state and local governments vary considerably. Some states tax personal income, others do not. Most depend on excise taxes, particularly a sales tax, but while one state may tax only luxury items, others will tax food and prescription drugs as well. Local governments impose different tax measures but usually draw upon revenues raised from taxing real and personal property. Although the federal government imposes gift, estate, and certain processing taxes, its most productive sources of revenue are personal income and corporate taxes, both of which are collected by the Internal Revenue Service.

Internal Revenue Service

The Internal Revenue Service (IRS) (http://www.irs.gov) is responsible for administering and enforcing federal tax laws and related statutes. Its activities include the determination, assessment, and collection of taxes; determination of pension plan qualifications and exempt organization status; and the issuance of rulings and regulations. In addition, it handles taxpayer complaints and provides taxpayer service and education. The IRS's service and education roles are particularly important to libraries, which may regularly acquire IRS forms and documents for their users and may occasionally refer them to regional and district offices for more specialized assistance.

The IRS will, for example, supply libraries with multiple copies of frequently used forms and instructions. Orders for such materials can be made by toll-free telephone or can be sent by mail to an IRS distribution center. In addition, the IRS publishes the following annual document that offers access to even more forms.

U.S. Department of the Treasury. Internal Revenue Service. **Reproducible Federal Tax Forms for Use in Libraries.** Washington, D.C.: Government Printing Office, 1980– . (IRS Publication 1132). Annual.

Reproducible Federal Tax Forms is a compilation of forms and accompanying instructions for libraries to lend to their users for photocopying. It includes different forms, or parts of forms, ranging from Form 1040EZ for single filers with no dependents to Form

9465 "Installment Agreement Request." Arrangement is by form number, with subject and title indexes. Certain specially printed forms are not included but may be ordered from the IRS forms distribution centers listed on the inside back cover of the volume.

The IRS also issues these forms in CD-ROM format and via the Web at http://www.irs.gov/formspubs/index.html. Those forms marked "info copy only" are exclusively available directly from the IRS. Also accessible at this site are forms to download and use on personal computers and an easy-to-use help section for locating the correct forms. (See figure 9.8.)

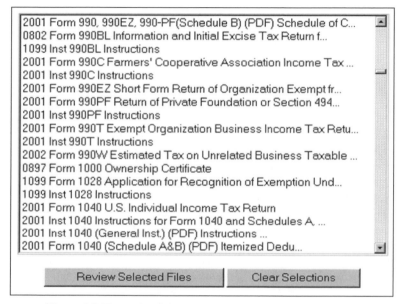

Figure 9.8. Example of listings downloadable from the IRS at http://www.irs.gov/formspubs/index.html.

Librarians would be well advised to retain superseded editions of *Reproducible Federal Tax Forms* as volumes for earlier years provide quick and convenient access to information and forms that might otherwise be difficult to find and are especially popular with patrons who need to file amended tax returns for previous years. These forms are also available from 1992 forward at the Web site. In addition to forms, the Internal Revenue Service publishes manuals, regulations, statistics, and decisions, some of which are discussed later.

The IRS offers free consultation by telephone regarding tax questions and problems. Telephone lines are often busy, however, particularly during the height of the tax preparing season, and callers are advised to be patient and persevere.

The Web site (http://www.irs.gov/) contains the latest tax information for individuals and businesses plus links to information on tax scams and a wealth of statistical data.

Other Government Agencies

Although the IRS is responsible for most of the federal taxes collected, another Treasury Department agency, the Bureau of Alcohol, Tobacco, and Firearms (http://www.atf.treas.gov/), is responsible for collecting revenues from the alcohol and tobacco industries.

In addition to federal agencies, each state has a department of taxation or revenue responsible for administering major taxes, including individual and corporate income taxes, and estate, sales, and other excise taxes. The names of state agencies, their tax rates, and the revenues they collect are included in several different sources, but one of the most convenient and readily accessible is *The Book of the States*. Even more detailed information is available in the *Multistate Corporate Tax Almanac.*

Council of State Governments. **The Book of the States**. Lexington, Ky.: The Council, 1935– . Annual.

Multistate Corporate Tax Guide. New York:Aspen Publishers, 1990– . Annual.

Schmidt Enterprises, LLC. **Tax and Accounting Sites Directory**. 1995–2003. http://www.taxsites.com/. (Accessed August 18, 2003).

In addition to chapters on state constitutions, branches of government, elections, management, personnel, and administration, *The Book of the States* includes one on state finances. It provides an overview of the states' budget procedures, their revenue sources, expenditures, and debts. It also includes a summary of recent trends in state taxation; lists agencies responsible for administering different kinds of state taxes; and presents tables showing by state excise tax rates, sales tax exemptions, and rates and exemptions on individual and corporate income tax returns. A short descriptive segment follows several sections, including that listing state amnesty programs.

The *Multistate Corporate Tax Guide* uses charts to compare different aspects of corporate taxation on a state-by-state basis, including such topics as S Corporations, Partnerships, Limited Liability Companies, and Limited Partnerships. In addition to charts, each section includes an analysis and description of trends. The *Guide* also features income, sales, and use taxation from the top state officials who interpret and apply the rules. This publication also includes a summary of key legislative and regulatory changes within states and charts that serve as a quick lookup service for questions on corporate taxation. This publication is also available on CD-ROM and via the Internet.

Just as taxes collected vary from one state to another, so also do services provided by state departments of revenue and taxation. At a minimum, however, most compile and publish pertinent statistics and, like the IRS, will make multiple copies of tax forms and instructions available to libraries as well.

Tax and Accounting Sites Directory is a superior listing of Web sites, with substantive information, in both accounting and taxation (see figure 9.9, page 218). The links range from the international to the local level. One can learn accurately what the European Union means by "Value Added Tax" or exactly which tax forms must be submitted to the state of North Carolina.

Extremely valuable to every user is the link to all states and then within the state to all the agencies involved with taxation. Any librarian or user with recourse to the Internet can now access copies of tax forms from any state and also discover the filing regulations. The *Directory* also links to local and municipal sites where available (see figure 9.10, page 219).

Tax and Accounting Sites Directory

Tax Sites

Tax Topics	Federal Tax Law	State & Local Tax	International Tax
Tax Forms & Pubs	Tax Software	Guides-Tips-Help	News & Updates
IRS Links	Rates & Tables	Tax Associations	Policy & Reform
Finance & Investing	Publishers & CPE	Tax Discussions	Academia
Tax Jobs	Firms & Careers	Tax Bookstore	Web Search

Accounting Sites

Financial Reporting	Auditing & Fraud	Managerial	Gov. & NFP
International	Information Systems	Software	AICPA Links
On-Line News	Regulatory Bodies	Associations	Certification
Firms & Careers	Government & Data	Publishers & CPE	Academia
Accounting Jobs	General Law	Web Services	Web Search

Tax and Accounting Jobs

Featured Jobs	Post Jobs

| Search | Add URL | About | Awards | Site Stats | Legal Disclaimer | Privacy Policy |

Copyright © 1995-2002 Schmidt Enterprises, LLC
Maintained by Dennis Schmidt
E-Mail: webmaster@taxsites.com

Figure 9.9. First screen of *Tax and Accounting Sites Directory*.
Reprinted with permission of www.taxsites.com.

Taxes collected by county, municipal, township, and special district governments vary so much that it is difficult to generalize about them. Some information is contained in the Census Bureau's *Census of Governments*, which includes data on taxable property values and tax assessment and on the finances of school districts, special districts, county governments, and municipal and township governments. The Census Bureau also publishes some surveys of state and local finance. All publications of the *Census of Governments* are available at http://www.census.gov/govs/www/index.html.

Tax and Accounting Sites Directory

North Carolina Tax Sites

State Tax Agency	**Legal Information**
Organizations	**Government Sites**

State Tax Agency

- Department of Revenue
    - Business Taxes
    - Corporate Income and Franchise Tax
    - Electronic Filing
    - Estate Tax
    - FAQs
    - **Forms and Instructions**
    - Gift Tax
    - Hot Topics
    - Individual Income Tax
    - Practitioner Page
    - Property Tax
    - Sales And Use Tax
    - Taxpayers' Bill of Rights
    - Withholding Tax

Legal Information

- Administrative Code
- Judicial Information
- Legislative Information
- Practitioner's Corner Tax Law
- Statutes
    - Corporate Tax Law
    - Individual Income Tax Law
    - Sales and Use Tax Law
    - Taxation
- Tax Bulletins
    - Corporate Franchise Tax
    - Corporate Income Tax
    - Individual Income Tax
    - Sales and Use Tax
- Tax Directives
    - Corporate Income Tax
    - Individual Income Tax
    - Sales and Use Tax

Organizations

- North Carolina Association of CPAs
- North Carolina Society of Accountants
- North Carolina Society of Enrolled Agents
- North Carolina Society of Tax Professionals

Government Sites

- State and Local Government Resources
- State Home Page

| Home | Search | Add URL | Legal Disclaimer |

Figure 9.10. ***Tax and Accounting Sites Directory*****, links to tax agencies and resources for North Carolina (http://www.taxsites.com/states/northcarolina.html).** Reprinted with permission of www.taxsites.com.

Federal Tax Law and Administration

Taxes imposed in this country's early history were limited primarily to excise taxes, which were repealed whenever the government had enough money to meet its rather limited needs. During the Civil War, income as well as excise taxes were levied, but it was not until the early 20th century that income tax became a permanent part of our lives. In 1909, Congress passed the Sixteenth Amendment to the Constitution, permitting the imposition of federal income tax. In 1913, after ratification by three-fourths of the states, it became law.

All three branches of the federal government are actively involved in the enactment and administration of tax law. The Joint Committee on Internal Revenue Taxation and the House Ways and Means and Senate Finance Committees are responsible for gathering information and holding hearings, which may eventually be reported to Congress and culminate in the passing of new or amended tax legislation. Federal tax laws are referred to collectively as the Internal Revenue Code, or Tax Code.

The Treasury Department is responsible for administering the Tax Code. It issues interpretations of the Tax Code, called Treasury Regulations, which are available in many regional depository and law libraries.

The Internal Revenue Service, in addition to collecting taxes, enforcing tax law, and issuing rulings in response to requests for guidance, interprets Treasury Regulations and negotiates disputes with taxpayers.

In the event that disputes between taxpayers and the IRS are not successfully negotiated, they can be taken to court. The Tax Court, federal district courts, and the Claims Court are empowered to hear cases involving the interpretation of tax law and its application in specific situations. Appeals are directed to U.S. Circuit Courts and to the U.S. Supreme Court.

The activities of these agencies of the federal government are important, because each is involved in amending or interpreting tax law. As amendments, rulings, regulations, interpretations, and court decisions are issued, they become part of the body of tax law and are in turn succeeded by rulings, regulations, interpretations, and court decisions pertaining to them. Such issuances are of vital concern to accountants, lawyers, and other tax professionals, who generally use either loose-leaf or electronic services to keep informed.

Tax Publications and Information Sources

A wide range of frequently revised publications pertaining to taxation are available. Some are aimed at the general public, others at tax specialists. Clearly, the selection and inclusion of such publications in any library collection will reflect the interests and needs of its particular clientele. This section considers some of the main types of printed and electronic sources of potential interest to library users.

Dictionaries

In many libraries, the accounting and general business and economics dictionaries on hand will be sufficient to handle requests for definitions of tax terms. More specialized tax dictionaries do exist, however. The titles listed below are typical.

Minars, David, and Richard A. Westin. **Shepard's McGraw-Hill Tax Dictionary for Business.** New York: McGraw-Hill, 1994. 478p.

U.S. General Accounting Office. **A Glossary of Terms Used in the Federal Budget.** January 1993. http://www.gao.gov/. (Accessed August 19, 2003).

Shepard's McGraw-Hill Tax Dictionary for Business is an abridged version of a text widely used by tax attorneys, *Shepard's 1992–1993 Tax Dictionary*. It lists and defines 6,000 legal, technical, and accounting terms, with entries ranging in length from a single sentence to a paragraph or more. It is directed at both tax professionals and the layperson who wants to clarify tax concepts. References to the Internal Revenue Code, Treasury Regulations, and case law are frequently included, as are cross-references to related terms in the dictionary.

Although not nearly as comprehensive, *A Glossary of Terms Used in the Federal Budget* offers clear, brief definitions, intended for use by agencies, professionals, and the layperson. Although the primary scope is budget terms, accounting expressions are also defined. Terms are grouped by category, with cross-references from one section to another. In addition, the *Glossary* includes a brief description of the federal budget process, appendixes, and a solid index. It is available in pdf format from the Web page and can be found by putting the title into the search box.

Income Tax Guides

Issued annually to reflect current tax practice, income tax guides help individuals, accountants, lawyers, and others to identify, interpret, and prepare the necessary forms to be filed with federal and state agencies. Most are fairly general, summarizing federal income tax requirements as they apply to individuals, businesses, corporations, and organizations. Others have a narrower focus. They may be similar to those pertaining to federal tax but may deal with tax laws in specific states, or they may emphasize tax practices that apply to specific occupations or professions.

General guides fall into three categories: those published by the Internal Revenue Service itself, those issued by publishers of major loose-leaf tax services, and popular guides. Some of the best are listed below.

U.S. Internal Revenue Service. **Your Federal Income Tax**. 2001. http://www.irs.gov/formspubs/index.html. (Accessed August 19, 2003).

Your Federal Income Tax is an IRS booklet that describes the types of tax returns that can be filed by individuals, including for each return step-by-step instructions and comments. It explains the tax laws that cover salaries, interest and dividends, capital gains, and other types of income, and discusses itemized deductions. Sample forms and schedules are included, as are numerous examples showing how tax law applies in certain situations. In addition, the booklet briefly summarizes important tax law changes. The IRS prepares many similar booklets (see figure 9.11, page 222), and all are obtainable from the Web site at http://www.irs.gov/forms_pubs/pubs.html. Libraries that supply tax information can now print any publication needed by patrons.

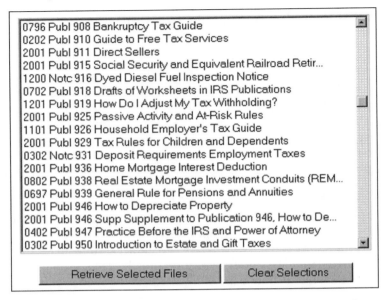

0796 Publ 908 Bankruptcy Tax Guide
0202 Publ 910 Guide to Free Tax Services
2001 Publ 911 Direct Sellers
2001 Publ 915 Social Security and Equivalent Railroad Retir...
1200 Notc 916 Dyed Diesel Fuel Inspection Notice
0702 Publ 918 Drafts of Worksheets in IRS Publications
1201 Publ 919 How Do I Adjust My Tax Withholding?
2001 Publ 925 Passive Activity and At-Risk Rules
1101 Publ 926 Household Employer's Tax Guide
2001 Publ 929 Tax Rules for Children and Dependents
0302 Notc 931 Deposit Requirements Employment Taxes
2001 Publ 936 Home Mortgage Interest Deduction
0802 Publ 938 Real Estate Mortgage Investment Conduits (REM...
0697 Publ 939 General Rule for Pensions and Annuities
2001 Publ 946 How to Depreciate Property
2001 Publ 946 Supp Supplement to Publication 946, How to De...
0402 Publ 947 Practice Before the IRS and Power of Attorney
0302 Publ 950 Introduction to Estate and Gift Taxes

Retrieve Selected Files   Clear Selections

Figure 9.11. More forms and publications available from the IRS.
Taken from the Web site at http://www.irs.gov/formspubs/lists/0,,id=97817,00.html.

Major publishers of loose-leaf tax services also issue tax guides. As compared to those mentioned above, they are more technical, and may include citations to their corresponding loose-leaf services or to the Tax Code itself. The two most commonly used guides are published by Commerce Clearing House, and the Research Institute of America.

U.S. Master Tax Guide. Chicago: Commerce Clearing House, 1943– . Annual.

Federal Tax Handbook. New York: Research Institute of America, 1975– . Annual.

Although there are some differences, these guides are quite similar in arrangement, format, and content. Each includes tax tables and schedules and a summary of recent developments. Like their loose-leaf counterparts, each uses numeric paragraph designation rather than page numbers to refer to specific topics, and each is arranged by broad topic. All have detailed subject indexes and, in addition, include footnotes citing references to more detailed information offered by the loose-leaf and online services. In addition, the *Federal Tax Handbook* includes editorial observations, notes, and warnings about specific tax practices. These guides are quite inexpensive and in many settings provide information sufficiently detailed to answer most tax-related inquiries. Libraries in which the need for information is more specific or highly specialized will, of course, need to subscribe to one or more of the loose-leaf or online services.

The third major type of general tax guide consists of popular guides written for laypeople. Such guides are in heavy demand at public and some academic libraries, particularly after major tax reform has been enacted. The quality of these guides can vary considerably, but two of the best are listed below.

Bernstein, Peter W., ed. **The Ernst & Young Tax Guide**. New York: John Wiley, 1992– . Annual.

H & R Block . . . Income Tax Guide. New York: Simon & Schuster 1990– . Annual.

The Ernst & Young Tax Guide is the only such guide issued by a Big 4 accounting firm. The *Guide* is well organized, and the information is comprehensive, including explanations, examples, tax-saving tips, and tax planning suggestions. A popular feature is a guide to the strategies to help plan the next tax year. Much of this material is also contained in the publication from *H & R Block,* but one special addition is the "Encyclopedia of Tax," a listing from A to Z of questions, tax problems, and issues.

Specialized tax guides include those focusing on taxes levied by specific states or on tax practices most likely to be of interest to a specific professional or occupational group. The titles that follow are typical.

CCH Tax Law Editors. **Guidebook to North Carolina Taxes**. Chicago: Commerce Clearing House, 1972– . Annual.

Tax & Financial Guide for College Teachers and Other College Personnel. Washington, D.C.: Academic Information Service, 2002– . Annual.

The *Guidebook to North Carolina State Taxes* is representative of commercially published state tax guides. Intended as a quick reference source, it describes general provisions of state tax laws, regulations, and administrative practice, and includes tax tables and explanatory paragraphs. References are made throughout the *Guidebook* to relevant sections in the state tax service, *CCH's North Carolina Tax Reports*. Included are "Highlights of Tax Changes," a detailed table of contents, "Law and Regulations Finding Lists," and a topical index. Similar guidebooks are published for other states.

The *Tax and Financial Guide for College Teachers* focuses on tax laws, rulings, procedures, and forms most likely to pertain to academicians. Although it lacks the footnotes and legal references included in the guides issued by loose-leaf publishers, it is more detailed than the popular guides and is often comprehensive enough to serve the needs of individual faculty preparing returns. Included is specific information on such topics as sabbaticals, honoraria, and rulings for graduate students. This publication belongs in all academic collections.

Directories

Although there are few tax directories per se, many business, accounting, and government directories list tax practitioners and organizations. The *United States Government Manual*, for example, lists key officials and regional and district offices of the IRS.

There is, however, a special directory that is used whenever information on tax exempt organizations is needed: the annual *Cumulative List of Organizations*, compiled by the IRS.

U.S. Department of the Treasury. U.S. Internal Revenue Service. **Cumulative List of Organizations Described in Section 170(c) of the Internal Revenue Code of 1986, Revised to September 30, 2001.** Washington, D.C.: Government Printing Office, 1954– . Annual.

The *Cumulative List* is a roster of organizations to which contributions are tax deductible. Each entry includes the organization's name and the city and state in which it is located. A coding system is also used that identifies each organization by type and the limitation on deductibility. Three cumulative quarterly supplements update the annual *List* by citing organizations to be added. The IRS also distributes this information via an online database at http://www.irs.gov/exempt/display/0,,i1%3D3%26genericId%3D15053,00.html. The database can also be found by entering *"Cumulative List of Organizations"* into the search box at the home page of the IRS (http://www.irs.gov). (See figure 9.12.)

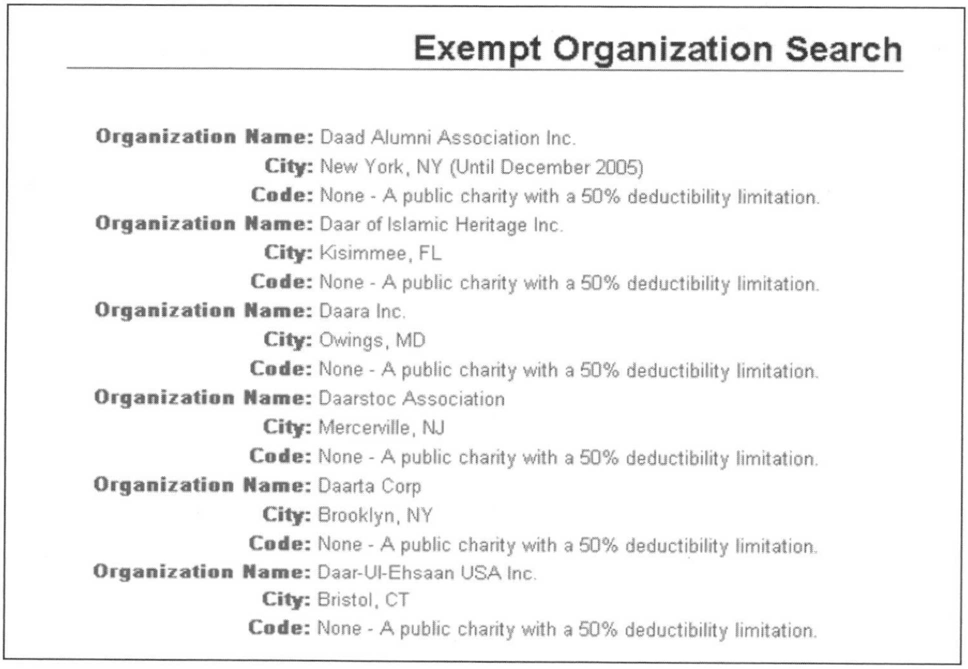

Exempt Organization Search

Organization Name: Daad Alumni Association Inc.
            City: New York, NY (Until December 2005)
           Code: None - A public charity with a 50% deductibility limitation.
Organization Name: Daar of Islamic Heritage Inc.
            City: Kisimmee, FL
           Code: None - A public charity with a 50% deductibility limitation.
Organization Name: Daara Inc.
            City: Owings, MD
           Code: None - A public charity with a 50% deductibility limitation.
Organization Name: Daarstoc Association
            City: Mercerville, NJ
           Code: None - A public charity with a 50% deductibility limitation.
Organization Name: Daarta Corp
            City: Brooklyn, NY
           Code: None - A public charity with a 50% deductibility limitation.
Organization Name: Daar-Ul-Ehsaan USA Inc.
            City: Bristol, CT
           Code: None - A public charity with a 50% deductibility limitation.

Figure 9.12. Typical listings, *Cumulative List of Organizations*.
Taken from http://www.irs.gov/charities/page/0,,id=15053,00.html.

Periodicals, Newspapers, and Indexes

Since professional tax assistance is most frequently provided by accountants and lawyers, many serials in those fields contain articles on tax law, theory, and practice. In addition, almost every type of periodical described in chapter 3 regularly features tax-related articles. These articles are most evident in January issues and whenever major tax reforms are enacted. Taxation also has special periodicals of its own, ranging from special interest publications such as the *Church Treasurer* and *Divorce Taxation* to serials with a much broader scope. Three such titles are discussed below.

National Tax Journal. Columbus, Ohio: National Tax Association—Tax Institute of America, 1948– . Quarterly.

The Journal of Taxation. New York: Warren, Gorham & Lamont, 1954– . Monthly.

Tax Features. Washington, D.C.: Tax Foundation, 1957– . Monthly.

The National Tax Association is an association of accountants, economists, attorneys, government tax officials, academicians, and others with an interest in taxation. One of its major goals is to promote the scientific, nonpolitical study of taxation, and one of the key publications that it uses to meet this goal is its quarterly periodical, the *National Tax Journal*. The most scholarly of the titles discussed in this section, the *National Tax Journal* features articles by scholars and practitioners that report research; analyze and evaluate current national, state, and local tax policy; and treat other issues pertaining to government finance. Articles, which deal with topics as diverse as tax evasion by small businesses to corporate income and the impact of state taxation on infrastructure services, include abstracts and bibliographies and frequently contain formulas and graphs.

The *Journal of Taxation* is written by and for tax practitioners and focuses more on technical and methodological concerns. It provides up-to-date information on the latest tax law changes, court decisions, revenue rulings, and administrative actions Articles are grouped by broad topic such as "Accounting" and "Compensation & Benefits," and each issues includes new rulings. The *Journal of Taxation* is indexed in most business and many general periodical indexes. Details about the online version of this journal are available at http://www.riahome.com/estore/.

Tax Features, published monthly by the Tax Foundation (http://www.taxfoundation. org/), is available free in the United States to public and university libraries, teachers, government officials, and members of the working press. It is a newsletter that presents news and analytical articles on taxation and government spending.

Tax articles are included in *Business Source Elite*, *Business Source Premier*, *ABI/INFORM Global*, the *Wall Street Journal*, and most other business periodicals' online collections. In addition, Commerce Clearing House publishes a loose-leaf service that indexes and summarizes articles on federal taxation.

Federal Tax Articles. Chicago: Commerce Clearing House, 1968– . Loose-leaf, with monthly updates.

Federal Tax Articles is an annotated listing of articles, comments, and notes published in 250 tax, accounting, legal, and other professional journals. The summary of each article includes the highlights of the main points plus citations to applicable cases, rulings, and regulations, which enables the user to quickly find primary materials. Articles are grouped together under the section(s) of the Internal Revenue Code to which they apply. Further access is provided by topical and author indexes.

Loose-leaf Services

Taxation is a complex field, made particularly so by the diversity of taxes collected at each level of government and by the voluminous and frequently changing laws, regulations, and other government issuances pertaining to them. As a result, it is an area in which loose-leaf and online services are abundant.

Although the nature and extent of these services will vary from one library to another, many business reference collections will include at least one of the comprehensive federal tax services listed below. These multivolume services present and analyze tax law, court cases and decisions, and IRS administrative rulings.

Federal Tax Coordinator 2d. New York: Research Institute of America, 1970– . Loose-leaf, with biweekly updates.

Standard Federal Tax Reporter. Chicago: Commerce Clearing House, 1913– . Loose-leaf, with weekly updates.

The overlap between the *Federal Tax Coordinator 2d* and the *Standard Federal Tax Reporter* is considerable. Both include topical indexes, case tables, and numerical finding lists, permitting research by subject, case name, and numerical citation. Each, however, has certain unique characteristics and, as a result, has its own loyal following.

The *Federal Tax Coordinator 2d* has thorough coverage of income, FICA, FUTA, estate, gift, and excise taxes organized by subject.. Each chapter deals with a fairly broad topic, such as income tax deductions or estate tax, and each occupies its own volume. Further, each chapter begins with a description of the taxes normally collected, followed by a detailed table of contents. It, in turn, is followed by descriptions of problems in the designated area. Frequently the tax explanations include illustrations, observations, recommendations, and cautions. Citations to supporting authorities are included in footnotes at the bottom of each page. Following the explanatory section is a verbatim reprint of all pertinent Tax Code and Treasury Regulation sections.

While the *Federal Tax Coordinator 2d* may be particularly popular with novice tax researchers, professionals more often turn to the *Standard Federal Tax Reporter*. Arranged by Internal Revenue code section, this service includes statutes, regulations, notes of court and administrative decisions, other administrative documents, some legislative history, and commentary. Finding aids include lists of Revenue Rulings, cases, Treasury Decisions, and Private Letter Rulings, all linked to the relevant paragraph numbers. This service tends to offer greater detail and more thorough analysis. It is available as a 25-volume loose-leaf service and as part of the *Federal Tax Libraries* section of the *CCH Internet Tax Research Network* (http://www.cch.com).

Space does not permit detailed consideration of these services' respective contents, format, and arrangement, but such information is readily available in the descriptive information, and through the list of contacts and request for information tags available on the Web sites of their publishers.

In addition to the multivolume, comprehensive loose-leaf services described above, a number of smaller, more highly specialized tax services are also available from the same publishers. These include titles that focus on a specific type of tax, such as sales or estate and gift tax, or that present state tax law in all 50 states or in a single state.

Government Publications and Services

Federal tax publications generally fall into three broad categories: (1) income tax guides and instructional booklets published by the Internal Revenue Service; (2) statistics compiled from tax returns; and (3) congressional publications, tax laws, regulations, and court decisions. Although there is no government-issued bibliography that provides a full listing of all such publications, a Superintendent of Documents' subject bibliography lists current publications.

Government Printing Office. **Taxes**. (Subject Bibliography 195). November 20, 2001. http://bookstore.gpo.gov/sb/sb-195.html. (Accessed August 19, 2003).

Taxes, available from http://bookstore.gpo.gov/sb/sb-195.html, lists and sometimes annotates tax-related publications issued by the IRS, the Congress's Joint Committee on Internal Revenue Taxation, and other federal agencies. Emphasis is on titles of potential interest to researchers and tax practitioners rather than to the general public; lists of IRS tax information publications are not included. As with other bibliographies in this series, prices and Superintendent of Documents classification and stock numbers are also included.

Although the Government Printing Office has also compiled a list of Internal Revenue Cumulative Bulletins (Subject Bibliography 194) (http://bookstore.gpo.gov/sb/sb-066.html), the IRS offers information that is both more current and more comprehensive at http://www.irs.gov.

Many of the most important IRS guides and instructional publications have been discussed in earlier sections of this chapter. Compilations of tax statistics, the second major type of federal tax publication, are described in the section that follows. Finally, while discussion of the myriad of laws, regulations, and court decisions that comprise the third major type of federal tax information is more appropriate to a legal text, a few such publications should be noted.

U.S. Department of the Treasury. Internal Revenue Service. **Internal Revenue Bulletin.** n.d. http://www.irs.gov/business/lists/0,,id=98230,00.html. (Accessed August 22, 2003).

———. **Internal Revenue Cumulative Bulletin**. n.d. http://www.irs.gov/business/lists/0,,id=98230,00.html. (Accessed August 22, 2003).

The *Internal Revenue Bulletin* lists and announces official IRS rulings and procedures, and publishes Treasury Decisions, Executive Orders, Tax Conventions, legislation, court decisions, and other items pertaining to taxation. Each issue is divided into four main parts: rulings and decisions based on the provisions of the 1986 Internal Revenue Code; treaties and tax legislation; administrative, procedural, and miscellaneous; and items of general interest. The highlights of each issue are described on its cover, and the first Bulletin for each month features an index to the preceding month's issues. Published in paper since 1954, all Bulletins, since 1996, are now free on the Web.

Twice a year, the weekly issues of the *Bulletin* are consolidated into a permanent, indexed source, the *Internal Revenue Cumulative Bulletin*. Each *Cumulative Bulletin* follows the same general arrangement as the weekly *Bulletin* but also includes a subject index, finding lists, a. cumulative list of announcements relating to Tax Court decisions published in the *Bulletin*, and a list of tax practitioners (primarily attorneys and CPAs) who have been disbarred from or voluntarily consented to suspend preparing tax returns for a specified time period. Published since 1969, the issues for 1995 onward are available on the Web.

Statistics

Tax statistics generally fall into two main categories, those published by the government and those issued by other organizations, including trade associations, research organizations, and commercial publishers. Statistics published by the government are frequently summarized or presented in condensed form in the *Statistical Abstract of the United States* and many of the statistical compilations described in chapter 6. There are, however, sources compiled by the IRS's Statistics of Income Division that provide more detailed information on federal taxes.

U.S. Department of the Treasury. Internal Revenue Service. **Statistics of Income Bulletin.** Washington, D.C.: Government Printing Office, 1981– . Quarterly.

———. **Tax Statistics**. c2000. http://www.irs.gov/taxstats/article/0,,id=97067.html. (Accessed August 22, 2003).

The *Statistics of Income Bulletin* provides published annual financial statistics from various tax returns filed with the Internal Revenue Service. These statistics are presented in the *Bulletin*'s "Selected Statistical Series" section, which includes current and historic statistics on individual income rates and business tax returns, as well as returns submitted by sole proprietorships, partnerships, and corporations. Other tables highlight gross IRS collections and receipts, excise taxes, and projections of returns. In addition, the *Statistics of Income Bulletin* includes articles on a wide range of subjects, including demographic characteristics of taxpayers, high income tax returns, and environmental taxes. (See figure 9.13.) The *Bulletin* is also available on the Web at http://www.irs.gov/taxstats/display/ 0,,i1%3D40%26genericId%3D16810,00.html or by clicking on Tax Stats at http://www.irs.gov and then checking the list of publications.

Selected Occupations, by Sex, 1998 Estate Tax Decedents
[All figures are estimates based on samples--money amounts are in whole dollars]

Occupation	Male decedents			Female decedents		
	Number	Percent of all male decedents [1]	Average gross estate, date of death	Number	Percent of all female decedents [1]	Average gross estate, date of death
	(1)	(2)	(3)	(4)	(5)	(6)
Managerial and professional specialty occupations:						
Executive, managerial	16,335	30.0	2,675,886	5,187	20.6	1,890,390
Engineers, architects, surveyors	4,209	7.7	1,516,743	102	0.4	1,224,626
Healthcare	3,996	7.3	1,934,376	1,853	7.4	1,245,455
Teachers, librarians, curators	2,067	3.8	1,364,344	5,175	20.6	1,482,169
Lawyers, judges	2,368	4.3	2,601,075	143	0.6	2,531,771
Writers, artists, entertainers, athletes	853	1.6	2,342,885	1,048	4.2	1,999,665
Technicians	799	1.5	1,208,524	412	1.6	1,214,519
Sales supervisors	5,838	10.7	2,529,903	1,473	5.9	1,906,510
Insurance sales	821	1.5	1,655,154	136	0.5	1,063,652
Real estate sales	687	1.3	2,053,182	610	2.4	1,367,420
Securities and financial services	592	1.1	2,971,197	119	0.5	1,387,493
Other sales occupations	2,844	5.2	1,582,394	786	3.1	1,210,227
Administrative support	1,189	2.2	1,373,765	5,328	21.2	1,266,137
Service occupations	752	1.4	1,276,952	737	2.9	1,371,066
Farm	4,210	7.7	1,373,738	729	2.9	1,650,123
Precision production, craft, repair	3,018	5.5	1,281,955	216	0.9	1,361,007
Operators, fabricators, laborers	1,774	3.3	1,471,482	309	1.2	1,163,374

[1] Decedents for whom an occupation was not reported, including those who were homemakers or retired, were eliminated from this analysis.

Figure 9.13. Federal estate tax returns from the *Statistics of Income Bulletin* (Spring 2002).

Most of the information available from the IRS is contained in the Statistics of Income series, which includes separate sections for individual, partnership, and corporate income tax returns. The data, reports, and research studies are available from http://www.irs.gov from the *Tax Statistics* section (see figure 9.14).

Privately published compilations of tax statistics include those made available in the *Book of the States*, the *Multistate Corporate Tax Almanac*, and other commercially published sources. The Tax Foundation issues another useful compilation.

Facts and Figures on Government Finance. Washington, D.C.: Tax Foundation, 1941– . Biennial.

Facts and Figures on Government Finance contains about 300 tables providing current and historical data on government revenues and expenditures at the federal, state, and local levels. Each table cites the source(s) from which data were gathered and frequently date back for several years; some date back as far as 1902. A glossary and subject index are also included.

Many trade associations, particularly those representing industries that must pay special taxes, include relevant tax statistics in their publications or at their Web sites. Typical of these are the American Trucking Association (http://www.trucking.org/) and the Distilled Spirits Council of the United States (http://www.discus.org/). Such industry-specific data can usually be identified by consulting the *Statistical Reference Index*.

Internal Revenue Service The Digital Daily

DEPARTMENT OF THE TREASURY

Home | Tax Stats | About IRS | Careers | FOIA | The Newsroom | Accessibility | Site Map | Español | Help

Search IRS Site for:
[   ] GO

Search Forms and Publications for:
[   ] GO

Search Help

contents

Individuals
Businesses
Charities & Non-Profits
Government Entities
Tax Professionals
Retirement Plans

resources

e-file
Forms and Publications
Where To File
Contact My Local Office
Frequently Asked Questions
Taxpayer Advocate

Home > Tax Stats

Tax Stats

Tax Statistics - Produced by the Statistics of Income Division and other areas of the Internal Revenue Service

Announcements
Brief descriptions of recent major additions to Tax Stats are shown here.

Tax Stats at a Glance
The Statistics of Income (SOI) program produces data files compiled from samples of tax and information returns filed with the IRS. There's a wealth of information about the financial composition of individuals, business taxpayers, tax exempt organizations and more. Look here for some summary statistics from these files, as well as files from other IRS sources.

IRS Statistical Overview
Locate here information on the number of returns filed with IRS, as well as the collections received by, and the refunds paid by, the IRS. There's also statistics on examination activities, taxpayer assistance provided by IRS, and criminal enforcement activities.

Statistics by Topic
Look here for your specific topic. It could include individuals, corporations, or tax exempt organizations. Or, perhaps you're interested in employment, estate, or excise taxes. There's even more, like the international area.

Statistics by Form
Look here for data on your specific topic using these selected IRS form numbers and titles.

Statistical Publications
Find links here for the IRS Data Book, the Statistics of Income Bulletins, and other SOI publications. You can also access projections data and research bulletins.

Statistics of Income
Learn about the Statistics of Income program, which produces most of the IRS statistics. This area includes information on SOI studies, products, and services. It also discusses careers with SOI and provides links to SOI Bulletins.

Papers
Look here for papers written by members of the Statistics of Income Division of IRS and presented at various conferences, as well as papers written by other IRS employees and others at IRS Research Conferences.

Tax Stats Dispatch Mailing List
Do you want announcements covering the most recent tax statistics? Then join our mailing list.

Questions or Comments
If you have a question about TAX STATS ONLY, here's the place to send it to us. We will promptly get back to you.

PDF Documents
PDF is a common format used here and it allows you to view documents on-line electronically for most computers. This area will link you to the freely available Adobe Acrobat reader that is required to view and print PDF files.

Figure 9.14. Listing of statistical tables provided by the IRS at http://www.irs.gov/taxstats/index.html.

Notes

1. Martin Rosenberg, *Opportunities in Accounting Careers* (Lincolnwood, Ill.: VGM Career Horizons, 1983), 2.

2. Ordering information available at http://www.aicpa.org/edu/candpubl.htm.

3. Wendy McKenzie, *Financial Times Guide to Using and Interpreting Company Accounts* (London: Prentice Hall, 1998), 11.

4. Steven A. Moscove, *Accounting Fundamentals for Non-Accountants,* rev.ed. (Reston, Va.: Reston Publishing, 1984), 7.

5. James E. Kristy and Susan Z. Diamond, *Finance without Fear* (New York: AMACOM, 1984), 45.

6. RMA presently uses both SIC and NAICS codes but plans on switching by the fall of 2004 to NAICS codes only. (Information on the Web page at http://www.rmahq.org/Ann_Studies/asstudies.html.)

7. Risk Management Association, *2001/2002 RMA Annual Statement Studies*. (Taken from the Web page at http://www.rmahq.org/Ann_Studies/ratiodef.html.)

8. Description and ordering information available from Risk Management Association at http://www.rmahq.org/Ann_Studies/asstudies.html.

9. Dick Levin, *Buy Low, Sell High, Collect Early and Pay Late: The Managers Guide to Financial Survival* (Englewood Cliffs, N.J.: Prentice-Hall, 1983), 102.

10. These can be ordered for a small charge from http://bookstore.gpo.gov/sb/about.html or can be obtained free upon request from:

> Superintendent of Documents
> U.S. Government Printing Office
> Washington, DC 20402

11. *Accounting & Tax Database* is available from:

> ProQuest
> 300 North Zeeb Rd.
> PO Box 1346
> Ann Arbor, MI 48106-1346
> Phone: (734) 761-4700
> Toll free: (800) 521-0600
> E-mail: info@il.proquest.com
> Web: http://www.proquest.com/

10

Money, Credit, and Banking

The availability of money and credit has a profound influence on the way business is conducted. Whether a company chooses to expand operations or lay off employees, whether retail stores maintain large or small inventories, or whether real estate sales soar or plummet is to a very large extent determined by money supply, interest rates, and the financial institutions and government agencies responsible for both. This chapter begins by considering briefly the basic characteristics of money, monetary measures, and foreign exchange. It next covers commercial and consumer credit, then proceeds to discuss such financial institutions as commercial banks, savings and loan associations, and credit unions, as well as such government agencies as the Federal Reserve System and the Federal Deposit Insurance Corporation. It concludes with the identification and description of key reference and research sources.

Money

One of the characteristics that distinguishes advanced cultures from more primitive ones is the widespread use of money, rather than barter, for the exchange of goods and services. Although one culture may designate wampum or fur pelts as money and another may choose gold and silver, money serves three major functions regardless of the forms it takes. First, money serves as the accepted medium of exchange; it is a tool to facilitate transactions. Second, it serves as a standard of value. In the United States, for example, librarians' salaries and television sets are priced by assigning dollar values to them. Finally, money serves as a store of value; it can be saved to permit future purchase of goods and services.

Money in the United States has evolved from such commodities as tobacco and gunpowder to the coins, paper currency, and demand deposits (checking accounts and other checkable deposits held by banks and thrift institutions) presently in use. Although most laypeople think of currency as comprising the bulk of our money supply, demand deposits are the most common form of money. Most payments today are made by check or by electronic transfer of funds from one account to another; few individuals or businesses use cash to pay for major purchases. Demand deposits and their role in the nations' money supply are discussed at length in the section on banks.

Monetary System

Most countries have a monetary system comprising the various kinds of money (for example, coins, currency, and demand deposits), the rules and regulations regarding their issuance and control, and the organizations responsible for them. The Constitution of the United States, for example, grants Congress the power to coin money and regulate its value. Congress has in turn delegated this money power to the Department of the Treasury and the Federal Reserve System and, through it, to commercial banks.

Monetary Measures

As economies become more complex, so also do their monetary systems, which is reflected in the way money is measured. The Federal Reserve System is responsible for collecting and publishing data on money supply in the United States. To do so, it has created a series of measures, M 1, M2, M3, and L, that it uses to determine just how much money there is. Although this book does not delve deeply into the characteristics and uses of these alternative measures, please note here that the measures progress from MI, the narrowest definition of money supply, to L, the most inclusive, and that all are listed and defined in the Federal Reserves' most important periodical, the *Federal Reserve Bulletin*.

Foreign Exchange

The growth of foreign trade and travel is reflected in the increasing number of questions that librarians and researchers must answer regarding foreign money and its value relative to the dollar. Although any number of sources list foreign currencies, one title is particularly useful for detailed information.

Cowitt, Philip P., ed. **World Currency Yearbook**. Brooklyn, N.Y.: International Currency Analysis, 1955– . Annual. (Formerly *Picks' Currency Yearbook*.)

For each country listed in the *World Currency Yearbook*, a discussion of its currency's history, transferability, recent developments, and administration is included, supplemented by annual statistics covering the past decade for currency circulation and official, free market, and, when applicable, black market exchange rates. Annual exchange rates are useful for tracking changes over time.

Frequently, however, the need is for more current information. In such instances, the daily foreign exchange tables published in newspapers or on the Web are the best place to begin. Although not all countries are represented in such tables, those in which trading is heaviest are included. One of the best currency converters available on the Web is maintained by OANDA.com (http://www.oanda.com/convert/classic). This site provides exchange rates for 164 currencies. The noon buying rates are also supplied by the Federal Reserve Bank of New York (see figure 10.1).

Country	Monetary Unit	Noon Buying Rates
+ European Monetary Union	Euro	0.9752
+ Australia	Dollar	0.5468
Brazil	Real	3.1510
Canada	Dollar	1.5737
China, P.R.	Yuan	8.2770
Denmark	Krone	7.6228
Hong Kong	Dollar	7.8000
India	Rupee	48.5200
Israel	Shekel	N/A
Japan	Yen	119.7800
Malaysia	Ringgit	3.8000
Mexico	Peso	9.9700
+ New Zealand	Dollar	0.4700
Norway	Krone	7.5823
Philippines	Pesos	N/A
Singapore	Dollar	1.7576
South Africa	Rand	10.6480
South Korea	Won	1194.1000
Sri Lanka	Rupee	96.1000
Sweden	Krona	9.4255
Switzerland	Franc	1.4960
Taiwan	N.T. Dollar	34.3000
Thailand	Baht	42.5200
+ United Kingdom	Pound	1.5544

Figure 10.1. Federal Reserve Bank of New York, sample of daily exchange rates
(http://www.ny.frb.org/pihome/statistics/forex12.shtml).

Credit

Credit, usually defined as the promise to pay in the future in order to buy or borrow in the present, is an integral part of our economy. Consumers, corporations, businesses, even governments use credit on a regular basis. This section examines credit from two different perspectives: What a bank or other creditor looks for when deciding whether to grant credit, and what the prospective recipient, or debtor, seeks.

Creditworthiness

One of the major elements in determining whether to extend credit is the creditworthiness of the individual or organization seeking it. The granting of credit, in other words, is based on the creditor's confidence in the debtor's ability and willingness to repay the loan in accordance with the terms of the agreement. To determine creditworthiness, the creditor begins by considering three factors, sometimes called "the three Cs": capacity, capital, and character.

Capacity is the debtor's present and future ability to meet financial obligations. In determining the capacity of a small business person to repay a loan, the creditor may take into account the applicant's business experience, general background, and demonstrated ability to operate a business profitably. Someone seeking a consumer loan, on the other hand, would be quizzed about his or her employment history and present level of debt.

The second factor is capital, the assets held by the debtor. Capital includes such items as savings accounts, securities portfolios, insurance policies, pension funds, and property, any of which might be used as collateral to secure the loan.

Capacity and capital help creditors to determine an applicant's ability to repay a loan. Equally important, however, is the applicant's willingness to repay, designated by creditors as character. Although character lends itself less easily to objective measurement than capacity or capital, certain factors such as the person's reputation, known associates, and credit history are considered to be important components of character. Of these, the most important to creditors is credit history.

Credit Reports

Creditors rely heavily on credit histories—records of how past debt obligations were handled—to make decisions about applicants. Such histories are contained in credit reports sold to banks and other organizations by credit bureaus and credit reporting services. Most credit bureaus are local. The credit reporting services, on the other hand, are large, national operations.

Dun & Bradstreets' *Business Information Reports* is one of a series of confidential ratings that presents credit histories and other information on companies and businesses. A report may range in length from 1 or 2 pages to 20 or more, but it includes the credit history, which notes outstanding debt, bills past due, late payments, and related data, as well as brief descriptions of the business and its key officers, current financial conditions, and banking information. In addition, special events such as burglaries or executive changes are noted, as are such public civil filings as lawsuits and tax liens. A credit rating assigned by Dun & Bradstreet is also included.

Two points about the *Business Information Reports* and other, similar credit reports should be noted. The first, and most important for libraries, is that such reports are sold only to financial organizations, businesses, and individuals with legitimate needs for them. They are not made available to business competitors, and they are not intended to be accessible to the public. As a result, except in libraries where access to the public is restricted, they are not a part of library collections.

The second is that while the credit history itself is based on data supplied by creditors, the company being rated supplies some of the remaining information, such as the description of current financial conditions, and is under no obligation to provide full or even accurate information.

There are also compilers of personal credit reports. Many of them are prepared or at least sold by local credit bureaus. Whether they are prepared locally or at some distant location, such reports generally include the person's name, address, and Social Security number; credit history; details concerning current and past employment; and such personal information as date of birth and number of dependents. Like their business counterparts, personal credit reports are intended primarily for financial institutions and other creditors and are not available in libraries. The two major companies who supply these reports are Experian (http://www.experian.com/) and EQUIFAX (http://www.equifax.com/). Consumers may access a free copy of their credit reports from these agencies. If the report is found to be in error, the issuing agency must amend it and submit the revised version to the creditor(s) or consumer who originally requested the report.

Interest

While creditors are most interested in culling creditworthy applicants from those who are not, those same applicants are concerned with getting the best terms possible. Although the terms of a loan may include such factors as loan fees and service charges, the single most important item is interest. Interest is the price that borrowers pay to lenders for credit over specified periods of time; it is, in effect, a rental fee paid for the use of money. The amount of interest paid is based on a number of factors: the amount of the loan, the length of time involved, the repayment schedule, the interest rate, and the method used to calculate interest.

Interest rates usually depend on the supply of loaned funds and the demand for those funds. In addition, the rates may vary depending on the borrower. Two rates that are frequently referred to in business publications and broadcasts are the discount rate and the prime interest rate. Neither is available to ordinary borrowers. The discount rate, described further in the section on the Federal Reserve System, is the interest charged on short-term loans made by Federal Reserve Banks to commercial banks that are members of the Federal Reserve System. The prime interest rate, on the other hand, is the rate commercial banks charge preferred customers, usually large corporations and business enterprises. Both discount and prime interest rates have an impact on the interest rates charged for all other types of loans, and both are regularly reported in the *Federal Reserve Bulletin* and other financial statistics sources.

By itself, however, the annual interest rate is not always an accurate indicator of what a loan really costs. More useful for comparative purposes is the annual percentage rate, or APR. The APR is the true cost of a loan and in some instances may be considerably higher than the annual interest rate. Suppose, for example, that someone wants to borrow $1,000 for one year at 6 percent interest. The most favorable terms for the borrower would be based on a single, annual simple interest payment; at the end of the year, the borrower would repay the creditor the $1,000 plus $60 interest. In this instance (and whenever the interest being paid is simple annual interest), the APR and the interest rate are identical.

If, however, the same person were offered a "discount" or an "add on" loan, the APR would exceed the annual interest rate. A discount loan is one in which the annual interest is deducted from the principal of the loan before the borrower receives it. The borrower, in other words, receives less than the principal but is being charged interest on the full amount:

> Lets' borrow that same $1,000 for a year but this time from a bank. Say the annual interest rate is the same as you paid your friend, 6%. The bank would probably take out the $60 in the 6 % annual interest -in advance. This is called a discount loan. Now, for openers, you receive only $940. Then you pay off $83 monthly to liquidate (pay off) the loan. Therefore, your true cost or APR is 11.8% on $1,000. Puzzled? Well, you were paying interest on $1,000 but had use of only $940, and not even that for the full year. Moreover, with your monthly payments reducing the principal amount of the loan, the average amount of your money at your disposal during the course of the year was $470.[1]

"Add on," another method of calculating interest, adds the annual interest to the principal at the outset and is thus somewhat more advantageous to borrowers than a discount loan, but less so than a simple interest loan. Once again, the APR is greater than the annual interest rate; the loan costs more:

In this case, the 6% or $60 annual interest rate would be added to your principal sum of $1,000 at the outset. You pay back $88.30 a month, and your APR is 11.1 %. Your monthly payments are a little bit higher, but your APR is slightly lower, and you have the use of more money—$1,000 versus $940—than you did with the discount loan.[2]

The point to be made here is not how to compute the APR but to stress its importance. Creditors are required by law to disclose the APRs for all prospective credit transactions so that borrowers can compare the terms offered by one financial institution with those extended by another.

Banks, Thrifts, and the Financial Services Industry

The various business organizations offering services relating to financial resources are generally referred to as the financial services industry (see figure 10.2). A number of these organizations—commercial banks, savings and loan associations, savings banks, and credit unions—serve as intermediaries, accepting the deposits of some and extending credit to others. They are classified as depository institutions. Although the distinctions between the different types of depository institutions and other components of the industry have become increasingly blurred, each was originally formed to serve different functions and still retains certain emphases. This section concentrates on two main types of depository institutions—commercial banks and thrifts—and considers briefly other financial service organizations.

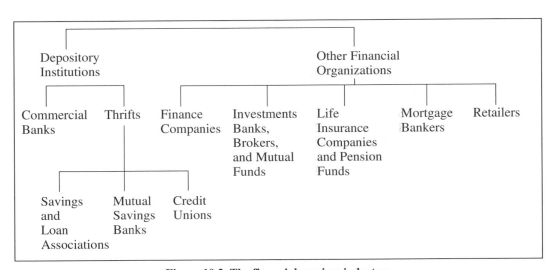

Figure 10.2. The financial services industry.

Commercial Banks

In the year 2000 there were 8,315 FDIC-insured commercial banks in the United States, ranging from small, nonspecialized operations to giant financial "department stores," with billions of dollars in deposits. All, however, share certain characteristics. First, each is a business whose main goal is to achieve profit by lending and investing the funds placed at its disposal:

The individual commercial bank has much in common with the business firms with which it deals. Like many of them, the bank is a corporation. It has applied for, qualified for, and received a charter from the proper national or state government agency, empowering it to do business as stipulated in the charter. . . . The bank performs certain productive activities for which others are willing to pay; and in so doing, it incurs certain costs. In order to remain a going concern, it must experience a cash inflow from productive services rendered and from other sources that is sufficient for meeting all obligations as they become due, including all costs of doing business. Furthermore, its activities must provide an acceptable rate of return on investment. Usually a large fraction of a banks' income is in the form of interest on the claims it holds, particularly loans; while the two leading classes of bank costs are wages and salaries and interest paid on time deposits, that is, deposits not subject to check.[3]

Second, banks perform three functions: (1) They receive and hold deposits of funds from others, (2) they make loans or extend credit, and (3) they transfer funds by written orders of depositors.

Deposits of currency, checks, and bank drafts constitute the main source of funds available to commercial banks. Deposits are categorized as time or demand. A time deposit is one in which the funds deposited can be withdrawn only after a specified lapse of time or designated future date. Although a number of types of time deposits are available, the two best known are certificates of deposit and savings accounts.

Demand deposits, on the other hand, can be withdrawn at any time. They are available upon demand for immediate spending on goods and services and are thus considered to be part of the nation's money supply. Checking accounts are the most common type of demand deposit; a depositor simply writes a check on his or her account to transfer funds to the organization or person requiring payment. With depositors writing and depositing checks every day, funds continuously flow into and out of banks.

Banks are not, however, required to keep on hand the full amount deposited. Under what is known as the fractional reserve system of banking, they must keep only a designated percentage of their deposits in cash and reserve accounts. The remainder can be used for investments and loans, commercial banks' major profit-making activities. Such activities are important not only to banks but to the economy as a whole, because they permit the creation of new demand deposits and thus contribute to the money supply.[4] To illustrate, the following example is borrowed from Znet (http://www.zmag.org/Instructionals/GlobalEcon/id9_m.htm).

You deposit money into a bank account for safety, convenience, and the interest that banks pay on deposits. The bank accepts your deposits so it can loan out your money at a higher rate of interest than it paid you. The bank does not simply introduce lender to borrower and then collect a fee if the two decide to consummate the loan. Instead, the bank takes your deposit, according you the legal right to withdraw any or all your money whenever you want. Then the bank turns around and loans to a borrower who is under no obligation to repay the principle, much less the interest, until a specified date in the future.

Although banks can create new demand deposits by making loans, their ability to do so is greatly affected by the Federal Reserve System, which can increase or decrease legal reserve requirements (the percentage of total deposits that banks are required to keep available to make payments on demand) and can thus decrease or increase excess reserves available for lending and investing. This role is discussed further in the section on the Federal Reserve System.

Commercial banks traditionally have emphasized the credit and deposit needs of businesses rather than individuals. Further, since the bulk of a bank's money comes from demand deposits rather than savings accounts and other time deposits, the focus is on short-term loans rather than on long-term loans such as mortgages. Although commercial banks are now competing vigorously for individuals' business, other financial organizations have historically emphasized the banking and credit needs of individual consumers.

Thrift Institutions

Thrift institutions, or thrifts, received their name from the purpose for which they were originally established: to encourage thrift among the working class by providing places for them to deposit their savings and take out loans. Such organizations, accordingly, concentrated on savings accounts, residential mortgages, and other types of consumer credit. Three main types of thrift institutions evolved, each of which is considered briefly below.

Savings and Loan Associations

The savings and loan association, or S & L, is the predominant type of thrift institution. The first S & Ls, known as building and loan associations, were founded in the 19th century to help workers become homeowners. People formed an association and regularly deposited their savings. As deposits grew, the association's members bid for mortgage funds:

> In early associations, members agreed to purchase shares of stock in the amount that they wished to borrow. The shares were paid for by regular, mandatory payments. When enough money was collected to make a loan, the loan was auctioned off among the associations' members. The loan carried a fixed rate of interest, usually 6%, and the member bidding the highest number of discount points got the loan. . . . Meanwhile, each member continued to pay for his shares and, with the interest from the first loan, another was soon made.[5]

Although they no longer require that borrowers be members, savings and loan associations remain a major lender for the purchase of homes and related types of real estate loans. The Office of Thrift Supervision (OTS) (http://www.ots.treas.gov/) supervises all federally chartered and many state-chartered thrift institutions, which include savings banks and savings and loan associations.

Mutual Savings Banks

Mutual savings banks are the oldest thrift institutions in the United States. Like savings and loan associations, they were established to promote financial security and thrift among workers and have been active mortgage and real estate lenders. Whereas savings and loan associations have developed throughout the country, however, mutual savings banks have been concentrated largely in the northeastern United States. Further, while S & Ls, like commercial banks, can be either federally or state chartered, until a few years ago all mutual savings banks were chartered solely by state agencies.

Credit Unions

Credit unions are similar in many respects to the other thrift institutions already described. Like them, credit unions came into being in the United States in the 19th century to meet the needs of workers. However, unlike savings and loans and mutual savings banks, credit unions will give loans only to members, who must share some common bond, such as place or nature of employment or institutional affiliation. Credit unions may be federally or state chartered, and most are also insured by federal or state agencies. Today, over 10,000 credit unions with over $480 billion in assets serve more than 79 million people in the United States.[6] The National Credit Union Administration (http://www.ncua.gov/) is an independent federal agency that supervises and insures approximately 6,000 federal credit unions and insures approximately 3,300 state-chartered credit unions.

Other Financial Institutions

Depository institutions, however, are not the only components of the financial services industry. Other organizations include finance companies; investment banks, securities brokers, mutual funds and investment companies; life insurance companies and pension funds; mortgage banks; and retailers.

Finance Companies

Finance companies fund both households and business firms and are, in fact, classified by the types of loans they make. Sales finance companies, for example, specialize in installment loans for the purchase of automobiles, home appliances, and other consumer durables; GMAC Financial Services, a General Motors unit that makes loans for the purchase of the company's automobiles, is an example of a sales finance company. Personal finance companies make personal loans, and business finance companies generally extend credit to business based on accounts receivable or sales of equipment. As a rule, loans made by finance companies are short term.

Investment Banks, Securities Brokers, and Investment Companies

Although the subject of investing is covered in the chapters that follow, it is worth noting here that three of the organizations most directly involved in investing are integral parts of the financial services industry.

Investment banks underwrite securities when they are first offered. When, for example, a corporation or government wants to raise money, it often issues stocks or bonds. These newly issued securities are then sold to investment banking firms, which in turn sell them to the public at a slightly higher price. Investment banks, in other words, buy large blocks of securities at wholesale prices and resell them at retail prices.

Securities brokers act as agents for clients interested in the purchase or sale of stocks, bonds, and other securities. In recent years, some brokers have begun to offer new services that compete with commercial banks. Large, full-service brokerage houses, for example, now offer financial products that combine the features and benefits of credit cards, checking accounts, money market funds, and traditional securities trading accounts. They have, accordingly, become an increasingly powerful segment of the financial services industry.

Investment companies and mutual funds are organizations that pool the funds deposited by individual investors to buy diversified securities portfolios. They have dramatically increased their business in recent years and are now frequently in direct competition with commercial banks, having siphoned off some of the business formerly handled by banks.

Life Insurance Companies and Pension Funds

The primary purpose of life insurance companies and pension funds is to provide financial security to individuals and households. Participants make periodic payments over long periods of time, in return for which they or designated beneficiaries will receive future payments. Insurance companies and pension funds, in turn, invest the money they receive in securities or use it to make loans.

Federal Reserve System

Although it is by no means the only government agency involved in the regulation of banking activities, the Federal Reserve System is the most important. This section examines its structure, the services it provides, and its impact on the economy.

Organizational Structure

The Federal Reserve System (http://www.federalreserve.gov/), often referred to as "the Fed," was established in 1913 by Congress to serve as the country's central bank. At the head is the chairman of the central governing body, the Board of Governors. Based in Washington, D.C., the board consists of seven members appointed by the president with the advice and consent of the Senate. Each is appointed for a 14-year term and must represent a different Federal Reserve District, thus ensuring fair representation of regional interests. The president appoints one member of the board as chairman and another as vice chairman, each for four-year terms. Behind the scenes, financial experts, economists, and other support staff assist the Board of Governors. (See figure 10.3.)

The Board's duties include overseeing the operations of the 12 Federal Reserve Banks, supervising state-chartered member banks, sharing the responsibility with the Reserve Banks for discount rate policy, and setting reserve requirements for member banks. In addition, the governors serve on the Federal Open Market Committee, described below. The board also regulates the implementation of certain consumer credit protection laws and carries on public information activities, including publication of the monthly *Federal Reserve Bulletin*, staff economic studies, and other materials.

The Federal Open Market Committee (FOMC) (http://www.federalreserve.gov/fomc/) is the Fed's most important policy-making body. Composed of all seven members of the Board of Governors and 5 of the 12 regional Federal Reserve Bank presidents, this committee has become the forum at which monetary policy matters are discussed and decisions made:[7]

> Before each regularly scheduled meeting of the FOMC, system staff prepare written reports on past and prospective economic and financial developments that are sent to Committee members and to nonmember Reserve Bank presidents. Reports prepared by the Manager of the System Open Market Account on operations in the domestic open market and in foreign currencies since the last regular meeting are also distributed. At the meeting itself, staff officers present oral reports on the current and prospective business situation, on conditions in financial markets, and on international financial developments. In its discussions, the Committee considers factors such as trends in prices and wages, employment and

production, consumer income and spending, residential and commercial construction, business investment and inventories, foreign exchange markets, interest rates, money and credit aggregates, and fiscal policy. The Manager of the System Open Market Account also reports on account transactions since the previous meeting.[8]

Chairman, Board of Governors	The Chairman (and the Vice Chairman) of the Board are named by the President from among the members and are confirmed by the Senate. They serve a term of four years.
Board of Governors	The seven members of the Board of Governors of the Federal Reserve System are nominated by the President and confirmed by the Senate. A full term is fourteen years. One term begins every two years, on February 1 of even-numbered years. A member who serves a full term may not be reappointed. The Board sets reserve requirements and shares the responsibility with the Reserve Banks for discount rate policy. In addition, the Federal Reserve Board has regulatory and supervisory responsibilities over banks that are members of the System, bank holding companies, international banking facilities in the United States, Edge Act and agreement corporations, foreign activities of member banks, and the U.S. activities of foreign-owned banks. They meet frequently with Treasury officials and the Council of Economic Advisers to help evaluate the economic climate and to discuss objectives for the nation's economy.
Federal Open Market Committee	The Federal Open Market Committee consists of twelve members: the seven members of the Board of Governors of the Federal Reserve System; the president of the Federal Reserve Bank of New York; and, for the remaining four memberships, which carry a one-year term, a rotating selection of the presidents of the eleven other Reserve Banks.
12 Regional Reserve Banks	Federal Reserve Banks operate under the general supervision of the Board of Governors in Washington. Each Bank has a nine-member Board of Directors that oversees its operations.
Boards of Directors	Reserve Bank boards of directors are divided into three classes of three persons each. Class A directors represent the member commercial banks in the District, and most are bankers. Class B and class C directors are selected to represent the public, with consideration to the interests of agriculture, commerce, industry, services, labor, and consumers. Class A and class B directors are elected by member banks in the District, while class C directors are appointed by the System's Board of Governors in Washington. All head office directors serve three-year terms. The directors appoint the Reserve Bank presidents and the first vice presidents to five-year terms, subject to approval by the Board of Governors. The Reserve Bank directors also appoint all officers of the Bank.

Figure 10.3. Structure and responsibilities of the Federal Reserve System.

The FOMC is, in fact, considered so important that committee members are not the only ones in attendance. The seven remaining Federal Reserve Bank presidents not serving on the committee, Board of Governors staff members, and senior staff economists regularly attend the meetings, which are held every five to eight weeks.

The next level of the Federal Reserve System consists of the regional Federal Reserve Banks and their branches (see figure 10.4). In all, there are 12 banks and 25 branches. Each bank serves a designated district of the country, providing banking services to member banks in its district. Like the Board of Governors, each bank also provides an assortment of information materials, ranging from sophisticated statistical studies to comic books and filmstrips intended for grade school students.

Finally, the last tier of the system is composed of commercial banks. All nationally chartered (that is, those with federal or national in their title) and most large state-chartered banks are members. Banks are required to comply with the Federal Reserve's regulations (http://www.federalreserve.gov/bankreg.htm) covering banking matters but are entitled to certain services as well.

Figure 10.4. The 12 Federal Reserve Districts.
Reproduced from the Web page at http://www.federalreserve.gov/otherfrb.htm.

Services

The Federal Reserve System is a sort of "banker's bank," providing to member banks and the federal government services similar to those offered to the public by commercial banks. Federal Reserve Banks and their branches, for example, serve banks in their districts by holding their cash reserves and making short-term loans to them, charging the discount interest rate. The Reserve Banks also move currency and coin into and out of circulation:

> When Congress created the Federal Reserve System, it recognized that the demand for cash by the public and the banking system varies from time to time. This demand increases or decreases directly with the level of economic activity and with the seasons of the year. For example, consumers' demand for currency typically increases during holiday seasons, and farmers' demand increases during

planting and harvesting seasons. The additional currency and coin put into circulation to meet seasonal demand is eventually returned to depository institutions by merchants and other business owners.[9]

Federal Reserve Banks issue Federal Reserve notes, the most common type of currency in circulation today. These notes are backed by assets held by Reserve Banks, which primarily consist of government securities and gold certificates.

The Fed also serves as a central check-clearing system. Each Reserve Bank receives checks from banks for collection, sorts them, sends the checks to the banks upon which they were written, and transfers payment for the checks through accounts at the Federal Reserve Bank.

Another service available to member banks is the national wire transfer of funds and securities using *Fedwire* (http://www.frbservices.org/), the Federal Reserve Communications System. In 2001 the average daily transfer of funds over the *Fedwire* network was $1681010 million (http://www.federalreserve.gov/PaymentSystems/FedWire/default.htm).

The Fed provides financial services to the U.S. government as well. The Federal Reserve System, through district Federal Reserve Banks, accepts deposits and issues checks for the U.S. Treasury. Payroll withholding taxes, for example, are deposited into the government's checking accounts at Federal Reserve Banks, while redemption fees for such items as U.S. Savings Bonds and food stamps are paid by transferring funds from the appropriate government accounts to the commercial banks at which they originally were redeemed. Finally, Reserve Banks handle the clerical work involved in selling and redeeming government securities such as Treasury bills, notes, and bonds.

The Board of Governors and each Federal Reserve Bank employs research staff to gather and analyze economic data and interpret economic conditions and developments. Such data and the accompanying interpretations and projections are used by the Board of Governors, Federal Open Market Committee, and Federal Reserve Bank officers to make important administrative and policy decisions. They also serve to keep the public well informed. Most regional banks publish a monthly or quarterly journal devoted to basic research and analysis of current economic issues. Publications and statistics are available from the Federal Reserve Bank at http://www.federalreserve.gov/publications.htm.[10]

Monetary Policy

Even more important than the services it provides, however, is the Federal Reserve System's role in formulating monetary policy. By setting monetary policy, the Fed regulates the flow of money and credit, or money supply. Money supply is a key factor in economic stability. Too much money may lead to inflation; too little, to recession. As was mentioned earlier, the Fed continuously monitors economic conditions in the United States. Based on the data it gathers and analyzes, it recommends actions to encourage or discourage the ability of commercial banks to extend credit by increasing or decreasing the amount of credit available and by raising or lowering the cost of credit. To accomplish its goals, the Fed uses three main tools: reserve requirements, the discount rate, and the purchase and sale of government securities.

Reserves, it should be remembered, represent deposits not available for lending. Increasing or lowering the amount of reserves that member banks are required to keep, the Fed can significantly affect the amount of credit that is available. For example, if the reserve rate is set at 15 percent, it will enable banks to lend 85 percent of their deposits, but if reserve requirements are raised to 25 percent, the amount of credit available will decline to 75 percent. Increasing reserve requirements reduces the amount of money available for loans and results in higher interest rates. Decreasing reserve requirements, on the other hand, allows banks to lend more and usually results in lower interest rates.

The discount rate charged by Reserve Banks on short-term loans to member banks can also affect lending. Raising or lowering the discount rate will discourage or encourage banks' borrowing from the Fed, which will in turn affect commercial banks' lending practices.

Finally, the Federal Reserve System, along with other organizations and individuals, buys and sells government securities in the open market. Unlike the others, however, the Fed does this to affect the supply of credit rather than for investment purposes. To illustrate, the Fed buys securities to increase reserves and stimulate lending and sells them to decrease reserves and lending.

In summary, to stave off inflation, the Federal Reserve System usually raises reserve requirements and discount rates and sells government securities that it holds. To fight against recession, that is, to expand credit and increase borrowing, the Fed acts by taking the opposite actions. It lowers reserve requirements and discount rates and buys government securities. By making the policy decisions that result in these actions, the Fed contributes to the country's economic stability and growth.

Other Federal and State Government Agencies

The United States has a dual banking system. Banks and thrift institutions may be either federally or state chartered. As a result, both federal and state government agencies are involved in regulating and monitoring their activities.

Federal Agencies

The Office of the Comptroller of the Currency (http://www.occ.treas.gov/), part of the Treasury Department, is integral to the national banking system. As the administrator of national banks, the comptroller is responsible for chartering all national banks, for the conversion of state-chartered banks into national banks, and for the establishment of branches by national banks. The Office of the Comptroller also supervises national bank operations and is responsible for overseeing the regular examination of all national banks. It also supervises the federal branches and agencies of foreign banks:

> The OCC's nationwide staff of examiners conducts on-site reviews of national banks and provides sustained supervision of bank operations. The agency issues rules, legal interpretations, and corporate decisions concerning banking, bank investments, bank community development activities, and other aspects of bank operations. National bank examiners supervise domestic and international activities of national banks and perform corporate analyses. Examiners analyze a bank's loan and investment portfolios, funds management, capital, earnings, liquidity, sensitivity to market risk, and compliance with consumer banking laws, including the Community Reinvestment Act. They review the banks' internal controls, internal and external audit, and compliance with law. They also evaluate bank management's ability to identify and control risk.[11]

All banks belonging to the Federal Reserve System are required to be members of the Federal Deposit Insurance Corporation (FDIC) (http://www.fdic.gov). The FDIC is an independent, self-supporting government organization that helps to promote the stability and safety of the banking system by insuring the deposits at commercial and savings banks.

Prior to the establishment of the FDIC, a bank failure meant that depositors lost all or part of their savings. Today, in the case of such failure, the FDIC takes over the bank. The claim of each depositor (up to $100,000) is paid, either as a result of the FDIC's sale of the bank's assets or its auction of the failed bank's assets and liabilities to the highest bidder, who then is responsible for operating the bank.

Another way in which the FDIC contributes to the safety of the banking system is by requiring the improvement of banks that examination shows to be improperly managed. If corrective action is not taken, the bank's insurance is terminated. Loss of FDIC insurance requires a national bank to give up its charter and a state bank to withdraw from the Federal System. Moreover, banks realize that public knowledge that they were no longer insured would be likely to lead to widespread deposit withdrawals and might culminate in bank failure.

Although commercial banks may be members of both the Federal Reserve System and the Federal Deposit Insurance Corporation, savings and loan associations, savings banks, and credit unions are excluded from membership. They are, however, served by other federal agencies patterned after the Fed and the FDIC.

The Federal Home Loan Bank System (http://www.fhfb.gov/) is to savings and loan associations what the Federal Reserve System is to commercial banks. Its primary purpose is to ensure that the banks remain adequately capitalized and able to raise funds in the capital markets. The system consists of three tiers: the Federal Home Loan Bank Board, 12 regional Federal Home Loan Banks, and some 8,000 member savings and loan associations.

The 12 regional Federal Home Loan Banks provide loans to member banks in their regions and help to stabilize the available supply of residential mortgage credit. Every federal savings and loan association and savings bank and every state-chartered savings institution insured by the FDIC is required to become a member of its regional Federal Home Loan Bank. Although the Home Loan Banks cannot regulate money supply as does the Federal Reserve System, they do lend funds, establish interest rates, and set other requirements for members. They are located in Atlanta, Boston, Chicago, Cincinnati, Dallas, Des Moines, Indianapolis, New York, Pittsburgh, San Francisco, Seattle, and Topeka.

Savings and loan associations and savings banks are covered by the Federal Home Loan Bank System, but credit unions are not. Federally chartered credit unions, however, are chartered, insured, supervised, and examined by the National Credit Union Administration (NCUA) (http://www.ncua.gov/).

It should be clear from this discussion that banks and thrifts are among the most heavily regulated and supervised institutions in the country.

State Agencies

State-chartered banks and thrifts come under the control of state authorities. Although the structure of banking agencies varies from one state to another, most are established as separate departments or are parts of state departments of finance or commerce. Like their federal counterparts, state banking agencies charter, regulate, and monitor the banks and thrifts under their control. In addition, each state has the right to prohibit certain kinds of banking activities, such as branch banking, within its borders.

Publications

The financial services industry is well represented by both print publications and other types of information sources. This section examines materials relevant to banking and credit. Other segments of the financial services industry are covered in the chapters that follow.

Bibliographies and Guides

Balachandran, M. **A Guide to Statistical Sources in Money, Banking, and Finance**. Phoenix, Ariz.: Oryx Press, 1988. 119p.

Lester, Ray. **Information Sources in Finance and Banking**. London: Bowker-Saur, 1996. 818p.

Still a useful publication, despite its date, is *A Guide to Statistical Sources in Money, Banking, and Finance*, a selected, annotated bibliography of sources that contain banking and monetary statistics. It is arranged by broad geographic categories (state, regional, national, foreign, and international), with a separate section for databases. Using it, one can identify printed and electronic sources that contain data on interest rates, consumer finance, bank deposits and loans, foreign exchange markets, and related topics. A directory of publishers and subject and title indexes are appended.

Information Sources in Finance and Banking is considerably broader in scope and covers available sources for finance and banking. Banking resources per se are a small subset of the information provided, which includes sources of data of a financial, banking, and economic nature. In addition to the work's title and publisher, each entry contains a brief annotation and specifies the language of publication, country or countries covered, approximate number of pages, and frequently the price or subscription rate. *Information Sources in Finance and Banking* is particularly useful for its coverage of publications that cover the United States, United Kingdom, and European Union. A heavily annotated list of banking sources is included in Chapter 5, "Financial Institutions and Markets."

Other sources are considerably more specialized, focusing on specific types of publications or selecting materials intended for certain audiences.

U.S. Superintendent of Documents. **Financial Institutions**. July 2, 2001. (Subject Bibliography 128). http://bookstore.gpo.gov/sb/sb-128.html. (Accessed August 28, 2003).

Like other titles in the Superintendent of Documents Subject Bibliography series, *Financial Institutions* selectively lists and annotates laws, congressional documents, and agency publications. For each item listed, title, number of pages, Superintendent of Documents classification, stock number, and price are included. A link is provided for online ordering.

Dictionaries and Encyclopedias

Dictionaries

Banking dictionaries can be divided into two main categories: those intended for practitioners and students and those written for consumers. Although a number of such dictionaries are available, the following are among the best.

American Banker Online. **Glossary**. ©2003. http://www.americanbanker.com/glossary.html. (Accessed August 28, 2003).

Newman, Peter, ed. **The New Palgrave Dictionary of Money & Finance.** New York: Stockton Press, 1992. 3vs.

Fitch, Thomas P. **Dictionary of Banking Terms**. 4th ed. Hauppauge, N.Y.: Barron's Educational Series, 2000. 529p.

Hales, Michael Gordon. **The Language of Banking: Terms and Phrases Used in the Financial Industry**. Jefferson, N.C.: McFarland, 1994. 169p.

Rosenberg, Jerry M. **Dictionary of Banking**. New York: John Wiley, 1993. 369p.

The American Banker *Glossary* is a handy online compilation of terms ranging from "ABO" to "zoning". Included are acronyms and cross-references. For those libraries and individuals who infrequently need a banking dictionary, this may suffice.

At the other extreme is *The New Palgrave Dictionary of Money & Finance,* which is an encyclopedic dictionary containing 1,080 signed essays, written by 800 contributors, that deal with a wide range of topics on money and finance. Almost all of these entries contain bibliographies. Entries are arranged alphabetically and contain cross-references. Each volume contains an alphabetical list of entries and a list of acronyms that appear in the text. *The New Palgrave* belongs in the collection of all academic and large public libraries.

Although the emphasis is on short explanations in the *Dictionary of Banking Terms,* some of the more complicated definitions are given an expanded entry. Depending on the context of the entry there may be several meanings, so each is treated as a subentry. Cross-references are abundant, and the *Dictionary* also includes a listing of abbreviations and acronyms as well as world currencies by country.

The *Language of Banking* has the least number of entries of any of the listed dictionaries, but its strength lies in the detailed descriptions of terms. For example, the description of *FEDWIRE*, the transfer service used by the Federal Reserve, covers a page, and the description of Bankers' Acceptances covers two pages.

The *Dictionary of Banking* is a standard reference work, presenting definitions for over 7,500 terms in banking. Although some of the definitions are original, many have been taken from basic banking reference works; in such instances, the definitions are attributed to the original sources, which are listed in the back of the *Dictionary.*

Encyclopedias

Three encyclopedias are considered standard reference works.

Woelfel, Charles J. **Encyclopedia of Banking and Finance**. 10th ed. Chicago: Fitzroy Dearborn, 1994. 1219p.

Allen, Larry. **Encyclopedia of Money**. Santa Barbara, Calif.: ABC-CLIO, 1999. 328p.

Markham, Jerry W. **A Financial History of the United States**. Armonk, N.Y.: M. E. Sharpe, 2002. 3vs.

The *Encyclopedia of Banking and Finance* is an authoritative, well-written source that combines brief definitions of basic banking terms with a series of encyclopedic articles on such varied topics as the Federal Reserve System and foreign bills of exchange. Statistics and bibliographies are frequently included, and definitions are often enhanced by examples illustrating proper usage. In addition, key concepts and terms from such related fields as finance and insurance are featured, and major banking legislation is described at length. *The Encyclopedia* is also available electronically as part of the *netLibrary* collection. It is a basic reference work that belongs in every business collection.

Less essential but still very useful is the *Encyclopedia of Money*. Directed at the general reader, it purports to cover the evolution of money and banking systems in the world. Entries are several paragraphs long and cover such topics as Bank Clearinghouses and the Gold Standard Act of 1900. Where the book is really useful and also at times fascinating is in its coverage of such historical topics as the Credole, warehouse warrants for grain that circulated as currency, and Yap Money, thick stone wheels used as money by the natives of one of the Caroline Islands in the South Pacific. Short bibliographies are included.

The three volumes of *Financial History of the United States* contain a history of finance in America. The first volume covers from the time of Christopher Columbus to the Robber Barons (1492–1900), the second from J. P. Morgan to the institutional investor (1900–1970), and the third from the age of derivatives into the new millennium (1970–2001).

Each volume is divided into chapters and each chapter into sections that are further subdivided. In volume III, for example, the first section of chapter 3 is "The Stock Market Crash of 1987," which is then divided into "New Wave Finance," "Meltdown Concerns," "The Market Crash," "The Aftermath," "Brady Commission," "Securities Market Problems," "More Market Volatility," "Futures Markets," and "The Chicago Sting Operation." Each section is clearly written and readable. Extensive bibliographies are included and there are both subject and name indexes.

Financial Manuals and Directories

Banking directories generally reflect the divisions between commercial banks, thrifts, and other financial service institutions. *Mergent Bank & Finance Manual*, however, is an exception.

Mergent. **Mergent Bank & Finance Manual**. New York: Mergent FIS. 1900– . 4vs. Annual, with semiweekly supplements. (Available electronically in *Mergent Online,* http://www.mergent.com/.)

Formerly known as Moody's Financial Information Services, Mergent has been publishing detailed business descriptions, corporate histories, and financial statements since 1900. The *Manual* is, in fact, both more and less than a directory. As a financial manual, it presents brief histories and descriptions of and current operating statistics for banks, thrifts, and other financial service organizations, far more information than most directories provide. Compared to the directories that follow, however, the *Manual* includes fewer banks and thrifts.

Volume 1 covers commercial banks and trust companies, mutual savings banks and savings and loan associations, and such federal credit agencies as the Federal Reserve System and the Federal Deposit Insurance Corporation. Volumes 2, 3 and 4 focus on other components of the financial services industry, including mutual funds and investment companies, real estate companies, real estate investment trusts, finance and insurance companies, and unit investment trusts.

For research on banks and thrifts, the first volume is most useful. In it, the largest banks are treated at length. Entries are often several pages long, and generally include a corporate history, lists of subsidiaries and affiliates, a description of the bank, the names of its officers and directors, balance sheet and income statement data, and information on stocks and dividends. Additional banks are covered in less detail in a separate section. This information is also included in *Mergent Online,* where one can search by SIC or NAICS code to get a list of certain types of banks within a state and then link to the full-text information. (See figures 10.5 and 10.6.)

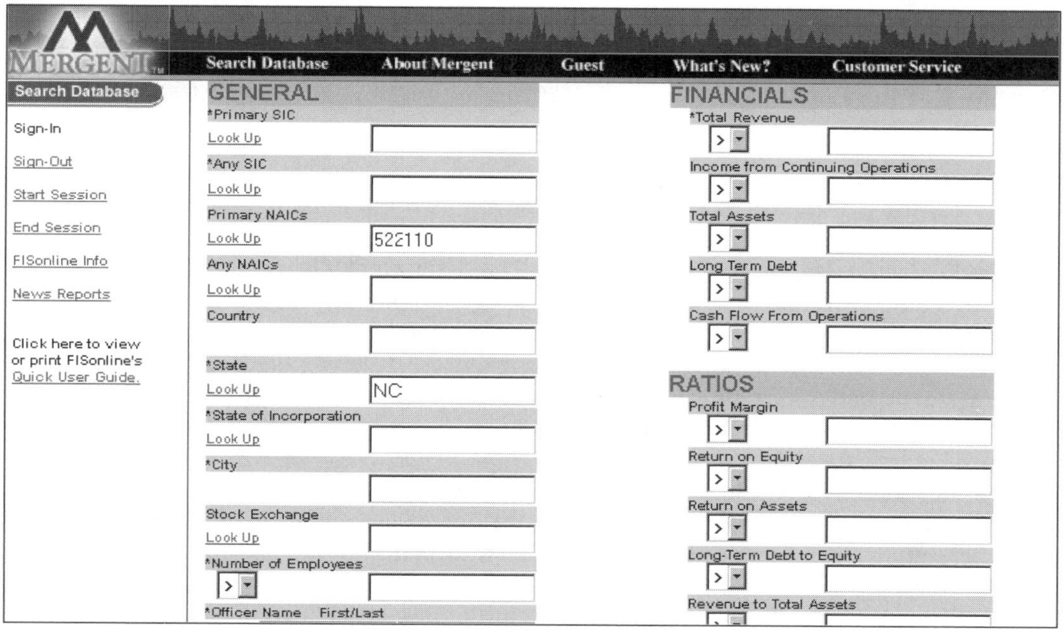

Figure 10.5. An online search for banks (NAICS 522110) in North Carolina using advanced search in *Mergent Online*. Reproduced by permission of Mergent © 2002.

Figure 10.6. Selected bank listings produced by searching in *Mergent Online*.
Reproduced by permission of Mergent © 2002.

For standard directory coverage other publications are generally consulted. Commercial banks, for example, are listed in the following titles.

The Bankers' Almanac. West Sussex, England: Reed Information Services, 1919– . 6v. Semiannual.

Directory of the World's Banks. 11th ed. Chicago: Fitzroy Dearborn, c1996. 1186p.

Thomson Bank Directory. Skokie, Ill.: Thomson Financial,2000– . 4v. Semiannual.

The Bankers' Almanac provides information on over 4,000 major international banks in 201 countries. To be included, the banks must hold a full banking license issued by the central bank or monetary authority in the country of domicile and must be able to supply a fully audited annual report and balance sheet. The first three volumes alphabetically list the banks by name, volumes 4 and 5 list the banks geographically, and volume 6 contains a brief alphabetical listing of over 20,000 other authorized banks. For each full listing in volumes 1, 2, and 3 information includes full addresses; the Telerate; bank code; Web address; Fitch, Mergent, and S&P ratings; corporate structure; merger information; a listing of directors; a list of correspondents; standard settlement instructions; and information from the consolidated balance sheet. Indexes are included. The *Almanac* is expensive, and it is unusual for any but the largest, most specialized, or most affluent libraries to have a subscription.

The *Directory of the World's Banks* also provides addresses and telephone numbers and at least the name of one contact person. The information is not as detailed as that in the *Almanac,* and the shorter listings are for 10,000 banks as opposed to 24,000. The arrangement is by continent and country, and indexes are provided. This volume is, however, held by most large libraries and so will be more accessible to researchers.

Thomson Bank Directory, formerly known by the well-recognized name *Polk's World Bank Directory*, profiles banks and their branch offices. Volumes 1 and 2 provide information for the United States, and volumes 3 and 4 cover the rest of the world. The arrangement in the first volumes is by state and town; in the world volumes it is by country and town. A number of entries provide some balance sheet information and principal correspondents. Most contain officer information. Various tables are listed, including the top 500 U.S. banks listed by assets, key financial information by state, credit ratings, and international offices of U.S. banks. This is one of the most popular directories and is held by most libraries. This publication and the *Savings Directory* are included in the *Thomson Global Banking Resource* (http://www.tgbr.com/), which is available online and as a CD-ROM. These directories are also included in the full LexisNexis service

Although the *Thomson Bank Directory* provides good coverage of commercial banks, it excludes savings and loan associations and credit unions. For listings of such institutions, other directories must be consulted.

Thomson Credit Union Directory. Skokie, Ill.: Thomson Financial, c1991. Semiannual.

Thomson Savings Directory. Skokie, Ill.: Thomson Financial, c1991. Annual.

Credit Union Directory. Washington, D.C.: Callahan & Associates, 1986– . Annual.

The two Thomson directories listed above provide a comprehensive listing by state and city for all active S & Ls, building and loan associations, cooperative banks, and savings banks in the United States. Although most entries lack the detailed financial data contained in the banking directories described above, they do include standard directory information and the location and addresses of branch offices.

Callahan's *Credit Union Directory* provides contact information and financial snapshots for all 10,366 credit unions in the United States. The Web page for Callahan & Associates (http://www.callahan.com/) has a directory that links to the Web pages of credit unions plus some free statistical information. All of these directories contain various tables and statistics.

The FDIC issues a free, online directory. The *Financial Institutions Directory* (http://www3.fdic.gov/idasp/index.asp) allows one to search for a holding company, an institution, or an office. One can also create, save, and retrieve custom peer groups of insured institutions and bank holding companies. Also retrievable are quarterly financial reports for each institution.

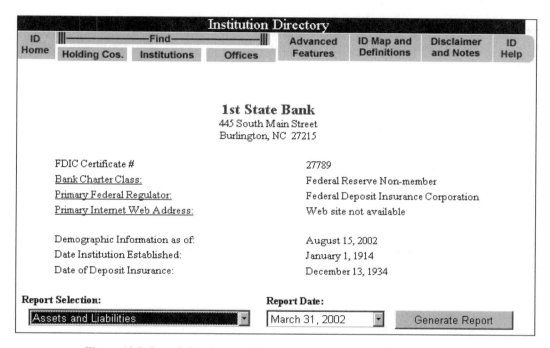

**Figure 10.7. Sample bank record from the *Financial Institutions Directory*,
http://www3.fdic.gov/idasp/index.asp.**

Bank Rating Directories

While Mergent, S&P, and Fitch company ratings are well known, Sheshunoff (http://www.sheshunoff.com/) specifically focuses on banking and its associated services and issues ratings. Sheshunoff publishes materials on regulatory compliance, implementing policies and procedures, bank security, and risk management. In fact every aspect of banking is covered in a manual, as a loose-leaf service, or as an online product. One that is particularly useful and found in libraries is described below.

The Bank and S&L Quarterly: Ratings and Analysis. Austin, Tex.: Sheshunoff Information Services, 1998– . Quarterly.

This publication looks at FDIC-insured institutions and gives a fast, easy snapshot of their overall health, compares each to its peers, and shows whether it is growing. This quarterly service provides easy-to-read data, in a simple format, on individual banks and S & Ls. Information is included on the size and growth of the bank, the loan exposure, capital adequacy, asset quality, earnings and liquidity. The *Sheshunoff* also rates each bank within its peer group. The publication is expensive, but the quality of the information is excellent and well worth the price.

Periodicals, Newspapers, and Indexes

Periodicals

Although personal finance magazines such as *Money* and general business periodicals such as *Business Week*, *Fortune*, and *Forbes* regularly report on the banking industry, most specialized banking periodicals are written for practitioners and scholars. Their number is impressive; over 350 banking and finance titles are listed in the *Standard Periodical Directory*. Although comprehensive coverage is impossible in a work of this sort, the titles that follow are standard banking periodicals.

ABA Banking Journal. Washington, D.C.: American Bankers Association, 1908– . Monthly.

The Banker. London: Financial News Ltd., 1926– . Monthly. (Some free information available at http://www.thebanker.com/.)

Journal of Money, Credit, and Banking. Columbus, Ohio : Ohio State University Press, 1969– . Quarterly. (Earlier volumes are available through JSTOR; later publications are online through MUSE.)

US Banker. New York: General Banking Division of Faulkner & Gray, 1977– . Monthly. Web version available at http://www.us-banker.com/.

The *ABA Banking Journal* is the official publication of the American Bankers Association, the premier association for the commercial banking industry. It emphasizes current operations and practices in banking, recent developments, bank management, government regulation and legislation, and ABA-sponsored activities and services. Interviews with banking executives and government officials are frequently featured, as are reports on the implications of legislation enacted or being considered. Other articles cover the introduction of new financial products and such management-related issues as personnel, customer relations, bank marketing, and security.

The *Banker* is a premier magazine for banking professionals. Each monthly issue covers a number of countries and topics such as banking services, markets, and global securities services. At the Web site http://www.thebanker.com/ are some free articles and a database of rankings where one can retrieve top banks in different regions and countries. Like the *ABA Banking Journal, The Banker* emphasizes practice rather than theory.

The *Journal of Money, Credit, and Banking* is scholarly and international in scope. The editors and contributors are usually university professors. Each author must provide any data and programs used in compiling the articles, and these are made available for researchers at http://webmail.econ.ohio-state.edu/john/IndexDataArchive.php. Recent articles have covered such topics as money supply, interest rates, and commercial credit.

US Banker covers more everyday and undoubtedly more popular subject matter. Topics covered recently include women and mortgages and the misdeeds of top executives. For those looking for a very readable glossy journal that will nonetheless keep them up-to-date with banking issues, this is probably an excellent choice.

The government's role in regulating and influencing financial activities is reflected in its periodical literature. The *Survey of Current Business* (http://www.bea.doc.gov/bea/pubs.htm), for example, publishes selective statistics on banking, credit, and money. Other government periodicals provide even more comprehensive coverage.

U.S. Board of Governors of the Federal Reserve System. **Federal Reserve Bulletin**. Washington, D.C.: Government Printing Office, 1915– . Monthly.

FDIC Banking Review. Washington, D.C.: Federal Deposit Insurance Corporation, 1988– . Quarterly.

The *Federal Reserve Bulletin* combines articles on the Fed and banking with the texts of reports and statements made by the Board of Governors to Congress; summaries of policy actions of the Federal Open Market Committee, staff research studies, current legal developments; and announcements of Fed policy changes. Its "Financial and Business Statistics" section is an excellent source of current data on money, bank reserves, Federal Reserve and commercial banks, financial markets, federal finance, securities markets and corporate finance, mortgages, consumer credit, and related domestic and international banking activities. This section is, in fact, one of the best sources in which to locate information on monetary and financial conditions.

In addition, each issue of the *Bulletin* publishes a guide to special tables and statistical releases and the issues in which they appear, as well as lists of current members and official staff of the Board of Governors, the Federal Open Market Committee, and two advisory councils. Other lists contain the names and terms of people appointed to the Board of Governors since its beginning in 1913, and the locations, addresses, and officers of Federal Reserve Banks, branches, and offices. Articles but not statistical tables are available online at http://www.federalreserve.gov/pubs/bulletin/default.htm.

The *FDIC Banking Review* provides original research on issues related to banking and deposit insurance. Recent issues have included articles on merchant banking, depositary institutions, and the savings and loan crisis. Most articles are written by staff of the FDIC. The *Review* is online at http://www.fdic.gov/bank/analytical/banking/.

Newspapers

Although major daily newspapers such as the *New York Times,* the *Wall Street Journal,* and the *Financial Times* devote considerable attention to money, credit, and banking, another daily is even more important.

American Banker. New York: American Banker, 1836– . Daily, Monday through Friday.

The *American Banker* (http://www.americanbanker.com/) is basic reading for most professionals in the financial services industry. It covers current news and developments; analyzes trends; and profiles key companies, executives, and officials. All aspects of the industry are covered. Many issues include special sections focusing on such topics as marketing or technology and financial networks. Ranked lists of the largest financial institutions are published regularly. A listing of the available special reports and rankings is available at http://www.americanbanker.com/specialreports.html.

Indexes

There is no longer a specific index for banking. Since the demise of *Banking Literature Index* in 1993, librarians and researchers have had the standard online database sources that were described in chapter 3. Many banking and financial journals are now part of such databases as *ABI/INFORM Global,* with the added advantage of being available in full text.

Government Documents

Government involvement in regulating and monitoring banking activities is reflected in its documents output. The diversity and sheer number of documents on banking and the financial services industry are immediately apparent to anyone scanning through the subject index of the print *Monthly Catalog of United States Government Publications* or using the free online catalog at http://www.gpoaccess.gov/cgp/index.html/. Titles range from guides for consumers, to shopping for loans, to congressional hearings on bank deregulation and Third World debt, from periodicals and news releases to statistical compendia. Although the need for such publications will vary considerably from one library to the next, the Web links that follow point to those found useful in many library settings.

The Federal Reserve System issues publications on actions taken by the Board, its staff, and the Federal Reserve Banks; enforcement actions; regulations; and legal interpretations, all available from http://www.federalreserve.gov/bankreg.htm. The Fed also provides information for consumers, such as *Consumer Handbook to Credit Protection Laws* (http://www.federalreserve.gov/pubs/consumerhdbk/default.htm) and *Home Mortgages: Understanding the Process and Your Right to Fair Lending* (http://www.federalreserve. gov/pubs/mortgage/morbro.htm). These and other publications are available by checking the Web site at http://www.federalreserve.gov/publications.htm. Not all are on the Web, but instructions for ordering print copies are included.

There is also a catalog of publications at http://app.ny.frb.org/cfpicnic/frame1.cfm. By checking on one of the subjects at the left of the screen a list of publications in that category will appear. One may order copies online. (See figure 10.8.)

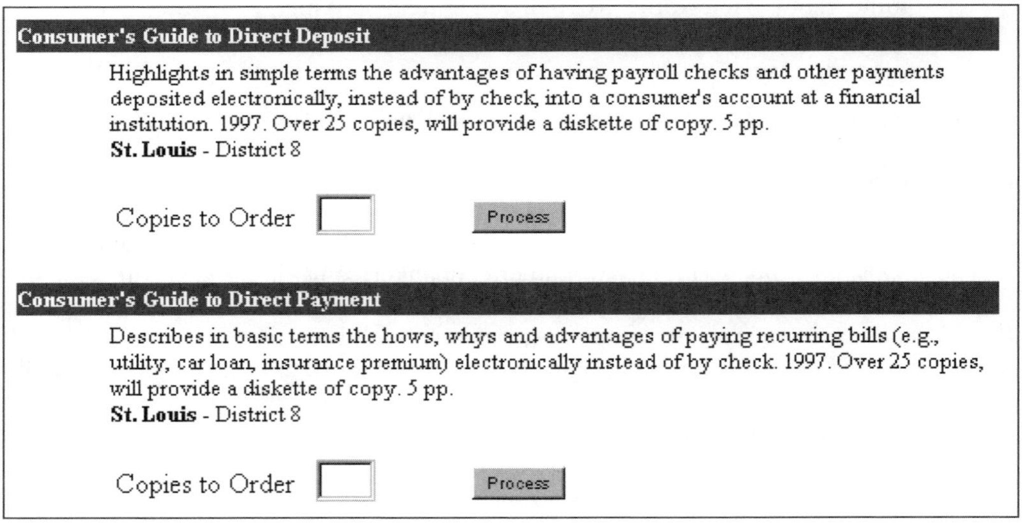

Consumer's Guide to Direct Deposit

Highlights in simple terms the advantages of having payroll checks and other payments deposited electronically, instead of by check, into a consumer's account at a financial institution. 1997. Over 25 copies, will provide a diskette of copy. 5 pp.
St. Louis - District 8

Copies to Order ☐ Process

Consumer's Guide to Direct Payment

Describes in basic terms the hows, whys and advantages of paying recurring bills (e.g., utility, car loan, insurance premium) electronically instead of by check. 1997. Over 25 copies, will provide a diskette of copy. 5 pp.
St. Louis - District 8

Copies to Order ☐ Process

**Figure 10.8. Example of publications available in the consumer banking category at
http://app.ny.frb.org/cfpicnic/frame1.cfm.**

The other agency much concerned with money and banking is the FDIC (http://www. fdic.gov/). Again, the Web site contains an important accumulation of information. The researcher can link to information on deposit insurance, regulations for bankers, electronic banking procedures, and more.

Much of the information that a researcher needs is now available on the Web. Not only the resources from the Fed and the FDIC but also bills, committee reports, and prints that involve the banking industry can be located online. The representative list of publications in figure 10.9 was retrieved by entering "banking" as a keyword at http://thomas.loc.gov. Each document is retrievable in pdf format by clicking on the house or senate number.

---

50 Bills from the 107th Congress ranked by relevance on *"banking"*.

50 bills containing your phrase **exactly as entered**.

Listing of **50** bills containing your phrase **exactly as entered**.

1 . Money Laundering Abatement Act (Introduced in Senate)[S.1371.IS]
2 . Community Savings and Investment Act of 2001 (Introduced in House)[H.R.1220.IH]
3 . Community Savings and Investment Act of 2001 (Introduced in Senate)[S.605.IS]
4 . National Bank Offshore Activities Act of 2001 (Introduced in House)[H.R.2273.IH]
5 . Consumer Banking Services Costs Assessment Act of 2001 (Introduced in House)[H.R.1061.IH]
6 . Consumer Affordable Transaction Account Act of 2001 (Introduced in House)[H.R.1059.IH]
7 . Microcap Fraud Prevention Act of 2001 (Introduced in Senate)[S.1985.IS]
8 . International Money Laundering Abatement and Anti-Terrorist Financing Act of 2001 (Placed on Calendar in Senate)[S.1511.PCS]
9 . American Wetland Restoration Act (Introduced in House)[H.R.1474.IH]
10 . Authorizing expenditures by the Committee on Banking, Housing, and Urban Affairs. (Reported in Senate)[S.RES.40.RS]
11 . Money Laundering Prevention Act (Introduced in House)[H.R.2978.IH]

Figure 10.9. Representative list of publications on banking from http://thomas.loc.gov.

Statistics

Government-issued publications, in a variety of formats, are some of the best sources of current statistical information. As was mentioned previously, the *Federal Reserve Bulletin* contains detailed monthly statistics on money, credit, and banking. Each of the Federal Reserve Banks publishes a monthly economic review and other titles as well. They are particularly useful for an overview of regional business and economic conditions. Similarly, each of the 12 regional Federal Home Loan Banks publishes information at its Web site that features analysis of area economic conditions as they relate to mortgage loans and the thrift industry. Articles in the *Bulletin* and in the Federal Reserve periodicals that contain statistics are indexed in the *American Statistics Index* (*LexisNexis Statistical*), which is one of the best sources of information on the statistical output of independent federal agencies. Links to each Federal Reserve District are at http://www.federalreserve.gov/otherfrb.htm, and the link to the Federal Home Loan Banks is at http://www.fhfb.gov/FHLB/fhlbs.banks.htm.

There is also a searchable online index for Federal Reserve economic research. This is known as the *Fed in Print* (http://www.frbsf.org/publications/fedinprint/index.html). This database is searchable by words in the title, author, and keyword, and can be limited by year and type of publication. An index is provided for all fields except keyword. Documents that are available electronically are linked; for those that are not there is reminder that a library may have them or one can order them directly from the Fed.

Twenty-four-hour access to regional and national financial and economic data is provided by *FRED®* (http://research.stlouisfed.org/fred/index.html#data). This site provides historical U.S. economic and financial data, including daily U.S. interest rates, monetary and business indicators, exchange rates, balance of payments, and loans. The *FRED®* data files are grouped into 12 categories, including one for commercial banks and one for monthly reserves data. "All files, except those that are compressed, are in ASCII format.

Compressed files are in .zip or self-extracting .exe formats. The compressed files contain all of the ASCII files within that category of data."[12] The "Commercial Banking" section has at least 50 years of monthly or weekly data on topics such as Bank Credit of all Commercial Banks, Consumer Loans at all Commercial Banks and Total Automobile Credit Outstanding. For these large data sets there are excellent instructions for downloading and converting into Excel spreadsheets. (See figure 10.10.)

This is an excellent source of statistical information on money and banking.

Commercial Banking   **FRED II:** Help\FAQ

Results 1-20 of 22   Next

Title	Units	Freq.	Seas. Adj.	Updated
Bank Credit of All Commercial Banks	Bil. of $	W	SA	2002-08-22
Commercial and Industrial Loans at All Commercial Banks	Bil. of $	M	SA	2002-08-20
Commercial and Industrial Loans of Weekly Reporting Large Commercial Banks	Bil. of $	W	SA	2002-08-22
Consumer (Individual) Loans at All Commercial Banks	Bil. of $	M	SA	2002-08-20
Other Securities at All Commercial Banks	Bil. of $	M	SA	2002-08-20
Real Estate Loans at All Commercial Banks	Bil. of $	M	SA	2002-08-20
Total Automobile Credit Outstanding	Bil. of $	M	NSA	1999-04-01
Total Automobile Credit Outstanding	Bil. of $	M	SA	1999-04-01
Total Commercial and Industrial Loans Including Foreign Related Institutions	Bil. of $	W	SA	2002-08-22
Total Consumer Credit Outstanding	Bil. of $	M	NSA	2002-08-13
Total Consumer Credit Outstanding	Bil. of $	M	SA	2002-08-13
Total Investments at All Commercial Banks	Bil. of $	M	SA	2002-08-20
Total Loans and Investments at All Commercial Banks	Bil. of $	M	SA	2002-08-20
Total Loans and Leases of Commercial Banks	Bil. of $	M	SA	2002-08-20

Figure 10.10. Sample listing of commercial banking statistics available from *FRED* at http://research.stlouisfed.org/fred2/categories/23.

FDIC Statistics on Banking (http://www.fdic.gov/bank/statistical/statistics/) is a quarterly publication that provides detailed aggregate financial information as well as number of institutions and branches for all FDIC-insured institutions. Aggregate statistics are retrievable from thefourth quarter of 1991 on balance sheets, income statements, and loans for commercial banks and savings institutions. (See figure 10.11.)

According to the Web site, "The FDIC has introduced a new feature that provides users with most of the financial information contained in the *Statistics on Banking* and allows them to dynamically generate customized reports for analysis. For instance, users can create reports that consist of any combination of single institutions or bank holding companies, standard peer groups of institutions, and custom peer groups of institutions and bank holding companies." This system is available at http://www3.fdic.gov/sdi/.

Other statistical compendia are published by professional and trade associations. Following is a representative list with Web addresses. All list available publications, and some free information is provided.

Table RC-13	**SECURITIES OF FDIC-INSURED SAVINGS INSTITUTIONS** Institutions Grouped by Asset Size and Insurance Fund Membership (Amount in Millions of Dollars)				
Calendar Year, 2001	**Total Savings Institutions**	**Less than $100 Million**	**$100 Million to $1 Billion**	**$1 Billion or More**	**INSURANCE FUND**
					BIF Member	**SAIF Member**
Securities (debt and equity)	285,117	5,470	55,648	224,000	94,496	190,622
Assets held in trading accounts for Thrift Financial reporters	1,821	1	57	1,763	50	1,771
Security contra accounts for Thrift Financial reporters	2	0	1	0	0	2
Total securities and trading accounts (included below)	286,940	5,471	55,706	225,763	94,546	192,394
By type:*						
US Treasury securities and US Government agency and corporation obligations	228,932	4,063	40,364	184,506	56,506	172,427
US Treasury securities	3,039	24	892	2,124	2,890	149
US Government agency and corporation obligations	225,894	4,039	39,472	182,383	53,616	172,278
Securities issued by states and political subdivisions	4,488	197	2,319	1,971	1,596	2,893
Other domestic debt securities**	43,294	497	8,003	34,794	30,894	12,399
Foreign debt securities**	27	0	21	5	27	0
Equity securities	10,199	714	4,999	4,486	5,522	4,676
Memoranda:*						
Pledged securities***	21,634	109	2,864	18,661	18,035	3,599
Mortgage-backed securities	196,512	2,759	28,361	165,391	62,190	134,321

Figure 10.11. Securities of FDIC-insured savings institutions. Generated from the Web site at http://www.fdic.gov/bank/statistical/statistics/sectione.html.

America's Community Bankers	http://www.acbankers.org
American Bankers Associatio n	http://www.aba.com
ATM Industry Association	http://www.atmia.com/
Bank Administration Institute	http://www.bai.org
Consumer Bankers Association	http://www.cbanet.org
Independent Community Bankers of America	http://www.icba.org

Banking Tables

Basic to any banking reference collection is the presence of at least one compilation of banking and financial tables. A number of such sources are available, but one of the most comprehensive and popular works is listed below.

Thorndike, David, and Donald S. Benton. **Thorndike Encyclopedia of Banking and Financial Tables**. 4th ed. Austin, Tex.: Thomson Financial/Pratt, 2001. 1v. (various pagings).

The *Thorndike Encyclopedia of Banking and Financial Tables* groups tables by six broad categories. A general explanation precedes each table and describes its use, and each table begins with a summary of the rates, terms, payments, and yields that are shown in the table. A dictionary of financial terms is also included. A yearbook brings the *Encyclopedia* up-to-date.

Databases

Many of the databases mentioned in previous chapters are relevant to the banking industry. *ABI/INFORM Global* and *LexisNexis*, for example, provide full text articles from banking journals, may of them complete with graphs and statistics. There are, however, other databases whose main emphasis ranges from banking regulations to bankruptcies. These databases are listed in directories such as the *Gale Directory of Databases*. There is one database that deals with all aspects of banking.

BANKSCOPE. Brussels, Belgium: Bureau van Dijk Electronic Publishing, 1998? http://www.bvdep.com/. (Accessed August 28, 2003).

Bureau van Dijk is one of Europe's leading publishers of electronic business information complete with manipulation software. *BANKSCOPE* is one module of *BvD Suite*, which can be purchased separately either as an online product or as a CD-ROM. It includes financial information on 11,000 banks worldwide. Subscribers receive up to eight years of detailed financial information on the top 6,500 European banks, the top 1,400 North American banks, 200 Japanese banks, the leading supranational banking and financial organizations, and more than 2,900 other major banks. Included in the subscription are Fitch, Moody's (Mergent), and S&P ratings; Economist Intelligence Unit (EIU) *Country Risk Ratings and Reports;* and *Country Finance Reports.* In-depth financial information can be extracted and generated in various formats. Although expensive, this is undoubtedly the best source of information for international banking.

Notes

1. Robin Gross and Jean V. Cullen, *Help! The Basics of Borrowing Money* (New York: Times Books, 1980), 41.

2. Ibid.

3. Thomas E. Van Dahm, *Money and Banking: An Introduction to the Financial System* (Lexington, Mass.: D. C. Heath, 1975), 48–49.

4. For simple descriptions of banking and credit, check the educational publications of the Federal Reserve Bank of Chicago at http://www.chicagofed.org/consumerinformation/index.cfm.

5. William Gobble and Bruce Harwood, *North Carolina Real Estate*, 2nd ed. (Reston, Va.: Reston Publishing, 1984), 245–46.

6. Taken from the Web page of the National Credit Union Administration at http://www.ncua.gov/indexabout.html.

7. The president of the Federal Reserve Bank of New York serves as a permanent member of the FOMC. For the remaining four memberships, which carry a one-year term, a rotating selection is taken from the presidents of the 11 other Reserve Banks.

8. Taken from the Web page at http://www.federalreserve.gov/pubs/frseries/frseri2.htm.

9. *Reserve Bank Studies* in pdf format are at http://www.federalreserve.gov/pubs/staffstudies.

10. Details of publications from 12 Federal Reserve District Banks are available at:

Boston	http://www.bos.frb.org/genpubs/
New York	http://www.newyorkfed.org/pihome/?expand=8
Philadelphia	http://www.phil.frb.org/publicaffairs/pubs/index.html
Cleveland	http://www.clev.frb.org/Pubs.htm
Richmond	http://www.rich.frb.org/
Atlanta	http://www.frbatlanta.org/
Chicago	http://www.chicagofed.org/publications/index.cfm
St. Louis	http://www.stls.frb.org/publications/index.html
Minneapolis	http://www.minneapolisfed.org/pubs/
Kansas City	http://www.kc.frb.org/home/subwebs.cfm?subWeb=7
Dallas	http://www.dallasfed.org/htm/pubs/index.html
San Francisco	http://www.frbsf.org/cgi-bin/addresses1.cgi

11. Taken from the Web page of the OCC at http://www.occ.treas.gov/aboutocc.htm.

12. Taken from the Web page at http://research.stlouisfed.org/fred2/.

11

Investments: An Introduction

As Americans become increasingly concerned with financial security, a growing number are seeking to find it through careful investment. The New York Stock Exchange's 2000 share ownership survey (http://www.nyse.com/pdfs/shareho.pdf) determined that over 84 million people owned stock in 1998, up from 69 million in 1995, which was up from 61.4 million in 1992 and 52.3 in 1989. One ongoing trend is the rapid growth of indirect methods of share ownership, such as ownership through investments in equity mutual funds or through 401(k) plans or defined contribution pension plan accounts. But stocks are not the only investment medium:

> Investment has many facets. It may involve putting money into banks, Treasury bills or notes, or common stocks, or paintings, or real estate, or mortgages, or oil ventures, or cattle, or the theater. It may involve speculating in bull markets or selling short in bear markets. It may involve choosing growth stocks, or blue chips, or defensive stocks, or income stocks, or even penny cats and dogs. It may involve options, straddles, rights, warrants, convertibles, margin, gold, silver, mutual funds, money market funds, index funds, tax exempt bond funds, and result in accumulation of wealth or dissipation of resources. Diversity and challenge characterize the field.[1]

In fact, as more people choose to invest, Wall Street has become increasingly ingenious in introducing new investment vehicles to the public. As a result, there are a myriad of investment opportunities for small, private investors. This chapter and the four that follow deal with the most common types of investments—stocks, bonds, mutual funds, futures, and options—and the basic types of information sources relevant to each.

Investors and Their Information Needs

Investors fall into two main categories: institutional and individual. Institutional investors include banks, insurance companies, mutual funds and investment companies, college endowment funds, corporate profit-sharing plans, and pension funds. They are organizations with considerable money to invest and large securities portfolios to manage. Frequently they have one or more departments that include securities analysts, portfolio managers, economists, and other experts to supply data and help make investment decisions. Individual investors, on the other hand, are private investors, people making their own, and comparatively small, personal investments. Generally they lack the expertise available to institutional investors and are not usually full-time investors.

To be successful, such investors must be well informed. The astute investor who is considering purchase of stocks, for example, will attempt to learn not only as much as possible about the company itself but also about the industry of which it is a part, the economy generally, and all of the factors that affect it. Some will look to their brokers to supply the needed information. Many others, however, will take a more active role, reading financial newspapers and business periodicals, advisory newsletters, and now gathering information from the Internet.

Investment information can be categorized in many ways. It can, for example, be classified as either descriptive or analytical. Descriptive investment information is factual; statistics comprise a large part of the data presented, and the focus is on the recent past or on the historical performance of the company, industry, or economic development being considered. Analytical investment information, on the other hand, does not limit itself to historical data but includes projections for future performance as well as investment recommendations. Both descriptive and analytical information sources belong in most business reference collections.

Before consulting these sources, prospective investors often need to learn more about specific types of investments. As a result, publications such as guides, encyclopedias, handbooks, and even textbooks are important because they provide broad coverage of the field.

Background Information Sources

Publications in this category introduce novice investors and librarians to specific types of investments, supply answers to quick reference questions, and often include lists and aids to further investigation. Although there are literally hundreds of such publications and Internet sites, the ones that follow are among the most highly regarded.

One good way to begin to understand the basics of investing in each of the major investment mediums is by consulting a personal finance guide.

Quinn, Jane Bryant. **Making the Most of Your Money; Completely Revised and Updated for the Twenty-First Century**. New York: Simon & Schuster, 1997. 944p.

Wiegold, C. Frederic, ed. **The Wall Street Journal Lifetime Guide to Money: Everything You Need to Know About Managing Your Finances—For Every Stage of Life**. New York: Hyperion, 1999. 624p.

Fool.com Fool's School. ©1995–2003. The Motley Fool (Producer). http://www.fool.com/school.htm?ref=G02A06, (Accessed August 28, 2003).

A well-known and easy to read personal finance manual is Jane Bryant Quinn's *Making the Most of Your Money*. It starts out by helping one determine exactly where one stands financially and then goes on to explain basic money management techniques. Next, Quinn offers comprehensive discussions about insurance needs, home ownership, college funding, investment planning, and retirement. This is a good book to start with for overall coverage before turning to other sources for more in-depth discussions. It is an up-to-date, comprehensive, and authoritative all-in-one resource that is not only helpful but also very readable.

The personal finance staff of the *Wall Street Journal's* "Money & Investing" division wrote another good introductory text, the *Lifetime Guide to Money*. Its 10 sections include planning, investing, insurance, benefits, family finances, estate planning, debt, real estate, taxes, money "mistakes," consumer fraud, and various "alternative" lifestyle situations. The information is organized according to the readers' ages and the situations with which they must cope.

The Motley Fool provides a humorous but knowledgeable look at some basic principles of investing. At the *Fool's School* (http://www.fool.com/school.htm?ref=G02A06) the investor can work through the 13 steps to investing, from "Settle Your Finances" to "Advanced Investing Issues" or simply plunge straight into "Investing Basics" (see figure 11.1, page 262.) In this section one can learn about the "joys of compounding," fixed income securities, stocks, mutual funds, and even how to choose an online broker. The founders of the Motley Fool, David and Tom Gardner, have also written four books: *The Motley Fool Investment Guide*, *You Have More Than You Think*, *The Motley Fool Investment Workbook*, and *Rule Breakers, Rule Makers*.

Although an experienced investor might consider these sources superficial or unsophisticated, they are a good starting point for librarians confronted for the first time with a reference question about the data contained in a stock quote or on commodities trading. As with most Web services, there are advertisements at the site; however, they are not too intrusive.

Encyclopedias and Handbooks

Handbooks and single-volume encyclopedias constitute still another source of background information. Usually each chapter deals with a different aspect of investing or with a specific type of investment and is often written by a specialist in the area being covered.

Currier, Chet. **The Investor's Encyclopedia: Tax Reform Edition**. 2nd ed. New York: Franklin Watts, 1987. 469p.

Blume, Marshall E., and Jack P. Friedman, eds. **Encyclopedia of Investments**. Boston: Warren, Gorham & Lamont, 1982. 1041p.

Downes, John, and Jordan Elliot Goodman. **Barron's Finance and Investment Handbook**. 5th ed. Hauppauge, N.Y.: Barron's Educational Series, 1998. 1396p.

Morton, James, ed. **The Financial Times Global Guide to Investing; The Secrets of the World's Leading Investment Gurus**. London; Washington, D.C.: Pitman Publishing, 1995. 748p.

Encyclopedia of Finance. ©2000. Ameritrade (Producer). http://www.ameritrade.com/education/html/encyclopedia/. (Accessed August 28, 2003).

The Investor's Encyclopedia treats a number of investment products, most of which are fairly traditional. The *Encyclopedia* is divided into three main parts: investment vehicles, tools and techniques, and strategies. Arrangement within the first section is alphabetical, ranging from annuities to zero coupon investments. Each entry is several pages long and includes a general description of the product, explains how and where to get investment information and how to invest, and discusses the costs of buying, owning, and selling. Investment risks and drawbacks are considered, as are the potential for income and capital gains.

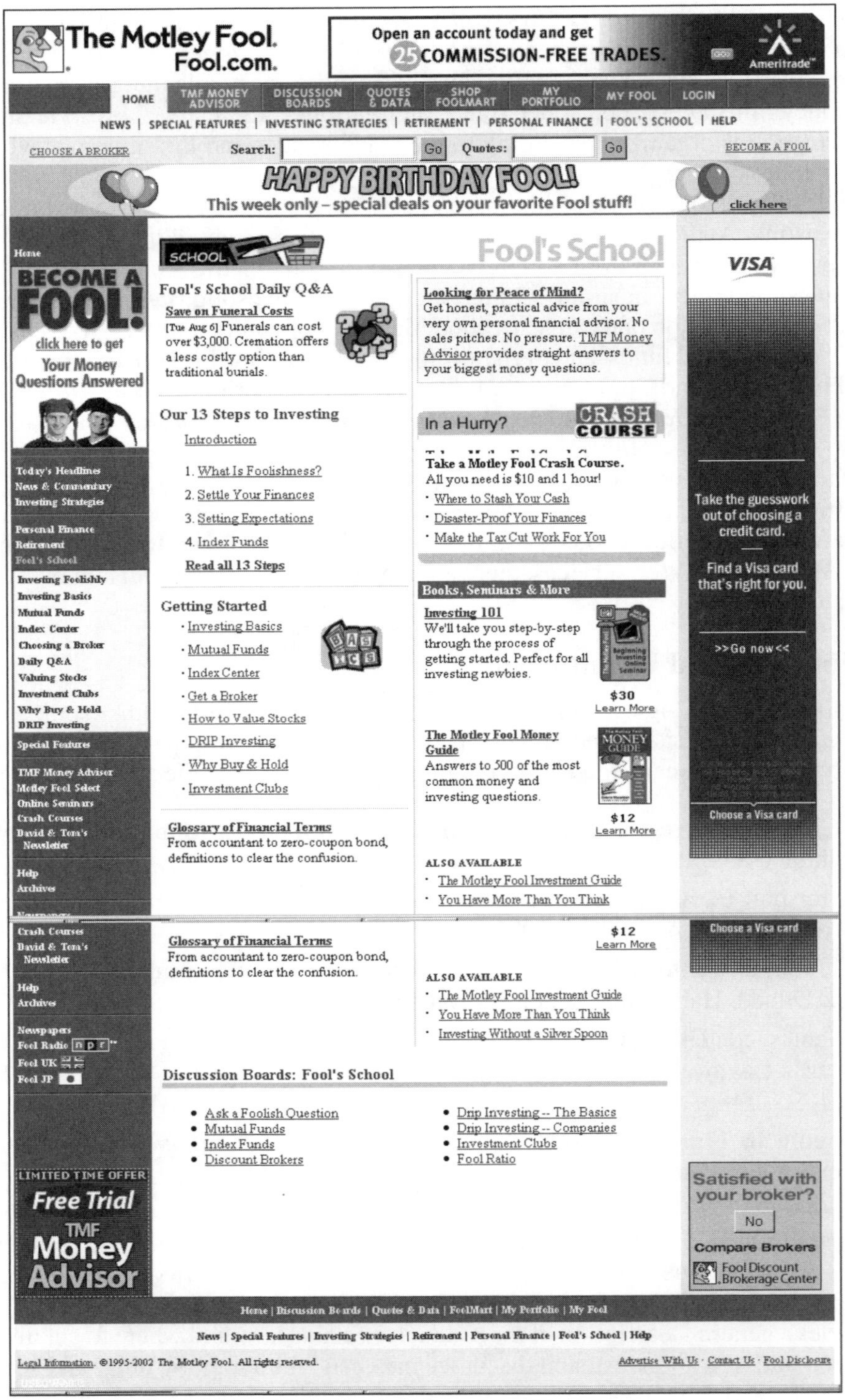

Figure 11.1 The Web page from *Fools' School* by the Motley Fool,
http://www.fool.com/school.htm?ref=G02A06.
© Copyright 1996–2000, The Motley Fool. All rights reserved.

The "Tools and Techniques" section describes such tools as investment advisory services and such techniques as fundamental and technical analysis, while the "Strategies" section covers hedging, index investing, investment clubs, social and ethical investing, and other topics. The *Encyclopedia* begins with a series of indexes that enable readers with certain investment goals—basic savings, maximum safety, current income, retirement, protection against inflation, liquidity, short-term gains, long-term growth, and tax advantages—to pinpoint the investment products, tools, techniques, and strategies most likely to be of interest to them. Although this book is now out of print, it is still a compendium of good information for the beginning investor and for librarians who need a short description of investment vehicles, and it is available in many libraries.

Although it is also intended for the general reader, the *Encyclopedia of Investments* is more scholarly and somewhat more technical than the *Investor's Encyclopedia*. Each chapter, written by an expert, covers a different type of investment and outlines the factors determining its market value, how to buy and sell, tax implications, and representative types of investors. Glossaries and reading lists are also included. *The Encyclopedia of Investments* is particularly useful for quick information on nontraditional investments. Chapters on art deco, rare books, foreign equities, collectibles, leasing ventures, and motion pictures, for example, are included as well as chapters on more traditional investment media. Both of the first two books are old, but much of the information is unchanged and the definitions and descriptions are especially useful.

The *Barron's Finance and Investment Handbook* is useful for both the novice and the more advanced investor. It provides a thorough overview of almost every type of investment, including bonds, annuities, life insurance, real estate investment trusts (REITs), and option contracts. It also contains lists of major financial institutions, historical data on leading indexes, as well as sections on how to read an annual report or financial pages and a comprehensive glossary of investment terms. It is probably the authoritative volume on investing, which is to be expected from Barron's.

The Financial Times Global Guide to Investing provides a complete perspective on the international world of finance and incorporates comprehensive coverage of all the areas for a successful investment strategy in international markets. It introduces the tools and language of modern finance and explains the role and behavior of the key players in the financial markets. More than a hundred of the world's most renowned "gurus" provide insight and advice on diverse investment topics ranging from government bonds to trading strategies. This book includes over 120 sections, each written by professional investors, and covers investment opportunities, strategies, tools, and techniques from seven categories, in over 60 countries. A bonus is Part 7, "Learning from Living Legends," a collection of articles by "the top ten global investors of the 1990s." Names in this group include Sir John Templeton, Dr. Martin Zweig, Mario Gabelli, Michael Aronstein, and Michael Price. Despite being packed with information, this is a very readable guide.

For those who want to quickly find an explanation of terms or a description of a process or strategy, the *Encyclopedia of Finance* is a good site to check. The Web page is divided into sections and then into units within each. The Stock section, for example, is divided into units that cover topics from "why do companies issue stock" to "buying and selling stocks." Although not as authoritative as the print volumes described, it is a quick way to find and deliver information to users.

Dictionaries

Many of the publications already described contain glossaries, but for more detailed definitions or for a more comprehensive listing of terms, it may be necessary to consult an investment dictionary.

Rosenberg, Jerry M. **Dictionary of Investing.** New York: John Wiley, 1993. 368p.

Scott, David Logan. **Wall Street Words: An Essential A to Z Guide for Today's Investor**. 2nd ed. Boston: Houghton Mifflin, 1997. 433p.

investorwords. 1996–2003. WebFinance, Inc. (d/b/a InvestorGuide.com) (Producer). http://www.investorwords.com/. (Accessed August 28, 2003).

The *Dictionary of Investing* lists and defines some 7,500 terms, abbreviations, and acronyms, with numerous cross-references included. It includes succinct but thorough definitions. *Wall Street Words* covers fewer terms, almost 4,000, but is more comprehensive in its descriptions. As well as the usual dictionary description, some entries are supplemented with "case study" paragraphs that provide actual accounts of concepts and strategies. For example, under the entry "microcap fund" there is a description of this type of fund, followed by a more detailed account including the risks of investing in this type of fund.

investorwords is one of the most comprehensive online glossaries available, providing solid definitions for over 6,000 financial terms, and includes 20,000 links between related terms. One can search by letter or within the 20 subject areas that include bonds, stocks, mutual funds, and trading. Searching for the word "options," one is given an exact explanation of the word but also the alternative of checking over 90 terms that include the word. One of the terms listed is "collar," and it has as one of its three definitions: "A combination of put options and call options that can limit, but not eliminate, the risk that their value will decrease." Further links are provided for the underlined terms. Perhaps best of all, this dictionary is provided free. (See figure 11.2.)

Figure 11.2. Screen capture of *investorwords.com*. Reprinted with permission of InvestorWords.com.

Many different types of publications—handbooks, textbooks, personal finance manuals, dictionaries—and Web pages provide needed background information for prospective investors. Similar information is also available in the pamphlets, booklets, and brochures published by brokers, stock and commodity exchanges, mutual funds, and investment companies, most of which are now available via the Web. Investment advisers are using new technologies to provide investment advisory services, to offer their services to prospective advisory clients, to obtain investment research, to facilitate portfolio management, and to communicate with their clients. It is therefore important to be able to identify these companies and to find their Internet addresses. To identify brokers and investment managers, one can consult the following publications.

Nelson's Directory of Investment Managers. Port Chester, N.Y.: Nelson Publications, 1988– . 3v. Annual.

Standard & Poor's Security Dealers of North America. New York: Standard & Poor's, 1922– . Semiannual.

The *Directory of Investment Managers* is one of a number of publications in the investment field from Nelson Publications (http://www.nelsons.com/dim.asp). It is also offered as part of a suite of information from Nelson. The management profiles are detailed and include the address of the company (and the Web address), the investment strategies of the company, the investment vehicles used, and a complete listing of professional staff by category of investment. Companies are listed alphabetically in the first two volumes, and the third contains nine indexes to the companies. These indexes include one by geography, three by investment specialties, three for managers, one by investment products, and one by minority and women owned. This publication is aimed primarily at institutional investors, and so the focus is primarily on this end of the market.

Standard & Poor's Security Dealers of North America has much shorter entries in its listing of U.S. and Canadian securities firms and is aimed at a more general audience. Arrangement is geographical, and the information provided for each firm includes its address, telephone number, identification number, and chief officers; for the firm's headquarters, it also includes the names of the exchanges of which the firm is a member and the types of securities in which it specializes. Also included in the *Directory* are the names and addresses of Canadian and U.S. exchanges and associations, major foreign stock exchanges, a listing of North American securities administrators by state and province, and a section listing firms that have been discontinued, that is, have gone out of business, moved, or changed their name, since the last issue of the directory was published.

There are two main types of brokerage firms, full service and discount. A discount brokerage firm is one that concentrates solely on executing transactions for its clientele, on buying or selling securities at the client's direction. No research is conducted, no advice given, no informational literature published. In return for this "no frills" service, clients can expect to pay some 30 to 50 percent less in commission fees than they would pay to traditional full-service investment firms. People who use discount brokers tend to be thrifty do-it-yourself-ers, and they often turn to the library and now the Internet for investment information.

Investment Advisory Services

Investment advisory services provide current information on general market conditions and/or specific companies. Some of these services are factual, and some are interpretive, making recommendations on the purchase or sale of specific securities. Quality, particularly of the newsletters that sell investment advice, varies tremendously. Some are respectable, and others are no more than hucksters' appeals to the gullible and greedy. There are literally hundreds of these publications, some of which are quite expensive. Each has its own, often vocal, following. Clearly, libraries must be highly selective and somewhat conservative in placing subscriptions to these publications. The service in vogue with investors one season may languish the next:

> Each quarter and each year, there are stars among the investment advisors and security analysts. These are individuals with a better record of picking winners than almost anyone else. Each year there are winners in the Irish Sweepstakes and the New York and Illinois state lotteries. No one, however, ever suggested that the winner of a million dollar grand slam prize in the Illinois state lottery had good insights. Few would pay for his advice on how to buy a winning ticket in the next year's lottery. The key question is whether the winners among the investment advisors have more skill and insight than the winners of the Irish Sweepstakes and the Illinois and New York Lotteries.[2]

The coverage in investment services varies. Some focus on particular types of investments, such as mutual funds or precious metals. Others use specific approaches or methods. Some rely on technical analysis, basing their recommendations on past patterns of market trading and price behavior. Some advocate "contrary opinion," theorizing that if all the other investment advisors are espousing a specific course of action, the sensible thing is to do the opposite. Perhaps one of the most unorthodox systems was that devised by Frederick Goldsmith, who based his recommendations on the actions of Jiggs, a character in the comic strip, "Bringing Up Father":

> If Jiggs was pictured with his right hand in his pocket, the market was a buy. If he was shown with two puffs of smoke rising from his cigar, this meant that the market would be strong in the second hour of trading. . . . When the strip showed Jiggs at the theater observing, "The intermissions are the only good thing about this show," Goldsmith advised his subscribers to buy Mission Oil.[3]

Almost anyone can publish an advisory letter. No special qualifications or preliminary tests are necessary. In fact, all that is required is that the publisher has no record of fraud and that he or she register with and periodically report to the Securities and Exchange Commission. It is mandatory that an annual report be filed with the SEC on the service's financial condition. This must include a brief description of the investment strategy being followed, information sources used, and methods of analysis employed. Publishers of such services have included people from a wide range of backgrounds, many of whom are not particularly well trained to give investment advice and who may not always hold their readers' financial well-being uppermost.

It is evident that library subscriptions to these services should be made with caution. Few publications, however, regularly list or evaluate advisory services. Articles can be found in some of the popular business journals, and descriptions are included in some of the periodicals and newsletter directories mentioned in chapter 3.

The most current and comprehensive source of information in this area is the *Hulbert Financial Digest (HFD)*, a monthly that tracks the performance of 165 investment letters, using a hypothetical $10,000 portfolio to gauge their individual success. This publication contains the rankings of top-performing newsletters, a listing of stocks and mutual funds that currently are most heavily recommended or shunned, and articles. The four top-performing newsletters are profiled in each monthly issue of the *Digest,* and custom profiles of all newsletters can be ordered from http://cbs.marketwatch.com/news/newsletters/overview. asp?siteid=mktw. These customized newsletters contain complete performance ratings and risk-adjusted ratings for the entire period for which the *Digest* has data and graphical analysis of each newsletter's average performance and of each of the individual portfolios the newsletter is recommending. There is a complete listing of all the newsletters included, and Internet links to each Web page, at http://cbs.marketwatch.com/news/newsletters/newsletters. asp?siteid=mktw&Dist=.

The cost, sheer volume, widely differing quality, and rapidly fluctuating popularity with the investing public of investment advisory services are some of the main reasons why most libraries do not support extensive collections of such materials. Factual services, that is, those focusing on past performance, both recent and historical, are likely to be better represented in library collections.

Other services, which have become available to investors because of the emergence of the Internet, are the monitored and unmonitored discussion groups. Many magazines and investment Web sites have an "ask an advisor" link, and then there are the news groups where individuals can share information. To find news groups one can either follow the links in a directory such as Yahoo! or go directly to *Tile.net* at http://tile.net/ and use a query such as "investment club" or "stocks".

Securities Quotations

Investors turn to quotations, brief, numeric price reports, to attempt to determine the present market condition for specific securities. Although the amount of information included in quotations varies, usually most include closing (the last price paid on a particular trading day) and bid (the price someone is willing to pay) prices, the number of units traded, dividends, and high and low prices paid over a designated time period.

Basic to providing good business reference service is the ability to decipher the newspaper tables that contain quotations. Quotations within most tables are arranged alphabetically by company name or abbreviation. The following publication is an extremely useful, compact, easy-to-understand volume that has everything one needs to master the vital information available in newspapers, in business publications, and on computers.

Passell, Peter. **How to Read the Financial Pages**. New York: Warner Books, Incorporated, 1998. 176p.

How to Read the Financial Pages offers clear explanations of basic statistics and translations of daily financial listings for the New York and American Stock and Bond Exchanges, Treasury and other government bonds, money market and mutual funds, and foreign exchanges. It should be consulted by any librarian or investor seeking to better understand the data contained in these tables.

Another publication which is useful to both investors and librarians is the interactive tour "How to Read The Wall Street Journal," available at http://info.wsj.com/college/guidedtour/index.html.

Newspaper abbreviations are not the only alternative designations by which a company may be known. In addition, each company is assigned a ticker symbol, a one- to five-letter designation used by the exchanges on which a company is traded, in ticker quotations, and in some publications and databases. The ticker symbol for the Cisco Systems, for example, is CSCO; for Microsoft Corporation MSFT. Ticker symbols are included, with other information, in many directories, investment services, exchange reports, and other publications, but they are not used in newspapers. Quick lookup services for ticker symbols exist on many business Web pages, including *Motley Fool* (http://www.fool.com).

Notes

1. Jerome B. Cohen, Edward D. Zinberg, and Arthur Zeikel, *Guide to Intelligent Investing* (Homewood, Ill.: Dow Jones-Irwin, 1977), 3.

2. Robert Aliber, *Your Money and Your Life* (New York: Basic Books, 1982), 107.

3. Myron Kandel, *How to Cash in on the Coming Stock Market Boom: The Smart Investor's Guide to Making Money* (Indianapolis, Ind.: Bobbs-Merrill, 1982), 89–90.

12

Stocks

Introduction

In the preceding chapter, basic investment guides were discussed. Before specific stock-related publications can be examined, however, it is first necessary to consider stocks themselves, the markets on which they are traded, and some of the ways in which stock market performance is measured.

Most companies issue stock to raise capital. Each share of stock represents part ownership in a corporation. An investor, after buying stock in a company, may get a handsomely engraved certificate testifying that he or she has, in effect, become part owner. The share of the corporate pie may be small, but the investor has, with the purchase, obtained that same fractional stake in everything the company owns, its plants and equipment, its patents and trademarks, even its management. Because stocks represent ownership, they are also known as equity securities, or equities.

Common and Preferred Stock

Stocks are either common or preferred. If a company issues only one type of stock, it is usually common stock. Similarly, unless the abbreviation pf or pfd follows a stock listed in a newspaper stock table, one can assume that it is a common stock.

With common stock ownership comes the opportunity to vote on corporate matters such as the election of company directors. Ordinarily each shareholder has one vote for each share held. This voting right is one of the ways in which common stock is different from preferred stock.

The other major difference pertains to dividends. A dividend is a payment, usually in cash, but occasionally in stock, made by a firm to its shareholders. Dividends are usually paid quarterly or semiannually. Newspaper stock tables and Internet services include estimates of annual dividends, usually based on the most recent quarterly or semiannual payment, in stock tables for each common and preferred stock traded on the national and regional stock exchanges.

The boards of directors determine dividends on common stocks. They are often, although not always, a direct reflection of how well the company has done in terms of earnings. A significant increase in company profits may well be reflected in an increased dividend to common shareholders. On the other hand, if the board decides to plow its profits back into company expansion or increased research and development, or if business is bad, dividends may be reduced or even eliminated. With common stock, there are no guarantees. The potential for profit or loss is much greater than with preferred stock.

Preferred stock is given preferential treatment over common stock. Preferred stockholders are entitled to their dividends, if any are forthcoming, before common stockholders are paid. Preferred stock, however, pays dividends at a specified rate, determined at the time the stock is issued; a holder of a preferred stock can expect no more than the specified dividend even if the company enjoys a banner year. In most corporations, preferred stockholders do not have the voting, or participation, rights enjoyed by common shareholders.

Convertible preferred stock is basically the same as regular preferred stock except that it can be converted into a certain number of shares of the company's common stock, determined at the time the convertible shares were placed on the market. To the investor, this is having the best of both worlds. The holder of the convertible preferred is promised a fixed dividend on the stock as long as he or she holds it and at the same time enjoys the prospect of being able, at a later date, to convert the shares to take advantage of a rise in the value of the common stock. This conversion privilege, however, can only be exercised once.

Earnings per Share

Investors use a wide range of measures to help determine the value of a stock and to compare it with other stocks. One such measure is earnings per share, or EPS, which translates total corporate profits into profits on a per share basis. A simple formula is used to derive earnings per share:

$$\text{EPS} = \frac{\text{Net profit after taxes} - \text{preferred dividends paid}}{\text{Number of shares of common stock outstanding}}$$

Dividend Yield

Another measure is dividend yield, derived by dividing annual dividends paid per share by the market price per share of stock. Unlike earnings per share, which is expressed in dollars and cents, dividend yield is expressed in percentage points. A company that paid $3 per share in dividends to its stockholders, and whose stock was trading at $30, for example, would have a dividend yield of 10 percent, while one paying $2 in dividends and whose stock is traded at $25 per share would have a dividend yield of 8 percent. Dividend yield is an indication of the rate of current income earned on the investment dollar and is one of the items reported in newspaper stock tables and in other stock-related information sources.

Price-Earnings Ratio

The price-earnings ratio, also known as the price-earnings multiple, multiple, p/e ratio, or p/e, is one of the most commonly used measures of stock value, particularly in comparison with other stocks in the same industry. The price-earnings ratio of a stock is simply the price of the stock divided by its earnings, normally its earnings for the past 12 months. The formula for this is:

P/E = Price of a share of stock

Earnings per share of the stock for the most recent 12-month period

Thus, a share of XYZ, selling for $35, with earnings of $7 per share in the past 12 months will have a p/e ratio of 5. In other words, the market is willing to buy a share of XYZ at a price five times greater than its current earnings.

Generally speaking, stocks in a given industry tend to have similar price-earnings ratios, and growth industries tend to have higher p/e ratios than more established industries. The p/e ratio is but one measure of stock value, but it is one of the most widely used. Price-earnings ratios are included in the newspaper stock tables for most exchanges.

Warrants

Warrants exist in a sort of financial netherworld. They are neither stock nor bond, have no book value, and pay no dividends. A warrant is a purchasable right that allows investors to buy corporate securities, usually common stock, for an extended time at a fixed price. When the designation wt. follows a corporate name (or abbreviation) in a newspaper stock table, it indicates that the security in question is a warrant.

Stock Exchanges

A stock exchange is a central marketplace where shares of stock and other securities are bought and sold, using the auction system. There are three national exchanges in this country as well as several regional exchanges (see figure 12.1).

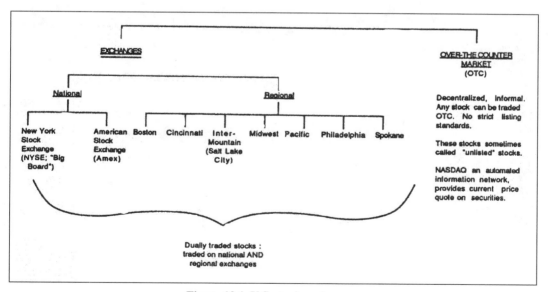

Figure 12.1. U.S. stock exchanges.

Each exchange is a private organization that sets its own standards for the securities it will list (or trade); only securities that have been admitted to a specific exchange can be traded there, and then only by exchange members or their representatives. The three largest exchanges are the national exchanges: the New York Stock Exchange, the American Stock Exchange, and the NASDAQ Stock Market.

New York Stock Exchange

The New York Stock Exchange traces its origins back to 1792, when a group of 24 brokers gathered under a buttonwood tree on Wall Street to devise rules of conduct for the trade of stock, hitherto unregulated, and to take buy and sell orders for those who wanted to trade. From these modest beginnings, the New York Stock Exchange has become the world's leading securities exchange, with more than 800 million shares of stock traded daily.

The standards for the stocks that it lists are also the most stringent. The NYSE requires that a company have an aggregate market value of publicly held shares of $60 million for companies that list at the time of their initial public offerings and $100 million for other companies. They must also earn at least $2.5 million annually and have at least 600,000 shares of publicly held common stock.[1] It is on this exchange that "blue-chip" stocks are traded, companies like GTE CORP, General Motors, IBM, and Maytag Corporation.

Membership on the exchange is costly and hard won. The number of "seats" or memberships on the exchange has been limited, since 1953, to 1,366, most representing brokerage firms. The price of a seat on the exchange fluctuates, but in August 1999 one seat sold for $2,650,000.[2] In addition, prospective members must be sponsored by two current members in good standing and must be approved by the board of directors.

The New York Stock Exchange offers a broad range of informational and educational tools (see figure 12.2).

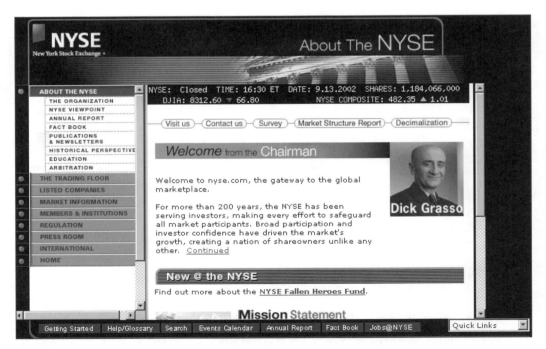

Figure 12.2. Example of the information available from Web page of the NYSE (http://www.nyse.com/about/).

Reprinted with permission of the New York Stock Exchange, ©2002.

Click on "About the NYSE" at http://www.nyse.com and then enter the education section. Here are found educational publications, an interactive education center, available outreach programs, and the educational curriculum section, which provides lesson plans at multiple grade levels. One of the publications available here is *A Guide to the World's Leading Securities Market,* which contains seven chapters, including a description of both the Trading Floor and monitoring for possible illegal trading, all of which are designed to enhance explanations and an understanding of the securities market. Another useful publication is listed below.

New York Stock Exchange. **Fact Book**. New York: The Exchange, 1956– . Annual. Also available in the "About the NYSE" section at http://www.nyse.com/.

The *Fact Book* is an annual compilation of current and historical statistics, with a summary of the previous year's activity and a description of the NYSE's organization and administration. It is an ideal quick reference source for people seeking answers to questions on the volume of shares traded, lists of stocks with largest market value, and the exchange's history.

American Stock Exchange and NASDAQ

The American Stock Exchange (http://www.amex.com) is the second-largest floor-based securities exchange in the United States. Like the NYSE, Amex, originally known as "The Curb Market," is strong on public relations and promotional activities. It makes publications and educational films available to libraries, schools, and prospective investors.

The NASDAQ (http://www.nasdaq.com) is the world's first electronic-based stock market and has become the model for developing markets worldwide. Today, about 5,000 companies, including small, growing companies, as well as many large corporations that have become household names, trade their securities on this electronic market.

On November 2, 1998, the National Association of Securities Dealers, Inc. (NASD), and the American Stock Exchange LLC (Amex) announced that they had merged. They still operate as separate markets but are both under the management of The Nasdaq-Amex Market Group, which is a subsidiary of NASD.

Both exchanges have excellent Web sites, which include histories, guides, screening options, investor resources, and a glossary.

Regional Stock Exchanges

In addition to the national stock exchanges, there are seven major regional exchanges in the continental United States: the Boston (http://www.bostonstock.com/), Cincinnati (http://www.cincinnatistock.com/), Intermountain (Salt Lake City), Midwest (Chicago) (http://www.chx.com/), Pacific (San Francisco and Los Angeles) (http://www.pacificex.com/), Philadelphia (http://www.phlx.com/), and Spokane. These exchanges were formed originally to help finance local corporations; because their standards are not as strict as those of the NYSE and Amex, many smaller companies are traded on the regional exchanges. At the same time, some stocks listed on the national exchanges are also listed on regional exchanges. These stocks are said to be dually traded.

Dually traded stocks are listed in the composite stock price tables for the New York and American Stock Exchanges in financial newspapers. Coverage of stocks that are traded only on regional exchanges, however, is rather sparse. It is limited for the most part to certain key issues, often no more than 10 or 20 for each exchange. More comprehensive information is, of course, available in the financial pages of the newspapers of the cities in which the regional exchanges are located and on the Web pages of the exchanges.

Over-the-Counter Market

The over-the-counter market (OTC) is unlike any of the stock exchanges. It is a decentralized, informal market, a network of thousands of dealer-brokers across the country who do most of their business by telephone and computer. Although NASDAQ stocks are frequently referred to as over the counter, NASDAQ is not the U.S. over-the-counter (OTC) market.

Over-the-counter securities are issued by companies that either choose not to, or are unable to, meet the standards for listing on the NASDAQ or any other stock exchange. Often stocks traded on the OTC market are said to be unlisted, that is, not traded on any of the national exchanges. It is on the OTC market that many small corporations sell shares to the public for the first time, and, as a result, investment in OTC-traded shares of these unproven companies tends to be more speculative than investment in companies listed on the organized exchanges.

The National Association of Securities Dealers, Inc.(NASD) also monitors the OTC market and sets standards for the ethical conduct of its members in much the same way the exchanges do. In 1971, the NASDAQ was created to automate and trade OTC securities. Prior to that, dealer quotations were disseminated by paper copy only. These copies were printed on pink-colored paper, and so the securities became known as "Pink Sheet" stocks. The "Pink Sheets" are still published weekly by the National Quotation Bureau. In addition, an electronic version of the Pink Sheets is updated once a day and disseminated over the Web at http://www.pinksheets.com/. This Web site is the best source available to obtain information about OTC securities (see figure 12.3).

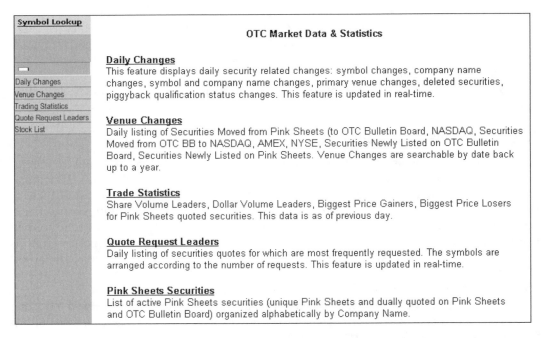

Figure 12.3. Information available from Pink Sheets (http://www.pinksheets.com).

International Stock Exchanges

Many publicly owned companies are increasingly international in both their operations and their ownership, so many investors need to find information on international investment. There are now available more resources, in both print and electronic format, which can guide the researcher in seeking out information on stock exchanges and their regulation.

Sheimo, Michael ed. **International Encyclopedia of the Stock Market**. Chicago: Fitzroy Dearborn, c1999. 1320p.

World Stock Exchange Fact Book. Round Rock, Tex.: Meridian Securities Markets LLC, 1995– . Annual.

The *International Encyclopedia of the Stock market* includes terms that are part of the vocabulary of the international stock market as well as terms specific to particular countries. They are fully defined to make them understandable to both the lay person and the business professional. The *Encyclopedia* also contains extensive information about individual countries' stock markets, including practices and regulation. Also provided are details on each country's leading regulatory agencies, its brokerage firms, and its most prominent practitioners.

By contrast, the *World Stock Exchange Fact Book* is a reference source that includes up to 25 years of data from more than 45 of the major stock markets worldwide. Arrangement is alphabetical by exchange, and each entry contains a mixture of text and statistics. The text includes information on clearing and settlements, commissions and fees, listing requirements, and investor protection, including regulatory agencies. The statistical information consists of historical tables containing as much as 25 years of data on number and value of shares traded, market indicators, including liquidity, and the market value index reported monthly as well as the much-sought-after market capitalization. A useful appendix contains details about the calculation of various indexes and other performance measures. Both publications are rather expensive and so may be beyond the reach of smaller libraries.

There are available on the Internet many Web sites with direct links to international exchanges. Using these one can audit whether companies are listed and check stock prices. One site that is very logically arranged is compiled and edited by Jonathan E. Halsey, Head of Compliance for Old Mutual Asset Managers (UK) Ltd. The exchanges page (http://www.compliance-exchange.com/) is by region and then by country, with direct links to stock markets and other exchanges (see figure 12.4, page 276). This Web site links not only to stock exchanges but also to associations, regulators, selected investment companies, journals, and educational resources (see figure 12.5, page 276).

Stock Prices

The price of a share of stock fluctuates. It is dependent on what buyers are willing to pay and sellers are willing to take, and that in turn is directly affected by corporate and industrywide developments, by the economy, by the current political situation, by foreign exchanges, and by many other factors. Stock price information is contained in many publications, ranging from the financial pages of newspapers to quote services available on the Internet or by linking directly to the stock exchanges via the Web.

Location	Exchange	Comments
Bahrain	Bahrain	There are about forty listed stocks here
Cyprus	Cyprus Stock Exchange	A few local companies are listed. Current market info is available
Iran	Tehran Alt. site	Daily trade table shows yesterday's prices. Company names are not listed in any recognisable order
Israel	Tel Aviv	Impressive array of multimedia
Jordan	Amman	Daily quotes on the Amman Financial Market
Kuwait	KSE	Kuwait Stock Exchange
Lebanon	Beirut	A small number of shares are listed here. The site is still under construction
Malta	Malta Stock Exchange	Check official list for the eight equities listed here. Also govt. bonds and some collective investment schemes
Oman	Muscat	The Muscat Securities Market site shows listed companies, listing rules and current and historic price data

Figure 12.4. Selected exchanges of the Mediterranean and Middle East. Reprinted with permission of http://www.compliance-exchange.com/.

Australia	Australian Securities and Investments Commission	ASIC (formerly named the Australian Securities Commission) is responsible for the conduct of business of Australian financial institutions
Australia	Australian Prudential Regulation Authority	APRA is responsible for the prudential regulation of Australian financial institutions. It came into existence on 1 July, 1998
Australia	Australian Financial Institutions Commission	AFIC is the prudential regulator for state-based Australian financial institutions. Copies of legislation are available for download
Australia	Australian Competition and Consumer Commission	ACCC administers legislation relating to anti-competitive and unfair market practices, mergers or acquisitions of companies, product safety/liability, and third party access to facilities of national significance
Australia	Financial Industry Complaints Service	FICS is a complaint resolution scheme for consumers who have a complaint about advice or loss as a result of consultation with a financial planner, stockbroker or investment adviser
New Zealand	New Zealand Securities Commission	Annual report available and some very general statements of principle

Figure 12.5. Extract of Web page showing some regulators for Australasia.
Reprinted with permission of http://www.compliance-exchange.com/.

Stock Tables

Most newspapers contain daily price information for stocks traded on the New York and American Stock Exchanges and the NASDAQ, as well as for the most active stocks traded on some regional exchanges. Stock prices from the previous day's trading are printed in tables in most newspapers Tuesday through Saturday, and the week's activity is commonly summarized on Sunday. These tables use an extremely abbreviated format, and basic to the provision of good business reference is an understanding of the items contained in a newspaper stock table. Figure 12.6 contains some of the most heavily used terms. Not all of this information is contained in every table; newspapers may leave out some of the columns listed, and it may be listed in a different order.

HI - LO	SYM	DIV	VOL	YLD	PE	HI – LO	CLOSE	NET CHG
47 – 37	WXYZ	1.80	315	5	10	43 - 40	423/8	+1

Column 1
> The high and low prices of this stock during the past year.

Column 2
> Shorthand for the company name.

Column 3
> Shows the annual rate of dividend payment, based on the company's most recent dividend declaration. In this example it is $1.80.

Column 4
> The volume of shares (in 100s) that were traded that day. On the date given it was 31,500.

Column 5
> Dividend yield, which is the current return on invested capital.

Column 6
> A key measure of a stock's underlying value. The P/E ratio compares the price per share to the earnings per share

Column 7
> The highest and lowest prices for trades on the last trading day.

Column 8
> The last price at which a share was traded.

Column 9
> Last trade yesterday compared to last trade of the day before. This is in dollars.

Figure 12.6. Hypothetical stock table.

Most newspapers also have Web sites that include a business section from which one can access a quote server that will give the latest stock price information. The added advantage of using the Internet is that the quotes are usually only 15 to 20 minutes delayed, at the most, and these pages will often link to current news stories about the stock being checked.

Sometimes historical stock prices may be required. Brokers, accountants, tax lawyers, and serious investors who need such data or want to study trends in the prices of specific stocks over a period of time can use either online or printed sources.

Daily Stock Price Record. New York: Standard & Poor's. Quarterly. (Available in separate editions: American Stock Exchange, 1962– ; New York Stock Exchange, 1962– ; and NASDAQ 1968– .)

Dow Jones & Co., Reuters Ltd. **factiva**. New York: Factiva, c2002– . Updated continuously.

Silicon Investor. 1995. http://www.siliconinvestor.com/. (Accessed August 28, 2003).

Each printed edition of the *Daily Stock Price Record* includes both daily and weekly stock prices and trading information for three-month periods. Separate volumes are issued each quarter for the American Stock Exchange, the New York Stock Exchange, and the NASDAQ. Although this publication may be too specialized for small and medium-sized libraries, librarians providing business reference service should know that it exists and that it provides a convenient alternative to online services.

Historical quotes are included in the *Companies/Markets* section of *factiva,* an online database that provides daily, weekly, monthly, and quarterly high, low, and closing stock prices for the past year, as well as stock trading volumes. The service also provides the ability to adjust for capital changes such as stock splits. The information can be produced in a formatted report, in an Excel spreadsheet, in a chart, or as a comma-delimited file.

For smaller libraries and researchers there is now available similar information free on the Internet from *Silicon Investor* (http://www.siliconinvestor.com). This service began as a discussion group forum but has evolved to provide research tools and resources that include company news, industry trends, and market commentary. Anyone can access the site, but to post to the discussion forum one must be a member. To get daily historical stock prices as far back as 1968, the user first enters the stock symbol of the company for which information is being sought. The quote that appears is for current data, and then there is an option to link to, for example, historical prices, a company profile, and earnings estimates.

Stock Price Indexes

Although investors are interested in the performance of specific stocks, they are also concerned with general stock market trends. Stock price indexes or averages give an overview of general stock market conditions. An index is a benchmark against which financial or economic performance is measured, There are several such market indicators, but the two best known are the Dow Jones Industrial Average and the Standard & Poor's Composite 500 Index.

Dow Jones Industrial Average

Anyone who watches network news has probably heard of the Dow Jones Industrial Average, which is given nightly along with other stock market information. The Dow Jones Industrial is a statistical compilation of the average prices of 30 well-known, blue-chip common stocks traded on the New York Stock Exchange. Although Dow Jones compiles averages for transportation and utilities as well, it is the Industrial Average that is Wall Street's most widely quoted measure of stock market performance.

Standard & Poor's 500 Index

More inclusive than the Dow Jones Industrial Average is the Standard & Poor's 500 Index, which measures the activities of 500 stocks considered to be a benchmark of the overall stock market. This index is composed of industrial, transportation, utility, and financial companies, with a heavy emphasis on industrial companies.

Other Indexes

Other indexes commonly referred to by market analysts reflect the behavior of stocks on each of the major markets on which they are traded. The New York Stock Exchange Composite (http://www.nyse.com/indexes/) includes all stocks listed on that exchange, and the NASDAQ Composite Index (http://www.nasdaq.com/) is composed of all stocks traded on NASDAQ. Another widely used index is the Russell 2000 (http://www.russell.com/US/Indexes/default.asp), which is the best-known of a series of market value weighted indexes published by the Frank Russell Company. The index measures the performance of the smallest 2,000 companies in the Russell 3000, and index of the 3,000 largest U.S. companies in terms of market capitalization. The Wiltshire 5000 Equity index is a market value-weighted index that includes all NYSE and AMEX stocks and the most active over-the-counter stocks and is used to measure a wider variety of investment styles. There are now over 7,000 stocks in the index. Stocks selected for the Wilshire 5000 must be headquartered in the United States and have readily available pricing data.

Stock Index Information Sources

Information on stock price indexes is easy to find, particularly for the more popular indexes. It is contained in financial newspapers, at most financial Web sites, and in sources that provide comprehensive stock market information. In addition to the standard statistical guides described earlier, a more specialized guide, useful despite its age, lists sources that contain stock price indexes and averages.

Bentley, Linda Holman, and Jennifer J. Kiesl. **Investment Statistics Locator**. Rev. ed. Phoenix, Ariz.: Oryx Press, 1995. 275p.

The *Investment Statistics Locator* lists by subject data available in 53 major investment serials. It cites the sources, for example, that publish half-hourly, hourly, daily, weekly, monthly, quarterly, and yearly versions of the Dow Jones Industrial Average. Less widely quoted market indicators and other types of investment statistics are also covered.

Each issue of the *Wall Street Journal Index* includes closing Dow Jones averages for the month or year being indexed, and Standard & Poor's *Daily Stock Price Record* series include three-month compilations of stock price indexes and averages in the first part of each volume. A brief explanation of each indicator is also provided.

When historical information is being sought, two publications are particularly helpful.

Pierce, Phyllis, ed. **The Dow Jones Averages, 1885–1995.** Chicago: Irwin Professional, 1996. 1v. unpaged.

Standard & Poor's Statistical Service. New York: Standard & Poor's Corporation, 1978– . 1v. Loose-leaf service with monthly supplements.

The Dow Jones Averages, 1885–1995 is useful for its description of the history and development of the indexes created by Dow Jones as well as for daily stock averages from January 16, 1885, through December 31, 1995. Each daily listing includes data on the Dow Jones Industrial, Transportation, and Utilities Averages as well as daily sales figures.

Standard & Poor's Statistical Service provides similar data for indexes developed by Standard & Poor's. The most recent information, included in the monthly "Current Statistics" supplements, also presents summary monthly information for the Dow Jones averages for the current and preceding years as well as weekly information for an array of Standard &

Poor's indexes for the same time period. In addition to the Standard & Poor's 500 Composite Index, for example, "Current Statistics" includes indexes for different types of stocks; capital goods versus consumer goods; high-grade versus low-price common stocks; and for such industry categories as aerospace, computer services, textile products, and toy manufacturers.

Data in the monthly "Current Statistics" section is enhanced by the *Security Price Index Record*, part of the *Statistical Service.* The *Record* presents the various S&P stock price indexes dating back to the 1920s, describes their history and development, and explains how they are computed. It is a key source of historical data for these and many other measures of stock performance and trading activity.

Corporate Reports

Astute investors require more than stock price and dividend information about the companies in which they are interested. They also want to know about company management, the products manufactured, and prospects for the future. Corporate reports, particularly those submitted to stockholders and the U.S. Securities and Exchange Commission, provide this information and are the primary data sources on which most published financial and investment advisory services are based.

Registration and Prospectus

The Securities and Exchange Commission (SEC) (http://www.sec.gov), established by the Securities Exchange Act of 1934, serves as the government watchdog over the securities industry. Two of its major functions are to require that publicly traded companies make detailed financial reports to it and to make the information contained in these reports accessible to the public so that it can make informed investment decisions. This begins with the company registration.

Before most companies can make a public offering of new securities, they must file a registration statement with the SEC.[3] This document includes general business information such as corporate history, products, sales, number of employees, and an assessment of competition. It also includes detailed financial statements and balance sheet information, a description of the security being offered, and information about management.

The prospectus, a document intended for prospective investors, contains the highlights of the registration statement. The SEC is careful to point out that while the information contained in the prospectus is accurate, its approval of the document does not imply that the security being offered is necessarily a wise and prudent investment choice. Four key areas in the prospectus deserve the would-be investor's concentration: (1) "Company Business," (2) "Recent Developments," (3) "Use of Proceeds," and (4) "Litigation." The prospectus is a very useful source of information on officer compensation.

A copy of the prospectus can be obtained from the company itself, from brokers selling the stock, and from the SEC database *EDGAR* (http://www.sec.gov/edgar.shtml).

10-K Report

The 10-K report, so called because it is submitted on form 10-K, is a detailed annual report that all publicly traded companies must submit to the SEC. It is the most exhaustive source of current corporate information. The report is divided into two sections, financial data and supporting data. The financial section includes a statistical summary of operations for the last five years, financial statements for each line of business, legal proceedings, and a list or diagram of parents and subsidiaries. The supporting data in the second section of the report include a list of principal stockholders, security holdings of management, and a list of directors with specific background information and term of office for each.

The information contained in 10-K reports is basic to investment analysis. Major business reference collections may include microfiche copies of 10-K reports for all publicly traded companies, for Fortune 500 companies only, or for some specially designated category (perhaps by industry or state). These reports are also available electronically from the SEC through the *EDGAR* (Electronic Data Gathering, Analysis, and Retrieval) system (see figure 12.7). Companies were phased in to *EDGAR* filing over a three-year period, ending May 6, 1996. As of that date, all public domestic companies were required to make their filings on *EDGAR*, except for those filings made in paper that had been given a hardship exemption. It should be noted that companies that have fewer than 500 investors and less than $10 million in total assets are not required to file annual and quarterly reports with the SEC.

General-Purpose Searches	Special-Purpose Searches
Search Companies and Filings NEW	**EDGAR CIK (Central Index Key) Lookup**
Find companies and associated filings	*Look up a company's CIK*
Show Latest Filings NEW	**Current Events Analysis**
List filings as they are processed by SEC	*Retrieve filings made on EDGAR during the previous week*
Quick Forms Lookup	**Mutual Funds Retrieval**
Webmasters note: *Quick Forms Lookup is temporarily unavailable. Please use the general Search Companies and Filings search function.*	*Search for mutual fund filings by name of fund and time period*
	Prospectus Search
Search the Historical EDGAR Archives	*Retrieve prospectuses and other "485" forms for a specified mutual fund*
Enter a keyword or phrase to search all header information (including addresses)	**Exhaustive Mutual Funds Search**
	Find ownership information (Schedule 13D) for all mutual funds on EDGAR

**Figure 12.7. Search choices on the *EDGAR* database at
http://www.sec.gov/edgar/searchedgar/webusers.htm.**

Comprehensive investment services routinely include information extracted from these reports. And in some instances, the companies themselves duplicate the contents of their 10-K reports in their annual reports to shareholders (known as an ARK). Finally, many libraries have online databases, such as *Disclosure,* that extract data from the 10-K and other SEC reports. The information contained in 10-K reports is easily accessible to all libraries and researchers.

Annual Report to Shareholders

Annual reports are free and generally available to libraries upon request; the only costs involved are for the postcards to request them, the staff time to process them, and the file cabinets in which to store them. Many are also available from company Web pages, although most companies only have current reports available. There are also services that will provide access to Web versions and hard copies of some current reports, including the following:

> *Public Register's Annual Report Service,* http://www.annualreportservice.com/

> *PRARS,* http://www.prars.com/cgi-bin/search.cgi

> *CAROL,* http://www.carol.co.uk/

Not all companies participate in these services, but if the information is available a direct link to the report is provided, which negates having to search company sites, and in some cases if a print copy is preferred it can be provided.

Historic collections of annual reports are also included in LexisNexis as part of the *NAARS* section and more recent years in the annual reports module of *FIS Online*.

Since annual reports to shareholders are not official SEC filings, there is considerable leeway in the depth of information they contain. One company's report may be little more than a glossy public relations effort; another's may essentially duplicate its 10-K report. Novice investors should be forewarned that annual reports do not always present the unvarnished truth.

Annual reports generally have two main parts. The first part summarizes the company's financial state, reviews its accomplishments for the past year, and discusses its plans and outlook for the future. The tone is positive, and problems or failures are seldom discussed. The second part of the report consists of the corporate financial statements or extracts from them, which are prepared by the company and verified by independent auditors. It is an excellent source of financial statistics, including current assets; property, plants, and equipment; liabilities; stockholders' equity; earnings; per share data; and for most companies, a 10 year summary of financial highlights.

The four reports that have been mentioned thus far—the registration statement, the prospectus, the 10-K report, and the annual report to shareholders—are rich sources of corporate information.

Other Reports

The reports described above are the most commonly consulted company filings, but they are not the only ones a company is required to make. Other reports must be filed with the SEC. The 8-K, for example, must be filed whenever unscheduled material events or significant corporate changes take place. Companies are also required to file listing application statements with national or regional stock exchanges whenever they propose to trade a new security on that exchange. A listing and description of these are available from the SEC Web site. Figure 12.8 gives examples of explanations of basic filings.

Finally, companies must file detailed reports with agencies of the state in which they are located. Three types of reports may be required:

1. *General corporate reports.* These will include the initial articles of incorporation (required in all states), notices of mergers and name changes, and, in most states, annual reports.

2. *Debt reports.* Under the Uniform Commercial Code, a company must file a report whenever it borrows against any of its assets. A separate statement is filed for each debt and will usually show the name and address of the debtor and the lender, along with a description of the property used as collateral and the maturity date of the loan.

3. *Security reports.* If a publicly traded company is listed on one of the national exchanges or if it is traded in more than one state, it must submit disclosure filings to the SEC. If its securities are traded in only one state, it is not required to report to the SEC but must file similar disclosure statements with the state in which it is being traded.

These state-filed reports are valuable information sources, particularly for smaller companies that are not traded on the national exchanges. Copies of these reports are usually available from the state agencies where they are filed.

10	This is the general form for registration of securities pursuant to section 12(b) or (g) of the '34 Act of classes of securities of issuers for which no other form is prescribed. It requires certain business and financial information about the issuer.
10-SB	This is the general form for registration of securities pursuant to Sections 12(b) or (g) of the '34 Act for "small business issuers." This form requires slightly less detailed information about the company's business than Form 10 requires.
8-A	This optional short form may be used by companies to register securities under the '34 Act.
8-B	This specialized registration form may be used by certain issuers with no securities registered under the '34 Act that succeed to another issuer which had securities so registered at the time of succession.
20-F	This is an integrated form used both as a registration statement for purposes of registering securities of qualified foreign private issuers under Section 12 or as an annual report under Section 13(a) or 15(d) of the '34 Act.
40-F	This is an integrated form used both as a registration statement to register securities of eligible publicly traded Canadian foreign private issuers or as an annual report for such issuers. It serves as a wraparound for the company's Canadian public reports.

Figure 12.8. The most widely used 1934 Act registration forms.
Taken from http://www.sec.gov/info/edgar/forms.htm.

Comprehensive Investment Services

Comprehensive investment services are used by people who want information about stocks and bonds and about specific companies and industries. Investment services fall into two categories. Some, which present facts and figures but contain no recommendations, are called investment and research information services. Others, which go one step further and advise readers regarding the investment outlook for the securities they list, are called investment advisory services. Investment and research information and advisory services, however, have several characteristics in common. Both are based on data compiled from the various SEC filings, annual reports, and other corporate releases, and may provide information on thousands of companies. Both are revised and updated on a regular basis. Finally, the cost of compiling these services is high, and as a result, subscriptions to them are expensive. Most are offered both as hard copy and electronic services.

Investment and Research Information Services

One product that most librarians and researchers know about is the collection of *Moody's Manuals,* now officially listed as *Mergent Manuals.* In 1998 Mergent, Inc. (formerly Financial Communications Company, Inc.) acquired the Financial Information Services division of Moody's Investor's Service. In this process it acquired "cornerstone" products that have traditionally been the *Manuals* and *Investment Guides.* Although Mergent has maintained these sources, it has focused its product development agenda on electronic technology and transfer of data. Both print copies and electronic products are described in this section.

Mergent FIS, Inc. **[Mergent] Moody's Manuals.** New York: Mergent. Annual. (8 different titles, described below.)

Mergent Online. New York: Mergent, 1998– . Computer file. http://www.mergent.com.

[Mergent] Moody's Manuals on Microfiche. New York: Mergent, 1909– . Annual.

Standard Corporate Descriptions. New York: Standard & Poor's, 1973– . Monthly with biweekly news updates.

Standard & Poor's NetAdvantage. New York.: McGraw-Hill, 1999– . Internet resource. (Search http://www2.standardandpoors.com.)

Mergent Manuals is the collective designation for a series of publications. Together, they cover approximately 25,000 American and foreign companies traded on the national, regional, and OTC exchanges, and some 17,000 municipal and government securities. These listings are consolidated by type into the following eight manuals, issued annually.

1. **Mergent Bank & Finance Manual.** New York: Mergent, 1955– . Annual. (Updated by Mergent Bank & Finance news reports at http://www.mergent. com/publish/news_reports.asp, July 1999– , which are cumulated monthly in: *Mergent Corporate News Reports*, July 1999– , 4v.) These volumes cover banks, insurance companies, real estate companies, real estate investment trusts, and miscellaneous financial enterprises.

2. **Mergent Industrial Manual.** New York: Mergent, 1954– . Annual. (Updated by *Moody's Industrial News Reports*, 1970–June 1999; by: Mergent news reports at http://www.mergent.com/publish/news_reports.asp, July 1999–, which are cumulated monthly in: *Mergent Corporate News Reports*, July 1999– , 2v.) Includes industrial companies traded on the New York, American, and regional stock exchanges. Although coverage varies, each company listing generally includes history and background, a description of the business, a list of subsidiaries and of principal plants and properties, and names and titles of officers and directors. Statistical data include income accounts, financial and operating statistics, and long-term debt and capital stock. The "Special Features Section," a blue paper insert in volume 1, includes a classification of companies by products and industries, a geographic index, and several tables pertaining to industrial securities, many of which go back 40 years or more.

3. **Mergent International Manual**. New York: Mergent, 1981– . Annual. (Updated by *Mergent International News Reports* at http://www.mergent.com/publish/ news_reports.asp, July 1999–, which are cumulated monthly in *Mergent International News Reports*, July 1999– .) Provides financial and business informa-

tion on more than 9,000 major foreign corporations and national and transnational institutions in 100 countries. The "Special Features" section includes a classification of companies by industries and products and selected financial statistics.

4. **Mergent OTC Industrial Manual.** New York: Mergent, 1970– . Annual. (Updated by *Mergent OTC Industrial News Reports* at http://www.mergent.com/publish/news_reports.asp, July 1999– , which are cumulated monthly in *Mergent Corporate News Reports*, July 1999– , 1v.) Information is very similar to that contained in the *Industrial Manual* except that the companies listed are those whose securities are traded over-the-counter.

5. **Mergent OTC Unlisted Manual**. New York: Mergent, 1986– . (Updated by *Moody's OTC Unlisted News Reports*, 1986–June 1999 and by *Mergent OTC Unlisted News Reports* at http://www.mergent.com/publish/news_reports.asp, July 1999– , which are cumulated monthly in: *Mergent Corporate News Reports*, July 1999– , 1v.) A collection of over 2,200 companies not listed on national or regional exchanges.

6. **Mergent Municipal & Government Manual**. New York: Mergent, 1955– . Annual. (Updated by *Moody's Municipal & Government News Reports*, 1986–June 1999 and by *Moody's Municipal & Government News Reports* at http://www.mergent.com/publish/news_reports.asp, July 1999– , which are cumulated monthly in *Mergent Municipal News Reports*, 1999– .) Includes federal, state, and local government bond issues.

7. **Mergent Public Utility Manual**. New York: Mergent, 1954– . Annual. (Updated by *Moody's Public Utility News Reports*,1986–June 1999 and by *Moody's Public Utility News Reports* at http://www.mergent.com/publish/news_reports. asp, July 1999– , which are cumulated monthly in *Mergent Corporate News Reports*, July 1999– .) Domestic and foreign public utilities are covered, including electric and gas utilities, gas transmission companies, and water and telephone companies

8. **Mergent Transportation Manual**. New York: Mergent, 1954– . Annual. (Updated by *Moody's Transportation News Reports*,1986–June 1999 and by *Moody's Transportation News Reports* at http://www.mergent.com/publish/news_reports.asp, July 1999– , which are cumulated monthly in *Mergent Corporate News Reports*, July 1999– .) Includes railroads and airlines as well as other fields of transportation such as bus and truck lines; water transport; oil pipelines; private bridge, canal, and tunnel companies; and car and truck rental companies. Its coverage of the railroad industry is outstanding.

The focus of each *Manual* determines the kind of specialized information it contains. Each listing, however, includes a history of the company or institution, a description of its business, its address, a list of its officers and directors, and basic financial data.

In addition to company-specific information, each *Manual* includes a blue "Special Features" section, which provides a wealth of current and historical statistical data and other information. This section in the *Bank & Finance Manual*, for example, lists stock splits and stock dividends, while the one in the *Transportation Manual* includes a comprehensive statistical and analytical survey of the railroad industry.

Each of the *Manuals* is updated by a newsletter, which may include interim financial statements, merger proposals, litigation, personnel changes, description of new debt and stock issues, and announcement of new financings. These are available online.

Mergent is a comprehensive service, and as a result, bonds as well as stocks and other securities are listed. For both bonds and preferred stocks, it assigns ratings so that relative investment qualities can be noted. For bonds, nine symbols are used, ranging from Aaa (highest investment quality, least risk) to C (lowest investment quality, highest risk). A variation of the bond rating symbols is used for Moody's (Mergent) preferred stock ratings, with **aaa** the designation for a top-quality preferred stock and **caa** the symbol for an issue that is likely to be in arrears on dividend payments. The blue pages in the front of each manual describe these ratings in some detail.

Moody's Complete Corporate Index, an index that is included with a subscription to the *Manuals*, is a convenient alphabetical index to the companies listed in the seven manuals that Moody's classifies as its corporate manuals. (*Municipal & Government Manual* is not included.)

Moody's Manuals on Microfiche, which includes all former titles, is a useful collection for historical research.

Mergent incorporates into *Mergent Online* historical and financial information as reported by the companies for over 10,000 U.S. public companies traded on the NYSE, AMEX, and NASDAQ stock exchanges as well as historical and financial information for approximately 17,000 non-U.S.-based companies from over 100 countries. Financials for 10 years (which will expand to 15 years) are "as reported" and can be downloaded to spreadsheet software such as Microsoft Excel. Financial information is given in either local currency or U.S. dollars. It includes links to EDGAR filings from 1993 to the present for U.S. companies, and annual reports in image format, archived from 1996, are also available. One can also retrieve lists of institutional holdings and insider trades.

In the basic mode, one may search by company name or ticker symbol. In the advanced mode, one may search for companies meeting specified criteria including selected SIC codes, geographical areas, revenues, and profits. The "build a report" function enables users to select, rank, and sort data items for companies. The database can be purchased in modules and added to as funds become available.

Standard Corporation Descriptions, the second comprehensive investment service, is roughly comparable to Moody's *Manuals*. It, too, lists companies traded on the New York and American Stock Exchanges and the larger unlisted and regional exchange companies, and the information it contains is extracted from company reports and SEC filings. *Corporation Descriptions*, now issued monthly, lists companies alphabetically rather than segregating them into broad industrial categories. Each issue contains an alphabetical index that includes name changes. Information for each company listed includes a description of the business, a list of plants and property, officers, and financial and operating data.

Standard & Poor's NetAdvantage includes electronic versions of nine S&P publications providing company, industry, and market specific information and data: the *S&P Bond Guides; Earnings Guide; Corporation Descriptions; Industry Surveys; Mutual Funds; S&P Outlook; Register of Corporations, Executives, & Directors; S&P Stock Guide;* and *Stock Reports.* As with *Mergent Online,* the data can be bought in modules and added to as funds allow.

Like Moody's (Mergent), Standard & Poor's rates bonds for their investment safety. The highest rating is AAA, which indicates that the capacity to pay interest and repay principal is extremely strong. D, the lowest rating, indicates that the company is in arrears of paying interest and/or repaying the principal.

In contrast to the Mergent's and Standard & Poor's investment information services, Value Line Investment Survey is an investment advisory service.

Value Line Investment Survey. New York: Value Line, 1936– . Weekly.

Value Line Investment Survey (Expanded Edition). New York: Value Line, 1995– . Weekly.

Like the others, *Value Line* includes investment information, but it goes beyond presentation of factual material to include advice regarding the investment outlook for specific stocks and industries. "The operation is stumbling," the would-be investor may be warned, or, on a more hopeful note, "This stock is a worthwhile speculation." In addition, *Value Line* numerically ranks the stocks it lists for investment safety, for probable price performance and yield in the next 12 months, and for estimated appreciation potential in the next three to five years. These rankings are one of the reasons why *Value Line* is such a popular service.

There are three main parts to *Value Line*: an index and summary section, a newsletter, and the company and industry reports section. The index includes the page citations to the companies listed. It also features tables for best and worst performing stocks, stocks with high three- to five-year appreciation potential, high yielding stocks, and lists of the companies whose stocks have been rated highest for safety and performance. Finally, for each company listed in the index, selected financial information, taken from the company reports section, is also included.

The second section, "Selection & Opinion," includes general stock market information, investment strategies, and an in-depth analysis of a specially recommended stock in its "Stock Highlight" feature.

The "Ratings & Reports" section, however, comprises the bulk of the service. In all, some 1,700 companies are covered in detail. (A sample listing is shown in figure 12.9, page 288.) Companies are grouped into broad industrial categories and then listed alphabetically. Particularly noteworthy for each company listing are the *Value Line* ratings; the "Insider Decision Index," which compares the purchase versus the sale of stocks in the company by its officers, directors, and other "insiders"; detailed statistical analyses, including historical data and projections; and beta. Beta, also known as the beta coefficient, is a measure of the sensitivity of a specific stock's price to overall price fluctuations in the New York Stock Exchange Composite Average. It is essentially an index of risk, in which the Composite Average is assigned a value of 1.0. Individual securities may be assigned betas that are less than, the same as, or more than the Composite Average. Generally, the higher the beta, the more volatile the stock. A high-risk stock thus has a high beta, a low-risk one a low beta. Although betas are included in a few other printed and online sources, *Value Line* is one of the most widely held publications containing betas.

Value Line, which is issued weekly, continuously analyzes the stocks it lists. Four times each year (or every 13th week), each stock is reevaluated, and a new analysis is printed. The *Expanded Edition,* which covers a further 1,800 stocks, follows, for the most part, the same layout, but the emphasis is on smaller and mid-cap stocks.

Unlike Moody's and Standard & Poor's, *Value Line Standard Edition* includes industry as well as company analyses. The listings for Coca-Cola and PepsiCo, for example, are preceded by a survey of the soft drink industry. Usually included in the industry analyses are a discussion of current political, economic, and technological developments that may affect the outlook for the industry; composite statistics; and *Value Line's* assessment of investment opportunities in the industry. It also includes explicit rankings of the industry investment prospects. In all, 93 different industries are covered, ranging from advertising to wireless networking.

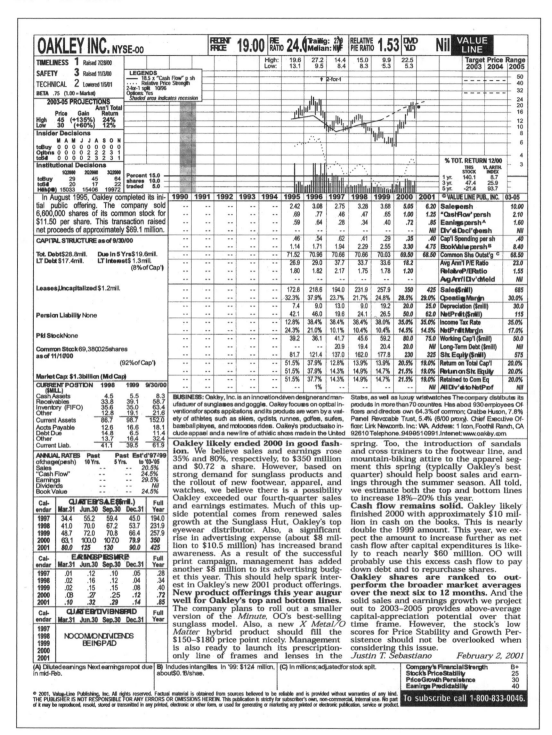

Figure 12.9. Typical listing, "Ratings and Reports" section, *Value Line Investment Survey*.
Reproduced with the permission of Value Line Publishers, Inc.

The standard edition of *Value Line* is available on CD-ROM, and both the standard and the expanded are available via the Web as well as in print. For many individual investors, the printed *Value Line* offers economical access to investment information. For those who would like to sort, screen, and graph individual common stocks, industry groups, or portfolios, the electronic versions are a worthwhile alternative.

Sources of Industry Information

Information on specific companies is vital to investors, but it should be supplemented with industrywide information. Someone contemplating a stock purchase in a large newspaper chain, for example, needs all available information about its financial well-being and the quality of its management but also needs to learn more about the outlook for the newspaper industry generally. Fortunately, there are many published industry studies. Depth of coverage varies but usually includes a review of the industry's recent performance, a description of the present situation, and projections for the future. A survey of the newspaper industry, for example, may discuss the effects that automation and consolidation of ownership have had on the industry, consider the implications of the shift of advertising dollars from newspapers to television, or speculate about the development of the Internet and whether electronic technology will fully replace print newspapers. Considerable statistical data may be included.

Industry Studies

The most comprehensive of all of the industry studies are the economic censuses published every five years by the federal government. The economic censuses are supplemented by monthly, quarterly, and annual surveys. Data from the 1997 census are published on the basis of the North American Industry Classification System, unlike earlier data, which were based on the Standard Industrial Classification (SIC) system. The census taken in 1997 is primarily available on the Internet (see http://www.census.gov/epcd/www/econ97.html), and only highlights have been issued in paper (see figure 12.10). One huge advantage of this method is that one may see quickly which reports are available, find the dates of publication for others, and link quickly to reports and tables. No longer does one have to check with a depository library to access the information.

Subject Series

Link to pdf	Series number	Title	Released
PDF	EC97F52S-LS	Source of Revenue	October 25, 00
PDF	EC97F52S-SZ	Establishment and Firm Size	November 28, 00
PDF	EC97F52S-SB	Miscellaneous Subjects	April 06, 01
PDF	EC97F52S-SM	Summary	April 11, 01

Figure 12.10. 1997 *Economic Census*: Some reports available in the insurance and finance sector. Taken from http://www.census.gov/epcd/www/97EC52.HTM.

In the preceding section, it was mentioned that *Value Line* contains industry as well as company analyses. Other sources, however, concentrate primarily on industry information.

Marlow-Ferguson, Rebecca, ed. **Encyclopedia of American Industries**. 3rd ed. Farmington Hills, Mich.: Gale Group, 2000. 2v.

Standard & Poor's Industry Surveys. New York: Standard & Poor's, 1973– . Weekly. (Supplemented monthly with *Monthly Investment Review* and *Trends Projections*.)

Mergent's Industry Review. New York: Mergent, 1989– . Loose-leaf, with biweekly updates.

U.S. Industry & Trade Outlook. New York: DRI/McGraw-Hill, Standard & Poor's; Washington, D.C.: U.S. Dept. of Commerce/International Trade Administration: [Supt. of Docs., U.S. G.P.O., distributor], c1998– . Annual. (Formerly *U.S. Industrial Outlook*. Washington, D.C.: Government Printing Office, 1960– . Annual.)

"Annual Report on American Industry." **Forbes.** In first January issue each year.

Standard & Poor's Analyst's Handbook. New York: Standard & Poor's, 1964– . Annual, with monthly supplements.

Encyclopedia of American Industries contains detailed essays on every industry in the Standard Industrial Classification (SIC) system, with each essay cross-referenced to the corresponding North American Industrial Classification System (NAICS) code. Volume 1 covers 459 manufacturing essays, and volume 2 contains 545 essays on service and other nonmanufacturing industries. The volumes contain both an alphabetical and an industry index and a list of contributors. The information on each industry appears under uniform headings such as industry snapshot, background and development, and industry leaders, and each entry contains a bibliography of both print and Internet sources. The essays incorporate major historical events, the organization and structures of the industry, statistics, government regulations, technological advances, and information on the leading companies within the sector. This title has quickly become a favorite of both librarians and researchers.

One of the most heavily used and well known titles in this area is *Standard & Poor's Industry Surveys.* This service includes, for 51 major industry categories, detailed analysis of each category and of the industries that it comprises. The categories are fairly broad and may include several subsets. In each survey, the investment outlook for the industry, comparisons of leading companies, and specific investment recommendations are featured, supplemented by statistical data, tables, and charts. A new *Survey is* issued weekly, so each industry should have a new publication at least once a year. These are updated by the *Monthly Investment Review,* which tracks the investment performance and prospects of 115 key industries each month.

The surveys include, for each industry, a report on the "Current Environment," an "Industry Profile," and a "Company Comparative Analysis." The narrative descriptions are supplemented with numerous tables and graphs, frequently cite relevant trade publications and government documents, and include summary financial statistics for major companies. A monthly supplement "Trends and Projections," is also included. It focuses on the current state of the economy, includes basic economic indicators, and presents industry and economic forecasts. Finally, both company and industry indexes are included. *Standard & Poor's Industry Surveys is* an excellent source of both factual and advisory information on many industries. This publication is available via the Internet as part of *Net Advantage* and other services maintained by Standard & Poor's. It will be necessary to contact the publisher to find which package is suitable for your institution's needs.

Mergent's Industry Review focuses on specific companies within designated industries rather than on the industries themselves. It contains financial information, operating data, and financial ratios for approximately 3,000 companies, arranged in 137 industry groups. Each industry listing includes comparative statistics, annual rankings of companies by revenue, net income, return on capital, yield, and other categories, as well as price scores for the most recent 12 months and for the past 7 years. A chart of composite stock price movements is also included.

The new *Industry & Trade Outlook* is the result of a public-private partnership between the U.S. government and McGraw-Hill. It was formerly published by the Department of Commerce as the *Industrial Outlook.* It provides coverage on over 220 industries, divided into 54 groups. The articles provide industry reviews, analyses, and forecasts; graphical snapshots of industry and trade trends; and comprehensive data from public and private sources. The U.S. Department of Commerce: provides historical data and forecasts on industry and trade activity, and McGraw-Hill's economic forecasting and consulting section provides forecast guidance and data

Unlike the *Industry Surveys* and *Mergent's Industry Review,* the *Outlook* does not cover companies. The data it contains, however, are extremely useful. More than 220 manufacturing and nonmanufacturing industries are analyzed. For each, a description of the industry is followed by an examination of recent developments, a discussion of its size, its trade position, and its growth history. Projections for the future are also included. Statistics abound, many of them taken from the economic censuses and other government sources. Other useful features include brief bibliographies at the end of most sections and the names, offices, and telephone numbers of the government experts who wrote the various industry reports, enabling librarians or library users to contact the specialists for additional information or for clarification. From http://www.ntis.gov/product/industry -trade-chgpters.htm one may also purchase and download individual chapters of this publication. The *Outlook*'s data have also become part of the *Statistical Abstract of the United States.*

Another industry information source, available in virtually all libraries, is the "Annual Report on American Industry," which appears in the first January issue of *Forbes* each year. Although coverage of industries is far more superficial than that in the preceding publications, it is useful. The report offers the profitability rankings of over 1,300 U.S. companies within their major industry. The rankings are based on return on earnings, return on capital, and debt/capital ratio. Rankings by growth, for the last five years, are also included. Finally, the last 12 months' sales, net income, and profit margins are included.

For historical information, the *Analyst's Handbook is* useful. It contains financial statistics from 1967 from the Standard & Poor's industry group stock indexes. More than 200 industry categories are featured, including aerospace/defense, footwear, paper and forest products, and life insurance companies. Coverage for each industry includes approximately 20 financial statistics, most of them on a per share basis. In addition, the *Handbook* contains selected financial ratios and income statement and balance sheet items for the past six years for most industry categories.

Commercial publishers and government agencies are not the only organizations that issue industry studies. Securities analysts and brokerage houses frequently publish substantial analyses of specific industries and companies. The following four sources are particularly useful for such information and are available at many libraries and organizations.

Nelson's Directory of Investment Research. Port Chester, N.Y.: Nelson Publications, 1976– . Annual.

Investext. Boston: Thomson Financial Networks, 19uu– . Computer file. Updated continuously.

Multex. New York: Mutex.com, Inc, 1995–. Updated continuously.

Reuters Business Insight. London: Reuters Group PLC, 19uu– . Updated continuously.

Nelson's Directory of Investment Research includes information on 17,000 analysts who work at more than 950 firms and analyze publicly traded companies and the industries they represent. Using it, research firms and key personnel can be identified, and the names and affiliations of analysts specializing in designated industries or U.S. and foreign companies can be determined. The *Directory* is useful for identifying specialists, but it does not list specific publications by name.

Investext is a full-text, online database that permits access to publications issued by investment houses, brokerage firms, and securities analysts. Although one can access *Investext* directly from Thomson Financial at http://www.thomson.com through *Research Bank Web,* it is also available from a variety of vendors including LexisNexis, Northern Light, and Dialog, and it is included as an add on in *Business & Company Resource Center* from the Gale Group. *Investext* provides full-text company, industry, and geographic research reports written by analysts from the leading worldwide investment banks, brokerage houses, and consulting firms. Coverage varies between vendors depending on the percentage of reports each one is allowed to access and on any time embargoes that may exist. There may be as long as a three-month time lag from some vendors. The complete *Investext* is available from Thomson Financial, and the latest issues for each industry group are listed on the Web site at http://www.tfsd.com/products/analyst/access.asp#I. This listing is free.

Multex supplies investment reports from over 500 leading investment banks, brokerage firms, and third-party research providers. It is accessible from http://www.multex.com/, where one may purchase single reports. From this page one may also access the "Telecomm Analyst" and the "Internet Module for Analysts," which provide free news reports, buy and sell reports, and an "analyst report."

With *Reuters Business Insight* one can read and download the full-page-image (pdf files) of some 300 Reuters' market research reports on a wide variety of industries. Reports are generally very extensive and lengthy; most are well over 100 pages and have lots of charts, tables, and graphs. Reports are grouped into five broadly defined areas: Energy, Consumer Goods, Finance, Healthcare, and Technology. A very basic search engine built into the site looks for any of the words you type into the search field and looks through both the title and body text of publications in its archive. This database is also international in scope.

From the Web page of *CorporateInformation.com* (http://www.corporateinformation. com) one can access international industry overviews. These include special reports from such agencies as the UN Food and Agricultural Organization, the UN Foreign Agricultural Organization, American embassies, and national governments. This site provides at no cost some excellent industry information.

Another Web company that provides investment reports is SkyMinder (http://www. skyminder.com). There are two parts to the service. The first, *SkyMinder.* provides access to in-depth credit and financial information plus business information on millions of companies and industries worldwide, but it does require an upfront payment from which purchases are deducted. The second, *SkyMinder Bit,* provides a quick overview of a company and an industry and is a pay-as-you-go service. This service is especially useful for reports on European companies and industries.

The federal government is a prolific publisher of industry studies. Government regulatory agencies produce detailed statistical analyses of the industries they monitor. Perhaps the most well known publications from the government are the *Current Industrial Reports,* listed by subject, available at http://www.census.gov/cir/www/alpha.html. Another resource from the government is the *EPA Sector Notebooks* (http://es.epa.gov/oeca/sector/), which provide an environmental profile along with regulatory requirements and pollutant release data.

There is also available on the Web a growing number of trade publications and trade associations that issue statistics, overviews, and articles. Information is also accessible from many of the periodical databases previously mentioned.

Other Publications

Published financial and investment information is a highly marketable commodity. The quantity, variety, and expense of material in this field is almost overwhelming. This chapter concludes by examining a few of the general categories of investment materials not yet considered. It should be emphasized that it is a representative and not a comprehensive listing.

Stock Reporting and Alert Services

Stock reporting services, although somewhat narrower in scope and less detailed than the comprehensive investment information services described previously, are useful for summary information and a quick overview of investments. Such publications are available in a variety of formats. Some are issued as loose-leaf services, others as paperback books or booklets. Stock reporting services are also available through an abundance of Internet sites.

Standard & Poor's Stock Reports: American Stock Exchange, New York Stock Exchange, NASDAQ, and Regional Exchanges. New York: Standard & Poor's, 1973– . 2v.

The *Stock Reports* provide current and background information on companies whose stock is traded on one of the national exchanges or on the OTC market. A few companies traded on regional exchanges are also included. In each service, a two-page company report highlights the company's business, its sales and earnings, per share data, beta, and related information. This service is also available via the Internet.

Other stock reporting services are available in paperback and are considerably less expensive.

Handbook of Common Stocks. New York: Mergent FIS, 1965– . Quarterly.

Handbook of Nasdaq Stocks. New York: Mergent FIS, 1997– . Quarterly.

Handbook of Dividend Achievers. New York: Mergent FIS,1979– . Annual.

Security Owner's Stock Guide. New York: Standard & Poor's, 1947– . Monthly.

The *Handbook of Common Stocks* (formerly *Moody's Handbook of Common Stocks* from 1989 to 1998 and before that *Moody's Handbook of Widely Held Common Stocks* from 1965 to 1989) gives basic financial information on nearly 1,000 NYSE stocks with high investor interest. The reviews of company background, recent developments, and investment prospects, supplemented by financial and operating statistics, make it particularly useful for a quick survey of the most popular stocks. Stocks are evaluated and assigned a rating of "High Grade," "Investment Grade," "Medium Grade," or "Speculative." The reviews of company background, recent developments, and investment prospects, supplemented by financial and operating statistics, make it particularly useful for a quick survey of the most popular stocks.

The *Handbook of Nasdaq Stocks* covers the fast-moving companies of the NASDAQ, with current performance and historical background for determining growth opportunities.

The *Handbook of Dividend Achievers* is a quick reference to more than 320 U.S. public companies that have increased their cash dividends annually for the past 10 consecutive years. Each company is profiled on a separate page, and information includes performance statistics, highest and lowest price-earnings (P/E) ratios, and seven-year financial performance indicators.

The *Security Owner's Stock Guide* is a monthly summary of investment information on several thousand common and preferred stocks. Each listing includes monthly high-low prices, volume traded, historical price ranges, dividends, earnings, and summaries of financial position. Althoughthe *Stock Guide* covers far more companies than Moody's *Handbook* and is updated more frequently, its format makes it less popular with many users, particularly novice investors. The *Guide* displays information for specific securities in a single line extending across two pages. People not familiar with it or the abbreviations used must frequently turn to the back of each issue for explanations of format and abbreviations. Although the emphasis in the *Guide* is on common and preferred stock, mutual fund issues are also covered.

Using any stock or newspaper quote service, one may link to the latest prices, but there are "alert" services that give any price changes, on designated stocks, as they occur. One free service, which only requires registration, is offered by Yahoo! at http://alerts.yahoo.com. One may activate the alert and receive alerts on any device that receives e-mail. Another service, which has a small monthly cost, is at http://www.cyberalerts.com. Using this service one can be alerted to changes in up to 30 stocks.

Charting

Most of the reference sources that have been discussed in this chapter favor what is called the fundamental approach to investment analysis, that is, basing investment decisions on the financial analysis of a company and examination of its management, the products or services it sells, and the general well-being of the industry of which it is a part. These data are used to help the investor make judgments about the worth of a particular stock.

Not every investor uses the fundamental approach. Some favor technical analysis, in which the focus is on timing: when to buy and sell stocks. Technical analysts follow fluctuations in stock prices and volume of trading rather than the considerations mentioned above and depend heavily on charts to help make investment decisions. Charts, the technicians contend, make it possible to tell in a glance what a stock's past performance has been and to make informed judgments about its future prospects.

In some libraries, patrons who are technically oriented may consider a financial collection that does not include at least one charting service inadequate. Although charts are included in several of the publications already mentioned, *Value Line,* and the stock reporting services, there are some sources that confine themselves to graphic presentation of stock and industry data. Typical of these is *Standard & Poor's/Trendline Current Market Perspectives,* a monthly publication that includes charts for over 1,500 stocks. Free charts can also be accessed through the Big Charts Web site at http://bigcharts.marketwatch.com/.

Obsolete Securities

Occasionally, librarians are asked to help patrons determine the value of shares in companies that are no longer in business. Someone who has unearthed a yellowing stock certificate for 200 shares of Yum-Yum International Restaurant may want to know whether to plan a world cruise or use it as kindling. A search of the standard business directories and comprehensive investment services may fail to yield information on the elusive Yum-Yum Restaurant chain. There are, however, several sources of information on companies that are no longer in business.

Directory of Obsolete Securities. Jersey City, N.J.: Financial Informamtion, 1927– . Annual.

Robert D. Fisher Manual of Valuable and Worthless Securities. New York: Robert D. Fisher, 1938–1975. Frequency varied.

The *Directory* lists companies and banks whose original identities have been lost because of name changes, mergers, acquisition, dissolution, reorganization, bankruptcy, or charter cancellation. Yum-Yum International Restaurant is listed in the *Directory*. "Charter cancelled and declared inoperative and void for nonpayment of taxes," the listing indicates, and assesses the current value of Yum Yum common stock at one cent per share.

Volumes 5 through 15 of the *Fisher Manual* list companies whose securities may have value or may be worthless. This reference superseded the *Marvyn Scudder Manual of Extinct or Obsolete Companies,* which was published by Marvyn Scudder in four volumes and included stocks from 1926 to 1937.

Stock Services on the Internet

Over the years there have been many books and articles printed and Internet sites founded that deal with stock information. It is easy for the individual investor, librarian, and researcher to gather information, but the amount of information available can be a problem. There are a myriad of stock services on the Internet, and it is easy to become overwhelmed.

A service (http://depts.washington.edu/balib/stocksites/) has been set up by Foster Business Library at the University of Washington that makes it easier to choose a Web service.

The *Stock Research Sites on the Web* "contains evaluations for free stock quote and investment research sites on the web. It does not contain any evaluations of brokerage or electronic trading site unless they have a significant research section that does not require a paid subscription or account with the company."

This service provides an alphabetical annotated list of the sites covered as well as comparative evaluations. Perhaps the best feature is the opportunity to "Screen for Sites" using the required criteria. (See figure 12.11, page 296.)

Using this screen, one can decide to see whether there is a site that will supply, for example, corporate information, an annual report link, news links, a 52-week H/L, competitors, and stock screening. The answer(s) appears along with a description, the date the site(s) was last evaluated, and the URL. This can answer a many questions and save a lot of searching time.

The electronic and print resources included in this chapter are only a fraction of those available. Along with publishers' catalogs, journals, and magazines, any researcher may need to frequently check online resources such as the *Free Pint* newsletter (http://www.freepint.com/issues/issues.htm) and *The Virtual Acquisition Shelf* (http://resourceshelf.freepint.com).

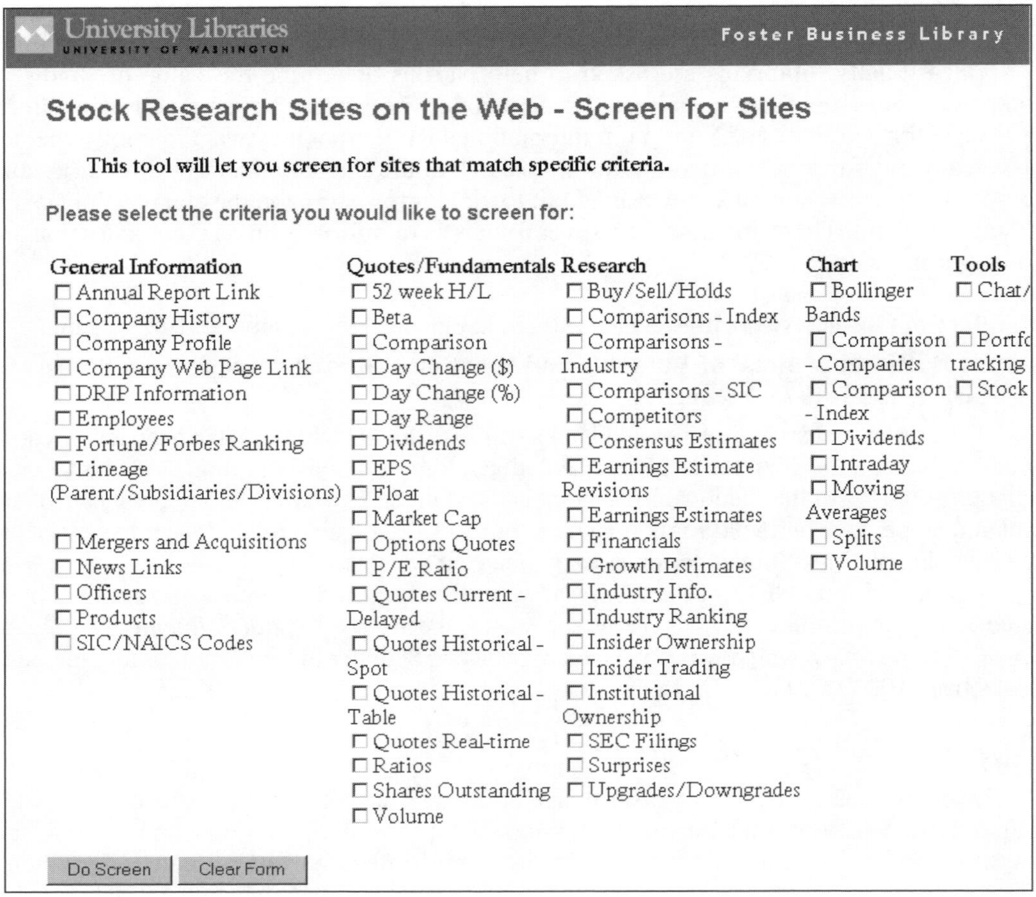

University Libraries
UNIVERSITY OF WASHINGTON
Foster Business Library

Stock Research Sites on the Web - Screen for Sites

This tool will let you screen for sites that match specific criteria.

Please select the criteria you would like to screen for:

General Information
- ☐ Annual Report Link
- ☐ Company History
- ☐ Company Profile
- ☐ Company Web Page Link
- ☐ DRIP Information
- ☐ Employees
- ☐ Fortune/Forbes Ranking
- ☐ Lineage (Parent/Subsidiaries/Divisions)
- ☐ Mergers and Acquisitions
- ☐ News Links
- ☐ Officers
- ☐ Products
- ☐ SIC/NAICS Codes

Quotes/Fundamentals
- ☐ 52 week H/L
- ☐ Beta
- ☐ Comparison
- ☐ Day Change ($)
- ☐ Day Change (%)
- ☐ Day Range
- ☐ Dividends
- ☐ EPS
- ☐ Float
- ☐ Market Cap
- ☐ Options Quotes
- ☐ P/E Ratio
- ☐ Quotes Current - Delayed
- ☐ Quotes Historical - Spot
- ☐ Quotes Historical - Table
- ☐ Quotes Real-time
- ☐ Ratios
- ☐ Shares Outstanding
- ☐ Volume

Research
- ☐ Buy/Sell/Holds
- ☐ Comparisons - Index
- ☐ Comparisons - Industry
- ☐ Comparisons - SIC
- ☐ Competitors
- ☐ Consensus Estimates
- ☐ Earnings Estimate Revisions
- ☐ Earnings Estimates
- ☐ Financials
- ☐ Growth Estimates
- ☐ Industry Info.
- ☐ Industry Ranking
- ☐ Insider Ownership
- ☐ Insider Trading
- ☐ Institutional Ownership
- ☐ SEC Filings
- ☐ Surprises
- ☐ Upgrades/Downgrades

Chart
- ☐ Bollinger Bands
- ☐ Comparison - Companies
- ☐ Comparison - Index
- ☐ Dividends
- ☐ Intraday
- ☐ Moving Averages
- ☐ Splits
- ☐ Volume

Tools
- ☐ Chat/
- ☐ Portfc tracking
- ☐ Stock

Do Screen | Clear Form

Figure 12.11. ***Stock Research Sites On The Web:*** **"Screen for Sites," at http://depts.washington.edu/balib/stocksites/screenform.cgi.**
Courtesy of Foster Business Library, University of Washington Libraries.

Notes

1. New York Stock Exchange, *Listed Company Manual,* available at http://www.nyse.com/listed/listed.html.

2. New York Stock Exchange, *Fact Book* (New York: The Exchange, 1956–),, 75. Available at http://www.nyse.com/about/about.html.

3. A full description of major filings with the SEC, including registration and prospectus, is available at http://www.sec.gov/info/edgar/forms.htm.

13

Bonds and Other Fixed-Income Securities

The preceding chapter examined stocks, the markets on which they are traded, and the use of stock-related publications by investors. This chapter deals in a similar way with another broad category of investments: bonds and fixed income securities.

How do these securities differ from stocks? Stocks are equity securities; they represent partial ownership in the issuing organization. Fixed-income securities, on the other hand, are debt securities, representing money lent to the issuing organization for a designated time period. They are, in effect, IOUs.

Usually, the issuing organization agrees not only to repay the principal at some future date but also to make regular, fixed interest payments for the use of the money. Some fixed-income securities are long-term loans, others are short term. Bonds fall into the first category.

Bonds

Bonds are long-term, fixed-income debt securities issued by corporations and governments to raise money. They can be as staid as U.S. savings bonds or as speculative as Mexican petrobonds paid in pesos, but most share certain characteristics. Bonds usually mature 10 years after they are issued, and some are issued for as long as 30 years.

When a bond reaches maturity, the issuing organization is required to repay the principal, or face value, to the bondholder. Usually bonds are issued in $1,000 denominations or in multiples of $1,000. There are, for example, bonds with face values of $5,000 or even $10,000; others, called "baby bonds," have face values of only $100 or $500. Most, however, come in $1,000 denominations.

Interest

Bondholders are entitled to interest, usually paid semiannually. The amount of interest paid is determined in advance and is a fixed percentage of the face value of the bond. A 71/8 percent $1,000 bond will earn its holder $72.50 per year, a 51/2 percent bond, $55.00. The important thing to remember is that the rate of interest is set at the time the bonds are first sold to the public and remains fixed for the duration of the bond's life. While the prime interest rate may skyrocket or plummet according to the state of the economy, the rate of interest paid on a bond remains the same for its entire life span. As a result, bonds provide a steady, predictable income.

With certain bonds, interest is collected by clipping one of the coupons attached to the bond and presenting it for payment. Thus, the interest paid on a particular bond is often called its coupon rate or coupon, and bonds with coupons attached are called coupon bonds. They are also called bearer bonds because the holder of the bond is presumed to be its owner. If someone loses a bearer bond, the finder can sell it or hold it, collect interest on it, and redeem it at maturity.

In contrast, a registered bond is registered in the name of the bondholder, and only that person can sell it, receive semiannual interest payments on it, or redeem it. No coupons are attached to a registered bond; interest payments are automatically sent to the bondholder when they come due.

There are also adjustable rate bonds. The rate on these is changed periodically to reflect interest rate indexes, such as that on Treasury bills. Zero coupon bonds may be bought at less than the face value, but the bearer will not receive periodic interest payments. For example, a bond with the face value of $20,000, which will mature in 20 years, may be bought for about $7,000. The difference in the face value and price paid is 51/2 percent interest compounded annually. Taxes must be paid on this annual interest although it is only paid at the end of the 20 years.

Prices

Although the interest rate is locked in for the life of the bond, the price of a bond fluctuates in much the same way as stock prices. What causes bond prices to rise or fall? Interest rates are the key.

When general interest rates rise, the interest rates on new bond issues must also be higher to attract investors. Interest rates on bonds already outstanding, however, are fixed and cannot be changed. As a result, an adjustment to the new interest rate takes place through a change in the prices of the outstanding bonds. When interest rates rise, the prices of outstanding bonds tend to decline. Conversely, if interest rates fall, bond prices rise.

If, for example, an investor paid $1,000 (face value or par) for an XYZ Corporation bond that paid 5 percent, and subsequently the XYZ Corporation offered 7 percent interest on its new bond issues, the resale market for the 5 percent bond selling at par (or $1,000) would be nonexistent. Why accept 5 percent interest when 7 percent is available? If, however, the 5 percent bond is offered for $850 instead of $1,000, the bond would be more attractive because the buyer would be earning annual interest of $50 on an $850 investment as well as a $150 profit when the bond matured.

Bonds selling for less than face value are said to be selling at a discount, while bonds selling at a premium are those selling for more than face value. Thus investment advice to buy "deep discounted bonds" simply means to buy bonds selling for considerably less than their face value.

Yield

There are two different ways of expressing yield, or return on an investment. The first, current yield, measures the annual return on the price that the buyer actually pays for the bond. Current yield is derived by dividing the interest rate by the price paid for the bond. If the bond was bought at par ($1,000), the interest rate and current yield are the same. If, however, the bond was bought at premium or discount, the current yield will be different from the interest rate.

The 5 percent XYZ Corporation bond purchased for $850, for example, has a current yield of 5.88 percent (5 divided by 850), while a 9 percent bond bought at premium for $1,050 would have a current yield of 8.57 percent (9 divided by 1,050). Current yields are calculated and usually included in the bond tables in financial newspapers.

Yield to maturity, the other expression of bond yield, is the effective rate of return to the bondholder if the bond is held to maturity. It takes into account the amount paid for the bond, its par value, the interest rate, and the length of time to maturity. For a given interest rate, maturity, and price, yield to maturity can be determined by using tables from reference books commonly called basis books or yield books. Although libraries generally do not include these highly specialized sources in their collections, yield to maturity is one of the data elements included in major bond publications such as Standard & Poor's *Bond Guide* and Mergent's *Bond Record*, which are discussed later in this chapter.

Call Provisions

When an investor buys bonds, he or she takes the risk that the issuing organization may default on interest payments or on repayment of the principal, or that spiraling inflation and general interest rates may make the long-term, fixed-interest bonds a poor investment. The investor may also have to risk recall of the bonds by the issuing organization before they reach maturity. This may result from two kinds of recall provisions, known as call and sinking fund.

A sinking fund is a pool of money put aside by the issuing organization so that, each year, it can recall and retire a certain percentage of the bond issue in advance of the actual maturity date. The rationale behind a sinking fund provision is that it is easier to retire the bond issue gradually than it is to pay the entire amount at maturity. If a bond issue has a sinking fund provision, a certain portion of the issue must be retired each year. The bonds retired are usually selected by lottery. The issuer usually has the option of buying the bonds on the open market or recalling them from bondholders. If the market price of the bonds is higher than the sinking fund call price, the issuer is entitled to recall a certain number of bonds from the bondholders and to redeem them at the stated sinking fund price. Usually there is a 5- or 10-year grace period before the sinking fund provision goes into effect.

Although establishment of a sinking fund provision at least theoretically reduces the likelihood of default on repayment of principal, it can also work to the disadvantage of the investor whose bonds are redeemed before maturity, because the prospect of a steady source of fixed-interest income has been eliminated. As a result, one of the things that many prospective investors want to know about a particular bond is whether it contains a sinking fund provision. Many printed investment sources identify bond issues containing sinking fund provisions with the letters s.f.

Other bonds have call provisions that permit the issuer, after a lapse of 5 or 10 years, to redeem the bonds at any time prior to their maturity, at a set price. Such bonds are labeled, appropriately, as callable bonds. Generally the issuer will exercise the call provision whenever the fixed interest rate for their outstanding bond issues is significantly higher than the interest rate at which they could issue new bonds. Bonds that are called in under this provision are redeemed at face value plus a fixed payment, often equal to one year's interest rate. Call prices are included for callable bonds in Mergent's (Moody's) *Bond Record*, Standard & Poor's *Bond Guide*, and many other investment publications.

Ratings

Investors pay close attention to the credit ratings assigned to bonds. The ratings most commonly consulted are those prepared by Mergent (Moody's) and Standard & Poor's. They represent an assessment of the issuing organization's ability to pay interest and repay principal to bondholders. Not every bond is rated, but the major ones are.

Slightly different rating symbols are used by Mergent (Moody's) and Standard & Poor's, as evidenced by their rating categories shown in figure 13.1. Lists and explanations of the various bond rating symbols are contained in many of the Moody's and Standard & Poor's publications described later in this chapter.

General Description	Mergent (Moody's)	Standard & Poor's
Highest Quality	Aaa	AAA
High Quality	Aa	AA
Upper Medium Grade	A	A
Medium Grade	Baa	BBB
Somewhat Speculative	Ba	BB
Low Grade; Speculative	B	B
Poor Grade, Default Possible	Caa	CCC
Poor Grade, Partial Recovery Possible	Ca	CC
Default, Recovery Unlikely	C	C

Figure 13.1. Bond rating categories.

Although each publisher is highly respected, some claim that Mergent surpasses Standard & Poor's in the value of its rating of municipal bond issues, whereas Standard & Poor's is more highly regarded for its rating of corporate bonds. In most instances, though, both services either assign the same rating to an issue or are within one rating level of each other. Neither service claims to be infallible.

Nevertheless, the ratings are useful. They give prospective investors an indication of the risk attached to each bond and carry enough weight so that bonds with higher ratings (that is, those with less risk) have lower yields than bonds with lower ratings. New issues with the same maturity and face value may offer different interest rates, based on their ratings. A triple A bond will have a lower coupon rate than a double A bond, and so on. Ratings can change, and if they do, announcements are featured in financial newspapers and other publications. One can also check the Web page of Standard & Poor's (http://www.standardandpoors.com), where recent changes are listed.

If the rating assigned to an outstanding bond changes, its price in the resale market (discussed in the next section) will reflect this change. A lower rating will usually result in the lowering of a bond's price, and vice versa.

Secondary Bond Market

Not all investors hold newly issued bonds to maturity. As a result, there is a secondary arena for bonds, with most of it centered in the OTC market, which is the primary market for the trading of outstanding government and municipal bonds, and for many corporate bonds as well. The New York Stock Exchange lists bonds, most of them corporate, although some government, international bank, and foreign bonds are also traded. Finally, some trading of bonds is also done on the American Stock Exchange.

Price and related trading information for many of the bonds traded in these markets is included in financial newspapers, bond-related publications, and Web sites. One example of a Web site with a quote center is *bonds online* (http://www.bondsonline.com/).

Money Market Instruments

Bonds are long-term debt obligations. Corresponding short-term loans to various borrowers, federal and local governments, corporations, and banks are known collectively as money market instruments.[1] These short-term obligations are issued by organizations with high credit ratings, are highly liquid (easily convertible into cash), and are generally of less than one year's duration. Typical money market instruments include Treasury bills, commercial paper (short-term IOUs issued by corporations), and commercial bank certificates of deposit.

Many of these securities require a substantial cash outlay and are thus of greater interest to institutional investors than to all but the wealthiest individuals. Commercial paper, for example, is sold in minimum denominations of $100,000. When interest rates are high, however, there is widespread interest in money market funds, which are a type of mutual fund. For as little as $500, an investor can buy into a money market fund, which pools investors' money and buys these expensive short-term obligations. Money market funds are discussed briefly in the next chapter.

Federal Government Securities

The federal government issues a wide range of marketable securities. Some, known as direct government obligations, are issued by the Treasury Department. These include Treasury bills, notes, and bonds. Others, such as the issues of federal agencies and government-sponsored agencies, are not considered direct obligations but enjoy credit ratings almost as impressive as those assigned to Treasury issues. The high rating given to government securities is based on the federal government's power to tax and print money. Risk of default on a U.S. government bond is nonexistent. As a result, government securities offer lower interest rates than do corporate debt obligations, which compensate for their greater risk by offering higher interest rates.

Trading of government securities is active, with billions of dollars' worth of short- and-long term securities bought and sold during a normal business day. Bills, notes, and bonds can be purchased over the Internet or phone, or by mailing a tender to a *TreasuryDirect*[2] office. Treasury marketable securities can be re sold through financial institutions and government securities brokers and dealers

Treasury Issues

One of the ways in which the Treasury Department finances the nation's debt is by issuing marketable securities. Three main types of Treasury issues, distinguished by their varying maturities, can be identified: Treasury bills, Treasury notes, and Treasury bonds.

Treasury bills (or T-bills or bills) are short-term securities, issued in maturities of 3, 6, and 12 months. T-bills do not pay interest. Instead, they are issued at a discount of their $ 10,000 face value. An investor may purchase a T-bill for $9,750, for example, and redeem it at maturity of one year for the full $10,000, thus earning $250. The price at which the bills are discounted is determined by the market, more specifically by the investors and dealers who submit competitive bids at weekly and/or monthly auctions of Treasury bills (see figure 13.2). The highest bids determine the discount. Most of the competitive bidders are dealers in government securities, commercial banks, and other institutional investors. For more information on types of Treasury issues one should investigate the Web page of the Bureau of the Public Debt at http://www.publicdebt.treas.gov/.

Security	Purchase Minimum	Purchase in Multiples Of	General Auction Schedule
4-Week Bill	$1,000	$1,000	Weekly
13-Week Bill	$1,000	$1,000	Weekly
26-Week Bill	$1,000	$1,000	Weekly
2-Year Note	$1,000	$1,000	Monthly
5-Year Note	$1,000	$1,000	February, May, August, November
10-Year Note	$1,000	$1,000	February, May, August, November
Inflation-Indexed 10-Year Note	$1,000	$1,000	January, July, October

Figure 13.2. Table of Treasury auctions (shows the general auction pattern for marketable Treasury securities). Taken from http://www.publicdebt.treas.gov/of/ofauctbl.htm (4/9/01).

There is an active secondary market for T-bills, and the *Wall Street Journal* and many other newspapers report the daily prices of Treasury bills. The quotations look like those in figure 13.3. Daily prices can also be found at http://www.investinginbonds.com and at http://www.bondsonline.com.

The table in figure 13.3 indicates that the buyer of a bill maturing on May 3, 2003, for example, earns 5.24 percent; that is, the asked price provides a yield of 5.5 percent. The 5.59 in the bid column refers to the yield someone selling the bills would reap. Actual dollar prices are not quoted in this table but can be determined by using a formula that takes into account discount rate and the number of days to maturity.[3] The last column, Ask/Yield, is investment yield, the figure to be used in comparing the return on Treasury bills with other types of investments.

Mat. Date	Days to Mat.	Bid	Asked	Change	Ask/Yield
May 25 '03	160	**5.59**	**5.55**	**−0.01**	**5.66**

Explanations:

Mat. Dat. Date at which Treasury Bill matures. There are 160 days to wait.

Bid The bid is the yield that someone **selling** the bill would earn. Someone **selling** a $10,000 T-bill maturing on May 25, 2003 would earn a yield of 5.59%.

Asked The yield the **buyer** would earn.

Change Change shows that yesterday's bid price was 5.60.

Ask/Yield The ask yield is the return the buyer would get if the ask price was paid and the bond was kept until it matures.

Figure 13.3. Example of a newspaper quotation for a Treasury bill.

Treasury notes and bonds have longer maturities than T-bills and are interest bearing. Bonds and notes come in denominations of $1,000, $5,000, $10,000, $100,000, and $1 million. Treasury notes range in maturity from 1 to 10 years, most falling in the 2- to 5-year range; Treasury bonds, on the other hand, generally mature in 10 years or more.

The Treasury follows essentially the same auction procedures for new note and bond issues as it does for bills. An offering is announced in advance of the issue date, and investors submit either competitive or noncompetitive bids and await the results.

Treasury notes and bonds are traded actively in the OTC market, and OTC bond and note prices are included in the financial pages of most newspapers. The sample in figure 13.4 contains most information likely to be found in a government securities table.

Rate	Maturity	Bid	Ask	Change	Ask/Yieldld
73/4	Feb. 02	105:12	105:14	103.12	5.5
53/8	Aug. 02	99:26	99:27		5.44

Explanation:

Row 1
Interest or coupon rate.

Row 2
Maturity date—the month and year in which the security matures. Securities are listed by date—first to mature is at the top of the list.

Row 3
Price at which an investor can sell the security. Prices in both the bid and asked columns are quoted in points, with one point equal to $10 for each $1000 of face value. A quote of 105 means that a security of $1000 is selling at $1050. The numbers after the colons represent 32nds. So :12 is equal to 12/32 (or 3/8) which is equal to $3.75. So the bid price of 105:12 means that the buyer is prepared to buy the security for $1053.75.

Row 4
The sellers ask price was 105:14 or $1054.38

Row 6
The yield that will be received by the buyer. This takes into account the price paid, the interest rate and the time to maturity.

Figure 13.4. Example of a quote table for Treasury bonds and notes.

The interest earned on Treasury securities is subject to federal income tax but exempt from state and local taxes. The same exemptions apply to federal agency issues.

Treasury securities are considered a "safe" investment and are actively traded. There is an abundance of information about them at the Web site http://www.publicdebt.treas.gov/ plus the ability to purchase the securities directly without using a broker. Each month the *Treasury Bulletin* (http://www.fms.treas.gov/bulletin/) issues a list of the estimated amount of public debt securities held by private investors (see figure 13.5).

End of fiscal year or month	Public debt securities, con. Held by private investors			Agency securities	Held by U.S. Government accounts and Federal Reserve Banks	Held by private investors
	Total (7)	Marketable (8)	Nonmarketable (9)	Total outstanding (10)	(11)	(12)
2001 - Jan	2,854,193	2,443,652	410,540	27,158	51	27,107
Feb	2,863,295	2,449,987	413,309	26,879	51	26,828
Mar	2,892,210	2,475,233	416,977	26,818	51	26,767
Apr	2,752,920	2,332,957	419,963	26,788	51	26,737
May	2,730,653	2,309,290	421,363	26,671	-	26,671
June	2,722,012	2,303,111	418,901	27,099	-	27,099
July	2,711,652	2,298,132	413,521	26,937	-	26,937
Aug	2,780,236	2,368,367	411,869	26,617	-	26,617
Sept	2,779,070	2,370,630	408,441	27,011	-	26,011
Oct	2,769,395	2,357,783	411,613	26,775	-	26,775
Nov	2,833,482	2,420,997	412,485	26,655	-	26,655

Figure 13.5. Estimated ownership of U.S. Treasury securities.
From *Treasury Bulletin* (March 2002), available at http://www.fms.treas.gov/bulletin/b12.html.

Federal Agency Issues

Federal agency securities are debt obligations of various U.S. government-guaranteed or government-sponsored entities. Included among these are the Small Business Administration and the Federal Home Loan Mortgage Corporation. Prime among these agency issues, or agencies, as they are collectively known, are those issued by the following organizations:

Small Business Administration

Federal Home Loan Mortgage Corporation (FHLMC or Freddie Mac)

Federal Farm Credit Bank

Federal National Mortgage Association (FNMA or Fannie Mae)

Government National Mortgage Association (GNMA or Ginnie Mae)

Student Loan Marketing Association (Sallie Mae)

Mergent's (Moody's) *Municipal & Government Manual* describes agency issues in some detail. For each listing, fairly detailed financial and organizational information is given, including description and rating of outstanding debt obligations. Daily quotations for many agency issues are included in the *Wall Street Journal* and other newspapers. The format used for reporting is very similar to that used for Treasury notes and bonds.

Municipal Issues

Issuance of debt securities is not limited to the federal government. State, city, town, and other units of local government and political subdivisions also issue bonds, referred to collectively as municipals or munis. They are also known as tax exempts because the interest earned on them is exempt from federal income tax and often from state and local income taxes where they are issued. Because of this tax-exempt feature, municipals can pay a lower rate of interest and still be competitive with taxable bonds paying a higher rate of interest. The Bond Market Association has on its Web page at http://www.investinginbonds.com/ a "Tax-Free vs. Taxable Yield Comparison Calculator." With this one can compare what one would need to earn on a taxable investment to match the tax-free yield of a municipal bond.

Municipal securities are issued to help finance new roads, highways, bridges, schools, hospitals, libraries, sports and convention centers, airports, sewers, utilities, and other facilities. Unlike federal government securities, municipals are not sold directly to the public. Instead, municipals are sold to investment bankers or underwriters who in turn make them available to investors. There are two basic types of municipal bonds, based on the source of revenue used to repay the bond.

General Obligation Bonds

General obligation bonds are secured by the full and unlimited taxing power of the government issuing the bonds. Also known as full faith and credit bonds, these securities are ranked second in safety only to federal government issues. This is because the issuer of a general obligation bond is required by law to exercise its taxing power so that bondholders can be paid. Income from property tax or other locally levied taxes is used to pay local general obligation bonds, while holders of state general obligation bonds are paid with revenues generated from income, sales, gasoline, tobacco, corporation, or business taxes. Theoretically, at least, general obligation bonds have first claim on the revenue of the state or local government issuing the bond. "By law," writes *Wall Street Week* sage Louis Rukeyser, "such bondholders are right up there with the school teachers and the policemen in their claim on the community; in fact, in Chicago, during the Depression, municipal employees generally got scrip, bondholders got cash"[4]

Revenue Bonds

Revenue bonds, on the other hand, are backed only by revenues from a specific project, such as the tolls, fees, or rents paid by the users of the facility constructed with the proceeds from the bond. A typical example would be a bond issued to build a toll road, backed not by local taxpayers but by the income generated, in the form of tolls, from the motorists who use the road. Because payments to holders of revenue bonds are not guaranteed by the unlimited taxing power of the issuing government, revenue bonds are generally considered riskier than general obligation bonds, and usually the investor is compensated for the added risk by receiving a higher rate of interest. Clearly the investor contemplating purchase of revenue bonds should learn all he or she can about factors that might affect the profitability of the facility being constructed. Although not common, default on revenue bonds does occur.

Sources of Information on Municipal Bonds

Information on municipals is not always easy to locate, and in some instances may be completely unobtainable from the standard printed sources available in most libraries or from Internet sources. Daily price quotations for municipal issues in the *Wall Street Journal*, for example, are limited to a few, select revenue bonds. The sheer volume and diversity of municipal bonds make it impractical for printed sources to list them all; the fact that many of them are serial bonds, each with a whole range of different maturities, makes it all but impossible. So, in many instances, an investor seeking current price and trading information for a specific municipal issue may well have to get it directly from a securities broker or a commercial bank.

Two major bond publications described later in this chapter, the *Mergent Bond Record* and *Standard & Poor's Bond Guide*, list many municipal issues, but the information given is limited to the rating assigned to each. Somewhat more detailed information is contained in the weekly bond advisory newsletters issued by both publishers. Standard & Poor's publication is *Credit Week;* Mergent's offering is the *Credit Survey*. Each includes fairly detailed analyses of a few issues, and each includes tables that briefly summarize new tax-exempt issues.

The most comprehensive source of information is *Mergent's Municipal & Government Manual*. Its arrangement is alphabetical by state, and then by city, town, and political subdivision. Information for each state includes a description of principal tax sources, financial, population, and industry statistics; a map of the state and its counties; and a list of outstanding issues.

After state government information is given, local government units are listed. The type of information provided varies according to the nature of the political subdivision. A town listing will include the name of the county in which it is located, date of incorporation, population in the most recent decennial census, assessed value of property, tax collected, the Mergent (Moody's) rating, overdue taxes, and the name of the bank making interest payments. A school district listing might include the district's location in the state, average school attendance figures, assessed valuation of property in the school district, the Mergent (Moody's) rating, and the name of the bank making semiannual interest payments to bond-holders.

The main drawback to *Mergent's Municipal* is that the information becomes somewhat dated as the year progresses. This is offset by the publication of a newsletter that updates the *Manual*. It includes listings of new and prospective issues, securities whose ratings have been changed or withdrawn, and a list of call notices posted by international, federal, and municipal organizations that are calling in some of their securities. The newsletter is available at http://www.mergent.com/publish/news_reports.asp.

There are also some excellent sources of information on the Web. One of these, mentioned previously, is maintained by the Bond Market Association and is available at http://www.investinginbonds.com/. The site includes *Investor's Guides* to all types of bonds. The guide to municipals describes the types of bonds and includes an explanation of safety factors, understanding market risk, calls, and taxes on the issues. The Web site also includes the daily report of transactions.

Corporate Securities

Corporations also issue bonds and other debt securities. As with government securities, corporate securities can be classified by length of time to maturity. Short-term corporate debt obligations, discussed in the section on money market instruments, are called commercial paper. Generally, commercial paper has a maturity of from 90 to 180 days, and since it is traded in minimum denominations of $100,000, is only indirectly purchased by individual investors via money market funds.

Corporate bonds, on the other hand, are usually issued in denominations of $1,000 or $5,000, making them a more likely target for the individual investor. As on many government and municipal bonds, interest is generally issued semiannually. Corporate bonds usually have maturities of from 20 to 30 years, and many of them contain the sinking fund and call provisions described earlier in this chapter.

Types of Corporate Bonds

Corporate bonds can be categorized broadly by the type of collateral put up to secure the bond. Some bonds are unsecured, with no collateral pledged as security. Others may pledge specific equipment, facilities, or their own portfolios of stocks and bonds.

Debenture bonds or debentures are unsecured loans, backed only by the company's "full faith and credit." In other words, all that stands behind repayment of the loan is the company's own word that it will repay the principal and make the requisite number of semiannual interest payments. Obviously, the financial and managerial well-being of a company issuing debentures should be of prime interest to the prospective bond buyer, and careful attention should be paid to the ratings assigned by Moody's and Standard & Poor's.

Other bonds may be backed by some specific, tangible asset against the possibility of default. If the company fails to make interest payments or to repay the principal, the asset can be sold so that the bondholders will be paid. Mortgage bonds, for example, are secured by a specific piece of fixed property such as a company plant or laboratory. Still other bonds pledge movable equipment as security. They are called equipment trust certificates and are generally issued by airlines and railroads. Finally, collateral trust bonds are those bonds backed by securities held by the issuing corporation. The collateral must have a market value at least equal to the value of the bonds.

Some bonds can be converted at the holder's option into a designated number of shares of common stock. These bonds are called convertible bonds or convertibles and offer the investor the chance to do a little financial fence-straddling. If the company fails to prosper, the convertible bondholder can choose not to exercise the conversion privilege and can instead collect semiannual fixed-interest payments much as he or she would on any other bond. (The interest rate will be less, however, than for straight, nonconvertible bonds issued by the same company.) On the other hand, if the company should prosper, the investor has the option of converting the bond into common stock at a previously specified conversion price. Assume, for example, that Placebo, Inc., a pharmaceutical company, issues a $1,000 convertible bond, giving its holders the option of converting the bond into 20 shares of its common stock. The conversion price per share of common stock would be $40, or $1,000 (the price of the bond) divided by 20 (the number of shares into which the bond can be converted). Suppose further that at the time the bond was issued, Placebo common was selling for $30 per share. No one would trade the bond for stock. But if Placebo should discover a cure for the common cold and its stock should zoom to $75 per share, the convertible bondholder would be able to tap into company profits by converting the $1,000 bond into 20 shares of stock, now worth a total of $1,500. Convertible bonds can be identified by the letters cv following the name, interest rate, and maturity date of bond listings in financial newspapers and other publications.

Trading of Corporate Bonds

Although the bulk of trading of corporate bonds is done on the OTC market, some corporates are also traded on the New York Stock Exchange. In fact more corporate bonds than stocks are listed on the NYSE. Daily trading activity on the NYSE is reported in the *Wall Street Journal* and *New York Times*. A look at the information contained in the daily bond quotation tables may be helpful. The sample shown in figure 13.6 is typical.

Company	Coupon	Mat. Date	Bid$	Yield%
BMO	7,000	Jan 28/10	106.55	6.04
BNS	5,400	Apr 01/03	101.56	5.95
Coke	5,650	Mar 17/04	99.59	5.80

Explanation:

Row 1
Abbreviated name of company issuing the bond.

Row 2
The coupon is the fixed interest rate that the issuer pays to the bearer.

Row 3
The date that the issuer will pay back the principal to the investor. Usually only the last two digits of the year will be given.

Row 4
The bid is the price someone is willing to pay. This is quoted in relation to 100, which is known as par. So BNS is trading at 1.56 % above par and Coke at .41 below par.

Row 5
The yield is the annual return until the bond matures or is "called." Yield is calculated by the amount of interest paid on a bond divided by the price.

Figure 13.6. Example of a corporate bond table.

Sources of Information on Corporate Bonds

Various company-issued reports, such as the annual report to shareholders and the 10-K report, will be of interest to investors, as will the comprehensive investment services described in the preceding chapter. The various *Mergent Manuals*, particularly the *Industrial, OTC Industrial, Public Utility, Transportation*, and *Bank & Finance* manuals with their detailed financial statements, company histories, and descriptions and bond ratings, are basic corporate bond information sources. *Mergent Online* also includes a separate module, *Bond Portraits,* which can be added to the basic product as budgets allow.

Mergent Bond Record and *Standard & Poor's Bond Guide* include lengthy sections on corporate issues. The *Bond Guide* lists over 6,800 domestic corporates, more than 560 Canadian and other foreign issues, and over 320 convertibles. General information is provided on each company, including its industry code and limited balance sheet data, as well as on each bond issued by the company. For each issue listed, data include the type of bond, the rating assigned to the bond, interest payment dates, coupon and maturity, information on redemption provisions, both current yield and yield to maturity, and other financial data. All of this information is packed into a single line, so abbreviations and symbols are heavily used. Detailed explanations are given on the front and back inside covers of each issue.

Convertible bonds are listed separately from the other corporate issues in the *Bond Guide*. Information given for each convertible issue includes coupon rate and maturity, Standard & Poor's rating, expiration date of conversion privilege, number of shares of common stock into which each bond can be converted, the conversion price per share of common stock, and the dividend income per bond. In addition, current stock data—market price, price-earnings ratio, and earnings per share—are included.

Mergent Bond Record provides similar information in a slightly different format and includes Canadian provincial and municipal obligations and international listings, as well as domestic corporate bonds, in a single listing. Otherwise, the information is virtually identical, with coupon rate and maturity, dates of interest payments, ratings, current price, sinking fund and call provisions, yield to maturity, and other financial data given for each issue.

As in the *Bond Guide*, convertibles are listed separately in the *Bond Record*. Data include the Mergent rating, conversion period and price, number of shares of common stock into which the bond can be converted, and current stock and bond data.

The bond advisory newsletters, discussed briefly in the section on municipals and at greater length in the forthcoming section on general information sources, include periodic in-depth analyses of specific corporate issues as well as brief tabular summaries of others.

General Information Sources

On the whole, information on bonds is more difficult to find than information on stocks. This is because of the diversity and complexity of bonds, because some bonds are traded only locally or have limited distribution, and because much of the published information is directed toward securities dealers and institutional investors rather than individual investors. Some publications are available mainly to bond dealers.

This is not to say information sources are not available; they are. The *Encyclopedia of Business Information Sources* lists publications, in a variety of formats, dealing with bonds. Most can be categorized as either factual sources that provide summary statistical data or as advisory services. Both are deserving of attention, but it should be kept in mind that while the few titles mentioned below represent the types of publications available, they in no way comprise a comprehensive list. The *Encyclopedia of Business Information Sources* lists major bond publications, and the librarian attempting to build a collection in this area would do well to consult them.

Factual Sources

Financial newspapers provide concise statistical data on bonds and other fixed-income securities. The *Wall Street Journal* has fairly comprehensive daily information on trading of federal government and corporate debt obligations, as does the *New York Times*. Weekly trading information is available in *Barron's*, *Commercial and Financial Chronicle* and *Media General Market Data Graphics*. Two publications issued by Mergent and Standard & Poor's contain monthly trading information. Although each has been referred to in earlier parts of this chapter, an overview of both is useful.

Standard & Poor's. **Bond Guide.** New York: Standard & Poor's, 1938– . Monthly.

Mergent Bond Record. New York: Mergent, 1932– . Monthly.

The *Bond Guide* is a monthly pocket guide to corporate, foreign, and municipal bonds. The bulk of each issue is devoted to corporate bonds, with 6,800 domestic corporates, more than 560 Canadian and foreign issues, and over 320 convertibles. Information in these sections is condensed into one-line summaries, which include detailed information on both the issuing companies and the specific issues themselves. The municipal section, which is so densely packed that the print is difficult to read, is limited to the ratings assigned by Standard & Poor's to each issue.

The *Bond Guide* also includes a directory of underwriters of corporate bonds, a description of the S&P rating scheme, and a digest of investment security regulations. It briefly lists corporate and municipal bonds whose ratings have changed and recent issues registered with the Securities and Exchange Commission. Because of its compact format, abbreviations and symbols are heavily used, and the inner covers of each issue explain each item included in the table in some detail.

Mergent's offering is the *Bond Record*, another monthly. Like the *Bond Guide*, it provides most information on domestic, Canadian, and some foreign bonds as well as Canadian provincial and municipal obligations. Convertible bonds are listed separately. In addition, it lists and rates commercial paper issued by companies. Separate rating and listing sections are also assigned to preferred stocks, industrial revenue bonds, environmental control revenue bonds, and municipal bonds and short-term loans. Finally, the *Bond Record* includes several charts: corporate bond yields by rating categories, yields of U.S. government securities, and weekly money market rates, among others.

Most small and medium-sized libraries will not find it necessary to subscribe to both the *Bond Guide* and the *Bond Record*. Both are good, basic guides, each with its own special features. Mergent's *Bond Record*'s format is more attractive and the print easier to read than that in Standard & Poor's *Bond Guide*. In addition, the *Bond Record*'s scope is broader; it provides information on short-term debt securities and government and federal agency obligations, whereas the Standard & Poor's publication does not. On the other hand, the corporate listings in Standard & Poor's *Bond Guide* feature more information about the companies themselves, assigning industry codes and including balance sheet figures and other financial data. Furthermore, the *Bond Guide* lists corporate underwriters. Clearly, the choice of one or the other of these publications will be a reflection of the library's budget, its clientele and their preferences, and the type of information requests concerning bonds most commonly handled.

There are also several Web pages on bonds. Perhaps one of the best is that of the Bond Market Association (http://www.investinginbonds.com), mentioned previously in this chapter. This contains descriptive guides for all types of bonds, a glossary of terms, a comparison calculator, and the ability to retrieve bond prices for the previous day and to sort them by CUSIP, ratings, issue, sector, coupon, maturity, yield, spread price, or size. This Web page also links to other resources through an annotated subject guide that includes listings for the asset-backed securities market, money market instruments, federal agency securities market, corporate bond market, municipal securities market, mortgage securities market, and treasury securities market. It is a well-organized site and up to this time the information is free.

Advisory Services

Like weekly stock advisory services, bond services provide their readers with general information about the economy, the investment climate, and market trends as well as with analyses of specific issues. Typical of these publications is *Credit Week.*

CreditWeek. New York: Standard & Poor's, 1973– . Weekly.

Value Line Convertibles Survey. New York: Value Line, 1970– . Bimonthly.

CreditWeek combines economic and credit market commentary with reviews and analyses of short- and long-term corporate issues, international bonds, and municipals. The "CreditWatch" section lists bonds and other fixed-income securities under special surveillance for possible changes in S&P ratings. A company merger, for example, may positively or negatively affect the credit standing of a corporation, while a voter referendum reducing local property taxes would have the same effect on municipal obligations.

Standard & Poor's is not the only publisher of bond advisory services. Fitch Investors Service (http://www.fitchibca.com/), a New York-based credit rating firm, rates municipal and corporate bonds, while *Value Line Convertibles* rates convertible bonds and preferred stocks. *Value Line Convertibles* ranks over 600 convertibles for potential risk and return, showing which convertibles make the best buys and which should be sold. Approximately 80 warrants, which are like options and are very risky, are also followed and evaluated. This service is available in both print and CD-ROM formats.

Since many libraries subscribe to one or the other or both of the library investment "packages" offered by Mergent and Standard & Poor's, their publications are the services most likely to be found in business reference collections.

For-Fee Databases

Many of the databases described in the preceding chapter contain information about bonds and fixed-income securities as well as stocks. General financial information, for example, is available in files produced by Dow Jones and Mergent. Some of the more specialized databases are described below.

Bond Buyer Full Text. New York: Bond Buyer. 1981– . Daily updates. Dialog File 626.

Fitch IBCA Ratings Delivery Service. New York: Fitch, 1998– . http://www.fitchibca. com/. (Accessed August 30, 2003).

RatingsDirect. New York: Standard & Poor's, ©1994–2003. http://www.ratingsdirect. com/. (Accessed August 30, 2003).

Value Line Convertibles Securities File. New York: Value Line, 19uu– . http://www. valueline.com. (Accessed August 30, 2003).

The *Bond Buyer* is the online, full-text version of the daily *Bond Buyer*. It focuses on fixed-income securities and includes statistics on bond yields, prices, and sales; articles on federal laws and regulations affecting tax-exempt financing; Internal Revenue rulings; and a complete record of municipal borrowings. Although the *Bond Buyer* is intended for institutional rather than private investors, the data it contains can be useful to scholars and researchers as well.

Fitch provides online, real-time ratings in the three sectors of corporate, asset-backed, and municipal bonds. These ratings, based on information obtained from issuers, underwriters, and their experts, are not recommendations to buy, sell, or hold any security. The Web site allows free access to recent press releases, presale reports, criteria reports, and all current ratings maintained by Fitch. For details about the ratings service and fees the user needs to check the Web site at http://www.fitchibca.com/. Fitch ratings are also made available through third parties, including Dow Jones, LexisNexis, and Interactive Data.

Standard & Poor's provides an integrated online service, *RatingsDirect,* which covers more than 6 million ratings, 248,000 issues, and 71,000 reports. The content includes ratings of specific securities and research, and analysis related to the supplied ratings. Subscriptions are available to information on all of Standard & Poor's global ratings activities or to information about a specific sector or region of interest.

The *Value Line Convertibles* is one of the largest sources of information available on convertible securities. It covers over 600 convertible bonds, preferred stocks, and warrants, with approximately 150 fundamental and proprietary data items on each. *Value Line*'s evaluations are included.

These fee-based services are expensive and are usually subscribed to by institutional investors, but librarians should be aware of them and the availability of the data for researchers.

Notes

1. The Federal Reserve Bank of Richmond issued in 1993 the seventh edition of *Instruments of the Money Market.* This book is no longer in print, but the chapters have been placed on the Web at http://www.rich.frb.org/pubs/instruments/.

2. *TreasuryDirect* is a program designed for investors who purchase Treasury bills, notes, and bonds and intend to hold them until maturity. Individual investors can establish a single *TreasuryDirect* account for all marketable Treasury securities with the same ownership and hold all their bills, notes, or bonds in the same account. Principal and interest payments are made electronically by direct deposit to an account at a financial institution designated by the investor.

More information can be obtained from

TreasuryDirect
P.O. Box 9150
Minneapolis, MN 55480-9150
Tel: 617-994-5500

3. The formula for converting the yield column to dollar price is

$$Price = \frac{100 - Yield\ (Maturity)}{360}$$

4. Louis Rukeyser, *How to Make Money in Wall Street* (Garden City, N.Y.: Doubleday, 1974), 161.

14

Mutual Funds and Investment Companies

Introduction

Stocks and bonds are for those who prefer direct participation in the investment market. Investment companies, that is, companies that sell shares in the investments held in diversified securities portfolios acquired with the pooled money of shareholders, are for those who prefer to relinquish responsibility for selection of securities and portfolio management to professional investment managers. The investor's responsibility ceases after he or she makes initial selection and purchase of shares in a chosen investment company, until such time as the investor decides to redeem the shares at current market value or switch to another fund.

The shares purchased may be in open- or closed-end investment companies. Open-end investment companies, known as mutual funds, are those that will sell an unlimited number of shares to all interested investors; they stand ready to issue new shares or redeem old ones on a daily basis. As the number of shareholders increases, the pool of money to be invested grows proportionally and the securities portfolio expands. The shares are sold, or repurchased, at prices reflecting the value of the underlying securities.

Closed-end investment companies,[1] on the other hand, issue and sell a fixed number of shares only once, at the time they are established. If new investors want to buy into a closed-end investment company, they must purchase some of the existing shares from another investor, using a stockbroker as an intermediary. Shares in these companies, also known as publicly traded investment companies, are traded on the major stock exchanges and over the counter, and their prices move up and down with investor demand. Shares in open-end investment companies, on the other hand, are sold directly to the investor by the issuing company. This distinction is an important one to the librarian doing business reference, because information for both types of investment companies may not be given in the same place. Daily share price information, for example, is given separately for open- and closed-end investment companies in financial newspapers.

Mutual funds and closed-end investment companies, however, have two basic operating principles in common: They pool money from their investors to buy a broad range of stocks, bonds, and/or other investment vehicles, and they have professional investment managers who take full responsibility for all investment decisions.

Mutual funds and closed-end investment companies offer certain advantages to the investor with limited resources. Prime among these is diversification of investments. Although all investors routinely are counseled to minimize risk by diversifying their investments in a wide range of companies and industries, few individual investors can hope to achieve the variety found in most investment company portfolios. The Janus (JANSX) Mutual Fund is a case in point. Its investment portfolio recently featured stocks of 20 companies in 12 different industries. For an individual investor to research and then vigilantly maintain constant oversight of this amount of information would be a full-time occupation

Professional management is another advantage, particularly for the inexperienced or anxious investor. The professional manager handles basic investment decisions. In addition, he or she takes care of all of the paperwork and administrative details, including the preparation and distribution of quarterly reports to shareholders. In return for these services, an annual management fee percent of the total is deducted from the company's assets.

A third advantage is that fund performance is subject to frequent reviews by various publications and rating agencies, making it possible to conduct comparisons between funds.

Mutual funds are attractive because in most instances they require only relatively small minimum investments, and dividends earned can be automatically reinvested in additional shares. Thus, it is possible for the small investor to steadily increase his or her holdings in a way that is difficult to match in other kinds of investments. Another significant advantage is the ease with which most investment company shares can be redeemed. This is particularly true of open-end investment companies or mutual funds, which stand ready to redeem shares at any time the securities markets are open. Shares are redeemed at net asset value, the value of the company's holdings minus its debt, divided by the number of shares outstanding. Net asset value is determined daily, so that market fluctuations in the price of the securities held by the fund can be taken into account. Closed-end investment companies, on the other hand, are traded on the securities exchanges, and their price is a reflection of supply and demand in the marketplace as well as of their net asset value.

Finally, many investment companies offer special services to their investors, including check writing privileges, special withdrawal plans, and the opportunity to switch from one company fund to another.

This is not to say that investment companies are without flaw. Some charge substantial sales commissions, some charge redemption fees, all levy management fees, and, in some instances, the return on these investments is not as great as one might earn from direct investment in stocks and bonds. Another disadvantage is that the investor exercises no control over what securities are bought or when they are sold. Still, for many the advantages they offer outweigh their drawbacks.

A mutual fund alternative is the unit investment trust (UIT). This is a registered investment company that buys and holds a relatively fixed portfolio of stocks, bonds, or other securities. "Units" in the trust are sold to investors, who receive a share of principal and interest or dividends. Many are collections of long-term bonds and therefore may remain outstanding for 20 or 30 years. Investors who choose bond UITs receive regular monthly income, and those who hold stock UITs receive dividend income, paid out monthly, quarterly, or semiannually, plus long-term capital growth potential. Unit investment trusts have a stated date for termination, and when they are dissolved, proceeds from the holdings are paid to the investors.

Another alternative is a hedge fund, which is an unregistered private investment pool that is subject to far less regulatory oversight than a mutual fund. With the exception of anti-fraud standards, they are exempt from regulation by the SEC under the federal securities laws, unlike mutual funds, which are regulated by the Securities Act of 1933, the Securities Exchange Act of 1934, the Investment Company Act of 1940, and the Investment Advisers Act of 1940. Hedge fund managers are not forced to disclose information about the hedge fund's holdings and performance. One drawback is that usually one must be prepared to invest $1 million or more.

Types of Investment Companies

Mutual fund investment companies, as we have seen, can be categorized as open- or closed-end. They can also be classified by the presence or absence of a sales fee, their investment objectives, and their portfolio contents. Each of these classifications merits further consideration.

Load and No-Load Funds

Some mutual fund shares are sold using stockbrokers or securities dealers as middlemen. They promote the funds, handle the paperwork, and make it convenient for the investor to buy shares. These services must be paid for, so for each transaction, a sales charge, or load, ranging from 11/2 to 81/2 percent is deducted from the initial investment. Thus, a $10,000 investment in a fund charging an 81/2 percent load is really only a $9,150 investment; the remaining $815 goes to the salesperson. Further, an investor who puts $10,000 into a load fund from which the $815 load immediately is deducted must earn $815 on his or her investment just to break even.

Other funds must be purchased directly from the issuing investment company. Because no middlemen are involved, often no sales commission, or load, is deducted, and these funds are called, appropriately enough, no-load funds. The total amount of the investment goes directly into fund shares, which means that, over the long run and given the same initial investment, shareholders in no-load funds come out ahead.

Let's assume two $10,000 investments, one in a load fund and the other in a no-load fund. In the case of the load fund, 81/2 percent or $815 is deducted; the remaining $9,150 is invested. If both funds grow at the same rate—10 percent per year, for example—the no-load fund will be worth $11,000 at the end of the first year, while the load fund will be worth only $10,065. The no-load investor is now $1,000 ahead; the load fund investor is about even. But let's look closer. Originally the no-load investor had $850 more working for him than did the load fund investor. Now the differential is $935 ($11,000 versus $10,065). What has happened is that the $850 paid out as commission in one case, but invested in the other, is also growing. And over the years this sum will continue to grow and compound, widening the differential. By the end of 20 years, the no-load investment will be worth $6,000 more.[2] For a comparison of the most popular load funds and their no-load equivalents see the "Tools" section of *FundAdvice.com* at http://www.fundadvice.com.

In terms of quality of professional investment management, neither the load nor the no-load fund is intrinsically superior. There are good, bad, and mediocre funds in both categories. Purchase of no-load funds, however, requires more investor initiative, since it is the investor who must identify potential no-load fund investments, contact each company for additional information, and initiate the actual purchase of shares. Although securities brokers are not ordinarily forthcoming with information on no-load funds, the investor can find these funds advertised in financial newspapers and publications and listed in some of the basic sources described later in this chapter. Another way in which no-load funds can be identified is through the Mutual Fund Education Alliance Web page,[3] which lists category leaders by investment objective and also has an alphabetical listing of more than 600 mutual fund companies and 12,000 mutual funds.

Investment Objectives

Investment companies can also be differentiated by their investment objectives. Some funds, which stress immediate income and invest primarily in corporate bonds or high dividend-yielding stocks, are income funds. Growth funds, on the other hand, look for long-term capital or income growth. Still other funds seek to attain a balance between income and growth. These are balanced funds. Many basic reference sources classify the various funds by their investment objectives; another source of this information is the prospectus issued by the fund itself. The 2001 prospectus for the Red Oak Technology Select Fund, for example, states that it is a nondiversified mutual fund whose investment goal is long-term capital growth and whose investment focus is U.S. common stocks. The fund strategy is to invest in common stocks of companies that rely extensively on technology in their product development or operations, or which the adviser expects to benefit from technological advances and improvements. The Fund is concentrated (invests at least 25 percent of its total assets) in "technology companies" thatdevelop, produce, or distribute products or services related to computers, semiconductors, and electronics. In other words, this is for people who are willing to risk investing in a fund that invests in relatively few companies in one industry.

Portfolio Contents

Varying objectives necessitate the purchase of different types of securities for each investment portfolio. As a result, another way in which investment companies can be categorized is by the types of securities they hold. Although there are several variations, the basic categories are as follows:

1. Bond funds
2. Equity (stock) funds
3. Money market funds
4. Balanced funds
5. Index funds

There is, of course, considerable variety within each of these categories. One bond fund, for example, may invest only in double and triple A-rated bonds, while another fund's portfolio may include a mix of high- , medium- , and low-rated bonds. Similarly, funds are often described by the kind of stocks they invest in. Funds that invest in growth stocks (stocks of companies with positive outlooks for growth) are described as growth funds. Funds that invest in value stocks (stocks of companies that are currently considered to be cheap based on fundamental data like earnings, revenue, and assets) are described as value funds. Some mutual funds invest only in stocks of foreign companies. These are called international funds, while global funds are those that invest in stocks of both foreign and U.S. companies. Sector funds are those that invest in stocks of a particular industry or area such as technology, real estate, or precious metals. Money market funds have relatively low risks compared to other mutual funds. They are limited by law to certain high-quality, short-term investments such as Treasury bills. Balanced funds mix some stocks and some bonds with money market instruments in an effort to provide growth, income, and conservation of capital. An index fund is a mutual fund that tries to mimic, as closely as possible, the holdings of a particular index. They are distinct from actively managed mutual funds in that they do not involve any stock picking by a fund manager; they simply seek to replicate the returns of a specific index, such as the S&P 500 or the Dow Industrial. Many of the basic reference sources give an indication of portfolio contents, and this information is spelled out in detail in individual investment company prospectuses.

As the economy changes, so also does interest in specific types of funds. In years of spiraling interest rates, for example, money market funds enjoy tremendous popularity, with a resulting proliferation of guides, directories, and advisory letters, many of which are in great demand by library users. Some of these titles are discussed later in the section on information sources.

Closed-end funds are divided into may of the same categories as mutual funds.

Current Per-Share Information

Mutual Funds

Mutual funds stand ready to redeem their shares at net asset value whenever the securities markets are open. Net asset value for each fund is determined daily and is listed in financial newspapers such as the *Wall Street Journal* and on various Web sites. Compared to stock and bond tables, those for mutual funds are relatively easy to decipher, and figures are in dollars and cents. A sample follows in figure 14.1.

MUTUAL FUND QUOTATIONS

XYZ Fund

Market Close Date	Aug. 2, 2001	Previous NAV	$18.20
Net Asset Value	$17.69	Ask	$17.69
Net Change	-0.51	% Change	-2.80%

1. Net Asset Value (NAV)
The market value of a fund share. In the case of no-load funs, the NAV, market price, and offering price are all the same figure, which the public pays to buy shares; load fund market prices are quoted after adding the sales charge to the net asset value. NAV is calculated by most funds after the close of the exchanges each day by taking the closing market value of all securities owned plus all other assets such as cash, subtracting all liabilities, then dividing the result (total net assets) by the total number of shares outstanding.

2. Net Change
The difference between today's last trade and the previous day's last trade. The difference between today's closing Net Asset Value (NAV) and the previous day's closing Net Asset Value (NAV).

3. Ask
The price at which a share can be purchased.

Figure 14. 1. Example of a daily online mutual fund table.

Thus, in the example shown in figure 14.1, the item listed, XYZ Fund, a load fund, could be redeemed for $17.69 per share, its current net asset value. The net asset value was down $.51 per share from the preceding trading day, which makes a –2.8 percentage change

Closed-End Investment Companies

Prices of shares in closed-end investment companies are shown in the stock tables of most financial newspapers. The *Wall Street Journal* on Mondays lists separate information on closed-end funds, including NAVs, market prices, and discounts or premiums. (See figure 14.2.)

Fund Name	Stock Exchange	NAV	Market Price	Premium/ Discount	52-Week Market Return/52-Week Yield
FGH Fund	NYSE	17.18	19 ½	+13.5	7.1

Column 1: Shows the name of the fund and usually the ticker symbol.

Column 2: The exchange on which the fund is traded.

Column 3: Net asset value of a share. Calculated by taking the fund's total assets: securities, cash, and any accrued earnings, less expenses and liabilities, and dividing the remainder by the number of shares outstanding.

Column 4: The final price of the stock at close of trading.

Column 5: The plus or minus figure shows the percentage premium (+) or discount (–) above or below the fund's NAV per share, at which the shares last sold.

Column 6: For stock funds this shows the 52-week percentage change in price plus dividends. For bond funds this shows the dividends paid during the last 52 weeks as a percentage of market price.

Figure 14.2. Hypothetical listing of a closed-end fund.

Information Sources

A wide range of printed and Internet sources exists to help investors select and monitor investment companies in which they are interested, ranging from prospectuses and reports issued by the companies themselves to guides, directories, and specialized advisory newsletters. Some major reference tools, representative of the various types of information sources available, are described below.

Prospectuses and Company Reports

Investment companies are required by law to submit a prospectus to all prospective investors. This document describes the fund's investment objective, portfolio, management, special services offered, assets and liabilities, and per-share income. This constitutes a summary of the registration statement filed with the Securities and Exchange Commission and provides an overview of a specific fund's investment philosophy and performance. Quarterly financial reports update the prospectus and pinpoint the company's current financial status.

These are readily available to anyone either from the SEC (http://www.sec.gov), from the Web page of the mutual fund company or, for those who want a print copy, directly from the company. This information comprises the primary source on which most basic investment company reference publications are based.

Most Web sites that give information on mutual funds offer tutorials on reading and understanding a prospectus. Among them is the Mutual Fund Education Alliance at http://www.mfea.com/GettingStarted/LearningTopics/Basics/ReadingProspectus.asp (see figure 14.3).

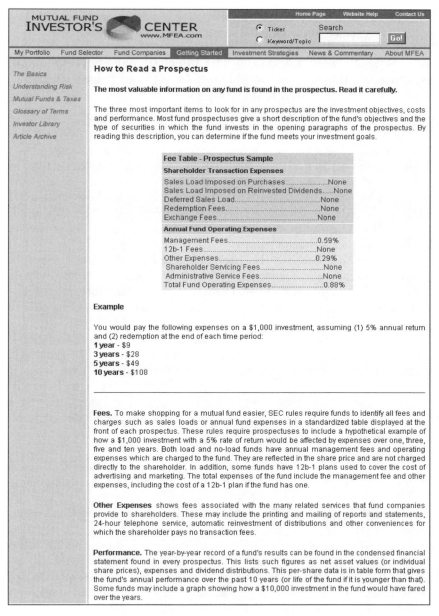

Figure 14.3. How to read a prospectus.

Encyclopedias, Guides, and Factbooks

Many of the general investment guides discussed in chapter 12 offer basic introductions to mutual funds and investment companies. More specialized guides are also available. Some are inexpensive booklets aimed at readers new to mutual funds. Others focus on specific types of mutual funds, such as money market funds or foreign equity funds. The type of mutual fund investment in vogue one season, however, may not be in the next, and these specialized guides may remain unread on library shelves for years after a brief period of popularity. Although such publications can be useful for the short term, libraries with limited book budgets should first acquire a core collection of general mutual fund guides or a core listing of Web sites that provide the same type of information.

Madlem, Peter W., and Thomas K. Sykes. **The International Encyclopedia of Mutual Funds, Closed-End Funds and Real Estate Investment Trusts.** Chicago: Glenlake Publishing; New York: AMACOM, 2000. 367p.

Investment Company Institute. **Mutual Fund Fact Book**. Washington, D.C.: The Institute, 1966– . Annual. (Available in pdf format at http://www.ici.org/stats/mf/index.html.

The *Encyclopedia* contains descriptions of every conceivable concept, term, fund category, and strategy as well as a huge array of individual funds and Real Estate Investment Trusts (REITs). The fund listings include the year it was offered, management tenure, minimum purchase, sales charge, five years of total returns, a beta, and how much a $10,000 investment has appreciated. The listings are given in sector groups, such as Municipal Bond Funds and National and Equity Income Funds. The tables are dense, but the information is well worth the effort it takes to read them.

The *Mutual Fund Fact Book* is very different in that it provides an overview of the mutual funds industry, including its history, growth and development, composite industry statistics, and a glossary of key terms. It is extremely useful for the researcher who wants to learn about mutual funds generally and does not require information on specific funds (see figure 14.4).

Several other useful investor guides produced by the Investment Company Institute and available free from the Web site include those shown in figure 14.5 (page 322).

These are only a few of the publications available from the Institute. It also produces materials on legislation, the economy and markets, retirement issues, and mutual fund developments and statistics. Any librarian wishing to acquire materials on mutual funds should visit the publications Web site at http://www.ici.org/statements/index.html to check what is freely available.

There are numerous Web sites, including those belonging to fund families, which include basic guides and information to the different funds. Several are listed below.

About.com. Mutual Funds. ©2003. http://mutualfunds.about.com/?once=true&. (Accessed August 30, 2003).

In the section "Mutual Funds 101," this site includes basic guides on the different types of mutual funds, guides to beginning investing in funds, and guides to asset allocation. Also collected on this page are links to fund families, index funds, charts, experts, investment fraud, and newsletters. This site is heavy on advice and guidance in all areas.

Table of Contents

Figure 14.4. Table of contents, *Mutual Fund Fact Book*, 2003 edition.
Reproduced with permission of Investment Company Institute, http://www.ici.org.

A Guide to Mutual Funds	http://www.ici.org/aboutfunds/bro_g2_mfs.html
A Guide to Closed End Funds	http://www.ici.org/aboutfunds/bro_g2_ce.htm
A Guide to Bond Mutual Funds	http://www.ici.org/aboutfunds/bro_g2_bmfs.html
A Guide to Unit Investment Trusts	http://www.ici.org/aboutfunds/bro_g2_uits.html
The Benefits of Diversification	http://www.ici.org/investing_for_success/diversification.html
Securing Your Retirement	http://www.ici.org/investing_for_success/retirement.html

Figure 14.5. Selected free publications from the Investment Company Institute.
Reproduced with permission of Investment Company Institute, http://www.ici.org.

Brill's Mutual Funds Interactive. ©1995–2003. http://www.brill.com/. (Accessed August 30, 2003).

The section "Funds 101" gives guidance on such topics as IRAs, Roth IRAs, simplifying your investment life, annuities, and taxes. This site also offers expert advice and links to mutual funds. The "Toolshed" provides the ability to screen for funds and get quick quotes or charts and a fund's prospectus.

The Motley Fool. **Mutual Funds.** ©1995–2003. http://www.fool.com/school/mutualfunds/mutualfunds.htm?ref'schAg. (Accessed August 30, 2003).

For those who prefer a more irreverent but still extremely useful look at mutual funds, this is the site to use. Information ranges from the "Boring Technical Stuff" to "Mutual Funds Performance Records." There is also an interesting look at the cost of mutual funds, including loads, expense ratios, taxes, and turnover and cash reserves. With free registration a user may take part in the online discussion board.

SEC. **Invest Wisely: An Introduction to Mutual Funds.** Modified June 2, 2003. http://www.sec.gov/investor/pubs/inwsmf.htm. (Accessed August 30, 2003).

The same kind of general information, included on other Web pages, is available, in a text format, from the SEC. A very useful link on this page is for consumers to register complaints about mutual funds. The link is at http://www.sec.gov/complaint.shtml. Frequently asked questions, including those on the regulation of funds, are available at http://sec.broaddaylight.com/sec/index.shtm.

Mutual Fund Investor's Center. ©1996–2003. http://www.mfea.com/. (Accessed August 30, 2003).

Another very usable site designed to help investors reach their financial goals. It contains a large collection of mutual fund company listings, as well as links to planning, tracking, and monitoring tools available on the Internet. One special feature is a section designed for women investors and the problems they may have. The tax section is also very extensive and includes tax articles that have been archived.

This is only a short selection of accessible Web sites. They were chosen because of the carefully written guides, the simplicity of the language, and the wealth of free information provided. There are many others available, and it is up to librarians to acquire or recommend those most useful for patrons.

For those who are interested in learning more about closed-end funds, an excellent source of information is the *Closed End Fund Center* Web page (http://www.closed-endfunds. com/) maintained by the Closed-End Fund Association (CEFA), the national trade association representing the closed-end fund industry. (See figure 14.6.)

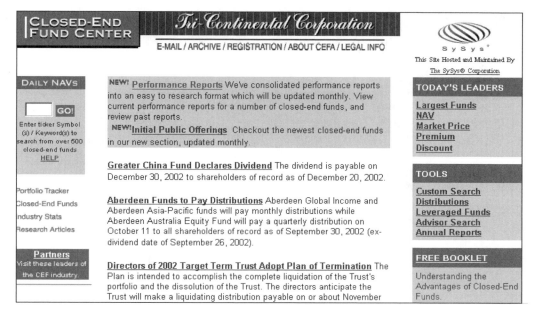

Figure 14.6. Home page of CEFA, showing some available information.
Reproduced with permission of Closed-End Fund Association, Inc. © 1999–2001. All Rights Reserved.

The CEFA Web page is a comprehensive collection of free information on the general composition of the funds, the advantages, and investment risk, as well as statistics, articles, and a fund tracker. Included on the page is information on buying and selling, dividends, discounts, and premiums, as well as the annual reports for over 200 closed-end funds and daily information on the industry's leaders. The information included encompasses both that needed by a beginner in investing and that needed by someone who has already invested in the funds. (See figure 14.7, page 324.)

Directories

Many investors feel more comfortable with print publications but still want composite information about open- and closed-end investment companies as well as details on specific funds. For them, the following title will be particularly useful.

Mergent Bank & Finance Manual. New York: Mergent, 1955– . 4v. Annual. (Supplemented by *Bank & Finance News Report,* Web version available at http://www. mergent.com/.)

Mergent Bank & Finance Manual is another source of detailed information. Volume 2 lists major U.S. and Canadian investment companies. Its entries contain detailed listings of portfolio contents and thorough company histories. *Mergent* also includes a listing of money market fund ratings. Volumes 3 and 4 contain information on UITs.

CLOSED-END FUND CENTER

TODAYS LEADERS

DAILY NAVS

[ ] GO!

Enter ticker Symbol(s) / Keyword(s) to search from over 500 closed-end funds

HELP

Portfolio Tracker
Closed-End Funds
Industry Stats
Research Articles

E-MAIL / ARCHIVE / REGISTRATION / ABOUT CEFA / LEGAL INFO

Top 25 closed-end funds based on net assets. NAV returns based on year-to-date as of most recent month-end results.

CLICK HERE to create your own custom list

Largest Funds		
Net Assets (Millions)	Based on net assets	YTD NAV Return
$2,363.40	Tri-Continental Corporation	-20.26%
$1,962.35	Nuveen Muni Value	5.05%
$1,815.85	DNP Select Income Fund Inc	-13.93%
$1,614.23	ACM Income Fund	4.56%
$1,478.04	Van Kampen Senior Inc Tr	-0.05%
$1,263.40	Nuveen Insured Muni Opportunity	9.60%
$1,262.31	Aberdeen Asia-Pacific Income Fund	17.00%
$1,234.93	Salomon Brothers Fund	-19.54%
$1,170.81	Adams Express Company	-17.82%
$1,013.30	Liberty All-Star Equity Fund	-23.30%
$1,008.88	Korea Fund	26.29%
$1,000.16	Gabelli Equity Trust	-20.19%
$953.19	Nuveen Prem Inc Muni	6.89%
$939.72	Mexico Fund	-9.32%
$935.29	General American Investors	-19.11%
$927.39	MFS Intermediate Income Trust	7.32%
$925.68	Nuveen Performance Plus Muni	8.96%
$920.79	Putnam Premier Income Trust	2.02%
$917.17	MuniYield Insured Fund	9.71%
$879.81	Nuveen Quality Preferred Income	N/A%
$875.70	John Hancock Bank & Thrift Oppty Fd	7.59%
$853.86	TCW/DW Term Trust 2003	3.67%
$823.75	Alliance World Dollar Govt Fund II	4.86%
$817.65	Nuveen Quality Inc Muni	8.21%
$773.75	Templeton Global Income Fd	9.47%

HOME
PortfolioTracker | Closed-End Funds
Statistics | Research Articles | E-Mail | Archive
Registration | About CEFA | Legal Info | Overview
Advantages | Types of CEFs | Buying & Selling
NAV's | Dividends & Distributions
Discounts & Premiums | Sources | FAQ's

Figure 14.7. Listing of largest closed-end funds.
Reproduced with permission of Closed-End Fund Association, Inc. © 1999–2001. All Rights Reserved.

Although *Mergent Bank & Finance Manual* provides information on both open- and closed-end investment companies, other publications are more specialized.

Although there are no widely held publications devoted specifically to closed-end investment companies, *Value Line* offers a quarterly summary of the investment company industry as well as detailed analyses of selected major closed-end investment companies whose shares are traded on national stock exchanges and over-the-counter.

Periodical Lists and Ratings

Many newspapers and periodicals regularly list and rate funds. One of the most comprehensive surveys is that offered by *Barron's*. Each week *Barron's* includes a weekly pull-out section on mutual funds that consists of articles on specific types of funds, investment strategies, and interviews with fund managers, supplemented by tables showing the Lipper mutual fund performance averages and weekly financial tables. In addition, each quarter, with the assistance of Lipper Analytical Services, a fund-rating organization, Barron's presents the *Lipper Mutual Funds Quarterly*, which includes "Leaders and Laggards," "Winners and Losers," as well as financial information for funds.

Other general business periodicals cover mutual funds as well, although not as often or as thoroughly as magazines devoted to funds. One of these is *Mutual Funds* (http://www.mutual-funds.com/), a monthly magazine that profiles funds and strategies for every life stage and investment goal.

Specialized Advisory Newsletters/Services

In addition to the periodic coverage of mutual funds and investment companies in such standard sources as *Barron's* and *Mutual Funds*, several advisory services and newsletters specializing in mutual funds are published. Although a comprehensive collection of such material is impractical for most libraries, many will include one or two such sources in addition to mutual fund directories and guides. A good guide to the newsletters follows.

The Hulbert Financial Digest. Washington, D.C.: Hulbert Financial Digest, 19uu– . Monthly.

HFD rates for actual performance most of the investment newsletters available. If a subscription is contemplated the user should first check *HFD* for the quality of a newsletter's effectiveness. This publication checks on approximately 160 newsletters and gives subscription details. The full list of publications covered is at http://cbs.marketwatch.com/news/newsletters/default.asp?siteid=mktw&dist=&). Each month there are reports on the top five performing newsletters plus a section on mutual fund newsletters. The *HFD* features in-depth profiles of four of the top-performing letters, presenting detailed analyses of their track records, strategies, and techniques, with graphs of their performances as far back as 1980. If one does not want to subscribe to the *HFD* newsletter one can contract to buy online a single newsletter or a single profile. Full subscription details and samples are available at http://cbs.marketwatch.com/news/newsletters/products.asp?siteid=mktw&dist=&. Several of the newsletters investigated are specifically concerned with mutual funds. *HFD* is now part of the Newsletter Center at *CBS MarketWatch* (http://cbs.marketwatch.com/news/default.asp?siteid=mktw).

Moneyletter. Holliston, Mass.: PRI Financial Publishing, 1980– . Biweekly. (For more information check http://www.moneyletter.com/.)

Morningstar Mutual Funds. Chicago: Morningstar, 1991– . Biweekly. Web version available at http://www.morningstar.com.

Mutual Fund Prospector. Moline, Ill.: Mutual Fund Prospector, 1998– . Monthly. Web version available at http://www.ericdany.com/.

Value Line Mutual Fund Survey. New York,: Value Line Publishing, 1993– . Monthly.

Moneyletter (http://www.moneyletter.com/) emphasizes funds likely to be of interest to individual investors and includes these in 10 model portfolios. Like the other services, it combines general information and investment advice with lists of top-performing funds, a fund scoreboard with recommendations, and coverage of specific investment companies.

Morningstar (http://www.morningstar.com), a Chicago-based fund-tracking company, provides data on more than 10,000 mutual funds and 8,000 stocks. Products are available in print, on the Internet, and on CD-ROM and can be customized for institutional or corporate clients. *Morningstar Mutual Funds* is one of the industry standards for rating funds, and uses a star (risk adjusted) rating system for each bond or stock fund. Funds are assigned anywhere from one to five stars, one being the least attractive and five considered the best. To obtain these ratings the first number Morningstar checks is the fund's rate of return. First all sales charges and redemption fees are subtracted from the performance of the fund being measured. Then the T-bill's return is subtracted from the fund's load-adjusted figure. This will give by how much the fund's return exceeded the risk free rate. A comparison is then made between that fund's return and other funds in its broad group. This is the return score. The groups used are U.S. stock, international stock, taxable bonds, and municipal bonds funds.

To get the risk score Morningstar analysts check the performance of a fund against the Treasury bill and compare this transaction against other funds in the group. The result is the risk score. The final part of the rating is to subtract the fund's risk score from its return. The results are then shown on a bell curve, with the top 10 percent given a five-star rating and the bottom 10 percent the one-star rating.

Many libraries buy *Morningstar* either as a print publication or as an online service, and individuals can take out a single subscription online at http://www.morningstar.com/. There is, however, a fair amount of free information at the Web site. This includes the rating of the fund, its top investments, and links to news stories. For those libraries that have researchers who need to perform a deeper level of analysis, the best product is probably the CD-ROM *Morningstar Principia*.

The *Mutual Fund Prospector* offers investment advice, timely information, and a model portfolio, whose performance is followed each month and which is available on the Web at http://www.ericdany.com/model_portfolio_performance.htm. When available, links are provided on the Web page to the funds that are followed in the newsletter.

Those researchers who have used the *Value Line Investment Survey* to follow stocks will be very comfortable using the *Value Line Mutual Fund Survey*. The first part of the *Survey* provides current rankings and performance data on 2000 funds; the second part contains over 150 full-page reports on individual funds. Included are historical returns (up to 20 years), top portfolio holdings, ratings, and risk. More information and a sample newsletter are available at http://www.valueline.com/productsamples.html.

There are numerous services and newsletters available, and just about every financial Web page has a section on mutual funds.

Notes

1. The Closed-End Fund Association (CEFA) is the national trade association representing the closed-end fund industry. Information about closed-end funds is provided at http://www.closed-endfunds.com/. The Web site provides general information, a list of all funds, plus links to annual reports and statistics.

2. Yale Hirsch, *Mutual Funds Almanac*, 11th ed. (Old Tappan, N.J.: The Hirsch Organization, 1980), 54.

3. The Mutual Fund Education Alliance™ is the not-for-profit trade association of the no-load mutual fund industry. The Web site at http://www.mfea.com/default.asp contains educational materials, a portfolio tracker, and listings of mutual funds with links to information.

15

Futures and Options

Stocks, bonds, and mutual funds are the most common investment mediums for individual investors, but they are by no means the only ones. This chapter focuses on other increasingly popular types of investments, specifically derivatives, examples of which are futures and options, and reviews of information sources relevant to them.

Derivatives

Derivatives are risk-shifting instruments. A derivative is a contract established by two or more parties where payment is based on (or "derived" from) some agreed upon value, which is established on the future value of an underlying asset, typically a commodity, bond, equity, or currency. Simply put, derivatives are instruments whose return depends on the return of other instruments. A derivative is a promise to transfer ownership at an agreed upon time in the future for an agreed upon price. A common property of many derivatives is that the asset itself is not exchanged, only the change in value of the asset. Derivatives include a wide range of instruments including futures and options (see figure 15.1, page 330).

The term most commonly associated with derivatives is *risk*. This is because most of us associate financial disasters such as Orange County, California,[1] or the collapse of Barings Bank,[2] with derivatives trading. Although the instruments themselves were blamed, it was more a lack of adequate internal and external controls that was to blame. As with all investments risk is involved, but an understanding of the risks being taken and an organization's exposure to risk is needed.

Most general business and financial encyclopedias will give an overview of derivatives, but many specialized sources also exist.

Guides

There are hundreds of books available that will give an in-depth analysis of derivatives. To find them one can search any library catalog or Web-based book service. Two titles that are useful and not too complicated are listed below.

• **Options.** An Option represents the right (but not the obligation) to buy or sell a security or other asset during a given time for a specified price (the "**Strike**" price). An Option to buy is known as a "**Call,**" and an Option to sell is called a "**Put.**" You can purchase Options (the right to buy or sell the security in question) or sell (write) Options. As a seller, you would become obligated to sell a security to, or buy a security from, the party that purchased the Option. Options can be either "**Covered**" or "**Naked.**" In a **Covered** Option, the contract is backed by the asset underlying the Option, *e.g.* , you could purchase a **Put** on 300 shares of the ABC Corp. that you now own. In a **Naked** Option, the contract is not backed by the security underlying the Option. Options are traded on organized exchanges and OTC.

• **Forward Contracts.** In a Forward Contract, the purchaser and its counter-party are obligated to trade a security or other asset at a specified date in the future. The price paid for the security or asset is agreed upon at the time the contract is entered into, or may be determined at delivery. Forward Contracts generally are traded OTC.

• **Futures.** A Future represents the right to buy or sell a standard quantity and quality of an asset or security at a specified date and price. Futures are similar to Forward Contracts, but are standardized and traded on an exchange, and are valued, or "**Marked to Market**" daily. The **Marking to Market** provides both parties with a daily accounting of their financial obligations under the terms of the Future. Unlike Forward Contracts, the counter-party to a Futures contract is the clearing corporation on the appropriate exchange. Futures often are settled in cash or cash equivalents, rather than requiring physical delivery of the underlying asset. Parties to a Futures contract may buy or write Options on Futures.

• **Stripped Mortgage-Backed Securities.** Stripped Mortgage-Backed Securities, called "**SMBS**," represent interests in a pool of mortgages, called "**Tranches**," the cash flow of which has been separated into interest and principal components.

Interest only securities, called "**IOs**," receive the interest portion of the mortgage payment and generally increase in value as interest rates rise and decrease in value as interest rates fall. Where the underlying mortgages for an **IO** carry variable ("floating") rates of interest, the value of the **IOs** tend to increase in periods of rising interest rates due to anticipated higher interest payments on the underlying mortgages. For **IOs** that have underlying mortgages at a fixed rate, the value of **IOs** also tends to increase in value during periods of rising interest rates because individual homeowners are less likely to refinance and prepay their mortgages. The value of the **SMBS** would therefore, tend to increase over the "life" of the mortgage instrument.

Principal only securities, called "**POs**," receive the principal portion of the mortgage payment and respond inversely to interest rate movement. As interest rates go up, the value of the **PO** would tend to fall, as the **PO** becomes less attractive compared with other investment opportunities in the marketplace.

Some **Tranches** may offer interest and principal payments in various combinations. Planned Amortization Classes "**PACs**," for instance, provide stable interest and principal repayments if the rates of prepayments on the underlying mortgages stay within a specified predetermined range.

Figure 15.1. Description of common financial derivatives. *Description of Common Financial Derivatives* by G. Philip Rutledge, Director and Rob Bertram, Counsel, Division of Corporation Finance, Pennsylvania Securities Commission. Copyright © Pennsylvania Securities Commission, February 1995, Second Edition. (http://sites.state.pa.us/PA_Exec/Securities/capital/derivatives.html).

• **Structured Notes.** Structured Notes are debt instruments where the principal and/or the interest rate is indexed to an unrelated indicator. An example of a Structured Note would be a bond whose interest rate is decided by interest rates in England or the price of a barrel of crude oil. Sometimes the two elements of a Structured Note are inversely related, so as the index goes up, the rate of payment (the "coupon rate") goes down. This instrument is known as an "**Inverse Floater.**" With leveraging, Structured Notes may fluctuate to a greater degree than the underlying index. Therefore, Structured Notes can be an extremely volatile derivative with high risk potential and a need for close monitoring. Structured Notes generally are traded OTC.

• **Swaps.** A Swap is a simultaneous buying and selling of the same security or obligation. Perhaps the best-known Swap occurs when two parties exchange interest payments based on an identical principal amount, called the "notional principal amount."

Think of an interest rate Swap as follows: Party A holds a 10-year $10,000 home equity loan that has a fixed interest rate of 7 percent, and Party B holds a 10-year $10,000 home equity loan that has an adjustable interest rate that will change over the "life" of the mortgage. If Party A and Party B were to exchange interest rate payments on their otherwise identical mortgages, they would have engaged in an interest rate Swap.

Interest rate swaps occur generally in three scenarios. Exchanges of a fixed rate for a floating rate, a floating rate for a fixed rate, or a floating rate for a floating rate. The "Swaps market" has grown dramatically. Today, Swaps involve exchanges other than interest rates, such as mortgages, currencies, and "cross-national" arrangements. Swaps may involve cross-currency payments (U.S. Dollars vs. Mexican Pesos) and crossmarket payments, *e.g.*, U.S. short-term rates vs. U.K. short-term rates. Swaps may include "**Caps,**" "**Floors,**" or Caps and Floors combined ("**Collars**").

A derivative consisting of an Option to enter into an interest rate Swap, or to cancel an existing Swap in the future is called a "**Swaption.**" You can also combine a interest rate and currency Swap (called a "**Circus**" Swap). Swaps generally are traded OTC through Swap dealers, which generally consist of large financial institution, or other large brokerage houses. There is a recent trend for Swap dealers to **Mark to Market** the Swap to reduce the risk of counter-party default.

Figure 15.1 (*Cont.*)

An Introduction to Derivatives. Singapore: New York: John Wiley. 1999. 212p.

Braddock, John C. **Derivatives Demystified: Using Structured Financial Products**. New York: John Wiley, 1997. 306p.

An Introduction to Derivatives, part of the Reuters financial training series, describes fundamental risk management tools and presents their application in trading, hedging, and arbitraging. This book is designed for a general audience and is one of the most basic primers available.

The Braddock publication, part of the Wiley series in financial engineering, breaks down a complex subject into manageable units that do not overwhelm the novice reader. Descriptions of instruments and products are clearly set out and the book also covers the responsibility and legal liability of companies and officers within the company. An added glossary is useful, and the indexing is fairly extensive.

Dictionaries

Most financial dictionaries contain at least some of the vocabulary of derivatives, but the following publication contains most of the specialized jargon as well as being a guide to the instruments in use. It is designed to provide more information, for each entry, than most typical dictionaries. The definition of "bull spread," for example, covers nearly two pages and contains diagrams.

Inglis-Taylor, Andrew. **Dictionary of Derivatives.** Basingstoke, England: Macmillan, 1995. 444p.

The second part of the *Dictionary* includes articles on exchanges that give the basic data about each including their histories, the instruments they trade, the contract months, and expiration dates.

Futures

In the futures market, investors trade futures contracts, which are agreements for the future delivery of designated quantities of given products for specified prices. This market is meant to provide an efficient and effective mechanism to manage price risk. The market can be described as a continuous auction market. Although futures trading in the United States began with agricultural commodities such as corn and wheat, items traded today are considerably more diverse. It is now possible to trade in precious and strategic metals, petroleum, foreign currency, and financial instruments as well as in such agricultural commodities as grain and livestock. During FY 2000, 580,414,437 futures and option contracts were traded on U.S. futures exchanges.[3]

Futures are usually divided into two broad categories: commodities and financial. (See figure 15.2.)

Commodities Futures

Commodities are sold in two different ways. Someone can buy sugar or wheat or pork bellies and take immediate possession of the product, which must be in a basic, raw, unprocessed state. Such a purchase is commonly referred to as a cash, or spot, transaction. Frequently, however, commodities are bought and sold for delivery at a later time by means of futures contracts. A commodities futures contract is a legal agreement between buyer and seller that a specified number of units of the commodity being traded on a particular futures exchange will be delivered at a certain place, during a certain month, for an agreed upon price. In July, someone who anticipates a rise in wheat prices, for example, may instruct his or her broker to buy one Kansas City Board of Trade (KCBT)(http://www.kcbt.com) wheat contract, to be delivered in December for $2.66 per bushel. If the market price of wheat rises from, say, $2.66 to $3.00 per bushel between the signing of the contract and the delivery date, the investor will make a profit. At this point, the purchaser of the wheat contract does not actually have physical possession of the bushels of wheat. The purchaser is not required to accept delivery; he or she can offset the transaction at any time before the delivery month. In fact, actual delivery occurs in less than 5 percent of all commodities futures transactions.

Someone who expects wheat prices to fall might instruct his or her broker to execute a contract to sell wheat at the current prevailing price. If prices fall, the seller of the contract to deliver will have earned a profit; if they rise, the buyer of the contract will come out ahead.

COMMODITY FUTURES		FINANCIAL FUTURES	
Grains and Oilseeds		**Interest Rates**	
Barley	Sorghum	Certificates of Deposit	T-bills
Corn	Soybean meal	Commercial paper	T-bonds
Flaxseed	Soybean il	GNMA Certficates	T-notes
Oats	Soybeans		
Rapeseed	Wheat		
Rye		**Foreign Currencies**	
		British pound	French franc
Wood		Canadian dollar	Japanese yen
Lumber	Plywood	Deutschemark	Mexican peso
		Dutch guilder	Swiss franc
Metals and Petroleum			
Aluminum	Petroleum		
Copper	Platinum	**Indexes**	
Crude oil	Propane	Consumer Price Index	Standard & Poor's 500 Index
Gold	Silver		
Heating oil	Unleaded gas	CRB Futures Index	Standard & Poor's 100 Index
Palladium		Municipal Bond Index	Standard & Poor's OTC Index
		NYSE Index	
Livestock and Meat			
Broilers	Hogs	NYSE Beta Index	U.S. Dollar Index
Feeder cattle	Live cattle	Value Line Index	
Pork bellies			
Food and Fiber			
Cocoa	Orange juice		
Coffee	Potatoes		
Cotton	Rice		
Eggs	Sugar		

Figure 15.2. Some major commodity and financial futures traded in the United States.

As indicated above, most traders choose to liquidate their contracts before delivery by arranging offsetting transactions to reverse the original actions. Buyers, in other words, liquidate their contracts by executing a similar number of contracts to sell the same commodity, and sellers offset theirs by purchasing an equal quantity of contracts to buy the product. The difference between the first transaction and the second transaction is the amount of profit or loss (excluding broker's commission and other expenses) accruing to the trader. Each commodities exchange has a clearinghouse that oversees all buy and sell transactions and stands ready to fulfill a contract in the event of buyer or seller default.

To this point, people who trade commodities have been referred to generically as investors. In fact, there are two main categories of commodities traders, speculators and hedgers. Speculators are traders who voluntarily assume high levels of risk in anticipation of equally high profits. The difference between speculating and investing is worth emphasizing. Whereas investing offers the opportunity for making reasonable profit over the long term, speculating focuses on short-term trading and may involve considerable risk in the attempt to realize high profits.

The other main type of commodities trader is the hedger. Hedgers are often producers or major consumers of commodities who use futures contracts very conservatively to reduce risk and to protect themselves against adverse price fluctuations.

Commodities futures contracts appeal to individual investors who are willing to assume considerable risk in the hope of making a substantial profit in a short period of time. The risks should not be minimized: Commodities prices fluctuate, affected by such unpredictable factors as world economic conditions, the weather, political developments, and the supply of the commodity being traded. Additional risk is introduced by the purchase of commodities futures contracts on margin. Margin simply means that the contract is not fully paid for in cash. Instead, the trader deposits earnest money, usually 5 to 20 percent of the cash value of the contract, with the broker. Buying on margin greatly increases the impact of commodities price fluctuations. With a 10 percent margin, for example, the commodities trader will realize a gross return of 50 percent if the futures profits are 5 percent. If, on the other hand, the prices move in the wrong direction and losses are 5 percent, the holder of a contract with a 10 percent margin will suffer losses of 50 percent. As a result, even minor price fluctuations may have disastrous consequences for some. Individual investors are usually counseled to avoid commodities futures trading unless they can absorb the losses and have a high tolerance for risk.

Futures Exchanges

Trading in commodities and financial futures is mostly conducted in the United States on 10 major exchanges. In many respects, commodities exchanges are similar to stock exchanges. Both are membership organizations. In commodities exchanges, most members are either individuals representing brokerage firms (through which nonmembers trade) or those who are directly involved in producing, marketing, or processing commodities.

Like the stock exchanges, each commodity exchange has its own governing board, which sets and enforces the rules under which the trading takes place, and like the stock exchanges, the commodities exchanges themselves do not buy or sell the product being traded or set prices.

Yet another similarity is the willingness of the exchanges to provide information to prospective investors about the mechanics of trading and about specific commodities. As a result, it is a fairly simple matter for a librarian wishing to build a comprehensive pamphlet collection to acquire an impressive number of publications from the exchanges, usually at no cost. The Web pages of the exchanges also contain much of the information either in pdf or html format, and these are probably the easiest places to begin a search for information. (See figure 15.3.)

Each exchange sets certain standards for the goods it trades; a Minneapolis Grain Exchange wheat contract is always for 5,000 bushels of spring wheat, while the coffee "C" contract is always for 37,500 pounds. The exchange also specifies delivery site(s) and the months in which delivery may take place. Figure 15.4 (page 336) summarizes the basic regulations set by the Chicago Board of Trade pertaining to corn futures contracts. Not included are the regulations for shipping. All CBOT regulations are available from http://www.cbot.com/cbot/www/page/0,1398,14+64,00.html.

Board of Trade of the City of New York (formed by a merger of the Coffee, Sugar and Cocoa Exchange and the New York Cotton Exchange)	http://www.nybot.com
Chicago Board of Trade	http://www.cbot.com/
Chicago Board Options Exchange	http://www.cboe.com/
Chicago Mercantile Exchange	http://www.cme.com/
Kansas City Board of Trade	http://www.kebt.com/
Minneapolis Grain Exchange	http://www.mgex.com/
New York Mercantile Exchange	http://www.nymex.com/
Philadelphia Board of Trade	http://www.phlx.com/

Figure 15.3. Major U.S. commodities and futures exchanges.

Each exchange also sets limits on the amounts by which prices can either rise or fall during a single trading day. An exchange temporarily suspends trading of a particular delivery month in a commodity when it reaches the daily limit established by the exchange, thus controlling some of the wide swings that might otherwise develop in commodities prices.

Contract Size
5,000 bu

Deliverable Grades
No. 2 Yellow at par,[1]
No. 1 yellow at 1 1/2 cents per bushel over contract price,
No. 3 yellow at 1 1/2 cents per bushel under contract price

Tick Size[2]
1/4 cent/bu ($12.50/contract)

Price Quote
Cents and quarter-cents/bushel

Contract Months[3]
December, March, May, July, September

Last Trading Day
The business day prior to the 15th calendar day of the contract month.

Last Delivery Day
Second business day following the last trading day of the delivery month.

Trading Hours
Open Outcry: 9:30 A.M.–1:15 P.M. Chicago time, Mon–Fri.
Electronic (a/c/e): 8:30 P.M.–6:00 A.M. Chicago time, Sun.–Fri.
Trading in expiring contracts closes at noon on the last trading day.

Ticker Symbols
Open Outcry: C
Electronic (a/c/e): ZC

Daily Price Limit[4]
20 cents/bu ($1,000/contract) above or below the previous day's settlement price. No limit in the spot month (limits are lifted two business days before the spot month begins).

Terms

[1]Par is the face value.
[2]Tick is the smallest allowable increment of price movement for a contract.
[3]Contract month is the specific month in which delivery may take place under the terms of a futures contract.
[4]Daily Price Limit is the maximum price set by the exchange cash day for a contract.

Figure 15.4. Some corn futures trading conditions.

Commodity Futures Trading Commission

Futures trading is regulated by the Commodity Futures Trading Commission (CFTC) (http://www.cftc.gov/cftc/cftchome.htm), an independent federal regulatory commission established by Congress in 1974. The mission of the CFTC is to

> regulate commodity futures and option markets in the United States. The agency protects market participants against manipulation, abusive trade practices and fraud. Through effective oversight and regulation, the CFTC enables the markets to serve better their important functions in the nation's economy—providing a mechanism for price discovery and a means of offsetting price risk.[4]

The CFTC also serves as an important source of commodities futures information, issuing periodic statistical compilations and reports on the trade in various commodities. In addition, it offers several publications, including a glossary of terms, for the individual investor considering trading in commodities. These are all downloadable from the Web page at http://www.cftc.gov/cftc/cftchome.htm.

Current Prices

Because of the volatility of the commodities market and its rapid price fluctuations, current price information is vital to traders. Professional investors may get up-to-the-minute information using tickers, wire services, and online databases. Small investors, on the other hand, may rely on the current daily price information found in the *Wall Street Journal*, *New York Times*, *Journal of Commerce*, and many local newspapers or may retrieve time-delayed (usually 20 minutes) data from sites on the Internet. A sample of the kind of information contained in daily futures tables is shown in figure 15.5 (page 338). In this table, the opening price for hog futures contracts maturing in December is 40.8 cents per pound, or $1,792,000 per contract.

Although prices for major commodities are easy enough to locate in key financial newspapers and on the Internet, there are many less widely traded for which information can be difficult to find.

Chapman, Karen J. **Commodities Price Locator**. Phoenix, Ariz.: Oryx Press, 1989. 135p.

Catherine Friedman, ed. **Commodity Prices**. 2nd. ed. Detroit: Gale Research, 1991. 630p.

Chapman's *Price Locator* provides access to prices reported in more than 150 publications. The main body of the book is an alphabetical arrangement by commodity name and there is also a sources guide and a list of abbreviations.

Commodity Prices lists over 180 sources that contain information on more than 10,000 agricultural, commercial, industrial, and consumer products. Many fairly specialized commodities are included in a list that ranges from abaca to zucchini. Each entry includes the price source, price frequency, units of measure, and type of price.

Although both books are dated they still contain invaluable information, and many larger libraries will have copies in the collection. The *Encyclopedia of Business Information Sources*, arranged by specific product, also lists sources of hard-to-find price information and has the advantage of being more current.

Tuesday October 26, 2000
Open Interest Reflects Previous Trading Day

	1	2	3	4	5	6 Lifetime		7 Open
	Open	High	Low	Settle	Change	High	Low	Interest
Hogs—	Live	(CME)	40,000	lbs.,	cents	per lb.		
Dec	44.80	44.97	44.20	44.45	−.20	47.45	39.00	12,784
Feb01	47.00	47.10	46.37	46.62	−.32	49.22	41.00	7,280

LIVESTOCK & MEAT

How to Read a Futures Table

General
Hogs—Live—name of the contract
CME—name of the exchange
40,000 lbs.—the size of the contract
cents per lb.—the cost per unit
Dec/Feb01—these are the contracts for December 2000 and February 2001. The first in the list is always the first contract due.

1. Open——Opening price for this day's trading (44.80)
2. High——-High price of the day for the December 00 Live Hog contract (44.97)
3. Low ——Low price of the day for trading the December contract (44.20)
4. Settle——-Closing price for this day's trading session. (44.45)
5. Change——-Net Change in the closing price from the prior day's trading session.
6. Lifetime High/Low——
    These figures show the highest and lowest trading figures since the contract began.
7. Open Interest——
    Indicates the number of open positions in that contract.
    Open interest reads 12,784 meaning there are 12,784 contracts still long and short in the market.
    When two people trade one contract that represents one open interest.

Figure 15.5. Example of a futures trading table.

Financial Futures

Although commodities futures trading has been practiced for generations, financial futures are relatively new. Financial futures trading began in the 1970s with the trading of futures contracts on selected foreign currencies and fixed income securities, such as Treasury bills. Since then, the diversity of products and trading volume has expanded considerably, and as with commodity futures contracts, traders can use financial futures for hedging.

Futures markets provide an arena in which companies that are dependent on prices of basic commodities, exchange rates, or securities markets can reduce the risk of unfavorable price swings. For example, if an importer needs to pay large bills three months into the future rather than take the risk that the currency markets will be favorable then, he could buy futures contracts to ensure that his prices will remain stable.

Financial futures can also be used for speculating. Someone who expects interest rates to increase can buy interest rate futures. If expecting the value of the Japanese yen to decline, the person can sell foreign currency futures. The most rapidly growing sector of the financial futures market, stock index futures, permits traders to try to profit from swings in the stock market by buying or selling futures contracts tied to such stock indexes as the Standard & Poor's 500 and the New York Stock Exchange Composite Index. Other index futures are tied to municipal bonds, the consumer price index, and commodity futures.

Financial futures are traded on the Chicago Board of Trade, Chicago Mercantile Exchange, Kansas City Board of Trade, and New York Board of Trade. Financial futures prices for major products are reported daily in futures price tables along with commodity price data and are also available on the Web from all of the commodity exchanges as well as private services.

Futures Information Sources

Futures traders require current information to help them make sound investment decisions. They may acquire this information through brokerage firms; by reading financial newspapers and magazines; or from commodity exchanges, government agencies, commercial publishers, and database vendors. While only the largest and most specialized institutions will have a comprehensive collection of relevant reference materials, virtually every library should include selected publications. This section examines certain basic works and some relevant Web sites.

Handbooks, Manuals, and Guides

Finding information on how futures trading works is easy. There are virtually hundreds of "how to" books for erstwhile traders, ranging from flamboyant rags to riches overnight sagas to weighty academic tomes, and almost all of them include descriptions of the mechanics of futures trading. Sometimes, however, a patron may want a brief introduction to futures trading. The titles listed below are particularly useful.

Bernstein, Jake. **How the Futures Markets Work**. 2nd ed. New York: New York Institute of Finance, 2000. 328p.

Chicago Board of Trade. **Commodity Trading Manual**. Chicago: The Board, 1999. 410p.

Chicago Board of Trade. **Trading in Futures: An Introduction for Speculators**. Chicago: The Board, 2000. 43p. (Avaliable at http://www.cbot.com/.)

Bernstein's book is intended for beginners and serves as a good introduction to the subject. Areas covered include the basic concepts of trading, hedging, and analysis, and it also contains a description of how an exchange works and how a trading floor is organized.

Published by the Chicago Board of Trade, the *Commodity Trading Manual* includes chapters on the history and development of commodities trading, basic operations and trading strategies, and federal and exchange regulations. The major exchanges themselves are described in some detail.

For each of the commodities covered, the *Manual* includes a summary of past production, performance, supply, and demand. It lists the exchanges on which each is traded (and includes each exchange's regulations pertaining to delivery months, trading units, price and position limits, grades deliverable, delivery sites, and exchange trading hours) and cites selected sources of commercial, government, and trade information. An extensive glossary is included, part of which is online at the Web page of the Board in the Knowledge Center section (http://ww.cbot.com).

Trading in Futures presents more detailed information on such technical aspects of futures trading as price forecasting, seasonal trends, and trading guidelines. Worksheets are included in this free publication.

The Board issues many useful and free publications, including *Investor's Guide to CBOT DJIA Futures and Futures Options, Agricultural Futures for the Beginner,* and *Managing the Reality of Risk.* The Internet has made these easier to track. A researcher needs only to access the Web site at http://www.cbot.com and then check the publications lists and order forms. If hard copy is needed it can be ordered online, or pdf versions can be downloaded (available at http://www.cbot.com/cbot/www/new_order_form/1,1969,,00.html).

To find comprehensive information on exchanges, trading houses, and finance institutions worldwide more specialized sources will be needed.

Battley, Nick, ed. **World's Futures & Options Markets.** Chichester, New York: John Wiley, c2000. 1425p.

Compaq Handbook of World Stock, Derivative and Commodity Exchanges. Welwyn Garden City, England: Mondo Visione, 2000– . Annual.

The *World's Futures & Options Markets* is a classified directory of 64 exchanges and 950 contracts. Information includes a profile of the exchange, addresses, key contact information, and information on specific contracts listed.

Previously known as both the *Bridge Handbook of World Stock, Derivative & Commodity Exchanges,* and the *MSCI Handbook of World Stock, Derivative & Commodity Exchanges,* the strength of the *Compaq Handbook* lies in its brief descriptions, which provide information for about 245 exchanges in 106 countries and regions. The information furnished includes a concise summary of exchange history, a summary of the organizational structure, and full addresses and contacts. Also included are the main indexes, aggregate trading data, and articles from industry figures. An online version of this book, with regular updates, is now available, although it is probably more useful, and affordable, for traders rather than libraries.

For students, researchers, and traders interested in finding out more about trading futures, detailed information will be needed on algorithms, indicators, and programs. One of the most detailed publications available on trading systems has been updated to contain information on the latest techniques.

Kaufman, Perry J. **Trading Systems and Methods.** 3rd. Ed. New York: John Wiley, c1998. 703p.

Not intended for the casual reader, *Trading Systems and Methods* consists of in-depth analyses of both new and classical trading systems and incorporates detailed explanations, heavily interspersed with both calculations and graphs.

Bibliographies

Malliaris, A. G., ed. **Futures Markets**. Brookfield, Vt.: Edward Elgar Publishing, 1997. 3vs.

Futures Markets is a compilation of some 70 of the most significant academic articles on futures. In three volumes, the work goes from the 1959 article by Leland Johnson, "The Theory of Hedging and Speculation in Commodity Futures" (*Review of Economic Studies*), to Stephen D'Arcy and Virginia Grace France's 1992 work, "Catastrophe Futures: A Better Hedge for Insurers" (*Journal of Risk and Insurance*). The volumes contain articles on such topics as why futures markets exist, the benefits of exchanges and market regulation, volatility, institutional hedging, hedging theories both in terms of specific contracts and groups of contracts, portfolio selection, and the price tendencies of single markets. This work belongs in most academic and large public libraries.

Dictionaries

Many of the publications that have already been described contain glossaries of key terms. In addition, the standard investment dictionaries listed in chapter 11 also include basic futures trading vocabulary. Another source is particularly useful for its coverage of commodities trading.

Steinbeck, George, and Rosemary Erickson. **The Language of Commodities**: A Commodity Glossary. New York: New York Institute of Finance, 1985. 198p.

The *Language of Commodities* defines terms ranging from abandonment to zero plus tick, some of which are too specialized to be included in standard business dictionaries. Explanations as well as definitions are frequently included, and both are enhanced by specific examples, charts, and see also references. Appendixes include "How to Read the Commodity Financial Quotes"; "Reference Guides," frequently used abbreviations for commodity exchanges and organizations; "Basic Calculations," which demonstrates the use of relevant formulas and calculations; and "How to Find a Commodity Factor," which explains how to translate data given in newspaper financial pages into factor, a component used in commodity formulas. There are also many glossaries available on the Web, including those at the Web sites of the various exchanges.

Periodicals, Newspapers, and Newsletters

Futures trading is covered to a certain extent in such general business periodicals as *Business Week* and *Forbes*, but these will be too dated to be of much practical use to professional traders. Most traders need immediate, unfiltered information.

There is, however, one specialized commodity periodical that is popular with traders and researchers alike.

Futures. Chicago: Futures Magazine, 1972– . Monthly. Semimonthly in January, June and September. (Online subscription and some free information are available at http://www.futuresmag.com/.)

Futures offers its readers a series of articles on different aspects of futures and options trading. An issue may contain as many as 20 different articles dealing with such subjects as trading techniques, government policy affecting trading, the economy, and developments at specific exchanges. It also includes a section on international markets and news. Each issue includes editorial comments; "Trade Trends," news of major exchanges; "Hot Commodities," which covers commodities; "Managed Money Review," discussion of funds trading in futures and/or options; and "Trader Profile," for biographical coverage of noted traders.

Although readers new to futures trading may find some articles difficult going, for the most part *Futures* is lively and well written and can be useful to novice investors as well as seasoned professionals. Since 1999 *ProQuest* has issued the full text of this journal in *ABI/INFORM Global*.

Each year *Futures* issues a directory supplement, the *SourceBook: Commodity and Financial Services International Directory*. The *SourceBook*, which can be purchased separately, contains the names and addresses of the major U.S. and non-U.S. brokerage, charting, computer, and advisory services, as well as publishers, consultants, and a complete list of worldwide industry regulators complete with contact information. The *SourceBook* is freely available at http://futuresmag.com/sourcebook/sourcebook.html.

Although not as popular as *Futures,* another periodical contains data of interest to academicians and other researchers.

The Journal of Futures Markets. New York: John Wiley in affiliation with the Center for the Study of Futures Markets, Columbia University, 1981– . Monthly.

Published in affiliation with the Center for the Study of Futures Markets of the Columbia Business School, The *Journal of Futures Markets* contains articles written by scholars on the technical and methodological aspects of futures trading and analysis. Each issue includes between four and eight signed articles. This journal is also available on the Web, from 1996 on, via the Wiley electronic journals collection.

Several financial newspapers contain information about commodities markets in addition to the price quotes that they regularly supply. The *Wall Street Journal*, for example, devotes at least one page of each issue to commodities, including features on specific products and the political, economic, industrial, and climatological factors that affect them, as well as summaries of significant developments in futures markets on the preceding trading day. *Barron's* column, "Commodities Corner," features analysis of recent developments in the trading of specific products, as well as more general information, including a listing of changes in the key commodity indexes.

It is the *Journal of Commerce*, however, that provides the most comprehensive financial newspaper coverage of commodities. The daily price tables it includes for both futures and cash markets list more commodities than comparable tables in other newspapers, with data on foreign markets, London metals, Tokyo gold, Singapore rubber, and Sydney steer, among others, as well as domestic markets. It also includes articles on individual commodities, reviews of past trading, and projections for the future, all of which are included in the first section of the paper and indexed on page 1. In addition, the *Journal of Commerce* covers all the major business and financial news that can affect commodities prices. Periodically, whole sections of the paper are devoted to specific industries, products, and commodities, or to special studies of supply and demand for each commodity. It is an important source of information for the serious commodities trader. This publication is available as a subscription Web product at http://www.joc.com/ and is available from various database vendors including Dialog (as File 637) and LexisNexis.

Other newspapers and journals specialize in futures trading, but the one most favored by brokers and traders is *Consensus*.

Consensus. Kansas City, Mo.: Consensus, 1971– . Weekly.

Consensus focuses on commodities. Each weekly issue includes digests of current market letters, special studies, buy and sell recommendations issued by major brokerage firms, daily price quotations, and detailed price charts. Whether the cost of a highly specialized publication such as *Consensus* is offset by its anticipated use by library users must, of course, be determined by each library. There is a subscription Web version of this publication with daily updates. From the site at http://www.consensus-inc.com one can view a sample issue of the publication and also check on some of the other services offered, such as access to the "Bullish Index Hotline" and links to the Web pages of other useful publications.

Commodities newsletters, weekly or monthly reviews of commodities trading and trends, are issued by several sources. Many are free, particularly those issued by banks, brokerage firms, and commodities exchanges. The titles listed below are typical.

Barclays Bank. Group Economics Department. **Barclays Commodities Survey**. London: The Bank, 1979– . Semiannual.

The Group Economics Department of Barclays Bank publishes a brief newsletter that surveys recent developments, makes five-year projections, and offers a sector by sector commodity review. It is intended for the layperson and is both authoritative and well written. It is available from the bank's Web page at http://www.newsroom.barclays.co.uk. The Kansas City Board of Trade makes available free of charge on its Web page at http://www.kcbt.com/ a series of reports on recent developments at the Board and in the products traded there. These are updated daily.

Statistics

A wide range of statistical publications is available, including those issued by commercial publishers, federal and state governments, and commodities exchanges. Some are highly specific, dealing with a particular commodity or group of commodities, such those provided by the U.S. Department of Agriculture, Horticultural & Tropical Products Division at http://www.fas.usda.gov/htp/comodlst.html. Others are more general and cover the whole gamut of futures trading. Of these general sources, one of the most widely used and highly regarded is the *CRB Commodity Yearbook* (formerly *Commodity Year Book*), the single most important source of current and retrospective statistical data, which should be in most library reference collections.

CRB Commodity Yearbook. New York; Chichester: John Wiley, 1939– . Annual. (Quarterly supplements.)

The *Commodity Yearbook* provides detailed statistical data on over 100 commodities, ranging from alcohol to zinc. Coverage for each basic commodity generally includes a review of the past year's supply and demand and the conditions affecting both; a list of the exchanges on which the commodity is traded in the United States; and several tables on world production, domestic price support programs, domestic price supply, distribution, production, prices, exports, volume of trading, and other statistics. Most tables give information for at least 10 years, and some date back as far as 14 years. The *Yearbook* also includes charts of cash prices for many commodities, with prices plotted on a monthly basis for the past 10 years. Each edition also features special research studies. The 2001 edition, for example, included articles on the cocoa market and technotrading. The *Commodity Yearbook* is produced by Commodity Research Bureau, a division of BRIDGE Information Systems,

Inc. (Chicago), which is one of the country's largest resources for financial statistics, historical data, and charting services. Its information is available online; in CD-ROM format; and through newsletters, charting services, and wire reports. It is closely associated with the Chicago Mercantile Exchange and the Chicago Board of Trade and is regarded as one of the leading sources of information on international and domestic commodity movements.

The Chicago Board of Trade, at http://www.cbot.com/, makes freely available both historical and current agricultural, financial and metal, futures, and options data.

More specialized information is also available, often in publications from trade associations and the federal government.

Metal Statistics. New York: American Metal Markets, 1908– . Annual.

U.S. Department of the Interior. U.S. Geological Survey. **Minerals Yearbook.** Washington, D.C.: Government Printing Office, 1932/1933– . 3v. Annual.

Typical of these is *Metal Statistics*, which compiles trade and production data on over 27 different metals, and the *Minerals Yearbook*, issued in three volumes by the U.S. Geological Survey. Volume I contains chapters on approximately 90 metals and minerals, mining, and quarrying trends, while Volume II reviews the information by state. An annual review of mineral production and trade and of mineral-related government and industry developments in more than 175 foreign countries is provided in Volume III. The USGS also makes available at http://minerals.usgs.gov/minerals/ information from the *Minerals Yearbook*, both current and historical (see figure 15.6). Also featured at this site is contact information by; commodity, state, and country.

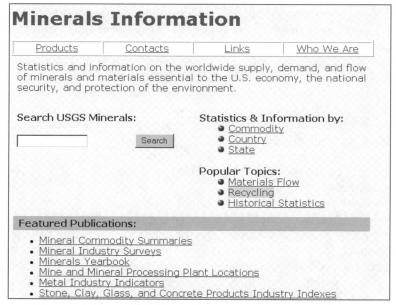

Figure 15.6. Image of the Web page for minerals information at http://minerals.usgs.gov/minerals/.

The U.S. Department of Agriculture is a major supplier of data on agricultural commodities. Much of this information is available through the USDA's *Statistics Service*, which, on the Web page at http://www.usda.gov/nass/pubs/pubs.htm, makes available agricultural statistics and issues special reports on specific commodities. (See figure 15.7.) The Web has made this information accessible to librarians and researchers as soon as it is compiled.

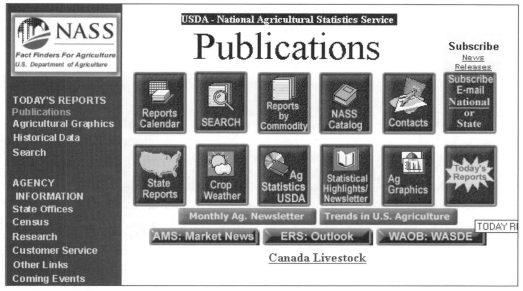

**Figure 15.7. Screen of the USDA National Agricultural Statistics Service
http://www.usda.gov/nass/pubs/pubs.htm.**

Other sources of general and specialized commodities statistics are the *American Statistics Index, Encyclopedia of Business Information Sources, Statistical Reference Index, LexisNexis Statistics,* and *Statistics Sources.*

Advisory Services

Another source of market information is the futures advisory services. There are many such organizations, most of which make their publications available on the Web because fast and current information is essential. As with all investment advisory services, cost and quality vary, as do user opinions about the merits of each. Major advisory services can be found using any Web search engine or by using a service such as the Open Directory, which lists some advisory services at http://dmoz.org/Business/Investing/Commodities,_Futures/ Advisory_Services/.

For many librarians, however, the decision will not be which of the many commodities advisory services to subscribe to, but whether to subscribe to any. The infrequent use of commodities advisory services by patrons compared to other investment services may mean that a subscription to such a publication cannot be justified, particularly with a limited serials budget.

Databases

Like the other investment media, a number of the general business databases contain information relevant to futures traders. Such files as *ABI/INFORM Global* and *Business Source Elite*, for example, often yield valuable background information. News and general index information is also available at http://www.bridge.com, but a subscription is needed to get information on the more than 300,000 stock options, commodities, futures, indexes, and currencies. Some academic business libraries will have a subscription to *Bridge Information Systems* or to another service, *Datastream*, but these are not generally accessible for public use. To find out more about available services the librarian or researcher can check in the *Gale Directory of Databases*.

Options

Options give their holders the right to buy or sell certain securities, traditionally common stocks in 100 share units, at a set price by a certain, predetermined date regardless of how high or low the price of the underlying stock may move during that time. An option holder may, for example, purchase the right to buy 100 shares of Acme Electronics for $60 per share anytime between date of purchase and, say, May. This means that, whatever the current market value of 100 shares of Acme may be, the holder can buy them for $6,000. If, for example, Acme shares soar to $106 (or $10,600 per 100 shares), the lucky option holder can either sell the option itself to another investor for a profit or can exercise the option and acquire Acme shares at a cost considerably below market value. If, on the other hand, the stock plummets to $50 per share (or $5,000 per 100 shares), the holder may choose not to exercise the option simply by allowing it to lapse; that is, by doing nothing until the contract expires in May. Why pay for the right to pay $6,000 for 100 shares of stock when it can be had for $5,000?

Holding an option is vastly different from owning the stock itself. Stock ownership represents part ownership in the issuing company, whereas an option merely gives its holder the right—which may or may not be exercised—to buy or sell stock at a predetermined price within a designated time period. An option holder has none of the rights of a stockholder; he or she cannot vote, owns no part of the company issuing the stock, and receives no dividends. Options are issued or written by individual investors and security dealers, who retain ultimate responsibility for carrying out the terms specified in the options contracts. They are not written by the companies issuing the underlying stock.

Options are attractive to many investors because they can be purchased for a fraction of the cost of the underlying stock and offer the opportunity for high profit with limited risk. Unlike the more speculative commodities trading, in options risk is limited to a predetermined amount, the amount paid for the option itself. If the market should go against an unlucky option trader, the worst that can happen is that the option will expire and become worthless. Finally, the action is fast. Most options expire at the end of three, six, or nine months.

Basic Features

Options contracts contain four basic features: (1) the striking price (also called the exercise price), or the price at which 100 shares of the underlying common stock can be bought or sold; (2) the exercise period, or the duration of the options contract; (3) the expiration cycle; and (4) the premium, or purchase price of the option itself. Each of these merits further attention.

The striking price, also known as the exercise price, is the price at which an option can be executed. In the above example, the striking price for a May option on Acme Electronics is $60 per share. (Note that while the striking price is listed on a per-share basis, the option contract itself is for 100 shares.) There are usually two or three different striking prices for options contracts expiring in a particular month.

The exercise period is the time during which an option can be executed. Listed options are written for periods of three, six, and nine months. For example, there are Acme options that expire in February, May, and August, and someone trading in Acme options could choose any of these exercise periods.

Closely allied to the exercise period is the expiration cycle. All options (other than LEAPS) are placed in one of three cycles created by the exchanges that list options. There is a January-April-July-October cycle, a February-May-August November cycle, and a March-June-September-December cycle. Prices are quoted for only three of the months listed in any cycle. For Acme, the February-May-August expiration dates would be quoted until the February options expired, then the May-August-November dates would be quoted, and so on.

The striking price, exercise period, and expiration date are all set at the time an option contract is written and do not change for the duration of the contract. The premium, or cost of the option itself, however, fluctuates from day to day, reflecting the current market value of the underlying stock and investor expectations about its future value. Option premiums are quoted in option tables on a per-share basis. If, for example, the premium for Acme is listed at 301/4, the cost of an options contract would be $3,025 or $30.25 x 100.

Puts and Calls

There are two basic forms of options: puts and calls. A call gives its owner the right to buy 100 shares of common stock at a specified price (the striking price) within a given time (the exercise period) before the expiration date. A put, on the other hand, is an option to sell 100 shares of common stock for the striking price, exercise period, and expiration date designated in the contract. The purchaser of a put expects the value of the underlying stock to decline, while the purchaser of a call expects the stock's value to increase.

Exchanges

Prior to 1973, all options were traded in the OTC market, with each option written to meet the specific requirement of the buyer. These conventional options were, in fact, so specialized that the secondary market for them was almost nonexistent. Holders of these conventional options could choose to exercise them and buy or sell the underlying stock at the striking price, or they could let the options expire; very seldom were they able to sell the options to other investors.

In 1973, the Chicago Board Options Exchange (CBOE) was opened by the Chicago Board of Trade, and listed options came into being. Unlike the conventional options traded over the counter, listed options are standardized, with systematic procedures for trading. As a result, there is a brisk secondary market in listed options, and although conventional options are still available in the OTC market, trading in listed options is far more active.

Although it was the first, the CBOE is not the only exchange that lists options. Puts and calls are also traded on theU.S. exchanges listed in figure 15.8, page 348.

American Stock Exchange Stocks, warrants, ratios	http://www.amex.com/
Chicago Board of Trade U.S. Treasury Bonds, German Government Bonds, Agricultural Futures and Options, Metals Futures and Options, Financial Futures and Options	http://www.cbot.com/
Chicago Mercantile Exchange Futures and options on agricultural products, currencies, indexes and interest rate products	http://www.cme.com/
Chicago Stock Exchange Stocks, warrants, notes, bonds	http://www.chicagostockex.com/
Cincinnati Stock Exchange Stocks	http://www.cincinnatistock.com/home.htm
Kansas Board of Trade Wheat, natural gas, and stock indexes	http://www.kcbt.com/
International Securities Exchange (ISE) Stocks	http://www.iseoptions.com/
Minneapolis Grain Exchange Spring wheat, shrimp	http://www.mgex.com/index.cfm
NASDAQ Security futures	http://www.nasdaq.com/
New York Board of Trade (NYBOT) Sugar, coffee, cocoa, cotton, currencies	http://www.nybot.com/
New York Mercantile Exchange Metals, energy	http://www.nymex.com/
New York Stock Exchange Stocks	http://www.nyse.com
Philadelphia Stock Exchange(PHLX) Sectors Index Options, currency	http://www.phlx.com/

Figure 15.8. Exchanges and the options traded.

Listed Options Quotations

Because options have such comparatively short life spans, and because the market for them can be extremely volatile, many professional traders follow price movements on an hour-by-hour or even a minute-by-minute basis. Smaller, private investors may find free options quotes, delayed by 20 minutes, at all exchanges, and a good place to start is the Chicago Board Options Exchange Web page at http://quote.cboe.com/QuoteTable.asp. One can obtain detailed or multiple quotes. For a small monthly fee any investor can become a member of this service and obtain "real time" quotes.

Options Information Sources

Decisions to purchase and trade in options are based primarily on the investor's opinion of the underlying stocks. As a result, the types of information sources described in chapter 12 will interest the person who speculates in options as much as the investor who buys stocks outright. Both will want to consult corporate reports, financial newspapers and journals, industry reports, stock charting, reporting and advisory services, and comprehensive investment services. There are, however, other more specialized publications.

Guides

Librarians and lay investors seeking to learn more about options trading can consult a wide assortment of introductory publications, ranging from pamphlets issued by brokers and exchanges to full-length texts outlining sophisticated trading techniques. In addition, sources that run the gamut of finance and investment often provide good basic information about options.

The Chicago Board Options Exchange (http://www.cboe.com/Home/Default.asp) includes free online tutorials, options basics, a bibliography of suggested reading, and a glossary. One may also download the "options toolbox," which allows one to simulate options strategies.

Exchange-issued information is revised fairly frequently and tends to more accurately reflect the constantly growing and changing options market. It is becoming necessary for all librarians to include Web links to training materials such as these because books that are only a year old may fail to indicate the breadth or volume of options trading today. One can also receive a list of free publications from *Futures* magazine at http://www.futuresmag.com/freestuff/freebies.asp. Included in this listing are pamphlets and books.

A specialized Web site for options is http://www.optionetics.com/. In the education section one can learn "How Options Work," "How to Use Options," or "What Affects Equity Option Prices." It is becoming more and more apparent that the way to provide up-to-date information on this rapidly changing field is to maintain constantly monitored Web links to instructional materials, tutorials, articles, and the relevant exchanges.

Periodicals and Newspapers

Options trading is covered periodically in *Business Week*, *Forbes, Money*, and other standard business serial titles. Some good current coverage of options trading can be found in *Barron's*. Along with articles that appear regularly is the column, "The Striking Price," which covers recent developments and trends in this fast-moving market. Articles on new developments, trading coups and fiascoes, and tax aspects of options trading are also regularly featured in the *Wall Street Journal*.

Statistics

Statistics on the options market are generally available from the exchanges on which they are traded. The easiest way to obtain these is to visit the Web pages of the various exchanges, where there are various listings as well as access to the annual reports.

Dictionaries and Glossaries

Many of the available dictionaries and glossaries are online. Some are prepared by university professors to help their students; others are made available by traders or investment centers. Following is a small example of what is available.

> *Futures & Options Glossary,* http://www.duke.edu/~charvey/Classes/glossary/g_index.htm. Prepared by Campbell R. Harvey, J. Paul Sticht Professor of International Business, Fuqua School of Business, Duke University.

> *Glossary,* http://www.riskglossary.com/. Prepared by Glyn Holtman, an independent consultant in financial risk management.

Other general financial dictionaries and glossaries, whether Web-based or available in hard copy, will also describe many of the relevant terms needed.

Advisory Services

Although prospective options traders may be content with some of the standard stock advisory services described previously, others may wish to consult special options services. Although there are not as many options services as there are stock services, their number is growing, reflecting the increased interest in this area.

One service that may be available in many libraries is supplied by Value Line.

Value Line Options. New York: Value Line, v. 12, no. 27, 1981– . Weekly.

Value Line Options is a weekly that ranks options performance and evaluates risk levels for both writers and buyers of puts and calls.

There are other options advisory services, some similar in scope and content to the *Value Line Options,* others that are more like newsletters in tone and format. Some of these publications are listed in *Futures* (http://www.futuresmag.com/resources/newlinks/advisory.html), and the librarian seeking to build a representative collection of options advisory services would do well to consult it.

Notes

1. For more information, see Mark Baldassare, *When Government Fails: The Orange County Bankruptcy* (San Francisco: Public Policy Institute of California, c1998, 317p.).

2. For more information, see Peter G. Zhang, *Barings Bankruptcy and Financial Derivatives* (Singapore; River Edge, N.J.: World Scientific, c1995, 166p.).

3. Taken from http://www.cbot.com.

4. Taken from http://www.cftc.gov/.

16

Insurance

This chapter describes basic concepts and identifies key information sources in insurance. It is an area in which information is sought by consumers as well as by investors and business people. Research inquiries may range from the investment performance of certain insurance companies to the computation of Social Security retirement benefits, from the number of unemployment insurance claims filed to the names of companies that insure against unusual risks. As a result, sources relevant to many different kinds of library users are examined.

Insurance Basics

We live in a world filled with risk. Headlines and news broadcasts daily announce disasters: explosions, droughts, floods, and crashes. Lives are lost, property destroyed. Modern technology brings with it a new array of real and potential disasters. To automobile wrecks and airliner crashes have been added nuclear reactor accidents, toxic waste, space shuttle explosions, and terrorist attacks. At the same time, many of our lives are touched by less dramatically newsworthy but equally devastating events: the untimely death of a spouse or family member, the loss of a job, floods or hurricane damage, or unexpected disease or disability. Almost all of these events have severe financial consequences for the afflicted. Many people turn to insurance to reduce such financial risk.

Characteristics of Insurance

Insurance is a social mechanism that allows individuals, businesses, and organizations to reduce financial risk by substituting a small but definite cost (the insurance payment, or premium) for a large, uncertain loss. Each of the insured pays a premium to the insurer for the promise that he or she will be reimbursed for losses up to the maximum amount indicated on the insurance policy.

Insurance, in other words, provides a certain measure of protection against major and minor catastrophes. It helps to protect against financial risk associated with death, disease, and property loss. It also may cover theft and embezzlement, professional malpractice, farm crops, ships' cargoes, satellite launches, movie stars, hijackings, product liability, and even the health of pets. Although different insurance companies (and government agencies) provide different types of insurance, certain characteristics are common to all.

The first of these is risk transfer. The insured pays premiums to the insurer, thus transferring financial risk within the limits stipulated by the insurance policy. The second is that of pooling. The premiums paid by all of the people cover the losses of the unlucky few to whom the insured-against disaster occurs.

Premium rates are in part based on the forecasts made by insurers regarding the number and severity of claims they will have to pay. Such forecasts are the responsibility of actuaries, experts in the mathematics of insurance. To determine premium rates, actuaries rely on the Law of Large Numbers and probability to predict the amount they will have to pay over a given period. The Law of Large Numbers is a mathematical principle that states that as the number of exposures increases, the actual results tend to come closer to the expected results; probability means that a given event will occur. For example, if one rolls a dice thousands of times, the number 1 will come up on the dice on the average of one out of every six times. So will the other numbers. In other words, according to the Law of Large Numbers combined with probability, the chances of a single event occurring, when there are six equal chances of it occurring, are one out of six:

> A practical illustration of the Law of Large Numbers is the National Safety Council's prediction of the number of auto deaths during a typical holiday weekend. Because millions of automobiles are on the road, the National Safety Council[1] has been able to predict with great accuracy the number of motorists who will die during a typical July 4th holiday weekend. . . . Although individual motorists cannot be identified, the actual number of deaths for the group of motorists as a whole can be predicted with some accuracy.[2]

In the insurance industry, the Law of Large Numbers means that as the number of people and organizations choosing to insure against certain financial risks increases, the number and extent of loss claims filed with the insurer will more closely approach those predicted. Using statistical data from mortality tables, for example, actuaries are able to predict with reasonable accuracy the number of people in a given population who will die within a specified period and whose beneficiaries might be expected to file life insurance claims.

A fourth characteristic of insurance is that policies enable the insured to be indemnified (either fully or partially reimbursed) for insured losses, but not to profit from such losses. The intent of this principle of indemnity is to eliminate or at least reduce the likelihood of intentional injury or destruction of property for profit. While the principle of indemnity does not, for example, preclude the possibility of arson to collect fire insurance, it means that fewer will be tempted to do so because the motive for profit will be missing.

The four basic characteristics of insurance, then, are that it transfers risk, pools losses, relies on the Law of Large Numbers to predict future losses, and utilizes the principle of indemnity to limit claims to no more than the actual losses incurred.

The terms of agreement between the insurer and the insured are set forth in the insurance policy, a legal contract that specifies types of coverage, amount and frequency of premiums, maximum coverage and amount deductible from coverage, exclusions, and the like. Although policies were once written in language unintelligible to all but lawyers and insurance professionals, many are now written so that laypeople may understand them more easily.

Types of Insurance

Insurance can be classified in many different ways. One of the most common is by type of insurer. As shown in figure 16.1, there are two groups of insurers, private and public. Private insurers are primarily commercial insurance companies that sell policies; public insurers are government agencies that provide compulsory or voluntary insurance Each of these kinds of insurers can, in turn, be categorized by the type of insurance they offer.

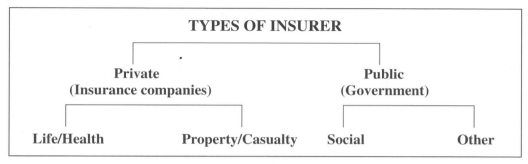

TYPES OF INSURER

Private
(Insurance companies)

Public
(Government)

Life/Health   Property/Casualty   Social   Other

Figure 16.1. Major types of insurers and insurance.

Insurance Sold By Private Insurers

Insurance sold by private insurers falls into two broad categories, life/health and property/casualty (see figure 16.2). Although some companies handle both types of insurance, many sell only one or the other. Life/health insurance and property/casualty insurance are, in fact, often treated as separate industries, as reflected in industry reports published in *Value Line* and Standard & Poor's *Industry Surveys.*

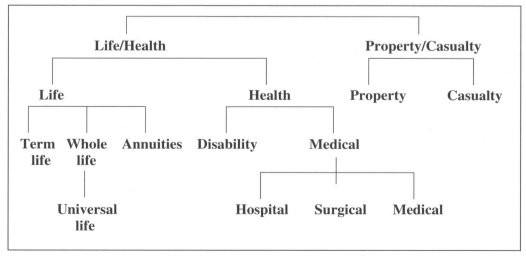

Life/Health   Property/Casualty

Life   Health   Property   Casualty

Term   Whole   Annuities   Disability   Medical
life   life

Universal   Hospital   Surgical   Medical
life

Figure 16.2. Types of insurance sold by private insurers.

Life Insurance

Life insurance offers financial protection against the death of a family member, usually the major wage earner(s) and/or the person responsible for running and maintaining the home. Although coverage varies, all life insurance policies generally pay money to the beneficiary upon the insured's death.

There are two basic types of life insurance, term and whole. Term life, which is the least expensive type of life insurance, is often compared by insurance companies to renting, rather than buying, a house. In return for the payment of premiums, the insured is covered for a specified period, or term. The term may be as short as one year or may extend for as long as 20 years or more. During that period, the insured is covered by the policy. Should he or she die while it is in force, the insurance company will pay the beneficiary the face amount of the policy. Should the insured live beyond the term covered, he or she will have to negotiate a new term life policy with the insurance company.

If term life is the insurance equivalent of renting, whole life is analogous to buying a house. Unlike the temporary coverage provided by term insurance, whole life provides insurance coverage over the entire life of the insured. There are other differences. The cost is determined by the insured's age at the time the policy is drawn up, based on actuarial tables that reflect the incidence and likelihood of death. Once the policy is in force, the premiums will remain the same, whatever the insured's health may be, or however long he or she may live.

Another difference between term life and whole life insurance is that the latter combines a forced savings plan with life insurance coverage. Part of each premium covers "pure" insurance, and part is diverted into a fund, called the cash value, which is similar to a savings account. The policyholder has two choices at any time: to continue paying the premiums at the rate originally agreed upon so that beneficiaries can receive death benefits or to terminate the policy and be given the cash value and its accumulated interest. The interest earned by the cash value in most whole life policies, however, is generally significantly less than the same money would earn in savings accounts, and consumers are frequently counseled to consider alternative forms of investment.

There are several other variants of whole life insurance. The first of these is universal or adjustable life, which offers adaptability in both premium payments and the death benefit a family receives. After the initial fixed payment, premiums can be paid in differing amounts, subject to certain rules fixed by the insurance company, and as a family's coverage, security, and asset accumulation needs change. Variable life provides death benefits and cash values that change with the performance of a portfolio of investments bound to the achievement of financial markets. As with any portfolio, the investor chooses the investment allocation from stocks, bonds, and other vehicles, and if the market does not perform well in the chosen segments the value of the policy may fall. This type of insurance policy will issue a prospectus. The final choice is a variable universal life policy, which combines features of variable and universal life policies. With this, the policy holder can have the investment risks and rewards attributed to variable life insurance, combined with the ability to adjust the premiums and death benefit, characteristic of universal life insurance.

Whereas the types of life insurance described above are intended primarily to cover the death of the policyholder and its financial consequences for the beneficiaries, life annuities focus on providing income payments to policyholders who have reached a certain age. Life insurance, in other words, provides protection for beneficiaries; life annuities are designed to provide income for old age.

An annuity is a series of income payments guaranteed for a number of years or over a lifetime. There are two main types of annuities. An immediate annuity is one that is purchased with a single, lump sum payment. The income starts one month from the purchase date if the income payments are to be made on a monthly basis, or one year from the purchase date if payments are made annually. Immediate annuities are usually purchased by the middle-aged or elderly who want annuity income to begin at once and to continue throughout the remainder of their lives.

A deferred annuity provides an income that begins at a future date. Although deferred annuities may be purchased with a single, lump-sum payment, more commonly they are paid for in installments over a number of years. The amount that the purchaser, or annuitant, receives is determined by the size of the premiums and the interest they earn as well as by the annuitant's age when payments to the insurance company began. The period of time between the first payment by the annuitant to the insurance company and the time the annuitant receives the first payment from the insurance company is known as the accumulation period. All interest earned on the accumulated payments during the accumulation period is currently tax-deferred; taxes are not levied on the interest until it is actually paid to the annuitant. This tax-deferred provision is one of the reasons that annuities are popular with many investors.

There are also two basic types of annuity contracts, fixed and variable. Money in a fixed annuity guarantees a fixed payment every month when withdrawals are begun. The equity indexed annuity is a variation of the fixed annuity. With this type of annuity, money accrues tax deferred at a minimum fixed rate of return, but the account also may earn additional interest based on the performance of an equity index such as the S&P 500. Money in a variable annuity promises no fixed payment, as it is invested in bond and stock funds, selected by the purchaser, and the value depends on how those funds perform. This type of annuity is also tax deferred.

Health Insurance

Just as the death of a family's key provider can cause severe financial hardship, so also can unexpected disease or disability. Health insurance deals with two major types of financial loss. The first helps to cover medical expenses, including the cost of hospital stays, surgery, regular medical bills, and the major medical expenses caused by catastrophic illness or injury. The nature and extent of coverage of such health insurance policies varies considerably; most have some restrictions, contain certain deductibles, and set limits on coverage. As a result, sources that permit some comparison between companies are vital.

The other major type of loss is that caused by disability. Disability insurance provides periodic payments when the policyholder is unable to work owing to a covered injury, illness, or disease. Although disability insurance helps to replace lost income, the principle of indemnity is very much in force. Companies, in fact, generally limit the amount of disability income to no more than 70 or 80 percent of the insured's earned income.

Although some health insurance policies provide both medical coverage and disability income payments, others offer only one or the other. Whatever the type of coverage offered, health insurance policies generally have certain provisions in common. The first of these is the continuance provision, which refers to the length of time that an individual policy may be in force and whether or not it will be renewed. A continuance provision may specify that the policy can be canceled by its holder or, alternatively, that the insurer can refuse to renew the policy. It can also specify that the policy must be renewed or that it cannot be canceled.

Many health insurance policies contain a preexisting conditions clause, which states that mental or physical conditions that existed in the insured prior to the issuance of the health insurance policy are not covered until the policy has been in force for a specified period, usually a year or two.

Some policies also have a probationary period immediately following their issuance, during which time sickness is not covered by the policy. The probationary period, which is intended to eliminate coverage for sickness that existed before the policy went into effect, does not extend to accidents, which are covered even during the probationary period.

Although much of the available health insurance is offered by private, commercial companies, they are by no means the only insurers in this field. Others include Blue Cross and Blue Shield and health maintenance organizations.

Blue Cross organizations are independent, membership corporations that provide protection against the cost of hospital care. Blue Shield organizations are similar in structure and membership but focus on medical and surgical costs. The Blue Cross and Blue Shield Association provides guidance and direction to the "Blues," setting and enforcing standards for their operation. Originally, Blue Cross and Blue Shield organizations were represented by separate associations. Following their merger into the Blue Cross and Blue Shield Association in 1982, many local Blue Cross and Blue Shield organizations also merged. Originally all were nonprofit organizations, but some have transformed themselves into for-profit companies.

Another alternative to traditional health insurance provided by profit and nonprofit insurance companies is the coverage offered through membership in health maintenance organizations. A health maintenance organization (HMO) is an organized system of health care that provides comprehensive health services to its members for a fixed, prepaid fee. By owning or leasing medical facilities, entering into agreements with hospitals and physicians to provide medical services, and hiring their own support staff, HMOs have greater managerial and financial control over the services offered. In return for a fee, usually paid monthly, HMO members are provided with a range of health services, most of which are covered in full, although coverage can be, and is, denied if an illness should need experimental medical treatments. All policies need to be carefully examined.

Another disadvantage is that although coverage is guaranteed to its members for the life of the HMO, not all health maintenance organizations survive. The membership in an HMO must be sufficient to support the cost of the services that are offered. When this is not the case (and sometimes, even when it is), HMOs may fail.

Another disadvantage is that members' selection of physicians and health care facilities is limited to those approved by the organization. Such limits to choice, some argue, destroy the traditional physician-patient relationship or result in poorer quality health care. In spite of these real and perceived disadvantages, HMOs have become a popular alternative to traditional health insurance.

Property/Casualty Insurance

While some private insurers specialize in life/health insurance, others protect against property damage or liability caused by negligence and are categorized as property/casualty insurers. Although the distinction between property and casualty lines has become increasingly blurred, each has its own focus. Property insurance provides financial protection against loss of or damage to property caused by fire, theft, riots, natural disasters, or other calamities. It covers buildings, equipment, and inventories, as well as losses caused by interruptions in business operations. Casualty insurance is designed to protect against legal liability for injuries to others or damage to their property. Property and casualty insurance are further divided into specific types of insurance, known as lines. Property insurance, for example, includes such lines as crop hail, ocean marine, and personal property insurance. Casualty insurance includes medical malpractice and product liability lines.

Property and casualty insurance can also be described as "first party" and "third party" insurance. Property insurance protects the policyholder, the first party, against damage to his or her property, whereas casualty insurance protects the policyholder from financial liability if he or she is held responsible because someone who is not a member of the household is injured on his or her property. Often both property and casualty coverage are provided in a single policy, as in automobile and homeowner's insurance.

Private insurers, as has been shown, can be classified according to the lines of insurance, life/health or property/casualty, that are written by them. Other classifications, based on the type of policyholder and the insurer's legal organization, are also possible.

Personal and Commercial Insurance

The first of these categorizes is insurance by the type of policyholder rather than by type of coverage, distinguishing between personal and commercial lines. Personal lines are sold to individuals; commercial lines, to businesses. Product liability insurance sold to a large pharmaceutical company is one of many commercial insurance lines. Many private insurers sell both personal and commercial lines.

Forms of Legal Organization for Private Insurers

Another way in which private insurers can be categorized is by form of legal organization. Most are either stock companies or mutual companies. Others are classified as fraternal benefit insurers, reciprocal insurance exchanges, and Lloyd's Associations.

Stock insurance companies are publicly traded corporations. Individual shareholders provide capital for the company in return for stock shares and the possibility of dividends. Most of the large property/casualty insurers are stock companies. The Travelers Insurance Corporation, for example, is traded on the New York Stock Exchange.

Mutual insurance companies, also known as mutuals, are owned by their policyholders rather than by shareholders. Just as shareholders earn dividends when stock companies have profitable years, policyholders benefit when mutuals have excess earnings, reaping benefits in the form of policyholder dividends or reduced policy renewal costs. While stock insurance companies are dominant in the property/casualty industry, mutuals are prevalent among life/health insurers.[3]

Although most private insurers are either stock companies or mutuals, there are also other forms of legal organization. They include fraternal insurers (originally formed in England as Friendly Societies), fraternal benefit societies such as the Knights of Columbus and Aid Association for Lutherans/Lutheran Brotherhood that write insurance for their members. A reciprocal exchange, on the other hand, is a form of cooperative insurance, an association in which members insure one another:

> To illustrate, assume each of ten business firms owns a building valued at $1 million. The ten firms could form an association and agree that each member would insure (and be insured by) each of the others in the amount of $100,000. If any of the buildings were damaged or destroyed the loss would be shared by all of the association members, each paying 10% of the loss. The advantage of this arrangement would be that each firm's loss exposure would be spread among the ten locations. Instead of standing to lose $1 million in a single loss, each would be exposed to a maximum $100,000 loss at each of the various locations. If the association grew to include 100 members the exposure of each would be lowered to $10,000 at each of the 100 locations.[4]

Another characteristic of reciprocal exchanges is that they are managed by an attorney-in-fact, an individual or corporation responsible for such administrative duties as collecting premiums, investing funds, handling claims, and seeking new members.

Insurance is also available through Lloyd's Associations, organizations comprising individuals who underwrite insurance on a cooperative basis. There are two types of Lloyd's Associations: (1) Lloyd's of London (http://www.lloydsoflondon.co.uk) and (2) American Lloyd's (http://www.lloydsoflondon.co.uk/america/index.htm).

Lloyd's of London is probably the most famous of all insurers. Most of the insurance that is sold at Lloyd's falls into property/casualty lines, and while it is best known for its unusual policies (covering, for example, the legs of *Lord of the Dance* star Michael Flatley for £25 million, and Betty Grable's legs for £1 million), most of its policies are written to cover somewhat more mundane risks. Lloyd's of London is not an insurance company. It is an insurance market, roughly analogous to a stock exchange. Just as the New York Stock Exchange neither buys nor sells stock but provides a location for and services to its members who do, so also does Lloyd's provide a marketplace for its members to sell insurance. It is, in effect, an association whose members, currently 123 underwriting syndicates, write and sell insurance, and it is unique in that its members accept, and are personally responsible for, risks as individuals rather than as corporations.

Lloyd's has a three-tiered structure, composed of underwriters, insurance syndicates, and members. If someone wants insurance through Lloyd's he or she must approach a Lloyd's accredited broker, who in turn will present a "slip," which sets out the terms of the risk, to an underwriter. The underwriter, who is employed by a syndicate, will either accept the whole of the risk or a percentage. If he or she accepts a percentage the broker will carry the slip to other underwriters until the whole risk is covered.

In 2000 there were 123 different syndicates, each specializing in certain insurance lines. Some, for example, write marine insurance, and others, aviation or product liability insurance. Lloyd's is operated by syndicates and underwriters but it is members, also known as Names, who provide the financial backing. Members' profits or losses depend on the percentage of the syndicate for which they are liable, and this in turn depends on the value of their investment. Each Name has unlimited personal liability and is expected to cover losses completely. Because of this unlimited liability, prospective members are carefully screened. In addition to having liquid assets of at least $550,000, such people must come recommended by Lloyd's members and must convince the admissions committee that they are suitable:

> To illustrate in a simplified fashion how Lloyd's operates, consider the following example. Jack Wilhoft is going into business and wants $1 million of products liability insurance on a new roller skate that he is manufacturing. An agent locates a company in the United States that will sell him $100,000 of products liability insurance. Since another American company cannot be found to underwrite the remaining insurance, the agent contacts a surplus line broker who arranges to place the remaining $900,000 of products liability insurance with Lloyd's of London. Information about Jack's roller skating business is submitted to a Lloyd's broker, who then presents the proposal to a syndicate specializing in high-risk products liability insurance. A lead underwriter then determines the initial premium rate. Let us assume that the lead syndicate takes $100,000 of the desired $900,000 of insurance. Each member of the syndicate will take his or her agreed upon share. The Lloyd's broker will then contact the other syndicates as well. The second syndicate may take $50,000, the third, $10,000, and so on, until the entire

$900,000 is placed. Each member of the various syndicates takes his or her share of the insurance, and pays his or her share of any loss. Finally, the policy is prepared, issued, and the insurance is in force.[5]

In 1989 the number of Names associated with Lloyd's was 31, 329, and there were 401 syndicates. It was at this time that a number of catastrophic events began to take effect in the insurance industry. These included Alaska's *Exxon Valdez* oil spill, huge asbestos claims, hurricanes, and pollution claims, including the company held responsible for Love Canal. Lloyd's was involved in all these insurance claims. The Names were held responsible for losses of £8 billion between 1988 and 1992, and as a consequence many bankruptcies and suicides[6] occurred. As a result there have been reforms in the operation of Lloyds. Corporations now account for about 80 percent of Lloyd's capacity, and the number of Names has diminished to 3,296 (figures taken from the Web site).

The United States is the largest overseas market for Lloyd's underwriters. The bulk of direct insurance business placed at Lloyd's from the United States covers "surplus lines," risks that cannot be insured by local companies. This could be anything from the value of a basketball player's legs to a private or public art collection. Lloyd's accredited brokers in the United States will work with Lloyd's underwriters in London.

Insurance Provided by Public Insurers

Although the private insurance industry handles billions of dollars annually, it is by means the only source of insurance coverage. Many federal and some state and municipal government agencies provide voluntary or compulsory protection against financial risk associated with unemployment, old age, death, and other perils. The insurance provided by public insurers falls into two broad categories: social insurance, such as Social Security, and other types of insurance, such as crop or flood insurance.

Many government benefit programs are listed at http://www.govbenefits.gov/jsp/ AgencyBenefitList.jsp, and many insurance programs are included. Checking those listed by the Department of Health and Human Services, one finds not only Medicare and Medicaid but also the State Children's Health Insurance Program (see figure 16.3).

Agency Partners	GovBenefits Programs
▪ Department of Agriculture	20 programs
▪ Department of Education	10 programs
▪ Department of Energy	1 program
▪ Department of Health and Human Services	18 programs
▪ Department of Housing and Urban Development	11 programs
▪ Department of Justice	1 program
▪ Department of Labor	16 programs
▪ Department of State	5 programs
▪ Department of Veterans Affairs	15 programs
▪ Federal Emergency Management Agency	3 programs
▪ Social Security Administration	10 programs
Total	**110 programs**

Figure 16.3. Government benefits programs.
Reproduced from http://www.govbenefits.gov/jsp/About.jsp.

Social Insurance

Social insurance is publicly financed insurance, usually compulsory, enacted into law to achieve certain social goals or to provide coverage that private insurers are unwilling or unable to offer. Social Security, for example, came into existence as an attempt to deal with the widespread unemployment and poverty of the Great Depression.

Certain characteristics distinguish social from private insurance. First, social insurance is based on law rather than contract, with eligibility requirements and benefits prescribed by law. Second, coverage is compulsory for all people to whom the law applies. As a rule, it covers only those who are or have been employed, their spouses, and their dependents. Third, social insurance programs are intended to be financially self-supporting, with specific payroll taxes designated to fund them. Fourth, social objectives are paramount. The purpose is to guarantee a minimum level of economic security, not to subsidize fully all living expenses:

> The philosophy is that, in an economic system that stresses free enterprise and individual initiative, people should not rely entirely upon governmental programs. Social insurance is designed to guarantee economic security at minimal levels; those who want more adequate benefits obtain them through personal savings and private insurance.[7]

Finally, benefits are paid as a matter of course to anyone who meets certain eligibility requirements; an eligible millionaire, for example, receives Social Security benefits whether or not he or she actually needs them.

The most important social insurance programs in the United States are the old age, survivors, disability, and health insurance programs, commonly known as Social Security, unemployment insurance, and workers' compensation.

Enacted into law as a result of the Social Security Act of 1935, Old Age, Survivors, Disability and Health Insurance provides most workers with retirement, survivor, disability, and Medicare benefits. Eligibility requirements for these benefits vary but are based to a very large extent on credit earned for the length of covered employment, with the amount of credit required in turn affected by the type of benefit being sought. Unemployment insurance programs provide short-term financial protection to workers who are involuntarily unemployed. Such programs pay workers weekly cash benefits; in addition, by requiring applicants for benefits to register for work at local employment offices, they help the unemployed find jobs. Each state has its own unemployment insurance program, subsidized by special payroll taxes paid by employers to the federal government. Workers' compensation programs are state-authorized social insurance programs that help to protect employees from the financial consequences of job-related injuries and disease. Workers' compensation provides medical care, disability income, rehabilitation services, and death benefits. Coverage varies from state to state. Most programs are compulsory, cover most occupations, and are limited to injuries or diseases that are job connected. Some states operate their own workers' compensation funds, while others allow approved employers to self-insure their workers or permit private insurers to provide coverage.

Other Government Insurance Programs

In addition to social insurance, the government oversees many other types of insurance programs. These include insurance on checking and savings accounts provided by the Federal Deposit Insurance Corporation and the Federal Savings and Loan Insurance

Corporation; federal crime insurance for property owners and businesses in high crime areas; and riot reinsurance, known as the Fair Access to Insurance Requirements (FAIR) plan, for property owners unable to obtain property coverage through private insurers. Further, the government offers some programs, such as life insurance for members of the armed forces and veterans, that are similar to coverage provided by private insurers.

Insurance Associations

The insurance industry is represented by several different associations. Some of the most important are the Alliance of American Insurers (http://www.allianceai.org/), the American Insurance Association (http://www.aiadc.org/), and the National Association of Independent Insurers (http://www.naiia.com/). In terms of the information they make available to the public and to libraries, however, two of the most important are the American Council of Life Insurance (http://www.acli.com/) and the Insurance Information Institute (http://www.iii.org).

The American Council of Life Insurance, the major trade association for the industry, serves almost 399 member companies, who handle 76 percent of the life insurance premiums and 75 percent of annuity considerations in the United States (information from the Web site). In addition to member services, this council lobbies legislators and government officials and collects and dispenses data about the life insurance industry. Its publications range from booklets for consumers to actuarial, economic, legal, social, and statistical research studies, most of which are available in pdf format from the Web site.

The Insurance Information Institute is the property/casualty industry's counterpart. Supported by major companies, it focuses on public relations, research, and publishing. Many of the booklets, statistics, and reports it publishes are available to the public and contain very useful industry data. Available at the Web site, for example, are links to an insurance glossary, industry statistics, industry financials, and special reports (http://www.iii.org/). A more general publication, *Financial Services Fact book*, not only covers insurance but also provides information on other services, including securities and savings; it is made available by the Insurance Information Institute at http://www.financialservicesfacts.org/financial/.

Regulation of the Insurance Industry

Government regulation of the insurance industry is intended to protect against insurer insolvency and fraud, to ensure reasonable premium rates, and to make insurance protection widely available. It is carried on at the state level by state insurance departments, usually under the direction of appointed insurance commissioners. In addition to the broad regulatory responsibilities outlined above, state insurance departments must review new kinds of policies, license insurance agents, and settle policyholder disputes. To find state insurance information, the Insurance Information Institute provides a link to all insurance departments and commissioners at http://www.iii.org/media/companies/state_org/insur_departments/.

The National Association of Insurance Commissioners (NAIC) (http://www.naic.org/splash.htm), a nonprofit association of state insurance commissioners, provides a forum on self-regulation of the insurance industry.

Insurance Information Sources

This section considers materials in a wide variety of formats, listing for each the key insurance information sources available.

Guides, Bibliographies, and Dictionaries

There is at this time no comprehensive guide to insurance. One source of fairly wide coverage is "Insurance and Real Estate," chapter 15 in *Business Information Sources*. In it, Daniells annotates key handbooks, textbooks, and services available in the fields of risk and insurance, and life/health and property/liability insurance, as well as bibliographies and indexes, law and legal services; sources of information about insurance companies; and statistics, periodicals, and directories. A list of insurance associations is also included. Unfortunately this publication has not been updated since 1993.

For insurance-related documents, the following bibliography should be consulted.

U.S. Superintendent of Documents. **Insurance**. Washington, D.C.: Government Printing Office, 2001. Subject Bibliography 294. Web version available at http://bookstore. gpo.gov/sb/.

Insurance selectively lists and annotates federal documents pertaining to health insurance and health care, liability coverage for small business, unemployment insurance, Medicare, Social Security, and related topics. As in all the subject bibliographies, GPO stock numbers and prices are included in addition to Superintendent of Documents classifications.

The following bibliography also selectively identifies current titles.

Special Libraries Association. Insurance and Employee Benefits Division. **Insurance and Employee Benefits Literature**. Washington, D.C.: The Division, 1950– . Bimonthly.

Insurance and Employee Benefits Literature lists and briefly annotates selected books, pamphlets, and documents. Arrangement is by subject, with both consumer- and industry-oriented titles included. Many of the publications cited are free.

Insurance vocabulary can, at times, baffle those within the profession as much as those outside it. There are specialized dictionaries and glossaries available in many libraries, and there are also many glossaries on the Web.

Rubin, Harvey W. **Dictionary of Insurance Terms**. 4th ed. Hauppauge, N.Y. : Barron's, c2000. 573p.

Clark, John Owen Edward. **International Dictionary of Insurance and Finance** Chicago: Glenlake Publishing Company, Fitzroy Dearborn Publishers, c1999. 342p.

The *Dictionary of Insurance Terms* defines terms and phrases as well as abbreviations and acronyms connected with all phases of the insurance industry. Arranged in alphabetical format, each term, concept, acronym, and proper name is clearly defined, often in great detail. Cross-references are included.

The *International Dictionary of Insurance and Finance* covers life, health, property, casualty, marine, disability, business interruption, and copyright and trademark protection, as well as other major insurance topics. Explanations are fairly short but contain many "see also" pointers. The explanations are weighted to the United Kingdom and United States rather than being "international" (as indicated in the title). This may also prove too expensive for small collections.

One Web glossary that is both browsable and searchable can be found at http://www.insure.com/glossary.cfm. Another, the *Field Guide for Property & Casualty Agents and Practitioners,* published annually by The National Underwriter Company, is available at http://www.imms.com/glossary/agloss.htm.

Handbooks and Consumer Guides

Insurance handbooks generally fall into two categories: those written for insurance professionals and those intended for laypeople. The following titles are representative of each.

Dionne, Georges. **Handbook of Insurance**. Boston: Kluwer Academic Publishers, 2000. 974p.

Social Security Handbook. U.S. Department of Health and Human Services. Social Security Administration. 2001. February 3, 2002. http://www.ssa.gov/OP_Home/handbook/ssa-hbk.htm. (Accessed August 30, 2003).

The *Handbook of Insurance* is volume 22 of the Huebner International Series on Risk, Insurance and Economic Security. It provides a single reference source that reviews the research developments in insurance that have occurred over the last 30 years. The *Handbook,* which begins with the history and foundations of insurance theory, contains peer reviewed chapters, written by leading authorities on insurance, on such phases of insurance as volatility and underwriting cycles, fraud, monopoly, liability, and loss reduction. Included is an extensive index.

The *Social Security Handbook* is the basic reference for social insurance programs and benefits, as well as social assistance programs, made available through the Social Security Administration. It describes federal retirement, survivors, disability, and black lung benefits; supplemental security income programs; health insurance; and public assistance programs. It also stipulates the evidence necessary to establish rights for specific benefits, lists the procedures for applying for benefits or filing claims, and describes the appeals review process. Each chapter covers a specific program or set of procedures and is subdivided into numbered paragraphs (see figure 16.4, page 364). An index, with citations to paragraph numbers, is also included. The official version of the *Social Security Handbook* is the version available on the Web at http://www.ssa.gov/OP_Home/handbook/ssa-hbk.htm

In addition to the handbooks described above, consumer guides periodically are published to help laypeople make decisions about insurance coverage or about specific insurance companies. Although the number of companies in the insurance business and the types of policies they write are too numerous to lend themselves to more than brief coverage in such sources, consumer guidebooks can nonetheless be useful for simplifying and providing a basic introduction to insurance. The Web is also an invaluable source of up-to-date information.

719.1 How do cost-of-living increases affect benefits?

Benefits may be automatically increased to keep pace with increases in the cost-of-living if laws for general benefit increases are not passed. Benefit increases depend upon the condition of the Federal Old-Age, Survivors and Disability Trust Funds. The increases are based on the smaller of either: (1) *the Consumer Price Index* as published by the Department of Labor; or (2) the average wage index, that is based on nationwide wages. Where the index for a current base quarter shows an increase over the same index for the last base quarter, the following happens: each PIA, each related maximum family benefit, each transitionally insured benefit and each special age 72 payment is raised to reflect the same percentage of increase (rounded to the nearest one-tenth of one percent). The base quarter is either: (1) the third calendar quarter of each year after 1982, or (2) a later calendar quarter within which a general benefit increase became effective.

719.2 When does the cost-of-living benefit increase become effective?

This cost-of-living benefit increase becomes effective beginning with December of the year that contains the base quarter for the index increase. The cost-of-living increase is published in the *Federal Register* on or about November 14 of the year preceding the year the benefits are payable.

Figure 16.4. Sample entry, *Social Security Handbook*.
Taken from the official online version at http://www.ssa.gov/OP_Home/handbook/ssa-hbk.htm.

Baldwin, Ben G. **The Complete Book of Insurance: The Consumer's Guide to Insuring Your Life, Health, Property, and Income**. Rev. ed. Chicago: Irwin Professional Publishing, c1996. 272p.

Learning Center. ©2000–2002. At *INSURANCE.COM*. February 15, 2002. http://www.insurance.com/profiles_insights/index.asp. (Accessed August 30, 2003).

The *Consumer's Guide* explains in simple terms the importance of insurance and the many types available. Each chapter is dedicated to a different category of insurance, including disability, life, real estate, vehicle, and long-term care. Also included are chapters on the kind of insurance available and how to choose appropriately. Throughout the book are sample letters and insurance tables, and glossaries are appended to each chapter. This book is useful for any library with a clientele interested in insurance.

INSURANCE.COM contains an excellent *Learning Center* that incorporates quality descriptions of the different types of insurance as well as articles on many topics such as the insurance of rental cars. One must always remember that this is a commercial site, so quotes and quote comparisons are offered for those who are interested. It is, however, easy to use this as just an information site.

Directories

Two directories dominate the insurance field.

The Insurance Almanac: Who, What, When, and Where in Insurance, An Annual of Insurance Facts. Englewood, N.J.: Underwriter Printing and Publishing, 1912– . Annual.

Who's Who in Insurance. Englewood, N.J.: Underwriter Printing and Publishing, 1948– . Annual.

The Insurance Almanac is a compilation of lists by categories of insurance companies and practitioners. Insurance companies, for example, are listed by form of legal organization and lines of insurance written. The company entries are fairly brief, including company address and telephone number, date and state in which the company was established, officers' names, types of insurance coverage written, and territory covered. Most entries also include the names of the executives in charge of advertising and claims.

The Insurance Almanac also lists agents and brokers in principal cities; insurance adjusters; and insurance inspection, investigation, and software development services. Finally, the *Almanac* identifies organizations related to various types of insurance, assigned risk plans and rating bureaus, and state insurance officials. It is a basic insurance reference work and belongs in most business reference collections.

Who's Who in Insurance provides biographical information on insurance officials, brokers, agents, and buyers. Each entry generally includes the biographee's address, educational background, positions held, club and association memberships, and other personal data.

Both *The Insurance Almanac* and *Who's Who in Insurance* are published by Underwriter Printing and Publishing, one of the firms dominating the insurance reference marketplace. Publications of two others, A. M. Best and National Underwriter, are discussed in the sections that follow on company and policy information.

Other biographical directories, published by professional organizations, include the *American Academy of Actuaries Yearbook* (http://www.actuary.org/yearbook/index.htm), the *Yearbook of the Society of Actuaries* (http://www.soa.org/yearbook/index.asp), and the Member Roster of the Life Insurance Marketing and Research Association (LIMRA) (http://www.limra.com/Directories/roster.asp). Such specialized lists of members are generally available free from the societies via their Web pages.

Information About Insurance Companies

One of the major considerations in selecting an insurer is the company's financial strength. All other things being equal, it is better to insure with a company that is financially sound-and likely to be so at some unknown time in the future, when a claim may be filed, than it is to buy insurance from a company that lacks financial strength or stability. As a result, publications that document and permit financial comparison of insurers are vital. Most reflect the traditional industry division between life/health and property/casualty insurers, but one does not.

Mergent. **Mergent's Bank & Finance Manual**. New York: The Service, 1900– . 3v. Annual.

Volume 2 of *Mergent's Bank & Finance Manual* permits comparison of some of the largest U.S. and Canadian insurance companies. As with the other Mergent (Moody's) manuals, length of coverage varies and to a certain extent depends on the fee paid by the company to Mergent. At a minimum, however, a listing includes the corporate address, number of employees, officers and directors, types of insurance written, and states in which the company is licensed to operate. Each entry also features comparative financial statistics for the current and preceding year, as well as investment and stock ownership information As with all *Mergent Manuals,* this information is included in the electronic version *FIS Online.*

The center blue pages provide data on the distribution and dollar value of assets (government securities, stocks, bonds, mortgages, real estate, and policy loans) held by U.S. life insurance companies and an interim earnings and dividend section.

Although *Mergent Manuals* provides useful financial and background information about many insurance companies, its coverage is neither as detailed nor as broad as that made available in more specialized sources. Some of the most widely used titles are described below.

A. M. Best Company. **Best's Insurance Reports: Life/Health**. Oldwick, N.J.: A. M. Best, 1906– . Annual.

A. M. Best Key Rating Guide: Life/Health. Oldwick, N.J.: A. M. Best, 1991– . Annual.

A. M. Best Company. **Best's Insurance Reports: Property/Casualty**. Oldwick, N.J.: A. M. Best, 1976– . Annual.

A. M. Best Key Rating Guide: Property/Casualty. Oldwick, N.J.: A. M. Best, 1976– . Annual

Best's Insurance Reports are published annually in two editions, one for the life/health industry and one for property/casualty insurers. The latest *Life/Health* edition provides detailed information on some 1,700 U.S. and Canadian life and health insurance companies. The latest *Property/Casualty* edition features more than 3,400 companies. Each report summarizes the company's history and describes its management and operation. It also presents key balance sheet and income statement data and includes statistics on the value of new business issued, insurance in force, and company development. Although each company report focuses on the past year's performance, many of the statistical tables provide historical data as well. In addition, most companies are assigned a financial size category and are rated on the basis of their financial strength and ability to meet contractual obligations. Company performance is compared to industry norms established by Best in the areas of profitability, leverage, and liquidity. In addition, Best's evaluation includes a qualitative review, focusing on such factors as "the amount and soundness of a company's reinsurance, the quality and diversification of investments, the valuation basis of policy reserves, and the experience of management."

Based on these factors, most companies are assigned ratings like those in figure 16.5.

A and A-	Excellent
B+ + . . . and B+	Very good
B and B-	Fair
C+ + . . . and C+	Marginal
C and C-	Weak
D	Poor
E	Under regulatory supervision
F	In liquidation
S	Rating suspended

Figure 16.5. Assigned ratings.

Companies not rated are assigned an NR in the report. Those that are excluded are usually either inactive, are too small, lack sufficient experience, or fall below minimum standards. In all, there are five main categories for exclusion, each of which is listed and described on the *Reports'* front cover and at http://www.ambest.com/ratings/guide.pdf.

People consulting *Best's Reports* for the first time are advised to read them with care. A certain amount of reading between the lines in company reports is necessary. Best seldom overtly condemns a company for bad management or investment policies. Either the comments are favorable, or none are included. As a result, Best's assessments must be interpreted with caution. (See figure 16.6.)

FCCI Insurance Group

FCCI INSURANCE GROUP

6300 University Parkway, Sarasota, FL 34240-8424
Web: www.fcci-group.com.

Tel: 941-955-2811
AMB#: 18290
Fax: 941-951-3709

BEST'S RATING

Based on our opinion of the group's Financial Strength, it is assigned a Best's Rating of A- (Excellent). The group's Financial Size Category is Class IX. Refer to the Preface for a complete explanation of Best's Rating system and procedure.

RATING UNIT MEMBERS

FCCI Insurance Group (AMB# 18290):

AMB#	COMPANY	RATING	
11257	FCCI Insurance Company	A-	g
03689	Monroe Guaranty Insurance Co	A-	g
12306	Brierfield Insurance Company	A-	r
10836	FCCI Commercial Insurance Co	A-	r
00719	National Trust Insurance Co	A-	r

RATING RATIONALE

Rating Rationale: This rating is based on the consolidated results of FCCI Insurance Company, its three substantially reinsured affiliates, National Trust Insurance Company (National Trust), Brierfield Insurance Company (Brierfield), and FCCI Commercial Insurance Company (FCCI Commercial), and its recently acquired subsidiary, Monroe Guaranty Insurance Company (Monroe Guaranty). The rating reflects the group's excellent capitalization, historically strong earnings performance produced by management, and high quality balance sheet. These positive rating factors are derived from the group's long standing leadership position in the Florida workers' compensation market which is further supported by its disciplined underwriting approach, strong medical management capabilities and extensive loss control procedures. The rating also acknowledges FCCI Insurance's exceptional business persistency rates fostered by its predominance of participating policies and its favorable policyholder dividend plan. In addition, through its reinsured affiliates, the group has positioned itself for better diversification as well as new growth opportunities in expanding states and through a larger product offering. Finally, the group's reorganization into a mutual holding company structure enhances its overall financial flexibility.

Offsetting these positive rating factors is the group's limited spread of risk due to both regulatory and product line concentrations in its core Florida workers' compensation market, recent deterioration in operating performance and aggressive premium growth in 2000. Additionally, the group faces a challenge to integrate the operations of Monroe Guaranty into the overall group. While the substantial growth in 2000 was largely accomplished through price increases, adding additional coverages to existing accounts and new growth in select books of business, the magnitude of this business combined with the untimely surplus drop creates some concern given the increased leverage position of the group. Nevertheless, given the group's continued focus on underwriting controls, claims management and conservative reserving, these recent expansion strategies should better position the group for sustainable growth, provide increasing stability to its risk portfolio and return the group to pre-2000 profitability measures in the longer term.

FIVE YEAR RATING HISTORY
Rating as of July 20, 2001: A-

Date	Best's Rating	Date	Best's Rating
05/31/01	A-	06/28/99	A-
05/30/00	A-	12/15/97	A-

KEY FINANCIAL INDICATORS ($000)

Period Ending	Direct Premium Written	Net Premiums Written	Pretax Operating Income	Net Income	Total Admitted Assets	Policyholders' Surplus
1996	408,723	386,890	23,795	18,642	1,006,313	263,451
1997	401,399	374,686	30,284	20,819	1,042,854	313,122
1998	401,507	356,494	1,307	9,736	1,082,236	371,568
1999	378,971	272,344	7,188	17,384	1,034,525	380,162
2000	473,321	436,336	-27,919	-12,598	1,113,050	287,750

Period Ending	Comb. Ratio	Inv. Yield (%)	Pretax ROR (%)	NA Inv Lev	NPW to PHS	Net Lev.	Overall Liq. (%)	Oper. Cash-flow (%)
1996	106.6	5.9	6.2	38.2	1.5	4.3	136.6	113.5
1997	105.4	5.7	8.3	43.5	1.2	3.5	144.7	100.2
1998	114.2	5.5	0.4	46.5	1.0	2.8	153.1	93.4
1999	115.6	5.1	2.7	47.6	0.7	2.3	160.6	83.8
2000	117.3	5.5	-6.8	47.5	1.5	4.2	135.5	120.8
5Yr	111.7	5.6	2.0	...	...	...	...	...

(*) Data reflected within all tables of this report has been compiled through the A.M. Best Consolidation of statutory filings. Within several financial tables of this report, this group is compared against the Workers Compensation Industry Composite.

CORPORATE OVERVIEW

FCCI Insurance Company (FCCI Insurance), domiciled in Florida, is the lead member of the FCCI Insurance Group (or the group). FCCI Insurance has been actively writing business in Florida since 1959, first as a trust, then as a mutual, and now as a stock insurance company. Numerous other members exist in the group, each ultimately owned by FCCI Insurance. The strategic plan of the group is focused on providing commercial property and casualty insurance products, with an emphasis on workers' compensation and employers' liability coverage in the southern Atlantic region of the United States. Other members of the group include established servicing and agency operations that perform third party administration functions, field investigation and surveillance, and brokerage services for a number of clients.

FCCI Services, Inc. (FSI), a subsidiary of FCCI Insurance, provides a broad range of marketing, loss control, underwriting, information systems, medical, actuarial and claims services for the insurance company operations of FCCI, self insured employers and other clients. Another entity, FCCI Agency, Inc., provides brokerage services for both clients within the risk bearing segment and service operation entities of FCCI.

In October 1997, FCCI Mutual Insurance Company (FCCI Mutual) applied to the Florida Department of Insurance (FL DOI) to reorganize in a mutual holding company structure. Under the plan filed with the FL DOI, FCCI Mutual Insurance Company was created. FCCI Mutual was converted to a stock insurance company and renamed FCCI Insurance Company, a wholly-owned subsidiary of the mutual insurance holding company. FCCI Mutual Insurance Holding Company is owned by the policyholders of FCCI Insurance who control 100% of the voting stock. The restructuring was approved by policyholders on August 27, 1998 and by the state on September 8, 1998.

Plans to geographically diversify operations through the utilization of FCCI Insurance's operating subsidiaries continued to move forward since their implementation a few years ago. National Trust's operations focus primarily on the writing of business outside of Florida, particularly in Alabama, Arkansas, Georgia, Kentucky, Mississippi and Tennessee. Also, National Trust writes other property and casualty coverage for policyholders of FCCI in Florida. In 1999, FCCI and Mississippi Insurance Managers, Inc. (MIM), an insurance management operation in Mississippi, created a domestic Mississippi property & casualty insurance company, Brierfield Insurance Company (Brierfield). Brierfield insures the business previously placed by MIM agents with other insurance companies. FCCI Commercial Insurance Company, previously a group self-insurance fund, had been in run-off since 1991 but received approval from the FL DOI to convert to a stock company in 2000. Also in 2000, FCCI Insurance Group merged a subsidiary holding company with the parent holding company of Monroe Guaranty Insurance Company, to diversify into new parts of the country and new product lines. The combined operations of FCCI Insurance, National Trust, Brierfield, FCCI Commercial, and Monroe Guaranty make up the rating unit for FCCI Insurance Group.

2001 BEST'S INSURANCE REPORTS—PROPERTY/CASUALTY

Figure 16.6. Sample entry, *Best's Insurance Reports: Life/Health*.
Copyright A.M. Best Inc., Oldwick, New Jersey.

In addition to detailed reports, *Best's Insurance Reports: Life/Health* lists state insurance commissioners, guaranty fund provisions by state, retired life-health companies, and data on the distribution of assets of U.S. life insurance companies and the growth of life insurance in the United States from 1880 to the present. *Best's Insurance Reports: Property/Casualty* also includes a listing of state officials and guaranty fund provisions as well as a ranked list of the largest 250 property casualty companies. (See figure 16.7, page 368)

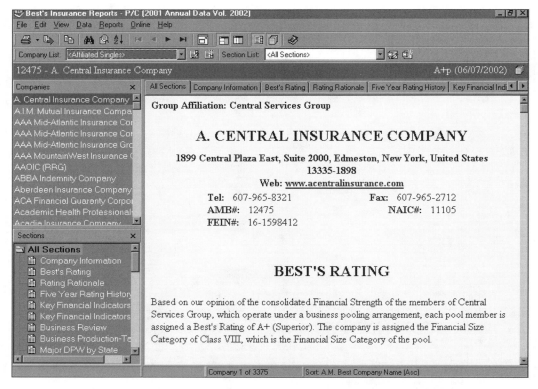

Figure 16.7. Sample entry, *Best's Insurance Reports* electronic version.
Copyright A.M. Best Inc., Oldwick, New Jersey.

The preface in both volumes describes Best's rating system and financial size categories in detail and explains each of the items contained in company reports. In addition, each edition includes the group affiliations of life/health and property/casualty insurers; lists legal reserve life insurance companies by state; and cites recent name changes, mergers, and dissolutions.

The print versions of *Best's Reports* are available in most larger libraries that need to answer general insurance questions. For those who need more specialized information or the added functionality of an electronic version, most Best's products are available on CD-ROM and as *Best Direct* via the Web. A CD-ROM subscription includes access to *Best Direct*. Users receive real-time e-mail notice of rating changes, news articles, and press releases for insurance companies of their choice. There is no limit on the number of companies that can be tracked. Detailed information about products is available from the Web page of A. M. Best Company (http://www.ambest.com). This page can also be used as a gateway to the Web pages of insurance companies. Enter a name in the search box to get the address and Web link to a company as well as news about the company. Registration is required for more information.

Best's Key Rating Guides are intended primarily for insurance professionals. They present summary financial information, operating ratios, and Best's ratings for some 3,200 property and casualty insurers and 1,400 life/health companies in tabular format. Other tables list insurance groups, states in which companies are licensed to do business, and companies and associations that have retired. As in *Best's Reports*, added functionality is gained by using the CD-ROM product.

Financial ratings are also available form other companies, most notably Standard & Poor's and Fitch. The ratings awarded by these companies can be obtained free of charge from the Web site of *insure.com* at http://www.insure.com/ratings/. An explanation of the ratings is on each page. For libraries with budget restraints this is an excellent site to gain information for patron questions.

Information About Insurance Policies

Requests for information about insurance policies generally fall into two categories: identifying companies that write policies offering special coverage and comparing policies written by different companies. An insurance agent, for example, may want to compile a list of companies writing ocean marine insurance or selling health coverage for hemophiliacs. The head of a family may want to compare the provisions of life insurance policies sold by Baltimore Life with those offered by Northwestern Mutual Life. Although precise comparison is impossible, the sources listed below provide a good base for identifying companies offering special coverage and for comparing the basic provisions of many insurance policies.

Who Writes What in Life and Health Insurance. Cincinnati, Ohio: National Underwriter. (Continued as a series of articles in *National Underwriter Life & Health* since 2001.)

The Insurance Marketplace. Indianapolis, Ind.: Rough Notes, 1962– . Annual.

Who Writes What in Life and Health Insurance was a listing of insurance companies and brokers that provide hard-to-place, unusual, substandard, or new types of life and health insurance coverage. This directory has been discontinued, but the information is now available as a series of articles in the *National Underwriter Life & Health,* a weekly publication also available online with daily updates. For all National Underwriter product and subscription information check the Web page at http://www.nationalunderwriter.com/.

The Insurance Marketplace identifies more than 640 categories of coverage and more than 800 providers that write policies for unusual or hard-to-place risks. This annual is a supplement to the December issue of *Rough Notes* magazine (http://www.roughnotes.com/); nonsubscribers can buy it separately or access it online from the company Web page. Information is supplied by region: Northeast, Southeast, Midwest, Southwest, and Western.

There are also various rating guides published by A. M. Best (http://www.ambest.com) and National Underwriter (http://www.nationalunderwriter.com/) These are more specialized publications to which most libraries would not subscribe, but details are available on the companies' Web pages.

Most of the Web sites mentioned previously will give some guidance on insurance policies. One more site, *All Insurance Guide* (http://www.all-insurance-guide.com/), gives lengthy descriptions of different types of insurance and some guidance about who may need them.

Insurance Periodicals

Periodicals relating to the insurance industry are generally either trade publications aimed at insurance practitioners or scholarly journals focusing on the study of insurance, risk management, and actuarial science. The titles that follow are typical trade publications.

Best's Review. Oldwick, N.J.: A. M. Best, 2001– . Monthly.

BestWeek. Oldwick, N.J.: A. M. Best, 2001– . Weekly.

National Underwriter: Life & Health/Financial Services Edition. Cincinnati, Ohio: National Underwriter, 1897– . Weekly.

National Underwriter: Property & Casualty/Risk & Benefits Management Edition. Cincinnati, Ohio: National Underwriter, 1896– . Weekly.

Each of the two major insurance publishers, A. M. Best and National Underwriter, publishes trade magazines for the insurance industries. Best's offering is *Best's Review*, an amalgamation of the *Life/Health, Property/Casualty* editions published since 1899. It contains news on industry and company developments and strategies, as well as prominent practitioners who have changed companies, been promoted, or retired. In addition, it covers regulation of the insurance industry, sales and marketing, and government policies as they affect insurance. Regular features include "Resources," which lists selected books, proceedings, software and educational resources; "Statistical Studies and Special Reports," which indexes the reports and "top listings" published by *Best's Review* in the last twelve months; and "Ratings," which provides new or recently changed *Best's* ratings. Each edition of *Best's Review* also includes a "Technology" section, which features technological advancements in the insurance industry and how these are changing everything from back office operations to distribution channels.

Further, each monthly edition of *Best's Review* provides more specialized coverage. Recent issues have included articles on how the World Trade Center disaster has affected the industry and changes in the needs of people investigating long-term care insurance. Each January edition includes an index to the articles included in the previous year's issues. This publication is also available online at http://www.bestreview.com, and subscribers to the print edition may access it by using the password provided in the paper copy.

Also available from this company are *BestWeek* and *BestDay*. *BestWeek* is published both in print (also downloadable in pdf format on Friday afternoon) and on the Web at http://www.bestweek.com. The weekly provides coverage of recent industry developments, interviews, financial news, and federal and legislative activity. *BestDay*, on the Web at http://www3.ambest.com/bestdaynews/BestDay.asp, provides breaking news in the insurance industry. Some of the stories are free to any visitor to the site, and subscribers to *BestWeek* have access to all the news. These publications will rarely be found in libraries as they are targeted to the insurance practitioner.

Similar coverage is provided in both editions of the *National Underwriter*, a weekly trade paper that reports on recent developments in the insurance industry. Articles may focus on commercial or personal insurance, group and employee benefits, sales, management, current legislation, and regulation. Special reports include markets, rankings, and financial reviews. Both these and other journals are accessible via the Web from http://www.nationalunderwriter.com. The *National Underwriter* and *Best's Reviews* are the most widely read and circulated of all such trade journals.

Scholarly treatment is provided in several periodicals; two of the most highly regarded follow.

American Risk Insurance Association. **The Journal of Risk and Insurance**. Athens: The Association, University of Georgia, 1932– . Quarterly.

The Society of Financial Service Professionals. **Journal of Financial Service Professionals**. Bryn Mawr, Pa.: The Society, 1946– . Bimonthly.

The Journal of Risk and Insurance is the most scholarly and quantitative of all insurance periodicals. Articles are usually written by academicians rather than insurance practitioners and frequently include formulas, statistics, and lengthy footnotes. Typical articles are "Optimal Asset Allocation Towards the End of the Life Cycle: To Annuitize or Not to Annuitize?" and "Life Insurer Financial Distress, Best's Ratings and Financial Ratios." Each issue also contains "Recent Court Decisions," which briefly describes important legal actions, and "Book Reviews," which features lengthier, signed reviews.

The *Journal of Financial Service Professionals*, formerly the *Journal of the American Society of CLU & ChFC*, publishes applied research in all areas of financial planning, including retirement planning, health care, economics, and information planning for the industry. A typical issue includes articles on estate, financial, and tax planning; information management; economic trends; and current ethical, legal, and social issues relating to the profession. The articles themselves are written by insurance professionals as well as by academicians and are generally less theoretical and quantitative than those appearing in *The Journal of Risk and Insurance*. The *Journal* is available online to members of the Society from the Web page at http://www.financialpro.org/.

Current information about the insurance industry is as important to consumers as it is to agents and brokers. Although no consumer-oriented serial is devoted entirely to insurance, some periodically describe or evaluate specific types of insurance coverage and insurance companies. *Consumer Reports*, *Business Week*, and *Money*, for example, frequently include articles intended to help consumers keep abreast of industry developments and make wise insurance decisions.

The above periodicals focus primarily on private, rather than public, insurance. One key government periodical, however, contains current information on social insurance programs provided by the federal government.

U.S. Department of Health and Human Services. Social Security Administration. **Social Security Bulletin.** Washington, D.C.: Government Printing Office, 1938– . Quarterly.

Each issue of the *Social Security Bulletin* includes summaries of recent research, notes and brief reports, and two or three articles treating some aspect of social insurance or public assistance. Recent issues, for example, have included articles on privatization of social security in Latin America, the pension status of divorced women at retirement, and a study on lifetime earnings patterns and the impact of pension reform. The articles are often written by the Social Security Administration research staff and usually include statistics, tables, and graphs. The *Bulletin*'s "Current Operating Statistics" section contains several pages of statistics pertaining to Social Security Administration programs as well as economic indicators relating to personal income and prices paid for medical care. An annual statistical supplement is included with the subscription. Articles from this publication are available at http://www.ssa.gov/policy/pubs/SSB/.

Periodical Indexes

Major insurance periodicals are indexed in such standard business sources as EBSCO*host*'s *Business Source Elite* or *Business Source Premier* and *ABI/INFORM* from

ProQuest. In many instances, these sources will suffice. There are, however, more specialized sources available.

Insurance Periodicals Index. Chatworth, Calif.: NILS Publishing, 1964–2000 . Annual.

Insurance & Employee Benefits Division (IEBD). **Guide to Insurance Research.** Washington, D.C.: Special Libraries Association, 2002– . Quarterly.

The *Insurance Periodicals Index,* now discontinued, indexed the articles, product announcements, book reviews, statistics, letters to the editor, and obituaries included in 53 major insurance periodicals and newspapers. The *Index* was arranged in two parts, a subject index and an author index. The *Insurance Periodicals Index* was originally compiled by members of the Special Libraries Association's Insurance and Employee Benefits Division from monthly lists in both editions of *Best's Reviews*. In 1982, the NILS Publishing Company joined with the division to help them develop the computerized database out of which the annual *Index* was then published. The contents of *IPI* are still a major source of information for the years that it covered.

The *Guide to Insurance Research* is prepared by members of the Insurance and Employee Benefits Division of SLA. At the time of writing only one issue has been published, but its aim is to selectively abstract journal articles, research reports, and books. The first issue contains reviews of 22 research studies from 2001. This publication is issued free of charge to members, but others interested in obtaining copies should contact the Division.[8]

Government Documents

Insurance is regulated at the state level. As a result, the federally published statistical compilations, consumer guides, and information sources so common to federally regulated industries are not generally available for private insurance. Congressional hearings regarding the insurance industry are held periodically and are subsequently published and distributed by the Government Printing Office. Most federal documents, however, deal with social insurance programs. Many are written for program beneficiaries. One such source, the *Social Security Handbook*, has already been described. Other booklets and brochures deal with specific types of social insurance coverage. Many of these publications are no longer issued in print form, but the information is available at the agency Web sites.

From the site maintained by the Social Security Administration one can read the history of social security, check the trustee's report, find answers to most questions, print copies of needed forms or fill them out online, and even calculate Social Security benefits. In figure 16.8 are some of the frequently asked questions with direct links to the answers. Information on laws, regulations and rulings, research and data, and services for business is also directly available.[9]

The Office of the Actuary, as part of its mission of monitoring the current and future soundness of the program, prepares reports on the financial outlook of Social Security and historical data on numbers of beneficiaries and average benefits. These can be requested from the Web page at http://www.ssa.gov/OACT/NOTES/actstud.html. Some of the more recent studies and notes are available for immediate printing from the same site.

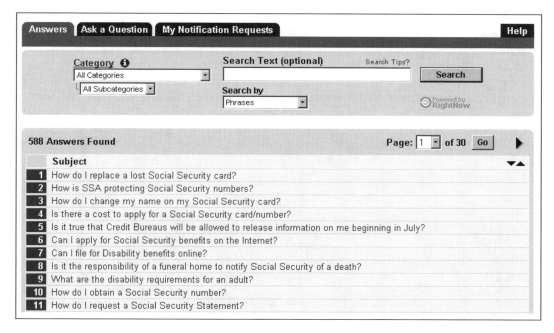

Figure 16.8. Example of the online help available from the Social Security Administration at http://ssa-custhelp.ssa.gov/cgi-bin/ssa.cfg/php/enduser/std_alph.php.

Medicare and You. Washington, D.C.: Government Printing Office, 1999– . Annual.

Medicare and You describes the Medicare program (http://www.medicare.gov) and the different plans available, lists medical care services and supplies included under or excluded from Medicare coverage, and includes a glossary of some of the words an individual may need to know. *Medicare and You* also focuses on situations in which it is advisable to obtain private insurance to supplement Medicare coverage, with tips for selecting insurers and supplemental insurance. These and other similar documents[10] are free from the Web site at http://www.medicare.gov/Publications/Pubs/pdf/pubcatalog.pdf or can be ordered online or by telephone. At this time the publications (see figure 16.9, page 374) are also available in Spanish and Chinese. Public and state-supported libraries can provide a useful service by providing access to patrons to the *Participating Physician Directory* at http://www.medicare.gov/Physician/Home.asp. As more of these materials become readily available from the Internet, librarians will need to be guides to the information in this medium or will need to have copies on hand in their collections

Although such consumer-oriented booklets are the most common type of federal document, other insurance-related sources are also available. Some present statistics relating to social insurance programs, others describe supplementary state programs, and still others, produced by the Small Business Administration, cover insurance as it relates to business. Again, most of this information is available from individual government Web sites, or one can use a search engine such as http://www.google.com/unclesam to find the appropriate data or publication.

Many state government agencies also issue insurance-related documents. They range from guides such as *Alaska Insurance Consumer Guide* and the Maine *Coping with the Aftermath of Weather Related Disasters Bulletin* to statistical compilations, fact books, and manuals. Such publications are frequently produced by state insurance departments and can be identified by checking the agency Web page. Some of the most detailed information on the insurance industry and on specific companies can be found in the annual reports issued by state insurance departments. The reports are available from the departments themselves, state document depository libraries, and through the SRI Microfiche Library. They are usually quite long, contain extensive statistical information, and are one of the primary sources from which data presented in the statistical sources listed in the following section are derived. A complete listing of the addresses and Web links to state insurance departments is provided by the Federal Consumer Information Center (FCIC) of the U.S. General Services Administration at http://www.pueblo.gsa.gov/crh/insurance.htm. These Web pages are an excellent way of keeping current with changes in the industry, insurance alerts, and listings of companies operating within a state.

Medicare and Home Health Care

Find out if you are eligible for home health care. Read this booklet to learn what Medicare covers and what kinds of questions to ask when choosing a home health care agency.

Available in English (HCFA Pub. No. 10969),
Spanish (HCFA Pub. No. 10969-S),
English Audiotape (HCFA Pub. No. 10969-RE),
Spanish Audiotape (HCFA Pub. No. 10969-RS), and
Braille (HCFA Pub. No. 10969-B).

Medicare Hospice Benefits

Hospice care is a special type of care for terminally ill patients. This booklet lists tips on how to find a hospice program, explains Medicare coverage, and tells you where to get more information.

Available in English (HCFA Pub. No. 02154),
Spanish (HCFA Pub. No. 02154-S),
English Audiotape (HCFA Pub. No. 02154-RE),
Spanish Audiotape (HCFA Pub. No. 02154-RS),
Braille (HCFA Pub. No. 02154-B),
English Large Print (HCFA Pub. No. 02154-LE), and
Spanish Large Print (HCFA Pub. No. 02154-LS).

Figure 16.9. Two publications listed in the Medicare catalog at http://www.medicare.gov/Publications/Pubs/pdf/pubcatalog.pdf.

Statistics

Insurance statistics are plentiful. Many of the sources already described contain valuable statistical information. Such trade publications as *Best's Review* regularly publish annual surveys of company and industry financial performance, while federal publications such as the *Social Security Bulletin* present detailed statistics on social insurance programs and benefits. State insurance departments publish statistics as well, based primarily on the reports submitted to them by insurance companies. Many of these current statistics are available from both government and association Web pages.

Although these sources are useful, they are by no means the only publications in which statistics are available. Although there is no single source that presents comprehensive information on all types of commercial and social insurance, several titles focus on specific insurance lines. Most reflect the traditional division between the life/health and property/casualty industries. Many libraries keep older editions of these publications so that historical statistics are obtainable.

The life/health industry is represented by several different sources. The two most widely consulted sources follow.

American Council of Life Insurers. **Life Insurance Fact Book**. Washington, D.C.: The Council, 1946– . Annual.

Health Insurance Association of America. **Source Book of Health Insurance Data**. New York: The Association, 1959– . Annual.

The *Life Insurance Fact Book* is a fundamental source. Based on data compiled from annual statements provided by life insurance companies, council surveys, and other organizations, it summarizes industry trends and developments, presenting information on life insurance purchases and ownership, annuities, life insurance and annuity benefit payments, pension and retirement programs, policy lapses and surrenders, life insurance assets, and other aspects of the life insurance business. For the most part it emphasizes the recent years, with data in tables, charts, and graphs supplemented by brief, narrative descriptions. Some historical data are presented. Additional sections identify key state insurance officials and present mortality tables, historic dates, and names and describe important trade and professional life insurance associations. A glossary and index are also included.[11]

Similar coverage is provided in the *Source Book of Health Insurance Data*. Like the *Fact Book*, it includes an index, glossary, and list of historic dates. Its main sections present tables on the extent of private health insurance coverage, benefit payments, premium income, government health care programs, medical care costs, disability and health care utilization, and health manpower. This publication is available from the Association at http://www.hiaa.org/.[12] Some of the research publications issued by the Association can be accessed free of charge from this Web site.

Although the *Fact Book* and the *Source Book* are perhaps the most widely used statistical sources, others are also available.

The Life Insurance Marketing and Research Association (LIMRA) (http://www.limra.com/) is one of the most prolific international publishers of statistics and reports on the life insurance industry. It conducts research, produces a wide range of publications, and is a principal source of industry sales and marketing statistics. It regularly surveys life insurance companies, agencies, agents, and brokers, and publishes its findings in such studies as *The Merge Factor*, *Maintaining Profitability Under Expense Pressures*, *Annuity Marketing*, and *Marketing to Hispanics in the U.S.* The research reports are available from the Web page, but to download the information, a membership is required. Freely obtainable are the newsletters (http://www.limra.com/Newsletters/default.asp), which contain information, and some statistics, on best practices, recruiting, and assessment. The membership roster is also freely accessible. By checking the press releases on the site one may also find some of the latest statistics.

The property/casualty industry is also well represented by statistical publications. Two of the most useful follow.

Insurance Information Institute. **Fact Book: Property/Casualty Insurance Facts.** New
 York: The Institute, 1961– . Annual.

A. M. Best Company. **Best's Aggregates & Averages: Property/Casualty**. Oldwick, N.J.:
 A. M. Best, 1976– . Annual.

The *Fact Book* is another association-published fact book. Like the others, it includes
detailed current and historic industry statistics, grouped under broad categories including
the Dollars and Cents of the Business, Factors Affecting Costs, Losses by Category, and
Laws Affecting Motorists. As a handy compilation of statistics this publication is extremely
useful and inexpensive. For those researchers needing to find free information, the statistics
and research reports section of the Institute's Web pages at http://www.iii.org/media/facts/
and http://www.iii.org/media/lateststud/ will provide some significant information.

Best's Aggregates & Averages: Property/Casualty includes composite industry data
as well as information on specific companies. It is particularly useful for researchers who
need to compare the performance of one company with others in the same line or with the
industry aggregate. It presents consolidated industry totals as well as totals for companies
categorized by type of organization and by predominant type of insurance written. Each of
these listings presents aggregate balance sheet and operating statistics, showing assets and
liabilities for the current and preceding year, average yield on company investments, premiums written, premiums earned and collected, commissions, expenses, and other operating
data.

In addition, *Best's Aggregates & Averages* features time series data on industry resources and operating results, loss and expense ratios, and an extensive "Lines of Business"
section that provides statistics on leading companies and insurance groups. Also included
are lists of leading companies and of underwriting expenses by company.

Other publications are more specialized. The Insurance Research Council (http://
www.ircweb.org), an industry-sponsored organization, conducts research, publishes the
findings, and makes them available to the public. *Uninsured Motorist*, for example, presents detailed demographic information on the characteristics of uninsured drivers and the
cars they drive, accident claims, and state laws on uninsured motorist coverage. From the
Council's Web page one can access the news releases or the abstracts of the publications to
find a few statistics free. Two industry-sponsored organizations, the Insurance Institute for
Highway Safety and the Highway Loss Data Institute (http://www.hwysafety.org/), publish
reports on theft, insurance losses, and collision coverage of automobiles, vans, pickup
trucks, and utility vehicles, as well as on accident-related injuries. The organization makes
all of its reports freely available from its Web site.

For a librarian looking to improve a collection of materials on insurance it would be
advisable to check all the Web sites of associations, organizations, and commercial publishers, as the amount of free information now available is extensive. The smallest public library can now provide some free statistics and ratings of insurance companies.

Notes

1. Some National Safety Council statistics are available at http://www.nsc.org/lrs/statstop.htm.

2. George E. Rejda, *Principles of Insurance* (Glenview, Ill.: Scott, Foresman, 1982), 24.

3 Although most property/casualty insurers are stock companies, there are some exceptions. State Farm Insurance, a mutual insurance company, is perhaps the most notable.

4. Frederick G. Crane, *Insurance Principles and Practices* (New York: John Wiley, 1980), 427.

5. Rejda, *Principles of Insurance,* 505.

6. Adam Raphael, *Ultimate Risk.* (London: Bantam Press, 1994), 11–16.

7. Frederick G. Crane, *Insurance Principles and Practices* (New York: John Wiley, 1980), 303.

8. Insurance & Employee Benefits Division (IEBD), 1700 Eighteenth St., NW, Washington, DC 20009-2508 USA, (202) 234-4700, Fax: (202) 265-9317.

9. Publications can be viewed or printed from the Web site at http://www.ssa.gov/. Contact information for local offices can be found by using the locator at http://s3abaca.ssa.gov/pro/fol/fol-home.html.

10. Publications can be viewed or printed from the Web site at http://www.medicare.gov/Publications/Search/View/ViewPubList.asp?Language=English (or access this page by using the site map). (Language can be changed to Spanish or Chinese at this site.) or by writing to:

> U.S. Department of Health and Human Services
> Centers for Medicare and Medicaid Services
> 7500 Security Blvd.
> Baltimore, MD 21244-1850
> Phone: 1-800-MEDICARE.

11. For more information on publications from the Council, check http://www.acli.com/, or write to:

> American Council of Life Insurers
> 101 Constitution Avenue, NW, Suite 700
> Washington, DC 20001-2133
> Phone: 202-624-2000.

12. Health Insurance Association of America, http://www.hiaa.org/.

> 1201 F Street, NW, Suite 500
> Washington, DC 20004-1204
> Phone: 202-824-1600

17

Real Estate

Previous chapters covered such traditional and speculative investments as stocks, bonds, mutual funds, commodities futures, and options. This chapter examines another investment medium, real estate. Its importance is difficult to overestimate:

> Each of us uses real estate every day. Real estate provides shelter, protection, comfort, convenience, privacy, and many other things. Business firms need a place of business -a store, office, plant, or other parcel of real estate-in order to carry on operations. Farms and ranches, of course, rely heavily on real estate. Governmental, educational, religious, and cultural institutions all make use of real estate. Our real estate resources-the homes, factories, office buildings, stores, shopping centers, farms, rights of way, roads, streets, parks, recreational areas, and other kinds-represent more than half of our national wealth.[1]

This chapter explains basic real estate concepts and describes reference sources of potential interest to homeowners, business people, investors, realtors, and real estate practitioners.

Basic Real Estate Concepts

Real estate means land and the attachments to it that are intended to be permanent. Such attachments, also known as improvements, may include fences, landscaping, bridges, and pipelines as well as buildings. Automobiles parked on the land or possessions stored in the buildings, however, are personal rather than real property. The distinction is an important one. Personal property includes items of a temporary or movable nature, and real property includes land and its permanent structures. Land includes more than the earth's surface. It begins at the earth's center and continues through to the surface and beyond it into space; rights to the subsurface, surface, and airspace for the same plot of land may, in fact, be separately held.

Categories of Real Estate

Real estate can be categorized in many different ways. It can, for example, be classed as urban or rural or as residential, commercial, or industrial. It can also be categorized as property purchased primarily for occupancy (a house, store, or factory) by its owner, or for investment purposes (an apartment building, a syndicated real estate partnership). A brief discussion of each of these classifications is in order.

As the population has grown and become increasingly urban, so also has the proportional increase of urban real estate. Even so, such real estate accounts for only 2.9 percent of the total land area in the United States, according to a report issued by the Economic Research Service of the U.S. Department of Agriculture (http://www.ers.usda.gov/Publications/ RCAT/rcat102/Rcat102k.pdf). Most other land can be classified as rural. It includes not only farms, ranches, and the land they occupy, but also commercial forests, wildlife refuges, reservoirs, and recreational and wilderness areas. Finally, some real estate can be categorized as both urban and rural; interstate highways and railroad rights of way fall into this classification.

Real estate is often described by the uses for which it is intended (see figure 17.1). Owner- and renter-occupied housing, for example, is generally referred to as *residentia property,* while real estate used for wholesale, retail, and service industries is considered *commercial property.* Shopping centers, office buildings, resorts, restaurants, and hotels and motels are all categorized as commercial property. Real estate used primarily for manufacturing or warehouses is referred to as *industrial property,* and includes factories, warehouses, and industrial parks.

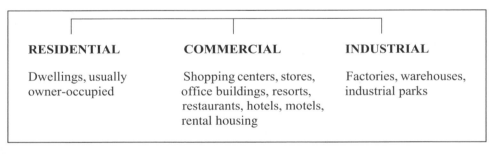

Figure 17.1. Types of real estate.

All real estate ownership represents investment, some of it considerable. Not all real estate, however, is purchased primarily for investment purposes. Although the homeowner hopes that his or her property will appreciate in value, usually the primary goal is to enjoy other benefits, such as shelter, privacy, convenience, and status, that home ownership may bring. The same is true for the small business person who owns the buildings and land occupied by his or her business. The emphasis in these situations is on ownership of real property for occupancy rather than for any immediate investment returns. Others, however, buy property primarily for investment. Land developers and contractors who routinely buy and sell real estate, and institutional investors, such as insurance companies that invest heavily in buildings and land, fall into this category. So also do a growing number of small, private investors. Some purchase real property directly; a person who has recently inherited money, for example, may choose to buy rental property rather than stocks or bonds. Other investors share ownership of real estate through limited partnerships and real estate investment trusts.

A *real estate limited partnership* enables member investors to share ownership in more extensive and diverse real estate holdings than they would be able to afford individually. Membership in such syndicates consists of limited and general partners. Limited partners put up the capital. General partners seek the investors, make the investment decisions, and act as the syndicate managers. In addition, general partners assume greater risk than limited partners; although limited partners chance loss of capital, their liability is limited to the amount of their investment. General partners, on the other hand, must personally assume all other liabilities of ownership and financing. In return for their services and their assumption of greater risk, general partners receive fees from the limited partners, much as investment company managers receive them from shareholders.

The partnerships may be either private (that is, not open to the public) or public. Public real estate limited partnerships, also known as master limited partnerships or MLPs, are publicly traded on the major stock exchanges and in the OTC market. Like other publicly traded securities, master limited partnerships are under the regulation of the Securities and Exchange Commission and are required to report to it on a regular basis.

Real estate investment trusts (REITs) are related investment media. Like limited partnerships, real estate investment trusts pool the money of several investors for the purchase of real property (or mortgages on such property) and are generally considered long-term investments. Like MLPs, REITs are publicly traded. REITs, however, are organized and function as corporations rather than partnerships; REIT investors are exempt from the risk of liability that limited partners must assume. By law REITs must be widely held and must distribute almost all their taxable income as dividends to shareholders. The best source of free and substantial information about REITs is available at the Web site of the National Association of Real Estate Investment Trusts (http://www.nareit.com/). Here one can obtain *About Reits* (http://www.nareit.com/aboutreits/index.cfm), *Guide to Reit Investing* (http://www.nareit.com/researchandstatistics/investing.cfm), statistics on the industry, and a link to companies and ticker symbols. Prospective investors are counseled to learn all they can about specific MLPs and REITs before they invest.

Real Estate Industry

Discussion of real estate to this point has focused on the property holder—the homeowner, business person, or investor—rather than on the business of real estate. Real estate is, however, a major industry. It includes a wide variety of businesses, most of which can be categorized as marketing, producing, or financing enterprises. In addition, several related industries and professions are frequently directly involved in the real estate industry.

Marketing

Marketing enterprises include two main types of business: brokerage and property management. *Real estate brokerage* involves selling, leasing, buying, or exchanging property for others on a commission basis. Brokerage firms, or real estate agencies, may range in size from small, one- or two-person operations to large national firms. They may handle all types of real estate or may specialize in residential, commercial, industrial, or farm property. All, however, serve as intermediaries, and all charge commissions. Owners and partners of brokerage firms are usually referred to as *brokers,* while other employees assisting in marketing real estate are usually called *real estate agents* or *salespeople.* Both brokers and agents must pass examinations to be licensed to practice in the states in which they are located.

Often the term *realtor* is used by laypeople to designate both *brokers* and *salespeople*. Not all such real estate practitioners, however, are realtors. A *realtor* is a broker who is affiliated with a local real estate board that is a member of the National Association of Realtors (NAR). The term is copyrighted by the NAR, and only those with the stipulated membership ties are allowed to use it.

The National Association of Realtors (http://www.realtor.org/), first organized in 1908, is the most important national real estate organization. It is composed of many local and state boards as well as such organizations as the Appraisal Institute (http://www.appraisalinstitute.org/), the Society of Office and Industrial Realtors (http://www.sior.com/links/linksmain.html), and the Realtors National Marketing Institute. The NAR performs many of the activities characteristic of trade and professional associations. It offers seminars and other continuing education opportunities, promotes the interests of the real estate industry, and has an active public relations program. The creation and support of its *Code of Ethics* (http://www.realtor.org/realtororg.nsf/pages/narcode) is generally regarded as its most important contribution to the profession and to the public. In 1916, the NAR voted to use the term *realtor* to designate member brokers and to distinguish them from other brokers who, it was felt, might not always adhere to the high standards set forth in the *Code of Ethics*. From the Association Web pages there are links for consumers, residential brokers, sales agents, and real estate specialties.

Property management is the other main type of real estate marketing enterprise. As the number of properties owned by absentee landlords and groups of people or organizations (including, for example, life insurance companies and pension funds, limited partnerships, and real estate investment trusts) increases, so also has the demand for professional property management. A property manager acts as the owner's agent; performing such duties as negotiating leases; collecting rent; supervising maintenance, repair, and upkeep of the property; and providing accounting and financial services. The property manager reports periodically to the owners and carries out any additional duties specified in his or her contract. These may include preparing and filing tax returns and arranging for insurance coverage. Although property management is available, usually through brokerage firms, for single-family dwellings, more often it is characteristic of larger properties such as condominiums and apartment complexes, shopping centers and stores, and office and industrial buildings. In return for such services, the property manager or the property management firm is usually paid a fixed percentage of rents collected from the occupants of the property.

Production

Another major functional division of the real estate industry is generally referred to as *production*. Production begins with land development. It, in turn, consists of three phases: preliminary analysis, implementation, and evaluation. During the first phase, the developer attempts to determine the market for a proposed development. This will include consideration of local economic conditions, demographic factors likely to affect demand, the existence and occupancy rates of similar types of property, and the availability of land for development. During this phase, developers may seek information from local government agencies, chambers of commerce, and trade organizations. Although sometimes overlooked, libraries can also provide valuable information. The *Economic Census*, the *Census of Population and Housing, County Business Patterns,* and many other government, trade, association, and commercial publications can help developers analyze the local market. If market research indicates that conditions are favorable, further study is required. It will include identification and analysis of possible tracts of land; subsequent selection of the site to be developed; and analysis of local, state, and possibly even federal government regulations that may affect the project.

During the second phase, the developer negotiates with and secures the approval of various government agencies, purchases and finances the land, and, with the aid of engineers and other specialists, draws up a complete layout and design for the tract. Someone developing land for a shopping center, for example, will use topographic maps, surveys, and the results of soil and drainage tests to designate space for the building itself and for parking, access roads, and landscaped areas. Implementation also includes the establishment of land use restrictions for future occupants, acquiring the necessary liability insurance and performance bonds to ensure completion of site improvements, and the actual installation of improvements on the site. The final step in the implementation phase involves marketing the new development to prospective buyers.

The third phase is feedback and evaluation. It involves assessment of development costs, sales performance, and other factors that helped the project succeed or fail. Following land development comes the building process. Many of the builder's tasks parallel those of the developer. Both begin with preliminary analyses. Like the developer, the builder wants to be certain that there will be a market for the finished product. Accordingly, the astute builder will also be interested in learning as much as possible about local market conditions and can benefit from consulting Census Bureau publications and other library information sources.

The preliminary phase also includes drawing up the building design and engineering plans. Other steps in the building process include securing the necessary financing, constructing the building(s), and, finally, marketing the finished product.

Sometimes the same company handles both land development and building. Whether the operations are combined or separate, however, the phases most closely tied to library resources and research are the preliminary planning phase when economic and demographic information is being sought and the phase in which the finished project is about to be marketed to prospective buyers or lessees. Both are marketing research-oriented, and many of the sources described in chapter 9 will be useful.

Financing

Few purchasers of real estate, whether they are individuals or businesses, have the capital to purchase property outright. Most must borrow from banks, savings and loan associations, or other financial institutions. These institutions, in fact, comprise the third main type of real estate enterprise: organizations involved in the financing of real estate purchases.

Although many lending institutions and practices are covered at length in previous chapters, certain special characteristics of real estate financing are worth noting. First, most real estate financing is long term; home mortgage loans, for example, may be for 20, 25, or even 30 years. Second, real estate loans are typically made with the property itself as collateral. For this reason, such loans require that the property be evaluated by a professional appraiser so as to arrive at an objective estimate of its current market value. Finally, the amount and terms of credit available for real estate financing are based to a large extent on the state of the economy and general money market conditions. When, for example, money is tight, real estate financing, particularly for residential properties, is more difficult to obtain.

The mortgage loan is the most common form of real estate financing. A *mortgage is* a legal instrument that allows the borrower to pledge the real property as collateral to secure the debt with the lender. It consists of two separate documents: the mortgage agreement, also known as the deed of trust, which sets forth the terms of the loan and pledges the property as security; and the promissory note, or deed of trust note, in which the borrower is made personally responsible for the debt.

Although the number and types of mortgage loans have increased tremendously in recent years, the two most common are the amortized loan and the adjustable rate mortgage.

An *amortized loan is* one that is spread out over a period of time and repaid periodically in payments that include both principal and interest. The loan, in other words, is paid off gradually. The payment is a fixed amount, and interest has first claim on the disbursement. With each payment made the amount of interest owed is reduced and so the amount paid off the principal increases.

Loan amortization tables are used to determine the size of the payments needed to repay a loan. Since library users often request such information, an examination of the amortization table shown in figure 17.2 is in order.

A loan amortization table, or schedule, includes four main pieces of information: the amount of the loan, the rate of interest being charged, the length of time to maturity, and the amount of the periodic payments. The table in figure 17.2, for example, shows the rates for a loan of $100.000 at 6.75 percent interest. The schedule is for monthly payments, and maturity is 15 years. This table was produced at http://www.interest.com/hugh/calc/mort.html. One can easily change mortgage amounts, years of the mortgage, and interest rates to see how much will be paid monthly. It must be noted that these tables do not include required insurance and property tax payments.

Loan amortization schedules are also available at banks and thrift institutions, and most libraries include one or two in their business collections as well. Two representative publications are listed below.

Estes, Jack. **Handbook of Loan Payment Tables**. New York: McGraw-Hill, 1976. 659p.

Thorndike, David. **Thorndike Encyclopedia of Banking and Financial Tables**. 4th ed. Austin, Tex: Thomson Financial, c2001. lv.

Although dated, the *Handbook of Loan Payment Tables* includes monthly amortization schedules for 329 interest rates from 5 to 25.5 percent, in increments of 8ths and l0ths of a percent. Terms are from 1 to 25 years in one-year increments, and then for 30, 35, and 40 years, and amounts covered in the *Handbook* range from $5 to $100,000. Many libraries still possess a copy in their collections.

The *Thorndike Encyclopedia of Banking and Financial Tables* contains a whole series of mortgage and real estate tables, including monthly and quarterly amortization schedules, constant annual percent tables, mortgage loan payment tables, percent paid off tables, and depreciation schedules.

The Internet is once again an excellent provider of information. Listed in figure 17.3 (page 387) are several free online calculators that can be used for mortgage computations.

Amortized mortgages are not the only types of mortgage loans that are made. Others are *variable rate mortgages,* in which interest rates fluctuate within a specified range; *balloon mortgages,* in which payments are initially low and repayment of the principal is made in one lump sum at the date of maturity; and *flexible payment mortgages,* which enable borrowers to adjust their payments so that they will be less in the beginning and will become progressively greater, reflecting expected increases in the borrowers' incomes.

For the given values:

Principal	**$ 100000**
Interest Rate	**6.75 %**
Amortization Period	**15** years
Starting month	**Jan**
Starting year	**2002**

The **Prin%** column shows the percentage of your regular payment that your principal payment is.

Your monthly payment will be $ 884.91

Year	Month	Prin	Prin %	Int	Balance
2002	Jan	322.41	36.434175	562.50	99677.59
2002	Feb	324.22	36.639117	560.69	99353.37
2002	Mar	326.05	36.845212	558.86	99027.32
2002	Apr	327.88	37.052467	557.03	98699.44
2002	May	329.73	37.260887	555.18	98369.71
2002	Jun	331.58	37.470479	553.33	98038.14
2002	Jul	333.44	37.681251	551.46	97704.69
2002	Aug	335.32	37.893208	549.59	97369.37
2002	Sep	337.21	38.106357	547.70	97032.16
2002	Oct	339.10	38.320705	545.81	96693.06
2002	Nov	341.01	38.536259	543.90	96352.05
2002	Dec	342.93	38.753026	541.98	96009.12
2002	TOTALS	3990.88	37.582762	6628.03	96009.12

Year	Month	Prin	Prin%	Int	Balance
2003	TOTALS	4268.76	40.199572	6350.16	91740.36

Year	Month	Prin	Prin%	Int	Balance
2004	TOTALS	4565.98	42.998585	6052.93	87174.38

Year	Month	Prin	Prin%	Int	Balance
2005	TOTALS	4883.90	45.992488	5735.01	82290.48

Figure 17.2. Sample loan amortization table using a Web calculator.
Copyright © Hugh U. Chou, http://www.hughchuo.org/. Reprinted with permission.

Year	Month	Prin	Prin%	Int	Balance
2006	TOTALS	5223.96	49.194850	5394.95	77066.52

Year	Month	Prin	Prin%	Int	Balance
2007	TOTALS	5587.69	52.620186	5031.22	71478.83

Year	Month	Prin	Prin%	Int	Balance
2008	TOTALS	5976.75	56.284021	4642.16	65502.07

Year	Month	Prin	Prin%	Int	Balance
2009	TOTALS	6392.90	60.202961	4226.01	59109.17

Year	Month	Prin	Prin%	Int	Balance
2010	TOTALS	6838.02	64.394769	3780.89	52271.15

Year	Month	Prin	Prin%	Int	Balance
2011	TOTALS	7314.14	68.878444	3304.77	44957.01

Year	Month	Prin	Prin%	Int	Balance
2012	TOTALS	7823.41	73.674308	2795.50	37133.60

Year	Month	Prin	Prin%	Int	Balance
2013	TOTALS	8368.14	78.804098	2250.77	28765.46

Year	Month	Prin	Prin%	Int	Balance
2014	TOTALS	8950.80	84.291065	1668.12	19814.66

Year	Month	Prin	Prin%	Int	Balance
2015	TOTALS	9574.02	90.160078	1044.89	10240.64

Year	Month	Prin	Prin%	Int	Balance
2016	TOTALS	10240.64	96.437738	378.27	-0.00

Year	Month	Prin	Prin%	Int	Balance

Where the final summary is

- Monthly Payment: **$884.91**

- Total Int.: **$59283.70** (No pre-payment)

- Total Int.: **$59283.70** (As given)

- **SAVINGS:** $0.00 Total interest saved, 0.00 Years shorter loan

- Avg. Int. each Month: **$329.35**

- **SAVINGS:** Normal Avg Int/Month: **$329.35, You Save $0.00**

Figure 17.2 (*Cont.*)

Mortgage Calculators	
Hugh's Mortgage and Financial Calculators	http://www.interest.com/hugh/calc/
Mortgage.calc	http://www.mortgage-calc.com/
HOMEPATH.COM (Fannie Mae)	http://www.homepath.com/cgi-bin/WebObjects-4/Home PathWOF.woa/wa/Calculator
MORTGAGE CALCULATORS Finance Center	http://mortgage-calculators.org/
MortgageMath.com	http://www.mortgagemath.com/

Figure 17.3. Some mortgage calculators available on the Web.

Frequently points are attached to mortgage loans. In finance, a point is 1 percent of the amount of the loan. On a $50,000 loan, a point is $500, on a $100,000 loan, $1,000. Points are used in real estate financing to increase the return on loans.

Financing for the purchase of real estate is available from both private and public organizations. In the private sector, thrift institutions such as savings and loan associations have been most important as sources of funds for the purchase of residential property, while commercial banks traditionally have provided commercial and industrial property loans. Since most commercial bank deposits come from checking rather than savings accounts, the emphasis is on short-term construction loans rather than on long-term mortgages. Life insurance companies also offer real estate financing, particularly for large-scale projects such as shopping centers, apartment complexes, and office buildings. Finally, two special organizations are involved in real estate financing. They are mortgage banking companies and mortgage brokers.

A *mortgage banking company* makes mortgage loans to borrowers and subsequently sells them as long-term investments to such institutional investors as life insurance companies, pension funds, savings institutions, and government agencies. The mortgage company handles the preliminaries: It assesses the creditworthiness of the borrower and the value of the property, prepares the necessary papers, and makes the loan. After it sells the mortgage, the mortgage company is usually retained by the purchaser to collect the monthly payments, handle additional paperwork, and deal with any borrower-related problems.

Mortgage brokers, in contrast, act as middlemen only. They neither lend money nor service the mortgages they help to arrange. Instead, they act as agents, bringing together prospective borrowers and lenders. In return, brokers are paid a fee, usually expressed in points, for each loan that they help to arrange.

In addition to the private organizations mentioned above, some federal government agencies are also either directly or indirectly involved in real estate financing. Although space does not permit consideration of all such agencies, two are particularly important to prospective home buyers: the Department of Veterans Affairs and the Federal Housing Administration.

The Department of Veterans Affairs (http://www.va.gov/) helps to finance home ownership by guaranteeing loans made by private lenders to eligible veterans. The Federal Housing Administration (FHA), a part of the Department of Housing and Urban Development (http://www.hud.gov/), insures mortgage loans made by private lenders against possible borrower default. By so doing, it lessens risk for private lenders and thus increases the supply of credit available for home financing. Veterans Administration and Federal Housing Administration-insured loans are known respectively as VA and FHA loans; loans made by private lenders without government backing or insurance are called conventional loans.

Discussion of real estate financing to this point has focused on what is known as the *primary mortgage market,* consisting of lenders and borrowers directly involved in the financing and purchase of real estate. In addition to the primary market, however, there is an active *secondary mortgage market,* in which lenders sell existing mortgages to other investors. The secondary mortgage market helps to increase the amount of credit available for real estate loans in all parts of the country.

Three government or quasi-government agencies and one private corporation are actively involved in the secondary mortgage market. The oldest of these is the Federal National Mortgage Association, also known as the FNMA or "Fannie Mae" (http://www.fanniemae.com/). Established by the government in 1938, the FNMA was rechartered as a private corporation in 1968 to provide secondary market support for the private residential mortgage market. Fannie Mae issues publicly traded stocks, bonds, and notes, and uses the funds from their sale to finance the purchase of FHA, VA, and conventional mortgage loans. FNMA encourages home ownership by buying more mortgages when money is tight, so that the original lenders can use the money from mortgage sales to issue new mortgage loans.

The Government National Mortgage Association (GNMA or "Ginnie Mae") (http://www.ginniemae.gov/) operates as a corporation within the Department of Housing and Urban Development and is responsible for two major secondary market operations. The first of these is its Tandem Plan, a subsidy program in which the FNMA buys government-insured and conventional mortgages at a discount from the GNMA and then resells them on the open market. The GNMA absorbs the difference between purchase and sales prices in order to subsidize mortgages that might not otherwise be marketable within the private sector and to stimulate housing production and purchase.

Another way in which the GNMA indirectly promotes home ownership is through its Mortgage Backed Securities (MBS) Program. Mortgages for similar types of property are pooled and used to back publicly traded GNMA securities. The securities pass through to the investors' monthly payments of principal and interest on mortgaged property held in the pool. The MBS Program's purpose is to increase the availability of mortgage credit by attracting new sources of funds for the mortgage market. Since its securities are backed by the full faith and credit of the U.S. government, the program has been successful in attracting both institutional and individual investors.

The Federal Home Loan Mortgage Corporation, also known as the FHLMC or "Freddie Mac," is a quasi-public corporation that provides for a secondary market for conventional mortgage loans.[2] It buys individual mortgages from savings and loan associations and banks that meet its requirements for loan applications and appraisal methods and that use standardized forms that it has developed. The loans are subsequently packaged into pools of several million dollars each and resold to institutional investors.

The Mortgage Guaranty Insurance Corporation (MGIC) (http://www.mgic.com/) also buys and sells conventional loans. Unlike the FNMA, the GNMA, and the FHLMC, the MGIC has no direct ties to the federal government; it is a private corporation. It does, however, share a common purpose with the FNMA, GNMA, and FHLMC: It attracts investors who might not otherwise invest in mortgage loans.

In summary, the real estate industry consists of three main elements: marketing, land development and construction (production), and financing. Financing, as has been shown, consists not only of providing direct loans to borrowers but also of participating in the secondary mortgage market.

Government and Real Estate

Private ownership and control of real estate in this country is a right that is subject to certain government restrictions. Although private citizens have the right to own buildings and land, the government has certain property rights as well: taxation, police power, and eminent domain.

Property taxes are levied to help support community services and facilities such as roads, sewers, schools, and libraries. To encourage citizens to pay such taxes promptly and in full, the government has the power to seize any property for which taxes are delinquent and to sell it to recover the unpaid taxes. Property taxes are collected primarily at the local level, and local property tax rates and assessed value of real property are published in the *Issuer Financials* volume of the *Mergent (Moody's) Municipal & Government Manual.*

Each state government has the right of police power, to enact and enforce laws and regulations for the common good. Such power can be exercised at the state level or delegated to local governments. Police power as it applies to real estate enables state and local governments to set minimum structural requirements for buildings by establishing building codes, to enact planning and zoning ordinances, and to draw up other related regulations. These might, for example, include regulations relating to the maximum height of buildings or to the minimum distance houses must be set back from the street. Since the right of police power affects how land can be used, it has a significant impact on property values. Local zoning laws, for example, may decree that land in a certain area be excluded from commercial or industrial use and will thus affect the value of that land as well as the uses to which it can be put.

Whenever the government or a public utility needs land for public use or for the construction of public facilities, it has the right to take ownership of privately held real estate. This right of eminent domain empowers the government to buy the property at fair market value whether or not its owner actually wants to sell it.

In addition to the activities tied to the rights of taxation, police power, and eminent domain, many federal, state, and local government agencies are involved with real estate. At the federal level, the Department of Housing and Urban Development (http://www.hud.gov/) is perhaps the best known of all such agencies.

The Department of Housing and Urban Development (HUD) was established in 1965 as the first cabinet-level department to oversee housing matters. It administers federal programs concerned with housing needs, fair housing opportunities, and community development. HUD also administers FHA mortgage insurance programs, facilitates construction and rehabilitation of rental units, and offers rent subsidy programs to low-income families. In addition, it oversees home buyer consumer protection and education programs and publications and supports neighborhood preservation and development programs. Many of the documents published by HUD are extremely useful to real estate researchers; some key titles are described later in this chapter.

Another important federal organization is the Federal Housing Finance Board (http://www.fhfb.gov/). An independent, self-sustaining agency, this board supervises and regulates savings and loan associations and operates the Federal Savings and Loan Insurance Corporation (FSLIC), which insures savings accounts in FSLIC-insured savings and loan associations. It also directs the Federal Home Loan Bank System, described in chapter 10.

Other federal departments and agencies are also involved in real estate. The Departments of Agriculture (http://www.usda.gov/) and the Interior (http://www.doi.gov/), for example, include agencies responsible for the nation's system of forests and parks, and the GNMA and the FNMA, as stated, are active participants in the secondary mortgage market. Other agencies are less directly involved or focus on some narrower aspect of real estate activity. Researchers seeking information on government involvement in real estate are advised to begin by consulting the *Monthly Catalog* or by using a Web browser such as http://www.google.com/unclesam.

State and local governments are similarly involved in promoting and protecting the public interest in real estate. Most states have agencies responsible for housing and land development programs, and many local governments have planning boards and related agencies. Much of this information is now available on the Web.

Real Estate Information Sources

The literature of real estate ranges from pamphlets for prospective home buyers to valuation manuals for real estate practitioners. Some sources, especially databases, are so specialized that they are not widely available. Other, more frequently consulted titles can be found in many different library settings and many others are available via the Web. The remainder of this chapter focuses mainly on sources that fall into this second category, listing and describing dictionaries and handbooks, directories, government documents, and statistical compilations in all available formats.

Dictionaries, Encyclopedias, and Handbooks

A wide range of general and specialized real estate dictionaries is available. Although space does not permit consideration of them all, the following are typical.

Shim, Jae K., Joel G. Siegel, and Stephen W. Hartman. **Dictionary of Real Estate**. New York: John Wiley, 1996. 307p.

Cox, Barbara., Jerry Cox, and David Silver-Westrick. **Prentice Hall Dictionary of Real Estate**. Upper Saddle River, N.J.: Prentice Hall, 2001. 314p.

Useful for both practitioners and laypeople, the *Dictionary of Real Estate* defines over 3,000 terms in real estate and allied fields. In addition to standard real estate vocabulary, the *Dictionary* includes abbreviations and acronyms that are adequately cross-referenced. Tables commonly used in real estate transactions are also featured, including monthly installment loan payments. Especially useful is the inclusion of diagrams and examples.

Although the *Prentice Hall Dictionary* and the *Dictionary of Real Estate* have many features and terms in common, there are enough differences that most libraries will hold both titles. Some terms are handled in detail in one book but not in the other, and although both contain tables and diagrams, these do not fully overlap. The appendixes in the *Prentice Hall Dictionary* contain a full diagram of the "Anatomy of a House" and a "Monthly Payment Matrix For a 30-Year Amortizing Loan," as well as instructions for various software packages; those in the *Dictionary of Real Estate* include "corner influence" and "present value of a dollar" tables.

Fisher, Jeffrey D., Robert S. Martin, and Paige Mosbaugh. **Language of Real Estate Appraisal**. Chicago: Real Estate Education, 1991. 290p.

The *Language of Real Estate Appraisal* is intended primarily for appraisers and other real estate professionals. Although the focus is on appraisal, terms in the areas of finance, statistics, and energy are also included. Definitions are generally brief, ranging in length from a sentence or two to an entire page. In addition, lists of acronyms, symbols, and abbreviations are included, along with tables for monthly and annual compounding. It features descriptions of and formulas for subdivision analysis, depreciation methods, and valuation models.

There are various dictionaries available on the Internet, include some specifically for the real estate industry. These can be found using any Web search engine, but the two listed below are especially useful.

Informedia Group, Inc. **Real Estate Glossary.** c2002 http://www.informediagroup.com/dearbuildernew/glossary/a1,htm. (Accessed August 30, 2003).

WebFinance, Inc. **investorwords.com.** c1997–2002. http://www.investorwords.com/cgi-bin/bysubject.cgi?18. (Accessed August 30, 2003).

Both *homeglossary.com* and *investorwords.com* contain a short description of most real estate terms. Many of the definitions contain links to related terms for easier understanding. *Investorwords.com* also has a list of "see also" terms at the end of each definition. For libraries without a strong interest in real estate these may provide adequate information.

More detailed information is available in encyclopedias and handbooks.

Arnold, Alvin L. with the assistance of Eric Stevenson, Marshall E. Tracht, and Paul D. Lapides. **The Arnold Encyclopedia of Real Estate**. 2nd ed. New York: John Wiley, 1993. 610p.

Abbott, Damien. **Encyclopedia of Real Estate Terms**. 2nd ed. London: Delta Alpha Publishing, 2000. 1430p.

The *Arnold Encyclopedia of Real Estate* lists, defines, and explains, in plain English, basic concepts in real estate, law, banking, and taxation. Arrangement is alphabetical, and the entries range in length from a sentence or two to several pages. Most, however, are one or two paragraphs long. Appended is a list of abbreviations.

The *Encyclopedia of Real Estate Terms* is an excellent guide to the meaning, use, and significance of over 8,000 real estate words and phrases. This edition is weighted to the North American market, but this is compensated for by reference to materials from Europe, Australia, Canada, Hong Kong, India, and New Zealand.. These references include case law and bibliographic references. The inside cover contains an extremely useful "Guide to the Encyclopedia," which shows the layout of individual entries. The appendixes contain a wide array of additional information, including: a 900-book bibliography listed by area; selected codes and laws; a listing of real estate organizations, complete with Web locations; tables of measurement; financial formulae; and a nine-page listing of acronyms. This is probably the most comprehensive, fairly inexpensive one-volume work available in this field.

Real estate handbooks are commonplace. For general information, the following cover different areas and complement each other.

Harris, Jack C., and Jack P. Friedman. **Barron's Real Estate Handbook**. 5th ed. Hauppauge, N.Y.: Barron's Educational Series, 2001. 828p.

Irwin, Robert, ed.-in-chief. **The McGraw-Hill Real Estate Handbook.** 2nd ed. New York: McGraw-Hill, 1993. 641p.

Barron's Real Estate Handbook is a compilation of information, including the definitions of over 2,000 terms, some with illustrations; "How to Read an Appraisal Report"; federal legislation; information on REITs; and a collection of useful mortgage and measurement tables.

The McGraw-Hill Real Estate Handbook presents 31 chapters, written by industry experts, classed under broad subject headings: Real Estate Taxation, Real Estate Business, Finance, and Buying and Selling. The *Handbook is* indexed.

Other guides focus on specific segments of the real estate industry. One area in which interest is particularly strong is the purchase and sale of real estate for investment.

Alvin, Arnold. **Real Estate Investor's Deskbook**. Boston: Warren, Gorham and Lamont, 1994. Various pagings.

———. **Real Estate Investor's Deskbook:** Annual Supplements. St. Paul. Minn.: West Group, 1997– . Various pagings.

McLean, Andrew James, and Gary W. Eldred. **Investing in Real Estate**. 3rd ed. New York: John Wiley, 2001. 311p.

Designed for use by both advisors and prospective investors, the *Real Estate Investor's Deskbook* is a comprehensive guide to all aspects of the process of investing in real estate. Both the *Deskbook* and its supplements are divided into 13 chapters that are further divided into sections. The chapters cover the strategies and techniques of acquiring, financing, and disposing of real estate. This is one of the most detailed sources available for investors and will probably be found in most libraries that cater to patrons interested in personal investment or to advisors who are helping them. The annual supplements, issued since 1997 by the West Group, have the same arrangement as the *Deskbook* and serve as a source to more recent developments that may affect investors.

Investing in Real Estate is intended for use by prospective investors rather than seasoned professionals. Written for the layperson, it discusses real estate as an investment medium and describes how to find properties, assess worth, and improve the value. Techniques for the analysis of specific investments are explained, and tax information is included.

Directories

A wide range of general and specialized directories is available. This section lists and describes some of the most widely used specialized titles and points to Web sites that list general realtors.

U.S. Real Estate Register. Wilmington, Mass.: Barry, Inc.,1985– . Annual.

Nelson's Directory of Institutional Real Estate. Port Chester, N.Y.: Nelson Publications, 1992– . Annual.

The *U.S. Real Estate Register* is designed for the professional to be able to quickly find services and properties. The *Register* is divided into four sections to make information conveniently accessible. Section One alphabetically lists the largest 1,200 companies along with contact information; Section Two is an alphabetical listing of 9,000 companies involved in all aspects of real estate from finance to utilities; Section Three lists currently available commercial and industrial properties that are for sale or lease; and Section Four is a classified index by state of all the listings.

Nelson's Directory of Institutional Real Estate has separate sections covering real estate investment management firms, real estate service firms, pension funds and foundations that invest in real estate, the 2,000 largest corporations with active real estate operations, and real estate investment trusts. Each entry includes an overview of the firm, names of key executives, and contact information. It is searchable geographically and by type of service offered. Coverage is mainly for the United States, but there are some entries for foreign entities.

There are many Web directories of realty and appraisal companies. One aimed at individuals and corporations or other organizations contemplating relocation in another part of the country is maintained by the Employee Relocation Council at http://www.erc.org/. Along with other information there is an online directory at http://www.erc.org/directory/index.shtml. One can search by geography to find both agents and appraisers who are members of ERC. Also featured is a listing of relocation service companies by area of specialization. All listings include full contact information.

Other links to realty companies and agents can be found at on the Web at most major real estate sites. Examples are REALTOR.com at http://www.realtor.com/ and HomeGain. com at http://www.homegain.com.

Periodicals and Periodical Indexes

The diversity of the real estate industry is reflected in such periodicals as *Appraisal Journal, Builder, Constructor, Journal of Real Estate Finance and Economics,* and *Journal of Real Estate Portfolio Management.* Although a comprehensive collection of such serials is rare in all but the largest or most specialized business collections, some real estate periodicals are more commonly held. They include the following titles.

Real Estate Forum. New York: Real Estate Forum, 1946– . Monthly

Real Estate Review. St. Paul, Minn.: West Information Publishing Group, 1971– . Quarterly.

National Real Estate Investor. Metcalf, Kans.: Primedia Business Magazines and Media, 1959– .Monthly, with an additional issue in July.

Real Estate Forum is a commercially published trade magazine that focuses primarily on recent developments in commercial and industrial real estate. A typical issue contains one or two articles; recent issues, for example, have included articles on the corporate sector and recovery. The bulk of each issue, however, consists of brief announcements in such regular sections as "Market Pulse," "National Leasing," "Global Digest," and "Finance." The February issue contains its annual "Deals of the Year," which examines major sales and leases across the country and identifies residential, commercial, and industrial markets that are unusually strong or weak.

While *Real Estate Forum is* essentially a news magazine, *Real Estate Review* contains more scholarly articles on a wide range of topics. Recent issues have included articles on such subjects as liquidity risk, conservation easements, and damage valuations. Contributors include real estate executives and practitioners as well as scholars, and the emphasis is on practical information and problem solving.

The *National Real Estate Investor* (http:www.nreionline.com) is another trade publication. It covers construction, development, finance, investment, and management, and combines news and announcements with articles. The magazine is divided into three major sections: the first is "Developments," which provides the latest news; the second section is more substantive and contains articles on the industry, the major players, and emerging trends. Finally, the third section, "Strategies," covers case studies, noteworthy problems, and regulatory issues. The Web site features the "Best of the Best," a set of regularly conducted surveys including "Industrial Trends," "Top Shopping Center Owners," and "Office Trends."

Some periodicals are particularly useful for the statistics they contain. Representative of these is *U.S. Housing Markets*.

U.S. Housing Markets. Canton, Mich.: Meyers Group, 1966– . Quarterly.

U.S. Housing Markets is issued in two parts, which can be subscribed to separately. The first part is the *Flash Report,* in which is published permit detail and history on all 330+ metropolitan areas approximately six weeks after the quarter ends. The second part is the *National Review,* published 10 weeks after the quarter ends, which surveys housing for all metropolitan areas in none regions and the United States as a whole. Data on private housing permits for single and multifamily units are provided, along with additional information on multifamily housing units completed or under construction, rental vacancy rates, household formats, and U.S. households by age groups. Also included are selected local data on total permits issued and listings of the busiest builders.

Many real estate periodicals are indexed and available full text in standard sources such as *Business Source Premier, Business Source Elite, and ABI/INFORM Global*. This makes it easier for even some of the smallest libraries to provide information in such specialized areas.

Government Documents

Federal real estate publications are rich and diverse. They include hearings on real estate development and financing, GNMA manuals for institutional investors, reports on new housing technology, statistics, and market analysis. The field is so broad that it is all but impossible to list even selectively documents likely to interest real estate brokers and sales people, developers, builders, financiers, and investors. Each library will want to collect documents or provide Web links to sources that reflect its users' interests and needs.

One area in which there is widespread interest in most public and many academic libraries is the purchase of residential property.

U.S. Department of Housing and Urban Development. **100 Questions & Answers About Buying a New Home**. December 10, 2001. http://www.hud.gov/offices/hsg/sfh/buying/buyhm.cfm#Dear. (Accessed August 30, 2003).

U.S. Department of Housing and Urban Development. **Buying Your Home**. Updated May 2, 2002. http://www.hud.gov/offices/hsg/sfh/res/sfhrestc.cfm. (Accessed August 30, 2003).

U.S. Federal Reserve Board. **Consumer Handbook on Adjustable Rate Mortgages**. n.d. http://www.federalreserve.gov/pubs/brochures/arms/arms.pdf. (Accessed August 30, 2003).

100 Questions & Answers About Buying a New Home is a guide for prospective homeowners. Sections discuss the advantages and disadvantages of owning a home, selecting a house, purchase contracts, home financing, the closing process, money management, and mortgage insurance. A glossary is appended. Although some will find the language and information simplistic, for many first-time buyers the simple layout and question-and-answer format is ideal. *Buying Your Home* contains information on home buying, home financing, and the settlement process. Information includes items such as "Shopping for a Loan" and "Specific Settlement Costs." This booklet is available in pdf format or MS Word, so those libraries that prefer can have a print copy available for patrons. For those seeking to understand the basics of an ARM a good source is the *Consumer Handbook*, a 27-page booklet, which will answer questions on what exactly they are and how they operate. Included are a mortgage checklist and a glossary.

Statistics

Statistics concerned with all aspects of real estate are abundant. They include data gathered and published by a wide range of sources and provide information on construction and sale of housing, growth of shopping centers and industrial plants, operating costs, and vacancy rates. In addition, general demographic, social, and economic statistics are of direct importance to real estate operations of all kinds. Although space does not permit coverage of every relevant statistic, some of the most important ones are discussed below.

On the most basic level, most people pay rent or monthly mortgage loan installments. Costs for housing are, in fact, one of the major components of the consumer price index, which presents data on rent, owners' equivalent rent, homeowners' or tenants' insurance, and maintenance and repair. Such information is included in the CPI *Detailed Report* and the *Inter-City Cost of Living Index*, both of which are described in chapter 6.

Data on construction and building costs are also compiled and reported. The information compiled by the government is issued in a *Value of Construction Put in Place*, now available at http://www.census.gov/const/www/c30index.html (see figure 17.4). This monthly item gives information on residential and nonresidential real estate as well as public utilities and farm construction. Additional sources of information are listed in the periodical.

There are several major construction cost indexes, some produced by the government, others by private organizations. The Census Bureau, for example, issues the *Index of New One Family Houses*. The Federal Highway Administration publishes indexes relating to highway construction, and the Department of the Interior issues a Bureau of Reclamation *Construction Composite Index* (http://www.usbr.gov/tsc/cct00-03.pdf), which measures the costs of constructing dams and reclamation projects sponsored by the department. The Federal Energy Regulatory Commission (FERC) issues a Federal Energy Regulatory *Commission Pipeline Index* (http://www.ferc.fed.us/oil/OilIndex.htm), which presents data on construction costs reported by pipeline companies regulated by the commission. (See also figure 17.5, page 397.)

Some of the most widely cited indexes are issued by private sources. Key among these are the *Boeckh Indexes*, which cover 11 building types in 213 cities throughout the United States and 53 cities in Canada. It has costs for 115 elements in each location. These consist of 19 building trades, 89 materials, and 7 tax and insurance elements. The *Engineering News-Record* (http://www.enr.com/), a trade paper for the construction industry, publishes national cost indexes for construction and building, which are available at the Web site. Others sources are the *Turner Construction Company Index*, which is based on selling prices in Eastern cities, and the *Handy-Whitman Indexes*, which present building costs for reinforced concrete buildings, gas plants, and electric light and power plants. Most of the indexes described are published annually on the Web by the U.S. Census Bureau at (http://www.census.gov/pub/const/C30/annindex.pdf).

Table 4. Monthly Value of Construction Put in Place—Seasonally Adjusted Annual Rate in Current Dollars—Con.

[Millions of dollars]

| Period | Total | Public construction | | | | | | | | | | | |
| | | Total | Buildings | | | | | Highways and streets[1] | Military facilities | Conservation and development | Sewer systems | Water supply facilities | Miscellaneous public[7] |
			Housing and redevelopment	Industrial	Educational	Hospital	Other public buildings[6]						
2000: April	178,351	81,160	5,353	1,183	42,063	4,313	28,248	56,185	2,280	5,845	12,013	6,920	13,939
May	173,394	81,473	5,139	1,059	43,538	4,255	27,483	51,603	2,329	5,314	10,515	6,979	14,881
June	168,152	80,489	5,210	1,078	42,641	4,131	27,428	49,431	2,262	5,814	10,809	6,491	13,888
July	164,520	79,082	5,132	1,161	41,911	3,998	28,981	49,628	2,195	4,818	9,945	5,961	12,800
August	173,311	81,970	5,342	1,308	43,038	4,055	28,236	52,777	2,388	5,568	9,719	7,137	13,747
September	176,559	82,233	5,275	1,099	43,751	4,042	28,067	53,923	2,509	6,425	9,617	7,156	14,866
October	175,969	85,163	5,517	1,116	44,020	3,805	30,705	48,764	1,983	6,815	9,703	7,000	16,640
November	175,680	84,673	5,575	1,177	44,776	4,151	28,994	48,858	2,629	5,789	9,831	6,989	16,911
December	177,883	86,184	5,578	1,201	46,745	3,643	29,016	50,189	2,107	6,339	10,009	6,950	16,105
2001: January	186,100	87,368	5,852	1,587	46,001	3,875	30,043	55,368	2,270	7,381	10,165	7,239	16,318
February	187,508	86,785	5,482	1,392	45,732	3,625	30,254	56,204	2,342	7,838	10,352	7,560	16,437
March	187,954	87,547	5,962	1,351	45,946	3,953	30,504	57,443	2,131	7,573	10,076	7,919	15,275
April	193,397	91,607	6,340	1,605	47,773	3,802	30,904	57,717	2,530	6,332	10,997	8,654	15,560
May	198,336	94,405	6,535	1,329	49,953	3,844	32,743	60,437	2,274	7,216	10,282	7,716	16,406
June	196,249	91,120	6,488	1,388	46,754	3,949	32,542	61,534	2,477	6,592	10,410	8,463	15,852
July	195,077	93,938	6,135	1,400	50,242	3,902	32,120	60,470	2,375	6,063	9,980	8,011	15,140
August	193,521	94,802	6,020	1,419	51,304	4,220	31,750	55,667	2,539	7,265	10,008	8,021	15,218
September	191,635	95,921	6,183	1,907	50,626	4,140	32,995	53,534	2,362	7,344	9,875	7,965	14,645
October	190,184	99,413	6,742	1,078	53,537	4,152	33,903	55,082	2,343	7,489	9,978	7,862	16,317
November	204,443	99,577	6,835	1,433	52,665	4,418	34,226	58,717	2,353	7,392	10,799	8,160	17,444
December	208,270	100,788	7,552	2,410	52,183	4,647	34,016	59,840	2,152	7,548	10,561	8,536	18,845
2002: January	216,178	102,747	7,037	1,490	53,624	5,444	35,151	66,014	2,223	8,668	10,950	8,360	17,225
February[r]	218,626	106,818	7,128	2,346	56,800	5,166	35,178	61,726	2,416	8,865	11,760	8,167	19,074
March[r]	208,626	104,052	7,258	1,875	54,624	5,170	35,125	58,245	2,321	8,715	11,057	7,799	18,837
April[p]	206,457	103,666	7,562	1,441	56,747	5,137	32,779	58,706	2,368	7,957	10,610	7,079	17,083
PERCENT CHANGE													
March 2002-April 2002	-1	(Z)	4	-23	4	-1	-7	1	2	-9	-4	2	-8

NA Not available, but estimates are included in totals. P Preliminary. R Revised. Z Less than 0.5 percent

[1] Includes farm nonresidential and other private categories, not shown separately. [2] Includes residential improvements, not shown separately. [3] Includes amusement and recreational buildings, bus and airline terminals, animal hospitals and shelters, etc. [4] Includes gas, electric, railroad, and petroleum pipelines not shown separately. [5] Includes privately owned streets and bridges, parking areas, sewer and water facilities, parks and playgrounds, golf courses, airfields, etc. [6] Includes general administrative buildings, prisons, police and fire stations, courthouses, civic centers, passenger terminals, space facilities, postal facilities, etc. [7] Includes open amusement and recreational facilities, power generating facilities, transit systems, airfields, open parking facilities, etc.

Figure 17.4. *Value of Construction Put in Place.* Reproduced from http://www.census.gov/prod/www/abs/c30.html.

Annual Construction Cost Indexes
(1996 = 100)

Year	U.S. Census Bureau One-Family Fixed-Weighted	Price Deflator	Turner	Federal Highway Adm Composite	Bureau of Reclamation	Handy Whitman Building	Handy Whitman Electric	Handy Whitman Gas	Handy Whitman Water	C.A. Turner Telephone	Engineering News Record Buildings	Engineering News Record Construction
1964	18.0	18.0	18	19.7	20	20	19	21	19	29	19.1	16.6
1965	18.6	18.6	19	20.5	21	20	19	21	20	30	19.6	17.3
1966	19.5	19.5	19	21.5	21	21	20	22	20	32	20.3	18.1
1967	20.1	20.2	20	22.5	22	21	21	22	21	33	21.0	19.0
1968	21.3	21.2	21	25.3	23	22	22	23	22	34	22.5	20.5
1969	22.6	22.6	23	28.5	24	24	23	24	23	36	24.7	22.6
1970	23.2	23.2	26	30.2	26	26	24	25	25	39	26.1	24.6
1971	24.5	24.5	29	31.5	28	28	28	28	28	40	29.6	28.1
1972	26.2	26.3	30	31.6	31	31	28	31	31	41	32.7	31.2
1973	28.8	28.8	32	34.8	32	34	30	35	33	44	35.5	33.7
1974	31.7	31.7	38	47.5	36	41	38	40	39	51	37.6	35.9
1975	34.5	34.5	39	47.6	42	45	42	43	43	53	40.8	39.3
1976	36.7	36.7	40	46.1	45	46	44	46	45	56	44.5	42.7
1977	41.1	40.6	41	49.0	48	49	47	47	48	59	48.2	45.8
1978	46.2	46.1	44	58.0	51	53	50	51	52	63	52.2	49.4
1979	52.1	51.7	49	70.1	56	59	55	55	57	70	56.8	53.4
1980	58.0	57.0	54	79.7	62	66	60	60	64	79	60.6	57.6
1981	62.1	61.0	60	77.2	68	68	66	66	68	80	65.5	62.9
1982	63.3	62.8	64	72.5	72	69	69	71	72	82	69.7	68.0
1983	66.1	64.5	68	71.8	73	71	71	73	72	79	74.4	72.3
1984	68.1	67.0	71	75.9	74	74	73	76	75	76	75.5	73.7
1985	69.8	68.3	74	83.6	75	76	74	75	76	76	75.8	74.6
1986	73.4	71.4	76	82.9	76	78	75	73	78	77	77.5	78.4
1987	76.8	74.7	79	82.0	77	79	80	75	79	78	79.3	78.4
1988	79.3	77.7	82	87.4	79	82	84	80	81	78	81.1	80.4
1989	82.2	80.8	84	88.3	82	84	86	84	84	85	82.2	82.1
1990	84.6	83.4	87	88.9	85	85	88	86	85	87	84.4	84.2
1991	84.8	84.1	89	88.1	88	83	88	87	85	87	85.9	86.0
1992	86.8	86.8	89	86.1	89	84	89	89	87	87	88.5	88.7
1993	90.0	90.0	91	88.8	91	91	92	91	91	89	93.5	92.7
1994	94.1	94.0	94	94.3	94	94	95	97	95	90	97.1	96.2
1995	98.1	98.1	97	99.8	98	97	98	99	98	96	97.1	97.3
1996	100.0	100.0	100	100.0	100	100	100	100	100	100	100.0	100.0
1997	102.9	102.9	104	107.5	103	103	102	102	102	102	105.0	103.6
1998	105.6	105.6	109	106.2	105	104	104	104	104	102	105.8	105.3
1999	110.4	110.4	113	111.9	107	107	105	107	107	101	107.9	108.3
2000	115.4	115.5	118	119.3	111	110	109	111	112	103	110.3	110.3
2001	120.6	120.5	121	118.7	112	113	113	114	116	106	111.6	112.8

Source: U.S. Census Bureau
Construction Expenditures Branch
Manufacturing & Construction Div.
Washington, DC 20233-6916

Figure 17.5. "Annual Construction Cost Indexes." Reproduced from http://www.census.gov/pub/const/C30/annindex.pdf.

Other indexes supply information on industrial vacancies and office vacancies. These are compiled by CB Richard Ellis (http://www.cbre.com/default.htm). Included in the free reports are metropolitan downtown suburban areas with the highest and lowest vacancy rates and the methodology for compiling the index. The reports are available at http://www.cbre.com/Research/Market+Reports/default.htm.

The most detailed and comprehensive statistics on the construction and housing industries are those published by the Census Bureau. Such data include a series of monthly, quarterly, and annual surveys, known collectively as "Construction and Housing Reports." These are available in both pdf and print format, and a sample listing is provided in figures 17.6 and 17.7.

CONSTRUCTION			
1997 Economic Census -- Construction Reports			
EC97C23A	Geographic Area Series	Document	Order
EC97C23I	Industry Series	Document	Order
EC97C23S-AS	Subject Series - Geographic Area Summary	Document	Order
EC97C23S-IS	Subject Series - Industry Summary	Document	Order
1992 Census of Construction Industries			
CC92-A	Geographic Area Series (Files are 3 Mb or less)	Document	Order
CC92-I	Industry Series	Document	Order
CC92-S-1	Subject Series	Document	Order
Construction Statistics			
C20	Housing Starts	Document	Order
C21	New Residential Construction In Selected Metropolitan Areas	Document	Order
C22	Housing Completions	Document	Order
C25	New One-Family Houses Sold	Document	Order
C30	Value of New Construction	Document	Order

Figure 17.6. Sample listing of construction reports. Available in pdf from
http://www.census.gov/prod/www/abs/cons-hou.html.

U.S. Department of Commerce. Bureau of the Census. **Factfinder for the Nation**. July 2000. http://www.census.gov/prod/2000pubs/cff-9.pdf. (Accessed April 24, 2002). (Accessed August 30, 2003).

The *Factfinder for the Nation,* a free Census Bureau guide, lists and briefly describes construction reports published by the Bureau and the type of information included.

U.S. Department of Commerce. Bureau of the Census. **Economic Census. Construction**. Washington, D.C.: Government Printing Office. Quinquennial, taken in years ending in 2 and 7.

The census information enumerates construction establishments that operate as general and special trade contractors, builders, and land subdividers and developers. It consists primarily of two main series, an *Industry Series* (http://www.census.gov/prod/www/abs/cciview1.html), which includes reports on different construction industries, and the *Geo-*

	HOUSING		
	Housing and Household Economic Statistics		
	American Housing Briefs	Document	Order
H171	Supplement to the American Housing Survey for Selected Metropolitan Areas, 1994, 1993, and 1992	Document	Order
H170/99-84	American Housing Survey for Selected Metropolitan Areas	Document	Order
H151/95-1	Supplement to the American Housing Survey for the United States: 1995 (2 Mb)	Document	N/A
H151/93-2	American Housing Survey Components of Inventory Change: 1980-1993 United States and Regions (2.2 Mb)	Document	Order
H151/91-2	American Housing Survey Components of Inventory Change: 1980-1991 United States and Regions (2.2 Mb)	Document	Order
H151/93-1	Supplement to the American Housing Survey for the United States in 1993 (2.1 Mb)	Document	Order
H150/99-75	American and Annual Housing Survey for the United States and Regions	Document	N/A
H131	Current Housing Reports: Characteristics of Apartments Completed: Annual Reports	Document	Order

Figure 17.7. Sample listing of housing reports. Available in pdf from
http://www.census.gov/prod/www/abs/cons-hou.html.

graphic Area Series (http://www.census.gov/epcd/www/97EC23.HTM), which presents data for selected metropolitan areas, all 50 states, nine census divisions, and the United States as a whole. *American FactFinder* (http://factfinder.census.gov/servlet/BasicFactsServlet) is extremely useful for compiling custom data using the *Industry Quick Reports* (http://factfinder. census.gov/servlet/IQRBrowseServlet). An example of this service is shown in figure 17.8.

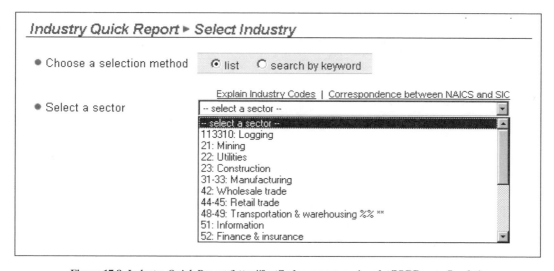

Figure 17.8. *Industry Quick Report* (http://factfinder.census.gov/servlet/IQRBrowseServlet).

Once a sector, for example construction, has been chosen, the next step is to chose a sub-sector and finally an industry, The report that then appears contains industry and financial data for the industry segment being researched. This step-by-step approach makes it easy for even a novice researcher or librarian to find needed data.

Most libraries can now provide access to the complete *Economic Census* and the various construction reports and statistics, as these are freely available on the Web, but quick access to many of the statistics is still available using the *Statistical Abstract of the United States.*

The Census Bureau also issues a series of statistical publications relating to housing. Key among these are the *Census of Population and Housing*, *Current Housing Reports*, and the *American Housing Survey.*

U.S. Dept. of Commerce. Bureau of the Census. **Census of Population and Housing**. Washington, D.C.: Government Printing Office, 1790– . Decennial.

Every 10 years, the Bureau of the Census collects detailed demographic and economic information about U.S. inhabitants and their dwellings. This decennial *Census* (http://www. census.gov/) presents housing and occupancy information. Both general and detailed housing characteristics are provided, supplemented by subject reports such as the *Survey of Market Absorption* (http://www.census.gov/hhes/www/soma.html), *Housing Vacancies and Home Ownership* (http://www.census.gov/hhes/www/hvs.html), and *Housing Affordability* (http://www.census.gov/hhes/www/hsgaffrd.html). By using the *Census* and the reports, researchers can obtain valuable information about the physical and financial characteristics of housing units. They can, for example, determine the number of condominium- and renter-occupied units, housing vacant and for sale, and housing lacking complete plumbing facilities. Data are available for each state and for designated metropolitan areas, as well as for the United States as a whole. As with other *Census* material the fastest way to develop custom reports is by using *American FactFinder* (http://factfinder.census.gov/servlet/ BasicFactsServlet). Using the "enter an address" option one can obtain information down to the block and tract level.

The *American Housing Survey* supplements the *Census* by providing current information on housing characteristics.

U.S. Dept. of Commerce. Bureau of the Census. **American Housing Survey**. Updated September 27, 2001. http://www.census.gov/hhes/www/ahs.html. (Accessed August 30, 2003).

The *Survey* is conducted by the Bureau of the Census for the Department of Housing and Urban Development. The American Housing Survey (AHS) collects data on the Nation's housing, including apartments, single-family homes, mobile homes, vacant housing units, household characteristics, income, housing and neighborhood quality, housing costs, equipment and fuels, size of housing unit, and recent movers. National data are collected in odd numbered years, and data for each of 47 selected Metropolitan Areas are collected about every four years, with an average of 12 Metropolitan Areas included each year. The national sample covers an average 55,000 housing units. Each metropolitan area sample covers 4,800 or more housing units.

The AHS returns to the same housing units year after year to gather data; therefore, this survey is ideal for analyzing the flow of households through housing.[3]

The government issues other statistics as well. The Bureau of Labor Statistics' monthly *Producer Price Index* highlights changes in the cost of such building materials as plumbing fixtures, lumber, and mobile homes. In addition, the *Federal Reserve Bulletin* presents information on primary and secondary mortgage market activity and on outstanding residential, commercial, and farm mortgage debt. In some libraries, however, the "Construction and Housing Section" of the *Statistical Abstract of the United States,* which contains excerpts from many of the sources described above, will suffice.

Contractors who submit bids on all types of construction projects need statistics and costs. They are routinely asked to submit estimates of how much it will cost to erect the proposed structure or remodel an existing one. These estimates are usually based on past experience and reflect anticipated labor and building materials costs. Sometimes published building cost estimators are also used. An extremely useful online source is the F. W. Dodge Web site (http://fwdodge.construction.com/), which provides analysis, forecasts and trends for the construction industry. The construction owner can also find plans and specifications and be alerted by e-mail to new projects out to bid. These are subscription databases, and it is unlikely that many libraries will have access. But researchers and librarians need to know about this source so that they can direct patrons to what is an extremely useful source of information.

Other publications provide operating statistics for different categories of commercial, industrial, or residential property, showing income and expense data for each. By consulting these sources, building owners, property managers, developers, investors, and others can compare their operations to the national, regional, or local norms for that type of property.

Institute of Real Estate Management. **Income/Expense Analysis: Conventional Apartments**. Chicago: The Institute, 1954– . Annual.

———. **Income/Expense Analysis: Condominiums, Cooperatives, and Planned Unit Developments**. Chicago: The Institute, 1978– . Annual.

———. **Income/Expense Analysis: Federally Assisted Apartments**. Chicago: The Institute, 1986– . Annual.

———. **Income/Expense Analysis: Office Buildings**. Chicago: The Institute, 1976– . Annual.

———. **Income/Expense Analysis: Shopping Centers.** Chicago: The Institute, 1991– . Annual.

Building Owners and Managers Association International. **BOMA Experience Exchange Report**. Washington, D.C.: The Association, 1920– . Annual.

Urban Land Institute. **Dollars & Cents of Shopping Centers**. Washington, D.C.: The Institute, 1961– . Annual.

Each year, the Institute of Real Estate Management (http://www.irem.org) compiles and analyzes financial operating data contributed by its members for over 7,700 buildings and developments. These data are published as separate titles: *Income/Expense Analysis: Apartments, Income/Expense Analysis: Office Buildings; Expense Analysis: Condominiums, Cooperatives, and Planned Unit Developments, Income/Expense Analysis: Federally Assisted Apartments,* and *Income/Expense Analysis: Shopping Centers.* Coverage varies, but each publication charts recent trends in building operations, covers income by source, and presents data for different building types. The *Apartments* report, for example, features information on such expenses as utilities, security, repairs, grounds maintenance, and real estate taxes, and presents median income and operating costs as dollars per square foot of rentable area and as a percentage of gross possible income.

Operating statistics for U.S. and Canadian office buildings are also available in the annual *BOMA Experience Exchange Report.* The *Report* presents income and expenses for different types of private and public office buildings and also includes building occupancy rates, year-end rent, and space per tenant and worker. Data on selected areas by zip code are included.

Dollars & Cents of Shopping Centers reports on shopping center operations. Based on responses made by shopping centers to periodic surveys by the Urban Land Institute, *Dollars & Cents* includes operating receipts and expenses, sales, rent, and detailed tenant information. Data are by type of shopping center (super regional, regional, community, and neighborhood) and cover the United States and Canada.[4]

Online Databases

Most of the general online business databases provide access to both the general and some leading industry publications in real estate and related fields. There are also databases and Web sites that will provide more specialized information.

U.S. Department of Housing and Urban Development. **HUD USER.** Updated March 18, 2003. http://www.huduser.org/publications/pdrpubli.html. (Accessed August 30, 2003).
    HUD USER includes reports, documents, and other sources dealing with affordable housing, housing finance, building technology, economic development, housing for special groups such as the elderly and disabled, energy conservation, assisted housing, and other topics. Although most of the titles are issued by the Department of Housing and Urban Development, documents from other government organizations and some journal articles are indexed as well. Most of the documents cited in *HUD USER* are available in pdf format and can be downloaded. For those that need to be purchased there are links to the online store.

U.S. Department of Housing and Urban Development. **Homes for Sale**. Updated February 26, 2002. http://www.hud.gov/homes/homesforsale.cfm. (Accessed March 22, 2002). (Accessed August 30, 2003).
    At this site one can link not only to HUD homes for sale but also to properties offered by other agencies such as the FDIC and IRS. Most are searchable by geography, and most of the information about the various properties is fully listed at the Web site.

There are other databases offered by associations such as the Appraisal Institute and Urban Land Institute, but these are very specialized and require subscriptions. Most libraries will not have access to these, but librarians should be aware of them so that they can direct patrons to them.

Notes

1. George F. Bloom, Arthur M. Weimer, and Jeffrey D. Fisher, *Real Estate,* 8th ed. (New York: John Wiley, 1982), 3.

2. Although the FHLMC buys some VA mortgages, it concentrates more on conventional loans.

3. Taken from http://www.census.gov/hhes/www/ahs.html.

4. Pricing and ordering information is available at http://www.uli.org/dk/uli_BookStore_fst.html.

Appendix A

Business Acronyms and Abbreviations

AACSB	American Assembly of Collegiate Schools of Business
ABA	American Bankers Association
ABC	Audit Bureau of Circulations
ABI	*Abstracted Business Information* (variant name for the database, *ABI/INFORM*)
ACCRA	American Chamber of Commerce Researchers Association
ACE	Active Corps of Executives
ACH	Automatic Clearing House
ADR	American Depositary Receipts
AGI	Adjusted Gross Income
AICPA	American Institute of Certified Public Accountants
AID	Agency for International Development (U.S.)
AIRAC	All-Industry Research Advisory Council (insurance organization)
AMA	American Management Association
AMA	American Marketing Association
AMEX	American Stock Exchange
APB	Accounting Principles Board
APR	Annual Percentage Rate
ARB	*Accounting Research Bulletin*
ARBA	American Reference Books Annual
ARF	Advertising Research Foundation
ARM	Adjustable Rate Mortgage
ARS	Annual Report to Shareholders
ASB	Auditing Standards Board (AICPA)
ASR	*Accounting Series Releases* (SEC)
ASI	*American Statistics Index*
ATM	Automated Teller Machine
B2B	Business to Business
B2C	Business to Consumer
BEA	Bureau of Economic Analysis (U.S.)
BLS	Bureau of Labor Statistics (U.S.)
BNA	Bureau of National Affairs, Inc.
BPA	Business Publications Audit of Circulation
BPI	*Business Periodicals Index*
BPI	Buying Power Index
BRASS	Business Reference and Services Section, American Library Association
BRS	BRS Information Technologies, formerly Bibliographic Retrieval Services, Inc.
CAGR	Compound Annual Growth Rate
CBOE	Chicago Board Options Exchange

CBT	Chicago Board of Trade
CCPA	Consumer Credit Protection Act
CCH	Commerce Clearing House, Inc.
CD	Compact Disk Certificate of Deposit
CD-ROM	Compact Disk, Read-Only-Memory
CEA	Council of Economic Advisers (U.S.)
CEO	Chief Executive Officer
CFTC	Commodity Futures Trading Commission (U.S.)
CFA	Chartered Financial Analyst
CFO	Chief Financial Officer
CIO	Chief Information Officer
CIS	Congressional Information Service, Inc.
CIT	Commission on Insurance Terminology (of the American Risk and Insurance Association)
CLU	Chartered Life Underwriter
CME	Chicago Mercantile Exchange
CMX	Commodity Exchange, Inc.
COGS	Cost of Goods Sold
COLA	Cost of Living Adjustment
CPA	Certified Public Accountant
CPI	Consumer Price Index
CPI-U	Consumer Price Index for All Urban Consumers
CPI-W	Consumer Price Index for Urban Wage Earners and Clerical Workers
CRS	Congressional Research Service (U.S.)
CSCE	Coffee, Sugar & Cocoa Exchange
Cv	Convertible Security (i.e., convertible preferred stock or convertible bond)
D & B	Dun & Bradstreet, Inc.
DCAA	Defense Contract Audit Agency (U.S.)
DDA	Demand Deposit Accounts
DOD	Department of Defense (U.S.)
DOL	Department of Labor (U.S.)
D-U-N-S	Dun's Universal Numbering System
EBI	Effective Buying Income
ECI	Employer Cost Index
ECOA	Equal Credit Opportunity Act
EPA	Environmental Protection Agency (U.S.)
EPS	Earnings per Share
ERC	Employee Relocation Council
ERS	Economic Research Service (U.S.)
ESA	Employment Standards Administration (U.S.)
ETA	Employment Training Administration (U.S.)
FAA	Federal Aviation Administration (U.S.)
FAIR	Fair Access to Insurance Requirements
FASB	Financial Accounting Standards Board
FCC	Federal Communications Commission (U.S.)
FCRA	Fair Credit Reporting Act
FDA	Food and Drug Administration (U.S.)
FDIC	Federal Deposit Insurance Corporation (U.S.)
Fed	Federal Reserve System (U.S.)

FERC	Federal Energy Regulatory Commission (U.S.)
FHA	Federal Highway Administration (U.S.)
FHA	Federal Housing Administration (U.S.)
FHLB	Federal Home Loan Bank
FHLBB	Federal Home Loan Bank Board
FHLBS	Federal Home Loan Bank System
FHLMC	Federal Home Loan Mortgage Corporation (U.S.) (Freddie Mac)
FICB	Federal Intermediate Credit Banks (U.S.)
FIFO	Firs In First Out
FNMA	Federal National Mortgage Association (U.S.) (Fannie Mae)
FOMC	Federal Open Market Committee, Federal Reserve System (U.S.)
FRM	Fixed Rate Mortgage
FSLIC	Federal Savings and Loan Insurance Corporation (U.S.)
FTC	Federal Trade Commission (U.S.)
GAAP	Generally Accepted Accounting Principles
GAAS	Generally Accepted Auditing Standards
GAO	General Accounting Office (U.S.)
GDP	Gross Domestic Product
GNMA	Government National Mortgage Association (U.S.) (Ginnie Mae)
GNP	Gross National Product
GPO	Government Printing Office (U.S.)
GSA	General Services Administration (U.S.)
HBR	*Harvard Business Review*
HMO	Health Maintenance Organization
HUD	Housing and Urban Development Department (U.S.)
HUT	Households Using Television
ICC	International Chamber of Commerce
IMM	International Monetary Market
IPC	Individuals, Partnerships, and Corporations
IPO	Initial Public Offering
IRS	Internal Revenue Service (U.S.)
ISBN	International Standard Book Number
ISSN	International Standard Serial Number
ITA	International Trade Administration (U.S.)
ITS	Intermarket Trading System
KCBT	Kansas City Board of Trade
LLC	Limited Liability Corporation
LIMRA	Life Insurance Marketing and Research Association
LMS	Labor Management Standards Office (U.S.)
LOMA	Life Office Management Association
MBS	Mortgage-Backed Securities Program
MGE	Minneapolis Grain Exchange
MGIC	MGIC Investment Corporation
MRDF	Machine-Readable Data File
MVMA	Motor Vehicle Manufacturers Association
NAIC	National Association of Insurance Commissioners
NAICS	North American Industry Classification System
NAR	National Association of Realtors
NAREIT	National Association of Real Estate Investment Trusts

NASD	National Association of Securities Dealers, Inc.
NASDA	National Association of State Department Agencies
NASDAQ	National Association of Securities Dealers Automated Quotations
NAV	Net Asset Value
NBS	National Bureau of Standards (U.S.)
NCHS	National Center for Health Statistics (U.S.)
NCUA	National Credit Union Administration (U.S.)
NLRB	National Labor Relations Board (U.S.)
NMS	National Market System
NTIS	National Technical Information Service (U.S.)
NYFE	New York Futures Exchange
NYME	New York Mercantile Exchange
NYSE	New York Stock Exchange
OASDI	Old Age, Survivors, Disability and Health Insurance
OBA	Office of Business Analysis (U.S.)
OMB	Office of Management and Budget (U.S.)
OSHA	Occupational Safety and Health Administration (U.S.)
OTA	Office of Technology Assessment (U.S.)
OTC	Over-the-Counter
PAIS	*Public Affairs Information Service Bulletin*
P/E	Price/Earnings Ratio
PIT	Preferred Stock
PFD	Preferred Stock
P-H	Prentice-Hall, Inc.
PPI	Producer Price Index
R&D	Research and Development
REIT	Real Estate Investment Trust
RELP	Real Estate Limited Partnership
RMA	Risk Management Association
ROA	Return on Assets
ROC	Return on Capital
ROE	Return on Equity
ROI	Return on Investment
ROS	Return on Sales
RPI	Retail Price Index
S & L	Savings and Loan Association
S & P	Standard & Poor's Corporation
SBA	Small Business Administration (U.S.)
SBW	Small Business Workshop (IRS)
SCORE	Service Corps of Retired Executives
SCSA	Standard Consolidated Statistical Area
SEC	Securities and Exchange Commission (U.S.)
SF	Sinking Fund
SFAS	Statement of Financial Accounting Standards
SIC	Standard Industrial Classification
SLA	Special Libraries Association
SMSA	Standard Metropolitan Statistical Area
S/N	Stock Number (U.S. Superintendent of Documents)
SRDS	Standard Rate & Data Service

SRI	*Statistical Reference Index*
SUDOCS	Superintendent of Documents (U.S.)
T BILL	Treasury Bill
TCE	Tax Counseling for the Elderly
USDA	Department of Agriculture (U.S.)
VA	Veterans Administration (U.S.)
VITA	Volunteer Income Tax Assistance
WSJ	*Wall Street Journal*
WT	Warrant

Appendix B

Federal Government Departments and Agencies Relevant to Business

Department or Agency	Function	URL
Agriculture	Works to improve farm income; develop markets for agricultural products; and help curb hunger, poverty, and malnutrition. Helps landowners protect soil, water, forests, and other natural resources. Through inspection and grading, ensures quality of daily food supply. Responsible for rural development, credit, and conservation programs.	http://www.usda.gov/
Economic Research Service	Provides economic information to aid in the development of agricultural policies and programs. Information made available through monographs, reports, situation and outlook periodicals, and databases.	http://www.ers.usda.gov/
National Agricultural Statistics Service	Prepares estimates and reports on production, supply, and prices of agricultural products.	http://www.usda.gov/nass/
International Trade Administration	Promotes world trade; strengthens U.S. international trade and investment position.	http://www.ita.doc.gov/
Patent and Trademark Office	Examines, registers, and administers national system of patents and trademarks.	http://www.uspto.gov/
Defense	Provides military forces needed to deter war and protect national security.	http://www.dod.gov/
Defense Logistics Agency	Works with current and potential suppliers of weapon systems and other DOD materials; administers defense contracts and other support services.	http://www.dla.mil/

Department or Agency	Function	URL
Education	Establishes policy for federal assistance to education; supports educational research.	http://www.ed.gov/
Office of Educational Research and Improvement	Focuses on educational research, development, demonstration, and assessment. Collects and disseminates statistics pertaining to U.S. and foreign education	http://www.ed.gov/offices/IES/NCES/
Energy	Coordinates and administers the government's energy functions, sponsors energy technology research and development, and administers energy data collection and analysis programs.	http://www.energy.gov/
Energy Information Administration	Collects, processes, and publishes data in the areas of energy resources and reserves, as well as energy production, demand, consumption, distribution, and technology.	http://www.eia.doe.gov/
Health and Human Services	Administers government programs in the areas of health, welfare, and income security; collects, analyzes, and publishes data relating to them.	http://www.hhs.gov/
Food and Drug Administration	Works to protect against impure and unsafe foods, drugs, cosmetics, and other hazards.	http://www.fda.gov/
National Center for Health Statistics	Collects, analyzes, and disseminates health statistics; promotes and conducts research in health data systems and statistical methodology.	http://www.cdc.gov/nchs/
Social Security Administration	Administers national program of contributory social welfare; conducts research relating to poverty, financial insecurity, and health care for the aged, blind, and disabled.	http://www.ssa.gov/
Housing and Urban Development	Responsible for programs concerned with housing needs and assistance, community development, mortgage lending and rent subsidies, and encouraging private home-building.	http://www.hud.gov/
Interior	Responsible for nationally owned public lands and natural resources, protects fish and wildlife, assesses mineral resources, and works to ensure that their development is in the public interest.	http://www.doi.gov/

Department or Agency	Function	URL
Geological Service	Identifies the nation's land, water, energy, and mineral resources; classifies federally owned land for minerals, energy, resources, and water power potential; investigates natural hazards; and conducts the National Mapping Program.	http://www.usgs.gov/
Justice	Enforces law in the public interest, including law relating to drugs, immigration, and naturalization. Promotes effective law enforcement, crime prevention and detection, and prosecution and rehabilitation of offenders.	http://www.usdoj.gov/
Federal Bureau of Investigation	Investigates all violations of federal law except those assigned to another agency.	http://www.fbi.gov/
Labor	Administers federal labor laws and monitors changes in employment, prices, and other measures of the national economy.	http://www.dol.gov/
Bureau of Labor Statistics	Collects, analyzes, processes, and disseminates data relating to employment, wages, and prices.	http://www.bls.gov
Employment and Training Administration	Fulfills DOL responsibilities relating to employment services, job training, and unemployment insurance.	http://www.doleta.gov/
Employment Standards Administration	Administers and directs employment standards programs dealing with minimum wages, overtime, farm labor, and nondiscriminatory and affirmative action for workers on government contracts and subcontracts.	http://www.dol.gov/esa/
Occupational Safety and Health Administration	Develops and promotes occupational safety and health standards, issues regulations, conducts investigations and inspections to determine compliance with safety and health standards, and issues citations and proposes penalties for noncompliance.	http://www.osha.gov/
State	Provides the president with advice in formulating and executing foreign policy.	http://www.state.gov/
Transportation	Establishes and administers national transportation policies and programs, including those relating to highways, mass transit, railroads, and aviation.	http://www.dot.gov/

Department or Agency	Function	URL
Federal Highway Administration	Operates and administers highway transportation programs relating to highway development and travel, transportation needs, and engineering and safety aspects.	http://www.fhwa.dot.gov/
Federal Railroad Administration	Promulgates and enforces rail safety regulations, administers financial assistance programs, and conducts research and development.	http://www.fra.dot.gov/site/
Maritime Administration	Administers programs to aid in the development, promotion, and operation of the U.S. merchant marine.	http://www.marad.dot.gov/
National Highway Traffic Safety Administration	Carries out programs relating to safety and performance of motor traffic vehicles, their occupants, and pedestrians.	http://www.nhtsa.dot.gov/
Treasury	Formulates and recommends economic, financial, tax, and fiscal policies; serves as the financial agent for the U.S. government; and manufactures coins and currency.	http://www.ustreas.gov/
Bureau of Alcohol, Tobacco and Firearms	Enforces and administers firearms and explosives laws, as well as those governing the production, use, and distribution of alcohol and tobacco products.	http://www.atf.treas.gov/
Internal Revenue Service	Administers and enforces internal revenue laws, excluding those relating to alcohol, tobacco, firearms, and explosives; determines, assesses, and collects taxes; and educates and advises the public.	http://www.irs.gov
United States Customs Service	Assesses and collects customs duties, excise taxes, fees, and penalties due on imported merchandise; seizes contraband; and processes persons, carriers, cargo, and mail into and out of the United States.	http://www.customs.ustreas.gov/

Appendix C

Federal Government Corporations and Independent Agencies Relevant to Business

Organization	Functions	URL
Commodity Futures Trading Commission	Regulates and oversees the trading of commodity futures and Commission options.	http://www.cftc.gov
Consumer Product Safety Commission	Protects the public against risk of injury from consumer products, develops uniform safety standards, and promotes research and investigation.	http://www.cpsc.gov/
Environmental Protection Agency	Protects and enhances the environment by controlling and abating air, water, solid waste, radiation, and toxic substance pollution.	http://www.epa.gov
Equal Employment Opportunity Commission	Responsible for compliance and enforcement activities relating to equal employment opportunities among federal employees; promotes voluntary action programs by employers, unions, and community organizations.	http://www.eeoc.gov/
Export-Import Bank of the United States	Facilitates and aids in financing exports of U.S. goods and services.	http://www.exim.gov/
Federal Communications Commission	Regulates interstate and foreign communications by radio, television, wire, and cable.	http://www.fcc.gov/
Federal Deposit Insurance Corporation	Promotes and preserves public confidence in banks; protects the money supply through provision of insurance coverage for bank deposits.	http://www.fdic.gov/
Federal Maritime Commission	Regulates waterborne foreign and domestic offshore commerce of the United States.	http://www.fmc.gov/

Organization	Functions	URL
Federal Mediation and Conciliation Service	Provides mediators to help labor and management settle work stoppages and other disputes.	http://www.fmcd.gov/
Federal Reserve System	Central bank of the United States; responsible for administering and policy making for U.S. credit and monetary affairs.	http://www.federal reserve.gov
Federal Trade Commission	Promotes the free enterprise system; ensures that it is not hindered by monopoly, restraints on trade, or unfair or deceptive trade practices.	http://www.ftc.gov/
General Services Administration	Responsible for providing the government with an economical and efficient system for managing its property and records.	http://www.gsa.gov/
National Credit Union Administration	Charters, insures, supervises, and examines federal credit unions.	http://www.ncua.gov/
National Labor Relations Board	Administers federal labor law; prevents and remedies unfair labor practices.	http://www.nlrb.gov/
National Mediation Board	Resolves air and railway disputes that might disrupt travel or threaten the economy.	http://www.nmb.gov/
National Science Foundation	Promotes science and engineering through the support of research and education programs.	http://www.nsf.gov/
National Transportation Safety Board	Investigates accidents, conducts studies, and makes recommendations on safety measures and practices.	http://www.ntsb.gov/
Nuclear Regulatory Commission	Licenses and regulates U.S. commercial power plants and the civilian use of nuclear energy.	http://www.nrc.gov/
Securities and Exchange Commission	Protects investors and maintains the integrity of the securities markets.	http://www.sec.gov/
Small Business Administration	Aids, counsels, assists, and protects the interests of small business.	http://www.sba.gov/

Organization	Functions	URL
United States Agency for International Development	Responsible for policy planning, policy making, and coordination of international economic issues affecting developing countries.	http://www.usaid.gov/
United States International Trade Commission	Furnishes studies, reports, and recommendations involving international trade and tariffs to the president, Congress, and other government agencies	http://www.usitc.gov

Appendix D

Representative Types of Business Information Published by State Government Agencies

Department/Agency	Information Provided
Agriculture	Crop production and demand, agricultural statistics, market surveys, consumer guides
Commerce/Business	Business and economic statistics, directories, surveys and assessments, economic indicators
Economic Development/ Planning	Promotional literature; directories; reports, forecasts, and projections
Education	Public and private education statistics, school enrollment, directories, reports
Energy	Energy statistics, alternative energy sources, energy conservation
Insurance	Annual reports, insurance statistics, lists of authorized insurance companies, consumer guides
Labor/Employment	Hour and wage statistics, cost of living, unemployment compensation, occupational safety and health, local labor market information
Taxation/Revenue	Income statistics, sales of certain taxed products, tax guides, statistical reports.
Tourism	Guides and brochures, maps, calendars of events.
Transportation	Traffic statistics, transit development plans, research studies, traffic safety

Appendix E

Key Economic Indicators

Indicator	Description	Government Agency	Frequency and URL
Balance of Payments	Difference in value of goods and services exported and imported by the United States.	Bureau of Economic Analysis	Monthly http://www.bea.gov/
Building Permits/ Housing Starts	Shows the number of permits issued and housing units begun. Used to check the economy, as construction is usually one of the first industries to show changes.	U.S. Bureau of the Census	Monthly http://www.census.gov/const/ www.newreconstindex.html
Consumer Price (CPI)	The measure of prices for a fixed basket of consumer goods. Used to measure inflation.	Bureau of Labor Statistics	Monthly http://www.bls.gov/cpi/
Gross Domestic Product (GDP)	The dollar value of the goods and services produced and consumed in the private, public, domestic, and international sectors. It is the broadest measure of economic output and growth.	Bureau of Economic Analysis	Quarterly http://www.bea.gov/
Interest Rates	Interest is the charge for borrowing money; and interest rates are the price of money. The rate is the interest per year divided by the principal and expressed as a percentage.	Federal Reserve Board	Weekly http://www.federalreserve.gov/releases/H15/

Indicator	Description	Government Agency	Frequency and URL
Personal Income	The income, from all sources, received by households. Used as a measure of purchasing power.	Bureau of Economic Analysis	Monthly http://www.bea.doc.gov/bea/dn/nipaweb/SelectTable.asp?Selected=Y
Producer Price Index	An index of commodity prices; it measures the average price over time received by domestic producers for their output.	Bureau of Labor Statistics	http://www.bls.gov/ppi/
Retail Trade	Provides the first indication of the strengths and weaknesses of consumer spending.	U.S. Bureau of the Census	Monthly http://www.census.gov/mrts/www/mrts.html
Unemployment	Percentage of the workforce that is involuntarily out of work.	Bureau of Labor Statistics	Monthly http://stats.bls.gov/news.release/empsit.toc.ht

Appendix F

Representative Web Sites for Business Information

General Sites and Search Engines

AllTheWeb. http://www.alltheweb.com/
This search engine uses dynamic clustering based on Open Directory. Basic Web search plus searching in real time news, pictures, videos, MP3s, and ftp files.

BRASS Best of the Best Business Web Sites. http://www.ala.org/brassTemplate/cfm?
Section=BRASS
A subject index to the "Best of the Best" created by members of the BRASS (Business Reference and Services Section of ALA) Education Committee.

Google. http://www.google.com/
A simple search in *Google* returns Web pages that contain all the words in the query, so narrowing the search is as easy as adding more words to the search terms. *Google* ignores common words such as "how". If the word is essential to the search add + (+how) or make the whole search a phrase. To limit searches to pdf add the words "filetype:pdf". Search areas include sets of images, news groups, and a directory. Based on Open Directory.

Librarian's Index to the Internet. http://lii.org/search/file/business
A directory of Web links. Sites are selected, indexed, and annotated by Californian librarians.

Yahoo. http://www.yahoo.com
Browsable directory of Web sites. One can search the whole Web or search within topic and region. If nothing is found in *Yahoo* the search defaults to *Google*.

Acronym Database. http://www.acronymfinder.com/
"The web's most comprehensive database of acronyms, abbreviations, and initialisms. 229,000+ definitions!"

Investorwords.com. http://www.investorwords.com/
Over 6,000 business definitions, each with appropriate cross-referencing.

Accounting and Taxes

CPA Directory. http://www.cpafirms.com/Firmlist/firmlist.cfm
A listing of U.S. CPA firms by region, state, or area code. This directory also contains about 300 international firms.

CPA JOURNAL Home Page. http://www.cpaj.com/
Table of contents of the current journal is available. There is also a link to archives of the journal available from the New York State Society of Certified Public Accountants Web Site. These archives when last checked covered 1989–2001.

CPAnet. http://www.cpanet.com/accounting.index.asp
The online community & Web site resource for accounting professionals. Links inlcude news, directories, articles, associations and software.

Rutgers Accounting Web—A Part of the International Accounting Network. http://accounting. rutgers.edu/
One of the largest accounting Web sites, with links to professional organizations, research, class outlines, and more.

Tax and Accounting Sites Directory. http://www.taxsites.com/
A fairly inclusive site, with links to forms, associations, publishers, rates and tables, career, and legal information. International, federal, and state links.

Banking

AAAdir Bank Directory—US and International Banks. http://www.aaadir.com/
A directory links to the Web pages of world banks. Also contains statistical information, links to stock exchanges, organizations, and dictionaries.

Bank Rate Monitor. http://www.bankrate.com/brm/default.asp
Rates for mortgages, home equity, car loans, cds, credit cards etc. Search by state and type of loan needed. Includes calculators.

Central Banking Resources Center—Mark Bernkopf. http://patriot.net/~bernkopf/
Links to all central banks, ministries of finance and economy, and currency boards.

FDIC Data. http://www.fdic.gov/bank/index.html
Analytical, statistical, and historical information on banks from the Federal Deposit Insurance Corporation.

Statistical Resources on the Web/Finance and Banking. http://www.lib.umich.edu/govdocs/ stecfin.html
Alphabetical list of links to statistics on international and U.S. banking. Maintained by the University of Michigan Documents Center.

Yahoo—Banks. http://dir.yahoo.com/business_and_economy/shopping_and_services/financial_services/banking/banks/
Alphabetical listing of banks, with links to the Web sites.

Bankruptcy

American Bankruptcy Institute World. http://www.abiworld.org/
The premier site for bankruptcy information on the Web. Contains statistics on both business and consumer filings.

Bankruptcy Courts. http://www.abiworld.org/chambers/courtdirs.html
Links to international, federal, and state bankruptcy courts.

InterNet Bankruptcy Library. http://bankrupt.com/
Information on conferences, local rules books, and periodicals. News section contains free articles from specialized periodicals embargoed for 90 days.

Bonds

Bonds Online. http://www.bonds-online.com/
Includes explanations of different types of bonds as well as quotes, yields, and outlook. A subscription is required for the more specialized information.

Brady Bonds—International Quotes. http://www.bradynet.com/
Leading provider of fixed income instruments for emerging markets. Includes Brady bonds, Eurobonds, and exotic debt.

Municipal Bond Yields—Bloomberg. http://www.bloomberg.com/markets/rates/index.html
Listing for triple-A rated, tax-exempt insured revenue bonds.

Standard & Poor's Rating Services. http://www.standardandpoors.com/
Good free information in the "Media Center" on changes in ratings.

T-bills, Notes & Bonds Online. http://www.publicdebt.treas.gov/sec/sec.htm
Information on T-bills, notes and bonds, including how to buy them online. Information on interest rates and expenses, STRIPS, security liquidations and current and historical public debt statistics.

The Bond Market Association. http://www.bondmarkets.com/
For the investor, provides free publications on types of bonds and investing as well as research reports and links to other bond sites. Regulatory information is also provided.

Yahoo's Bond section. http://dir.yahoo.com/Business_and_Economy/Finance_and_Investment/Bonds/
Another link to links on bonds.

Codes

Harmonized Tariff Schedule of the United States. http://dataweb.usitc.gov/SCRIPTS/tariff/toc.html

The *HTSA* provides the applicable tariff rates and statistical categories for all merchandise imported into the United States; it is based on the *International Harmonized System*, the global classification system that is used to describe most world trade in goods.

NAICS http://www.census.gov/epcd/www/naics.html.

The *North American Industry Classification System (NAICS)* has replaced the *U.S. Standard Industrial Classification (SIC)* system. *NAICS* was developed jointly by the United States, Canada, and Mexico to provide new comparability in statistics about business activity across North America.

NAICS (searchable index). http://www.census.gov/epcd/naics/framesrc.htm

Enter the term, or part of a term, being searched for.

Schedule B Export Codes. http://www.census.gov/foreign-trade/schedules/b/index.html

Trade transactions are classified under approximately 8,000 different products leaving the United States. Every item that is exported is assigned a unique 10-digit identification code. Every 10-digit item is part of a series of progressively broader product categories.

SIC (lookup system). http://www.osha.gov/oshstats/sicser.html

Search the 1987 version SIC manual by keyword, to access descriptive information for a specified four-digit SIC

Company Directories

Blue Book of Building and Construction. http://www.thebluebook.com/

Regional construction directories in most major markets throughout the United States. Over 1 million listings and profiles.

CorporateInformation. http://www.corporateinformation.com/

Over 350,000 quick company profiles and over 20,000 detailed company profiles and research reports. Searching is also available by state, country, and industry. Other information provided includes currency exchange rates and news stories.

Hoover's ONLINE. http://www.hoovers.com/

Basic capsule information is free; the free links to SEC filings and corporate news makes it a useful "one-stop" shop.

Also available:

> *Hoover's Online UK,* http://www.hoovers.com/global/uk/
>
> *Hoover's Online France,* http://www.hoovers.com/global/fr/
>
> *Hoover's Online Italia,* http://www.hoovers.com/global/it/fr
>
> *Hoover's Online EspaZa,* http://www.hoovers.com/global/es/
>
> *Hoover's Online Germany,* http://www.hoovers.com/global/de/

Kompass—International Directories. http://www.kompass.com
Worldwide search by company name or product. Basic directory information on 1.6 million companies is free.

Thomas Register of American Manufacturers Online. http://www.thomasregister.com/
Searching is by company or product. Directory information plus links to online catalogs are supplied. More than 72,000 product headings and over 170,000 companies listed.

Company Financial

Annual Report Service—The Public Register. http://www.annualreportservice.com/
Choice to view the online annual or to request a free hard copy. Free registration is required.

CAROL. http://www.carol.co.uk/
Company Annual Reports On Line. Scope is international. Free registration required.

CorporateInformation. http://www.corporateinformation.com/
Includes company profiles and research reports.

EDGAR Database of Corporate Information. http://www.sec.gov/edgar.shtml
Official Securities and Exchange Commission Web site. Financial filings from public companies.

SearchSystems.net. http://www.searchsystems.net/
Useful to check state sites to find the names of corporations that file only in that state.

Exchanges

American Stock Exchange. http://www.amex.com/
Access to current market and historical data, charts and tools, news, and educational resources.

Chicago Stock Exchange. http://www.chx.com
CHX trades equities only. Site contains volume information back to 1998, company listings, the annual factbook, and report.

Federation of European Stock Exchanges. http://www.fese.be/
Monthly statistics on the performance of European equity, bond, and derivative markets and special reports are provided at the site.

Futures & Options Exchanges. http://www.numa.com/ref/exchange.htm
Directory of exchanges by country. Maintained by NUMA Financial Systems.

NASDAQ. http://www.nasdaq.com/
Current information, guides, and links.

New York Stock Exchange. http://www.nyse.com/
Includes everything from the history of the NYSE to current quotes. The factbook is in the "About" section.

Philadelphia Stock Exchange. http://www.phlx.com/
Updated contract specifications on *PHLX*'s products, current news releases, text from publications, and newsletters.

stock point. http://investor.stockpoint.com/
Information about worldwide investing. Contains links, tools, commentary, and a streaming ticker board. The site can be personalized after registration.

Yahoo Stock Exchanges. http://dir.yahoo.com/Business_and_Economy/Business_to_ Business/Financial_Services/Exchanges/Stock_Exchanges/
Links to major stock exchanges of the world.

Futures, Options, Commodities

Bloomberg Active Futures. http://www.bloomberg.com/markets/commodities/cfuture. html
Current "most active" futures.

Commodity Futures Trading Commission. http://www.cftc.gov/cftc/cftchome.htm
Contains information on "how to trade," a listing of trader's commitments, consumer advisories, and enforcement bulletins.

Commodity Charts, & Quotes. http://tfc-charts.w2d.com/
Free source of daily commodity futures and financial charts.

Eaglewing Research Links. http://www.eaglewing.com/linkpage.htm
Links to everything you want to know on the gold market.

Futures and Options Resources on the Web. http://www.ace.uiuc.edu/ofor/resource.htm
Exchanges, Prices & Outlook, Research, Government Resources, and other Futures and Financial sites. Maintained by Department of Agricultural and Consumer Economics, University of Illinois at Urbana-Champaign.

Historical Futures Price Data. http://www.spotmarketplace.com/futures/prices/
Some historical prices and settlement data.

Options Industry Council (OIC). http://www.optionscentral.com/
Includes guides to all aspects of futures and options as well as quotes, volume data, links to SEC filings, and contract adjustments and product specifications.

USGS Minerals Information. http://minerals.usgs.gov/minerals/
Statistics and information on the worldwide supply, demand, and flow of minerals. For some of the commodities, data are reported as far back as 1900.

Industry

1997 Economic Census. http://www.census.gov/epcd/www/econ97.html
Latest economic census data. Scroll down the page to check the American FactFinder, which will provide Geography Quick Reports, Industry Quick Reports, and Data Sets.

Advertising Industry—Ad Age Dataplace. http://www.adage.com/datacenter.cms
Provides advertising and marketing industry data compiled by the Ad Age Research Department. Check also the Special Reports for useful information.

Country Analysis Briefs. http://www.eia.doe.gov/emeu/cabs/
Some country overview information and in-depth energy information.

Current Industrial Reports—US Census. http://www.census.gov/cir/www/
Timely, accurate data on production and shipments of selected products.

Hoover's Online. http://www.hoovers.com/
Click on Companies & Industries and then Industries at the left of the screen. There are some free *Industry Snapshots* and free sector analysis. At this time there is also a link on the front screen to *Industry Snapshots.*

ITA Basic Industries. http://www.ita.doc.gov/td/bi/
From the International Trade Administration. Contains foreign trade figures but also U.S. information. Some sections contain more than others.

Links from Fuld & Company Library. http://www.fuld.com/i3/index.html
The top of the site lists general links to useful tools for industry information. Scroll down the page to link to industry-specific information.

Newspaper Industry—Newspaper Association of America. http://www.naa.org/
Basic facts on newspaper distribution and sales as well as advertising data.

Pharmaceutical Industry—Ph RMA. http://www.phrma.org/
Useful industry information, but remember that PHRMA represents the country's leading research-based pharmaceutical and biotechnology companies.

Polson Enterprises Industry Home Pages. http://www.virtualpet.com/industry/mfg/mfg.htm
Links to publications and other sites for most major industries.

Initial Public Offerings (IPOs)

IPO Central—Hoover's Online. http://www.hoovers.com/global/ipoc/index.xhtml
Lists latest IPOs with company details. Includes an IPO scorecard listed by industry.

Insurance

A.M. BEST. http://www.ambest.com/index.html
Information on all aspects of the insurance industry. Includes the well known Best's Ratings.

Insurance Company Homepages—The Big List. http://insurance.about.com/blbiglist.htm?once=true&
Links to the Web pages of insurance companies. Also links to articles and a free newsletter.

Insurance Information Institute. http://www.iii.org/
Information on all types of insurance. Includes industry statistics, financials and outlook, hot topics, research studies, and a glossary.

insure.com. http://www.insure.com/index.html
Basic guides to all types of insurance and company information, including ratings from S&P and Fitch. Directory listings by state of insurance agents. Includes a lawsuit library. Free quotes.

International Links

Foreign Government Resources on the Web. http://www.lib.umich.edu/govdocs/foreign.html
Via University of Michigan, information on countries, constitutions, laws, treaties, news, and statistics.

Governments on the Web. http://www.gksoft.com/govt/
A comprehensive database that includes parliaments, ministries, offices, law courts, embassies, city councils, public broadcasting corporations, central banks, multinational organizations, political parties, etc.

Country Analysis Briefs. http://www.eia.doe.gov/emeu/cabs/contents.html
Substantive reports on individual countries and special topics provided by the Department of Energy.

Country Risk Analysis. http://www.duke.edu/~charvey/Country_risk/couindex.htm
Studies by Professor Campbell R. Harvey, Fuqua School of Business, Duke University.

U.S. Business Advisor. http://www.business.gov/busadv/maincat.cfm?catid=94
Scroll down the page to link to; Country Commercial Guides, Department of State Background Notes and CIA Publications and Handbook.

VIBES. http://library.uncc.edu/vibes/
"Provides over 1,600 links to Internet sources of international business and economic information that are in English and available free of charge."

Mutual Funds

Brill's Mutual Funds Interactive. http://www.brill.com/
A leading Web site for guides and information about mutual funds, plus links to funds.

MORNINGSTAR. http://www.morningstar.com/
Lots of free information about individual funds; ratings are included in the free information.

MUTUAL FUND INVESTOR'S CENTER. http://www.mfea.com/
An excellent site for general information and links to mutual funds.

Mutual Funds—advice from the SEC. http://www.sec.gov/investor/pubs/inwsmf.htm
The Securities and Exchange Commission's guide to investing in mutual funds.

Mutual Funds Facts & Figures—Investment Company Institute. http://www.ici.org/stats/
Site includes facts and figures, statistical reports, and the latest factbook.

Periodicals and Newspapers

Bizjournals. http://www.bizjournals.com/
Business news from 41 local markets and 46 industries.

Find Articles. http://www.findarticles.com/
Free articles from 1998 to the present from 300 journals. Searching is possible within subject areas.

Industry/Trade Publications. http://www.ecola.com/news/magazine/industry/
Alphabetical listing of journals plus links to journals listed by industries such as mining or metals.

MagPortal.com. http://www.magportal.com/
Search by subject for freely available online articles.

NewsLink. http://newslink.org/biznews.html
Links by state to business dailies and business magazines.

OnlineNewspapers.com. http://www.onlinenewspapers.com/
Listings, by country, of thousands of available newspapers.

Real Estate

Directory of Real Estate Centers. http://www.cba.uc.edu/getreal/center.html
List of real estate centers compiled by the University of Cincinnati.

Fannie Mae. http://www.fanniemae.com/
Information about mortgages and applications. Scroll down the screen and on the left find a link to the database of Fannie Mae properties for sale.

FDIC owned real estate. http://www.fdic.gov/buying/owned/index.html
FDIC properties for sale. Also calendars of special sales.

Glossary of Real Estate Terms. http://www.websiteupgrades.com/glossary/free/
Courtesy of Website Upgrades Inc.

Home Sales Information. http://classifieds.yahoo.com/reinfo/homecompsquery.html
Home sales information, including prices of homes in your area or an area in which you are interested.

Mortgage Calculators. http://www.bankrate.com/brm/rate/calc_home.asp
Find the monthly payment for a particular loan and calculate discount points.

PikeNet. http://www.pikenet.com/pike?func'showHome
Commercial real estate on the Web, with about 3,500 links to resources and service providers worldwide

Small Business

CELCEE—Center for Entrepreneurial Leadership Clearinghouse on Entrepreneurship Education. http://www.celcee.edu/
"CELCEE acquires information related to entrepreneurship education From diverse sources, including journal articles, websites, syllabi, conferences, pamphlets, curriculum guides, government publications, videos, books, computer software, and more."

Doing Business with Government. http://www.business.gov/busadv/maincat.cfm?catid=256
Buying from and selling to the federal government.

MoreBusiness.com. http://www.morebusiness.com/
Articles, guides, software downloads, and calculators.

Small Business Journal. http://www.tsbj.com/
Back issues and tables of contents.

US BUSINESS ADVISOR. http://www.business.gov/
Links to government resources for business. Includes financial, legal, and workplace information. The starting point for business. Check also http://www.firstgov.gov/.

US Small Business Administration (SBA). http://www.sba.gov
Everything for the small business owner. Advice, forms, legal information, sample business plans. The place to start for those opening a new business.

Statistics

1997 Economic Census. http://www.census.gov/epcd/www/econ97.html
The Economic Census profiles the U.S. economy every five years, from the national to the local level.

Bureau of Labor Statistics. http://stats.bls.gov/
Links to federal economic indexes, productivity and employment statistics, and publications.

County Business Patterns. http://fisher.lib.virginia.edu/cbp/
Provides county, state, and national level business data from 1977 to the most recent year available. Statistics include number of establishments, payroll (annual and first quarter), number of employees, and number of establishments by size class for two-digit SIC industry groupings.

Directory of Online Statistics Sources. http://www.berinsteinresearch.com/stats.htm
Directory lists online statistics sources, by subject, for quick reference. Links are provided to both free and fee sources.

FEDSTATS. http://www.fedstats.gov/
The gateway to statistics from over 100 U.S. federal agencies.

Statistical Resouces on the Web. http://www.lib.umich.edu/govdocs/stecon.html
Links to business, industry, trade, and economic statistics sites, maintained by the Documents Center at the University of Michigan.

Stock Quotes

Stock quotes are freely available on the Web at most newspaper and general business sites. Those listed below have more than basic quote information or are for smaller stocks.

411 Stocks. http://www.411stocks.com/
Current stock and indexes listings. Also included are earnings warnings, top gainer, and top loser.

cnnmoney. http://money.cnn.com/markets/
A major business site that gives not only stock quotes but also earnings reports, how-to guides, and news reports. One of the first places to begin looking for all kinds of business information.

pinksheets.com—OTC information. http://www.pinksheets.com/
The central resource for trading information on OTC stocks. Includes real time quotations.

Stock Research

Stock Research Sites on the Web—Foster Business Library, University of Washington.
http://depts.washington.edu/balib/stocksites/
"This site contains evaluations of free stock research sites on the Web. There has been no attempt to apply any qualitative or quantitative ranking to the sites, rather, this lists the features available on the different sites along with some evaluative comments on usability and design."

Stock Splits and Stock Dividends Equity Analytics, Ltd. http://www.e-analytics.com/ splitd.htm
Stock splits and dividends back to 1996, plus a calendar of upcoming splits.

YAHOO Historical Prices. http://chart.yahoo.com/d
Historical quotes back to the early 1970s. Dividend information is also available. Lists can be directly downloaded into a spreadsheet.

Title Index

The following conventions have been observed: In most instances subtitles are not used. When there is more than one entry, numbers in boldface indicate major coverage and the letter "n" following a page number indicates only minor coverage.

Subject Index

About the Author

RITA W. MOSS, Business/ Economics Librarian at UNC Chapel Hill since 1991, compiled the Business Economics section of the *Guide to Reference Books* (11th edition). She has presented numerous workshops for SOLINET (Southeastern Library Network) on business resources (1993–1996) and currently presents workshops for NC Live (North Carolina Libraries for Virtual Education) covering business databases and Web resources.